The Radical Orthodoxy Re

This Reader presents a selection of key readings in the field of Radical Orthodoxy, the most influential theological movement in contemporary academic theology. Radical Orthodoxy draws on pre-Enlightenment theology and philosophy to engage critically with the assumption and priorities of secularism, modernity, postmodernity and associated theologies. In doing so it explores a wide and exciting range of issues: music, language, society, the body, the city, power, motion, space, time, personhood, sex and gender. As such it is both controversial and extremely stimulating, provoking much fruitful debate amongst contemporary theologians.

To assist those encountering Radical Orthodoxy for the first time, each section has an introductory commentary, related reading and helpful questions to encourage in-depth understanding and further study.

John Milbank is Professor of Religion, Politics and Ethics at the University of Nottingham, the author of *Being Reconciled: Ontology and Pardon* (Routledge, 2003) and one of the editors of the Radical Orthodoxy collection of essays.

Simon Oliver is Associate Professor of Systematic Theology at the University of Nottingham and the author of *Philosophy, God and Motion* (Routledge, 2005) in the Radical Orthodoxy series.

The Radical Orthodoxy

Reader

Edited by

John Milbank and Simon Oliver

Routledge
Taylor & Francis Group

LONDON AND NEW YORK

First published 2009
by Routledge
2 Park Square, Milton Park, Abingdon, Oxon. OX14 4RN

Simultaneously published in the USA and Canada
by Routledge
270 Madison Ave., New York, NY 100016

Routledge is an imprint of the Taylor & Francis Group, an informa business

Typeset in Perpetua and FranklinGothic by
Taylor & Francis Books
Printed and bound in Great Britain by
CPI Antony Rowe, Chippenham, Wiltshire

British Library Cataloguing in Publication Data
A catalogue record for this book is available from the British Library

Library of Congress Cataloging in Publication Data
The radical orthodoxy reader / editors, Simon Oliver and John Milbank.
    p. cm.
Includes bibliographical references and index.
1. Philosophical theology. 2. Radicalism–Religious aspects–Christianity.
3. Postmodern theology. I. Oliver, Simon, 1971- II. Milbank, John.
BT40.R356 2009
230'.046–dc22   2008046103

ISBN10: 0-415-42512-3 (hbk)
ISBN10: 0-415-42513-1 (pbk)
ISBN10: 0-203-88921-5 (ebk)

ISBN13: 978-0-415-42512-4 (hbk)
ISBN13: 978-0-415-42513-1 (pbk)
ISBN13: 978-0-203-88921-3 (ebk)

Contents

Acknowledgements   viii
About this Reader   x

PART I
What is Radical Orthodoxy?   1

Introducing Radical Orthodoxy: from
participation to late modernity
SIMON OLIVER   3

1.   Radical Orthodoxy: a conversation
      ED. RUPERT SHORTT   28

2.   'Postmodern critical Augustinianism': a short
      summa in forty-two responses to unasked
      questions
      JOHN MILBANK   49

      FURTHER READING   62
      QUESTIONS   62

PART II
Theology and philosophy, faith and reason 63

    INTRODUCTION 65

3. Truth and vision
    JOHN MILBANK 69

4. Duns Scotus: his historical and contemporary significance
    CATHERINE PICKSTOCK 116

    FURTHER READING 147
    QUESTIONS 148

PART III
Theology and the secular 149

    INTRODUCTION 151

5. Spatialization: the middle of modernity
    CATHERINE PICKSTOCK 154

6. Political theology and the new science of politics
    JOHN MILBANK 178

    FURTHER READING 195
    QUESTIONS 195

PART IV
Christ and gift 197

    INTRODUCTION 199

7. Christ the exception
    JOHN MILBANK 202

8. The schizoid Christ
    GRAHAM WARD 228

    FURTHER READING 257
    QUESTIONS 258

PART V
Church and Eucharist   259

    INTRODUCTION   261

9.   Thomas Aquinas and the quest for the Eucharist
      CATHERINE PICKSTOCK   265

10. Transcorporeality: the ontological scandal
      GRAHAM WARD   287

    FURTHER READING   307
    QUESTIONS   307

PART VI
Politics and theology   309

    INTRODUCTION   311

11. "A fire strong enough to consume the house":
     The Wars of Religion and the rise of the
     nation state
      WILLIAM T. CAVANAUGH   314

12. The gift of ruling
      JOHN MILBANK   338

    FURTHER READING   363
    QUESTIONS   363

Afterword   365

    The grandeur of reason and the perversity of
    rationalism: Radical Orthodoxy's first decade
      JOHN MILBANK   367

    Index   405

Acknowledgements

The editors are grateful to the publishers and authors for permission to reproduce the following material:

- John Milbank, '"Postmodern Critical Augustinianism": A Short Summa in Forty-two Responses to Unasked Questions', *Modern Theology*, 7(3), 1991: 225–37.
- 'Radical Orthodoxy: A Conversation', in Rupert Shortt, *God's Advocates*, London: DLT, 2005.
- John Milbank and Catherine Pickstock, *Truth in Aquinas*, London: Routledge, 2001, chapter 2.
- Catherine Pickstock, 'Duns Scotus: His Historical and Contemporary Significance', *Modern Theology*, 21(4), 2005: 543–74.
- Catherine Pickstock, *After Writing: On the Liturgical Consummation of Philosophy*, Oxford: Blackwell, 1998, chapter 2: 47–74 (sections 1–5).
- John Milbank, *Theology and Social Theory: Beyond Secular Reason*, 2nd edn, Oxford: Blackwell, 2006, chapter 1.
- John Milbank, *Being Reconciled: Ontology and Pardon*, London: Routledge, 2003, chapters 5 & 6.
- Graham Ward, 'The Schizoid Christ' in idem., *Christ and Culture*, Oxford: Blackwell, 2005, chapter 2.
- Catherine Pickstock, 'Thomas Aquinas and the Quest for the Eucharist', *Modern Theology*, 15 (2), 1999: 159–80.

- Graham Ward, 'The Ontological Scandal', in *Cities of God*, London: Routledge, 2001, chapter 3.
- John Milbank, 'The Gift of Ruling', *New Blackfriars*, 85 (996), 2004: 212–38.
- William Cavanaugh, '"A fire strong enough to consume the house:" The Wars of Religion and the Rise of the Nation State', *Modern Theology*, 11(4), 1995: 397–420.

We also wish to express our great thanks to Lesley Riddle, Gemma Dunn and Amy Grant of Routledge for their kindness, assistance and infinite patience in the production of this Reader.

About this Reader

It is now more than ten years since the publication of the first collection of essays under the title *Radical Orthodoxy*. The original series of twelve books has since led to many more publications covering an extremely broad range of subjects, from work to the nature of the university and the craft of reading theologically. The three series *Veritas* (London: SCM), *Interventions* (Grand Rapids: Eerdmans Publishing Company) and *Illuminations: Theory and Religion* (Oxford: Wiley-Blackwell) continue this broad trend in ever-new and varied ways.

The literature which lies beneath the wide umbrella of Radical Orthodoxy is therefore very extensive and there is a large body of works which engages thoroughly with Radical Orthodoxy's key themes in more or less critical ways.[1] This Reader offers a combination of writings which seek to introduce Radical Orthodoxy alongside some of this sensibility's signature texts – those which have been most influential, definitive, enduring and provocative. While it is not possible to do justice to the sheer energy and breadth of Radical Orthodoxy in one volume, nevertheless it is hoped that this volume will provide a convenient quick point of reference for specialists and a guide for students.

This Reader is divided into six parts. The first part provides an introduction to Radical Orthodoxy which it is hoped will be particularly helpful for students. The remaining five parts each feature two texts which deal with a theme that is central to Radical Orthodoxy or an area which features some of Radical Orthodoxy's most original and provocative interventions. At the beginning of each part you will find a brief introduction to the texts. Some suggestions for further reading can be found at the end of each part. Those items in a shaded box indicate, where applicable, particularly important texts which have informed Radical Orthodoxy either positively or negatively (for example, passages from Plato or portions of Aquinas's *Summa Theologiae*), or texts where a core theme (for example, gift) is discussed in an important way. Where applicable, the best available English translation is cited. Those items in a clear box indicate texts which are particularly suitable for students at advanced undergraduate or taught graduate level. Remaining items in the lists of further reading are relevant for more detailed or specialist study. The inclusion of an item in the bibliography does *not* indicate that the text can be labelled 'radically orthodox'. Sometimes, the reverse is the case. These works are cited as important for understanding and clarifying the contribution of theologians whose sympathies more-or-less coincide with the sensibility which might be called 'Radical Orthodoxy'. For example, the lists of further reading frequently refer to works by philosophers and theologians of whom Radical Orthodoxy has been most critical. Finally, following the further reading can be found a number of questions for discussion which seek to focus the reader's attention on particularly important issues. Professors and teachers may find these useful in provoking class discussion.

At its heart, Radical Orthodoxy is devoted to what has become known as *ressourcement*, namely the renewed reading of the depths of the Christian tradition in order to inform a rigorous, critical and authentically theological reading of our own times. If the texts offered in this Reader do nothing more than encourage the reader to read again with renewed intensity the works of Plato, Aristotle, the patristic theologians, the Neo-Platonists, Aquinas, Scotus, Kant and many others, they will have served their principal purpose.

Note

1   A very comprehensive and regularly updated bibliography of material relating to Radical Orthodoxy is provided by James K.A. Smith, Shannon Schutt Nason, Kristen Deede Johnson and Jerry Stutzman at http://www.calvin.edu/~jks4/ro/ (accessed 1 September 2008).

PART I

What is Radical Orthodoxy?

Introducing Radical Orthodoxy: from participation to late modernity

Simon Oliver

'**O**nce, there was no "secular".' This is the opening statement of John Milbank's *Theology and Social Theory*. This book, launched with this sentence, is often cited as the beginning of the theological sensibility which has since become known as Radical Orthodoxy. During the almost twenty years since the publication of Milbank's groundbreaking work, Radical Orthodoxy has arguably become the most discussed and provocative tendency in Anglophone theology. Given that works in the Radical Orthodoxy genre are often ambitious in scope and purpose, engaging with classical, mediaeval, modern and late modern thought in order to read theologically the signs of our own times, the territory is vast. This introduction will provide an initial overview of some key themes before we engage with Radical Orthodoxy face to face. I am going to use John Milbank's introductory claim – that 'once, there was no "secular"' – as my own starting point. So what does it mean to state that there was once no secular, and how is Milbank's opening remark unfolded in a theology which claims to be radical and orthodox?

The invention of the secular

That we live in a secular society – particularly, but of course by no means exclusively, in western Europe and North America – is often taken for granted.

We are very familiar with journalists telling us that Europe is post-Christian with regular church attendance in inexorable decline, while the US, despite having by far the highest incidence of religious belief and practice in the West, constitutionally separates politics and religion. We might understand a secular society as one in which the *public* realms of politics, business and the law lack any reference to God or the transcendent. What residues of religious practice and common prayer remain in politics or the public sphere are merely faint echoes of a long forgotten world in which belief in God influenced every aspect of human living, both public and private.[1] Religious practice is now thought to be confined to a *private* realm in which people can indulge their personal beliefs so long as those beliefs do not infringe on the (publicly defended) rights of others. As well as thinking of the secular in terms of the confinement of religion and theology to the private sphere of 'personal belief', we might also think that the secular refers to a shift in perspective and understanding whereby we can answer fundamental questions about nature and humanity with no reference to God or any transcendent origin or purpose.

In *A Secular Age*, the Canadian philosopher Charles Taylor, in a work which is in many ways highly consonant with writings in the Radical Orthodoxy sphere, suggests a third way in which we might understand the secular, namely with reference to the shift from a situation in which belief in God is the largely unchallenged governing principle of human life and understanding to a situation in which belief in God is simply one option amongst many others.[2] It becomes just another 'world view'. As Taylor points out, this suggests that, despite high levels of religious participation, the United States exemplifies the secular: religion becomes a consumer product amongst many others with countless 'retailers' peddling their version of God in a free market.

In the debate surrounding secularism's origins and identity, most are agreed that, even though the seeds were sown centuries ago, it is relatively recent in our intellectual history and is part of the birth modernity. In the high mediaeval period in much of Europe, up to around the turn of the fifteenth century, all political and social practices were orientated around Christian feasts and fasts, the division of land into ecclesiastical parishes understood primarily as communities of prayer, and the rule of a monarch under God.[3] There was a shared conviction that the social body was ordered in and through the body of Christ, the Church. Nature and human society were understood to be bound together as creatures before God.[4] Of course, in practice this was no utopia – the world is, of course, fallen – but it was a society of worship which believed that violence and suffering were not the natural state of man (as modern political theorists were later to suggest) but an intrusion, and that common peace and flourishing were to be sought through hope and participation in 'divine society'.

Historians, sociologists, anthropologists, philosophers and theologians have offered countless explanations for the extraordinary shift from what is sometimes known as 'the mediaeval consensus' to the modern secular world. One of the more straightforward and popular accounts of the demise of the mediaeval consensus and the advent of secular modernity refers to the rise of natural science in the sixteenth and seventeenth centuries. What is this account of secular modernity's establishment? To understand it properly, we must return to the mediaeval West and the influence of the ancient Greek philosopher Aristotle (384–322 BC).

Following the introduction of his works into the Latin West from the late twelfth and early thirteenth centuries (via the Islamic philosophers of northern Spain), a version of the philosophy of Aristotle had gradually become dominant in Europe. His works formed the basis of the curricula in the new universities, and his natural philosophy, refracted through Christian theology, heavily influenced the way people thought about their relations with each other and their place in creation. Crucially, however, while Aristotle advocated the observation of nature in order to describe its workings, he did not advocate what we now call experimental science. Experiments do not involve simply the observation of nature; they involve the isolation, control and manipulation of natural process in order to measure outcomes. Performing experiments allowed natural philosophers (the term 'scientist' came later) such as Galileo to predict and therefore manipulate natural processes much more carefully. Coupled with great advances in mathematics in the seventeenth century, this gave the first natural scientists such as Newton the tools to discover the supposed facts about nature.

This provokes the characteristically modern sense that human knowledge is advancing inexorably as new discoveries are made. The old world of natural philosophy, Christian practice, the Bible and theology was being stripped away to reveal a more neutral world view which was apparently disinterested, objective and factual. While 'reason' of course had a prominent place in earlier thought as a participation in the reason – the *logos* – of God mediated through traditions and social practices, a new understanding of reason was to dominate this Enlightenment. This rationality was not particular to any tradition or subject matter, but common to all peoples and times.[5] This reason was to be dispassionate, standing independent of any cultural or historical influence.[6]

So the rise of the secular is understood in terms of the simultaneous retreat of religion and theology. This is sometimes referred to as 'desacralization'. This means that the question of humanity's (or creation's) ultimate origin and purpose is largely sidelined in favour of questions which concern the more immediate and immanent workings and functions of human beings and nature. Questions about the *facts* of nature were now divorced from questions of *value* or *purpose*.

This view of the transformation from the mediaeval consensus to the modern secular world is so straightforward that we often take it for granted. It is a view which sees the secular as the result of clearing away the debris of superstition, ritual and tradition which we imagine dominated mediaeval Europe to open new possibilities directed by the neutral hand of reason expressed most particularly in the natural sciences. The advent of the secular is therefore seen as the natural result of the inevitable progress of human knowledge and thinking.

As Milbank unfolds his opening claim that 'once, there was no secular', we see that he rejects this view of the emergence of the secular from the ruins of the mediaeval consensus. Why? Milbank argues that the secular is not simply that which is left behind once we have rid ourselves of religion and theology. The secular is not a neutral, dispassionate or objective view of ourselves and the world; it had to be *created* as a positive ideology. The secular view holds its own assumptions and prejudices concerning human society and nature which are no more objective or justifiable than those of the ancient and mediaeval philosophers and theologians.

> The secular as a domain had to be instituted or imagined, both in theory and in practice. This institution is not correctly grasped in merely negative terms as a desacralization. It belongs to the received wisdom of sociology to interpret Christianity as itself an agent of sacralization, yet this thesis is totally bound up with the one-sided negativity of the notion of desacralizing; a metaphor of the removal of the superfluous and additional to leave a residue of the human, the natural and the self-sufficient.[7]

So Milbank's crucial point is that the secular is not simply the rolling back of a theological consensus to reveal a neutral territory where we all become equal players, but the replacement of a certain view of God and creation with a different view which still makes theological claims, that is, claims about origins, purpose and transcendence. The problem is that this 'mock-theology' or 'pseudo-theology' is bad theology. Secularism is, quite literally, a Christian heresy – an ideological distortion of theology.

So we have a different picture: in the vacuum created by the confinement of God to the margins of human society and self-understanding in the period we call 'modernity' or 'the Enlightenment', something would enter to fill the void as a new theology in disguise. In other words, there would be some kind of transcendent principle or overarching narrative framework for understanding natural and cultural processes which would replace the mediaeval consensus. Milbank's key focus is on *power* as that which becomes the governing principle of modern thought.[8] The forces of nature and the forces of society – whether in the hands of a Newtonian, Darwinian, Nietzschean, Marxist or capitalist – are now understood as governed by competing claims to, or expressions of, power. To the extent that God was residually present in the new modern discourses of the seventeenth, eighteenth and nineteenth centuries, he was now an agent of power amongst other agents, albeit one with a newly conceived absolute power (*potentia absoluta*) which he could wilfully wield as a supplement to his ordinary power (*potentia ordinata*), this latter being, as it were, for everyday use.[9]

To refer to power is, however, only part of the story. Of course, pre-modern thought was much concerned with political and cosmic power. For Milbank, what changes in secular modernity is the *context* in which theories of power are articulated. Whereas the Christian theological understanding of creation understood *peace* to be 'ontologically basic' in expression of the eternal peaceful difference in the Trinity, now society and nature are understood to be characterized by an essential *violence* which must be controlled and tamed by the exercise of power. Creation comes to be seen as primordially or originally violent.

> Christianity, however, recognizes no original violence. It construes the infinite not as chaos, but as a harmonic peace which is yet beyond the circumscribing power of any totalizing reason. Peace no longer depends on the reduction to the self-identical, but is the sociality of harmonious difference. Violence, by contrast, is always a secondary willed intrusion upon this possible infinite order (which is actual for God).[10]

Of course it is the case that the mediaeval world knew much of violence and conflict, but, particularly following St Augustine of Hippo (AD 354–430), these were understood as *intrusions* into a created order in which peace is ontologically basic. Proper society was one which reflected such primordial peace. By contrast, in modern thought violence and conflict are seen to be basic characteristics of society and nature which we tame by the competitive exercise of power and the reduction of all differences to uniformity. God becomes just another agent of power – albeit a very powerful agent – in the project of *enforcing* peace.

An important concept which arises in the short quotation from Milbank above is 'difference'.[11] This reflects very clearly the character of Neoplatonic understandings of the order of the Church, society and cosmos which have heavily influenced Radical Orthodoxy's diagnosis of the character of modernity. For those prior to modernity who write in the broad tradition of Christian theology influenced by Neoplatonic thought, cosmos, Church and society are understood to be composed of a hierarchy of harmonious differences of natures, talents, characters, wills, desires and so on. This tradition receives perhaps its most influential expression in the works of the eastern Christian mystic Dionysius the Pseudo-Areopogite (c.AD 500), *The Celestial Hierarchy* and *The Ecclesiastical*

Hierarchy.[12] For Nicholas of Cusa (1401–64), who is perhaps the last mediae-val representative of Christian Neoplatonism, hierarchy was crucial because it embodied the difference of talents, skills, characters and so on, which should compose any body whose parts are mutually enhancing, whether it be the body of Christ (following the imagery given to us by St Paul in, for example, Romans 12.5 and 1 Corinthians 12.12–27), the social and political body, or the whole cosmic hierarchy. Within the hierarchical social or ecclesial body, an individual found a role, place and identity and, as such, was set free *to be a particular person* within a social or ecclesial whole. One's personal identity was under-stood more as a gift than a matter of the invention of the individual will. Simi-larly, within the cosmic hierarchy creatures find a place and identity. Each of these hierarchical unities was, crucially, more than the sum of its parts and just as real as any particular member of the whole. The identity of any indivi-dual member of the hierarchy was constituted in relation to other members. The celestial body was understood to be a real whole – genuinely a *uni*-verse, rather than simply a collection of individual things.

> But every concordance is made up of differences. And the less oppo-sition there is among these differences, the greater the concordance and the longer the life. And therefore life is everlasting where there is no opposition [that is, eternal peace]. On this basis you can perceive the basic principles of the most holy Trinity and Unity because it is a unity in trinity and a trinity in unity, and there is no opposition internally since whatever the Father is, so also are the Son and the Holy Spirit.[13]

Moreover, the ecclesial, social or cosmic hierarchies are not to be understood as 'top-down' with the those at the top distant from those at the bottom. God was understood by Nicholas of Cusa to be equally present to every point in the hierarchy: 'Thus one God is all things in all things.'[14] We also tend to think of hierarchy as necessarily authoritarian and the embodiment of inequality. In the end, for a thinker such as Cusa there was only one fundamental, irreducible difference within the hierarchy, namely that between God and creation. How-ever structured, authoritarian or differentiated the cosmic, social or ecclesial hier-archies might be, all are united as creatures before God. Humanity, as uniquely created in the *imago dei*, enjoys a collective equality before God. Moreover, for Cusa the more complex a hierarchy the more it contains within itself checks and balances in relation to power. Different parts of the political, ecclesial or cosmic body balance each other and ensure a measure of equality. To the extent that hierarchies become simple and 'flat', the opportunity for the accumulation and abuse of power in just one part of the hierarchy duly emerges.

In the modern period, difference – the difference between natures, cultures, viewpoints, desires, interests, skills, genders, wills and so on – came to be understood as harbouring the seeds not of mutually enhancing and harmonious unity, but of conflict. Difference could be regarded as the engine of friction, the source of envy, resentment and disagreement. This led to what is sometimes referred to as the 'flattening' tendency of modernity, namely the desire to era-dicate difference in favour of homogeneity and uniformity. The metaphor of 'flattening' is a deliberate contrast with the hierarchical and differentiated understanding of the Church, society and cosmos which dominated ancient thought and the mediaeval consensus.

An example of the flattening tendency of modernity in contemporary capitalist politics comes in the form of individualism which does not recognize society as anything more than a construct, or a haphazard, functional and incidental con-glomeration of individuals. This view of the dominance of the individual is often traced to the rise of nominalism in fourteenth- and fifteenth-century philosophy and political theory and it is the distant source of the individualism which is so often bemoaned in our culture today. Nominalism is the view that universals (such as 'society') are not real entities, but only the names for collections of individuals. Nominalism therefore suggests that 'society' is not real; there are only individuals who happen to coalesce in certain contingent ways *which are not essential to the nature and identity of those individuals*. However, such indivi-duals, who harbour different desires, needs, skills and the like, in pursuing their own self-interest which is not linked in any *necessary* way to the collective interest (because the collective – society – is not real), are always subject to violence and conflict insofar as those interests are mutually contradictory. So 'society' must be manufactured and, as William Cavanaugh argues, this is what occurs in the birth of the nation state in early modernity.[15] Social contracts are established whereby individuals give over to the central State or the monarch the means of violence and coercion (military and legal protection, the police) in exchange for the State's guarantee of the safety and rights of individuals. At its most minimal (and the politics of the right espouses above all things the rolling back of government), the State therefore exists to manage conflict between that which is most essential to human identity, namely the individual.

The tendency to see 'difference' as more a source of violence than the basis of collective peace can also be seen in the programmatic culture of early modern science. If reason indeed stood over and above the mediations of his-tory, culture or other circumstances, and was in principle straightforwardly accessible, then in principle approaches to truth, including the truths of nature, should be more univocal and uniform. So the culture of early modern science is at once concerned at any sense of contestable truths (matters of fact should be incontrovertible) while at the same time anxious to form social practices which minimize any potential source of disagreement, or at least manage its occasional appearance. Put simply, if what we mean by 'reason' and 'truth' does not depend on one's particular perspective, circumstances, background or history, but is a matter of objective and dispassionate indifference, disagreement simply should not arise. Thus Isaac Newton, David Hume and other key figures of the British Enlightenment were notorious for their abhorrence of disagreement. A culture of 'civility' arose in the form of a code of practice for the manufacture of matters of scientific fact which was designed to minimize the effects of 'difference'. The result was an intellectual culture which admitted to its membership only those of very particular social backgrounds, training and persuasion. Writing of the controversy between the seventeenth-century philosopher and political theorist Thomas Hobbes (1588–1679) and the natural philosopher Robert Boyle (1627–91), Stephen Shapin and Simon Schaffer comment that 'Managed dissent within the moral community of experimentalists was safe. Uncontrollable divisiveness and civil war followed from any other course.'[16]

Hobbes is perhaps the clearest example of a political theorists who understands violent conflict to emerge from a differentiated social body. In his great work *Leviathan*, published in 1651, Hobbes is struck by the natural state of conflict and self-interest which pertains between individuals.[17] He calls this the 'state of nature'. Hobbes does not mean that we are naturally selfish and lack any degree of altruism. His point is that, without government, there is no reason to act in any way other than to preserve one's own self-interest, most probably by violence. How, then, does one avoid the conflictual 'state of nature'? Hobbes argues that the only rational approach is to establish a social contract in which law (the courts) and violence (the armed forces) – the tools of protection – are handed over to a central, sovereign power, whether it be a monarch or government. That sovereign authority promises to keep peace through coercion in the form of law and punishment. Social relations are now mediated through politics, the law and economics, all made possible by the contract with the central, sovereign power. Religion becomes an entirely private matter and, indeed, the Church becomes a department of state and subject to the regulative and jurisdictional power of the sovereign. Leviathan swallows the Church.

Whether in the theological, political or natural scientific spheres, the modern period therefore regards 'difference' as politically and socially dangerous. It is the harbinger of violence and conflict, hence the need to 'flatten' difference. Milbank contrasts this modern opposition to difference with the theological understanding of creation as based on a supreme and peaceful harmony which is difference itself – namely the Trinity. Here we see an infinite and eternal difference which, *because* it is difference, is also harmonious *unity* (rather just a monadic 'thing'). In being an effect of this eternal harmonious unity, creation also exhibits a unity-in-difference, albeit faintly and analogously. In Milbank's work this leads to a critique of those modern forms of social thought which seek the flattening of difference and the violent imposition of peace understood as nominalistic uniformity. Difference is ontologically basic within creation and the character of the harmonious good. This is seen particularly in the visible realm in the differentiated body of the Church, the blend of harmonious gifts into a whole which is as real as its individual members.

In asserting the ontological priority of peace rather than violence, it is important to recognize the extent to which Milbank and those who have written under the Radical Orthodoxy banner are at this point reasserting an ancient doctrine of creation which is at once shared with the Jewish and Islamic traditions: first, that God creates *ex nihilo*, and secondly that evil has no positive foothold in being, but is rather the privation of the Good. Why are these important?

In his cosmological treatise *Timaeus*, Plato expounds a creation myth in which a demiurge orders a pre-existent chaos according to the eternal pattern of the Forms. Plato's successor Aristotle claimed that the cosmos is of everlasting time, and involves the bringing of order from chaos by means of desire for a final good. This ancient Greek cosmology, which had a huge influence on the later Christian doctrine of creation, nevertheless differed in one crucial respect from Judeo-Christian (and later Islamic) understandings of God's creative act: for the latter tradition, God creates from nothing. In other words, God does not have to master a pre-existent chaos. There is no primordial assertion of power or will by the divine. Unlike our acts of 'making', God is not constrained by any pre-existent material, and there is no 'before' and 'after' to God's creation (for God creates the 'before' and 'after' of time itself). The act of creation is a pure donation in expression of the infinite gratuity of God. It is therefore not an act of violent imposition upon a pre-existent chaos, but an act of pure peaceful donation. Within the theological tradition, the doctrine of creation *ex nihilo* is developed first as a doctrine of God: creation is an expression of God's sovereign, peaceful freedom. For the Christian tradition, the difference between God and creation inscribes the difference which lies at the heart of being itself, namely the Trinity.[18]

Parallel to the view of creation *ex nihilo* is the clearly Platonic and Augustinian notion that what is ontologically primary is the Good.[19] Evil is not something in itself, but only the absence of the Good, just as darkness is not something in itself, but merely the absence of light. St Augustine rejected the Gnostic and Manichean cosmology which understood good and evil to be on a kind of ontic plane of reality competing for power.[20] So any dualism of good and evil is rejected. It must be stressed that this is not a view of how we *experience* evil. Certainly we experience evil as powerful and real. It is, rather, a metaphysical view which recognizes that, before there can be evil, there must be the Good. This is to say that evil is entirely parasitic on the Good; it is a lack, or absence, of the Good, and therefore it is not some*thing* in itself. A chemical weapons silo, for example, is privative for it represents the absence of that which is primordial, intelligible, abiding and therefore real: true sociality and peaceableness.

Radical Orthodoxy contends that the Platonic–Augustinian doctrine of the primacy of the Good is replaced in modernity with a view that evil and violence are somehow primordial and have a share in reality.[21] In other words, evil is reified; it is turned into some*thing* alongside the Good. To the extent that this view of creation was already present in the ancient world in the form of a Gnostic and Manichean cosmology rejected by the ancient Church under the heavy influence of Augustine and the Platonic tradition, then modernity and secularism do not look quite so new. However, the Church was able to resist the tendency to think that evil is something, or that the cosmos features a fundamental duality of good and evil. How was it able to do so, and what changed so that our understanding of creation and our place therein became so focussed on violence and power in the form of a pseudo-theology? It is Radical Orthodoxy's contention that the shift in understanding is first and foremost theological; it is a change in the doctrine of God.

This leads us directly to one of Radical Orthodoxy's most important questions. If God had to be pushed to one side in order to be replaced by a fundamentally different and pseudo-theological understanding of human society and nature, how did this happen? What changed in our understanding of God such that God could be marginalized in our thoughts and practices? Those who have written under the banner of Radical Orthodoxy argue, along with many other twentieth-century theologians and philosophers, that it is theological shifts in late mediaeval thought which paved the way for the rise of the secular. In order to understand how this happened, we need to examine the understanding of God which was prevalent some time before the rise of the secular. So prior to the rise of modernity, prior to the fourteenth and fifteenth centuries, how did Christian theologians understand God, and how did that understanding form the core of the mediaeval view of the world? This is a tricky question, but answering it will bring into focus two of Radical Orthodoxy's key concepts: analogy and participation. I am going to shift perspective from the broad and sweeping description of Milbank's argument above to the much more detailed examination of a key text from the mediaeval theologian who has, more than any other, influenced Radical Orthodoxy, namely St Thomas Aquinas (c. 1225–1274/5). We will look first at what Aquinas has to say about the way in which we *speak* about God before we consider the way in which we understand creation's relation to God. As we will see, it is the change in the doctrine of God that later opens the space for the rise of the secular.

Analogy and participation

It is not at all obvious that we are able to speak of God. Why? Because our words are orientated towards finite things – the natural world, human beings and so on – and using those same words to refer to the infinity of God would surely stretch them beyond breaking point. Whenever we speak about God we would seem to use words more properly suited to creatures. Such speech must surely be futile, for God infinitely exceeds any thought or conception we might have of him. Yet we do speak about God, whether in schools, universities, seminaries or the liturgy of the Church. This observation – that we apparently cannot speak of God and yet we do speak of God – is the beginning of St Thomas Aquinas's consideration of theological language and the naming of God towards the beginning of his great *Summa Theologiae* (1a.13) written in the 1260s. How, for Aquinas, can we speak of God? In answering this question, Aquinas is not providing us with a theory of language which we might then deploy in speaking about God. Rather, he is beginning with some comments about how we happily get on with the business of speaking about God in prayer and worship.

There is one crucial observation which Aquinas makes prior to his consideration of theological language and it is important that we are aware of this context. However we speak of God, we must use words which we more commonly associate with finite creation. As Aquinas says, we name God from creatures. We are permitted to do this because of a principle which Aquinas accepts from Neoplatonism: effects resemble their causes. What does this mean? Think of a cause–effect relation, say a potter (cause) who makes a pot (effect). Does Aquinas mean that pots *look* like potters? Obviously not. He only wishes to say that any effect will express something of the character or 'style' of its cause. So a pot reflects the potter's skill, intention, imagination and creativity. In a somewhat similar sense (although of course qualifications apply[22]), because God is the cause of creation, creation will express *something* of the character of God, however faintly or tangentially. This is the basis on which we name God from creatures. At a more pragmatic level, Aquinas simply wishes to note that, when we speak of God, we use words which are more readily used of creatures. We know what it means to call a dog or a recipe 'good'; we should not be so quick to think that we can identity or define divine goodness, because such goodness is infinite and of a wholly different order. In order to identify what we mean by 'a good dog' or 'a good recipe', we must know what kind of thing a dog or a recipe is, for they exemplify goodness in different ways according to their natures. However, we do not know what God is, for God is not a type of thing. God is not just one amongst others, classifiable under genus or species. Yet because God is the cause of creation, creation will express something of its divine origin.

One of the most obvious ways in which we speak of God is figuratively or metaphorically. The Bible is replete with metaphorical speech about God, for example when we say that 'God is my rock'. We might understand metaphor in a number of ways, but most generally it should be observed that metaphors are *literally false* (God is not literally a rock). Yet they certainly carry a weight of truth which we would struggle to express in purely literal speech.[23] Metaphorical speech, in already being somewhat indirect and tentative, does not seem to present us with such an acute problem when used to refer to God for there is no pretence to be speaking literally or directly. Yet we clearly speak of God using more than metaphor. It is surely not straightforwardly metaphorical to call God 'good' or 'wise'. So how else might we speak of God?

There are two ways of speaking of God which Aquinas dismisses for a number of reasons. The first suggests that, when we make statements such as 'God is good', what we mean is simply that God is the cause of goodness. In other words, God is good because he causes goodness in others. This, however, is problematic: God is also the cause of bodies, yet God is not a body. Also, in claiming that 'God is good' means only that 'God causes goodness', the implication is that goodness belongs primarily to creatures, and only secondarily to God as the cause of that goodness. Aquinas avoids this approach because he wishes to maintain that goodness belongs primarily to God. Alternatively, we might think that when we speak of God we do so negatively. So when we say God is good we are not suggesting that we have any positive purchase on what it is for God to be good; we are merely saying that 'God is not evil'. Broadly speaking, this is the basis of what is sometimes known as 'negative' or 'apophatic' theology. At one level, Aquinas is deeply attracted to this tradition which refers to God not by a process of positive ascription, but by negating our conception of God due to its infinite inadequacy. However, Aquinas's reason for not opting wholeheartedly for the so-called *via negativa* is that in some instances we *do* speak of God positively, and we apparently mean what we say. So how might we best make sense of this positive speech about God?

Pursuing this question, Aquinas begins by pointing out that the words that we use of God might be deployed equivocally or univocally. When we 'equivocate', we use what is apparently the same word but in utterly unrelated ways. For example, we might refer to 'river bank' and 'high street bank', thus using the word 'bank' equivocally to the point where we might wonder whether we are, in any meaningful sense, using the same word. When we use words 'univocally' – literally 'with one voice' – the use is identical. For example, we might refer to 'John's wisdom' and 'Peter's wisdom', using the word 'wisdom' univocally. For Aquinas, when we speak of God we do not equivocate, but neither do we speak univocally. When we say 'God is good' and 'Samuel is good' we are using the word 'good' neither equivocally (in *completely* different senses) nor univocally (in identical senses). We are not speaking univocally because what it means for God to be good is not what it means for Samuel to be good, even though Samuel's goodness might be an expression of, or a faint reflection of, divine goodness. Does this suggest that there is an intermediate path between equivocation and univocation?

That middle path is known as analogy.[24] When we speak of God, we do so analogically. What does this mean? There are numerous theories of analogy which might meet Aquinas's needs in describing the way in which we speak of God, but we will consider those two which seem to have been most prominent in thirteenth century thought. The first is known as 'analogy of proper proportion'. On this view, when we speak analogically we do so in terms of two ratios or proportions. Thus we might say that 'as sight is to the body, so is the intellect to the soul'. This is a comparison of two relations (sight to body and intellect to soul) and might be expressed in terms of a mathematical proportion. For example, we might say that 'as 3 is to 2, so 6 is to 4'.

Is this satisfactory? No, and for two important reasons. First, if God is infinite, he cannot be subject to any meaningful ratio or proportion (as Nicholas of Cusa, the last representative of the Neoplatonic mediaeval consensus, made clear in the fifteenth century). Moreover, if God is to be subject to a proportion which can be compared to a proportion between two created things, this implies that God is essentially like creatures, only infinitely bigger. As we will see shortly, this presents serious problems. The second reason why analogy of proportion is problematic is because it seems to deal in identities or tautologies. In terms of the mathematical proportion mentioned above, 3 divided by 2 simply *is* 6 divided by 4. We appear to be saying the same thing twice rather than placing two different relations together in a revealing way.[25]

Although Aquinas does seem to discuss analogy of proper proportion in the *Summa Theologiae*, he clearly opts for what might better be described as analogy of attribution.[26] How does this differ from analogy of proper proportion? Imagine that you eat wholegrain bread for breakfast. We might call such bread 'healthy'. It is not, however, healthy *in itself*; it is called healthy by virtue of its relation to you because it makes you healthy. There is thus an analogy between healthy bread and a healthy human being. A human being is healthy *in himself or herself*, and health is *attributed* to the bread because it makes the human being healthy. The bread is not healthy in itself, but only by virtue of its relation to the person who eats it. Likewise, we might talk of a 'healthy complexion'. This is not healthy in itself, but is a sign of healthiness in someone. Similarly, we say that God is good *in himself*. I am good not in myself, but by virtue of my relation to God, for God enables me to be good and, in being a creature of God, I am a sign of God's goodness. Aquinas would say that the principal focus of the term 'good' is God, and all other things are analogously referred to as 'good' by virtue of their relation to this principal focus.

> This way of using words lies somewhere between pure equivocation and simple univocity, for the word is neither used in the same sense, as with univocal usage, nor in totally different senses, as with equivocation. The several senses of a word used analogically signify different relations *to some one thing* (*diversas proportiones ad aliquid unum*), as 'health' in a complexion means a symptom of health in a man, and in a diet means a cause of that health.[27]

There is, therefore, an analogy between my goodness and God's goodness whereby goodness is *attributed* to me by virtue of my relation to God.[28] It is not the case that goodness is attributed to me simply because God causes my goodness (Aquinas has already rejected this view), but rather because my goodness is a sign of God's goodness. In my goodness one somehow sees, albeit faintly and through a sign, divine goodness. Put another way, we might say that the question is not 'Is God good?', but rather 'In what sense, if at all, can I be called good?'

> When we say he [God] is good or wise we do not simply mean that he causes wisdom or goodness, but that he possesses these perfections transcendently. We conclude, therefore, that from the point of view of what the word means it is used primarily of God and derivatively of creatures, for what the word means – the perfection it signifies – flows from God to the creature.[29]

Aquinas is here stating that perfection terms – such as good, wise, living – are predicated primarily of God and secondarily of creatures. In other words, God is these perfections *in himself*. We have these perfections *attributed* to us by virtue of our relation to God.

For Aquinas, the matter does not end here. God also exists in himself. God is said to be simple, meaning that it is of his essence to exist. Whereas creatures are composed of many aspects or parts which we might or might not possess (and are therefore 'complex'), God is not *composed* in this way: God *is* his goodness, wisdom and so on. God *is* existence itself. We only have existence *attributed* to us by virtue of our relation to God as creator. Just as bread is not healthy in itself, neither do I exist in myself (I might, after all, not exist). Put another way, we might say that, in creatures, there is a *real distinction* between essence (*what* things are) and existence (*that* things are). So even existence, or 'being', is analogical in the sense that creaturely existence is due to a relation with the source of being itself, namely God. This is the basis of what later became known as the *analogia entis*, or the analogy of being. On this view, we only exist or have being *by virtue of a relation with being itself*, namely God.

However, analogy of attribution does present potential problems. On this view, only God exists *in himself*. To put the matter in Aristotelian terms, God is the only real substance.[30] All other existents – all creatures – are merely accidental or only exist in a secondary sense. This seems to imply something like pantheism. Pantheism is often identified as the theological view that the universe is 'God's body'. More generally, we can identify pantheism as the view that there is only God and that creation is not 'real' in any meaningful sense in itself. So as well as pantheism being associated with the view that the universe is 'God's body', it might also be associated with the view known as theological idealism, namely the idea that creation exists only and exclusively as an *idea* in the mind of God. No matter how we look at it, because analogy of attribution suggests that creation does not exist in itself, it seems that we are forced to concede that there is only God. Creation is a chimera, just a dream. That would be pantheism.

It is at this point that John Milbank, Catherine Pickstock and many others, following various Platonic and Neoplatonic readings of Aquinas, point to the crucial piece of the jigsaw which will complete the high mediaeval view of God and the concept which many see as lying at the heart of Radical Orthodoxy: the metaphysics of participation. The notion of 'participation' extends back to Plato and is no doubt crucial to Aquinas's view of creation's analogical relation to God. Following Aquinas, Milbank and Pickstock claim that there are still substantial entities in creation, but only insofar as they *participate* in the gratuity of God's *gift* of being. God bestows upon creation a finite participation in his own substantiality. In other words, creation does not have an existence by virtue of itself, but only and always because of the gratuity of God. The radical implication of this view of participation is that creation has no autonomous existence. Creation does not stand alongside God as another focus of being or existence, neither does it lie 'outside' God. When God creates the universe, there is not one 'thing' (God) and then, suddenly, two 'things' (God + creation).

> Creatures, for Aquinas, beneath the level of patterns of granted relative necessity and subsistence, are radically accidental. But not thereby, of course, accidents of the divine substance: rather they subsist by participation in it.[31]

In Platonic thought, the concept of participation is used to describe the relationship between the visible realm of becoming and the realm of being represented by the Forms. The former participates in the latter and has no autonomous existence outside this relationship, hence Radical Orthodoxy's emphasis on participation yields a non-dualistic reading of Platonic thought.[32] The visible realm of becoming does not stand alongside or in juxtaposition to the Forms in a way that might imply two foci of existence or being (dualism). Rather, the realm of the Forms and the realm of becoming are 'interwoven' in such a way that the visible, created realm which we inhabit perpetually 'borrows' existence from the Forms (and ultimately the Form of the Good) which are more real, eternal and stable. Plato uses many words to describe this relationship: *mixis* (mixture), *symplokē* (interweaving), *koinonia* (coupling), *mimesis* (copying), *methexis* (participation). All of these preclude any sense that the realm of becoming is autonomous.

Along with a number of other commentators, including recently Rudi te Velde and Fran O'Rourke, Milbank and Pickstock see a Neoplatonic participatory ontology at the heart not only of Aquinas's writing on language, but of his whole theology.[33] This is not, however, a straightforward recapitulation of Plato's scheme. Christian theology introduces the notion of creation as a gift of grace. At every moment, creation is *ex nihilo*, 'from nothing'. Its existence is a continuous and gratuitous divine donation in the form of an 'improper' participation in God's own substantiality. This participation is improper in the simple sense that it is not *proper* to creation. In other words, there is no sense in which creation has a self-subsistent 'right' to existence; at all times, creation 'is' only because of the gratuity of God.

Participation therefore avoids what might otherwise be a risk in understanding creation's relation to God through analogy of attribution, namely the pantheistic view that the only really subsisting thing is God. Participation asserts that creation is real, but it also asserts that creation's reality is not autonomous, but is a constantly arriving gracious gift of self-subsistent being, namely God. Creation is not simply a 'given'; it is 'gift'. A corollary of this is that creation *ex nihilo* does not refer to some kind of primordial temporal instant where God simply willed everything into being and stood aside. At every moment, creation is *ex nihilo*.[34]

The view that there are not two foci of being, and that creation has no self-subsisting autonomy but only exists by God's gift of participation in his own substantiality, is echoed in various ways throughout the corpus of Radical Orthodoxy writings. This doctrine of God and creation even governs the properly theological understanding of the relationship between human discourses such as theology, philosophy and the sciences.

> Participation, however, refuses any reserve of created territory, while allowing finite things their own integrity. Underpinning the present essays [in the collection *Radical Orthodoxy*], therefore, is the idea that

every discipline must be framed by a theological perspective; otherwise these disciplines will define a zone apart from God, grounded literally in nothing.[35]

How can this be so? Let us begin with theology whose subject matter is God and all things in relation to God. In so far as *everything* is fundamentally related to God (according to the metaphysics of participation, nothing created is wholly autonomous or self-standing), we might follow Aquinas and stipulate that theology therefore has no *specific* subject matter because nothing is autonomous from God.[36] Theology could be about anything, because everything is fundamentally related to God. We could not even say that theology's subject matter is 'revelation' because revelation is not itself bounded. Until the advent of modern theology, revelation is not understood as a discrete 'thing' or a packet of information; creation itself is revelatory of God.[37] So in a moment of apparently outrageous temerity, we might even say that theology 'tries to say something about everything', for everything is related to the divine.

In contrast to theology, other discourses do have clearly delineated and mutually exclusive subject matters. History deals with the past, the natural sciences with nature, medicine with the naturalized human body, psychology with behaviour and emotion, and so on. We might say that these discourses try, however improbably, 'to say everything about something'. Because the Christian doctrine of creation, expressed in terms of participation, stipulates that the *subject matters* of such discourses, because they are aspects of creation, are not autonomous from God, so neither can these discourses be autonomous from that discourse which pertains to God, namely theology. In other words, human discourses have to attend to the realization that their subject matters point beyond themselves to the transcendent. In so far as the subject matters of non-theological discourses are fundamentally related to God the creator, so those non-theological subject matters will be related to theology itself. The nature of that relation would require very careful and sophisticated articulation, but the central point for Radical Orthodoxy is that no discourse which seeks truth can count itself as wholly autonomous from issues of transcendent origin and purpose – that is, the issues of theology. However, this is most certainly not to suggest that other discourses are thereby collapsed into theology any more than it is to suggest that, within the framework of participation, creation collapses into God. We might even say that, in some sense, all human discourses 'participate' in theology by attending to the fundamentally *created* nature of their subject matters. Just as the metaphysics of participation points to the proper existence of creation which yet owes its created being at every moment to that which is being itself (God), so too the peculiar character of non-theological discourses must be maintained while denying that those discourses are self-standing and autonomous from, or indifferent to, theological considerations.

It is to this that Milbank refers when he makes the very provocative and now oft-quoted claim that

> If theology no longer seeks to position, qualify or criticize other discourses, then it is inevitable that these discourses will position theology: for the necessity of an ultimate organizing logic [that is, a '(pseudo-) theology' of some kind] ... cannot be wished away.[38]

It is also the basis for Radical Orthodoxy's refusal to admit the autonomy of any discourse, including philosophy, from theology.[39] Again, it is *not* the case that Radical Orthodoxy has thereby turned everything into theology under different guises. The refusal of the language of autonomy is instead the refusal of the possibility of indifference to the transcendent. In other words, it is the refusal of the idea that God is in any way irrelevant to the truth of anything.

The intimate relationship between theology and other discourses also mirrors Radical Orthodoxy's claim that faith and reason are inextricably intertwined, and that at no point does one enter a realm of faith having kicked away the ladder of reason. Why? Because having maintained that one cannot be indifferent to the transcendent – to God – one must equally maintain that *one cannot be indifferent to immanence and our created nature* to which belongs the reason that is peculiar to our nature. In other words, we do not see with a 'God's eye' perspective as the privileged recipients of a self-contained revelation accessed by an autonomous faith, but rather always understand from the perspective of reasoning created beings. Thus theology does not sit in pristine isolation from other human discourses, particularly and most obviously that to which it is most clearly related owing to the breadth of its subject matter, namely philosophy. The consequence of this view of the nature of theology is its constant and critical engagement with other disciplines. This is why Radical Orthodoxy, from its inception, has seemed to be a very ambitious sensibility which deals critically and theologically with an often bewildering array of subjects. It is also why Radical Orthodoxy often does theology 'tangentially' by discussing topics well outside those traditionally thought of as 'theological', from economics to physics to the body.

It is Radical Orthodoxy's contention, however, that in its peculiarly modern guise theology has become just another discipline alongside others. On the one hand, neo-orthodox and conservative theologies (exemplified by the early Barth) have tended to shore up theology's identity and legitimacy by defining a peculiar subject matter, usually revelation. On the other hand, liberal theologies have tended to dissolve theology into apparently more fundamental disciplines in such a way that theology becomes merely the religious dimension of history, natural science, anthropology, sociology or philosophy. This is part of what Milbank calls theology's 'false humility' whereby it attempts to take its place alongside other disciplines and discourses, thus leaving behind a vacuum which is filled by the pseudo-theology of power and violence. This is the invention of the secular.

How did we move from an analogical participatory doctrine of creation in which there was no secular space – no arena devoid of reference to the divine – to a situation in which theology and religion are the marginal preserve of the credulous and weak-minded, and the pseudo-theology of secular late modernity, with all its attendant arbitrary assumptions, holds sway? It is Radical Orthodoxy's contention that the beginnings of this shift are to be found in the forgetting of participation in the late Middle Ages and the rise of the view that there are two foci of existence sharing a common being. In other words, creation comes to be seen as existing autonomously in such way that it becomes possible to be indifferent between finite and infinite being. How did this come about?

Univocity of Being and the creation of secular space

In the generation following Aquinas, his analogical understanding of the relation between God and creation was radically recast. Radical Orthodoxy, following the lead of numerous prominent scholars of mediaeval theology and philosophy, has seen the work of John Duns Scotus (c.1265–1308) as of particular – although by no means exclusive – importance. Scotus ushered in two important moves away from the Neoplatonic–Aristotelian consensus: the univocity of being and an understanding of knowledge as representation. I will address these briefly in turn.

As we have seen, for Aquinas there is no abstract 'being' separate from God; the divine is *ipsum esse*, or 'being itself'. In God, being and existence wholly coincide and hence God is known as one and therefore simple. Created being, or *esse commune* ('being in common') is *composed* in the sense that essence does not coincide with existence; any creature might not be, and thus essence (*what* something is) and existence (*that* something is) are not one but 'mixed'. Created being exists analogically because being is predicated primarily of God (God *is* being) and is *attributed* to creatures by participation. There are myriad implications of this understanding of the relation between finite and infinite which will be explored later in this Reader. For now it is important to note that 'being' is not an abstract concept common to creator and creature. Rather, insofar as all creatures 'are' because they participate in being itself (*esse ipsum*), creatures are known pre-eminently as they exist in the divine *logos*.

This metaphysics of participation is radically re-thought by Scotus in a highly complex fashion. To put things very simply, Scotus conceives God and creatures as falling under a common concept of 'being'. This 'being' applies to finite and infinite *in the same way*, hence Scotus calls this concept *univocal* between God and creatures. For Aquinas, God and creatures are sheerly different (the former being 'self-subsistent being', the latter sharing mysteriously in that being by 'participation'), this later becoming known as 'the ontological difference'. For Scotus, on the other hand, this 'difference' between finite and infinite is rethought. God now has a more intense and infinite being which is possessed to a lesser extent, but in essentially the same way, by creatures.

Why does this matter? Imagine that, as a creature, you wish to 'ascend' to God. Commencing from finite creaturely being, you begin to traverse the 'space' between creaturely, finite being and infinite divine being. If God's being is now understood as infinitely greater than creaturely being but essentially the same, that space between God and creatures will itself be infinitely great. Can one traverse that infinite space between God and creatures? No, because no matter how far one travels, there will still be an infinite distance to traverse. Paradoxically, whereas we might think that placing God and creation under a single univocal concept called 'being' might make God less 'other' or less 'distant', the opposite occurs. An infinite quantitative 'sea of sameness' (that is, univocal being) is established between God and creation. The consequence of this shift in the doctrine of God is that God becomes a distant object who can only be the focus of a superstitious faith which is separate from reason.

The interpretation of Scotus on this point is controversial and complex, and the essay by Catherine Pickstock in this volume seeks to do justice to this complexity (see Chapter 4). Even where commentators nuance Scotus's position and articulate his reasons for rejecting the metaphysics of participation and analogy of attribution in favour of some form of univocity, the valuation of this shift varies enormously. For Radical Orthodoxy, Scotus's work marks a crucial staging post in the move towards what is often referred to as 'the bracketing' of God, which is characteristic of the modern period. Here, the question of God and theology becomes marginal ('bracketed') because God is understood to lie at the far side of an untraversable infinite sea of being. Thus God is distant, and this distance opens up the possibility of a space for which God is largely irrelevant. This space is autonomous, self-standing and self-governed. This is the invention of the secular.

At the same time, because God is understood univocally as 'good' or 'just' in the same way as you or I might be 'good' or 'just', only infinitely more so, God comes to be understood in anthropomorphic terms as rather like an infinitely large person, a cause alongside other causes in the universe, or an object amongst other objects in the field of our attention. This is the God of modern theology and philosophy. It is the contention of Radical Orthodoxy that the God in whom people do not believe today is this God of modernity, not the God of orthodox, pre-modern Christian theology.[40]

Another aspect of Scotus's thought which is rather less controversial amongst commentators concerns knowledge as representation. To what does this refer? For those prior to the fourteenth century who lie within the broad tradition of Christian Platonism, knowledge is understood in a particular way in terms of abstraction. For example, as I know a tree it is clear that the matter of the tree cannot enter my mind. However, my mind can abstract the *form* of the tree. The tree, as it were, 'repeats itself' in my intellect. My intellective soul in turn refers this abstraction to the Form or Idea of 'tree' – namely, what a tree truly is in the mind of God.[41] Thus I know the particular object in front of me as a tree and not a boat, and as a certain tree of particular beauty. The crucial point in this rather strange understanding of knowledge is that the form of the tree really does enter the intellect of the knower, and thus knowing the tree is as much an aspect of the life of the tree as it is of the knower. Moreover, my knowledge of the tree is not just a *representation* of the tree; it really is the form of the tree.

For Scotus – and few would claim that this is not an important element in his thought – knowledge is understood in terms of representation. My knowledge of a tree is rather akin to my mind taking a snapshot of the tree as if my mind were a camera. So what I know is not the tree itself, but *only a representation of the tree*. This is significant for two reasons. First, representations can be the cause of mistrust. In other words, my representational knowledge of the tree can be called into doubt because it is only a representation – a picture or snapshot, if you like. Understood in this way, the knowledge which comes from our senses can be the object of suspicion and doubt, and hence knowledge as representation is often regarded as the beginnings of a peculiarly modern form of scepticism. A corollary of this provides the second reason why knowledge as representation in Scotus is important. Because knowledge is now somewhat problematic, the focus for philosophy shifts from *what* we know (in which ontology (the what) and epistemology (the knowledge) are intertwined) to *how* we know what we know. This therefore marks the invention of an autonomous and particular variant of philosophy which has become of almost exclusive concern in the modern period, namely epistemology – the study of how we know what we know. It also marks the point at which we can know things without what Catherine Pickstock calls 'real ontological elevation'. Under the Platonic scheme outlined above, created beings are known by reference to the divine – that is, fundamentally, theologically through 'elevation' towards participation in God's own knowledge. With knowledge understood as representation (as Milbank makes clear in Chapter 1), created beings are known without reference to God and simply are *as they appear to be to us*, in our representation of them (this being the beginning of the long road to the modern philosophies of thinkers as diverse as Kant and Locke). We do not know things in themselves (however falteringly or partially), but only *representations* of those things. What we see of creation is rather like flicking through a family album of holiday snapshots rather than being on holiday in person.

Radical Orthodoxy therefore contends that the invention of the secular – namely, a space understood as autonomous from the transcendent, and subject matters which make no reference (or idolatrous reference) to the transcendent – begins with *theological* shifts many centuries ago and cannot be accounted for in terms of bald human progress or the dismantling of religion by the force of a new science or rationality. Moreover, because the secular – in particular, modern philosophy understood as metaphysics which prioritizes being as indifferent as between finite and infinite – finds its genesis in theological shifts, it cannot diagnose either the nature of its own beginnings or the solution to its own problems. Hence, as Milbank so provocatively claims, 'only theology overcomes metaphysics'.[42] Does this therefore suggest a nostalgic return to the theology and politics of the high middle ages? No. Rather, Radical Orthodoxy, in being another movement of *ressourcement*, argues that the riches of the orthodox Christian tradition of faith and reason, theology and philosophy, can be deployed not only as *a* possible solution to the problems of late modernity, but as *the only* solution. That application will provoke some very radical conclusions concerning the signs of our times and the renewal of society.

This introduction is very far indeed from a complete characterization of Radical Orthodoxy. The texts of this Reader seek to demonstrate the variety of ways in which the riches of Christian orthodoxy are brought to bear on the problems of late modernity in radical ways. For example, we will see in many of the contributions to this volume the narrative and Christological understanding of truth which are equally definitive of Radical Orthodoxy, as well as the ways in which Radical Orthodoxy regards our condition of late modernity as an opportunity to think again about the possibility of a genuinely Christian imagination.

Notes

1   See Eamon Duffy, *The Stripping of the Altars: Traditional Religion in England 1400–1580*, New Haven and London: Yale University Press, 1992; John Milbank, Catherine Pickstock and Graham Ward (eds), *Radical Orthodoxy: A New Theology*, London: Routledge, 1999, p.1; Simon Oliver, 'What can Theology offer Religious Studies?' in Simon Oliver

and Maya Warrier (eds), *Theology and Religious Studies: An Exploration of Disciplinary Boundaries*, London: T&T Clark, 2008.

2   Charles Taylor, *A Secular Age*, Cambridge, MA, and London: The Belknap Press of Harvard University Press, 2007, pp.1–22 and passim.

3   Duffy (see Note 1); John Bossy, *Christianity in the West 1400–1700*, Oxford: Oxford University Press, 1985.

4   On the separation of nature and culture in modernity, see Simon Oliver, 'The Eucharist before Nature and Culture', *Modern Theology* 15(3) (1999), pp. 331–53.

5   Alasdair MacIntyre, *After Virtue*, London: Duckworth, 1984, and ibid., *Whose Justice? Which Rationality?* London: Duckworth, 1988.

6   See Stephen Toulmin, *Return to Reason*, Cambridge, MA: Harvard University Press, 2003. See also chapter 2 of this volume.

7   John Milbank, *Theology and Social Theory: Beyond Secular Reason*, 2nd edn, Oxford: Blackwell, 2006, p.9.

8   In this sense, it would not be off the mark to see Milbank's early work as a protracted critical response to Christianity's most trenchant critic and theoretician of power, namely Nietzsche and his successors.

9   See Amos Funkenstein, *Theology and the Scientific Imagination from the Middle Ages to the Seventeenth Century*, Princeton, NJ: Princeton University Press, 1986, p.124. This shift can be seen very clearly with reference to divine action. For theologians influenced by the Neoplatonism of the Church in antiquity to the high Middle Ages, God is the primary cause of creation in whom all secondary and tertiary causes participate. In other words, God sustains creation in existence at every moment and makes possible causation within creation. God is the *primary* cause of this book being written (in the sense that God created and sustains its authors), but the authors are nevertheless real and potent *secondary* causes of the book being written. God's causing this book is *not* the same as (not univocal with) my causing this book. Put simply, were it not for God I would not be here to write this book. In the modern period, God becomes a cause amongst other causes, exercising his power in a (univocal) way which competes with natural causes ('did I do that, or was it God?'). This leads to some very unhelpful discussions concerning whether or not God causes certain events to happen. On the hierarchy of causes, see St Thomas Aquinas, *Commentary on the Book of Causes*, trans. Vincent A. Guagliardo, OP, Charles R. Hess, OP, and Richard C. Taylor, Washington, DC: The Catholic University Press of America, 1996. On Newton's understanding of God as 'pantakrator' (the all-powerful), see Simon Oliver, *Philosophy, God and Motion*, London: Routledge, 2005, ch.6.

10 Milbank, *Theology and Social Theory* (see Note 7), pp.5–6.

11 This might momentarily remind us of Jacques Derrida's concept of *différance*. While it is certainly related, it must be remembered that Derrida's concept has a very specific purpose in the context of his philosophy of speech, writing and presence. *Différance* (with an 'a') is, of course, not a word: it a neologism of sorts which is related to the verb *différer* (which means both to defer and to differ), *la différence* (the difference) and *différant* (the verbal adjective – the condition of differing, or deferring). Derrida is pointing to the meaning of language in terms of the difference between terms and the constant deferral of meaning. For an introduction to Derrida's importance for theology (positive or negative), see Graham Ward, 'Why is Derrida Important for Theology?', *Theology* 95 (1992), pp.263–70.

12 See Pseudo-Dionysius, *The Complete Works*, trans. Colm Luibheid, New York: Paulist Press, 1987.

13 Nicholas of Cusa, *The Catholic Concordance*, trans. Paul E. Sigmund, Cambridge: Cambridge University Press, 1991, Book 1 para. 6.

14 Ibid., Book 1 para. 4.

15 See chapter 11 of this volume.

16 Steven Shapin and Simon Schaffer, *Leviathan and the Air-pump: Hobbes, Boyle and the Experimental Life*, Princeton, NJ: Princeton University Press, 1985, p.152. See also

Steven Shapin, *A Social History of Truth: Civility and Science in Seventeenth-Century England*, Chicago and London: University of Chicago Press, 1994; and Catherine Pickstock, *After Writing: On the Liturgical Consummation of Philosophy*, Oxford: Blackwell, 1999, pp.146–58.

17 Thomas Hobbes, *Leviathan*, ed. J. C. A. Gaskin, Oxford: Oxford University Press, 1996, part 1 ch.13.

18 Milbank, *Theology and Social Theory* (see Note 7), p.431; Simon Oliver, 'Trinity, Motion and Creation *Ex Nihilo*', in Carlo Cogliati, David Burrell, Janet Soskice and William Stoeger (eds), *Creation and the God of Abraham*, Cambridge: Cambridge University Press, 2009.

19 The following comments certainly apply to the whole of Milbank's *Theology and Social Theory* (see Note 7), and are made more explicit still in his *Being Reconciled: Ontology and Pardon*, London: Routledge, 2004.

20 See Gillian Evans, *Augustine on Evil*, Cambridge: Cambridge University Press, 1982. A good contemporary cultural example of Manichean dualism can be seen in the *Star Wars* films.

21 See Milbank, *Being Reconciled* (see Note 19), pp.1–24 and *Theology and Social Theory* (see Note 7), pp.438–40. See also Conor Cunningham's crucial work *Genealogy of Nihilism*, London: Routledge, 2000, in which he argues that the advent of modernity inaugurates a nihilistic ontology – an ontology of 'lack' or 'absence' – which at once reifies the *nihil*.

22 As David Burrell points out when writing of Aquinas on religious language:

> We cannot speak of God at all, in other words, unless it be under the rubric of 'the first cause of all'. Yet such a cause leaves no proper traces since its *modus operandi* cannot conform to the ordinary patterns whereby effect resembles cause ... None the less, Aquinas claims that certain expressions can be trusted to 'signify something that God really is', in the face of the two-fold manner in which we know 'they signify something imperfectly'. His claim appears to turn on a special class of expressions: 'words like "good" and "wise"'. Since this class is defined by the capacity of its members to function appropriately across quite diverse genera, these expressions have been singled out as analogous terms (David Burrell, *Aquinas: God and Action*, London: Routledge, 1979, pp.60–61).

In other words, analogous (perfection) terms (unlike the metaphorical) have a very broad frame of reference, sufficiently broad to refer to the divine (but not, of course, univocally).

23 Of course it is the case that metaphorical speech is not really the primary problem; it is far from clear how we might speak *literally* of anything, let alone God.

24 St Thomas Aquinas, *Summa Theologiae*, 1a.13.5.

25 John Milbank and Catherine Pickstock, *Truth in Aquinas*, London: Routledge, 2001, p.50.

26 We need to be very careful with terminology. In Greek, 'analogy' literally means 'proportionality'. Hence when Aquinas follows the broad tradition of Aristotle in his discussion of religious language and uses terms such as *proportiones* we might think that he is espousing a variant of analogy of proportion. However, this would not be true to Aquinas's text since he does not propose an understanding of religious language as proportional relationship amongst a range of uses.

27 Aquinas, *Summa Theologiae*, 1a.13.5.

28 In addition to being referred to as 'analogy of attribution', this variant of analogy is sometimes known as 'analogy by reference to one focal meaning', or, as Aristotle termed it, *pros hen* ambiguity (meaning 'in relation to one').

29 Aquinas, *Summa Theologiae*, 1a.13.7.

30 In Aristotelian terms, 'substance' (*ousia*) does not mean some kind of material stuff. The metaphysics of substance is extremely complex. Generally, a substance is something which exists in itself rather than through another. Whiteness, for example, is not

a substance, for it only exists in white things. A dog, however, may be considered a substance.

31   Milbank and Pickstock (see Note 25), p.35. Some may note the link with Pickstock's reading of Aquinas's doctrine of transubstantiation in *After Writing* (see Note 16), pp.259–66. Aquinas uses the concept of 'accident' in a very unAristotelian fashion when he claims that the accidents of bread and wine which persist after the consecration do not qualify the substance of the body and blood of Christ. They are, paradoxically, 'free-floating'. In a sense, the Eucharist is a recapitulation of creation: creation is an accident, but not an accident of the divine substance. It is, by grace, 'free-floating'. The transubstantiation at the Eucharist is therefore a Christological reassertion that creation itself is an act of pure grace.

32   Pickstock (see Note 16), pp.3–46.

33   See Rudi te Velde, *Participation and Substantiality in Thomas Aquinas*, Leiden: Brill, 1995 and *Aquinas on God: The Divine Science of the* Summa Theologiae, Aldershot: Ashgate 2006; Fran O'Rourke, *Pseudo-Dionysius and the Metaphysics of Aquinas*, Notre Dame, IN: University of Notre Dame Press, 1997.

34   This is what distinguishes the theological doctrine of creation *ex nihilo* from so-called Big Bang cosmology. Creation *ex nihilo* does not privilege any particular moment as being 'the moment of creation'. At every moment, creation is 'suspended' over nothingness.

35   Milbank et al., *Radical Orthodoxy* (see Note 1), p.3.

36   How Aquinas identifies 'theology' is, of course, a matter of contention. There is that theology which pertains to philosophy and that theology which pertains to *sacra doctrina*, or the 'holy teaching' of the Church. Here I refer to the latter which in turn participates in *scientia divina*, God's own knowledge.

37   See John Montag's very important essay 'Revelation: The False Legacy of Suarez' in Milbank et al., *Radical Orthodoxy* (see Note 1).

38   Milbank, *Theology and Social Theory* (see Note 7), p.1.

39   See chapter 3 of the present volume.

40   This is the particular contention of Michael Buckley's highly influential *At the Origins of Modern Atheism*, New Haven and London: Yale University Press, 1987.

41   On Ideas in the mind of God, see St Thomas Aquinas, *Summa Theologiae* 1a.15.

42   John Milbank, 'Only Theology Overcomes Metaphysics' in idem., *The Word Made Strange*, Oxford: Blackwell, 1999, ch.2.

Chapter 1

Rupert Shortt (ed.)

Radical Orthodoxy: a conversation

SHORTT: No survey of contemporary Anglophone theology can leave Radical Orthodoxy out of the picture. Though it has divided the critics, at times sharply, there's
ready agreement about the momentousness of the movement inaugurated by you,
John, in association with Catherine Pickstock, Graham Ward and others, in the
early 1990s. We'll naturally need to consider the cavils in some detail, but I'd like
to set the scene with a stripped-down account of your work.

Close to the heart of Radical Orthodoxy lies the immodest, but in your view
vital, belief that Christian thought has to give a plausible and self-confident account
of the whole world. You are saying that unless theology can evoke a coherent universe
in which other things fit, then it becomes a dreary kind of ecclesiastical house-
keeping or settles down into what Donald MacKinnon used to call ecclesiological
fundamentalism. One just talks about the Church. And although Radical Orthodoxy is sometimes thought of as a very Church-dominated or in-house discourse, it
could be argued that the opposite is true.

But how can this be done in a highly secular climate like ours? Your answer derives
from the argument that much modern atheism is parasitic on bad theology. In particular, you maintain that somewhere in the late Middle Ages the whole doctrine of
God went badly wrong, because God got sucked into the business of running the

universe. The utter difference, the utter gratuity, of God's action was overlaid, and that led to what you see as two very ambiguous effects, intellectually and culturally: the Reformation, which tries to re-enshrine the difference of God, but does so at the expense of a robust idea of participation in the divine life; and then the Enlightenment, where a challenge is placed against unaccountable authority and tradition, precisely because authority and tradition are seen as inner worldly phenomena. From this springs a strong current of unbelief conceived as rebellion against the celestial headmaster.

A prime villain in your narrative is Duns Scotus. The specific charge against him is that he divorced philosophy from theology by declaring that being could be considered independently from the question whether one is thinking about created or creating being. Eventually this gave rise to an ontology and epistemology abstracted from theology. In the late Middle Ages and early modernity philosophers became preoccupied with the pursuit of such an ontology and epistemology, and the Reformation failed to halt the trend. On this reading of history, the sundering of philosophy and theology meant that theology lost its concern with reality as a whole. It fragmented, grounding itself on certain revealed facts, and issued in the authoritarianism associated both with Protestant Biblicism and ultramontane Roman Catholicism. Western culture thereby lost the patristic and early medieval sense that reason and revelation are not opposed concepts. As you put it in *Radical Orthodoxy*, your programmatic collection of essays:

> In the Church Fathers or the early scholastics both faith and reason are included in the more generic framework of participation in the mind of God. To reason truly one must be already illuminated by God, while revelation itself is but a higher measure of such illumination.[1]

I hope this introduction helps clear the ground a little, especially over the question of why the movement seeks to harness the apparently opposed categories of 'radicalism' and 'orthodoxy'. John, I wonder if you could take up the story by saying something about your background and evolution.

MILBANK: I think your report touches on the heart of what we're concerned with. We're not necessarily putting forward any one specific Christian metaphysic, but we definitely believe that in the end Christianity is going to be unconvincing if it's not connected to an entire coherent intellectual vision. Not a totalised vision in which all the details are set rigidly, but a vision in which all religious belief and practice connects with, say, nature, or the way you read history, or the way you act in society. And I think there is a fundamental conviction among all the people who inaugurated the movement that there's something unreal about a lot of quite sincere religious belief and practice at the moment, that too many people are looking at nature and society in a basically secular way, with spirituality tacked on. It's therefore right to point to Donald MacKinnon's suspicion of pietism as in fact a kind of secular phenomenon: this has had a very profound effect on me. In an almost Victorian manner he wanted to link Christian doctrine with a rigorous philosophy, and was very impatient of shortcuts and pretences.

SHORTT: He didn't teach you, did he?

MILBANK: He didn't. And in fact I've probably exchanged about two words with Donald MacKinnon in my life, but I went to his lectures and I would say that in an era when the norm in many theology faculties was disbelief in the Trinity and the incarnation, he successfully sustained an older kind of High Church tradition that had a profound understanding of orthodoxy. He was also linked, albeit critically, with many of the groups in the 1930s like the Christendom movement, and he was one of the last people really to understand the logic of Anglican divinity – in so far as this has truly existed.

SHORTT: What about your earlier career? You studied for a while at Westcott House, the Cambridge theological college, in the early 1980s, but decided against ordination. While there you were taught by Rowan Williams and another patristics expert you've identified as an important influence, Mark Santer. This was followed by the publication in 1992 of your book *Theology and Social Theory*,[2] one of the foundational texts of the Radical Orthodoxy movement.

MILBANK: Yes. After Westcott I did a doctorate on Vico, and later went to Lancaster University as the Christendom Fellow. It was a very exciting period to be in the religious studies faculty there, and I also interacted with perhaps the best sociology department in the country at that time – people like Scott Lash, John Urry and Russell Keat. I wrote *Theology and Social Theory* at Lancaster. Radical Orthodoxy extends the approach taken in that book, where I was calling into question the idea that the right way forward, if you're relating theology to other disciplines, is to see them as having their particular areas of expertise, and theology as having its own discrete sphere of competence, and then to bring them together. My argument was that the social sciences, if you dig into their history, may have already taken all kinds of theological or anti-theological decisions that you need to be aware of. And conversely, I was influenced by Nicholas Lash's view that theology doesn't have its own special subject matter: it's much more a question of the way in which the epiphany of God makes a difference to everything. That's why you can't detach theology from a certain view of society.

In the 1990s I and other younger theologians shared a concern that even some people we admired – others in the MacKinnon-influenced tradition I've spoken of – were slightly too caught up in questions of linguistic usage deriving from

Wittgenstein, and not sufficiently prepared for a full-blooded engagement with metaphysics. It was not that we wanted to abandon the linguistic concerns – far from it – but more that we felt that they were being dealt with in a manner that implicitly assumed that language or grammatical structures operated rather like a set of Kantian pre-given transcendental categories. This meant that a modern predominance of epistemology over ontology – of knowledge as knowledge of our mode of knowing rather than of things known – was still surreptitiously in place. To the contrary, one can argue that if one takes the linguistic character of thought yet more seriously and recognises that the linguistic mediation of reality always exceeds any determinations of a priori structures, including those which try to fix what language is capable of, then it becomes at least possible to suppose that our mode of knowing is continuously reshaped by what there is to be known. The 'question of metaphysics', in MacKinnon's phrase, then resurfaces in a way that does not take the 'critical' character of the Kantian critique for granted.

SHORTT: This was what propelled you to take Continental thought more seriously, given its greater concern with ontology in the wake of figures such as Hegel and Heidegger?

MILBANK: Yes. And although we didn't want to baptise some secular theory or other, as so much twentieth-century theology has done, we still found it very interesting that postmodernism was calling humanism into question by suggesting that there's very little mileage in trying to explain things in terms of purely human concerns or what human beings imagine is going on – including Kantian attempts to have a stable grasp of the processes and criteria of human understanding. Instead you have to look at wider inhuman forces at work, at that which flows through us, operates in, with and despite us. And, while these theories are obviously often nihilistic and naturalistic rather than religious, nevertheless there's a certain parallel between them and the theological desire to go beyond mere humanism.

Perhaps even more importantly, I think that many postmodern theories – perhaps in the wake of modern physics – have questioned the idea that you can get determinate meaning and clear certainty in any human field. So there has been a strong insistence all the time that when you think you've got definite meaning, or some clearly grasped area of value, you're deluding yourself, and in fact you're suppressing the questions, the ambiguities that always remain. And part of our case involves the claim that theology is on the side of indeterminacy, and of a certain authentic and inescapable vagueness, because if we live in a created universe which only reflects in multiple finite ways an infinite plenitude of meaning, then there is a sense in which everything is always somewhat partial and uncertain, veiled, fragmentary and never foreclosed. I think that's a theme which also arises in Rowan Williams's writings very strongly.

SHORTT: One of the corollaries you draw from this is that perhaps only theology can question whether a recognition of indeterminacy necessarily results in either scepticism or nihilism.

MILBANK: That's true. Only theology can teach us to live with uncertainty, because of our corresponding belief that we also have some remote approximation to the truth and hope for a final disclosure of mystery which will nevertheless not cancel out its unfathomable depths. And I've become increasingly aware that to some degree this isn't just a theological attitude, but that in many ways it informs some of the most sophisticated philosophical traditions. I know little about Eastern schools of thought, but certainly in the case of Platonists and Neoplatonists, we gradually became aware of the way in which notions of revelation, grace, gift, faith, myth, significant history and epiphanic ritual saturate their writings, and not just the works of the Christian theologians among their ranks. And so Radical Orthodoxy very much wants to learn from the researches of people like Jean Trouillard or Pierre Hadot and point out that philosophy was a religious practice in antiquity, and the Middle Ages were at least half aware of this. Philosophy, in other words, was not thought of as something done in a vacuum. In the Middle Ages, when you did stop, as it were, at philosophy, that was often linked to certain techniques of the liberal-arts faculty or certain regional areas, such as logic or astronomy. But when you look at the full range of issues dealt with by philosophy in antiquity, the borderline with theology becomes extremely blurry, because there's no real abandonment of the Augustinian sense of an integral wisdom under which all thinking and, indeed, all human life are only possible through divine illumination.

But this observation does not mean, as some people imagine, that Radical Orthodoxy takes Christianity to be a mere refinement of Neoplatonism. We have continuously acknowledged that the biblical legacy introduces a radical sense that God is personal and loving, that he creates, brings about developments within time, and orientates us towards an eschatological future. If, with other contemporary thinkers like J.-L. Chrétien, we tend to point out ways in which these new aspects were nonetheless remotely foreshadowed in Platonic tradition, and equally ways in which the Bible balances historical concerns with interests in cosmology, epiphany, mediating hypostases and participation, then that simply shows a concern to follow the latest scholarship in qualifying certain unhelpful dualities of the 'Hellenic' and the 'Judaic'. We also would wish to stress how Christianity is revolutionary with respect to both these legacies: eschatology becomes something already realised as well as yet to come; the final mystery becomes something concretely present in our midst, as well as something infinitely distant.

On our view, however, a sense of integral wisdom embracing both reason and revelation, both the perennial and the historical, does come gradually adrift, and, as you've said, Scotus is a pivotal figure.

SHORTT: Your critics, including other contributors to this book [*God's Advocates*] such as Christoph Schwöbel, say that your approach to Scotus is simplistic,[3] that he's an exceptionally complex figure. How do you answer this charge?

MILBANK: Scotus is indeed unbelievably sophisticated, and we've tried increasingly to do justice to that — those interested should read Catherine Pickstock's detailed responses to our critics.[4] We also think that there are many other strands in this sundering of reason and revelation. It certainly begins before Scotus with Avicenna, Gilbert Porreta, Roger Bacon, Henry of Ghent, Bonaventure and others. Nevertheless, there is a justified consensus amongst historians that the shift reaches its most consummate focus in Duns Scotus.

The overall upshot of this shift is threefold. First of all, there's the point outlined in your introduction: people start to think that you can talk about being before you come to talking about God. There's a marked contrast here with Aquinas, who says that only God exists of himself. Only God has the plenitude of being. When you're talking about created beings, you can never talk about them as simply existing, full stop. Only God exists without qualification; by contrast creatures, as Augustine taught, are a kind of blend of being with nothingness. And by the time you get to Duns Scotus there's been a switch to a different outlook, according to which something either simply exists or it doesn't; so finite things fully exist, and they fully exist in just the same sense in which God exists. The shorthand for this view is known as 'the univocity of being'. It means that we can speak in a univocal sense about God's being and the being of creatures because (despite many nuances in Scotus's writings at this point) at some fundamental level both God and creatures 'exist' in the same way, even though the manner of their existing in the concrete is drastically and even unmediably diverse.[5]

SHORTT: Thus from Scotus onwards, the tendency is towards the idea that creation is outside God in the way that the quadrangle through the window is outside this room.

MILBANK: That's right. And sure enough, if you look at Scotus's treatment of causality and grace and so on, there is a drift towards the idea that somehow creation makes a contribution that is all of its own, that it adds something to God's action, and this is definitely problematic. Admittedly, if the classical view is right and God is the source of all reality, and omnipotent, it's very difficult then to understand how there is a place for something else. But I think the tradition tends to leave that as a mystery. The risk on the Scotist view is that you've started to idolise God. You've started to treat God as if he's a very big thing, and it's undeniable that people do eventually start talking about God as coming under the category of an individual, which isn't the case in classical tradition.

Nevertheless, I think it's important to concede that the 'exemplarist' view to which Radical Orthodoxy is committed does, as I've just indicated, raise the question of why God bothers to create if things exist in him in a more eminent (meaning eminently different as well as eminently 'similar') manner. In the face of this question it can become tempting to insist that creation fully exists outside God's existence. However, the Scotist idea that creation embodies quantitatively finite degrees of the same goodness that is infinite in God leaves one with the same problem: Why add the finite to the infinite? One needs perhaps to say that in some sense the experience of finitude, of lack, of weakness, mysteriously 'adds' something to plenitude itself. It's a bit like the way the dependency of childhood is not just a deficiency, but something positive, later lost. But I think that thinking of this notion in a participatory, analogical context rather than a univocalist one would allow one to suggest, after someone like Sergei Bulgakov, that in some fashion God himself is still 'there' in this finite weakness, in this emptying out of plenitude, and that this is the ground of possibility for incarnation. If in future Radical Orthodoxy reintroduces kenosis, or divine self-emptying, as an aspect of methexis, or participation, our overall ontology will become better balanced.

A second way in which you can see Scotus's legacy relates, as I've said, to the shifting treatment of causality. In earlier notions of causality which were very much informed by Neoplatonic tradition, causality was seen in terms of 'influence' – literally a flowing-in – so that the operation of lower causes was caused by the operation of higher causes at an entirely different level. But under the model favoured by Scotus and some of his contemporaries, you have two factors exerting a shared influence, so that the sense of the meaning of the word 'influence' becomes different. You get the idea that divine causality is not simply operating at a higher level, but that it descends to the lower level and contributes a bit alongside the secondary cause that's contributing a discrete bit of its own.

SHORTT: Which in turn gives rise to some pretty unhelpful views about divine action?

MILBANK: It does. And part of our case here is that much modern philosophy is built on what appears to be a very unsophisticated and unmystical account of God: you can't talk in the normal vocabulary of facts and objects when you're dealing with transcendent reality. That's part of the argument of Michael Buckley, who's done so much to explore this subject with books like *At the Origins of Modern Atheism*.[6] At the same time though, it's important to say that Enlightenment thinkers can't be held entirely responsible for their misunderstandings, for the reason you've already given – that they were in many cases reacting against bad theology. And the third shift I would instance is towards something like an epistemology of representation. In the traditions of thought inherited from antiquity and sustained in the early

Middle Ages (in Anselm and Aquinas, for example), the idea is that when you know something, in a sense you are part of that reality, but in a different way. In your knowing the tree, the tree is, as it were, 'treeing' in you: thinking the tree belongs to the life of the tree, if you like. There's a famous book by Owen Barfield, a member of C. S. Lewis's circle, called *Saving the Appearances.*[7] While the scholarly detail in it is often wrong, I think the substance of Barfield's argument is very much borne out by recent research indicating that there was a shift in the Middle Ages from knowing by identity with the thing known (via the transmission of 'form' from the material object to our mind), to the modern notion that the knower is completely detached. This is the idea that when one knows the tree, one is in a sense taking a snapshot of it, developing it in one's brain. It's the notion that Richard Rorty calls 'the mirror of nature'. I think that when you combine that with this new idea of a univocal ontology, what you tend to land up with is a drift from ontology towards epistemology, because if all we know are the snapshots that we take, and if you can know something adequately without referring it to God, then you're on the road to Kant – to saying that what we know is merely how we know things, not a knowledge of how things are in themselves.

And I think it's very important to say at this point that none of us in Radical Orthodoxy is all that original in terms of our historical judgements. We're just trying as theologians to do our amateur best to make sense of the finest research done by philosophers and historians of medieval thought – people like Ludwig Honnefelder in Germany, Jean-François Courtine, Olivier Boulnois and Jean-Luc Marion in France – and they are increasingly saying that the whole Kantian turn is in many ways a complex and subtle footnote to the Scotist revolution, and therefore that it has deep roots in the Middle Ages. Terminology can get very complex here: Marion tends to insist, for very good reasons, that one should describe as 'ontology' and as 'metaphysics' only those approaches that were historically given those names. That means univocalist treatments of being were in general undertaken prior to theological considerations ('natural' or 'revealed'), from roughly the late sixteenth century onwards and actually no earlier (even though the ground for such comprehensive pre-theological 'systems' had long been prepared, as I have already tried to indicate).

The implication of this is, then, that Kant did not really understand what he was doing, for all his brilliance. He was not overturning all of Western thought up to that point: only completing a very recent mode of reflection by reversing it. This means that to call Kant into question is not conservatively to go back to the pre-critical, but to question the whole idea of pre- and post-critical pigeonholing, and I'd suggest that the real break came earlier with univocity. If that is the case, then the truth or otherwise of this break can be assessed only by theology as well as philosophy. Modern philosophy then has no autonomous ability to assess the conditions of its own genesis. This is the most radical and fundamental of all the claims made by Radical Orthodoxy.

SHORTT: Simon, you were taught by John as an ordinand in the mid-1990s and your first book, *Philosophy, God and Motion*, appeared in 2005 as the final instalment in the twelve-volume *Radical Orthodoxy* series from Routledge.[8] How have you been shaped by the movement?

OLIVER: I'd like to develop what John said much earlier about theology's relationship to other discourses, and theology itself becoming much more self-contained as a discourse in modernity. When I was studying philosophy, politics and economics as an undergraduate at Oxford, we read a good deal of British empiricism and Descartes, but with very little sense of the narrative behind philosophical thought that John's just outlined. The analytical and ahistorical treatment of philosophy places a very strong emphasis on the idea that reason is transparent and untraditioned – that is, something into which philosophy can directly enquire, and that stands over and above history, culture, practices and traditions.

After going on to Cambridge to study theology, I read the moral philosophy of Alasdair MacIntyre. This has been very influential on Radical Orthodoxy and on Stanley Hauerwas, another figure whose work has inspired many of us a good deal. MacIntyre's *After Virtue*[9] taught me that reason – in particular, for MacIntyre's concerns, moral reason – itself belongs within particular discourses; that ideas about it change over time; that therefore there isn't a reason held in pristine autonomy by philosophy or by science to which theology has to appeal, and that this insight can give theology a new kind of confidence. Studying the Fathers, Aquinas and more recent theology and continental philosophy with John, Graham Ward and Catherine Pickstock gave me a much more exciting theological perspective on fundamental issues. Catherine Pickstock's reading of Plato and the Neoplatonic tradition was a particularly important influence while I did doctoral research under her supervision. Although we rarely conversed, another influential figure was Nicholas Lash, whose seminars on religious language influenced countless Cambridge theologians. I remember a pithy comment of his which John has already alluded to – that theology says something about everything, while other discourses often seek to say everything about something.

SHORTT: And, as John has also suggested, this has implications for theology's relations to other disciplines.

OLIVER: Yes. What has proved very attractive for a number of younger contributors to Radical Orthodoxy who have often come from philosophy or other disciplines into theology is a refreshing confidence in tackling concepts that have traditionally been held solely within the purview of other subjects: for example, the concept of motion in my own work, or society in John's, or space, or time, or illumination. All these subjects were interpreted theologically up until the High Middle Ages: you find them being examined in Augustine, Aquinas, Anselm, Grosseteste and many others. Without being unduly nostalgic, I think there is something to be recovered in their vision of those concepts which is authentically theological and radical. It can't and shouldn't necessarily supplant the accounts given in other discourses, but it can certainly complement or challenge them. For example, the understanding of motion might properly belong to physics, and yet there could be other kinds of motion analogically related to the local variety which properly belong within the purview of theology, like the motion of learning or thinking.

MILBANK: Motion is a very good example. For a long time theologians, along with everybody else, would have assumed the final truth of the Newtonian laws of motion – that physical motion is all uniform, and approximates to an abstract paradigm that describes an ideal frictionless reality. Then along come physicists themselves and start to diversify the reality of motion once more, link it back to physical realities such as light, and deny its ideal reversibility. So it seems quite legitimate for somebody like Simon, then, to ask: Well, doesn't that mean that we should look at some earlier attitudes to motion within philosophy and theology, and relate those to what's now happening? I think it's a good example of the way theology can be wrong-footed if it simply assents to what the secular world takes for granted, especially as Newton's ideas were very much informed by theological assumptions – and assumptions of quite a strange kind, in his case.

OLIVER: Yes. Perhaps I could add some detail. If the universe is saturated with motion, and God is beyond all qualifications of motion and change, how does one have a proper sense of divine action within such a view? Newton, and countless others before him and since, struggled to find an answer to this critical question. Motion (which theologians and philosophers before modernity understood in very broad terms as both local and qualitative change) was seen as something that should not 'infect' the Godhead, because God should not be subject to the vagaries of change. One answer to the question of divine action is to place some kind of buffer between God and the universe, thus protecting God from the fluctuations of the cosmos. This is Newton's solution (a strategy adopted by many before him). He rejected the doctrine of the Trinity, and he understood Christ as the created 'viceroy' of God, putting into action the dictates of the supreme divine will. Christ is pictured as the bridge which keeps the universe from God.

Meanwhile – and this is a clear instance of an overlap between Newton's substantial, although largely unpublished, theological work and his physics – the absolute space which is so integral to Newton's *Principia* begins to take on the characteristics of an orthodox understanding of Christ. Newton speaks of absolute space as 'eternal in duration and immutable in nature, and this because it is the emanent effect of an eternal and immutable being'.[10] He also describes space as God's *sensorium* – his sensory medium, through which he might peer at the universe. One can see that God is detached from such a universe, and one of Michael Buckley's contentions is that Newtonian physics ushers in the separation of theology from questions of cosmology. After Newton, God is bracketed from our (scientific) thinking about the universe. Nature, including motion, is now within the purview of a wholly autonomous natural science. Science and theology are separated because they have their own discrete subject matters.

One might suggest that Newton's theology is simply eccentric, and peripheral to his natural philosophy. But this is simplistic. In *Philosophy, God and Motion*, as well as examining Newton's work, I attempt to outline the way in which, for Aquinas in particular, motion is not something from which God must be preserved. Rather, motion is the means of creation's perfection, and a participation in the eternal dynamic exchange of love between the persons of the Trinity. Of course, Aquinas is clear that God does not change (there is nothing that God could 'become' or which he could 'acquire'), yet this does not mean that God is a kind of static object. God is an exchange of love, and this exchange is reflected, albeit faintly and analogically, within the motions of the universe. So motion can be understood as a participation in the eternal dynamism of God. Meanwhile, far from postulating a detached divinity, Aquinas has a view of God's action which is utterly intimate and yet allows genuine causal power to created beings.

So the account of motion in physics and the account of motion in theology will not be univocal, but as I've argued, there may be analogical similarities and points of genuine tension. The same might be said of many other concepts: light, space, time, society, language and so on. It's not an interdisciplinary outlook which claims that theology must in some sense fit itself into other discourses by finding banal similarities, nor one that seeks accommodation with the rationalities, priorities and conceptualities of other discourses, as was true of much liberal theology in the 1960s and 1970s. Rather, this approach allows us to question fundamentally the very histories of the concepts that many forms of discourse so often take for granted and deploy unreflectively.

MILBANK: But nor are we locking ourselves into a kind of a laager in the way that some Protestant neo-orthodoxy has rather tended to do, simply inhabiting a universe of biblical or ecclesiastical discourse. Reintroducing an emphasis on mystery, and challenging the anthropomorphism of certain strains of theology, might represent some kind of advance, but it's not enough if it simply drives Christian thought into a fideistic ghetto. Nor does it explain how you get religious revelation and language in the first place. Take John Montag's essay on this subject in the *Radical Orthodoxy* collection."[11] He's resisting the idea that one should think of revelation as a bolt from the blue, or as a discrete datum that you could get hold of. On the medieval view, revelation always involved a special illumination of the mind which was also connected with a remarkable external event, or series of events. In this way revelation was still in continuity with ordinary reasoning processes – even if it also took these by surprise. For at this period all knowledge was seen as involving the synthesis of external with internal light.

And I think that both in the Reformation and the Counter-Reformation there's sometimes a danger of losing hold of this view, although I would want to say very strongly that we're not proposing some simplistic view of the Reformation. Both Luther and Calvin attempted to restore, against the later Middle Ages, a participatory vision to Christology, if not more generally, and the treatment of grace and faith was made once again more Christ-centred, compared with later scholasticism. Calvin, in particular, can be read in different ways. Unlike Luther, who remains basically a nominalist thinker, Calvin doesn't really have much of an ontology or a philosophy. Some later Calvinists – Ralph Cudworth or Jonathan Edwards, for example – in fact took Calvin in a way that we would regard as very sympathetic. So we wouldn't want to be read as saying that Calvin was simply part of a wrong turn.

SHORTT: I think you've now either anticipated or directly answered some of the criticisms made of the movement, but let's nevertheless turn more specifically to the queries, because there are some fairly entrenched ideas about what you're alleged to be saying. The unease, even among some of your admirers, centres on the audacity of painting with so broad a brush: they tend to say that the painstaking engagement with difficult and uncooperative detail can be absent from your canvases, notwithstanding the qualifications you've given. Another perception is that you don't allow enough for what Rowan Williams terms 'the sinfulness, the provisionality and the muddle of the Church: all subjects on which an Anglican may be expected to have eloquent views'. He adds that both the Reformation and the Enlightenment 'are unhappy episodes in the Radical Orthodoxy world, and while I'm no uncritical supporter of either, I would say that they're both, if you like, dialectically necessary worlds'.[12] In other words, the idea that authority has to defend itself, has to argue, isn't a bad idea in itself. Rowan Williams and others are also a bit sceptical of the idea that there was just one great theological fall in the Middle Ages, and instead acknowledge a need to ask questions all along the way. You've touched on this already, but might want to say more, given that the point crops up a good deal.

MILBANK: I'm not sure that Rowan is saying anything that really goes against our basic argument. I'm not trying to say that the kind of meta-history that we're talking about captures everything that matters. Far from it. Nevertheless, as I've suggested, I do think that a shift away from a participatory attitude, and a move towards epistemology and the turn to the subject, viewed as self-sufficient and autonomous, are things that one can see as very long-term trends. I entirely agree with Rowan that it's important that authority be asked to give an account of itself – this was indeed far more the case for theology and the Church in the patristic period than in the Middle Ages. Often eighteenth-century Anglicans perceived in the circumstances of their day a return to that more rigorous and desirable state of affairs – which tended to include also more of a refusal of any sort of coercion to embrace the truth. But this immediately implies that such desirable attitudes were not the unique property of the Enlightenment. In questioning the Enlightenment, Radical Orthodoxy is not primarily insisting on the need for authority and tradition: here we advocate only a kind of counter-authority and counter-tradition, which we perceive authentic Christianity to be. In doing so we expose the concealed but actually extreme authoritarianism of 'Enlightenment' as such. There's a link between advocacy of the absolutely autonomous free individual as the ultimate norm, and the subtle growth of totalitarian politics. How can one human will find room for itself alongside others save by the imposition of arbitrary formal rules by a central authority that requires unbounded power in the absence of tacitly shared social principles? Here one has the individual autonomous subject writ large as state sovereignty. The apparent advocacy of pure reason without the intrusion of emotional prejudice is always secretly the promotion of a cold will to power. Moreover, despite the eighteenth-century critique of 'the Middle Ages' (a fiction of course, just as much as the Enlightenment break is itself a fiction invented in a later era), it actually sustained and extended the voluntarism of late scholasticism.

SHORTT: I think that a possible difference between Rowan Williams and you, John, is that he is more favourably disposed towards Hegelianism.

MILBANK: Yes. I'm afraid that Hegel, for all his sophistication, is too much of a rationalist for me, and I don't really accept his kind of historicism, with all its unfolding, dialectically necessary moments. I continue to think that Vico offers a more subtle and more Augustinian – as well as more interestingly bizarre – historicist alternative. It's always a temptation to think that events are, from a human perspective, more than a complex set of contingencies, and I'm strongly opposed to the Whig view of history. So I don't think of the Reformation as something that was always likely to happen. There had consistently been drives within parts of the Church towards reform, simplicity, personal religion and so forth, but these cropped up among the Lollards, the friars, the humanists and elsewhere. Something quite other and more genuinely Catholic and mystical might have emerged, and indeed for a time, especially in Spain, certainly did. If Europe had seen the triumph of a kind of pan-Erasmianism, then it is not just likely, but probable, that a quite different sort of modernity might have emerged – one perhaps where the formalities of liberty, equality and fraternity were balanced by the constant attempt socially to incarnate the virtues of faith, hope and charity, rather in the spirit of Thomas More.

Again, if the Enlightenment is essentially rejecting bad theology, and yet also sustaining some of the assumptions of that theology (one can see both things going on, for example, in its treatment of 'natural theology'), talk of its being 'dialectically necessary' doesn't seem to mean very much. Yet Rowan is absolutely right if he wishes to insist that the Enlightenment properly took further demands that personal freedom, social equality and the fraternity of the human race be legally recognised and protected. But one can say this and also see Enlightenment social norms as a thinned-out version of Christian social principles. These principles entail, in addition, a vision of our inherent relationality, of the social realm as the constant exchange of gifts within one socially material body (as for St Paul), of creation as a gift that cannot be possessed, and of a possibly realisable peace of consensus and harmony linked with the belief that all reality participates in the infinite harmony of God. Without such faith, how can we ever trust that the Enlightenment-rooted demand that 'the freedom of each presupposes the freedom of all' is capable of fulfilment? Or perceive that it has already been anticipated for us by the incarnation?

Having said all this, I take Rowan's point to this degree. Late medieval philosophy produced a tide of extremely sophisticated, rigorously logical rationalism, and I don't think that when that's happened you can simply go back to what went before. But I don't think that critics of such rationalism – Pico della Mirandola, Nicholas of Cusa, or later figures such as Pierre Bérulle, Ralph Cudworth or Vico or Hamann or Coleridge – are simply harking back to a pre-lapsarian era. What they are commending are philosophical visions that diagnose the limits of rationalism. Although they can be read as in essential continuity with, say Aquinas, they can also be read as tacitly saying that without a better grasp of the role of metaphor, the imagination, narrative, language, history and human creativity, the slide into univocity, nominalism and epistemology is inevitable because an uninflected reason will be bound to favour these trends. In order to defend someone like Aquinas within modernity, one has to bring to the fore elements that were at best latent within his reflections. At the same time, the thinkers I have mentioned also showed how the notion of an 'uninflected' reason, taken apart from emotion, sign and symbol, and historical conditioning, was in itself a rationally unjustifiable fiction.

SHORTT: They see, more emphatically than in the Middle Ages, that it's not rational simply to think that only reason discloses the world?

MILBANK: Yes. Reason combined with ethical, aesthetic and poetic impulses may be what discloses the world. And once you become more conscious of that possibility, you have to allow that the imagination may be playing an enormous role. This is why I think that the counter-Enlightenment thinkers, in that they're stressing far more the role of the imagination, of art and narrative and poetry and so on, are quite different from medieval thinkers whom I admire, like Aquinas, or even Augustine (although in many ways he already inaugurated such 'humanism' with his reflections on music and language).

SHORTT: Again, you've partly anticipated another criticism that's sometimes made of Radical Orthodoxy, namely that the movement represents a failure of nerve masquerading as a recovery. This is the view of people who distinguish more sharply between philosophy and theology, both in their readings of figures such as Aquinas, and in their view of the methodology appropriate to Christian thought today. Could you comment further on your approach to theological reasoning?

MILBANK: I think Newman gets it right in *A Grammar of Assent*.[13] Argument will take you only so far. As soon as we get on to the issues that really matter to anybody existentially, we're into an area where argument serves an incredibly important purpose in trying to get everything consistent and in persuading people by saying: If you think this, then that would mean you thought that, and you don't really think that. This is what Socrates does all the time. But it goes only so far. For Newman, it's the mind that thinks, and we can trust the mind because it's a function of the soul, and the soul is linked to reality. This is what you have to believe if you believe in God, or in a transcendent ground. For if the ultimate reality is self-establishing spirit, then a share in this spirit must be his initial gift to creation, which is received by humans, among other spiritual entities. This may be shocking in the contemporary world, but if we're serious about our theological vision, we will be committed to strong accounts of the soul.

OLIVER: Another way of thinking about it would be to say that syllogism and argument are put to work very differently in someone like Aquinas, because he doesn't assume that syllogism is going to get him from nowhere to somewhere, which is essentially Descartes's move. In Aquinas, by contrast, there is already a vision or a memory. Indeed, memory is particularly important. A central theme in the work of John and Catherine Pickstock has been to address 'the aporia of learning' which one finds in Plato's *Meno*: how do we know what we don't know about? Plato's answer to this difficulty is that, when we come to know, we are recovering a memory, something that is primordially present in us. The issue is complex, but one might think of it as analogous to a sculptor drawing the sculpture from the marble in which it is latently present. Similarly, when we come to know, our knowledge is not written onto a blank canvas by reason. Rather, it is drawn from us by persuasion. Then we realise that in some dim sense we knew all along.

MILBANK: And even Aristotle has his own version of this when he says that the order of discovery is the reverse of the order of being. He also assumes that you've got some dim inkling of what the result's going to be.

OLIVER: This is why the notion of knowledge as illumination is increasingly important for Radical Orthodoxy. Our knowledge is corrigible, not because it's simply either right or wrong in a black and white sense, but because it's illuminated, but only to a certain degree. So our knowledge is always partial: it's dimmer or brighter, and in the end it's always illuminated from a single source. Crucially, there's only one guarantee of truth — only one source of light — which is God's own knowledge.

MILBANK: And in a sense, truth is self-authenticating. Otherwise it would just be a trivial truth like, you know, following the rule of one plus one all the time.

SHORTT: I hope that readers who aren't that familiar with Radical Orthodoxy will have got a clearer sense not only of what the movement is saying, but why it matters. It might be helpful now to turn the soil to explore some of the implications of your arguments a bit further. As we've seen, one of your core claims is that the separation of philosophy and theology held to have been triggered by Duns Scotus led to an impoverishment of both subjects. It eventually issued in a philosophy neglectful of the big questions about human destiny, and a theology locked in the prison of revealed facts, as I reported earlier.

One of the escape routes you commend most enthusiastically comes from the French *nouvelle théologie* of the mid-twentieth century: its pioneers, such as von Balthasar and de Lubac, also question the modern separation of faith and reason by recovering the patristic sense that to reason truly one must be illuminated by God. In other words, there is no human nature not already graced. Now it's this that's so dangerous in the eyes of some Protestants, given the Reformers' distinction between grace and nature, and their insistence that a corresponding gulf lies between 'Athens' (namely, Platonism and other forms of pagan reasoning) and 'Jerusalem' (that is, the purportedly very different outlook grounded in scriptural revelation). As we've seen, you both want to question this distinction. But in the eyes of those who wish to preserve it, de Lubac was downplaying the process of salvation; and contemporary Protestants have not been shy about bringing a similar charge against Radical Orthodoxy.

This debate might still seem abstruse to some, but in fact it has a crucial bearing on ways of understanding the relation between form and content in Christian proclamation, and thus for debate about the relation between the Church and the world.

I'd like to quote Fergus Kerr at this point, who sums up very eloquently the multiple identity problems faced by Roman Catholics – and by extension, other Christians too:

> is the way to be a Catholic these days to do your best to rethink Catholicism, to recreate Catholic sensibility, devotion, liturgy and so forth, absorbing positively … everything that is right and good and true and beautiful in Protestantism, the Enlightenment, and modern thought? Surely what happened at Vatican II was that at last the Roman Catholic Church accepted the truth of the Reformation? … Or, to continue this rough sketch, do you say that enough is enough, that we have taken on board more than enough … Karl Barth pointed out in *Ad Limina Apostolorum* that with these Catholic attempts to be modern … we have only bought into liberal Protestantism, with its concomitant individualism. On this reading, modernity is just too dangerous to assimilate … Look at what has happened to the liturgy, now entirely constructed around rationalist ideals of intelligibility, and, paradoxically, favouring rampant emotionalism. On this version of events, the only solution is for the Church to go post-modern – meaning by that, of course, a return to the pre-modern.[14]

At this point the picture becomes further complicated, because Radical Orthodoxy seems to lend itself to conflicting interpretations. Bridging the gap between Athens and Jerusalem is a strategy associated not only with yourselves, but also with liberalism – hardly a natural ally of your movement. Conversely, however, going 'premodern' in Kerr's sense places you alongside Barth, another unlikely bedfellow. Would you clear a path through the thicket here?

MILBANK: Continuing to try to make these issues less arcane, let's think of the situation of the Church, especially the Roman Catholic Church today, when it tries to speak in the public realm about moral and political issues. The dilemma is: do you speak on the basis of a natural law that should be available to everybody, whether or not they're recognising God, in which case it's very doubtful whether you're talking about any kind of natural law that the Middle Ages could have recognised; or do you, on the other hand, say that our positions are grounded in our entire Catholic vision, and here the obvious risk is that people will ask why they should listen. But you might also say that that's the only possible alternative course because, in fact, what we say only makes sense in terms of our entire vision.

I think that, by contrast, the route de Lubac's legacy points to would actually fall between those two stools, because for him it really does cut both ways: that throughout human history there is some remote glimmering of grace, there is some calling of God going on, and, on the other hand, the revelation we're headed towards is the consummation of an ontology of the human person, of the human spirit. So that kind of perspective would say that, speaking in the public realm, we should latch onto things that aren't completely unchristian, or that to some extent remain residually Christian. People still talk about forgiveness, reconciliation and mercy, and the idea that each person matters as much as everyone else, in a way that pagans, on the whole, didn't. And therefore we don't need to speak within a completely natural law-based kind of discourse: we can get people to try to see more deeply the implications of what they already think. This includes getting them to recognise that their vision isn't completely cut off from something that in the end resembles a religious vision; but it also doesn't mean that one has to start by overwhelming them with one's entire Christian metanarrative and ontology.

This implies that our discourse is always situated in a kind of in-between realm, which was where de Lubac and von Balthasar often sought to operate. Their approach is very easily summed up. I think they're saying that without God there really can't be any humanism, or humanism will always turn sinister, because if you try to take standards simply from what's given to our humanity, in the end that will come down to something like an extension of human power and pride. But, on the other hand, all theological discourse has to entail a form of humanism. It has to be an increased vision of what we are capable of as human beings under grace, and what is within our scope and capacity to see as human beings through divinisation.

So I return to the idea of a Christian humanism as an alternative Reformation and an alternative modernity. And here one can pick up again the relation to postmodernism: with it, Radical Orthodoxy refuses mere humanism; beyond it, it shares in the project of theologically saving humanism.

SHORTT: Let's look more at the future. Simon, what further ground would you like Radical Orthodoxy to cover?

OLIVER: It's certainly true that the *Radical Orthodoxy* collection of essays and the books we've referred to have been only a beginning. And, as John has said, while critics have thought that the movement has put together a totalising vision, that was never the intention. I think we've laid down a distinctive view of the relationship between theology and philosophy, and theology and other discourses. I'd like to see this area developed a little more carefully.

SHORTT: John has already mentioned the soul. Is this another area that calls for more work?

OLIVER: Yes, and I think that a much more sophisticated view of the soul has obvious implications for the mind–body debate, but a return to the soul is a natural progression of the rejection of knowledge as representation. John said earlier that representational knowledge treats the mind as if it's just a tableau onto which things are stamped. If we can stop thinking of the soul in Cartesian terms as a human 'hard drive', then I think there could be very interesting and radical implications for theological anthropology more generally. There might also be a connection with contemporary science in this regard, because physicists claim that observation makes a difference to what is seen, at least at a quantum level. As we've suggested, many medieval theologians envisage a genuine mutual interaction between the observer (the soul) and that which is observed.

I would also like to see Radical Orthodoxy engage more particularly with scientific culture, because this tends to set the agenda of so many debates within politics, economics and ethics. My own work is currently concerned with teleological understandings of the natural, namely the idea that nature is orientated towards specific ends or goals. This ancient view has clear connections with Christian eschatology – the 'end times' towards which we move, yet which are intimated in the present. For the past two centuries teleology has been largely rejected by natural science, yet it now seems to be provoking renewed interest.

The contributors to the *Radical Orthodoxy* series have provided fresh readings of, for example, Plato or Aquinas, precisely through not reading them through the lens of modernity and rationalism. So much Anglo-American Aquinas scholarship has nullified his thoroughgoing theological, radical and inspirational edge because he has been restricted to the agenda set by modern analytic philosophy. Nevertheless, it would be beneficial for Radical Orthodoxy to reflect further on methodology and engage once again with philosophical and theological texts right through the tradition with a degree of attentiveness and care.

MILBANK: I agree. At the same time I would want to add that many people who accuse us of being simplistic tend to be rather vague. They never say where we're wrong.

OLIVER: That's certainly true. Underlining what John has already said, I think it's also very important to remember that, although Radical Orthodoxy has produced genealogies, we're not concerned simply with looking for devastating crux moments in the history of theology or metaphysics. Scotus's univocity of being or representational theories of knowledge are very important, but the claim that they are important moments is always qualified. Intimations of these crucial shifts can be seen much further back. But I don't think our sense of history is so bound to finding 'singular moments when the rot set in', as if everything before that moment had been pristine. Rather, one tries to identify stages when broad, long-lasting and complex trends reach some kind of clear articulation and distillation.

MILBANK: More generally, we're telling theologians to take courage. Secular thought is not something that you have to receive in a fearful and trembling fashion (reserve that attitude for divine epiphanies!). It's something that you can come to terms with and comprehend and call into question. The trouble is that if you say that you don't want theologians to have false humility, then immediately you're accused of arrogance and triumphalism. On the contrary, all we are doing is trying to work out what would make theology even minimally plausible by not accepting its ghettoisation – which is partly the result of separating off the biblical from the Greek legacy throughout our Christian culture. (This is less true, perhaps, of Jewish culture.) But, of course, we're sinful beings; so we probably do need to be more hesitant in some ways. Not probably: certainly.

OLIVER: One thing that Radical Orthodoxy has reinstated is a medieval sense of the massive intellectual demands of doing theology. The movement is often criticised for the scale of its ambition. But I think the ambition and scope of the many and various projects that might come under the banner of Radical Orthodoxy are warranted. Otherwise, theology gradually becomes consigned to a ghetto where it becomes much more straightforward, delineated in its aims and, ultimately, parochial and dull. Radical Orthodoxy has blown that apart and said that we've got to realise just how demanding and varied the subject is. A moment ago John mentioned the need for hesitancy. Maybe also a degree of humility is in order. But John says quite clearly in the opening page of *Theology and Social Theory* that this humility should not be false. In other words, we should not be humble before other discourses or the assumptions of the secular, but humble before God and our task.

MILBANK: There are a lot of difficulties about that, because you run the risk of having excessively tight parameters. I would prefer it if people could express partial allegiance to the movement or rather to the ideas it seeks to promote. Inevitably it has been seen in party terms to some degree, but I think we're trying to move away from this. There are obviously several cognate movements that have a lot of sympathy with Radical Orthodoxy. There's the Yale School and other groups in the United States, or the people in Britain who are influenced by Lash and MacKinnon and Williams, besides many influenced by currents in phenomenology or in Thomism. In relation to the latter two, Radical Orthodoxy has maybe been exercising something of a mediating role. Recently I heard David Tracy of Chicago giving a paper in which he pretty much accepted the Radical Orthodoxy genealogy, and disavowed his earlier liberalism. So you get to the point where you've had your 'influence' and you've done one stage of your work and the hope is that it flows into a broader river. I think it was appropriate that the *Radical Orthodoxy* series stopped with twelve fairly polemical books, and that we're now going on to our new 'Illuminations' series,[15] which will feature a wider range of authors. The series includes people very sympathetic, partly sympathetic, and even hostile to us. It's trying to take this debate forward, and I hope to extend it also to cover the history of religions more than we've done hitherto.

Notes

1   John Milbank, 'Knowledge: The Theological Critique of Hamann and Jacobi' in John Milbank, Catherine Pickstock and Graham Ward (eds), *Radical Orthodoxy: A New Theology*, London: Routledge, 1999, p.24.
2   John Milbank, *Theology and Social Theory: Beyond Secular Reason*, 2nd edn, Oxford: Blackwell, 2006.
3   See Rupert Shortt, *God's Advocates: Christian Thinkers in Conversation*, London: DLT, 2005, p.97.
4   Catherine Pickstock, 'Reply to David Ford and Guy Collins', *Scottish Journal of Theology* 54.3 (2001), pp.405ff.; and 'Modernity and Scholasticism: A Critique of Recent Invocations of Univocity', *Antonianum* 78.1 (2003), pp.3ff.
5   See, for example, Duns Scotus, *Opus Oxoniense* I, distinction III, Questions I and iii, available in Allan Wolter (ed.), *Philosophical Writings*, London: Hackett, 1987, pp.4–8, 14–33.
6   Michael Buckley, *At the Origins of Modern Atheism*, new edn, New Haven, CT: Yale University Press, 1990.
7   Owen Barfield, *Saving the Appearances: A Study in Idolatry*, 2nd rev. edn, Middletown, CT: Wesleyan University Press, 1988.
8   Simon Oliver, *Philosophy, God and Motion*, London: Routledge, 2005.
9   Alasdair MacIntyre, *After Virtue: A Study in Moral Theory*, 25th anniversary edn, London: Duckworth, 2007.
10 Isaac Newton (ed. and trans. A. R. Hall and M. B. Hall), *Unpublished Scientific Manuscripts of Isaac Newton: A selection from the Portsmouth collection in the University Library, Cambridge*, Cambridge: Cambridge University Press, 1962, pp.132–6.
11 John Montag, 'Revelation: The False Legacy of Suárez' in John Milbank, Catherine Pickstock and Graham Ward (eds), *Radical Orthodoxy: A New Theology*, London: Routledge, 1999.
12 Rowan Williams, in an unpublished interview. See also Rupert Shortt, *Rowan Williams: An Introduction*, London: DLT, 2003.
13 John Henry Newman, *A Grammar of Ascent*, Oxford: Oxford University Press, 1985, ch.8, 'Inference'.
14 Fergus Kerr, OP, 'A Catholic Response to the Programme of Radical Orthodoxy', in Laurence Paul Hemming (ed.), *Radical Orthodoxy? A Catholic Enquiry*, Aldershot: Ashgate, 2000, pp.57ff.
15 Three further book series have succeeded *Illuminations: Theory and Religion* (Wiley-Blackwell), *Veritas* (SCM) and *Interventions* (Eerdmans Press).

Chapter 2

John Milbank

'Postmodern critical Augustinianism'

A short summa in forty-two responses to unasked questions

1. The end of modernity, which is not accomplished, yet continues to arrive, means the end of a single system of truth based on universal reason, which tells us what reality is like.

2. With this ending, there ends also the modern predicament of theology. It no longer has to measure up to accepted secular standards of scientific truth or normative rationality. Nor, concomitantly, to a fixed notion of the knowing subject, which was usually the modern, as opposed to the pre-modern, way of securing universal reason. This caused problems for theology, because an approach grounded in subjective aspiration can only precariously affirm objective values and divine transcendence.

3. In postmodernity there are infinitely many possible versions of truth, inseparable from particular narratives. Objects and subjects are, as they are narrated in a story. Outside a plot, which has its own unique, unfounded reasons, one cannot conceive how objects and subjects would be, nor even that they would be at all. If subjects and objects only are, through the complex relations of a narrative, then neither objects are privileged, as in pre-modernity, nor subjects, as in modernity. Instead, what matters are structural relations, which constantly shift; the word 'subject' now indicates a point of potent 'intensity' which can re-arrange given structural patterns.

4. The priority given to structural relations allows theology to make a kind of half-turn back to pre-modernity. One can no longer commence with modern inwardness:

this is only marked negatively as 'intensity' or potential, and the things that can truly be spoken about are once again external. However, this externality is no longer, as for pre-modernity, an organised spatial realm of substances, genera and species, but rather a world of temporary relational networks, always being redistributed, with greater and greater 'freedom', as one passes from mineral to vegetable to animal to cultural animal. So the point is not to 'represent' this externality, but just to join in its occurrence; not to know, but to intervene, originate.

5. Externality is therefore a kind of process. One cannot look at this process as a whole, but one can try to imagine what it means, its significance. All cultures, all 'religions', in effect see their temporal processes as microcosms of the whole process. Of course, postmodernism denies the point of doing this, except as a game. Yet to understand one's own proffered words or actions as just arbitrary, itself implies a speculation on the arbitrariness of the process in general: its universal production of the merely contingent. Christian theology, by contrast to nihilistic postmodernism, yet with equal validity, imagines temporal process as, in its very temporality, reflecting eternity, as the possibility of a historical progress into God, and as something recuperable within memory whose ultimate point is the allowing of forgiveness and reconciliation. This speculation is utterly unfounded, is inseparable from a narrative practice of remembering, and yet, in postmodern terms, it is just as valid or invalid as claims about supposedly universal human needs, desires or modes of interaction. Modernity dictated that a sensible theology would start from 'below'; postmodernity implies that conceptions of the 'below' – of human subjectivity and relationship – are only constituted within the narrative that simultaneously postulates the 'above'. Once the epistemological approach from the subject is shown to be as foundationalist as pre-modern metaphysics, the latter makes a strange kind of return: but as a necessary 'fiction' concerning the unseen relation of time to eternity, not as a record of 'observation' of this relationship.

6. Postmodern theology does not, therefore, begin with an account of the subject, for this is not neutrally available. By the same token, it is not seriously challenged by modernist discourses claiming to narrate a universally fundamental genesis of the subject in individual lives or in human history: Freudianism, Marxism, sociology. On the other hand, it faces a new and perhaps more severe challenge from the implications of a more thoroughgoing perspectival historicism which is what intellectual postmodernism is really all about. If Christianity is just one of many possible perspectives, then why believe any of them? Is not each perspective a strategy of power, every discourse but the means to assert that discourse? Postmodernism seems to imply nihilism, albeit of a 'positive' kind, embracing contingency and arbitrariness as the real natural good.

7. Whatever its response may be to nihilism, postmodern theology can only proceed by explicating Christian practice. The Christian God can no longer be thought of as a

God first seen, but rather as a God first prayed to, first imagined, first inspiring certain actions, first put into words, and always already thought about, objectified, even if this objectification is recognised as inevitably inadequate. This practice which includes images of, talk about, addresses to, actions towards 'God', can in no way be justified, nor be shown to be more rational, nor yet, outside its own discourse, as more desirable, than nihilism.

8. But is this really all that can be said? That Christianity is just 'on a level' with other practices, other discourses? Not quite. First, it may be argued that Christianity can become 'internally' postmodern in a way that may not be possible for every religion or ideology. I mean by this that it is possible to construe Christianity as suspicious of notions of fixed 'essences' in its approach to human beings, to nature, to community and to God, even if it has never fully escaped the grasp of a 'totalising' metaphysics. Through its belief in creation from nothing it admits temporality, the priority of becoming an unexpected emergence. A reality suspended between nothing and infinity is a reality of flux, a reality without substance, composed only of relational differences and ceaseless alterations (Augustine, *De Musica*). Like nihilism, Christianity can, should, embrace the differential flux.

9. Yet here arises the second point regarding whether Christianity is just 'on a level'. For nihilism, the flux is a medium of perpetual conflict, a pagan *agon* where the most powerful rhetoric will temporarily triumph, only to succumb to an apparently or effectively more powerful discourse in the future. Because there are no fixed categorical areas for different discourses/practices, they ceaselessly overlap and contest for influence. Lyotard and others rightly do not envisage a peaceful coexistence of a plurality of discourses without mutual interference. The best that can be hoped for is some mitigation of the severity of conflict, a set of formal rules of engagement such as is provided by the market or bureaucracy – forms which can survive many changes in the actual content of 'truth'. For this reason, postmodern nihilism remains in continuity with liberalism and the Enlightenment. Christianity, however, unlike many other discourses, pursued from the outset a universalism which tried to subsume rather than merely abolish difference: Christians could remain in their many different cities, languages and cultures, yet still belong to one eternal city ruled by Christ, in whom all 'humanity' was fulfilled. In this way it appears as a 'precursor' of enlightenment, and any claim of outright Christian opposition to enlightenment is bound to be an oversimplification. But the liberty, equality and fraternity latent as values in Christianity do not imply mere mutual tolerance, far less any resignation to a regulated conflict. On the contrary, Christianity is peculiar, because while it is open to difference – to a series of infinitely new additions, insights, progressions towards God – it also strives to make of all these differential additions a harmony 'in the body of Christ', and claims that, if the reality of God is properly attended to, there can be

such a harmony. And the idea of a consistently beautiful, continuously differential and open series is of course the idea of 'music'. In music there must be continuous endings and displacements, yet this is no necessary violence, because only in the recall of what has been displaced does the created product consist. Violence would rather mean an unnecessarily jarring note, a note wrong because 'out of place', or else the premature ending of a development. Perhaps this is partly why, in *De Musica*, Augustine – who realised that creation *ex nihilo* implied the non-recognition of ontological violence, or of positive evil – put forwards a 'musical' ontology. Christianity, therefore, is not just in the same position as all other discourses vis-à-vis postmodernity; it can, I want to claim, think difference, yet it perhaps uniquely tries to deny that this necessarily (rather than contingently, in a fallen world) entails conflict.

10. Explication of Christian practice, the task of theology, tries to pinpoint the peculiarity, the difference, of this practice by 'making it strange', finding a new language for this difference less tainted with the over-familiarity of too many Christian words which tend to obscure Christian singularity. The idea that this practice is essentially 'music' would be an example of this 'making strange'. And, as a second example, this music implies 'community' in a very particular sense. For Christianity, true community means the freedom of people and groups to be different, not just to be functions of a fixed consensus, yet at the same time it totally refuses *indifference*; a peaceful, united secure community implies *absolute* consensus, and yet, where difference is acknowledged, this is no agreement in an idea, or something once and for all achieved, but a consensus that is only in and through the inter-relations of community itself, and a consensus that moves and 'changes': a *concentus musicus*. Christianity (and not even Judaism, which postpones universality to the eschaton, a final chord) uniquely has this idea of community: this is what 'Church' should be all about (Lash).

11. Unless it reflects upon the singularity of Christian norms of community, theology has really nothing to think about. For Christian practice, like every practice, is all external, a matter of signs and actions interpellating 'persons'. The tradition already insisted that 'God' is only spoken about with reference to certain historical happenings and memories; a postmodern emphasis will add that God is never seen, never looked at. The response to God is response to the pressure of the unknown, and if Christians ask what God is like, then they can only point to our 'response' to God in the formation of community. The community is what God is like, and He is even more like the ideal, the goal of community implicit is its practices. Hence He is also unlike the community, and it is this inexpressible reality that the community continues to try to respond to.

12. If God can only be given some content through community, then speaking of God is not just a matter of words, but also of images, and bodily actions. These all articulate 'God'.

13. The community as substantive peace, as musical difference, is actually performed, ideally imagined, and in both these aspects, contemplated.

14. Augustine already put the idea of the peaceful community at the centre of his theology; thought of God, of revelation from God, was for him inseparable from the thought of heaven, of words and 'musical laws' coming down from heaven. The heavenly city meant for Augustine a substantial peace; but this peace could also be imperfectly present in the fallen world, in the sequences of time, and time redeemed through memory.

15. One way to try to secure peace is to draw boundaries around 'the same', and exclude 'the other'; to promote some practices and disallow alternatives. Most polities, and most religions, characteristically do this. But the Church has misunderstood itself when it does likewise. For the point of the supersession of the law is that nothing really positive is excluded – no difference, whatsoever – but only the negative, that which denies and takes away from Being: in other words, the violent. It is true, however, that Christians perceive a violence that might not normally be recognised, namely any stunting of person's capacity to love and conceive of the divine beauty; this inhibition is seen as having its soul in arbitrariness. But there is no real exclusion here; Christianity should not draw boundaries, and the Church is that paradox: a nomad city.

16. The religions and polities that exclude, characteristically seek to identify one thing that must be removed: a scapegoat, which can become in some ambiguous fashion 'sacred', because of the efficacious effect of its expulsion, bearing away all that is undesirable, together with all the guilt of the community. At the same time, the relationship of the community to the transcendently divine often demands further acts of distinction in the form of 'sacrifice'. The divine demands an offering, the violent separation, by fire or knife, of spirit from body, a purging off, to send up to heaven. Originally these were human sacrifices, then later commuted to symbolic ones, but still, frequently, in addition, the lives of those fallen in holy wars, or else the sacrifice of a pure ascetic spirit that has become indifferent to disturbing emotions.

17. Instead of multiple difference, there is dualism here: the banished, the purged off, against the included, the subsumed. The law of this dualism implies an ever-renewed conflict both within and without the city gates. This is the *traditional* mode of violence, whose existence must certainly be noted, though it is different in kind to modern/postmodern regulated and 'indifferent' conflict. Of course, legal monotheism, and Christianity when it has failed to escape this mode, remains half-trapped by this dualism. Whereas a Christianity true to itself should oppose all modes of violence: the pre-modern violence of law, the modern violence of norms of subjective 'rights', the postmodern violence of a total lack of norms. Yet the rejection of dualistic violence

grows throughout the Bible: monotheism and creation out of nothing eschew the idea of a 'chaotic' realm over against the divine, in eternal conflict with it. And the Jewish idea of law aspires to the idea of a law at one with life, with Being. But there is still some exclusion of the positive, some attempt to secure in a code the harmony of Being, and no complete recognition that perfect, divine rule is beyond all coercion. In a sense, this is a failure to have a perfect monotheism, and exhibits residues of dualism; in another sense monotheism alone is inadequate, as it cannot think of God as primarily the openness of love to the other.

18. Where there is a positing of a sacred over against a chaotic other, then the supremacy of the sacred can always be deconstructed, for it appears that there is something more ultimate that includes both the sacred and chaos, that governs the passage between them. Is not this passage itself chaotic? Hence there is a hidden connection between pre-modern pagan dualism and postmodern dualism. The latter's self-proclaimed paganism is a kind of deconstructed paganism, for the real pagans were always hoping to subordinate the admitted conflictual diversity of the gods to a harmonious order; an open celebration of the finality of the *agon* was only latent. But Christianity, which is not dualistic in this fashion, and already admits the flux of difference, is therefore outside the reach of deconstruction (in precisely Derrida's sense).

19. If pre-modern religions and postmodern nihilism are secretly akin, indeed, different moments of a 'dialectic' (postmodernism claims to refuse dialectic, but this is the instance of its failure to do so; it is right to make the effort), then, by contrast, one can trace in the Bible the slow emergence of opposition to the common factor of violence in all human norms. For it gradually takes the part of the scapegoat, and starts to place a ban on revenge against those who first violently excluded their brethren (the protection of Cain by God). The Hebrews were originally nomads, and chance and prophecy constantly recalled them to their nomad status (Girard).

20. In the course of this nomadic history, sacrifice is also commuted. Finally, in Christianity, God is thought of as asking only for the offering of our freewill, in a return of love to him. This is no longer in any sense a self-destruction, or self division, but rather a self-fulfilment, an offering that is at the same time our reception of the fullness of Being. It is receiving God: 'deification'.

21. In a world dominated by evil and violence, self-offering, to God and others, inevitably involves suffering. This is why there is suffering at the heart of Christ's perfect self-offering to God.

22. This is not, of course the offering of a blood-sacrifice to God. Before the cross, comes the preaching of the kingdom. The kingdom is really offered by Christ to

humanity, and the cross is the result of a rejection of this offer. However, this very rejection tends to suggest the 'original' character of human sin; to sin, theology has speculated, is to refuse the love of God, and so to render oneself incapable of recognising God, by substituting the goals of human pride in his place The putting to death of God shows what evil is: its nihilistic pointlessness, its incomprehensibility (Schwäger).

23. This speculation continues: evil cannot fully see itself as evil, therefore only the uncontaminated good, God himself, can fully suffer evil – not in eternity, which is beyond suffering, but in the human creation: hence the necessity for the *Deus Homo*. Such a speculation is an important part of Christianity, a theoretical component which a postmodern approach can recognise as actually 'taking off from the narrative sources, as *not* fully grounded in them, and yet as validated merely by the profundity of the picture of God which results, merely by the pleasing shape of the conceits which it generates. However, at the same time a postmodern approach must do more justice to the narrative, practical, social level than in the past. For if Jesus's perfect suffering belonged to his 'interiority', then how can it make any difference to us, how would we know about it? Much past theology has seemed to suggest that there is a change, consequent upon the atonement, in the divine attitude towards us, a change to which we are just 'extrinsically' related, and which is just 'positively' revealed to us. However, if the perfect character of Jesus's suffering is recognised by us, then this can only mean that it is more present 'on the outside', in his deeds, and words, and even in the words used by others which compose the record of Christ; for it is only the recorded, interpreted Christ who saves us, and this mediation does not conceal some more original, 'self-present' Christ – that would be a mere asocial phantom. The speculation about atonement is grounded in a narrative relation to which we must constantly return: the Church considers that in all its actions it can learn to suffer truly (and thereby perceive our previous original sin of unperceived egotism) from the story of Jesus, so that its plot can be fulfilled universally. Does this practical situation imply the finality of Jesus, his identity with the divine word? The more subtle reply is, not quite, for practice cannot claim to 'know' the finality of what it treats as final. Even a theoretical, speculative discourse conceived as having a 'second order', 'regulative' function is finally excessive (in a positive sense), and makes its own peculiar contribution to the content of Christianity, thereby insinuating itself back into first-order discourse from which it is only relatively distinguished (as all speech both orders and regulates, and regulates only in giving new orders). Thus, in the New Testament itself, speculative considerations about the atonement are celebrated in poetic, devotional terms. Already the metaphors and mythical 'metanarratives' implying incarnation and atonement are 'somewhat in excess'; they not only secure the first-order level of 'historical' narrative recitation, they also go speculatively beyond this to suggest a particular 'mythical' picture of God as becoming incarnate,

suffering in our stead. Nothing justifies this speculation except itself, and the way it then enriches the stories told and redoubles the perceived significance of Christian practices.

24. For the traditional speculation, God cannot endure the contradiction of sin; creation must offer itself back to God; evil prevents it from doing so; therefore God must offer creation back to God, through the incarnation of the *Logos*, who includes all things. Yet for early Christianity, it is clear that God suffers a contradiction until all make for themselves the offering already made by Christ. The 'incarnation' has no meaning, therefore, except as 'the beginning', the foundation of the Church, a new sort of community of charity and forgiveness, as a space for the possibility of this offering. For Augustine, it is the *Church* that is the adequate sacrifice to God – in other words the realisation of perfect community. The centrality of incarnation and the cross in no way contradicts the truth that the central aspect of salvation is the creation of perfect community.

25. Christianity is primarily about this hope for community. But it offers more than hope: it also remembers perfect community as once instantiated by the shores of Lake Galilee; this is a memory compounded only of words and images. But there should be no pathos here, and Christianity has too often been sunk in this pathos. It is not that we have a few fragments of memory in lieu of the 'real presence' of the resurrected Christ, but that these fragments are the real saving presence; they provide us – within the whole network of tradition within which they belong – with a new *language* of community. The Christian claim is that the narratives about Christ show what love – a difficult and demanding practice requiring more subtlety, style and correct idiom than mere 'well-meaning' – is. That here is the *logos*, the lost harmonic pattern of genuine human life, which can now be re-appropriated.

26. What are we to make of the fact that a 'resurrection' forms a part of this memory? Resurrection is no proof of divinity, nor a kind of vindication of Jesus' mission. And no very good 'evidence' survives, only the record of some strongly insisted-upon personal testimonies. What we have is the memory of community, of 'ordinary' conversation, of eating and drinking, continuing beyond death. Without this element, there could not really be a memory of a moment of 'perfect' community, for this is normally inhibited by the forces of nature as we know them, and by death, especially.

27. To remember the resurrection, to hope for the universal resurrection, is a 'political' act: for it is the ultimate refusal of all denials of community. The return of all the dead in reconciliation – the innocent, the guilty, the oppressed and the oppressors – is looked for (Peukert).

28. The resurrection is about the persistence of the ordinary, and the doctrine of the incarnation locates God in the ordinary, even if this is an ordinariness 'transfigured'. Although this doctrine is a radical speculation, which was only gradually articulated, it is also a rebuke to attempts to formulate metaphysically the divine perfection; one can make groping attempts, but finally God's perfection is most like this particular life, historically obscure, almost lost to view.

29. God is most to be found in this life recognisably like our own, yet also recognised as uniquely 'other', because we take it as judging all other lives.

30. The doctrine of the incarnation – of Jesus's 'identity' with the divine *Logos* – secures this practical relation of the Church to Jesus, yet also goes beyond and reinforces it in the way suggested above. Its real validation is in allowing us to imagine a peaceful, totally charitable God, who cannot force us, and yet cannot let us go. Also, by returning us to the narrative, by tying us to contingency, it suggests that divine goodness is no generalised intention, but always takes a very particular 'form'. That it is inseparable from aesthetic harmony.

31. Yet in the memory of Christ we are given the language of salvation, and not formulas for how to use this language. For the universal offering to be made, the Church must creatively construct her own response to Christ. This is why there is a work of the Spirit that can be distinguished from that of Christ, even though this response itself is ideally and infinitely fulfilled within the Godhead.

32. For if evil is truly overcome in the perfect harmony of Christ's life in community with his followers, and in the language of this community which we remember, this still does not mean that here we possess a *gnosis*, in the sense of a given formulaic wisdom that we must just recite or magically invoke. Instead, this language allows us to *escape* from the dominating effects of human discourses which totally subsume all differences, new occurrences, under existing categories. Atonement means that the flux is permitted to flow again, that the *Logos* only really speaks with its real intent in the ever-different articulation of our responses. The Holy Spirit is associated with this diversity of answers. But they all form the continuous unity of the body of Christ.

33. The doctrine of the Trinity is a statement of faith that God is, 'in himself', as he has been imagined by us to relate to human history. Here we imagine him to speak once as a word that unifies all other words, and as continuously achieving that final unification of all other words by articulating a manifold response to the one word. So God involves not just the first difference of expressive articulation of content (inseparable from content), but also the second difference of interpretation of expression

(inseparable from expression, making expression always already conversation). With-out this second difference, we would be tempted to think that the expression just carried us back to a pre-formed content, or else that God was but a single *ratio*, which would be little better than seeing him as but a single person. With this second difference, one truly has a moment of response to expression in God which goes beyond, is 'excessive' in relation to the expression. Hence the love that subsists between Father and Son is communicated as a further difference that always escapes, or, as Stanislas Breton puts it, 'an *infinite* relation' (Derrida and Labarriére).

34. God as Trinity is therefore himself community, and even a 'community in process', infinitely realised, beyond any conceivable opposition between 'perfect act' and 'perfect potential'. A Trinitarian ontology can therefore be a differential ontology surpassing the Aristotelian *actus purus*.

35. 'In the image of the Trinity' means that 'human beings' are moments of particu-larly intense and adaptive 'recollection' within the temporal process, although such recollection is constitutive of the temporal process itself. For a present moment 'is' in its repetitive holding of the past, yet in this 'remembering' it escapes at one level the temporal continuum and arrives as a 'meaning' which has a free capacity for adaptation and expansion (Augustine, *Confessions*; Deleuze).

36. The human mind does not 'correspond' to reality, but arises within a process which gives rise to 'effects of meaning'. It is a particularly intense network of such effects. Our bodily energies and drives (for Augustine in *Civitas Dei* the *ingenium* which images the power of the divine Father) are made 'present' and articulate (so alone constituted and sustained) through the happening of linguistic 'meaning', which is also the event of a 'truth' which cannot 'correspond'. For Augustine this second moment is the cultural training of the artist's *ingenium*; it is also that active memory by which we constantly learn through repeating our individual and collective bio-graphies. Knowledge 'surfaces' as the process of learning, which is true if divinely 'illumined' – it is not a knowledge of an object outside that process (God being this process, in its infinite plenitude).

37. The mind is only illumined by the divine *Logos*, if also our 'preceding' energies, and our 'emergent' desires, correspond to the Father and the Spirit, respectively. We know what we want to know, and although all desiring is an 'informed' desiring, desire shapes truth beyond the imminent implications of any logical order, so ren-dering the Christian *logos* a continuous product as well as a process of 'art'. Moreover, if all that 'is' is good and true, then no positive reality can be false as a 'mistake', or as 'non-correspondence', but only false as deficient presence, embodying the shortfall of an inadequate desire. Now desire, not Greek 'knowledge', mediates to us reality.

38. All desire is good so long as it is a restless desire (a more-desiring desire) which is moved by infinite lack, the pull of the 'goal'. Such desire is nonviolent for it could only be content with the unrestricted openness, non-possessiveness and self-offering of resurrected bodies. Yet this is not the cold 'detachment' (both in relation to creatures and away from creatures) of a 'disinterested' *agape* sundered from eros. This would imply that finite reality, as for Neoplatonism, by always lacking, always being unworthy of erotic attachment, must always be evil. For Augustine, Christianity goes beyond this by conjoining to 'the goal' also 'the way', which means a constant historical determining that desire is well ordered, not just through its deference to infinite fruition, but also by a particular selective pattern of finite use. The *appropriate* preferences of *eros*, the 'right harmonies' within a musical sequence, alone ensure that this sequence 'progresses' towards the infinite goal. For every new act, every new word, may be either enabling or inhibiting, and although inhibition is mere negation, this can only be registered by the 'fine judgement' which recognises an aesthetic distortion (*De Trinitate*).

39. 'The way' is not theoretically known but must be constituted through judgement in the repeated construction and recognition of 'examples', which cannot be literally copied if they are to be genuinely 'repeated'. The first example, Christ, by being first, inevitably defines the way, because this way is considered to be a single way (if not single we are back in agonistics: this is the only reason its singularity matters). Because Christ is remembered as a *founder*, whose character is by definition not representable in terms of prior cultural orders, it is inevitable that his character will *entirely coincide* in its representation with the new categories of the new ecclesial society. Hence as founder, Christ is also the total realised collective character of the Church which is yet to come, and will itself include all cosmic reality. It follows that the *topos* Christ-founder surprisingly bears in itself the elements of a 'high' Christology. The correspondence of Christ to God, or the identity of the entire 'pattern' of his life (which is what *persona* really implies, not any substantive 'element') with the *Logos*, only makes sense within the broader context of the correspondence of the ecclesial 'way' to God. For the 'pattern' of Jesus's life is only provisionally and canonically complete; as the 'context' for the new society it cannot 'belong' to an 'individual' and this is why one should hold onto, but re-interpret, the Chalcedonian insight that Jesus possessed no human *hypostasis*. For the 'patterns' or 'coherencies' of our lives never belong to us, are not 'completed' at our deaths, and can be repeated, or even more fully realised, by others: this is supremely true of a pattern that is taken to be canonically normative, as eschatalogically coinciding with the identities of all of us, as omni-repeatable and, so, as 'divine'.

40. Furthermore, 'the way' is not defined solely as such a repetition. Were this the case, then we would be remaining within the logic of parts and wholes which characterised Greek thinking both about the individual and society, and tended to exile individual awareness and expression to the asocial realm of *theoria*. By contrast, as

Augustine saw, the primacy (or equal primacy) of desire implies that 'individuality' arises only through the constant rupturing and 'externalisation' of the subject. To contemplate is now to desire the other, to enter further into relation both with God and with human beings and angels. And the way is a community, not just Christolo-gical supplementation, but from the outset the inclusion of interpretative response in the relations of Mary, of John the Baptist, and the disciples to Christ. This is why there is a historical happening of Christ not *just* as the image of the Father, but also as the relation to the father, which as invisible, and indeed only 'imagined' in language, can only be made present as the inner-relatedness of the Church, including its 'initial' relation to Jesus in his own relatedness to the traditional imagining of a Father–God. Desire exceeds even the Christian *logos*, and yet fulfils it and therefore does not after all exceed it (according to the logic of 'substantive relations'), because the *usus* of the cultural product, understood 'aesthetically' as a work of art, is not exhausted even by a sympathetic judgmental attentiveness to its 'perfect' specificity. Desire, through re-application, both respects this perfection and undoes it through joining the work to the continuous musical series. Hence the way is Christ, but equally the Church. And both are 'real' as the cultural happening of 'meaning'; 'liberal versus conservative' debates about the historicity of the resurrection, etc., will have no place in a postmodern theology.

41. 'The way', which is redemptive, is only the proper occurrence of creation. This is why Augustine is right to think that the 'economic' Trinitarian series of Paternal voice–Christ–Ecclesia discloses to us a Trinitarian ontology which allows us to describe the universal happening of humanity in and through time. In this account of participation in the Trinity (presented as 'Trinitarian vestiges' in the soul) the his-torical mediation of the Trinity is upheld by Augustine *more* than by others, precisely because he makes this process the metahistorical context for all historical reality, and so wisely and necessarily obscures its singularity: it is not just one revelatory event within an order that is quite otherwise (*De Trinitate*).

42. Creation is always found as a given, but developing, 'order'. As the gift of God, creation also belongs to God, it is within God (together with the infinity of all articulations that there may be) as the *Logos*. But existing harmonies, existing 'extensions' of time and space, constantly give rise to new 'intentions', to movements of the Spirit to further creative expression, new temporal unravelling of creation *ex nihilo*, in which human beings most consciously participate. Yet even this movement, the vehicle of human autonomy, is fully from God, is nothing *in addition* to the divine act-potential, and not equivocally different in relation to him. The latter conception would be 'pagan', 'gnostic', 'Cabbalistic', whereas it is God himself who is differentia-tion, ensuring that this process is 'music', not the ceaseless rupture and self-destruction of a differentiation poised 'univocally' (Deleuze) between an 'indifferent'

transcendence and an anarchic finitude. The trust that in our linguistic and figurative creations we can constantly recognise, when it arises, the aesthetically 'right' addition, which is, in its specific content, a criterion of self-validation, is now the mode of recognition of a transcendental/ontological possibility of 'participation' (Kant). And so translates for us, 'faith in the triune God'.

Bibliography

St Augustine, *The City of God, De Trinitate, Confessions, De Musica.*

Balthasar, Hans Urs von, *The Glory of the Lord: A Theological Aesthetics, Vol. I: Seeing the Form*, trans. E. Leiva-Merikakis, Edinburgh: T. and T. Clark, 1982.

Deleuze, Gilles, *Logique du Sens*, Paris: Editions du Minuit, 1969.

—— *Différence et Répétition*, Paris: Presses Universitaires de France, 1972.

—— (with Felix Guattarai), *A Thousand Plateaus*, trans. Brian Massumi, London: Athlone, 1988.

Derrida, Jacques, *Of Grammatology*, trans. G. G. Spivak, Baltimore, MD: Johns Hopkins University Press, 1982.

Derrida, Jacques and Pierre-Jean Labarriére, *Alterités*, Paris: Osins, 1986.

Girard, René, *Of Things Hidden Since the Foundation of the World*, trans. Stephen Bann and Michael Metteer, London: Athlone, 1987.

Kant, Immanuel, *Critique of Judgement*, trans. Werner S. Pluhar, Indianapolis, IN: Hackett, 1987.

Kierkegaard, Søren, *Repetition*, trans. H. V. and E. H. Hong, Princeton, NJ: Princeton University Press, 1983.

—— *Philosophical Fragments*, trans. H. V. and E. H. Hong, Princeton, NJ: Princeton University Press 1985.

Lash, Nicholas, *Easter in Ordinary*, London: SCM, 1989.

Lyotard, Jean-François, *The Postmodern Condition*, trans. Geoff Bennington and Brian Massumi, Manchester: Manchester University Press, 1984.

—— *The Différend: Phrases in Dispute*, trans. Georges van den Abbeele, Manchester: Manchester University Press, 1988.

Milbank, John, *Theology and Social Theory: Beyond Secular Reason*, 2nd edn, Oxford: Blackwell, 2006.

Peukert, Helmut, *Science, Action and Fundamental Theology*, Cambridge, MA: Massachusetts Institute of Technology Press, 1986.

Schwäger, Raymund. *Der Wunderbare Tausch: Zur Geschichte und Deutung der Erlosungslehre*, Munich: Kosel, 1986.

Further reading

Hemming, Laurence Paul (ed.), *Radical Orthodoxy? A Catholic Enquiry*, Aldershot: Ashgate Publishing, 2000.

Milbank, John, Catherine Pickstock and Graham Ward (eds), *Radical Orthodoxy: A New Theology*, London: Routledge, 1999.

Montag, John, 'Radical Orthodoxy and Christian Philosophy', *Philosophy and Theology*, 16(1), 2004.

Smith, James K. A. and Olthuis, James H. (eds), *Creation, Covenant, and Participation: Radical Orthodoxy and the Reformed Tradition*, Grand Rapids, MI: Baker Academic, 2005.

Burrell, David, 'Radical Orthodoxy: An Appreciation', *Philosophy and Theology*, 16(1), 2004.

Hyman, Gavin, *The Predicament of Postmodern Theology: Radical Orthodoxy or Nihilist Textualism?*, Louisville, KY: Westminster John Knox Press, 2001.

Long, D. Stephen, 'Radical Orthodoxy', in Kevin Vanhoozer (ed.), *The Cambridge Companion to Postmodern Theology*, Cambridge: Cambridge University Press, 2003, pp.126–45.

Shakespeare, Stephen, *Radical Orthodoxy: A Critical Introduction*, London: SPCK, 2007.

Smith, James K. A., *Introducing Radical Orthodoxy: Toward a Post-Secular Worldview*, Grand Rapids, MI: Baker Academic, 2004.

Questions

1. What seems to be particularly characteristic of Radical Orthodoxy as a theological sensibility?
2. How does Radical Orthodoxy understand the relationship between theology and other disciplines? What is distinctive about Christian theology?
3. How does Radical Orthodoxy understand 'reason' and its relation to 'revelation'?
4. How does Radical Orthodoxy understand postmodernity's (or, more suggestively, late-modernity's) relation to modernity?
5. In what ways does Radical Orthodoxy reflect an Augustinian legacy?

PART II

Theology and philosophy, faith and reason

Introduction

Radical Orthodoxy is clearly committed to the view that faith and reason are intimately and always intertwined. There is no 'dualism'; that is, there is no sense in which there are two orders of knowing standing over and against each other, one based on faith, the other on reason. Of course, there is a tendency to associate 'faith' with the discourse of theology, and 'reason' with philosophy. As faith and reason are intertwined, so too are theology and philosophy.

The debate concerning the relationship between faith and reason, and theology and philosophy, is frequently undertaken with reference to Aquinas's understanding of the relationship between *sacra doctrina* – the holy teaching of the Church which brings *salus* or salvation – and philosophy. This is the focus of the next essay by John Milbank. How is the relationship between *sacra doctrina* and philosophy understood?

The matter is complicated, not least because our categories of 'theology' and 'philosophy' do not map clearly and directly onto the categories which Aquinas considers: *sacra doctrina* on the one hand, and 'that theology *which is part of philosophy*' (what we might call philosophical theology). There are a number of ways in which the distinction between *sacra doctrina* and philosophy has been understood. Milbank's interpretation of Aquinas is very Augustinian and Neoplatonic. He regards *sacra doctrina* and philosophy as involving different intensities of illumination along a single spectrum of knowing. In other words, philosophy – which always includes its own dimension of faith – is a participation in the light of knowledge radiating from God the creator. This is, however, a faint illumination; in *sacra doctrina*, that illumination is ever more intense but arrives as something genuinely new. This suggests that the boundary between philosophy and *sacra doctrina* is very delicate indeed, rather like the boundary between the shadows of a leafy tree and the open sunlight. For Milbank, philosophy is not autonomous from – does not lie *outside* – the principal source of being and knowledge, namely God, any more than creation is 'autonomous' from God (see the introduction to this Reader, pp. 17–18). Philosophy always has a theological horizon. Meanwhile, *sacra doctrina* involves not only the deployment of philosophy in the articulation of the meaning and implications of holy teaching, but also philosophy's transformation or consummation. As Aquinas would put it, referring to the miracle of the turning of water into wine at the wedding in Cana, 'those who use philosophical texts in sacred teaching, by subjugating them to faith, do not mix water with wine, but turn water into wine' (Aquinas, *Commentary on the* De Trinitate *of Boethius*, 2.4.ad 5). At a most fundamental level, Radical Orthodoxy resists the notion that there is more than one source of knowledge and truth, namely God himself.

For some critics, the notion that *sacra doctrina* and philosophy are different intensities of a single illumination seems to preclude any sense that our knowledge is genuinely *ours*. Yet Milbank's point in his interpretation of Aquinas is that my knowledge does not stand to God's in the way that my knowledge stands to your knowledge. In other words, we do not have an autonomous 'chunk' of knowledge which stands alongside another 'chunk' of knowledge which is God's. Our knowledge, in both philosophical reason and *sacra doctrina*, is a participation in God's own knowledge, the *scientia divina*. Our ability to know as humans – in freedom – is itself a divine gift, but no less genuinely ours for being a gift. In fact, it is *more ours* in being a gift. But the implication is that the knowledge attained to by philosophical reason is not properly spoken of as 'autonomous', as if it stands outside a definitive relation to God and God's continual self-disclosure in creation.

If Radical Orthodoxy sees theology and philosophy as intimately intertwined in a theologian such as Aquinas, it sees that certain theological moves in the succeeding generation brought about the separation of theology and philosophy, and eventually the sundering of faith from reason. There is a long tradition of regarding John Duns Scotus's (1266–1308) move towards the univocity of being as crucial in the story of the separation of faith and reason. 'Being' is now a third term shared in the same way (univocally) by God and creatures. Rather than understanding God as *being itself* in which creation participates, the univocity of being suggests that God and creatures share a common being, only God is infinite and creation is finite. Invoking Scotus in this way has proved very controversial (and has dominated debates concerning Radical Orthodoxy to a very surprising degree), so, despite the technical and very complex nature of the arguments, Catherine Pickstock's most extensive and intricate treatment of the key issues is included here.

As Pickstock remarks, the matter may not concern the interpretation of Scotus so much as how one values the move to univocity in the history of Western thought. Many philosophers celebrate this innovation, regarding it as the first move on the road to modern liberty. Why? Because being is rendered not hierarchical, but always the same and therefore in some sense 'equal'. These arguments are put forward in some of the contributions to the journal issue in which Pickstock's article first appeared (*Modern Theology* 21(4), October 2005). For the moment, one way of understanding the central issue concerns the infinite extent of God's being which separates God from creation. For Aquinas, God can be understood as 'enveloping' creation with an infinite intimacy; there is no danger of God collapsing back into creation because God is simply *sheerly* different. Under a univocal ontology, God's being cannot be 'reduced' lest he begin to look like just another finite being. So God must stand 'at a distance', on the far side of an infinitely wide 'chasm of being'. God then becomes an object of superstition and one requires a 'leap' over the chasm to reach God. This is the leap of faith, and it involves leaving reason behind. Faith deals with God on the far side of the chasm; reason deals with finite being.

Pickstock's essay addresses the complex nature of Scotus's thought and the objections to Radical Orthodoxy's interpretation of this phase in the history of theology and philosophy. For the moment, I will address one perhaps obvious objection to Milbank's essay which might emerge from a reading of Pickstock on Scotus. In regarding philosophy and *sacra doctrina* as lying on a single spectrum of illumination by the divine, is Milbank advocating a univocity of philosophy and *sacra doctrina* (suggesting that they are essentially the same kind of discourse) which he will not allow to their subject matters? The subject matter of philosophy is 'being' (not any particular kind of 'being', but just 'being' in a most general and abstract sense). The subject matter of *sacra doctrina* is God. If philosophy and *sacra doctrina* are essentially the same *kind* of discourse, does this imply that their subject matters – 'being' on the one hand, and God on the other – are also the same kind of thing? Does this imply that God is studied as if God were just one more instance under the general category 'being'? This is a complex matter. Put simply, we must remember that both philosophy and *sacra doctrina* participate in a yet higher science with which they are *not* univocal, namely the *scientia divina*, God's own knowledge. This is often lost in discussions of Aquinas's understanding of the relation between theology and philosophy: *sacra doctrina* is not the highest science or anything like a 'zap' from God which simply delivers information. It continues to be mediated within creation and through our modes of thought (this, after all, is what the revelation of God *in the incarnation* is all about). This is why Radical Orthodoxy continues to regard theology as speech about God in which we speak of God 'tangentially' by always speaking of other things (creation, humanity, society and so on). Milbank sees that, at its very height, *sacra doctrina* may even include an intuition of God (Aquinas hints at this in many places), and this is the juncture at which *sacra doctrina* reveals its most intense participation in the light of God's own knowledge. Nevertheless, *sacra doctrina* is not a bizarre kind of knowledge lying outside our natural ways of knowing, but intensifies our natural ways of knowing. It turns philosophy into wine.

Chapter 3

John Milbank

Truth and vision

I

If truth, for Aquinas, is inherently theological, then is the theology involved an affair of reason or of faith? Or is it first an affair of reason, and later an affair of faith?

In the most usual interpretations, Aquinas is seen as espousing a sharp distinction between reason and faith, and concomitantly between philosophy and theology. Furthermore, this distinction is viewed as both benign and beneficial: on the one hand, it safeguards the mystery and integrity of faith; on the other hand, it allows a space for modern secular autonomy, while discouraging the growth of political theocracy and hierocratic control of knowledge.

The present chapter will, however, argue that this dualistic reading of Aquinas is false. Dualism concerning reason and faith emerges not from Thomas, but rather from intellectual and practical tendencies within the late mediaeval and early modern periods (even if they were somewhat enabled already by the Gregorian reforms with their sharper divide of the lay from the clerical). Moreover, its consequence was not benign, but instead itself encouraged, with and not against early modernity, a theocratic and hierocratic authoritarianism.

For the more science and politics were confined to immanent and autonomous secular realms, then the more faith appealed to an arational positivity of authority invested with a right to rule, and sometimes to overrule, science and secular politics, whose claimed autonomy, being construable as pure only in formalistic terms, was by the very same token open to substantive breaching. Theocracy required the 'other' realm of the secular in order to have something over which to exert its sway: thus the most theocratic construals of papal authority emerged only in the later Middle Ages, as physicalist theories of the rights of a finite power legitimated by absolute power over lesser powers enjoying, intrinsically, only a limited sway. Quite shortly afterwards, similarly theocratic theories were deployed by absolute monarchs, and the resulting blend of theological voluntarism and physicalist theory of the rights of *de facto* power is not without echo in the later articulation of totalitarian philosophies.[1]

Moreover, the neo-Thomistic promotion of papal power in the nineteenth and twentieth centuries was likewise predicated upon gnoseological dualism, not monism. In order to combat the sway of idealism and positivism, nineteenth-century Catholic thinkers such as Joseph Kleutgen argued, inaccurately, that mediaeval Christian thinkers had developed a purely autonomous philosophy, more rationally sound than the philosophies of modernity, whose conclusions were nonetheless in strict harmony with those of faith.[2] The outcome of this new reading of the Middle Ages was to lend the Roman Catholic hierarchy a double support; on the one hand, it received the supposedly neutral acclaim of reason (underwriting its authority in the educational and scientific sphere), but, on the other hand, its claims to speak in the name of something beyond reason were thereby rendered more plausible. Moreover, just as a supposedly 'Thomistic' reason was often in fact contaminated by empiricism and positivism (in overreaction to idealism), so likewise a faith regarded as entirely other to reason was grounded on revealed 'facts' and literalistic decrees of appointed authority. Here again, the strong concessions to reason only led to a final and unquestionable trumping of reason by faith. And if, so often, theological 'liberals' ascribe to something like this framework, then they need to be aware of just this genealogy.

However, if the dualistic legacy of neo-Thomism is in this way sinister in its consequences and implications, can one really dissociate it from the teachings of Aquinas himself? How is one to deny, in Thomas, first of all, the presence of his clearly stated view that we can know many things in God's Creation by rational attention to it, without the assistance of faith? And how is one to deny, in the second place, the role in his work of a purely philosophical theology, as opposed to that of *sacra doctrina*, which appeals to revelation?

Let it be said straightaway that it is possible to cite passages in Aquinas which appear incontrovertibly to support these positions. Thus he does indeed say that we can know many things by the light of natural reason without appeal to faith.[3] And he does indeed say that the theology pursued by philosophy is able, by the natural light of reason alone, to know God as first cause, which is to say as creator, if nothing more.[4]

However, exegesis is easy; it is interpretation that is difficult. And Aquinas, more than most thinkers, requires interpretation. Some thinkers, like Heidegger, appear on the surface to be obscure and deep, but on analysis are revealed as offering all too clear and readily statable positions. But as Rudi te Velde very well intimates, with Aquinas the opposite pertains.[5] Only superficially is he clear, but on analysis one discovers that he does not at all offer us a decently confined 'Anglo-Saxon' lucidity, but rather the intense light of Naples and Paris which is ultimately invisible in its very radiance – rendering the wisest of us, for Aquinas after Aristotle, like owls blinking in the noonday.[6] Of course it is true that Aquinas does indeed refute shaky positions with supreme economy, simplicity and clarity of argumentation, but the arcanum of his teaching lies not here. It resides rather in the positions he does affirm, often briefly and like a kind of residue, akin to Sherlock Holmes's last remaining solution, which must be accepted with all its implausibility, when other solutions have been shown to be simply impossible. Often this conceptual residue is prefaced by a revealing *quoddamodo* 'in a certain sense' and we are left contemplating, not a discursive chain, but a bare single word such as *proportio* [proportion], *convenienter* [consistently or suitably], *claritas* [clarity] or *ordo* [order] and must attempt to fathom its conceptual depths in relation to other 'remaining' concepts and locutions. At the heart of Aquinas's thought, commentators discover highly problematic notions – the real distinction of *esse* and *essentia* in creatures, the primacy of act over possibility, the intrinsic perfection of *esse*, 'proper accidents', 'active potential', 'real relations', 'intelligible being', the distinction of 'first' from 'second act', the nature of *ens commune* as distinct from *esse*, and the relation of participation to substance in his overall ontology – all of which exhibit a certain profound obscurity that resists easy interpretation or analysis.

Bearing these general procedural remarks in mind, our claim in the present case is that Aquinas's apparently clear avowal of an autonomous reason and philosophical theology cannot be rendered consistent with certain other crucial passages in his writings and therefore must be reinterpreted. In the light of other passages, we shall argue, the distinctions between reason and faith, on the one hand, and 'philosophical' theology and *sacra doctrina*, on the other, can only be considered as relative contrasts within a more fundamental gnoseological [of, or pertaining to, types of knowledge, such as faith and reason] situation embracing the two poles, in either case. For both instances (reason/faith; philosophical theology/*sacra doctrina*) we will make this claim in two stages. First of all, we will establish that the distinguished approaches can at the very most be thought of only as distinct phases within a single gnoseological extension exhibiting the same qualities throughout. Then we will further establish that even the phases are not clearly bounded in terms of what can or cannot be achieved. To the contrary, it will turn out that the single extension has an equally single 'intension' stretched between its beginning and end and accessible at any point along the continuum, although in different degrees of concentration, giving varying 'intensities'. Having established these points concerning Aquinas's method, we shall then show how his 'rational' treatment of Creation is informed by faith, while his exposition of the revealed Trinity is in fact highly demonstrative. Throughout we hope to show how a 'radically orthodox' position (primarily characterized by a more persistent refusal of distinct 'natural' and 'supernatural' phases and a consequent assault upon an autonomous naturalism as 'nihilistic'), can indeed be rendered as an attentive reading of Aquinas.

II

There can be no doubt that Aquinas distinguishes between faith and reason. The difficult issue, though, is just how. For it is equally clear that they are but phases within a single extension. Thus Aquinas declares that both the natural powers of thought and the superadded powers given in grace and glory both operate through participation in the uncreated and intelligible light of the divine intellect.[7] In the case of the former, natural powers, the *intellectus* or 'higher reason' enjoys a certain very remote approximation to the divine intuition, or immediate intellectual vision, which operates without recourse to discursive unfolding.[8] Hence it enjoys some vision of the pure divine form without matter only known to our *modus cognoscendi* [way of knowing] as the diverse transcendentals of Being, Unity, Truth, Goodness and Beauty. By way of this vision it permits the 'lower reason' in its higher scientific aspect (as identified by Aristotle) to discern by judgement in some measure the 'simple essences' of finite substances as (literally) conveyed into the human mind by way of the senses. Concerning those essences it cannot be deceived in such a way that here it partakes infallibly of the divine power of intuitive recognition. (John Jenkins has recently refuted Lonergan's denial of this aspect of intellectual vision in Aquinas.)[9] However, since in concrete reality no simple essences subsist (or else they would rival God in their simplicity),[10] no pure scientific cognition is ever exercised by us without discursive mediation: no cognitive 'sight' without cognitive 'language'. And in the case of the higher reason's partial grasp of undivided transcendental principles, it is all the more the case that this arises through and after our comprehension of material divided things. Moreover, even in perceiving the contingent combinations of finite essences, we can, indeed, unlike God, be deceived, and must always exercise judgement by questioning just what we do see, and in allowing for deceptive appearances.[11] Here the subordinate discursive aspect of the lower reason comes particularly into play.

This discursive aspect of the lower reason, while assuming certain scientific principles that are in turn judged in the light of the higher reason's gaze upon the eternal, itself calls again upon the higher light of judgement (by way of analysis), to make its specific intentional pronouncements upon evidence and probable coherencies. In such a circular fashion, *ratio* and *intellectus*, while distinguished, nonetheless operate as a single power.

Thus, when making pronouncements about the truths of external things and in further realizing these truths within itself (since Aquinas holds that truth resides primarily within the intellect, but secondarily within things),[12] the mind continues to be informed by the intellective vision of truth, goodness and beauty. This is essential because Aquinas holds that the truth residing in things is not simply their ontological manifestness (though this is crucial, and rules out any epistemological approach to truth, since what if it were universally the case that all beings absolutely hide themselves?) but also a truth to themselves or degree of realization of their own perfection, or own goodness.[13]

In this way, a thing is 'true' to the degree that it participates in the divine standard for its own realization. Hence, in pronouncing on and manifesting the truth of a thing, the human intellect itself assesses it in the light of this standard, and its sense of how manifest a thing is, or how manifest ('true') the intellect can make it, is inseparable from its sense of its perfection or appropriate goodness. Moreover, as we further concluded, this assessment is itself a registering of the inscrutable 'proportion' that pertains between the being of things and the human intellect – an analogical proportion which Aquinas specifically identifies as a participation in transcendental beauty.[14]

In contrast to many presentations, therefore, it can be seen that Aquinas's entire treatment of truth must be brought within the domain of his philosophical theology. It is not the case, for Aquinas, that one can be sufficiently assured of some specific truth merely by attending to a feature of the divine Creation, without necessarily recognizing it as created. On the contrary, for Aquinas, one can pronounce no judgement of truth without assessing a degree of appropriate participation in the transcendental attributes proper to divinity (though this is not to say that such an assessment need always be carried out with full reflexive consciousness of the *proportio* between creature and creator). Were one to attempt to comprehend a finite reality not as created, that is to say, not in relation to God, then no truth for Aquinas could ensue, since finite realities are of themselves nothing and only what is can be true.

If *intellectus* offers a certain measure of direct cognitive vision – though never, for now, apart from the discursiveness of *ratio* – then the 'light of faith' is for Aquinas simply a strengthening of the *intellectus* by a further degree of participation in the divine light. This strengthening shifts the balance of thought slightly away from discursivity and further towards the divine pure intuition – since an increase of 'light' means an increase in the relative immediacy of understanding.[15] In the case of the operation of reason, we have seen in the first chapter [of *Truth in Aquinas*] that Aquinas's continued Augustinian and Neoplatonic construal of truth as inner *illuminatio* can nonetheless incorporate (as it could already in Augustine, Proclus and Dionysius, if not Plotinus) an essential Aristotelian detour through the truth embodied in finite creatures and conveyed to us only via the senses. And while faith involves an intensification of participation in divine intellectual intuition, the same fusion of inner and outer is sustained in the knowledge accessible by faith (although it is just this fusion which is undone in later neo-scholastic accounts of revelation).[16] Here, also, for faith as for reason, the passive intellect marries the infallible witness of intellectual light to the infallible intuition of the senses (infallible so long as nothing contrary to the ordinary run of nature, such as a mirage, intervenes to distort their deliverances). Thus the paradigmatic scene of revelation, for Aquinas, is represented by the instance of prophecy. Here a supernatural supplement of infused cognitive light is inseparably conjoined with some extraordinary sensory vision, miraculous event, or at least novel historical occurrence.[17] Since all these latter three may only, as finite instances, mediate the divine in the shape of enigma, the visions which they offer are partial and can be disclosed in their meaning – and so fully seen – only through acts of inter-pretation (beginning with the prophet himself), as essential for faith as for reason. Thus, while an approach to pure vision is strengthened by faith, it still does not constitute a moment isolatable from discursive mediation.

It follows that, for Aquinas, revelation offers the extraordinary only in a very qua-lified fashion. Even the miraculous must be apprehended by the senses in the normal way, and is in continuity with the usual operation of nature insofar as what ultimately matters about both is the meanings they convey, not the equally limited realities which they instantiate. And the extraordinary is indeed confined to the manner or means of disclosure of meaning, since the meaning disclosed is simply divine reality. Thus, if reason leads us up to a God unknowable in this life, faith leads us to the same destination, and with the same restriction. It is only in post-Baroque conceptions of revelation that faith appears to answer to something 'more' – to new disclosures of information about God and about what God has done. Paradoxically, such newness can appear to throw into relief and to substantiate the pure autonomy of reason. But where, as with Aquinas, 'revelation' denotes simply God's self-disclosure, then no new domain other than that of reason is opened up since, as we have seen, we are only able to think at all within the arena of the divine self-disclosure and our partial grasp of the divine *reditio ad seipsum* [return to self] in which he substantially consists. Thus instead of reason's autonomy being thrown into relief by faith, reason itself, and the goals of reason, are further fulfilled by faith.

It follows that reason and faith are at the very least construed by Aquinas as suc-cessive phases of a single extension always qualitatively the same. That is to say, always conjoining inner illumination of the active intellect by God with formation of the passive intellect by species received from creatures whose being, equally with our intellect, is formed and measured by participation in the divine understanding.

III

There can equally be no doubt that Aquinas distinguishes between the theology that pertains to philosophy, on the one hand, and *sacra doctrina* [the 'holy teaching' of the Church], on the other. But again the difficult issue concerns exactly in what manner.

In this case, however, there would seem on the face of things to be a clearly made distinction. Breaking with Aristotle's alternations and aporias, Aquinas declares that the prime subject of metaphysics is being and not the first cause.[18] By 'being' as subject matter, Aquinas means here its transcendental properties such as 'substance', which need not inhere in matter (rendering them metaphysical) and excludes the 'causes of being' (only secondarily dealt with), which are its first principles, including the first cause: these cannot inhere in matter. One is tempted to say that with this development metaphysics has become a fundamental ontology; however, this transformation was yet to come (with Scotus). In Aquinas's case the subject matter of metaphysics is not being in its entirety, but *ens commune* [being in common], that being which is 'common' to finite creatures and distinguished from their natures or essences; being which is entirely secondary and created. God only enters into consideration for this newly restricted metaphysics insofar as it is obliged, like any science, as part of its procedure, to inquire into the causes of its subject matter.[19] As with any science, however, this inquiry must be very incomplete since (for Aquinas's set of Platonic/Aristotelian assumptions) the cause of a subject matter must necessarily transcend it and so be 'higher' than the effect it produces. By this token, the cause invoked necessarily belongs to the domain of a higher science, above the one being pursued. Hence, in the present instance, metaphysics is able barely to indicate the cause of *ens commune*, to pronounce it 'God', and to indicate negatively the properties of inconceivable absolute and simple power and undividedness it must possess in order to be able to bring forth actuality.

But concerning God as he is in himself, his 'whatness', it must remain silent. Such matters are the concern (according to the exposition in the opening question of the *Summa Theologiae*) of a higher science, above metaphysics. However, this higher science, uniquely, is beyond the capacities of human reason, since it concerns the spiritual and infinite, and human reason is attuned only to material finite things, not even to disembodied intelligence and still less to infinite reality. Therefore, in this case uniquely, there is a science that can be possessed properly only by that which it is the science of – God, who, being simple, is of course absolutely identical with his own self-understanding.[20] The only possible mode of access for human beings to this final science is in consequence by divine self-disclosure, upon which *sacra doctrina* is based. Like other restricted sciences, *sacra doctrina* borrows its assumptions and first principles from a higher science, but here this is the absolute science possessed by God and the blessed alone.[21]

The new Thomist restriction of metaphysics and consequent confinement of metaphysical knowledge of God to the *an est* [what is], reserving to *sacra doctrina* the exposition of the *quid est* [who is][22] – insofar as some remote intimation of this has been revealed to us – opens, of course, a tempting possibility for mediation between Barth and Aquinas on a post-Kantian basis.[23] For if one suggests, as one validly can, that the metaphysical knowledge of God as first cause in Aquinas is both thin and tentative, then the way lies open to stress that for him, as for Barth, all certainty regarding God derives from scripture. Now this stress is by no means false, but it can tend to ignore the fact that, for Aquinas, in an unBarthian fashion, scripture records the event of the augmentation of human intellect through a deepened participating in the divine simplicity. Thus, for Aquinas, it is less that metaphysics is abandoned by reflection on scripture, and much more that it is fulfilled in its intention, but beyond its own understanding of this intention. It is both suspended and subsumed. And we shall soon see that this continued deployment of metaphysics by *sacra doctrina* in fact calls into question the neat division of cognitive range between *an est* and *quid est*. The post-Kantian mediation between Thomas and Barth will turn out to be false, because the weak analogical recourses of metaphysics which reason to God only as first cause are in fact the only terms in which *sacra doctrina* can receive and comprehend the revelation of God as he is in himself. Since metaphysics can in this way be elevated, its limitations for Aquinas do not amount to the drastic ones perceived by Kant.

However, in terms of the apparently sharp *an est/quid est* division, it would seem that Aquinas authorizes, if not a fusion of Kantian philosophy and Barthian theology, then at least a clear division of theological subject matter between a doctrine of Creation accessible for metaphysics, on the one hand, and the rest of the credal teaching – supremely the doctrine of Trinity – accessible only for *sacra doctrina*, on the other.

Were matters as simple as this, then one would expect Aquinas to have divided up his substantive teaching accordingly. But he does not do so. Specifically, it is by no means clear that he ever engages in 'metaphysics' in his own right, as opposed to commenting on metaphysical treatises in a context which virtually equates metaphysics with 'pagan teaching'.[24] The nearest he comes to this might be the explicitly apologetic *Summa Contra Gentiles*, wherein he does indeed treat of God in relation to creatures by way of rational 'ascent' in the first three books, and then of God in himself by way of revelatory 'descent' in the fourth book, which includes an account of the Trinity.[25] This is not, however, necessarily regarded by Aquinas as an ideal scheme according to the intrinsic demands of the subject matter, and since the scheme is abandoned in the *Summa Theologiae*, there is every reason to assume (as Aquinas indeed indicates)[26] that it is adopted for reasons of apologetic strategy. Of course, that it can be so adopted is highly significant, and might seem to betoken the clear-standing independence of a metaphysical approach to God. However, throughout the first three parts scripture is cited (if with discrimination) and, more decisively, the doctrines of the beatific vision and of grace are dealt with, despite their (fully acknowledged by Aquinas) Christological and Trinitarian presuppositions. It is as if Aquinas's approach to apologetics was in fact highly pragmatic, in such a way that, in the 'broadly monotheist' first three parts, he included not only metaphysical considerations, but also doctrinal matter that might not appear so immediately alien to Muslims and Jews.

However, the *Summa Theologiae* should be taken as a more realistic guide at once to Aquinas's purely theological and to his most mature understanding (especially if it is intended for 'beginners' only in the sense of standing at the commencement of the most advanced stage of theological learning).[27] Here the treatment of the triune God is inserted after the exposition of divine unity (so concluding a single continuous treatment of God at the outset) and before a later reverting to more 'philosophical' topics (for example, concerning ethics). Moreover, in the *Summa Theologiae* it is clearer than with the *Summa Contra Gentiles* that the work throughout belongs to *sacra doctrina*. If God's unity and perfection are 'demonstrated', they are nonetheless also treated as revealed by scripture and testified to by tradition[28] (while, inversely, merely probable arguments are offered for the Trinity). Moreover, scripture primarily, and Christian tradition secondarily, are seen as contributing far more compelling evidence for the intellect (that is to say, as providing much stronger, because immediately apparent, *reasons*) than the even more weakly intuitive deliberations of philosophy.

Michel Corbin has pointed out another crucial difference from the *Summa Contra Gentiles*.[29] In the latter work, metaphysics operates within *ratio* and *scientia*, while the province of *sacra doctrina* tends to be that of *similitudo* – an imagined likeness of the divine intellect scarcely amounting to science. Correlatively, metaphysics here offers through all its *rationes* a mere *similitudo* of *sacra doctrina*.[30] However, in the *Summa Theologiae*, both metaphysical theology and *sacra doctrina* are brought firmly within the domain of *scientia*.[31] This is not at all, as Corbin rightly insists, merely in terms of a structural isomorphism. The latter was, indeed, all that was involved in Aquinas's initial understanding of *sacra doctrina* as *scientia* in the *Commentary on the Sentences*; here it meant simply that theology, also, makes deductions from first principles. Now, however, theology participates in the divine science, the mind of God, which includes in immediate indivision both 'principle' and 'derived conclusion', these being only distinguished according to our *modus significandi*. This is the new theory of *sacra doctrina* as a 'subalternate' science, borrowing from the conclusions of a higher science somewhat as music borrows from mathematics[32] – though the analogy can be, for Aquinas, only a remote one since mathematics does not 'pre-contain' music, nor in principle swallow it up without remainder, as the *Scientia Dei* so subsumes *sacra doctrina* in both instances.

If, however, in the *Summa Theologiae*, there is a much more integral relation between divine self-understanding and sacred theology, there is also a much more integral relation between sacred theology and metaphysics. The 'preliminary' role of metaphysics on its own as establishing God as first cause is now barely gestured towards,[33] and instead the focus is upon the need for *sacra doctrina* itself to deploy philosophical arguments.[34] Moreover, no longer does metaphysics offer vague similitudes of theological similitudes (in a fashion which tends to suggest more of a cleavage between discursive reason and the positive authority of faith). Instead, theology has direct recourse to metaphysical *scientia* – its unarguable principled insights and its discursive arguments – because it is in itself simply the deepening and strengthening of science. This recourse is not at all necessary because of any innate deficiency on the part of *sacra doctrina*, since, in principle, as the grasp of divine self-knowledge, it is not cognitively deficient in any respect whatsoever – not in relation to philosophy as metaphysics ('first' philosophy), nor in relation to philosophy as the various liberal arts. Rather, it is necessary on account of the innate deficiency of human reason, which cannot, short of the final vision of glory, grasp what is in itself most intelligible, but must explicate this in terms of reasonings clearer to humanity, but in themselves less clear, which is to say less rational.

Thus, as Corbin establishes, in the *Summa Theologiae*, philosophical theology figures much less as an independent phase with procedures and assumptions other than those of *sacra doctrina* (its role being now that of *manuductio* [leading]). To the contrary, it seems that within the scope of a single consideration (whether of, for example, the divine truth, or the persons of the Trinity), one passes imperceptibly from the relatively discursive to the relatively intuitive, as we more nearly approach the pure divine insight. Therefore, it is not at all here the case that reason offers certainty, and faith a clinging to uncertainties. Instead, there is one continuous passage of reason/faith from illusory relative certainty to obscurely envisaged absolute certainty. In addition, one can point out that in the realm of metaphysics, even the relative certainty proffered by reason is very weak. For scientific demonstration proper depends, for Aquinas after Aristotle, on a univocity of terms answering to a univocity between causes and effects. For Aquinas, this contention disallowed a transgeneric 'science' in the strictest sense, since the community of being (which Aquinas terms 'analogical'), permits no clear conception of a distinct operating substance (what is being outside its community?), nor of specific differentiation which constitutes scientific definitions (as nothing can be added to being, and it is no more nor less being in all its categorical and individualized manifestations).[35] Since, however, Aristotle placed the first mover within the genus of substance as the 'highest genus' that is 'immutable substance', and even saw it in its underived self-standing as paradigmatic of a substantive being, he was able to speak scientifically of 'God'.[36] Aquinas, however, by identifying God with non-generic *esse*, and by specifically excluding God from genus and from substance in the sense either of distinct essence or self-standing individual (though not in the sense of self-subsistent),[37] also ensures that there can only be an analogical and not strictly scientific approach to the divine. Hence, for example, his 'demonstrations' of God's existence can only be meant to offer weakly probable modes of argument and very attenuated 'showings'.

It is here significant that, despite Aquinas's supposedly more *a posteriori* and cosmological bent, he does deploy, almost as much as Anselm, an Augustinian 'logic of perfection'. Indeed, after the consideration of divine simplicity and being in the *Summa Theologiae*, the consideration of divine perfection and goodness immediately follows.[38] This is required, since a projection of what must belong to the perfect alone allows one to establish God's further attributes, given that he is radically unknown (and indeed it is actually presupposed by Aquinas even for simplicity and being). This primacy of perfection in Aquinas cannot simply be a matter of his empirically observing that in nature the relatively perfect precedes the relatively imperfect, since there is no available sensory information that will confirm this pattern in the most sublime height. Here, indeed, it might seem that we only know the most perfect (or absolute good) 'to be' because we respond to a certain pre-ontological insistence of the ideal (Plato's Sun of the Good beyond Being which itself discloses Being).

Thus *a posteriori* demonstration from creatures plays a weak role in Aquinas, and there is in fact much more Augustinian *a priori* (so to speak) argument – in terms of 'what must' belong to perfection – than is usually allowed. It is even the case that we only know God to be the fullness of *esse* without particular essential limitation, or restriction to this or that possibility of unrealized actuality, because we also know all finite beings under the aspect of *bonum*, or their always more or less desirability, and therefore cannot conceive of any bare 'fact' that does not incite some sort of assessment. (The idea that something 'either exists or not', without degrees of intensity of existing, is impossible for Aquinas, as it must still be for theology, since it implies a neutral, inert, meaningless and uncreated existing as belonging to a thing in its own right.) While, for Aquinas, in terms of substance, a thing primarily is said 'to be', and secondarily is said 'to be good' (since mere existence is also good), in terms of its operation it is primarily regarded as 'good' (since operation involves teleology) and secondarily as 'existing'. Yet (as we shall see) the 'second act' of operation is, for Aquinas, itself a superadded degree of *esse* that is more hyperessential than the 'original' given substance. This suggests strongly that we only grasp *esse* in its most intense aspect of superaddition to original substance (and essence) under the aspect of goodness (although of course the apprehensions of *esse* and *bonum* are only distinct for finite understanding).[39] Nonetheless, it suggests equally that, for Aquinas, the guiding apprehension of perfection is not after all of a pre-ontological formal possibility (as it soon became for Duns Scotus) but rather is a dim and remote perception of a plenitude of infinite actuality. The insistence of the ideal is, after all, as much ontological as pre-ontological.

Therefore Aquinas does not really have recourse to an *a priori* vision of the Good in the sense of a Kantian epistemological reflection on the structures of finite understanding, but to a Platonic and Augustinian ontological recollection of something real and eternal. If this recourse indicates the limits of Aristotelian cosmological aspirations in Aquinas, it is equally the case that, like Augustine, he refuses (as he thinks, against Anselm) any purely *a priori* philosophical theology, or argument from the conception of the highest perfection to the necessity of its existence. On the contrary, Aquinas does not regard perfection as self-evident when reduced to bare possibility, and therefore is able to entertain (apparently) equally a nihilistic possibility: although the highest good would have to *be*, there need not be a highest good.[40] Hence, after all, the only thing that authenticates perfection (and, indeed, the only thing that defines it) must be some sort of experience of its actuality. And this is indeed implied by Aquinas's repeated insistence on God's partial communication of his good to creatures in such a way that their goods can only be understood as good in their pointing away from themselves to the perfection they hint at (their own partial perfection consisting in just this hint).[41] That which clinches his exposition of the divine attributes is neither the ascent from effect to first cause nor the *a priori* grasp of the latter, but rather the (Dionysian) reading of the divine signs and symbols as disclosed in the hierarchies of participating creatures.[42] Such an hermeneutic space is, in metaphysical terms, highly elusive and unstable, since it is grounded neither in firm *a posteriori* evidences, nor in solid *a priori* necessities. Given this conclusion, it is not surprising that in the *Summa Theologiae* Aquinas asserts the tentative character of all philosophic deliverance about God in the face of revelation, and claims that even philosophic 'certainties' are confirmed more strongly, or can even be overruled by, *sacra doctrina*.[43]

If metaphysical theology is so uncertain that it enjoys, at best, a weak autonomy, this is not at all to say that, for Aquinas, by contrast, *sacra doctrina* is triumphantly disclosive. Here, instead, we discover that the contrast of the two theologies now further breaks down, but this time from the opposite direction. For, while it is said of metaphysical theology that it can only know that God is (as first cause), what he is not, and by no means what he is, exactly the same restrictions are placed on *sacra doctrina*.[44] It is after all, therefore, not the case that for Aquinas philosophy knows God barely to be, while theology proper declares his nature. To the contrary, it seems that both can do the former, and neither can do the latter. So what does *sacra doctrina* add, and why are there two theologies?

At this point another temptation arises, and one somewhat succumbed to by those, in the wake of Henri Trouillard, wishing to slant Aquinas in a henological rather than ontological direction.[45] This is to suppose that what revelation discloses is an absolute degree of divine unknowability, a *deus absconditus* at a 'distance' absolutely removed even from the causal apex of being arrived at by philosophy, and so from intellection, actuality, unified mind and personality. One problem with this position is that it seems to leave the finite symbolic and historical vehicles of revelation stranded in a pure positivity, just as the gulf which it imposes between infinite and finite must tend to a quasi-Manichean refusal of finitude.[46]

Such a second temptation – a radicalization of the first Kantian one, since it renders the beyond-limits an empty sublime – should also be resisted. For, in his *Commentary on Boethius's De Trinitate*, Aquinas explicitly follows Gregory the Great's as it were 'Hegelian' deconstruction of a 'Kantian' distinction between the *an est*, taken as a bare acknowledgement that there exists an ultimate noumenon (to speak in Kantian terms), and the *quod est*, taken as knowledge of God 'in himself'.[47] Aquinas, after Gregory, insists that one cannot know that a thing is without having some dim inkling of what it is, since nothing is ever manifest or judged as manifest in entirely neutral anonymity. This applies, one might interpolate, even in this extreme limit situation, since to glimpse any boundary, even an absolute boundary, must be to see, however inchoately, beyond that boundary, else one's gaze would pass right through it and one would register no boundary after all. One can also point out the crucial but unstated and merely implicit coherence here with Aquinas's refusal of the ontological argument, as detailed above. For one might indeed be able to acknowledge a bare absolute cause without content were such a possibility existentially self-authenticating, but, if this is not the case, then indeed one will only affirm such a cause if in some manner (it is very difficult to say how) its reality is manifest to us and we know incoherently what it is. (This is an actual theoretical presence of course deemed impossible by Kant, but on the basis of a non-problematization of limits which Aquinas had already surpassed. Also one can note here that the Kantian 'practical' postulation of God runs from 'ought' to 'can' to 'is', and so, in effect, is the ontological argument denied in theoretical reason. And, since, for Kant, only practical reason observes fully the priority of the possible, and is thus for his rationalism much more rational than the-oretical reason, which is taken to be too much in slavery to actuality, the ontological argument is, in Kantian terms, much more properly 'practical'.[48] Thus Jacques Mar-itain (however much he has been sneered at) was absolutely right as against Gilson and others to claim that there is some inchoate temporal knowledge of the divine essence in Aquinas.[49] And two other considerations support this conclusion. First of all, philosophical reason for Aquinas concludes to God (the ground of causation) as *esse ipsum* [being itself], but, since God's essence is 'to be', to arrive in this fashion at an apparently bare existential affirmation is, uniquely in the case of God, to arrive also at some recognition of essence, albeit with the strict proviso that we no more comprehend what it is simply 'to be' in the infinitive (without tensed, pronomical or other mode of inflection) than we comprehend the divine *essentia*. However, the recent scholarship of Rudi te Velde and others has insisted that form and essence do not collapse into *esse* in God for Aquinas, but rather *esse* and *essentia* absolutely coin-cide in God in such a way that God is superformal, 'most formal of all' and infinitely determined (not emptily existential). This reinforces the view that to encounter — in some fashion — God as *esse* is to encounter him in some small degree as he in himself.[50]

The second consideration concerns Aquinas's view of causality. Aquinas consistently takes a Neoplatonic view according to which an effect is like its cause, indeed pre-eminently exists in its cause. As Jean-Luc Marion astutely suggests, this causal origin is really for Aquinas less Aristotelian 'cause' than the Dionysian 'requisite' (*aitia*), or attribution to the original source of the 'gift' of the effect in its whole entirety as effect.[51] For this view (which entirely circumvents David Hume's correct critique of the metaphysics and physics of causality), a cause does not really 'precede' an effect, since it only becomes cause in realizing itself as the event of the giving of the effect.

Thus, for Aquinas, in the case of divine causality, the decision to create and the 'eminent' reality of creatures are included in the eternal uttering of the Logos.[52] Inversely, an effect does not really come after a cause, since only the effect realizes the causal operation and defines it. In other words, there is always a Humean surplus of pure inexplicable 'succession' which is the apparently random surplus of a new event over the event which precedes it, unless a cause is more than a cause, but rather the entire gift of the effect and the emanation of the effect, which itself defines the cause as cause. (One can see how the Trinity perfects this conception.) Hence the doctrine that effects resemble their causes is not an embarrassing metaphysical residue in Aquinas, but an intrinsic part of an essentially non-metaphysical (!) transmutation of cause, since metaphysics tends to view cause as straightforwardly prior to, and independent of, its effects. As Marion indicates, a reduction of causality to efficient causality fulfils the metaphysical aspiration, and does not withdraw from it, as is usually thought. Given this understanding of causality in terms of requisition and participation, to know God as cause – as supreme form, as supreme goal, as the supreme being, perfection and manifestedness of things – must mean to enter more deeply into effects in such a fashion that one starts to know more of them also in their source and origin.

Thus, instead of insisting that, for Aquinas, not even *sacra doctrina* knows the divine essence in this life (though this is largely true), it is much more important to insist that even philosophical theology knows something of this essence (and one can note that, for Aquinas, even knowledge of finite essences is merely partial).[53] The question is, how can this be, without idolatrous impiety, and this will be answered in the next section. For now what is clear is that the *an est/quid est* contrast entirely fails to distinguish the two theologies. Corbin is quite correct to note that interest in any such distinction fades away in the *Summa Theologiae*.

Moreover, when one brings into juxtaposition (as Aquinas explicitly does not), the presentation of 'metaphysics' in the *Commentary on Aristotle's Metaphysics*, and the presentation of *sacra doctrina* in the *Summa Theologiae*, then one is struck by the fact that both are subordinated, albeit in different manners, to an inaccessible *Scientia Dei*. As we have seen, the subject matter of metaphysics for Aquinas is unequivocally being (whereas for Aristotle it was aporetically and ontotheologically either being-in-general or the first-being [God], in such a way that in a circular fashion God is an instance of being in general and yet being in general is paradigmatically defined in terms of the perfect substance which is God).[54] However, the ultimate goal of investigation of a subject matter, according to Aquinas, is discovery of its cause, and hence God as cause of *ens commune* is a secondary concern of metaphysics. Here, though, one might ask, what is the relation between concluding to a cause which is the subject of a higher science (God's own) in metaphysics, and deriving the first principles of one's science from a higher science (Gods own) in *sacra doctrina*? For are not, for Aquinas as for Aristotle (as not for post-Kantian philosophy), epistemological principles identical with ontological causes? Is not the end here also the beginning? To be sure this does not necessarily mean that higher causes/principles are always adequate grounds of effects/consequences – this constitutes the 'Humean' deficiency already alluded to. Hence the realities of mathematics (abstractable from specific matter, not from any matter) are certainly principles and causes of physical realities (only present in specified matter) and yet they do not 'account for' physical motion (the heart of physics after Aristotle) any more than mathematics fully 'accounts for' music. However, Aquinas speaks of the need for a science fully to account for the genus of its subject matter, citing the physical investigation of 'natural bodies'.[55] Now physics, for Aquinas, fully accounts for motion, the heart of such realities, in terms of an appeal to the first mover, God. And this pushes us nearer to a cause not simply 'prior' (certainly not temporally, but also in a certain sense already described, not even ontologically), a cause which can alone be adequate, fulfilling the 'requisite'.

The 'first mover' emerges as the conclusion of a consideration of the subject matter of 'moving things'. But as Aquinas's arguments for a first mover (all the five ways, taken together) show, they only work because motion is understood from the outset as being undergone with a purpose, or for a reason, and on account of a goal in accord with a nature. Therefore, if all these motions are themselves unmoved, their very motions – which is to say their purposes, reasons, goals, and natures – are themselves illusory.[56] In knowing motions, therefore, which are all aims towards perfections (while the latter are only knowable as participations of the supreme end, the supreme good), the first mover is really radically presupposed. The conclusion to a cause only works because of an initial dim apprehension of the cause as principle.

So must not something similar apply in the case of metaphysics? Are not its argued-to causes also secretly initially presupposed principles? One could, however, argue here that Aristotle, unlike Plato, discovers principles purely immanent to finitude in the shape of real abstract universals not situated at a distance from the particulars from which they are abstracted: specifically the principles of substantive form (uneasily and aporetically poised between concrete individual and general essence). One could further argue that Aquinas renders those principles more independent (compared with Aristotle) of any paradigmatic appeal to the unmoved first mover. On this understanding (which has some plausibility), Aquinas would have moved halfway towards a Scotist pure ontology independent of theology, by allowing for a complete prior knowledge of finite essence and substance innocent of later queries as to origins. However, such a position would assume, like Scotus, that finite things univocally 'are' as much as the infinite, whereas Aquinas affirms that they only 'are' in a derived, approximate, analogical sense. Since he also takes pure being, *esse*, to be alone absolutely self-subsistent (in such a way that its individuating 'is' is its general nature and vice-versa, as if Socrates 'were' humanity – although God is neither 'individual' nor 'general'), it follows that finite things are also only substantive in a derived sense. Hence Aquinas speaks of metaphysics as concerned with *passiones entis* or the 'proper accidents' of being (*ens commune*) which are the several predicaments, including sub-stance.[57] The point here is that finite being is not on its own account subsistently anything, but is only granted to be in various ways, although these include the mode of finite necessity and the mode of (relative) substance. Moreover, these accidents are 'proper', since finite 'common' being can only be through these characteristic modes, and only these accidents paradoxically grant it the various things proper to itself which essentially define it.

Nothing, therefore, for Aquinas, in the finite realm properly 'is' of itself, nor is 'subsistent' of itself, nor is essentially formed of itself. If it is true (as commentators all acknowledge), that being is an *adveniens extra* which is 'superadded' to essence or form as an 'accident' (a locution Aquinas never altogether abandons),[58] then it is equally true that, since Aquinas holds that *forma dat esse* [form gives being],[59] form or essence are also superadded, and essence cannot be a kind of independent receiving finite 'base'. (Erich Przywara worried about this in Aquinas, but almost needlessly, although essence/form never, for Aquinas, quite holds parity with *esse*.) As Rudi te Velde points out, were this so, then essence would appear to be an element positively proper to finitude and outside participating emanation, whereas Aquinas affirms that all finite being emerges from nothing only as, and through, its likeness to the divine. In keeping with this perspective, he holds that the higher in the scale of being things are (advancing, after Augustine, as we saw in the first chapter, from being through life to intelligence), the more they are defined in their essence not through their 'first act' of subsistent existence such as the 'burning' of fire, but rather through their properly accidental 'second act' (or second perfection) of effective operation (which is also a more intense existing, so that second act is more to be characterized as *esse*, first act more as *essentia*) – such as the heating and drying and liquefying caused by fire.[60] At the *telos* of this operation, things are also defined through a 'third perfection' which is the ecstatic attaining to 'something else' that is yet one's goal, one's rest. Supremely, under this scheme, thought is not the substantive essence of soul, since soul is the form of an animal, and its thinking power in humanity may be dormant, but rather a mere 'power' of the soul, even if – as a proper accident – it is 'consequent' upon the essence of the soul. And yet the 'actively potential', and properly accidental emanation of this power, is nonetheless what most defines the human animal.[61] With his effortless cunning (although it is the cunning of Proclean Neoplatonism itself), Aqui-nas fuses Aristotelian naturalism with Neoplatonic participation – this non-essential, mere thinking-tool owned by an animal is nonetheless the superadded descending *palladium* which renders us superessentially as we are, more than we are.

If *esse* and *essentia* are superadded, then so is subsistence. It is true that existentially 'to be' and essentially 'to be something' and substantively 'to be something in this' (e.g. human only by being Socrates or whomsoever) are only distinguished in finite crea-tures and therefore in one sense (as affirmed by Jean-Luc Marion in the case of being),[62] it is only creatures who are, or have natures or substances. However, in another equally or even more crucial sense, 'something' cannot fully be except by being absolutely all realized possibilities (for in this way it cannot not be and it cannot be more than it is); nor can something be fully defined except through an infinite operation; nor can something fully subsist unless it combines the self-standing of an individual with the self-determination of an essence and the repletion of unqualified *esse*.[63] Thus, while God is beyond substance as given foundation, individual or universal, it is also the case that in none of these three finite modes (there being for Aquinas no original matter to supply a pure foundation) is true subsistence to be found, as it is in God. Creatures, for Aquinas, beneath the level of patterns of granted relative necessity and subsistence, are radically accidental. But not thereby, of course, accidents of the divine substance; rather they subsist by participation in this substance.

Nevertheless, Aquinas proclaims that metaphysics most of all treats of substance.[64] What can this mean, if metaphysics is now primarily about *ens commune*, not God, and yet subsistence is alienated to God? Is it that Aquinas's metaphysics moves in an ontotheological circle after all? No: it is rather that to look for the cause of *ens commune* (or *esse commune*, as sometimes phrased), finite essence, and finite substance, is to recomprehend this 'subject matter' in its own fundamental depth of origin from *esse* identical with *essentia* and *subsistentia*. In this causal referral, no surplus of integral effect remains, unlike the case of physical motion in relation to mathematics and geometry, or music to mathematics. But, at the same time, one must be referring all to a cause already dimly grasped as principle, since *ens commune*, finite essence and finite substance are only comprehensible as faint adumbrations of the one divine formal archetype. This is theoontology, not ontotheology, for, in order to comprehend this archetype, it did not need first to be situated in a 'general discourse' about being, essence and substance, indifferent to finite and infinite, as later articulated by Scotus.[65] Therefore, in referring its subject matter to a higher cause and a higher science, metaphysics must for Aquinas be moving (unlike physics or music) towards its own abolition. This is not, of course, because he espouses a theological arrogance, but merely because nothing can be added to the divine knowledge or divine power. Any philosophical additions which continue to be required are a consequence of our continued (but potentially ever-diminishing) imperfection, not of a kind of divinely decreed division of intellectual labour.

But the more radical implication of the above analysis is that the metaphysical argument from subject matter to alien higher cause is structurally indistinguishable from *sacra doctrina*'s derivation from alien higher principles. It seems, then, that metaphysics as self-abolishing and self-evacuating (in order to fulfil itself), is already, in some weak sense, *sacra doctrina*: indeed Aquinas explicitly affirms that all speculative sciences participate in and anticipate the light of glory – an assertion which is equivalent to such a claim, since what constitutes *sacra doctrina* is precisely this participation and anticipation.[66] And, after all, how can metaphysics remain as 'the architectonic science' if there is a still higher, more architectonic science which is nonetheless radically unknown? This being the case, in order to fulfil its architectonic role, metaphysics must seek revealed guidance from above, thereby becoming merely artisanal, subordinate and no longer metaphysical. Inversely, therefore, *sacra doctrina* now articulates the real metaphysics, the real ontology, theology, gnoseology, and so forth. And just as the causes found by metaphysics at the end were really the principles known at the beginning, so, counterwise, the principles revealed to *sacra doctrina* at the outset are really the causes sought at its conclusion. For *sacra doctrina* does not add consequences drawn by human science to principles derived from divine science, as music might infer harmonies from mathematical ratios. On the contrary, since the divine principles include immediately in all their simplicity all the 'consequences', or, rather, since here there are only principles,[67] *sacra doctrina* seeks to penetrate more and more the consequential effectiveness or causal potency of the divine principles of knowledge which are equally the divine principles of action (since in God theory and practice are identical). Just like metaphysics, only with more intensity, it begins improperly with created effects and refers them in their entirety – removing them from their own nullity to their divine letting-be – to the divine cause, which exceeds *sacra doctrinal* powers of comprehension. Thus, as with faith and reason, the difference between the two theologies in Aquinas is at most one of degree and of different phases within a single extension.

IV

However, in the case of both pairs, even this distinction of phases is not so clear. First of all, let us return to the issue of faith and reason.

In the first question of the *Summa Theologiae*, Aquinas asks why, if God can be naturally known, he has to be discursively inferred, and is not immediately apparent. In reply, however, he affirms that there is, indeed, an inchoate ordering of all human reasoning to the beatific vision, the final intellectual intuition of God.[68] Thus, beneath the distinction of *fides* [faith] and *ratio* [reason] along our temporal ways, lies the much more fundamental contrast between *in patria* and *in via*. According to this contrast, both faith and reason are dim anticipations of the final vision of glory. One here finds confirmed the view that, for Aquinas, since *a priori* reasonings to God are refused, and straightforward *a posteriori* inductions are equally impossible, discursive reasoning about God must presuppose a disclosure of God to our *intellectus*, which enjoys a very remote participation in the divine immediacy of vision. In the passage cited, Aquinas compares this remote glimpse to a first sight of 'Peter' in the distance before we know that it is, indeed, Peter who approaches. It is therefore clear that Aquinas, like Augustine before him, associates our continuous approach to the beatific vision with 'the Meno problematic', or the need already to know something before one can possibly come to know it – for how else will one in the first place seek to know it at all? And the same problematic (with the added example of the child first addressing all men vaguely as 'father') is alluded to in the passage in the *Commentary on Boethius's de Trinitate* already discussed, where it is directly associated with the assertion that we must in some way already know the divine essence in order to affirm God's existence.[69]

From Augustine and Anselm, therefore, Aquinas has inherited a deep identification of the Platonic problematic of knowledge with Christian eschatological tension. For the first two thinkers, reason itself is faith seeking understanding, since for thought to get going it must not only trust its first sight of a man in the distance, but must first believe the reports of others that this is to be called 'man'. And if, for all these thinkers, reason for now can only be faith, then, inversely, faith for now can only develop its insights rationally and discursively, while finally it is destined to be pure *intellectus*, when we shall see as we are seen (though not enjoy any Hegelian 'comprehension' of the absolute). Once freed from our bodily carapace, the contrast between object seen and medium-seen-by disappears (here Aquinas is Aristotelian and Neoplatonic since he refuses an alleged Platonic 'polytheistic' diversity of many forms 'illumined' by the sun of the Good), and we see only what we see by the uncreated light, though we receive it still only in part, and also as created.[70]

However, Aquinas introduces a yet more dramatic association of knowledge in general with eschatological vision. In the middle of part one of the *Summa Theologiae*, he executes the most extraordinary *chiasmus*. For in expounding the divine attributes, one might expect Aquinas to proceed, after his treatment of being, simplicity and perfection (goodness), quite shortly to transcendental truth and intellection. Instead, before anything has been said of divine intellect or will (approaching 'personhood'), Aquinas details God's presence to creatures, under the heading of divine substance.[71] This drastically indicates that God's omnipresence simply is God himself, and that there cannot really be any being 'other' than God. Such omnipresence is seen as the direct effect of divine goodness, and elsewhere Thomas cites Dionysius's 'daring to say' that God on account of his goodness exists 'as it were outside of himself'.[72] For only this impossible self-exteriorization will explain how there can be something other to God participating in God, when God is in himself the repletion of being. This impossible conjecture is the most that can be said. In part one of the *Summa Theologiae*, however, it is added that God is especially and uniquely present to intellect, where 'he dwells as if in his own temple'; also it is made clear that intellect simply is this more intense presence, and that this presence is only by grace.[73] Thus at the heart of the chiastic reversal – Creation and humanity dealt with under divine substance – grace appears for the first time, and in the midst of what some have taken to be an exercise in purely rational theology. One could interpret this to mean that, for Aquinas (and here we press perhaps beyond the *nouvelle théologie*), all creatures subsist by grace in the sense that they only subsist in their constant 'return' to full divine self-presence, while intellect simply is the consciousness of this return.[74] Thus not only is the intellect grace; it is in a sense simply the site of manifestation of the creature, and so of grace. Because we are mind, humans specifically are destined to be deified.

It is only after this description of mind as the event of divine kenotic descent, that Aquinas redescribes it as also the event of eschatological ascent: in other words, his account of the beatific vision is deliberately placed quite shortly after his account of divine omnipresence. In this account, as de Lubac pointed out (thus continuing and recommencing the real theological revolution of the twentieth century),[75] Aquinas argues that reason has a natural urge to see the divine essence, since science is unsatisfied till it knows the nature of a cause. And, since nature cannot be frustrated, he further argues that this urge must be capable of fulfilment.[76] On the other hand, he equally affirms that such a supernatural fulfilment surpasses the capacity of human nature in such a way that reason can only fulfil its aspiration by grace.[77] Today, Catholic conservatives like J.-H. Nicolas, who wish to back away from de Lubac's revolution, try to claim that only the fulfilment is granted by grace, while the impulse to the beatific vision is purely natural.[78] Yet this cannot be the case, because a nature is fulfillable as a nature; it demands as of right fulfilment, and hence, if we are naturally orientated to the supernatural, this can only be because our original and 'most proper' nature is a paradoxically superadded nature (a supreme instance of 'second act'), giving us more than our due as our due, and pulling us naturally beyond our nature in an *ecstasis* [beyond oneself] at the outset.

But since our mind cannot fulfil its own rationality, except through knowing the divine essence, and since otherwise it would not 'see' that the highest imaginable perfection 'is', whereas it might not be, rendering the world without order or meaning (and imagination mere fiction), there simply would be no 'reason' whatsoever, outside the orientation to beatitude. Mind is the continuing event of this orientation, suspended between the already of a pre-discursive glimpse of the final vision of God and the not yet of the full realization.

It might, however, be contended that these passages which seem to render reason as faith (and whose drastic implications are still resisted by much conservative and liberal Catholic theology within their shared assumptions) are confusing aberrations, not hermeneutically decisive. But in reply one can point to the cruciality of the context of the passage on orientation to beatitude: namely the chiastic *interruptus* (also present in a different way in the *Summa Contra Gentiles*)[79] of the treatment of divine substance. The chiasmic reversal is completed when, after the treatment of the creation and finite mind under divine substance, Aquinas proceeds to treat divine truth and intellect under divine operation. Thus, to the elevation of our being into the divine substance, answers God's foreshadowing, within himself, of a proceeding beyond himself. And surely this chiasmic structure implies that Aquinas is advancing from an 'impersonal' knowledge of God as One and Good, shared with pagans like Proclus, to a more Christian apprehension of God as intentional mind and will and so as personal. Also, that while the first knowledge may be relatively a matter of rational ascent, the second is only granted through the radical descent of grace (even if Aristotle was able to anticipate fully divine nous). Moreover, intellection as a more intense presence of God, already suggests that God must first be disclosed if he is to be desired, and thus that in us, as in God, logos must precede will (in God the Holy Spirit) — while only a gracious right-willing and desiring allows us to recognize what appears as a horizon of aspiration.

Thus it would appear that reason is not even a 'phase' distinct from faith — though it may offer a lesser degree of intensity — since it is situated in the same 'intense' suspension between time and eternity, and Aquinas affirms, as has been said, that all speculative sciences participate obscurely in the beatific vision. And this interpretation is confirmed by Aquinas's treatment of the historical perspective. Before the fall, reason was perfected by an original grace and righteousness which included an anticipation of the Incarnation in its aspect of glory (as Bruce Marshall has rightly insisted).[80] From this we can see that the beatific orientation is always, also, a Christological one. After the Fall, humans lost this original righteousness, and became incapable of obeying the natural law: Aquinas is quite clear, we cannot do any genuinely 'natural' good.[81] Equally, as Bruce Marshall has also pointed out, Aquinas declares that the 'partial' knowledge of God enjoyed by the pagans is no knowledge at all since, given the divine simplicity, to know only some of the divine attributes is not to know any of them properly (and we shall see later that the exposition of the Trinity completes the account of divine simplicity).[82] However, as Eugene Rogers has stressed, since God's creative action is not to be thwarted, the original righteousness becomes, after the fall, immediately available again as redeeming grace, already present in natural and historical typological anticipations of Christ.[83] For Aquinas, indeed, 'the invisible things of God' in Romans always made visible everywhere suggested precisely a manifestation of the divine essence, which can only be made available by grace.

V

If faith and reason are not distinct phases, then neither are the two theologies. In fact, this has already been more or less demonstrated in section III, since there it was seen that metaphysics self-collapses into *sacra doctrina*, while the latter, as *in via* [on the way' to the perfection of knowledge] must remain in the unsatisfactory transitional state which is 'metaphysical'.

Now, however, we wish to underline Aquinas's transmutation of the idea of an architectonic science, and his undermining of metaphysics' independent architecture. The vital issue here is the handling of the transcendentals, and, in particular, Being. Can metaphysics, for Aquinas, really sustain a treatment of being as transgeneric? And is *ens commune* (the subject of metaphysics) like *esse* (a divine attribute) genuinely transgeneric? Commentators tend to dismiss Aquinas's occasional description of *ens commune* as a genus as a vague locution, but this may be too hasty.[84] For when discussing whether God enjoys knowledge of particulars, unlike our abstracting mind, Aquinas refuses one Arabic position according to which God only knows creatures under their 'being in general'.[85] This does, indeed, suggest that *ens commune*, since it is really distinct from creaturely *essentia* (for creatures might not be), is a kind of abstracted, 'bare' existential. (Here one might note that, for Aquinas, 'being' does not coincide with 'real', since for him 'real' stands in contrast with 'intellectual' or 'formal', not with nullity: hence mathematical entities 'are', but are not 'real'; reality denotes a more intense degree of being.)[86] It would follow that if metaphysics examines the accidental predicaments of *ens commune*, it cannot properly deal with *esse* which, as transgeneric, is just as fully instantiated in the concrete individual as the universal essence, or in an accident as in a substance. So what may be unstated by Aquinas, and is yet everywhere implicit, is that there is a radical inconsistency between Aristotle's claim, on the one hand, that metaphysics is the science of being which is transgeneric, and his claim, on the other, that as an architectonic science it only lays down an abstract ground plan, leaving the details of intellectual treatment to other sciences whose narrower scope is yet beyond its own competence. For if metaphysics deals with being, then surely it should deal with all there is. Surely it should be as variously artisanal as it is architectonic? At this juncture a formal/material distinction becomes deconstructible: the most general categories which we must presuppose – being, unity, truth, goodness, etc. – can only be formally denned through the endless empirical task of material description and redescription of an infinite number of particulars: metaphysics here becomes also history.

God's self-knowledge, as simple, is at once formal and material, and therefore exceeds the metaphysical as the ground of the historical. For whereas the self-thinking of the Aristotelian first mover is abstract, and does not extend to material particulars and so is 'metaphysical', the self-thinking of God, for Aquinas, includes all the exact details of every way in which he can be participated.[87] Therefore it is only architectonic to the degree that it is also artisanal, and only lays down the formal ground plan as the ideal comprehensive *esse* of the entire construction: since God's *theoria* is also practice, his 'preceding' idea is only realized with the completed 'work' of his emanating *verbum* [word].[88] Thus, even for God, a pure seeing is also an immediate judging articulation. And, since God is *esse*, he does indeed immediately contain in a unified expression which is also a single intuition[89] an infinitude of participated knowledge. In this way God's science corresponds to the transgeneric status of *esse* – the impossibility of hierarchically dividing it, or of qualifying it by addition – in a way that metaphysics as merely foundational and preliminary simply cannot. (This also shows that Aquinas, by rendering God's science equally and ecstatically present to the lower as to the higher, breaks with Aristotle's psycho-political paradigm for metaphysics – referred to by Aquinas in his *Proemium* to his commentary on the Metaphysics – which appeals to the need for self-government, or rule of lower parts of a whole by a higher.) It is in consequence clear that, as Marion now rightly declares,

Aquinas entirely alienates *esse* to God.[90] But in that case, since the divine essence which is *esse* is only disclosed to *sacra doctrina*, he also alienates *esse in toto* to *sacra doctrina* (and likewise subsistence, form and essence, since these also, as shown in section III, belong properly to God alone and are superadded along with *esse*).

Now it may seem that this Platonic and theoontological reading of Aquinas is at variance with his Aristotelian recognition of a level of abstraction of universal form which does not involve elevation and separation. Aquinas makes this recognition because he accepts Aristotle's argument that forms situated eternally apart from finite things cannot really be the substantial forms of those things, or in other terms do not account for their separate subsistent existence.[91]

However, Aquinas's Aristotelian criticisms of Plato with respect to theology (for example in the *Commentary on the de Causis*)[92] again and again involve: (1) the refusal of many forms as inconsistent with monotheism; (2) the refusal of forms prior to the intellect as inconsistent with a personal God; and (3) the refusal of matter as privative as inconsistent with Creation. In other words, the Aristotelian critique of Platonic theology (as Aquinas supposed it to be) is basically a bolstering of a Christian critique. And the same thing can even be said of his defence of Aristotelian finite substance, since this secures the independent reality and goodness of the Creation. However, in his early *Commentary on Boethius's de Hebdomadibus*, Aquinas, after Boethius, faced a dilemma: if created substances are only good as receiving good from God, that is, by participation, then how can they be said to be good at all, good in themselves, good in their substance?[93] Solving this dilemma in part motivates Aquinas's switch of emphasis from *bonum* to *esse*: for he argues that it is subsistent existence, as a participant in *esse*, that is itself the most fundamentally participatory thing. Hence, a thing can be good of itself and yet also good only by borrowing since its very own being is the most borrowed thing of all. But, at the same time, and inversely, that which is lent by God, granted to be participated in, is primarily the gift of relative self-standing, in accord with the Dionysian idea that God's goodness is his 'standing outside of himself'. Both these notions reconstrue participation as grace and kenosis, but they do not add grace and kenosis to participation.

However, since relative individual self-subsistence, always open to the super-essential addition of second act, is now itself radically participatory, Platonism trumps Aristotelianism in Aquinas in such a way that, instead of the most general and abstract being removed from material things, it is rather individual material things which are paradoxically removed from themselves – referred beyond themselves in order to be recognized as themselves (and this may well be the real Plato, as Aquinas could not have known).[94] But this concrete material unity which is thus referred upwards is also equally a general formal unity and being, in such a way that the transcendentals, unlike *genera*, are fully present in each one of their instantiations. Therefore the upward referral of unities in their transcendental unity, which is not that of diverse species, is not in danger of diversifying the divine in a 'polytheist' fashion.

It follows that there can indeed be no secure, immanent, Aristotelian consideration of either being or substance for Aquinas, since metaphysics will not answer to the transgeneric manifestness of being (nor even of substance taken in a fully transcendental sense, according to which even an accident must have a certain secure integrity: for Aquinas, accidents 'are' through substance).[95] Only God's own science, and then *sacra doctrina*, can so answer. Thus *sacra doctrina* as meta-architectonic is really only architectonic as also artisanal and bumpkin-like. It does not, declares Aquinas, in apparent deficit of metaphysics, supply any principles to subordinate sciences; however, in excess of metaphysics, it can judge the conclusions of all subordinate sciences.[96] This must follow since *sacra doctrina* is the true transgeneric science of *esse* and can in principle further illuminate being in all its instantiations. Thus, although it deals with the real under the aspect of *revelabile* (as sight with reality under the aspect of colour), when anything discloses God it must, since it has its entire being from God, disclose itself more intensely and without remainder. God knows all things in their eminent reality — therefore it is clear that a disclosure of this science does not, in principle, require supplementation by other sciences, and can, in principle, as Aquinas insists, revise all their conclusions. However, this is not a programme for the extermination of other faculties, since for now theology continues to be mediated by metaphysics, and even more by the philosophical liberal arts, as those disciplines concern concrete specificities to which theology proper (*sacra doctrina*), unlike metaphysics, extends. One could even say that theology only exists in its infusing inflection of the arts and not somehow 'in itself'. Philosophy as metaphysics, however, because of its inadequate response to its own subject matter, as detailed above, does have a tendency to be 'evacuated' by *sacra doctrina*.[97] (For this process, Aquinas offers military as well as chemical comparisons.)[98]

But why, if *sacra doctrina* judges even conclusions, does it offer no principles? The answer is astutely offered by Corbin: it is because theology as science in Aquinas redefines the very idea of science, away from discursivity and towards pure intuition, on its way to the beatific vision.[99] Thus to receive, obscurely, the first principles of divine science from God, is also to receive obscurely all the conclusions of divine science, which are the principles, since God only sees (although he sees through making, and through making sees). So, as Corbin argues, even though *sacra doctrina* is now conceived as more 'scientific' than previously, this now implies that it receives divine principles/ consequences with a greater non-discursive immediacy. But since we, as embodied creatures, can only enjoy an intense intuition via the senses, we now aspire higher only by attending more closely to the lower sensory realm to which God condescends. As metaphysics is now for *sacra doctrina* history, our reasoning must occur much more through images, narratives and liturgical offerings. Above all, it is *sacra scriptura* [sacred scripture] as read, manifested and performed (for it was not yet a discrete, foundational and merely written text), which now shows us science at its most scientific.[100]

Metaphysical theology and *sacra doctrina* are not then discrete phases since for Aquinas there is only one never fully realized temporal passage from metaphysical discursivity with its incapacities fully to think the transgeneric (or to comprehend the formal as the material and vice versa), to the perfect vision of the divine self-understanding. But the mark of progress along this *via* is increasingly to see such historical development as itself the cognitive goal – itself the continuous manifestation of the transcendental. This is to look in history for the complete divine descent which can alone correct our wilfully wayward vision (which cannot see the invisible that is fully manifest in the visible) – a descent always presupposed as the only possible sustaining of original righteousness, but a descent which, much more emphatically, we are always yet to arrive at, even *anno domini*, as our final conclusion.

VI

Is it not the case, however, that Aquinas considers that natural reason can know God as one, and as creator, whereas faith is required to know God's inner life as triune? The first half of this contention must be considered false: first, because we have seen that the understanding of God as intellectual and willing, and so as creative, presupposes grace; and, secondly, because creatures are causally referred to the divine *esse*, which as transgeneric and inclusive of all reality is revealed as a divine name, not infallibly inferred.

In addition, it has been seen how not only Creation as a whole is a gift for Aquinas, but each creature is ceaselessly reconstituted through supplementation, in such a way that the 'more' and 'later' is taken paradoxically to define it. These instances of proper accidents arising through the second act of operation also involve the constitution of 'real relations' (as, for example, between a thing causing and a thing caused) in such a way that relations entered into in time can nonetheless be included in the definition of what a thing essentially is.[101] Here, also, one can see how the transcendentally non-generic character of the most fundamental predicaments extends now for Aquinas to event. And it is within the field of relation that the transcendentals 'Good' and 'True', along with willing and knowing, are instantiated. For the Good concerns the intrinsic proportionate ordering of one thing to another, a real relation, while the True concerns the presence of one thing in another: a merely one-sided relation *secundum dici* with respect to the thing known, but a real relation with respect to the knowing power and its expression of its knowledge of the other.[102]

It is surely clear that this new theological ontology of constitutive supernatural supplementation and ecstatic relationality reveals a cosmos already in a sense graced, and in such a fashion that the supplement of grace will not seem in discontinuity with existing principles of ontological constitution.

However, such ontological revision, undertaken by theology, would appear to be ruled out if one takes it to be the case (ignoring the aporias of the transgeneric) that one can draw up a list of categorical presuppositions once and for all, since their 'formality' is uncontaminated by material 'event'. This, however, is claimed by many Catholic theologians and philosophers. Nicholas Lash, for example, insists that metaphysics has gone wrong when it has mistakenly supposed categories like 'being' to be substantive, while those thinkers from Aristotle to Wittgenstein who insist on the formality of the categorical are all saying essentially the same thing.[103] But, surely, the realization that the categories we must presuppose in order to think or speak at all are not 'things', in the sense of ordinary 'objects', is more the beginning of perplexity than it is the dissolution of an illusion? For if they are not entities, then are they merely convenient and unavoidable fictions, as for nominalism? Or else, are they somehow universally real and entitative, yet not in the normal thing-like mode of entities, existing primarily in the mind but also somewhat in specified individuals (as for Aquinas)? Or are they psychological biases (Hume, Nietzsche)? Or else subjective yet necessary pre-conditions for the display of phenomena (Kant)? Or alternatively preconditions enshrined in an objective logical universe (Bolzano, Frege)? Or, yet again, are they embodied in a hard-to-disentangle mixture of animal and cultural ritual behaviour (Wittgenstein)? None of these construals crudely hypostasize the categorical, but they are all very different, and are ultimately perhaps rooted in different visions of the world, beyond the reach of argumentation. But in such a situation it is surely valid to imagine that a theological vision will have its own interpretation of the need for, and presentation of, categorical presuppositions.

Indeed, the consequence of theology not doing so is likely to be idolatry, as witnessed by the case of the late medieval and early modern scholastics. Since they on the whole came to regard transcendental being in purely philosophical terms as an empty, univocal category of mere existentiality, and no longer as an attribute of perfection, they could make no real sense of God as hypostasized *esse*.[104] And in consequence of this inability to grasp a subtle sort of hypostasisization, they were indeed forced to reduce the divine *esse* to the status of a thing, since the only conceptual resource left open to their theology was to conceive God as 'a' being, however supreme. The empty univocal concept of being which became the groundwork of modern metaphysics arises from elevating the logical grasp of being – a thing simply 'is' or 'is not' – over the ontological grasp, for which all actuality manifests more or less intense existence according to its innate perfection. The prior logical or formal grasp is then permitted to structure ontology in such a fashion that this is really an ontology of the virtually real, and no true ontology at all. Too often in the twentieth century such a strategy has been read back into Aquinas in order to secure a dimension of pure metaphysics in his writing which will be compatible with the modern metaphysical edifice – always erected, ever since Suarez at least, on a logical/ formalist and later transcendentalist base.

Thus Bernard Lonergan contended that, for Aquinas, a metaphysician is simply a sort of more powerful logician. Actually, in the context cited, what Aquinas said is that metaphysics is more powerful than logic since the latter deals with the predicaments only as intellectual entities, beings of reason, whose truth is merely probable – since their degree of ontological subsistence is rather weak – while the former deals with real actualities and as a result possesses a greater certainty.[105] This entirely ontological conception of logical reality is clearly at variance with any mode of semantic access to phenomena after Bolzano and Frege since, for Aquinas, logical possibility is only a faint version of real substantive actuality. It is designed to 'intend' this actuality, and guaranteed only by this actuality. For example, the 'logical' identification of Socrates with white in the mind in the phrase 'Socrates is white' – which taken literally identifies one genus with another – is only designed to disclose the inherence of the accident 'white' in Socrates' substantial being (if this is indeed the case in actuality).[106] Otherwise, logic would be trapped inside a nonsense world where Socrates really was identical with whiteness, given that we have to see how an accident inheres in a substance, and logic of its own capacity cannot conceive this. Therefore, were the metaphysician merely a more powerful logician, we would, for Aquinas, be ushered into a mad universe where everything could be identified with everything else.

The primacy granted to logic in the structuring of ontology by Lonergan correlates with his hostility to any notion of intellect as vision, or to intellectual intuition in the sense of encounter with the real presence of the ideal, which we have shown to be fundamental for Aquinas. Lonergan subscribed to something akin to a neo-Kantian/phenomenological notion of the *a priori*, as not once and for all accessible, but rather as continuously unfolding in the presence of phenomena, and in its open horizon somehow pre-assuming an orientation to the divine (but not as encounter with participated divine light, as for Aquinas). However, he insisted that this unfolding discursivity involves 'explanation' beyond Husserl's mere description, and this seems to correlate with his refusal of intellectual intuition, since what judgement grasps is a kind of necessary coherence of structure in the given, not the sheer 'presence' of things.[107] To this scheme, however, Lonergan conjoined, quite arbitrarily, a certain realism, in such a way that intellect is completed by a genuine 'insight into phantasm' mediated by the senses (and in this reduced sense he accepts a certain 'intellectual intuition'). The conjoining appears arbitrary, since the 'look' of the senses or the imagination is not confirmed for Lonergan by an intellectual gaze, but instead the judgement can only grasp the supplied insight within logical and self-consistent structures of holding-together which it grasps by unfolding its own latent powers of comprehension.[108] Absolutely nothing prevents one from taking this philosophy more consistently as an immanently confined idealism in which the human mind does not grasp anything of 'things in themselves'.

For certain later semanticist transpositions of Lonergan's transcendental Thomism, the unfolding *a priori* is located in the more objective sphere of language as constrained by logic and transcendental grammar. For this perspective, if it is possible coherently to use words to refer to God (in some remote sense), then this must be a possibility enshrined *a priori* in the logic of language and its use, a possibility within whose limits theology is confined. Here analogy is not thought initially to presuppose any account of participation in being. Rather it is seen as a 'comment on our use of certain words'. Here, once again, it appears that a specifically theological and revisionist construal of reality, and how we refer to it, is ruled out of order and falsely associated with the approach of Aquinas.

One immediate problem with this semanticist proposal is that if analogy is sundered from metaphysics in this fashion, then, by the very same token, it is sundered from *sacra doctrina* since, if analogy is a transcendentalist theory of the possibility of human language, it cannot be, first and foremost, as it is for Aquinas, an exposition of the Dionysian revealed descent of certain mysterious 'divine names' primarily disclosed in scripture.

A second problem is contextual: Aquinas immediately precedes the question on the divine names with an account of how the vision of God in glory is dimly anticipated by some vision of God in his effects, consequent upon their participation in the divine *esse*.[109] This strongly suggests that analogy is predicated upon the metaphysics of participated being.

A third problem is terminological. Yes, to be sure, the term *analogia entis* was coined long after Aquinas, and only made generally current in the twentieth century by Erich Pryzwara. But this does not render it necessarily inappropriate, so long as it does not connote a post-Scotist 'Thomistic' analogy within being, taken as indifferent to infinite and finite, God and creatures. Clearly it is not entirely inappropriate because Aquinas does speak of univocal causes (within the same species), equivocal causes (between different species – since despite the shared genus, specific differences are, from a generic perspective, unmediably distinct, like 'man' and 'tiger'), and analogical causes extending from *esse* to *genera*.[110] And one can note here that Aquinas specifically says that analogical likeness is more distant than equivocal (non)resemblance, yet also affirms analogy as mediating between equivocity and univocity.[111] This is because the transgeneric height of remoteness (all we know is even more unlike pure being, pure unity, etc., than one species or genus is unlike another) is nonetheless an equal closeness to everything, which reveals a hidden bond between finitely remote things and categories. In this way, for Aquinas, analogy discloses its elusive 'medium' status by abolishing any ontological equivocity whatsoever. Analogy is more equivocal than equivocation, because equivocal difference is after all only a weak degree of analogical resemblance. How could there be any equivocity, since all differences derive from transcendental unity?

This is the theological metaphysics which the theology of the divine names assumes. Aquinas is quite explicit: names stand for ideas in the mind which refer to things, and our minds can only grasp finite things by the mediation of the senses.[112] Thus, unless things themselves can be read as signs of God, names cannot be used analogically of God. The limits or unlimits of grammar reflect the limits or unlimits of the created order. But things can only be signs of God if the divine perfections are remotely visible in created perfections – or, rather, if to see a created thing as possessing any perfection is to grasp its faint conveying of a plentitude of perfection beyond its scope. In other words, the metaphysics of participation in Aquinas is immediately and implicitly a phenomenology of seeing more than one sees, of recognizing the invisible in the visible.

This has to be affirmed, because Aquinas disallows any *a priori* proof 'that there must be the highest perfection', in such a way that we could just formally take it to be true that created perfections pointed to this, without experiential registering of this being the case. Inversely, it cannot be for Aquinas that analogy involves (at least initially) merely a projection from the possibilities of words that possess implicitly a range beyond what we can presently grasp – as with perfection terms such as 'beauty' which 'anticipate' artistic styles as yet unknown. For, without ontological guarantee, this range might be merely equivocal save for human delusion – in such a way that relativists might say that the recognized 'beauty' of one era has nothing to do with the 'beauty' of another. In addition, the semanticist *a priori* understanding of analogy as projection from implicit linguistic resources can only issue in a purely agnostic rendering of analogy which is not Aquinas's. For the surplus of possible unknown goodness indicated by the use of the word 'good' must be, for an *a priori* consideration, simply a radically unknown Kantian sublime horizon, or a good entirely absconded. It can validly suggest from its own resources only that God possesses his own, absolutely unknown perfection which is the efficient causal source of perfection in creatures. However, Aquinas refuses such an agnosticism: for him, we do not refer to the 'good' or 'life' of God because he is the source of good or life in creatures; rather we refer to the good or life of creatures because they manifest a good which is pre-eminently precontained in God in an exemplary and more 'excellent' fashion.[113] This pure light of perfection is, for Aquinas, after Dionysius, displayed in 'the many coloured veils' of Creation. Only through such 'colours' do we see pure white light, but we do somehow see this, else we should not see colours at all, since they are, exhaustively, light's refraction.[114]

Thus analogy presupposes not just a metaphysics of participation, but also a phenomenology of participation, although this is not to say that the latter founds the former.[115] This is not the case, because there is, for Aquinas, no indefeasible original intuition of participated *esse* outside a (discursively mediated) judgement that this is the case, expressed within an entire conceptual and linguistic apparatus handed down to us from tradition. Thus for him, as for Augustine, the 'vision' of Peter approaching from the distance will be initially also a received report of his approaching, the witness of others which conceptually frames our expectations of what we will come to see. For us, intuition is never prior to judgement supplemented by argument, which is preformed by language and tradition; there is no 'raw experience'.[116] Indeed, to ignore the non-visual dimension of oral report, historicity and judgement, which fractures and yet essentially informs vision, is to reduce vision to a post-Ramist and Cartesian art of precise survey, which overlooks the truth that we only cognitively see in the light of an unseeable intellectual sun – all those obscure yet essential 'assumptions' which alone clarify everything else. For this problematic lacuna of darkness within the visible itself – which, nonetheless, for all creatures constitutes the visible – discursivity must seek to substitute by rendering itself the means of showing the unshowable which illuminates.

And yet, if all being is only apparent though linguistic mediation, it is nonetheless the case that all language must be taken as only 'the showing forth' of being. If, to the contrary, one affirms that language, as relative and constricted, never discloses, this very assertion pre-constrains language within an *a priori* framework itself independent of linguistic contingencies. Thus a linguistic turn construed agnostically, and as preventing ontological disclosure (even where this is disclosure of the divine *esse*), undoes also the insight that we remain always within linguistic mediation.[117] By contrast, if we take it on trust that language does disclose, we can remain within radical linguisticality since, if language (or any pattern of symbolical mediation) discloses as well as articulates, we do not require in addition another disclosure. Hence only theology remains with the linguistic turn, because (after Hamann) it understands speaking to be also a seeing or linguistic philosophy to be also phenomenology, and vice versa in either case.

In this respect, it is a mistake for theology to build on a linguistic turn construed as prior to theology since this will always degenerate into a non-linguistic and dogmatic apriorism, which exalts an uncatholic *Deus Absconditus*. The tendency will be to construe the apophatic strategy as gesturing outside transcendentalist bounds of possible experience, and the range of constitutively meaningful linguistic expression.[118]

In this way, a bias to verbal foundations which denatures language into an *a priori* tends to engender an agnostic construal of analogy. But, curiously, a foundational phenomenology based on supposedly pure passive intuitions prior to linguistic interpretation can issue in just the same effect. For a foundational intuition must be undeniably manifest, and this can only be plausibly imputed to bounded, concrete things. The most one can say of the manifestation of the unbounded is that it is implied by bounded things as their ground. Such an implication will then be taken as a kind of minimal manifestness so that, if one's criterion for the real is appearance-to-intuition, one will take the negative showing of the unbounded as the latter's essence. Thus, in Heidegger's phenomenology, Being in itself as not this or that being can only be equated with an originating nothingness 'concealed' in ontic presence, which must in turn be denied and annihilated if one is authentically to confront the absolute. Theologians working within phenomenological assumptions tend, therefore, to assume that the horizon of being alone will issue in nihilistic conclusions and to resist Heidegger in the name of 'the beyond being' (which must also somehow be apparent) taken as both Neoplatonic Unity (in the wake of Trouillard) and transcendental

Charity. But this manoeuvre can appear to hand this world over to being as construed by Heidegger, and therefore in a Manichean fashion to nihilism after all. Thus Jean-Luc Marion insists that, for Aquinas, Being in even the ontological and not ontic sense (the former identified by him with *ens commune*) is created by God, and that *esse* is a more-or-less empty name, selected (he now concedes) as the primary transcendental by Aquinas on account of its maximum indeterminate openness.[119]

Now, Marion is perfectly right to say, against Etienne Gilson, that appeal to the ontological difference alone will not secure transcendence since it can well be construed nihilistically, as by Heidegger. Moreover, he is also right to see the ontological difference as in a sense internal to Creation since in Aquinas's case it sunders existence from essence in finite creatures, whereas (as we have seen) the divine *esse* is also infinite *forma* and *essentia* – rendering God, in a sense, the site of the collapse of the ontological difference. Aquinas's divine *esse*, unlike Heidegger's crossed-out Being, does not obliterate, but eternally confirms the ontic (as not 'other' to the ontological). Nevertheless, one can be uneasy about any straightforward identification of *ens commune* with the ontological, or any consequent sense that the ontological is, also, simply 'created'. We have seen that *ens commune* may denote being in a weakly 'generic' fashion, and in consequence one could argue that, for Aquinas, divine *esse* as participated ceases to be fully transgeneric, and so ceases to be fully ontological, since it now divides into a being in general and a specified being in this and that. And even in the case of Heidegger, since his Being is distinguished from the ontic only as empty and therefore general, one may wonder whether one truly has the transgeneric: Heidegger, also, is all too philosophical, all too metaphysical. So while, in a sense, Marion is right, and *esse* exceeds even the ontological difference, in another sense, being (*ens commune*) that is divided from essence or from the ontic is itself, as somewhat generic, still somewhat ontic, and fails to arrive at the difference of Being from a being or of *esse* from *ens* (in Thomist terms). By contrast, only the *esse* which exceeds the ontological difference in fact attains the ontological difference. This is surely confirmed by the fact that the real distinction in the creature is not defined as simply one between *essentia* and *ens commune*, but rather as between *essentia* and *esse*, suggesting that, for the creature, the latter is what is received of the divine self-subsisting perfection in the individual being which causes it to exist in a unique fashion. For if the ontological difference is finally the creator/created difference, then each creature is internally constituted out of nothing as that difference.

It follows that *sacra doctrina* offers a reading of the ontological difference other than that of Heidegger's, and does not take his for granted, thereby handing being and the world over to futility, boredom and nullity. Certainly Marion is right against Gilson: the ontological difference is not necessarily an ally of Christian transcendence. But he is wrong to see it as a barrier against it since it is not a difference intuitively manifest in only one way, but manifest in different ways according to judgement. Nevertheless, of course, the judgement that we make of it (Christian, Heideggerean, or otherwise) is adopted as, for us, the most compelling, the most manifest, the most intense. The highest intensity, the highest perfection of pure infinitude[120] must needs be simultaneously expressed in judgement and shown to mental vision.

However, where intuition is conceived as prior to judgement, it will tend to halt at the circumscribably perceptible, and for this reason there is no paradox in the fact that it is specifically phenomenology (Levinas, Marion, etc.) which sometimes comes to regard the invisible as truly and authentically manifest only as invisible and so tends to demonize all visibility as idolatry.[121] Thus, for Marion, since *esse* is an empty name, all analogical predication must be a purely apophatic gesturing to a divine distance, whose giving, in order to preserve its purity as disinterested, is so impersonal that it becomes hard after all to distinguish it from pure arrival from the abyss. (Here one may note that divine 'distance' is both absolutely affirmed and absolutely denied by Aquinas.)[122] He is of course right to say that, in Aquinas, analogy concerning God is a matter of two-term *proportio*, not of four-term *proportionalitas* between two compared ratios. He is also right to say that, in subordinating the latter kind of analogy, Aquinas refuses the idea that there is any ratio in God we can grasp as univocally the same as some ratio between creatures. However, proportionality, if formally dogmatic, is substantively agnostic (and is so deployed by Kant) since the God who is good in relation to his being, as we are good in relation to our being, is also the God whose good is an unknown cipher.[123]

By contrast, if we do not see God as a ratio comparable to a finite ratio, we can only see God at all through a finite perfection, assuming that in some fashion a finite perfection only exists by disclosing that ideal actual perfection which is its exemplar. This must be the case because, in two-term *proportio*, meaning resides more properly in one pole then another, and yet where this pole is God we are forced to begin at the wrong end. So how could we grasp any analogy if the higher divine perfection were not actually shown through the lesser perfection?

It is therefore clear that Aquinas does not build from transcendental grammatical foundations, but starts beyond the beginning with a theological supplementation which is both a metaphysics of the superadded as paradoxically the most proper, and a phenomenology of seeing more than one can see if one is to see truly at all. Both the metaphysical judgement (or 'speculation') and the phenomenological vision are necessary and co-primary for *sacra doctrina*. Is there an intuition of Being involved here? Not in the old ontologist sense of absolute immediate grasp of the most fundamental ontological category, without the need for reflective abstraction from the differentiated. However, it *is* involved in the sense that all thought is a remote anticipation of the final beatified intuition of God, who as *esse* is also pure intellect in act identical with absolute intuition. Such anticipation is always apparent only for reflection, but apparent through reflection for all that. No doubt many will imagine that we have here reverted to Baroque delusions and fail to realize that Aquinas and Kant share the same non-Baroque intellectual chastity.[124] But, to the contrary,

Baroque metaphysical rationalism is grounded in the sundering of metaphysics from *sacra doctrina*, and thus is inevitably fulfilled in metaphysics-as-epistemology before and with Kant, since finite being, supposedly fully apparent to reason (as univocal), must quickly turn into being that is only a projection of the structures of reason. Because, with Kant, reason no longer 'sees' into the realities of finite being (beyond appearances which are given merely to sensory perception), it *a fortiori* may not see through and beyond these realities. Loss of intellectual intuition therefore does not result from the critique of metaphysics (as Kant thought), but from the fulfilment (with Kant) of an entirely dogmatic metaphysics.[125]

VII

In the above fashion our preceding claim that Aquinas offers a theological ontology can be defended. As earlier set out, the leading characteristic of this ontology is a grasp of creation in the light of grace, as itself graced or supplemented, and so as a preparation for human deification. This is reinforced by evidence of anticipation of a Trinitarian structure in his account of the created order. Thus, as we have seen, relationality is integral to supplementation, and the two most intense modes of relationality concern the True and the Good. It is also the case that Aquinas regards 'life' and 'intellect' as superadditions to being which offer more being because there is more intensity of perfection and more self-sufficiency. And this can be related to his account of Trinitarian traces at *Summa Contra Gentiles* 4.11 where 'life' which exhibits emergence or emanation from the inner to the outer (whether as plant growth or animal movement) thereby shows some approach to pure inner emanation and substantive relation, while 'intellect', which exhibits an emanative movement that differentiates yet remains within, exhibits one yet stronger.[126]

However, if in this way we can see that 'faith' already informs Aquinas's ontology of Creation, it must be said in reverse that 'reason' equally informs his theology of the Trinity. Despite his explicit disavowal of the possibility of natural reason discerning the Trinity, he in fact argues for the Trinity in much the same way that he argues for the divine attributes. We have already seen that the reason he gives for disallowing merely rational approaches to the Trinity is a rather weak one: human reason can offer only remote analogies, although this is just as true for divine unity, and so forth. One can only conclude that perhaps, since the Trinity is a harder matter to grasp, its manifestness is relatively a matter of descent rather than ascent; but as Aquinas makes clear in the *Summa Contra Gentiles*, the way down is always also the way up,[127] or in the terms of the *Summa Theologiae*, the *revelabile* only fully disclose themselves with 'the helping hand' of argumentation.[128]

In arguing for the Trinity, Aquinas claims, first of all, that personhood, or a certain radical 'incommunicability', is a higher perfection of pure subsistence found in the

Creation, and therefore an excellence which cannot be absent from God.[129] He further claims, in the second place that the human intellect, in forming an intention,
utters a conceptual word, which is neither the thing understood (since a thing is not
the idea of a thing) nor yet simply (as for Aristotle) the act of understanding by
which it is inseparably carried since a thought is more than the unfolding of the
structures of mind, but rather the construction of a contingent intention either
towards a contingent existing thing (even if that thing is oneself) or a contingent
thing-to-be-done or produced.[130] In forming this intention, the mind does (again, see
Chapter One [of *Truth in Aquinas*]), in a remote analogical sense, 'move',[131] and
something really does inwardly 'emanate' from the mind, in such a way that it stands
in a real relation to its own concept.[132] Mark Jordan has comprehensively demolished
(citing multiple texts) Lonergan's work in *Verbum*,[133] which attempted, in the face of
Aquinas's explicit terminology, to deny his Neoplatonic and Augustinian supplements
to Aristotle's theory of knowledge; hence Lonergan argued that the 'issuing' of the
verbum from the mind does not apply to the pre-reflexive grasp of simple essences
(though Lonergan's apriorism turns this into a kind of rough initial adumbration of a
concept), and involves in judgement only the development of implications from a
previous thought, and not a real ontological production of something 'other' than
oneself within oneself. For Aquinas, however, as Jordan shows, it clearly applies to
intellective grasp of essence as well as to discursive judgement, and therefore to
ontological production as well as epistemological implication. If it did not involve the
former, it clearly could not serve as an analogue for anything other than a modalist
theology. Aquinas claims, in the third place, that, since God is simple, and his act of
intellect equals his being, or equally his being equals his act of intellect (since the
latter is more intense being and is compared to the power of mind as *esse* to *essentia*),
and every act of intellect involves emanation of the *verbum*, then the *verbum* must be
substantive in God. It must as much embody Godhead as the Father, and is therefore
also the 'Son' of the Father, since sons are equal to fathers in nature and self-subsistence, whereas cognitive intentions are not so equal to minds.[134]

In this way, Aquinas has speculatively established the Son. He holds, in general, that
the thought of the True as a perfection is accompanied by desire for it as an end to
be obtained.[135] However, desire in creaturely persons also extends to their relation to
others and to goals outside themselves, without which they would have no ontological
'relation of order'. Such a perfection of desire must also be present in God, although
because it is here removed from exteriority, and because good ends desired are 'true'
as existing – just as the true is an end to be desired – it is present in God in substantive relation with the expression of truth, and, of course, as divine and simple, is
equally personal and substantive.[136] In this way, Aquinas speculatively establishes
the Spirit.

What is more, Aquinas does not leave the register of 'one divine essence' with all
the transcendental attributes, on the one hand, as simply distinct from 'three divine

persons' with their relations and 'notions' (the five aspects of origin and relationality within the Trinity), on the other. To the contrary, he goes some way towards integrating these two registers. Thus, in the first place, one can note that the essence and the persons are only distinct according to our *modus significandi* [way of signifying], in just the same fashion as being is only so distinct from goodness.[137] This should indeed give pause to over-enthusiastic hyper-Trinitarians (Moltmann, Gunton, etc.) in our own day. For it suggests that when Aquinas speaks first of all of the divine unity and simplicity (following Dionysius, not Augustine), he is not simply speaking of the one essence, but rather (already as Eckhart) of a divine depth of unity beyond our perceived distinction of essence and relation – but of course just as much relational as essential. The same point of indifference between relations and essence is, in fact, for Aquinas, as for Augustine, marked by the persons themselves – they are not identified *tout court* with the relations, even though they are the relations; instead, they slide uneasily between the relations and the essence, being identical with both.[138]

Secondly, we have already seen that *verbum* which is also *ars*, as an intrinsic aspect of intellection, has become 'convertible' with all the transcendentals. This means that, inversely, they are convertible with the emanation of the *verbum*, which now can be taken to convey the divine simplicity as much as anything else. Thus, thirdly, Aquinas says that if the persons of the Trinity, and in particular the Son, are identical with *essentia*, then they are so as *esse* manifesting the *essentia*.[139] Fourthly, Aquinas at times seems prepared to equate the Father with *subsistentia*, or 'the one understanding'; the Son with *essentia* (as absolute expressed *forma* or 'the intention understood'); and the Spirit with *esse* (as the completed end of the 'act of understanding').[140] This seems to correlate with that trace of Trinity which he locates even in non-intellectual creatures, as discovered in their subsistence, form and the 'relation of order' to other finite beings.[141]

From these fragmentary suggestions, one can develop a point concerning Trinitarian ontology that is only latent in Aquinas. The Augustinian ascending triad, being/ life/intellect (where the two later degrees represent more intense being) is qualified in its hierarchy at the point where, within intelligent creatures, the orientation of the will towards the Good picks up again the motion of life towards a goal outside itself, whereas the intellect fulfils itself as relation to the other within itself. In this way 'life' sustains a certain ecstasy as it were 'beyond' reason, as is suggested by Aquinas's other triad of first, second and third acts (or perfections), where a superessential reach to the other as goal is superadded even to the superessential superaddition of operation to substance. The Trinitarian trace of substance, form (which can extend to operation) and 'relation of order', appears to tally with the latter scheme, while the tension of both (and of the Trinitarian psychic vestige of memory, understanding and will together with the triad substance/essence/act of being), with the ascending triad being/life/intellect (where knowledge, not ecstatic movement is the culmination), suggests a Trinitarian hesitation between the 'priority' of *Logos* to which desire must submit and the 'finality' of desire, which conveys also, and always already, truth. Since desire, which is the highest intensity of life as will to the Good, is found also within the divine simplicity, even the emanation of the Logos which remains within God must pass, as life, to an end beyond itself, yet still within God, as the Holy Spirit.

Thus if a faith-perceived Creation points to the Trinity through an ontology of descending and relational supplements, and indeed of 'double supplementation' where end-is-added-to-operation-is-added-to-substance, then a rationally perceived Trinity confirms this pattern. In particular, it does so by implying that the supplementations received from on high by creatures are not simply abandonments of their manifold diversity in order to receive an alien simplicity. This is not the case because it turns out that this descending supplementation is grounded in a kind of 'reverse supplementation' in God which, instead of receiving, like a creature, unity in its manifoldness, receives manifoldness in its unity, as the Father is 'reversely constituted' by the Son and Spirit who express and desire (with simplicity) all manifold divine actuality, including the Creation, which God has decided shall exist apart from him. It is this reverse supplementation in God which finally assures us that we do not need to escape from the fact that the supernatural additions of participated unity can only arrive to us through the relationalities of space and time. For, if we do receive descents leading us from diversity to unity, nevertheless, after all, also for us this is through a reverse supplementation as we pass from achieved unity into renewed dispersal, renewed ecstatic being for others – in which alone, however, transcendental as opposed to numerical unity can be intensified.

In this fashion, the 'Meno problematic' structure of our being able to search to know only what is already known is no mere deficiency, but itself reflects God's uttering of the *Logos* only through the Spirit's desiring 'anticipation' of truth, which in God (as just discussed) is somehow both 'before' and 'after' it. This structure indeed appears to inform Aquinas's proceeding in the *prima pars* from God's being and goodness to his intelligence and truth, but then from truth to the divine will. And thus one can see just why commentators have offered apparently conflicting interpretations of Aquinas as 'existentialist', 'intellectualist', or even as primarily pivoted on 'the Good' (Marion). These are all legitimate readings, since he offers us what is ultimately a Trinitarian metaphysic. Here one can read Aquinas in either direction: the Trinity as the most intense being, or finite beings as weak participations in the relations of understanding and desiring.

In this light one can suggest (beyond, but with Aquinas) that if the *Verbum* and the *Donum* [gift – the Spirit] are also transgeneric as much as *esse*, then *analogia entis* is also *analogia trinitatis*. In other words, that to see the invisible in the visible is simultaneously to develop horizontally in space and time productive cognition and ecstatic reaching which both show and further realize the lateral harmonic and analogical *proportiones* by which alone we can penetrate the vertical *proportio* to God. Here again *theoria* is *poesis*, although *poesis* is *theoria*.

But what can this speculative reach to the Trinity betoken? Does it not suggest that one should re-express a non-dualism of reason and faith in 'Hegelian' terms as a naturalizing of the supernatural, in which theology succumbs to philosophy? Surely, no, because Aquinas's discursive arguments about the Trinity are ultimately confirmed by, and subordinated to, both intuition and performance. As arguments from created perfection, they are like other such arguments, grounded neither *a priori* nor *a posteriori*, but rather to be taken as expressions of a vision of the infinite in the finite. Hence there may be absolute personhood, pure relation, perfectly interior emanation, transcendental *Verbum* and *Donum*, but only if there is absolute perfection, and the possibility of such will not guarantee its reality nor even identify it. Only its actuality can do so, and this must be dimly perceived in order to be known. If such analogical receptions are flickering and uncertain, then this suggests that some uncertainty also hovers over our assumption that our minds do indeed relate to intentions of real being, do indeed construct and manifest the truth, do indeed desire a true good that is really to be had. Any lack of the highest perfection, which logically includes Trinity, must corrode backwards also perceived finite perfection into the remnants of illusion.

The reasoning to the Trinity may, therefore, be logically inviolable, but only if there is perfection, objective teleology and ontological truth. And sin renders our finite vision of infinite perfection vague and uncertain. Indeed, so blinded are we, that our vision can only be restored by the descent of perfection in time, in such a way that here we see the infinitely perfect entirely in the finite with our sensory eyes as performed thought which is also the personal substantive Son, who both realizes and lets proceed a true desire manifest in the substantive Eucharistic community. It may appear shocking that, for Aquinas, as for Augustine, the Trinity is seen as speculatively apparent in the Creation, but this is to miss the point that for both (in different ways), this speculation points us back to the fulfilment of speculation in lived history. To be sure, the Incarnation and the giving of the Spirit in time are first of all the implicit presuppositions of speculation – since these events alone have fully cleansed our minds to be able to see the Trinity in the created order (while these events themselves can only show the Trinity in terms of that order). And yet, much more radically, these events are themselves the achievement of speculation as vision and performance which is only for us attainable through a return to the sensorially imagistic and concretely immediate: a collective *conversio* ad *phantasmata*. For this reason Aquinas argues *to* Christology and the sacraments and not (or not so fundamentally) from them.

There is an additional and equally important reason for resisting the idea that Aquinas transforms Trinitarian theology into Trinitarian philosophy. This concerns the exact character of the highest perfection that is conceived and imagined. Is it simply an idealist completion of thought as a logical process, thought thinking itself and returning to itself? Werner Beierwaltes and Wayne Hankey both suggest that the basis of Trinitarian reflection lies in a Neoplatonic structure of the One reflecting on its own simplicity and thereby entering division, which is, nonetheless, cancelled, with simplicity restored, through a perfection of reflexivity.[142] Aquinas, however, identifies *reditio ad seipsum* as a metaphor (albeit a necessary and accurate one) for self-subsistence. Since Trinitarian relations are for him themselves subsistent and auto-sustaining, he cannot possibly think of these relations only in terms of outgoing and return, or of reflexivity. On the contrary, the idea of reflexive *nous* as compatible with absolute unity (perhaps present in Porphyry) is an extremely shaky one, and is rejected by Plotinus, Proclus and Iamblichus.[143] These three rigorously insist that thought in its 'doubling' character – of being showing itself to itself – is non-simple and non-unified, and therefore to be characterized as only the first emanation from that which is most absolute and radically non-cognitive. Exactly the same demotion of mind (yes!) is affirmed by Fichte, the early Schelling and even Hegel, and in all three it forms the basis for a philosophy of absolute being which, as nothing, must become finite in order to be, but again as absolute must return to nothing, leaving the finite in its pure naked contingency to show forth the untrammelled freedom of reality. In Faith and Knowledge, Hegel names this absolute idealism 'nihilism' (positively embracing Jacobi's insult), and protests that Fichte is not nihilistic enough because he refuses to say that the absolute is fully thinkable, that is to say, as graspable in its emptiness.[144] (Yes – they were all postmodern already.)

Perfection as rational reflexivity, therefore, offers only a formalism which engenders nihilism, since mind constituted as actually reflecting on its own self-consistency cannot be simple and original; both actuality in its definiteness, and thought in its mirroring reflectiveness, must fade before the abyss. It follows that neither Aristotle, nor mere monotheism, manage to render mind consistent with the absolute. To the contrary, only the concept of the Trinity does this, because here thought is not a doubling of being in mirroring, but rather it *is* being, which only consists in an 'original supplement' of self-disclosure through self-constitution. Thus, whereas reflection involves a 'doubling', substantive relation, by contrast, can be just as simple and transcendentally unified as substance. In this way, it is only the highest truth of faith – the Trinity – which establishes the absoluteness of reason.

But since this mental constitution of being in the relation of self-manifestation is not a mirroring nor a mimesis, but rather that expression through which alone being is at all, this expression, though absolute, and therefore more necessary than any conceivable necessity, is still not logically necessitated, as is an imitation or an echo, constrained to observe identity. To the contrary, the *Logos* is generated in the freedom of the Spirit, which expresses its *Donum* as the exchange between Father and Son, and yet as an exchange which overflows to a third, precisely because its return is not a return in pure identity, forming a closed circle which would be such that the Spirit might as well express only the will of the Father, rather than also the 'ever-new' utterance of the Son. Thus while charity for Aquinas denotes reciprocity,[145] he also declares that 'gift', following Aristotle, denotes non-return;[146] a 'moment' of unilaterality, since the circle spirals always through the same-as-different. (In this way a gift-as-exchange view is protected from Hegelian 'return'.)

Since the *Logos* is reasonable, and does not merely convey a capricious divine will, and yet cannot, as we have seen, be logically necessitated, its rational expression is essentially an aesthetic expression (as David Burrell and Gilbert Narcisse have both argued), responding to the inner necessity of the lure of beauty which it at once constructs and envisages. Thus Aquinas never suggests, like Leibniz, that God grasps perfection through pure ratiocination, but he still affirms God's response to perfection (which is himself) as something objective. Likewise, he does not think, again like Leibniz, that God could work out what is 'the best of all possible worlds' to create, since God as infinitely perfect could always create the more perfect. So in deciding, with perfect reason, upon this perfection, he must respond to something like an aesthetic prompting to do 'this, now, here' (to use entirely inappropriate analogues).

Hence, in thinking the perfection of the Trinity, argument finally yields to the intuition of the necessity of the inner divine *ars* (its, as it were, 'elective necessity'), which we dimly see and dimly echo in our own creativity, which is incapable, of course, of real 'creating' of being *ex nihilo* [from nothing], but is nonetheless, for Aquinas, able continuously to bring about new being 'in this' or 'in that'.[147]

VIII

It has been shown how, in three ways, Aquinas's *sacra doctrina* bends metaphysics into history: transgeneric *esse* fulfilled in theology converts the formal into the material; the redefined science of *sacra doctrina* grasps divine intuition only through descent to sensory intuition; finally, the 'reversed supplementation' of the Trinity validates history as the horizontal route of our vertical ontological supplementation: here truth is slowly engendered through our desiring anticipation of our final goal. And indeed, beneath even this initial turn towards our mode of animal 'life', divine grace which is the gift of the Spirit first meets us as a kind of quasi-physical 'motion', revealing here also the artisanal reach of divine knowledge beyond the architectonic sway of metaphysics. On the basis of the second consideration (and we can add the first and third), Michel Corbin argues that Aquinas deliberately fulfils speculation in its surpassing, as a reflection upon, and liturgical re-offering of, sacred history.[148] One might support this argument by suggesting that Aquinas here follows through the Dionysian legacy of theurgic Neoplatonism. For this tradition (Proclus and Iamblichus), since the forms are only 'recollected' through ever-renewed reminders in time, the soul cannot be elevated above time and the body (as for Plotinus, less faithful to Plato's texts and the esoteric traditions of the academy). Therefore, in order to encounter the divine, we must rely less on theoretic ascent than on a divine descent, which nonetheless is partially enticed through certain regular ritual performances. Here the contingently encountered triggers of recollection are as it were 'assured' through the non-identical repetition of the liturgical cycle. (Moreover, it is arguable that the idea of a Trinitarian grounding, even for the temporal and diverse anticipatory motion involved in recollection, is itself foreshadowed in Plato's own oral teaching – as indicated in several places in the dialogues and letters about the ultimate 'one' and equally ultimate manifold 'two', and the interplay between them.) In worship, supremely, we at once make and see, envisage in performing, thereby realizing Aquinas's vision of actuality as light.[149] Since God is not an object in the world, he cannot be available to us before our response to him, but in this response – our work, our gift, our art, our hymn – he is already present. Moreover, such poetic, theurgic, sacramental presence is for Christianity, as not for Neoplatonism, also a fully theoretical, intellectual presence since, with the Trinity, Christianity has succeeded in thinking thought as absolute and simple, precisely because it no longer thinks of it as reflexion, but as relation, *poesis* and vision. (It is orthodox Trinitarianism and not Neoplatonism, nor German idealism, as we have seen, which is intellectualist.)

Hence, in Part Three of the *Summa Theologiae*, Aquinas turns speculation into a kind of re-offering of Christ, and concludes with detailed recommendations for liturgical practice (to be discussed in the fourth chapter) before re-presenting (though this was never completed) the beatific vision as resurrection of the body and final judgement. In a sense, this suggests a very anthropological approach to Christology – not of course a Rahnerian one built on anthropological foundations, but a concluding to Christ as the realization of the human *telos* which is only here shown, beyond humanity. And Michel Corbin has further argued that the *Summa* does not follow Chenu's purported *exitus*/*reditus* scheme, since Part One concerns God, with much about descent as we have seen, while Part Two concerns humanity, with much about ascent through grace.[150] This suggests that Part Three is not about the foundation for return in Christ and actual return via sacramental grace, but rather concerns a kind of 'synthesis' (Hegelian but without Hegel's nihilism) of Parts One and Two, a treatment of God and Man at once, in such a way that God, in executing the perfect descent of his goodness in Christ, also allows humanity in Christ to fulfil its theological speculation as perfect theurgic practice which is both miraculous and sacramental.

Notes

1   See John Milbank, 'Theologie Politique', in J.-Y. Lacoste (ed.) *Dictionnaire Critique de Theologie*, Paris: Editions du Cerf, 1998.

2   See John Inglis, 'Philosophical Autonomy and the Historiography of Mediaeval Philosophy', *British Journal of the History of Philosophy* 1997, vol. 5, no. I, 21–53; ibid., *Spheres of Philosophical Inquiry and the Historiography of Medieval Philosophy*, Leiden: Brill, 1998.

3   For example, Aquinas, *Summa Theologiae* (hereafter, '*S. T.*') I. Q. 1 a. 2 AD. 2, and II. I. Q. 109 a. 1.

4 For example, *S. T.* I. Q. 2 a. 2; Q. 12 Q. 12 resp: Aquinas, *In Boeth De Trin* [Commentary on Boethius's *De Trinitate* [On the Trinity]] Q. 5. a. 4; Aquinas, *Summa Contra Gentiles* (hereafter, 'S. C. G.') I. 3(2).

5 Rudi te Velde, *Participation and Substantiality in Thomas Aquinas* Leiden: Brill, 1995, pp. ix–xiv.

6 For example, *S. T.* I. Q. I a. 5 AD. 1; Aquinas, *In Boeth de Trin* Q. 5. a. 4 and Aquinas, *Super Libr. De Causis Expos* [Commentary on the 'Book of Causes'], lect. 1, after Aristotle, *Metaphysics* 11.4.1070a 31.

7 *S. T.* I. Q. 12 a. resp: 'Hence also the intellectual power of the creature is called an intelligible light, as it were, derived from the divine light, whether this be understood of the natural power, or of some perfection superadded of grace or glory.'

8 *S. T.* I. Q. 79 a. 4: 'Now the human soul is called intellectual by reason of a participation in intellectual power; a sign of which is that it is not wholly intellectual but only in part.' Were the human soul entirely intellectual it would always be in the act of completed thought, enjoying pure intuition, whereas to the degree that the soul's thinking is intermittent this thinking is merely discursive. Aquinas further describes participation in pure intellect at *S. T.* I. Q. 84 a. 5: resp: 'For the intellectual light which is in us, is nothing else than a participated likeness of the uncreated light, in which are contained the eternal types.' (Hence there must be for Aquinas in some sense an intuition of *esse* along with all the other transcendentals and divine attributes.) Aquinas continues, 'By the seal of the Divine light in us, all things are made known to us.' Further clear evidence that for Aquinas the human intellect enjoys a share of the divine intuition (divine intuition being identical with the immediacy of divine light) is provided *In Boeth de Trin* Q. 6 a. 1 resp (c): 'intellect first contemplates a truth one and undivided and in that truth contemplates a whole multitude, as God, by knowing his essence, knows all things.' Also *S. T.* I. Q. 12 a. 11 AD. 3, where, commenting on Augustine (DeTrin, xii), Aqunias writes, 'even in this life we see God himself'. Furthermore, he states, 'All things are said to be seen in God and all things are judged in Him, because by the participation of this light, we know and judge all things.'

9 John I. Jenkins, *Knowledge and Faith in Thomas Aquinas*, Cambridge: Cambridge University Press, 1997, pp. 107–11.

10 In relation to 'rivalling God' see Aquinas, *In Boethius de Hebdomadibus* [Commentary on Boethius's *De Hebdomadibus* [commentary on the seven days of creation]] 3 for the parallel point that creatures cannot be good by substance without possessing divinity. On division and indivision see *S. T.* I. Q. 85 a. 8 resp and *S. T.* I. Q. 16 a. 2.

11 *S. T.* I. Q. 79 a. 7, a. 8, a. 9.

12 *S. T.* I. Q. 16 a. 1; and Aquinas, *De Veritate* [On Truth] I. Q. 1 a. 4 resp.

13 See *S. T.* I. Q. 16 a. 1 resp.

14 See *S. T.* I. Q. 5 a. 5 AD. 1: 'beauty relates to the cognitive faculty; for beautiful things are those which please when seen. Hence beauty consists in due proportion ... Now since knowledge is by assimilation, and similarity relates to form, beauty properly belongs to the nature of a formal cause.'

15 *S. T.* I. Q. 12 a. 13 resp: 'human knowledge is assisted by the revelation of grace. For the intellect's natural light is strengthened by the infusion of gratuitous light; and sometimes also the images in the human imagination are divinely formed, so as to express divine things better ... while sometimes, sensible things, or even voices, are divinely formed ... ' And see John Montag, 'Revelation: The False Legacy of Suarez', in J. Milbank, C. Pickstock and G. Ward (eds) *Radical Orthodoxy: A New Theology*, London: Routledge, 1999, pp. 38–63.

16 Montag (see Note 15).

17 *S. T.* II. Q. 171 a. 1 AD. 1; a. 2 resp; a 3 resp; I. Q. 12. a. 13 AD. I.

18 Aquinas, *In Metaph. Proemium* [Commentary on Aristotle's *Metaphysics*] and see J.-F. Courtine, *Suarez et le système de métaphysique*, Paris: Presses Universitaires de France, 1990, pp. 31–99.

19 Jenkins, *Knowledge and Faith* (see Note 9)and *In Boeth de Trin*, Q. 5 a. 4.

20 *S. T.* I. Q. 14 a. 4.

21 *S. T.* I. Q. 1 a. 2 resp.

22 *S. T.* I. Q. 12 a. 12. resp; ad. 1; AD. 3; *In Boeth de Trin*, Q. 6 a. 1 (c) ad. 2; *S. C. G.* 1. 3(3).

23   See, for example, Nicholas Lash, 'Ideology, Metaphor and Analogy', in *Theology on the Way to Emmaus*, London: SCM, 1986 pp. 95–120, esp. pp. 107–8.

24   See John Inglis, 'Philosophical Autonomy' (n.2). Inglis shows how not only Aquinas, but even Scotus and Ockham simply ignore certain more purely philosophical aspects of Aristotle's treatment of the soul which do not relate to theology. See also Inglis's *Spheres of Philosophical Inquiry* (see Note 2), p. 267 where he stresses that Aquinas did not think a Christian could live the life of a philosopher since he regarded philosophy as an essentially pagan practice as well as theory, belonging to a long-distant past.

25   On ascent and descent see *S. C. G.* 4. 1(11).

26   *S. C. G.* I. 9(2) and (3).

27   See Jenkins, *Knowledge and Faith* (see Note 9) and Michel Corbin, *Le Chemin de la théologie chez Thomas d'Aquin*, Paris: Beauchesne, 1972, p. 685.

28   *S. T.* I. Q. 1 a. 5 resp: 'other sciences derive their certitude from the natural light of human reason, which can err; whereas this one (*sacra doctrina*) derives its certitude from the light of the divine knowledge, which cannot be misled ... ' See also *S. C. G.* 19(2).

29   Corbin, *Le Chemin* (see Note 27) pp. 677–80, 713–27.

30   *S. C. G.* I. 8(1).

31   *S. T.* I. Q. 1. a. 2 resp, I-II. Q. 109. a. 1.

32   *S. T.* I. Q. l. a. 1 resp.

33   *S. T.* I. Q. 1 a. 8 and Q. 5 AD. 2.

34   *S. T.* I. Q. 5 AD. 2.

35   *S. T.* I. Q. 2. a. 2. ad. 2, ad. 3.

36   Aristotle, *Metaphysics E* 1.1026a. 28–32.

37   *S. T.* I. Q. 3 a. 3: '[God] must be his own Godhead' (that is to say, as individual and nature in one, he is really neither in our sense); see also, *S. T.* I. Q. 3 a. 5: God is here said not to be in a genus and at ad. 1 it is declared 'that God is not in the genus of substance' because (one has to interpret here a difficult passage) he is neither 'a' general sense, nor 'an' individual over-against others. Nor, of course, is he an 'underlying' substance to which accident could be added. However, elsewhere he is allowed to be 'subsistent' in the sense of being absolutely without prior cause or dependency.

38   *S. T.* I. Q. 2–6.

39   *S. T.* I. Q. 5 a. 1, a. 2. a. 3. In the *responsio* to article 1 Aquinas says: 'viewed in its primal (i.e. substantial) being a thing is said to be good relatively (i.e. insofar as it has being), but viewed in its complete actuality a thing is said to be relatively and to be good simply'. On this basis it is at least arguable that Aquinas grants a co-primacy of good alongside being.

40   *S. T.* I. Q. 2 a.1 AD. 2.

41   *S. T.* I. Q. 6. a. 4.

42   For Aquinas and Dionysius, see Fran O'Rourke, *Pseudo Dionysius and the Metaphysics of Aquinas*, Leiden: E. J. Brill, 1992.

43   *S. T.* I. Q. 1 a. 1: : 'Even as regards those truths about God which human reason could have discovered, it was necessary that man should be taught by divine revelation; because the truth about God such as reason could discover, would only be known by a few, and that after a long time, and with the admixture of many errors.' And a. 6 AD. 2: 'Whatsoever is found in other sciences contrary to any truth of this science [*sacra doctrina*] must be condemned as false: Destroying counsels, and every height that exalted itself against the knowledge of God (2 Cor. x. 4–5).'

44   For example, *S. T.* I. Q. 1 a. 7 AD. 1: 'Although we cannot know in what consists the essence of God, nevertheless in this science [*sacra doctrina*] we make use of His effects, either of nature or grace, in place of a definition.' See also Q. 2. a. 2 resp. and especially Q. 12. a. 13 AD. 1: 'Although, by the revelation of grace in this life we cannot know of God what He is, and thus are united to Him as to one unknown, still we know Him more fully according as many and more excellent of His effects are demonstrated to us ...'

45   For an account of the French Catholic attempt to refound Catholic thought on a Neoplatonic henological rather than Aristotelian/Thomist ontological basis, and the various influence of this on Stanislas Breton and Jean-Luc Marion (and the convergence with Levinas), see Wayne

Hankey, 'Denys and Aquinas: antimodern cold and postmodern hot', in Lewis Ayres and
Garth Jones (eds) *Christian Origins*, London: Routledge, 1998, pp. 139–85.

46   For a critique of Marion along these lines, see D. Bijou-Duval, 'Dieu avec ou sans L'Être',
Revue Thomiste, Jan.–Mar. 1995, TXCV, no. 1, 547–66.

47   *In Boeth de Trin*, Q 6. a. 3.

48   See Graham Priest, *Beyond the Limits of Thought*, Cambridge: Cambridge University Press,
1995, esp. pp. 94–123.

49   Jacques Maritain, *Distinguer pour unir*, Paris: Desclée de Brouwer, 1941, pp. 827–943; Etienne
Gilson, *Le Thomisme*, Paris: Urm, 1972, p. 126.

50   Rudi te Velde, *Participation and Substantiality*, pp. 201–33; Aquinas, *De Potentia Dei*, Q. 5 AD.
1: '*nam quantum uniciuque inest de forma, tantum inest ei de virtute essendi*', translated by te Velde
as 'the more of form each thing has, the more intensely it possesses being'. On p. 233 te
Velde says 'the form can be said to be distinct from God, not as an independent principle
besides God but insofar as in each particular form God (= Being itself) distinguishes himself
in a particular way from the simple identity of his essence. Form is something "of God" in
things created by God.' See also *S. T.* I. Q. 7 a 3 for the equation of *esse* with *forma*: 'Since
God is himself form, or rather himself being. He cannot be in any way composite.' Also Q. 17
a. 3: 'Just as the thing has being by its proper form, so the knowing faculty has knowledge by
the likeness of the thing known.' Finally a passage at *S. T.* I. Q. 8 a. 1 rules out any notion
that Thomist *esse* is a Kantian non-predicamental existential qualifier: 'Being is innermost
(*magis intimum*) in each thing and most fundamentally inherent in all things (*quod profundus
omnibus inesi*) since it is formal in respect of everything found in a thing.'

51   Jean-Luc Marion, 'Saint Thomas d'Aquin et l'onto-théo-logie', in *Revue Thomiste*, Jan.–Mar. 5
1995, TXCV, no. 1, pp. 31–66.

52   *S. T.* I. Q. 34 a. 3 resp: 'the word of God ... is both expressive and operative of creatures.'

53   *S.C.G.* 4.1(3).

54   See the Boulnois–Marion discussions in *Revue Thomiste*, Jan.–Mar. 5 1995, TXCV, no. 1, pp.
31–66.

55   Aquinas, *In Metaph. Proemium*. Regarding the latency of conclusions within principles, see
Aristotle, *Posterior Analytics* 71a 24.

56   *S. T.* I. Q. 2 a. 3. And II. I. Q.109 a. 1 resp.

57   *In Metaph.* L. IV. I IV. 574.

58   See Note 50, and *De Potentia Dei* Q. 5 a. 4 AD. 3.

59   See Note 50.

60   *S. T.* I. Q. 6 a. 3 resp: 'the first perfection of fire consists in its existing, which it has through
its own substantial form; its secondary perfection consists in heat, lightness and dryness and
the like; its third perfection is to rest in its own place. This triple perfection belongs to no
creature by its own essence; it belongs to God alone, in Whom alone essence is existence, in
Whom there are no accidents ...'

61   *S. T.* I. Q. 79. a. 1 resp: '... the intellect is a power of the soul, and not the very essence of
the soul. For then alone the essence of that which operates is the immediate principle of
operation when operation itself is its being: for as power is to operation as its act, so is the
essence to being. But in God alone this action of understanding is His very Being. Wherefore
in God alone is His intellect His essence: while in other intellectual creatures, the intellect is
a power.'

62   Marion, 'Saint Thomas d'Aquin' (see Note 51).

63   *S. T.* I. Q. 3. a. 3, a. 4 and a. 6.

64   *In Metaph. Proemium*.

65   Here, if we understand him right, we are slightly more inclined to attribute to Aquinas a
thoroughgoing Platonic theoontology than is Olivier Boulnois (see Note 54).

66   *S. T.* I. Q. 3. a. 6. resp: Q. 3 a. 7: '... just as in sensible forms there is a participation of the
higher substances, so the consideration of speculative sciences is a certain participation of
true and perfect happiness'.

67   *S. T.* I. Q. 1. a. 7.

68   *S. T.* I. Q. 2. a. 1 AD. 1.

69   *In Boeth de Trin*, Q. 6. a. 3.
70   See the whole of Q. 12 of the *Summa Theologiae*.
71   At *S. T.* I. Q. 8. a. 1–4.
72   *S. T.* I. Q. 20. a. 2 AD. 1.
73   *S. T.* I. Q. 8 a. 3 resp: 'God is said to be in a thing in two ways; in one way after the manner of an efficient cause; and thus He is in all things created by Him; in another way He is in things as the object of operation is in the operator; and this is proper to the operations of the soul, according as the thing known is in the one who knows; and the thing desired in the one desiring. In this second way God is especially in the rational creature, which knows and loves him actually or habitually. And because the rational creature possesses this prerogative by grace, as will be shown later (Q. 12), He is thus said to be in the saints by grace.' Note here that the 'especially' indicates some sort of gracious or teleological eschatological presence to all creatures, while as to humanity 'the saint' is ontologically normative.
74   See my remarks in Note 73.
75   The overcoming of a grace/nature duality (with Blondel, de Lubac and, in a very flawed manner, Karl Rahner) finally arrived at a theologically 'postmodern' questioning of modern assumptions, whereas Karl Barth remained basically within those assumptions and so within modernity. See Henri de Lubac, *The Mystery of the Supernatural*, trans. Rosemary Sheed, London: Geoffrey Chapman, 1962.
76   *S. T.* I. Q. 12 a. 1.
77   *S. T.* I. Q. 12 a. 4 resp: '… the created intellect cannot see the essence of God, unless God by his grace unites Himself to the created intellect, as an object made intelligible to it.'
78   Jean-Hervé Nicolas, 'Les Rapports entre la nature et le surnaturel dans les débats contemporaines', *Revue Thomiste*, July–Sept. 1995, TXCV, no. 3: 399–418.
79   *S. C. G.* 1 28–37.
80   Bruce Marshall, 'Faith and Reason Reconsidered: Aquinas and Luther on Deciding What is True', *The Thomist*, Jan. 1999, vol. 63, no. I: 1–49. And see *S. T.* II-II. Q. 2. a. 7; Q. 5. a. 1; III. Q. 1 a. 3.
81   *S. T.* I-II. Q. 93 a. 6 resp.
82   See Marshall, 'Faith and Reason Reconsidered' (see Note 80) and *S. T.* II.II. Q. 2 a. 3 AD. 3.
83   Eugene F. Rogers, Jnr, 'Thomas and Barth in Convergence on Romans I', *Modern Theology* 12: 1, Jan. 1996. See also Hermann Pesch, *Die Theologie der Rechtfertigung bei Martin Luther und Thomas von Aquin*, Mainz: Matthias Grunewald, 1985.
84   See, for example, *In Meta. Proemium c.*
85   *S. T.* I. Q. 14 a. 6 resp.
86   See, for example, *In Boeth de Trin*, Q 5. a. 3 esp. ad. 1.
87   *S. T.* I. Q. 14 a. 5, a. 6, a. 11; Q. 15. a. 3.; Q. 1. a. 5.
88   *S. T.* I. Q. 14 a. 16; Q. 16 a. 6; Q. 34 a. 1, Q. 1 a. 4; a. 2, a. 3. Also Q. 15 a. 2 AD. 2. 'By wisdom and art we signify that by which God understands.'
89   See John Milbank and Catherine Pickstock, *Truth in Aquinas*, London: Routledge, 2001, ch. 1.
90   Marion, 'Saint Thomas d'Aquin' (see Note 51).
91   *S. T.* Q. 84 a. 1 and Q. 15 a. 3 AD. 4.
92   See *Super Librum de Causis Espositio* commentaries on propositions 1–6. And see *S. T.* I. Q. 14 a. 1 AD. 1, 2 and a. 3 AD. 3.
93   *In Boeth de Hebdom.* 3–5; Rudi te Velde, *Participation and Substantiality*, pp. 87ff. and passim. See also L. Bruno Puntel, *Analogie und Geschichtlichkeit I*, Freiburg: Herder, 1969.
94   See, in particular, Catherine Pickstock, *After Writing: On the Liturgical Consummation of Philosophy*, Oxford: Blackwell, 1998, ch. 1.
95   *In Boeth de Trin*, 4. a. 4: 'Thus the principles of accidents are reducible to the principles of substances.'
96   *S. T.* I. Q. 1 a. 6 AD. 2. See also, and for what follows, Note 43.
97   Corbin, *Le Chemin* (see Note 27), p. 726; commenting on the first question of the Prima Pars, Corbin says that metaphysics '*semble ici englobée*'.
98   At Q. 1 a. 7 AD. 2, Aquinas cites 2 Cor. x. 5: 'Bringing into captivity every understanding unto the obedience of Christ.' John Inglis points out that, in the thirteenth century, members

of the Dominican order were forbidden to study Arts and Logic as such at the University, and could only study philosophy under special dispensation. This indicates at least some hesitancy about the study of the Arts as an autonomous discipline outside a theological context and also shows that the Dominican order at this time did not envisage any study of philosophy as a living independent discipline as opposed to the deployment of philosophemes within theology. See John Inglis, *Spheres of Philosophical Inquiry* (see Note 2), p. 267.

99   Corbin, *Le Chemin* (see Note 27), pp. 714ff.

100   Ibid., pp. 724, 793, 800ff.

101   *S. T.* I. Q. 13 a. 7 resp.

102   *De Veritate*, I. Q. 1 a. 1 resp.

103   See Nicholas Lash, 'Ideology, Metaphor and Analogy' (see Note 23). Here he cites David Burrell, *Aquinas: God and Action*, London: R.K.P., 1979/Scranton: Scranton University Press, 2008, p. 48: 'commenting on Aristotle's metaphysics, Aquinas reflects that a metaphysician differs from a logician only by his power. Not by a separate faculty; a metaphysician is distinguished only by the astuteness with which he employs those faculties we all share and which logic can help to refine. The mode of metaphysics is not intuitive for Aquinas, but logical.' The present authors agree with Burrell that there is no separate metaphysical 'faculty'. However, it is hoped that our analysis above in the text, and citations in the notes, show that, for Aquinas, all our thought, in order to be thought, is primarily intuitive, albeit in a very weak degree, and so *in toto* 'metaphysical' or rather 'theological'. What has to be said here is that while ontologist intuitionism represented one Catholic rejection of Kant, the neo-Thomist purging of Augustinian illuminationist elements from Aquinas was itself a rejection of anything that might be tinged with Kant's idealist legacy. Thus (ironically) Lonergan's 'Kantian' and transcendentalist suspicion of vision and intuition is itself also a perpetuation of neo-Thomist misreadings of Aquinas, just as it is ultimately allied to Baroque Thomist reliance on a univocalist ontology prior to theology, which itself eventually generated Kant and idealism. See Eric Alliez, *Capital Times*, trans. G. van den Abbeele, Minneapolis: Minnesota University Press, 1996, pp. 240–41. However, Burrell's truly inspiring work on Aquinas and medieval philosophy since *Aquinas: God and Action* abandons his earlier transcendentalist–semanticist premises.

104   See Courtine, *Suarez et le système de métaphysique* (see Note 18), passim.

105   *In Metaph.* L. IV.I.IV. 574.

106   See the subtle and vital arguments of Aquinas's *De Ente et Essentia*. Only after Scotus did logic emphatically cease to be concerned with the actual mode of things in the mind and become instead to do with 'algebraic' possibilities.

107   Bernard Lonergan, *Insight: A Study of Human Understanding*, New York: Harper and Row, 1978, pp. 320, 323, 412–15.

108   Bernard Lonergan, *Verbum: Word and Idea in Aquinas*, Notre Dame, IN: Notre Dame University Press, 1967, pp. 25, 49, 50–51, 64, 197.

109   *S. T.* I. Q. 12 a. 11, a. 12, a. 13. esp. a. 12 AD. 2: 'God is known by natural knowledge through the images of His effects' and a. 13 AD. 1: '[by grace we know God] more fully according as ... more excellent of His effects are demonstrated to us ...' This provides the ontological presupposition for the account of 'divine names' in Q. 13.

110   Here is the text which confirms that one may speak of *analogia entis* in Aquinas and disallows analogy as primarily a reflection on language: *S. T.* I. Q. 4 a. 3 resp: '... if there is an agent not contained in any genus, its effects will still more distantly reproduce the form of the agent [their generic, equivocal agency] not, that is, so as to participate in the likeness of the agent's form according to the same specific or generic formality, but only according to some sort of analogy, as existence is common to all.' In this way all created beings, so far as they are beings, are like God as the first and universal principle of all being. See also Q. 4 a. 2; Q. 6 a. 1. The same primary interest in causality and participation is perpetuated in Q 13: see Q. 13 a. 2 resp and Q. 13 a. 5. resp and AD. 1.

111   *S. T.* I. Q. 13 a. 5. resp.

112   For example, *S. T.* I. Q. 13 a. 10 sed contra; citing Aristotle, *Perihermeneias* I: 'The idea in the intellect is the likeness of what is in the thing.'

113 *S. T.* I. Q. 13 a. 2 resp.

114 Aquinas identifies actuality with light: *Super Libr. De Causis Expos.* Proposition 649(4–5).

115 On this matter, see Emmanuelle Gabellieri, 'Saint Thomas: une ontothéologie sans phenom-enologie?', *Revue Thomiste*, Jan.–Mar. 1995, TXCV, no. 1, 150–92.

116 Nicholas Lash, *Easter in Ordinary: Reflections on Human Experience and the Knowledge of God*, Charlottesville: University Press of Virginia, 1998.

117 Here, as elsewhere in the chapter, we are indebted to conversations with Phillip Blond, David Hart and John Betz. See also Conor Cunningham's crucial essay 'Language: Wittgenstein after Theology', in Milbank et al., *Radical Orthodoxy* (see Note 15), pp. 64–91.

118 This confused blending of Kant with the *via negativa* is pervasive in recent theology.

119 Marion, 'Saint Thomas d'Aquin' (see Note 51).

120 See Fran O'Rourke, 'Intensive Being in Pseudo-Dionysius and Aquinas', *Dionysius*, vol. XV, Dec. 1991, 31–81.

121 On this, see Phillip Blond's decisive analysis of Levinas, 'Emmanuel Levinas: God and Phe-nomenology', in Phillip Blond (ed.) *Post-Secular Philosophy*, London: Routledge, 1998, pp. 195–229.

122 Marion, 'Saint Thomas d'Aquin (see Note 51). 'Distance' between humanity and God is denied by Aquinas at *S. T.* I. Q. 7 a. 1 AD. 3: 'Hence nothing is distant from Him, as if it could be without God in itself', although the locution is allowed elsewhere.

123 See John Milbank, 'A Critique of the Theology of Right', in Milbank, *The Word Made Strange: Theology, Language, Culture*, Oxford: Blackwell, 1997, pp. 7–35.

124 See Lash, 'Ideology, Metaphor and Analogy' (see Note 23).

125 For the background to this, see once again, Courtine, *Suarez et le systéme de métaphysique* (see Note 18).

126 *S. C. G.* 4, the whole chapter 11. And see Gilles Emery, *La Trinité Créatice*, Paris: Vrin, 1995.

127 *S. C. G.* 4. 1(1) and (2).

128 *S. T.* I. Q. 1 a. 4 AD. 2; Q. 1 a. 8 resp. and ad. 2.

129 *S. T.* I. Q. 29 a. 3.

130 *S. T.* I. Q. 34 a. 2.

131 For example, *S. T.* II-II. Q. 109 a. 1. and Q. 79 a. 9 resp: 'for the act of reason is, at it were, a movement from one thing to another'.

132 *De Veritate* 1 Q. 4 a. 2.

133 Mark Jordan, *Ordering Wisdom: the Hierarchy of Philosophical Discourse in Aquinas*, Notre Dame, IN: Notre Dame University Press, 1986, pp. 31–9. At *S. T.* I. Q. 34 a. 2 resp. Aquinas says categorically that the 'word ... signifies that which emanates from another'. Some other texts speaking variously of 'intuition', 'manifestation', 'expression', 'procession', 'emanation' are *De Veritate* Q. 4 a. 1 resp. and ad. 5; *S. C. G.* 4. 11(6), (16); 12(5); *S. T.* I–II. Q. 93 a. 1 AD. 2; *S. T.* I. Q. 28 a. 4 a. I; Q. 34 a. 2.

134 *S. T.* I. Q. 34 a. 1, a. 2.

135 See *De Veritate*, I. Q. 1 a. 1.

136 *S. T.* I. Q. 37 a. I, a 2.

137 *S. T.* I. Q. 39 a. 1.

138 *S. T.* I. Q. 29 a. 4. resp.

139 *S. T.* I. Q. 34 a. 2 AD. I. And S.C.G., 4. 11(11).

140 *S. C. G.* 4. 11(13).

141 *S. T.* I. Q. 45 a. 7.

142 See Wayne Hankey, 'Denys and Aquinas' and 'Stephen Menn's Cartesian Augustine'(a review of Stephen Menn, *Descartes and Augustine*, Cambridge: Cambridge University Press, 1998), *Animus* 3 (available at http://www.mun.ca/animus); Werner Beierwaltes, 'Unity and Trinity in East and West', in B. McGinn and W. Olten (eds) *Eriugena: East and West*, Notre Dame, IN: Notre Dame UniversityPress, 1994, 209–31, and 'Cusanus and Eriugena', *Dionysius*, vol. XIII, Dec. 1989, 115–52.

143 See Hankey, 'Stephen Menn's Cartesian Augustine' (see Note 142), and Gregory Shaw, *Theurgy and the Soul: The Neoplatonism of Iamblichus*, Pennsylvania: Pennsylvania State University Press, 1995.

144 Hegel, *Faith and Knowledge*, trans. Walter Cerf, Albany: State University of New York University Press, 1997, p. 168.

145 *S. T.* II-II. Q. 25 a. 7, a. 8.

146 *S. T.* I. Q. 38 a. 2.

147 *S. T.* I. Q. 44 a. 5, a. 8. Although Aquinas reserves the capacity for 'creation' to God alone, since no instrumental help can possibly be given in the bringing about of being as such, Aquinas does in effect say that we are 'co-creators' (participating in the creative act), since we do communicate *esse* in limited ways.

148 Corbin, *Le Chemin* (see Note 27), pp. 800ff.

149 *Super Libr. De Causis. Expos.* Proposition G 49(45).

150 Corbin, *Le Chemin* (see Note 27), pp. 788ff.

Chapter 4

Catherine Pickstock

Duns Scotus: his historical and contemporary significance

In recent years, there has been a remarkable increase in focus upon interpretations of the theology and philosophy of Duns Scotus. Much of this focus has centred upon an attempt to place the crucial shifts in the direction of modern philosophy not with Descartes and Kant, but in the Middle Ages. Duns Scotus has been seen as central to this change, but by no means its instigator or sole contributor. Other important figures are often cited: Avicenna, Gilbert Porreta, Roger Bacon, Peter Olivi, Bonaventure, Henry of Ghent, William of Ockham, Jean Buridan. Moreover, the shift is not presented as a crude "before" and "after". Even if it is the case that the movement away from an analogical worldview became most marked in the fourteenth century, nevertheless it is clear that tendencies in this direction had been put in place from at least the twelfth century. One should see the change as part of the plurality of the Middle Ages themselves, and the divergent intellectual visions on offer. Indeed, in some ways, Aquinas can be seen as a conservative defender of positions which were already being challenged.

A crucial aspect of the recent focus upon these issues concerns the relationship between philosophy and theology. The suggestion that Duns Scotus rather than Kant is the caesura in the history of philosophy involves a revision in the understanding of the importance of theology in the history of philosophy, because Duns Scotus's philosophical and theological reflections are connected in a complex way. As we will see, his central thesis of the univocity of being is subtly linked to his understanding of the consequences of the Fall. Philosophers and theologians are considering the significance of this revised history (Ludwig Honnefelder, Jean-François Courtine and Olivier Boulnois in particular).

In response to this new development, one can isolate four main reactions. First, there are those who say that if one understands modern thought not just as "Kantian" but also as "Scotist", one can show how modern approaches to epistemology and politics are more compatible with a classical Christian vision than some have suspected. This is a very serious and coherent position, and it will be given consideration below. The second reaction, common to certain French phenomenologists such as Jean-Luc Marion and Olivier Boulnois, is more ambivalent. On the one hand, Scotus's univocity is seen as a commencement of an idolatrous ontotheology, and a loss of the mystical discourse on the names of God. On the other hand, it is seen as making way for a post-metaphysical theology focussed upon charity rather than knowledge. The third tendency is that of so-called postmodern thinkers such as Gilles Deleuze who argue that the Scotist shift towards a univocal ontology is more fundamental for modern thought than the shift to the subject and to epistemology. The fourth reaction which has come to be associated with Radical Orthodoxy, but has far older roots and a far wider contemporary adherence, holds that the shift towards a univocal ontology, knowledge as representation, and causality as primarily efficient, is philosophically questionable and has negative implications for the upholding of a Christian vision and for the synthesis of theology and philosophy.

In what follows, I will try to clarify why Duns Scotus has come to have such contemporary significance. In addition, I will attempt as far as possible, within the very brief compass of this essay, to give consideration to the different assessments just outlined, while explaining some of the arguments in favour of the fourth view.

1. The problem of epochs

In his book *We Have Never Been Modern* the French philosopher of science Bruno Latour exposes the falsity of the myth that there are absolutely irreversible breaks in cultures through time.[1] This observation bears strongly upon the theme of the present essay for, in tracing certain theoretical transformations from the later Middle Ages to the early modern period, one can see that aspects of late mediaeval theological thought underpin later characteristically "modern" ideas, even though much in the Enlightenment may also be seen as a qualified reaction against these changes. It has been common to account for the origins of modernity in terms of the vague edifice of "the Enlightenment", and to see modernity as co-extensive with the rise of the secular modern state needed to quell the Wars of Religion, together with the rise of systematic organisation of medical, educational and penal institutions. But given that attempts to improve society in a secular way via the state and the market have so visibly failed, then perhaps this revised genealogy which stresses the legacy of a distorted religious theory could also point us indirectly towards a more serious alternative future polity than the liberal and postmodern critiques.

But one can even go further than this. Against the one-dimensional "modern" vision of progress without a genuine *novum*, postmodern philosophers and cultural theorists have protested in the name of the diverse, the more than human, the incommensurable. In doing so, some of them (in particular Gilles Deleuze, Alain Badiou and Jacques Derrida) have explicitly appealed to Duns Scotus for their alternative vision. They regard his levelling of the infinite and the finite to a univocal being, his unleashing of the virtual and unmediably discontinuous, as permitting a radical break with a totalizing rationalism. But it has recently been argued that these Scotist innovations themselves lie at the inception of modernity. How then can they provide the key to a break with modernity? Surely they betoken a radicalisation of, and a return to, the very origins of modernity?

Duns Scotus's flattening out of actual necessity (an "aesthetically" necessary order shown only in actual existence, not proceeding from logical possibility) to pure virtuality and of being to the bare fact of existence, which are modern rationalist moves (and which undergird the primacy of epistemology over ontology), do indeed suggest a radicalisation of the modern in a more anarchic direction which renders all possibilities in their limitless range equally valid, and all existence merely phenomenal and ephemeral, lacking altogether in depth, or any symbolic pointing beyond itself towards either eternal truth or abiding human values. This suggests that one way to understand the postmodern is as the "late" modern, or the intensification of certain trends established within modernity. The invocation of Duns Scotus and the later Middle Ages by Gilles Deleuze, Alain Badiou, Jacques Derrida and many others is a crucial part of what is best understood as a revised understanding of the nature of modernity itself.

In the philosophical sphere, modernity used to be characterised by the turn to the subject, the dominance of epistemology and the guaranteeing of secure knowledge by the following of a reliable method. Today, following tendencies beginning early in the twentieth century with the work of Étienne Gilson, and climaxing in the rigorous scholarship of Jean-Luc Marion, Jean-François Courtine and Olivier Boulnois, we have become aware of the way in which both the Cartesian and the Kantian moves depended upon shifts within Latin scholasticism to such an extent that one can now validly say that both Descartes and Kant remained to a degree "scholastics".[2]

In particular, it can be seen that these two thinkers did not simply transfer allegiance for objectively critical reasons from an unwarranted claim to know being as it really is, to an attempt to define true knowledge and even being in terms of the unequivocally graspable and internally consistent. Rather, a prior change in the understanding of being, a prior re-orientation of ontology, was necessary in order to make possible the move from ontology to epistemology. As long as the Greco-Arab and then Western Catholic synthesis of Aristotle with Neoplatonism remained in place, a turn towards epistemology could have possessed no critical obviousness. Within this synthesis, every abstraction of properties – such as "being" or "truth" or "good" or "entity" – from the real, was still concerned with their instance *as* universal elements within the real (as opposed to logical abstractions), while even the act of abstraction was regarded as an elevation towards that greater actuality and perfection which characterised a more purely spiritual apprehension. The working assumption was that the finite occurrence of being (as of truth, goodness, substance, etc.) restricts infinite being in which it participates. When knowledge grasps finitude in its relatively universal aspects, it does not simply mirror finitude, but rather fulfils its nature in achieving a certain elevation of its reality.[3]

To conceive of knowledge, by contrast, as a mirroring, or as "representation", requires that one think of the abstraction that is clearly involved in all understanding in an entirely different fashion. To abstract must not involve any elevation but rather a kind of mimetic doubling. It is now regarded as a demand of rigour that one keep a "transcendental" universality strictly distinct from "transcendent" height and spirituality, logical abstraction from spiritual ascesis. This is what Duns Scotus achieves by reading pseudo-Dionysius and Augustine in his own fashion, in which he was sometimes alert to ambiguities within their texts and at other times seemingly almost wilfully perverse. His new and explicit deployment of perfection terms as "common" both to God and creatures was nonetheless anticipated by Bonaventure, and was decisively undergirded by central elements of the metaphysical views and positions attributed at the time to Avicenna.[4] For Scotus, being and other transcendental categories now imply no freight of perfective elevation.

Instead, finite creatures, like the infinite creator, nakedly "are", as opposed to "not being" in a punctiliar fashion – they are "the same" *in quid* as regards existing which belongs to them as an essential property, just as substance and accident, genus, species and individuality all exist in the same fashion, *in quid*. Only *in quale* – as regards specific differences of a qualitative kind, including the difference between finite and infinite, and the differences between the transcendentals (since Duns Scotus denies their full convertibility: being is not of itself entirely true, etc.)[5] – is there no univocity, but rather, it seems, something like pure equivocity. This provides a very complex and notoriously subtle picture, but, put briefly: as regards the pure logical essence of *esse*, there is univocity between all its instances, while as regards ultimate differentiating qualitative properties there is equivocal diversity. Thus, although *esse* is univocal *in quid*, as regards its being directly predicated of a subject in which qualities inhere, in the fully determined quidditive instance (which is for Scotus *in quid* in another more fundamental sense) there is always something formally present that is over and above pure univocity and appears indeed to be entirely "different". Nevertheless, because differences are only instantiated in things that are, Scotus declares that uncreated being and the ten genera of finitude are all included "essentially" within being as univocal and as a quasi-genus. (It is not a proper genus, for Scotus, because for him genera only divide the finite, and not because, as for Aquinas, being cannot, like a genus, be extrinsically determined.) Moreover, even the specific differences of finitude, the property of infinitude and the *passiones* or transcendentals are "virtually" included within being as univocal. This makes it clear that while, indeed, univocity is for Scotus a semantic thesis regarding the constancy of meaning through diverse predications, all the same he tends to semanticise the field of ontology itself, through his thesis of essential and virtual inclusion.[6] In effect this implies that being as a semantic or logical unit is also a formal element of the make-up of any existential reality; although Scotus does not explicitly speak of a "formal distinction" between being and essence, later Scotists developed a clear logicist formalisation.

When Scotus speaks of analogy, as Boulnois concludes, this seems to reduce either to the equivocal, or to degrees of "intensity" upon a quantitative model.[7] Although, indeed, Scotus allows that an infinite degree transcends the quantitative, this excess is once again conceived in an equivocal fashion, while the model of intensive ascent itself remains quantitative in its paradigm, as is shown by Scotus's insistence that the idea of "more good" does not – *contra* Augustine – affect our grasp of the meaning of "good".[8] The position of the analogical, as a third medium between identity and difference, whereby something can be like something else in its very unlikeness according to an ineffable co-belonging, is rejected by Scotus because it does not seem to be rationally thinkable.[9] What remains is a semantic world sundered between the univocal and the equivocal. Scotus's refusal, in contrast to Aristotle and Aquinas, to conceive of a semantic analogy within grammar and logic inevitably influences his conception of the metaphysical field also, since the new autonomy which he grants to the semantic is itself a metaphysical move: purely logical existence, including purely punctiliar essential univocal being *in quid* now belongs entirely to the real and can always be "virtually distinguished" within its more complex concrete binding together with other elements *in quale*. Far from this outlook displaying an unquestionable rigour, it would seem that the idea that abstraction opens upon its own neutral quasi-ontological realm of virtuality that is independent of any ascent to the concretely spiritual amounts simply to the following through of one hermeneutic option.

Since finite being is now regarded as possessing in essence "being" in its own right (even though it still requires an infinite cause), when the mind abstracts being from finitude, it undergoes no elevation but simply isolates something formally empty, something that is already in effect a transcendentally *a priori* category and no longer transcendental in the usual mediaeval sense of a metaphysically universal category which applies to all beings as such, with or without material instantiation. For this reason, it now represents something that is simply there, without overtones of valuation, although it also represents something that must be invoked in any act of representation, and is in this new sense "transcendental". Scotus here echoes the supposed Avicennian view that the subject of metaphysics is being and not the first principle (as Averroës held), for being can now be regarded as (for our understanding) transcendentally prior to, and also as common to both God and creatures.[10] In one sense, this inaugurates ontotheology and so is "modern" and not "postmodern".

But, in another sense, Scotus opens up the possibility of considering being without God, and as more fundamental (supposedly) than the alternative of finite versus infinite, or temporal versus eternal. And this space is as much occupied by Heidegger, Derrida and Deleuze as it was by Hegel. Here, Scotus's proto-modernity involves also the "postmodern".

Something similar applies to the Scotist impact upon theology. As a "proto-modern" thinker, Scotus's contributions had implications for the alliance between theology and the metaphysical (in the broad sense of pre-Scotist Platonic–Aristotelian philosophical realism, not in the sense of ontotheology). For within the prevailing theologico-metaphysical discourse of participated-in perfections, there was a ready continuity between reason and revelation: reason itself was drawn upwards by divine light, while, inversely, revelation involved the conjunction of radiant being and further illuminated mind. Here, as we have seen, to rise to the Good, before as well as within faith, was to rise to God. But once the perceived relationship to the transcendentals has undergone the shift described above, to abstract to the Good tells us nothing concerning the divine nature. To know the latter, we wait far more upon a positive revelation of something that has for us the impact of a contingent fact rather than a metaphysical necessity.

One can interpret the latter outcome as modern misfortune: the loss of an integrally conceptual and mystical path. Already before Duns Scotus (even in Bonaventure, perhaps), the business of naming God was beginning to change; it was gradually losing the accompanying element of existential transformation of the one naming. This tends to be a consequence of an aprioristic reading of Anselm by the Franciscans, for which perfection terms already start to denote abstraction rather than elevation.[11] But, with Scotus, the mystical dimension is lost, and Augustinian divine illumination of the intellect (in all human knowing) is reduced to the divine causal instigation of the natural light of the agent intellect (more so than for Aquinas, for whom the entirely created light of the individual human agent intellect was still a self-exceeding light).[12] In this way a path was opened for an historical transition from Platonic recollection (in its many mutations) to modern apriorism.

2. Duns Scotus and the end of onto-theology

The above verdict on Scotus is strongly contested by Orlando Todisco and Isiduro Manzano.[13] These writers do not question the "Radical Orthodoxy" view that Scotus stood at the centre of a paradigm shift in the thirteenth century. The argument here concerns evaluation rather than exegesis. What Radical Orthodoxy writers would tend to view negatively, they view positively.

In particular, Todisco and Manzano reject my (and others') interpretation that Scotus's ideas led to a diminution of the scope of theology. For Todisco, just the opposite is the case: by reducing metaphysics to a bare ontology which defines the *ens* in terms of the law of excluded middle, Scotus ends rather than inaugurates onto-theology and ensures that thenceforward our discourse concerning God and his rela-tion to the world will be much more radically derived from the sources of revelation. The Radical Orthodoxy writers are, furthermore, guilty of ignoring the fact that even univocity of being is a theological as well as a metaphysical thesis. Because of our fallenness, *in statu ipso* the first object of knowledge seems to be a material creature, mediated to us by the sensorily imagined phantasm. Only revelation of our previous unfallen condition opens up the hidden truth that by its original, integral nature our intellect is attuned to the metaphysical before the physical: that it properly grasps first the *ens qua ens*, in abstraction from either material or spiritual designation. In this way, and on account of this neutral abstraction, revealed theology itself paradoxically makes available the space for metaphysics as a science in its own right, purified of any Aristotelian co-reference to God as subject matter along with being. Conversely, a metaphysics redirected towards thinking about *ens* as such, in indifference as to cause and relation, reciprocally opens the space of revealed theology in two different ways. First, it helps to show the contingency of our perverse fallen condition, where, con-trary to natural governance, the senses lead the mind. Secondly, it reveals a natural precondition for the reception of supernatural grace – namely, the neutral possible orientation of our mind as much to infinite as to finite being.

Both Todisco and Manzano rightly consider that this indeed subtle and creatively brilliant scheme allows for a kind of benign dividing and ruling. Strict reason is more fully acknowledged than with Aquinas, since univocity permits a proof of God's exis-tence without reference to a higher cause beyond our grasp, and so within the terms of strict maintenance of a mediating identity as required by syllogistic proof: one can see with certainty that infinite being must be ontologically prior to finite being only because the middle term "being" retains a univocal identity. By contrast, Aquinas, following Averroës, knows that his always somewhat "physical" (though also meta-physical, unlike Averroës) "proof" of a first highest cause falls short of strict demon-stration.[14] In the Proclean derived *schema* of analogy of attribution and metaphysics of participation, a mystical supplement to pure reason would appear always to be required. However, Scotus goes further in seeing this *schema* as rationally deficient: he argues that it violates the law of excluded middle. Thus, one may contend, partici-pated *esse* at once is and is not the divine *esse*: if a thing is "like" what is higher than it, and this is irreducible to its being like in some ways (univocally) and unlike in other ways (equivocally), then it must be at once present as something that exists and yet also present as not this thing – and in the same way and the same respect.

On the other hand, reason is more chastened for Scotus than for Aquinas. Our fallen reason is properly attuned to the finite, and for this reason finite causes form a closed system, otherwise they would disperse into uncertainty (the foreshadowing of Kant is clear). God cannot be demonstrated from physical causes, and the ontological proof of his existence concludes only to a bare infinite without further determination purely *qua* infinite (whereas for Aquinas the infinite in its simplicity also equals *esse* and all the other transcendentals). Above all, for Scotus, the ontological difference between *esse* and *ens* will not capture the difference between Creator and creature, since this difference cannot logically and so (for Scotus) ontologically be construed in terms of participation. *Esse* is nothing in itself (a "vicious abstraction" as Richard Cross terms it) and is exhaustively instantiated in the same way in all the punctual occurrences of *entia*. The latter do not share an eminent elevation but something common and equal which they alone determine. Nevertheless, Todisco argues, this shared ontological dimension much better reveals the ontological distance of God than does the Thomist real distinction of *esse* from *essentia*. For, as we have seen, of the infinite one cannot rationally know its eminence or causality or excellence.

In this way, univocity unlike analogy – which can only open upon distance by also insinuating a likeness – leaves us radically open to divine grace. No extrinsicism is involved here for Todisco, since, quite to the contrary, Scotus saw the extrinsicist dangers of Aquinas's view of cognition: reason that is naturally (and not just *pro statu ipso*) confined to the *conversio ad phantasmata* is not at all prepared for the reception of grace. Nor does univocity encourage an arbitrary voluntarism: what it favours is charitable gift, not tyranny. For Aquinas the sharedness of *esse*, whereby divine omnipresence concerns a certain emanation of his *esse* as such, suggests a necessitating of God in creation, and indeed the divine reason for Thomas takes precedence over his will. In the Thomist cosmos some realities – like the orbiting stars – are "necessary", and only some others purely contingent. Likewise creatures possess "natural ends" which it seems they arrive at ineluctably. By contrast, for Scotus, the creation is pure willed free gift. It is incited, beyond reason, not by a will-to-dominate but by charity, which freely gives a space of freedom to the other. In the Scotist cosmos every creature *qua* creature is contingent, and, in being what it is, reveals that it might have been otherwise. Instead of possessing "natural tendencies", human creatures are endowed with open capacities (recognised by the doctrine of univocity) to which divine grace may condescend.

Corresponding with the new primacy of charity, however (and here Todisco and Manzano are in a kind of negative agreement with the Radical Orthodoxy authors), is a certain arena of created autonomy. This shows clearly that all parties agree that while univocity is rooted in formal logic, it has ontological and theological consequences. Univocity of being allows for Scotus a reading of divine/human concurrence in freedom in terms other than those of Aquinas – whose notions of a fully determined creaturely freedom can seem contradictory: just what, after all, is an entirely determined freedom? Even if, for Scotus, the divine election is irresistible, our response still has some formal space of its own, its own integrity grounded in the logical law of identity (just as, as one might mention, for the Franciscan tradition culminating in Ockham, property rights are a matter of absolute formal ownership and not built upon "appropriate use" as for Aquinas – in such a way that the life of religious poverty requires the abandonment of material ownership by a will which nonetheless "owns itself"). Since God freely gives gifts of finite being to us as others, he can also enter into covenanted bonds with us that are sensitive to our freedom.

One can note here as a supplement to the reflections of Todisco and Manzano that this concursus account of divine–human co-operation is one instance of Scotus's modified view (shared with Peter Olivi and Bonaventure) of the working of causality – and especially divine causality – in terms of the category of influential.[15] The latter is no longer seen as equivalent to a Neoplatonic processio, or as a higher total cause which by an "inflowing" gives rise to an equally total cause at a lower level (such as the human will under grace). For the older view of "influence", which followed the metaphorical contour of the term itself, a lower cause could retain its full integrity and yet be the "gift" of a higher cause with which it was in no sense properly commensurate. For Scotus, however, this radical integrity no longer applies, paradoxically because higher and lower cause now contribute respective shares on the same ontic plane, like two men drawing a single barge, to use a later frequently deployed analogy.

This shift in understanding of cause is another consequence of a univocalist ontology, for which all cases, as equally instances of bare existence as subjects, must be at the deepest level commensurable. At the same time, the idea that a higher cause in its descending influence abandons its higher incommensurable dignity also helped reciprocally to reinforce the apparent obviousness of such an ontology (as with the case of knowledge as representation).

Nevertheless, one might want to agree with Manzano and Todisco that the revised view of influentia as extrinsic, rather than in-flowing, might be defended as both more rationally comprehensible and more permitting of the exercise of human freedom in a more apparently non-paradoxical fashion. For Scotus, it is as free that human beings especially exhibit the image of God. This is because they are granted a certain authentic self-origination which remains at the most fundamental ontological level. By contrast, for Aquinas, at the level of Esse, freedom is itself radically predestined without remainder. Just for this reason, the Scotist God primarily characterised by freedom is no despot. Indeed, one can, following Todisco and Manzano, throw back such a charge upon Thomas. Is not the specifically Thomist potentia absoluta left dangerously undetermined and so only rendered just and true under the auspices of potentia ordinata? For Scotus, however, one can claim, the two potencies display one single will to charity – both in what God actually does and in what He might do.

The same formal goodness is shown in human beings: they do not require extrinsic teleological determination in order to be accounted good by nature, nor do they await any mode of cultural determination. Aristotelianism, to the contrary, requires that human beings be teleologically fulfilled in the life of the polis. But for Scotus human beings are not political or social animals as they are for Aristotle and Aquinas. Instead, they are able to negotiate culture as a work of freedom, and the only "common good" one should recognise is a contractually produced state of empirical peace. This Scotist "proto-liberalism", on Manzano's account, meshes exactly with his proto-empiricism and modest rationalism. Scotus maintains both the latter two elements because he also foreshadows (one can add to Todisco and Manzano) a Baroque division of knowledge between "truths of fact" and "truths of reason" confined to the little that follows from the law of identity.

According to the perspective which Todisco and Manzano present, with great lucidity, an extremely attractive theological programme is offered. If one takes modernity back to its Scotist roots (and even where they protest this thesis, their own exegesis tends to confirm it), one can retain what is valid in the modern world purged of its secularity. Thus empiricism, a strict use of reason and political liberalism all sit nicely with an apophatic attention to revelation and a theology focussed upon charity and the gift.

It is a very "Anglo-Saxon" programme, and why should some contemporary British and American authors question it? If, for the moment, I were permitted to be somewhat expansive, I would say that this is in part because of doubts about the "modern" Anglo-Saxon project which have arisen from within this project itself. Wilfrid Sellars, W. V. O. Quine, Richard Rorty and John McDowell have all questioned the possibility of empiricism and rationalism by questioning the possibility of distinguishing the sources of our knowledge as clearly either fact or reason, synthesis or analysis, or fact or value.[16] The epistemology of "representation" whereby the mind can image reality (in either an empiricist or rationalist/idealist variant) has been in this way challenged. Likewise, the liberal politics of "representation" of supposedly originally isolated and fully autonomous individuals through the objective artifices of contract, money, politeness and parliamentary election has been challenged by the work of Alasdair MacIntyre and Michael Sandel and many others (MacIntyre's work being Thomistic in inspiration).[17] So if, as both Radical Orthodoxy and Todisco with Manzano seem to agree, epistemological representation and political liberalism have roots in univocity, then an "Anglo-Saxon" questioning of univocity is not so surprising: it would appear logically to be next on the post-empiricist agenda. And, one might add, to conclude this digression, that it may be a welcome sign of the recovery of a truly European culture that British defenders of a South Italian Norman find themselves in debate with Latin defenders of a man born in a small town in the Scottish borders ...

3. The theological dimension of univocity

Can this defence of Scotism be adequately answered? In response, it is important to stress that one is not simply advocating the autonomy and wide compass of theology. Rather, the present critique of Scotus has more to do with the separation of faith from reason, grace from nature, will from reason and theology from metaphysics and physics.

One cannot (as most contemporary commentators agree) really exonerate Scotus from the charge of ontotheology. The distance of the infinite is not difference from the ontic, and univocity requires that God and creatures "are" in the same albeit spectral ontic fashion. Scotus's treatment of a vast range of issues from human freedom (as we have just seen), to questions concerning Adam, Christ, Grace and the Eucharist all tend to show that this logical/ontological minimum still makes a considerable conceptual and practical difference. Common to all these instances is the idea that a being as self-identical and so recognisable must be free from all internal relations (to adopt a later terminology). It must be thinkable in abstraction from all that has caused it, and from its constitutive co-belonging with other realities. It is this position which tends to encourage both epistemological and political atomism. If each finite position does not occupy the problematic (even, one can admit) contradictory space of participation, then it is identical with its own space, and univocity involves necessarily a logic of self-possession which may be at variance with the theological notion that being in its very existence is *donum* and not the mere ground for the reception of a gift – even for the gift of determination of this *ens* as finite. For even the latter reception allows a certain formal ground to persist outside gift, as in the case of the Scotist conception of the human will. This self-possessed space is frequently considered by Scotus as if *per impossibile* God did not exist, and so *etsi Deus non daretur*. Being can be treated purely "metaphysically" (for the first time) in abstraction from "physical" issues of cause and moving interactions. Yet does not this approach in some slight way impugn divine omnipotence and render God a being alongside other beings, even if this "alongside" is a non-negotiable gulf (and even because it is a non-negotiable gulf)? Todisco and Manzano do not engage this issue. Todisco in particular obfuscates the point that while, for Scotus, being and not God is the subject of metaphysics, God is nonetheless included in the first subdivision of this subject matter, as infinite being, whereas, for Aquinas, God, as cause of *ens inquantum ens* (and not just of being *qua* finite), can only be invoked as the inaccessible principle of the subject matter of metaphysics, unknowable by metaphysics itself.[18]

If, in this fashion, God is somewhat reduced to ontic status and included within the consideration of metaphysics, then the greater autonomy allowed by Scotus to theology in relation to metaphysics appears ambivalent. In particular, the conceptual space for revelation is predetermined in its nature by philosophy – just as much (and arguably more so) as with analogy of attribution. Since revelation is seen to be removed from every mode of compellingly intelligible necessity, it has to fall within the scope of pure contingency and pure factuality. It will inevitably favour the "truths of fact" pole within a facts/reason *a priori* alternative supplied solely by philosophy. The danger is clearly one of revelational positivism: that we know in advance that all that God can show us is positive facts and unambiguous information. For example, it does not seem good enough to say, with Manzano, that only by divine freedom are bread and wine appointed to be sacramental vehicles. Of course this is true, but it does not preclude a certain insight into their "convenience" or "aesthetic necessity" – how otherwise should spiritual writers be able to meditate, for example, on the significance of the colour, liquidity and intoxicating power of the wine? It is hard to make sense of this sort of limited but real insight into revelation without invoking certain ideas about analogical ascent (and also extending those notions to encompass theories of metaphor).[19]

Univocity appears to encourage dualities without mediation: God is unknowably and equivocally remote as regards His being *in quale*; this gap can only be bridged by positive revealed disclosures, yet this means that the space of revelation is philosophically predetermined as a space of facts or empirical propositions. By contrast, while it seems that analogy already by reason intrudes upon the space of revelation (since any rational advance is ultimately lured forward by a grace-granted anticipation of the beatific vision), nevertheless the paradoxical presence of unlikeness within likeness in analogy, which also governs revealed discourse, ensures that the mysterious unlikeness of the revealed truth is sustained, not just with regard to content, but even with respect to formality. An analogical participating reality is neither simply a reason nor simply a fact; neither simply universal nor simply particular. The participating analogue cannot exhibit a full rational account of its cause (cannot furnish us with a syllogistic proof of its cause) but only a partial one, by way of its concreteness as an effect, its very factuality which declares its cause by exhibiting more clearly its own concrete character. And yet this fact, in pointing towards its more excellent cause, embodies a kind of reason. This analogical perspective ensures that *revelata* are not reduced to objects or items of information. It allows more scope to revelation than does univocity, since *revelata* now bear with themselves not just their own historical contingency but also their own logic which reason without revelation cannot fully anticipate. To put this another way, the space for the *Logos* to amend even our logic may be somewhat lacking on Scotist premises.

So might it be that analogy more than univocity presents the autonomy of the logic of revelation? One can note that it was Aquinas and not Scotus who wrote many commentaries upon scripture imbued with the principles of fourfold allegorical exegesis. This is not at all to deny that for Scotus univocity is a theological as well as a metaphysical category. It does indeed have profoundly to do with Scotus's theology of grace, as Todisco notes. Since, for Scotus, we are fallen, we have lost the possibility of our orientation to the infinite in the beatific vision. At the same time, redeeming grace permits us a minimal recovery in neutral terms of the natural orientation of the intellect to being – but without yet allowing us, like Adam, by grace to see angels and God as easily as we might trees and rocks – and facilitates our re-orientation via grace to the infinite. Nevertheless, this beguiling circle relies heavily upon Scotus's supposedly Avicennian (and somewhat Plotinian) view that knowledge is not for us naturally mediated by the senses.[20] And this would appear to qualify the verdict that Scotus more than Aquinas allows this world to be true to itself within its own terms, since here something that clearly belongs to our embodiment – our conceptual grasp only of the sensorily mediated – is re-evaluated. Everything that depends upon this mediation – science, the arts, philosophy, even the sacramental practice of religion – must partake of this re-evaluation. The sphere of culture, like politics, for Scotus can only figure as a kind of semi-sinful emergency measure.

By contrast, Aquinas was able to combine a certain materialism with our natural orientation to a supernatural end. His affirmation that, even in Eden, we first understand the materially instantiated *ens*, requires no extrinsic supplementation in the order of grace (as Scotism suspects) because Aquinas also thought that being as such was the first object of the human understanding. The co-primacy depends entirely upon Thomas's *esse/essentia* metaphysics as supervening upon his form/matter, spirit/body metaphysics. Since every essence participates in *esse* and discloses it, the material thing renders being as partially transparent to our gaze just as much as does the spiritual thing. In this way the embodied creature can be as near and as far from the beatific vision as the angelic one. It is for this reason that Aquinas, elaborating upon several of the Fathers, could so vividly grasp that the degraded following of our senses by reason after the Fall was subverted by the Incarnation into the instrument of our redemption. Here it is Scotus who permits a pathway to extrinsicism because of his cognitive Plotinianism: Adam was not by nature orientated to the beatific vision but only by special grant of grace; Christ's humanity did not possess grace intrinsically but only by special fiat; Christ's dead body in the tomb was divine by virtue of the formal distinction and so separability of his body from his whole substance (whereas for Aquinas it was divine by virtue of its substantive inclusion via the *persona* of the *Logos* and single *esse* granted by the *Logos* instead of the normal unity of substantive form); our natural desire for beatitude is only for Scotus more than a vague non-cognitive probing, not by enticement by the supernatural goal itself, but rather under the historical impact of actual grace.[21]

The theological dimension of univocity tends to problematise rather than assist an integral vision. But, leaving questions of revelation aside, does logic nevertheless ineluctably commit us to a univocal vision, whatever the consequences for the theological realm? Todisco argues that this is the case. One can concede to him that our finite minds are inclined by their very *modus cognoscendi* to thinking that everything that "is", including God, "is" in the same fashion. The forms of language which we are obliged to use tend to imply this, and it is impossible for our logic altogether to escape such a conception. This circumstance, as both Aristotle and Aquinas recognised, is part of the categorical boundedness (at once ontological and logical) of our finite circumstances. However, this inescapable univocal moment concerns being as fully transparent to our logic, or mode of thinking. But this does not mean that logic by itself obliges ontology to follow its lead, unless one has already assumed an ontological priority of rational possibility over actuality. Just because, for the most transparent logic, existence is an either/or and the notion of "degrees of being" makes no sense, it does not follow that actual existence necessarily enshrines this logic. More-over, disclosures of being other than the logical – in aesthetic, ethical and con-templative experience – may suggest to us that being can undergo a qualitative intensification. For actual existence – the circumstance that there is anything at all – exceeds the *a priori* notion of existentiality as the condition of the possibility for things being this or that. Although everything that is given to us is a being, this still involves a disclosure that existence itself is a given mystery. And since the *a priori* grasp of *ens qua ens* as bare possibility cannot of itself generate a single actuality, we cannot know what being itself is, nor that it is predatory upon the prior repertoire of the possible; on the contrary, since the possible is always only the possibility of the actual, it makes more sense to assume the ontological primacy of actuality.

For these sorts of reasons, Aristotle's metaphysics asks what is being, and in what diverse ways can it occur? Neoplatonism dealt with the resulting *aporia* – is being primarily a first causal source or primarily the most general categorical circum-stance? – with the notion of a scale of processions, construed (especially by Proclus) as participations and imitations (albeit finally of the One beyond Being).[22] Without this resolution, one is left with two options: either the notion of a highest ontic being, which does not explain being as such and invites infinite regression, or with an Avi-cennian/Scotist notion of an acausal being in general which tends towards the mys-tery of an original *res* indifferent as to something or nothing. In the long run this allows the possibility of "Scotist" nihilism as evidenced by Deleuze. The Proclean (but also Augustinian, Dionysian and Thomist) hierarchy of participation and attribution avoids both of these problems. But is it merely senseless? Here one can venture that no finite logic can rule out the idea that the actuality of finite being includes always a greater and lesser intensity. Indeed, according to a certain traditional logic, only the instance of a lack in appropriate being at any given level makes sense of notions of falsity and evil. Likewise, according to a certain traditional ontology, only the notion of degrees of being makes sense of the facts of autonomous life which can accom-modate more being and exhibit a "self-advancing" being, and the comprehensive powers of cognition which "is in a manner all things" according to Aristotle. Most crucially, the doctrine of Creation forbids theology to think in terms of "bare exis-tence". If being as such is created, then to be a finite being is causally to receive a measure of being, and this donation of a participation in *esse* by God is beyond the causal reach of any finite creature. No creature can bring about being as such (though it can participate in the arrival of new being through processes such as the diffusion of light or the uttering of a thought, processes which exhibit some analogy with the immediacy of creation but remain within the ontic level of the modification of form: see Note 33 below). This is because *esse* in its original actuality as God is a simple plenitude, and other realities can only be as diversely refracting this simplicity in various degrees. By contrast, to say that one can think being univocally outside the realm of causality has implications for the doctrine of Creation. If one thinks of finite being only as a logical possibility and without reference to how it has causally arisen, when one does think of it in causal terms, one will assume that the causing of *esse* or the act of creation resides within the capacity of the finite creature. This is because "to be" is now just a bare existential, indifferent as to simplicity or complexity. Hence in the wake of Scotus a residue of Avicennian Neoplatonism resurfaces in Ockham: for the latter, at least in principle, the angelic intelligences may fully create beings below their own level.[23] The idea that created being is only a gift bestowed by infinite *esse*, not an *a priori* something/nothing that any creature might posit, is here dismissed, in such a fashion that the notion of the ontological omnipotence of God (for which to cause to be lies within the divine scope alone) as something that He himself cannot will away, is here abandoned. God's power comes to be regarded idolatrously as in effect but a supreme degree of ontic power, for which the mark of power is always that one might abandon one's power.

Logic does not oblige us to assume a univocal ontology. However, does analogy in logic violate the principle of non-contradiction? One must concede to Todisco that it appears to do so. Scotus was rigorous and correct in this respect, but maybe this is why Nicholas of Cusa, who sought (unlike the Baroque "Thomists") to salvage the Proclean heritage in the face of Terminism, decided to question the law of identity itself? The recourse to *coincidentia oppositorum* seems justified because of the ontological difference, which is also for Aquinas the infinite/finite difference. Just as there can only be pure identity and simplicity in the infinite – since finite things are always composed and shifting – so, inversely, there can be no mere logical identity in the unlimited, since this notion only makes sense by reference to limitations. For Aristotle (for whom it was still a relatively ontological, and not purely logical, principle), the law of excluded middle applies because there is such a thing as (for him always limited) "substance" (even though inversely the law also ensures that there can be such a thing).[24] If God, as according to Aquinas, lies beyond limited substance, then the law loses its field of application.

In a similar fashion, the law of excluded middle cannot readily apply to participation of the bounded in the unbounded. For the finite to enter into participation in the infinite is to enter into identity and non-identity, and this coincidence is reflected and doubled in the circumstance that the finite here becomes both finite and infinite at once. (And the finite can be construed either as the complex and non-identical or as the bounded self-identical.) This provides the contradictory dynamism of analogy which exceeds that of Hegelian dialectics (also indebted to Proclus) since the contradictory tension is not really a conflict in search of an elusive return to formal identity, but a higher harmony beyond logical opposition which inspires an increase and intensification of a tension which mediates and resolves in and through its apparent contradictoriness. One may protest that here language has taken a very long vacation indeed. But does it make any more workaday sense that God is omnipresent and yet the world is not God? That for Augustine we are "of ourselves" nothing and only something from God and yet are not God? That (as for Aquinas) our created freedom is entirely determined in the very formality of freedom and yet is incomprehensibly determined as free since God is the absolute author of the existential, including the existentiality of freedom? (If he is not, then, as David Burrell has argued, there is a competition between God and creatures in a "zero sum game" which loses divine transcendence in an ontic parity).[25]

The doctrine of Creation seems to impose these mysteries and the incomprehensible logic of analogy seems sensitive to them. According to a Scotist perspective, however, they undergo a demystification. This perspective appears to prioritise the mystery of freedom; yet pure freedom is so open as to cancel mystery. It is already emptily determined as the supposed opposite of rational determination, but this only allows to the divine absolute freedom the status of a pure free "thing" alongside us in so far as our reason can comprehend this. Every voluntarism is but the reverse face of a rationalism: what one has here is not a benign dividing and ruling, but instead a collusion generated by a questionable dualism. This dualism tends not to allow God the status of a freedom that is equally (and incomprehensibly) something rationally determined and also (again incomprehensibly) able to allow "another" space of freedom which is still *non aliud*. Inversely, reason and determination, once robbed of a freedom intrinsic to their being, are left to their own merely formal and ultimately tautologous devices. The mediation of the beautiful between goodness and truth is here impeded, and, whereas an aesthetic is always fundamental for Aquinas (as also for Bonaventure and other Franciscans), in Scotus it tends to be converted into an empirical aggregate (a consequence of the Avicennian view that there can be a multiplicity of forms in a single substance) and to analysable proportion. (This somewhat anticipates the later eighteenth-century tension between empirical and rationalist approaches to aesthetics, neither of which was capable of capturing the Beautiful: a circumstance which helped precipitate the romantic reaction against the Enlightenment.)[26]

One can say in opposition to this that unless we can formally distinguish truth and goodness in God, our use of these words no longer makes any sense. But this confines theological discourse to the inert and non-mystical. The Thomistic counter to this objection is that we already partially integrate in our lives the co-belonging of truth and goodness, and by mystical advance we are asymptotically but essentially drawn to the divine point where the difference between the two really vanishes.

Moreover, the Scotist determination of the divine difference by infinity is ontologically insecure once the infinitisation of the finite opens to view in the Renaissance (though this was anticipated by another great British Franciscan, Robert Grosseteste, in *De Luce*). Once this has happened, Scotus's ontological primacy of the infinite over the finite (which may be a true thesis) is perfectly compatible with a pantheistic immanentism. At this point it was only a continued subscription to attributive ascent and to ontological difference (between simple *complicatio* and composed *explicatio*) which prevented Cusa from becoming a Bruno or a Spinoza. (Alternatively there is a direct passage from Scotism to a Spinozistic postmodernism.)[27] As Cornelio Fabro has argued, only participation secures simultaneously transcendence and immanence. But only the God who is simultaneously both is the transcendent God, since infinity without participation, and so simply "beyond" and "outside" the finite, can be recruited to pure immanence alone. So participation is not merely a "Greek" thesis alien to the Biblical legacy; it is a framework perfectly compatible with free creation *ex nihilo.*[28]

Nor does Aquinas's idea that certain created structures are relatively "necessary" and others relatively contingent negate the freedom of the divine creative act. It rather augments our sense of divine freedom to point out that he can build into creation such a distinction. For the free contingency of the creation is ontological and not ontic and therefore more transcendentally free. This means that even the most apparently necessary structures within the cosmos are nonetheless contingent in their ontological dependency, just as the most apparently free creatures in the cosmos are fully determined in their existentiality. To say, by contrast, with Scotus, that all creatures are equally contingent in their ontic instance, thereby taking contingency always to mean that "a thing might have been otherwise" rather than to mean (ontologically) "a thing did not have to be" is to reduce the actual to our logical apprehension and to claim too much insight, despite the apparent mood of empirical piety or pious empiricism. How do we know that water, trees, fire and so forth merely instantiate "possibilities" from an infinite repertoire? Might they not instead disclose to a small degree the mysterious (not simply rational) necessities of the divine mind and will – which two realities Aquinas never separates, unlike Scotus, for whom a formally distinct will in the human instance is open to the possibility of an incomprehensible "pure" choice, altogether without inspiring reasons.

In the foregoing, we have explored some of the negative consequences of univocity and its alliance with the formal distinction of will from reason. But is there nothing in the idea that the reduction of metaphysics to a minimal ontology actually frees theology to be a practical discourse about charity that is truer to the priorities and exigencies of the Christian life? Certainly this perspective allows Scotus to articulate a rich theology from which valuable insights may sometimes be gleaned. Nevertheless, as both Todisco and Manzano reveal (inadvertently or not), the danger here is of a drift into formalism. If God's will is inherently charitable and this quality enjoys a certain subtle priority over, and independence from, his intellect (with which indeed it harmonises, yet does not altogether coincide) then what is the content of charity? It will tend to become a free respecting of the freedom of the other; the gift will be simply of freedom, and such giving will be set at variance with the mutual agreement of covenant and contract. (Even though for Scotus the second table of the Decalogue republishes the natural law, its extra force as direct divine law still depends on willed institution and formal agreement.)[29]

This secures what one might see as a typically modern duality of private "free" gift over against contract, and Manzano appears to endorse (though to evaluate differently) the reading of Scotus which allies him with an emerging market society and the rise of the nation state. But why should Christian theology endorse with Todisco (and Scotus?) the assumption that people properly pursuing their own legitimate interests will naturally be in a hostile relation to one another? Is this compatible with Augustinian frameworks of the natural harmony of the creation and the possibility of a substantive (not just formally and contractually contrived) human peace? And why, for Manzano, are notions of "the common good" any more obscure than the shared values of the public library, or the shared pleasures of the public *piazza* – and why allow Oxford Professors (in this case J. L. Austin) with their remarks about trousers, cats and teacups ("the common good" is an ambiguously forking "trouser phrase") to deprive us of such palpable actualities? Does not the shared *piazza* exhibit an irreducibly collective good in so far as it involves a kind of state of charity, a reciprocal give-and-take within a shared horizon, rather than the empty one-way gift of freedom and the contractual achievement to enjoy such gifts in solitary self-pleasuring? Such an exchange of freedom amounts to a reduction of gift to contract, since the gift is given only within the mutual agreement to respect each other's freedom; by contrast, a contract is like the passing in the night of two "free" gifts that never acknowledge each other or discover a mutual appropriateness.

Manzano's abandonment of Catholic social teaching (for which the notion of "the common good" is scarcely dispensable) in favour of the today still emerging liberal market-state must ensure that the realm of human cultural choices has little relevance to transcendent goodness and truth. If indeed Scotus went this far in the direction of contractualism, then the thesis concerning the secularising tendency of univocity is all the more confirmed.

I am not at all contending instead, as Manzano suggests, for "natural law fundamentalism". To the contrary, he takes the view that Aquinas's natural law, beyond the minimum that we share with animals (self-preservation, care of the young and so forth) concerns the prudential judgement of equity and not the reading-off of norms from a pre-given nature (a perspective which may indeed result in prejudicial views concerning women, as Manzano suggests). To deny, with Manzano, our natural orientation to sociality beyond the family does nonetheless appear to ignore certain facts (such as the fundamental role of sympathy, for example, as noted by that other philosophical Scottish lowlander, David Hume). But the fact of our orientation to agreeable association can nonetheless only be interpreted by increasing theoretical and practical insight into the value of association and just what it is that makes it agreeable. Teleology is not closure, if it equally avoids formal openness. But then, even the eschaton can be somewhat anticipated, otherwise it may as well be threat as promise.

Neither Aquinas nor Scotus possessed an adequate ontology of culture or history.[30] However, the semi-voluntarist perspective of the latter promises less in this domain than the semi-intellectualism of the former. If culture is merely the work of will, then it is irrelevant to reason; it is still irrelevant to reason if it is half the work of will and half the work of a rational *mathēsis*. For neither is intrinsically cultural. Culture is only taken seriously where it is seen that both reason and desire are only possible in terms of language and other humanly constructed products which in turn construct humanity. The Scotist denial that human knowledge naturally concerns primarily sensorily intuited things cannot support this sort of insight. Much is made of Scotus's "historicist" attention to the *status lapsus*. Yet this exhibits only a concern with salvific metahistory, whereas the denial of the materiality of knowledge before the Fall is also by implication a denial of the natural historicity of human understanding, namely, the rootedness of our thoughts in concretely embodied occasions and circumstances.[31] By contrast, the Thomist model of both human and divine understanding seems more promising. God's intellect at one with his will responds to a kind of intrinsic aesthetic necessity, since Aquinas does not yet subscribe to anything like Leibniz's idea of God as submitting to sufficient reason and a calculus of the best possibilities. This necessity is only present in the Trinitarian emanation of the *Verbum* and the procession of the *Donum*. (Although this embodies the *potentia ordinata*, it properly expresses the *potentia absoluta*, which coincides with divine wisdom, although this infinite potency and wisdom cannot be adequately embodied in any particular finite order. Nevertheless, since the particular ordained order perfectly expresses an infinitely wise absolute power, the latter does not virtually suspend the finitely incomparable "justice" of the actually ordained order. In contrast to Scotus, it avoids reducing it to a mere possible instantiation of an infinite repertoire.)[32]

For Aquinas our utterance of the inner word and directing of desire participates in the Trinitarian processions. Likewise, in the *Prima Pars*, he says that the former remotely approximates, as does the diffusion of physical light, to the divine act of creation, since there is a simultaneity between the "being made" of the word and the "is made" of the word (Aquinas's own locutions). This echoes the way in which, in the economy of creation, "being created" is identical with "is created" and no transition or movement appears to be involved. This suggests that there is for Aquinas an internal construction of expressive signs which is co-original with thought and reflective of divine emanation and outward creation (since for Aquinas the divine creative act is eminently included within the generation of the son).[33] In the seventeenth century, the Portuguese Dominican John of St. Thomas (Juan Poinsot) expanded the theory of the concept as inner word into an account of our necessary cognitive deployment of culturally instituted signs which were nonetheless in continuity with natural signs. The Trinitarian reference was preserved through a recognition that a sign like the Trinitarian person falls under a "real relation" within the domain of *esse intentionale* and is as objective as a real relation in the substantive universe (material or angelic). This means that for Poinsot (making use of the category of real relation which Scotism and Terminism had tended to reject), human knowing and willing are only possible within the cultural and yet objective edifice of signs which itself participates in the divine *Verbum* and *Donum* and so in divine *esse*.

(Poinsot's grasp of participatory metaphysics and analogy was not strong, but his account of signs is Thomistic and compatible with such a metaphysics.)[34]

One could argue that the potential of Thomism to generate an ontology and theology of culture is linked with its Proclean dimension. Proclus, as a "theurgic" Neoplatonist, insisted that recollection of the transcendent realities was possible only via their descent into culturally instituted ritual forms; in his treatment of geometry he insists on the technological and pragmatic mediation of geometric theorems.[35] I would concur with Benedykt Huculak's stress upon an Aquinas–Proclus alignment versus a Scotus–Plotinus alignment.[36] However, Proclus' stronger interest in recollection (despite Huculak's denial of this and conflation of Proclus with Plotinus at this point) and insistence upon the abiding of the finite soul in time seem closer to Plato than does the Plotinian legacy. It is partly on this basis that one might see Aquinas as "more Platonic" than Scotus. One could also add that Augustine had also reacted to Plotinus in a manner somewhat analogous to that of Proclus: in the *Confessions*, although the soul measures time since time is its own distension, it nonetheless remains dispersed within created time which is not itself the work of the human soul; recollection plays a role in Augustine's articulation of divine illumination, re-invoking the *Meno* problematic of seeking for what we somehow already know; God must descend in the Incarnation and the Eucharist if we are to see the divine ideas; "interior" vision is contained within the vision of a sacral cosmos.

Are the usual alignments and contrasts (Plato versus Aristotle; Plotinian Augustine versus Proclean Aquinas) really reliable? Can we not sometimes read Aquinas as more Augustinian than mediaeval "Augustinians" much influenced by Plotinus via "Avicenna Latinus"? This is not necessarily to deny that Franciscan mediations of Augustine can balance Aquinas's perhaps not always sufficient stress on intellect as intrinsically desiring. However, Augustine was himself far more Platonically intellectualist than the standard interpretations often suggest.[37]

4. Scotus and postmodernism

It is declared by Scotus that the way of denial, or *via negativa*, only removes finite imperfections from a positively known quality which is infinity, deemed to be properly "convenient" for God in a more absolute sense even than intellect and goodness and so forth.[38] By this concept of a positive infinite, one "grasps" an absolute void of mystery. Within the framework of Pseudo-Dionysian and Thomist negative infinitude, by contrast, one does not grasp mystery, but one might say that one is positively initiated into it, according to the Pseudo-Dionysian dialectic of the apophatic and cataphatic which mystical theology embraces. The comprehended infinite void is akin to the Plotinian-tinged Avicennian infinite One, taken by Scotus as formally preceding the divine qualitative perfections ("good", "true" and so forth), which themselves formally precede the divine intellection: at *Quodlibetal Questions* 5 a 3 Scotus speaks of these orderings as "quasi-emanations". (It is this ontological priority of a positive infinite over any substantive qualities which seems more or less to legitimate the use of the term "void" here.)

To say, as many do, that Scotus retains, in his own fashion, a form of apophaticism, is somewhat misleading. For Augustine and Aquinas, negativity introduces us to a mysterious and yet palpable darkness, which in refusing our analysis, still welcomes us. This remains the case even when perfection terms are negated, as with Pseudo-Dionysius and Eriugena, because this negation is always driven by a super-exceeding rather than a sceptical suspension.[39] But Scotus offers us instead the positive presence of a kind of fetishised infinite absence. This could be seen as an anticipation of the Kantian sublime which is alien to an infinitude of the *forma* of the beautiful. Such a shift in the mystical component towards the absolutely empty effectively delivers theology over to the ineffable authority of the Church hierarchy, and, later, alternatively, to that of scripture.[40]

One can also read Duns Scotus as offering a theological anticipation of postmodernity: by foreclosing the scope of theological speculation, he demoted intellect in general and opened up theology as the pure discourse of charity. We receive the loving will of God, and respond to this with our answering will.[41] Between the reading of Scotus as surrendering the mystical heart of Catholicism and the reading of Scotus as inaugurating a kind of Pascalian way of charity, recent French historians of philosophy seem to hesitate – and with perfect legitimacy. There is certainly a sense in which the Scotist distinguishing between the ethical goal of happiness and the goal of pure justice, linked with an obedient and correctly intending will, rather than a beatified intellect, leads not only towards Kant, but also (as he at least once recognised) towards Jean-Luc Marion's disinterested charity and unilateral gift. In like fashion, Scotus's separation of revelation from mystical ascent points towards both Barth's hermeneutics of the pure word of God and Marion's phenomenology (without metaphysics) of the revealed word. Both seem to be linked to a loss of the mediating vision of analogy, even though, contradictorily, Marion's defence of the Pseudo-Dionysian *via antiqua* against the Scotist inauguration of ontotheology, seems to require the *via antiqua* alliance of revelation with metaphysics in the broader sense, and a more emphatic sense of analogy and participation than Marion affirms (although establishing his position on this is very difficult indeed).[42]

It becomes illogical to uphold the "postmodern" Scotus while denouncing the "modern" Scotus, and this applies both in philosophy and theology. If one cannot countenance Scotist ontotheology, one must also question a "pure" philosophy concerned with a non-divine being, since this is ultimately grounded in univocity and the refusal of analogy in any sense consistent with the Pseudo-Dionysian naming of God. In this way, Heidegger comes into question. Likewise, if one is wary of the Scotist separation of abstraction from elevation, or, rather, his particular refusal of the

mystical, one must be wary also of his semi-voluntarism. For the very same separation, applied by Duns Scotus to Augustine's discourse on the Trinity, ensures that one
must interpret the divine intellect and divine will as univocally similar in character to
the human intellect and will. Such a predilection is reciprocally reinforced by Scotus's
Franciscan rejection of a distinguishing of the persons of the Trinity by substantive
relations.

This rejection is allied to an Avicennian assumption that divine essence, and then
intellect, and later still divine will, are "quasi-emanations" which precede in some
fashion the entire Trinity. This tends to disallow the idea that the *Verbum* simply "is"
an original aspect of the divine intellect in conjunction with the *Donum*, which in turn
simply "is" an original aspect of the divine will. Duns Scotus sees the *Verbum* as
"declaring" an understanding fully present in the Father as Father, in principle not
requiring any generation in order to be understanding; likewise with the Holy Spirit
in relation to paternal and filial volition.[43] This is inevitable, because if essence and
intellect and will are all "prior" to the Trinity, and formally separate from it, then all
three realities are essentially non-relational.

If relation has no root in the divine essence, then the persons which spring from
the divine essence, understanding and will cannot have their most fundamental identity in relation. They require instead some preceding respective principles to ground
their distinctive personhood. For Scotus, such principles are found in originating
essence, intellect and will. The divine intellect for Scotus, in contrast to Aquinas, can
only be intellectual if it represents something that precedes it: because what it
represents are the divine perfections (in contrast to the absolute simplicity of the
divine infinite essence), the latter being formally distinct from the divine intellect as
well as the divine essence. For Aquinas, by contrast, divine ideas do not abide outside
the divine intellect any more than outside the essence.[44] Because the intellect is
ineluctably compelled by the perfections, it is a "natural" response, and the *Verbum* is
said to proceed *per naturam*. For Scotus, this compulsion is formally independent of
the will, and this inaugurates a separation of judgement from teleology. Concomitantly,
the divine will in Scotus is separated from the inner lure of desire, and the procession
of the Spirit is grounded in a pure non-natural and, it would seem, arbitrary procession
per voluntatem.

Without recourse to substantive relation in identifying the persons of the Trinity,
the attribution of intellect to the Son, and will to the Spirit, ceases to be remote
analogical naming – since we cannot really grasp pure relationality – and becomes the
means of literal distinction. The Son proceeds *per naturam* (in "declaring", as words
do thought, the Father's ineluctable representations) but the Spirit *per voluntatem*. In
this way, God is psychologised in an unequivocal fashion foreign to Augustine, yet
scarcely because of western "perversions", since neither substantive relation nor the
filioque is anywhere in sight. Indeed, a reading of Scotus tends to show that none of
the typical textbook categorisations of the history of Trinitarian doctrine is valid: for

example, Scotus has a strong doctrine of the paternal *monarchia* as prior to generation and spiration because he also has a strong view of the divine *essentia* as characterising the Godhead, rather than Trinitarian relations. Such a view is found neither in Augustine nor in Aquinas who have weak (but sufficient) accounts of the *monarchia*. The oft-trumpeted Franciscan "alternatives" in Trinitarian theology, it seems, result from the subordination of the Christian Trinity to a Neoplatonic trinity lurking in the ontological shadows.

The Scotist mode of distinguishing the persons by the natural/voluntary contrast in turn ensures that will is regarded as a movement of pure spontaneity outside the heteronomy of the laws of motion (a movement is always from another, according to Aristotle) and independent of the recognitions of the intellect.[45] If the latter now simply represents a neutral being, without evaluation, then concomitantly "will" begins its career of the pure positing of values without foundation. This is the inauguration at once of pure piety and pure irresponsibility.

The issue does not involve a contrast between the modern and the postmodern. It is rather that both represent "a certain Middle Ages" (with roots which reach back before Duns Scotus in his Franciscan forebears) within which our culture still mostly lies, and whose assumptions we might want to re-examine.

It is not that the postmodern aspect of Scotism is now to be perceived as the most fundamental one. So far, this essay has pursued such an argument, but this is too one-sided. It is true that the reign of representation (or epistemology) assumes univocity of being, but it is also true that the latter assumes representation. In reality, one cannot assign a priority, either in logic or in historical fact; not in logic, because while representation assumes the formality of abstraction which univocity guarantees, this univocal formality is reciprocally established when it is assumed that the mind's ability to abstract something common mirrors something in the real, rather than doing something to the real. Not in historical fact, because the moves towards univocity were permitted by the Avicennian and later Franciscan doctrine that there can be many substantive forms within the entity, rather than merely subordinate forms integrated under one overriding form, as for Aristotle. This position arises because a new ontological weight is accorded to the mind's ability to isolate and abstract different elements – the source of the Scotist "formal distinction". In addition, Olivier Boulnois has shown how Roger Bacon's reception of Arab optics (or "Perspective") encouraged the view that physical realities are generated through an exact imaging or copying of prototypes, in a fashion that tends to reduce the Arabic stress on *convenientia* – or ineffable aesthetic rapport of all beings to each other (a theme taken up by Aquinas) – to exactly measurable proportion and equivalence.[46] This account of optics encouraged Bacon's account of the linguistic sign either as assisting a mental copying of something either real or imagined, or as arbitrarily invoking an ontic equivalent in algebraic fashion without the mediation of reflective understanding (so resisting the Aristotelian sequence of sign $\rightarrow$ concept $\rightarrow$ external thing understood). Such a perspective tended to unseat the Aristotelian view of knowledge as "realising" spiritually a materialised form, and this shift is sustained through Scotus up to William of Ockham.

We have seen that the paradigm of representation had another source. This may be equally or more fundamental. This is in relation to the *divine* intellect. As we have seen, Scotus shifts notions of divine understanding away from simple identity with essence, and, in consequence, away from the idea of its being archetypal art – a supreme "maker's knowledge" – rather than a kind of self-mirroring. For Scotus, the divine ideas of the divine perfections which are the first exemplars only arise as representations of perfections that in some sense precede cognition. So, just as, for Aquinas, finite knowledge by identity (the species of a thing being realised in our understanding) is grounded in the supreme divine identity that is simplicity, so, for Scotus, finite knowledge by representation is grounded in divine self-representation. In this double fashion, realism gradually gave way within the Middle Ages to modes of empiricism, scepticism and even idealism (though there were many examples of hybrids of knowledge by identity and knowledge by mirroring).[47]

The complex and gradual shift towards representation also tended to render less distinct cases of mere logical predication from real invocation. As we have already seen, the domains of logic and semantics began to dominate and predetermine that of metaphysics. This process was in certain ways begun by Avicenna himself: for the latter, logic deals with universals, and physics with particulars, while metaphysics concerns pure forms or essences indifferent either to universal or particular. But this tends to turn the subject of metaphysics into certain inherently abstract entities which hover in a no-man's-land between the logical and the real, the mental and the actual. Inevitably, this suggests a further logic of that which is not necessarily universal, and metaphysics is here placed on its Kantian course of concern with a transcendental logic. (Perhaps Kant – the pre-eminent "modern" – also remained within "a certain Middle Ages"?)[48]

Another way to express this would be to say that Scotus increased the tendency to logicise and semanticise metaphysics. Prior to his writings, being had usually been considered to be univocal within logic, equivocal within physics and analogical within metaphysics. It is true that Aquinas's theological analogy plays subtly between metaphysical and logical analogy, where the former (*ad unum ipsorum*, or proportionality) denotes a real ineffable sharing in one principle through *convenientia* by two other realities (as substance and accident share in being), and the latter (*ad unum alterum*, or proportion or attribution) denotes a mysterious link strictly in terms of semantic priority with no necessary foundation in the real – as both medicine and the body are healthy; the latter primarily so, yet the former in a causal manner. Nevertheless, attribution still assumes, following the Proclean legacy, an ontological foundation: as in this case the matter of occult sympathies, etc. Thus Aquinas also talks of *proportionalitas*, a parallel sharing in "health" between medicine and the animal body.[49] Without this metaphysical dimension, attribution would collapse into equivocity. In theology, for Aquinas, the metaphysical aspect of analogy preserves the real affinity, while the logical aspect preserves the dimension of mystery: how is God good? And how is medicine healthy? Yet the ontological assumption is made that God is pre-eminently good.

In this way, Aquinas begins somewhat to qualify metaphysics with logic in theology. His analogy, as Alain de Libera has suggested, can be seen as analogical to a second degree, since it lies between the relative univocity of metaphysical analogy and the relative equivocity of logical analogy.[50] Nevertheless, the interweaving of a logical moment tends to favour the metaphysical interpolation of participation within the schemes of ordered proportionate causality.

Scotus also gives logic and grammar a newly accentuated place in theology. But he goes further. Earlier in his career, he had presented being as logically equivocal; and later as logically univocal, mainly under the pressure of the need to ground the possibility of predication by finite creatures concerning the infinite, once participated-in perfections had been abandoned. The univocity of being within logic is here held to govern also the character of being as a transcendental formality. Every existing thing, whether finite or infinite, is univocal *in quid*, where being is taken to mean an essential "not not-being". Specific and virtual differences remain, however, as we have seen, purely equivocal. Gilles Deleuze was right: univocity releases equivocal difference, but it suppresses analogy.[51] Ultimately, the warrant for this move is not objectively rational; rather, it is grounded in the refusal of any existential and evaluative freight to the process of abstraction.

This essay has been an attempt to explore the relation of the Scotist legacy to modernity and postmodernity. In this light, the latter seems but an advanced version of the former, in which the inseparability of univocity, representation and flattened causal interaction on a single plane becomes more fully realised. One might also contend that according to this post-Scotist perspective, there is no modern phase at all, and so also no pre-modern to which one might nostalgically make appeal. Instead, there is "a certain Middle Ages" which has never ceased to be dominant, even now in the twenty-first century. Where, in the midst of all these epochs, which turn out not to be straightforward epochs after all, are we to look? Perhaps, as many people – from southern European Catholics to Midwestern-exiled evangelicals (such as John Hare) – seem to suggest, we need to retheologise modernity by returning it to its roots in Avicenna, and Henry of Ghent, Bonaventure and supremely Duns Scotus? But then, if so, how should one describe Aquinas's challenge to Avicenna (deploying Averroës, Pseudo-Dionysius, Proclus, and a de-Avicennised Augustine rather than Avicenna's Plotinus)? Not, surely, as an invocation of the pre-modern, but as something like an avant-garde innovation against the modern already begun in the name of a deepening of the Patristic tradition? To invoke such a project is not to return to the past.

Rather, it is the re-assuming of the newest and most innovative thing, scarcely known of at all.

Notes

1   Bruno Latour, *We Have Never Been Modern*, trans. Catherine Porter, New York and London: Harvester Wheatsheaf, 1993.

2   It has become fashionable to contest any interpretation of Duns Scotus which seeks to place him in any instrumental relationship with the kind of genealogy traced in the present essay; see for example David Ford's review of *Radical Orthodoxy* (London: Routledge, 1999) in *Scottish Journal of Theology*, Vol. 54 no. 3 (2001), pp. 385–404, 423–5. See also my response essay to his review in the same issue of that journal (pp. 405–22). It is my contention that the interpretation of Duns Scotus and his historical significance put forward in this essay, especially in relation to Aquinas, is scarcely controversial: see further Etienne Gilson, *Jean Duns Scot: Introduction à ses positions fondamentales*, Paris: Librairie Philosophique J. Vrin, 1952; but, more explicitly, Olivier Boulnois, "Quand commence l'ontothéologie? Aristote, Thomas d'Aquin et Duns Scot", *Revue Thomiste*, Vol. XCV no. 1 (January–March, 1995), pp. 84–108, and *Être et Representation: Une généalogie de la méthaphysique moderne à l'époque de Duns Scot*, Paris: Presses Universitaires de France, 1999 and *Duns Scot: sur la connaissance de Dieu et l'univocité de l'étant*, Paris: Presses Universitaires de France, 1990; J.-F. Courtine, *Suarez et le système de la métaphysique*, Paris: Presses Universitaires de France, 1990; Éric Alliez, *Le Temps Capitaux*, Paris: Editions du Cerf, 1999 II.i; Michel Corbin, *Le Chemin de la théologie chez Thomas d'Aquin*, Paris: Beauchesne, 1972; Jean-Yves Lacoste, "Analogie", in Jean-Yves Lacoste and Paul Bauchamp (eds) *Dictionnaire Critique de théologie*, Paris: Presses Universitaires de France, 1998; Bruno Puntel, *Analogie und Geschichtlichkeit*, Fribourg: Herder, 1969; G. Prouvost, *Thomas d'Aquin et les Thomismes*, Paris: Editions du Cerf, 1998; C. Esposito, *Introduzione a Suarez: meditazioni metafisiche*, Milan: Rusioni, 1996; David B. Burrell, *Knowing the Unknowable God: Ibn-Sina, Maimonides, Aquinas*, Notre Dame, IN: University of Notre Dame Press, 1986; Ludger Honnefelder, "Metaphysik zwischen Onto-Theologik, Transszendental-wissenschaft und universaler formaler Semantik. Zur philosophischen Aktualitat der mittel-lalterlichen Ansatze von Metaphysik", in Jan A. Aertsen and Andreas Speer (eds) *Was ist Philosophie im Mittelalter?*, Acts of the Tenth International Congress for Mediaeval Philosophy of the International Society for the Study of Mediaeval Philosophy, Berlin and New York: Walter de Gruyter, 1998, pp. 48–60; Mark D. Jordan, *Ordering Wisdom: The Hierarchy of Philosophical Discourses in Aquinas*, Notre Dame, IN: University of Notre Dame Press, 1986, and *The Alleged Aristotelianism of Thomas Aquinas*, Toronto: Pontifical Institute of Mediaeval Studies, 1992; John Inglis, "Philosophical Autonomy and the Historiography of Medieval Philosophy", *Journal of the History of Philosophy*, Vol. 5 no. 1 (1997), pp. 21–53, and *Spheres of Philosophical Inquiry and the Historiography of Mediaeval Philosophy*, Leiden and Boston: E. J. Brill, 1998; H. Möhle, *Ethik als Scientia Practica nach Johannes Duns Scotus: Eine Philosophische Grundlegung*, Munster, 1997. The significance of Duns Scotus's contribution is not that he is the sole inaugurator of transformations in theoretical speculation, but rather that he is one figure among many – although a crucial one – in a general shift away from a focus upon the metaphysics of participation (which he tended to reduce to a matter of external imitation rather than intrinsic "sharing in"), and he is noteworthy in particular because he gave attention to these issues in a comprehensive fashion. No scholar could deny that such a shift occurred: see for example such diverse figures as Gilles Deleuze and Richard Cross: Gilles Deleuze, *Différence et répétition*, Paris: Presses Universitaires de France, 1968; Richard Cross, *The Physics of Duns Scotus: The Scientific Context of a Theological Vision*, Oxford: Clarendon Press, 1998, and *Duns Scotus*, Oxford: Oxford University Press, 1999. Richard Cross is a critic of my own interpretation of Duns Scotus, although it is not so much that the two analyses of Duns Scotus stand in a hostile relation, but that the negotiations of these analyses differ greatly; see, for example, Cross's critique in "Where angels fear to tread: Duns Scotus and Radical Orthodoxy", *Antonianum* Annus LXXVI Fasc. 1 (January–March, 2001), pp. 7–41. See especially pp. 13–14 n. 40. Whatever one's position with regard to specific texts, one must perhaps take a position in relation to this generally acknowledged shift away from participation and its relative importance or otherwise. Put briefly, my own position is that

Duns Scotus and his successors, within an approach seeking (after the post-1270 condemnations) for complex reasons to emphasise the sovereignty of God and the primacy of
scripture, opened a space for univocal treatment of finite being without regard to theology,
rational or revealed. Although this space was not immediately exploited in a secularising
fashion, in the long run this came to be the case.

3   Duns Scotus, *Ordinatio*, I d 8 q 3 nn. 50 and 86, and I d 3 q 3 and see Boulnois, *Duns Scot:
     sur la connaissance de Dieu et L'Univocité de L'Etant*, Paris: Presses Universitaires de France, 1990,
     p. 379 nn. 192 and 193; Boulnois, *Être et représentation* (see Note 2), pp. 308–14, 457–505.

4   Alain de Libera, *La philosophie médiévale*, Paris: Presses Universitaires de France, 1994, pp.
     404–6; Alain de Libera and Maurice-Ruben Hayoun, *Averroës et l'averroësme*, Paris: Presses
     Universitaires de France, 1991; Alain de Libera, *Penser au Moyen Age*, Paris: Editions du Seuil,
     1991; Boulnois, *Être et représentation* (see Note 2), pp. 293–327. Richard Cross seems both to
     admit and to evade the issue concerning the shift in the meaning of removed universality and
     perfection terms. He rightly says that for Aquinas the concept of being was not an abstrac-
     tion, but a matter of concrete elevation and participation ("Where angels fear to tread" (see
     Note 2), p. 13). However, he also says that for both Aquinas and Scotus the concept of Being
     (and other transcendental terms) constitutes a concept "common" to both God and crea-
     tures: "there is a concept under whose extension both God and creatures fall, just as there is
     a concept under whose extension both cats and dogs fall" (p. 18). Once things are set up in
     this fashion, Scotus is bound to seem the more lucid thinker. Demonstrative theology
     requiring common concepts will clearly require univocal ones. However, since Aquinas admits
     that demonstration in general requires univocity, one can only assume (unless uncharacter-
     istically he overlooked something rather crucial) that for him, as for Averroës, demonstration
     of God is not genuinely apodeictic (related to syllogism) but more dialectical (allowing of
     probable assumptions). Likewise for Aquinas the only "common" concept of being is that of
     ens commune which applies to created being alone. (Cross neglects to note that for Aquinas, as
     for Scotus, "God" does not fall directly under the subject of metaphysics, which, after Avi-
     cenna's modification of Aristotle, they see as concerning *ens inquantum ens*: for Aquinas this is
     ens commune, for Scotus, univocal *esse*, conceptually indifferent as to created and uncreated).
     For Aquinas, the conceptual transition from creatures to God works (ontologically and
     epistemologically) through the ineffable *convenientia* of analogy of attribution, without any
     isolatable, univocal medium which can be considered to be "in common". (God himself is the
     ultimate ground of what is held in common between beings, so he cannot himself be an item
     within this set.)
         This means that for Aquinas the mode of signification/thing signified contrast as regards
     knowledge of God distinguishes between the divine *res* or reality which is also infinite
     thought, on the one hand, and our *modus* or limited access to this reality which is at once
     cognitive and existential, on the other hand. But Cross reads this distinction in post-Fregean
     terms as somewhat like a distinction of focal sense and multiple existential contexts. Without
     textual warrant this gives "being" and not *Deus/Esse* as the *res*, and then variable finite or
     infinite *modi*. But this scheme already allows being to be abstracted without perfective ele-
     vation – and of course, if one thinks in these terms, Scotus is likely to appear superior to
     Aquinas. But the important point is that Scotus inaugurates the conceptual sphere in which
     Fregean logical universes and Kantian transcendental categories (etc.) can orbit.
         Cross ensures that Scotus must beat Aquinas at a Scotist game. His disdain for historicism
     in this instance of profound epistemic transformation arguably prevents him from consider-
     ing a viable philosophical alternative. Nor is Cross consistent in this disdain. He indicates that
     he knows well that most thinkers up to and including Aquinas did not regard "being" as merely
     a "vicious abstraction" – for reasons bound up with notions of abstraction as involving real
     ontological elevation. It seems rather as though Cross thinks of the alternative view of the
     concept of "being" as simply not worth discussing. Fortunately, it would seem, Scotus put a
     stop to all this nonsense. Yet if he did call a halt to obfuscation, then it would seem that,
     indeed, "Radical Orthodoxy" is right to see him as a revolutionary – at least in this respect.
     Cross is again inconsistent about whether or not he is prepared to acknowledge historical
     change in relation to the question of analogy (another aspect of the handling of perfection

language). In places he seems clearly to allow that for Aquinas analogy is grounded in participation (p. 14), while in other places he asserts (p. 28) that for Aquinas "the likeness of analogy is just the likeness of imitation". For Cross, the reduction of participation to imitation is in line with nominalist common sense (participation "confuses" the essence of a property with its imitability: p. 14), but he fails to reflect that this common sense, if it be such, is also idolatry. Creation cannot simply be "part" of God, since God is not a divisible object, but nor can it simply "imitate" God, since there can be no third real medium between God and creatures that could confirm the truth or falsity of this copying. Only God himself provides the medium. Hence to imitate (somehow) God is also to share (somehow) in God, since God alone establishes and confirms the veracity of the imitation. For this reason, traditional "participation language", from Plato onwards, hovers between literal *mimesis* and literal "being a part of". Thus, for Aquinas, "[t]o participate is to take a quasi-part", *In Boeth. De Hebdom.*, 2.24. Yet Cross insists that the tradition was always secretly nominalist and adhered to the criteria of Anglo-Saxon common sense – reducing a real sharing-in to an empirically observable "likeness".

This is no more than anachronism, whatever one's opinion as to the coherence of "participation language". Moreover, Scotus's innovation in reducing participation to imitation is seen in his reduction of the language of *imago Dei* to an intensified instance of *vestigium*, in the context of his discussion of Trinitarian theology. By contrast, Aquinas had seen the *vestigium* (always seen as more like an empirically observable causal imprint of literal but relatively "thin" likeness: a "footprint" showing mainly God's might) as a weak instance of the *imago* (which is an ineffable showing-forth in a weak degree of the divine essence). See *Ordinatio*, I d 3 Pars 2 q unica; Aquinas, *Summa Theologiae (S. T.)* I q 93 a 2.

5   See for example *Ordinatio*, I d 3 q 1 and d 8 q 3 nn. 112–15.

6   Ibid., I d 3 q 3, nn. 31–151.

7   Boulnois, *Être et représentation* (see Note 2), pp. 290–91.

8   *Ordinatio*, I d 3 q 4 nn. 358–60.

9   Duns Scotus, *In Elench.* q 15 para [8] (22a–23a); *In Praed.* q 4 para [5] (446b–7a) and para [6] (447a); see also Boulnois, *Être et représentation* (see Note 2), pp. 246–7.

10   Boulnois, *Être et représentation* (see Note 2), pp. 327–405, 457–93.

11   Alain de Libera, *La philosophie médiévale* (see Note 4), esp. ch. 9.

12   Thomas Aquinas, *De spiritualibus creaturis*, a. 10: "Now it does not matter much if we say that intelligible things themselves are participated in from God or that the light that makes them intelligible is participated in from God." And see Jacob Schmutz, "La Doctrine Médiévale des Causes et la théologie de la Nature Pure (XIIIe–XVIIIe siècles)", *Revue Thomiste*, Vol. C no. 1–2 (January–June 2001), special issue, Surnaturel, pp. 217–64.

13   Orlando Todisco OFM CONV, "L'univocità scotista dell' ente e la svolta moderna", *Antonianum*, Annus LXXVI Fasc.1 (January–March, 2001), pp. 79–110; Isidoro Manzano OFM, "Individuo y sociedad en Duns Escoto" in the same issue pp. 43–78.

14   Libera, *La philosophie médiévale* (see Note 4), pp. 116ff.

15   On property rights, see Oliver O'Donovan, *The Desire of the Nations*, Cambridge: Cambridge University Press, 1996, p. 248: "Promoting a mendicant idea of absolute poverty [the Franciscans] posited a 'right of natural necessity' (Bonaventure) or a 'right of use' (Ockham). Though dissociated from real property, the right still carried proprietary overtones. Gerson invoked the term *dominium* to describe the right of self-preservation and indeed initiated the tradition of conceiving freedom as a property in one's own body and its powers." O'Donovan here radicalises the discussion of the ambiguity of Franciscan poverty in John Milbank, *Theology and Social Theory*, Oxford: Blackwell, 1990, p. 16. On the shift in meaning of *influentia*, see Jacob Schmutz, "La Doctrine Médiévale (see Note 12).

16   John McDowell, *Mind and World*, Cambridge, MA: Harvard University Press, 1995; Wilfrid Sellars, *Science, Perception and Reality*, London: Routledge & Kegan Paul, 1963; Willard Van Orman Quine, "Two Dogmas of Empiricism", in Quine, *From a Logical Point of View*, Cambridge, MA: Harvard University Press, 1994, pp. 20–47; Richard Rorty, *Philosophy and the Mirror of Nature*, Oxford: Blackwell, 1980.

17   Alasdair MacIntyre, *Whose Justice? Which Rationality?* London: Duckworth, 1988.

18   In defense of Scotus on this matter, see Leonardo Sileo OFM "I 'soggetti' della teologia e il 'soggeto' della metafisica", *Antonianum* Annus LXXVI Fasc. 2 (April–June, 2001), pp. 207–24. See also Boulnois, *Être et représentation* (see Note 2), pp. 457–505.

19   Gilbert Narcisse, *Les raisons de Dieu : argument de convenance et esthétique théologique selon saint Thomas d'Aquin et Hans Urs von Balthasar*, Fribourg, Suisse: Editions universitaires, 1997.

20   Boulnois, *Être et représentation* (see Note 2), pp. 55–107.

21   Olivier Boulnois, "Duns Scotus, Jean", in Jean-Yves Lacoste and Paul Bauchamp (eds) *Dictionnaire critique de Theologie*, Paris: Presses Universitaires de France, 1998; Rowan Williams, "Jesus Christus III: Mittalalter", *Theologische Realenzyklopadie* Vol. 16, New York, NY: Walter De Gruyter, Inc., 1987, pp. 748–53; Cornelio Fabro, "Participation", in *New Catholic Encyclopedia* Vol. X, New York: NY: McGraw-Hill Book Co., 1967.

22   Proclus, *Elements of Theology*, trans. E. R. Dodds, Oxford: Oxford University Press, 2000, Propositions 13, 25, 29, 55.

23   William of Ockham, *Quodlibetal Questions*, 1.1.

24   Aristotle, *Metaphysics*, 1005B 16–1009A 37.

25   David Burrell, *Freedom and Creation in Three Traditions*, Notre Dame, IN: University of Notre Dame Press, 1993, p. 94.

26   Duns Scotus, *Opus oxoniense*, 1 d 17 pars 3 q 13. See also Umberto Eco, *Art and Beauty in the Middle Ages*, New Haven, CT: Yale University Press, 1986.

27   Nicholas of Cusa, "On Learned Ignorance", in *Selected Spiritual Writings*, trans. L. H. Lawrence Bond, New York, NY: Paulist Press, 1997.

28   See II Peter 1:4 where human beings are said to be "sharers in the divine nature".

29   Duns Scotus, *Rep. Paris.*, 1 IV d 28 n 6.

30   Javier Andonegui OFM, "Escoto en el punto de mira", *Antonianum* Annus LXXVI Fasc. 1 (January–March, 2001), pp. 145–91.

31   This might seem to be contradicted by Scotus's assertion that there is an individuating factor in things – *haeccitas* – beyond negative material determination, which the intellect can intuit. See here Antonio Conti, "Alcune note su individuazione e struttura metafisica della sostanza prima in Duns Scoto", *Antonianum* Annus LXXVI Fasc. 1 (January–March, 2001), pp. 111–44. However, the Scotist account of individuation involves a somewhat incoherent "formal" element in matter (as if it could potentially exist of itself in an unformed state) and an ineffable principle of haecceity. One could here agree with Gilson that the Thomist account of the concrete act of *esse* supervening upon essential form gives a more adequate account of individuation (and a more relational one). However, Conti argues against Gilson that since being is the act of essence (the entire nature of a thing) and not of form (which is an aspect of the thing insofar as it informs matter), this leaves Aristotelian individuation which concerns the activation of matter by form – matter supplying negatively the individuating factor – unaffected. Hence Gilson's argument that the concrete existence of the thing gives a new primacy to the individual beyond Aristotle will not work. However, one might argue that the equal creative actuation by *esse* of matter and form, substance and accident, etc. ensures that material individuation only occurs "through" its share in *esse*. This tends to turn the negative individuation into something positive. Moreover, Aquinas makes it clear that the *esse/essentia* dimension is not just a topmost "added on" layer. Its analogical economy extends to the interrelations of genus, species and individual. See Fabro, "Participation" (see Note 21). It is also the case that the frequent expression in Aquinas *forma dat esse* suggests some equation of *forma* with *essentia*. The "negativity" of matter seems the best way to understand it and, compared with Aristotle, Aquinas accentuates its non-positivity: matter exists through form. This leaves external (non-angelic) limitation itself a gift or created mystery.

32   *S.T.*, I q 25 a 5 *resp.*

33   *S.T.*, I q 45 a 2 AD 3.

34   John of St. Thomas (Juan Poinsot), *Artis Logicæ secundæ pars* 581B 24–582A 16 and 574B 35–575A 5; John Deely, *New Beginnings: Early Modern Philosophy and Postmodern Thought*, Toronto: Toronto University Press, 1994, pp. 65–109; Jacques Maritain, *The Degrees of Knowledge*, trans. Gerald B. Phelan, Notre Dame, IN: University of Notre Dame Press, 1995, pp. 75–145.

35 Proclus, *A Commentary on the First Book of Euclid's Elements*, trans. E. R. Morrow, Princeton NJ: Princeton University Press, 1970; Jean Trouillard, *La Mystagogue de Procles*, Paris: Les Belles Lettres, 1982; Gregory Shaw, *Theurgy and the Soul*, Philadelphia, PA: University of Pennsylvania Press, 1995, "Introduction".

36 Benedykt Huculak, "De mature Augustiniano opere Joannis Duns Scoti", *Antonianum*, Vol. LXXVI Fasc. 3 (July–September, 2001), pp. 429–79.

37 Huculak (ibid.) cites Fabro as saying that Thomist participation proved incompatible with Augustinianism. However, the passage cited concerns merely the Thomist refusal of the "Augustinian" idea that finitude equates with materiality, Augustine's view here being arguably more complex than this characterisation. On Augustine's intellectualism, see James Wetzel, *Augustine and the Limits of Virtue*, Cambridge: Cambridge University Press, 1992.

38 *Ordinatio*, 1 d 8 q 3 n 49.

39 On illumination, see *Ordinatio*, I d 3 q 3 a 5. On negation, see *Ordinatio*, I d 8 q 3 n 49, and nn. 70–86. On the formal distinction of divine perfections and divine intellect, see *Ordinatio* I d 3 q 4. See also Olivier Boulnois, *Sur la connaisance de Dieu et l'univocité de l'etant*, Paris: Presses Universitaires de France, 1988, pp. 111–181 and *Être et représentation* (see Note 2), pp. 308–14, 457–505.

40 Duns Scotus, *Quodlibetal Questions*, 5 a 1. See George Tavard, *Holy Writ and Holy Church*, New York: Harper and Row, 1959, *passim*.

41 Duns Scotus, *Ordinatio*, I d 8 q 4; and see Olivier Boulnois, "Duns Scotus, Jean" (see Note 21).

42 See Jean-Luc Marion, "Une époque de métaphysique" in *Jean Duns Scot ou la révolution subtile*, Paris: Editions Radio-France, 1982, pp. 62–72.

43 *Ordinatio*, I d 3 q 4 n 387 and d 13 q 1 n 45; *Quodlibetal Questions*, q I a 3.1 57–80; q 8 a 1.27; Boulnois, *Être et représentation* (see Note 2), pp. 107–14.

44 Aquinas, *S.T.* I q 14 a 4 *resp.*; a 5 *resp.*; Scotus, *Ordinatio*, I d 30 q 1 nn. 11–53; Boulnois, *Être et représentation* (see Note 2), pp. 405–32.

45 See Boulnois, *Être et représentation* (see Note 2), pp. 107–14. *Ordinatio*, d 3 q 3 a 4. See also *Quodlibetal Questions*, q 1 a 3; q 2 a 2; q 3 a 2; 5 a 3.

46 Boulnois, *Être et représentation* (see Note 2), pp. 55–107. Richard Cross interprets the formal distinction in terms of the idea of features distinguishable within an entity but not separable from it. The present author wonders, however, whether this somewhat misses the point. For Aquinas such features are either really distinct in a certain way (like one's arm from the rest of one's body) or only intellectually distinct (like God's truth from God). Scotus, however, presents this in a different way: an intellectual distinction without total separation must have some real foundation of separability as well as holistic unity. For Scotus the arm is no mere real part: in one (over?) holistic respect, the "arm" is pulled back into ineffable *haeccitas*, where its separability lies dormant. In another (over?) atomistic respect, the arm is a kind of virtual prosthesis, ready to take on a life of its own. In relation to God there is only the latter danger: divine simplicity is compromised by Scotus. His Neoplatonic language of "quasi-emanations" to describe the ontological succession of formal distinctions in God tells against Cross's reading of this doctrine.

47 Boulnois, *Être et représentation* (see Note 2), pp. 17–107, 405–53. Cross speaks of Scotus's epistemic theory as if it simply followed common sense. However, once again he equivocates: at times Aquinas is also supposed to have a representational theory of knowledge, yet finally Cross concedes that Scotus innovates in shifting to *esse representivum* as the basis for knowledge, and that this inaugurates a modern epoch in thought about thinking.

48 Hannes Möhle, *Ethik als Scientia Practica nach Johannes Duns Scotus: Eine Philosophische Grundlegung*, Münster: Aschendorff, 1995; Etienne Gilson, *Jean Duns Scot: introduction à ses positions fondamentales*, Paris: Librairie Philosophique J. Vrin, 1952. A similar anticipation of a transcendental approach can be found in Scotus's account of time. He tended not to regard time as a real aspect either of moving things ("Aristotle") or of the distended life of the soul ("Augustine"). Rather, time for Scotus was a pure duration in its abstract measurableness, as if an abstract virtual clock were counting units of time at every moment. It is in this context that he redefines *aevum* (previously regarded as a concept embracing both angelic and

material duration) as pure finite resistance with indifference as to motion and its various modes. Hence *aevum* is said to apply as much, and in the same univocal fashion, to an angel as to a stone: *Ordinatio*, II dist 2 p I q 4 para. 182. Richard Cross (loc. cit. pp. 39–40) has argued that the present author is mistaken in *After Writing* in presenting Scotus as anticipating Newtonian and Kantian notions of abstract time. And yet for Scotus, even if there were no movement of the heavens, their repose could be potentially measured by that time which would measure their movement if it existed: *Opus oxon.* II dist 2 q 11. Other interpreters of Scotus have come to similar conclusions. See, for example, P. Ariotti, "Celestial Reductionism Regarding Time: from Albert the Great and Thomas Aquinas to the end of the Sixteenth Century", *Studi Internazionali di Filosofia* Vol. 4 (1972), p. 113: "Time as *aevum* is continuous, indivisible, independent of motion. It is tempting to see in Scotus' concept of *aevum* the roots of Newton's concept of absolute time." See also Alliez, *Le Temps Capitaux*, II.i, pp. 71–121.

49   St Thomas Aquinas, *S.T.* I q 13 a 5 *resp.*
50   De Libera, *La philosophie médiévale* (see Note 4), pp. 408–11.
51   Gilles Deleuze, *Différence et répétition*, Paris: Presses Universitaires de France, 1968.

Further reading

St. Thomas Aquinas, trans. Thomas Gilby, *Summa Theologiae*, 1a.1 (vol.1), Cambridge: Cambridge University Press, new edn 2006.

St. Thomas Aquinas, trans. Timothy McDermott, *Summa Theologiae*, 1a.2–11 (vol.2), Cambridge: Cambridge University Press, new edn 2006.

St. Thomas Aquinas, trans. Herbert McCabe, *Summa Theologiae*, 1a.12–13 (vol.3), Cambridge: Cambridge University Press, new edn 2006.

Scotus, John Duns, trans. Allan Wolter, *Philosophical Writings*, Indianapolis, IN: Hackett Publishing Company, 1987.

Bauerschmidt, Frederick Christian, *Holy Teaching: Introducing the* Summa Theologiae *of St. Thomas Aquinas*, Grand Rapids, MI: Brazos, 2005.

Cross, Richard, *Duns Scotus on God*, Aldershot: Ashgate, 2005.

Jordan, Mark, 'Theology and Philosophy', in Stump, Eleonore and Kretzmann, N., *The Cambridge Companion to Aquinas*, Cambridge: Cambridge University Press, 1993.

Kerr, Fergus, *After Aquinas: Versions of Thomism*, Oxford: Wiley-Blackwell, 2002.

Montag, John, 'Revelation: The False Legacy of Suárez', in Milbank, John, Pickstock, Catherine and Ward, Graham (eds), *Radical Orthodoxy: A New Theology*, London: Routledge, 1999.

Velde, Rudi te, *Aquinas on God: The Divine Science of the Summa Theologiae*, Aldershot: Ashgtate, 2006.

Williams, Rowan, *Arius: Heresy and Tradition*, London: SCM, 2nd edn 2001, pp. 215–29. [*This includes an excellent discussion of analogy and participation.*]

Boulnois, Olivier, *Duns Scot: sur la connaissance de Dieu et l'univocité de l'étant*, Paris: Presses Universitaires de France, 1990.

——*Être et représentations: Une généalogie de la métaphysique moderne à l'époque de Duns Scot*, Paris: Presses Universitaires de France, 1999.

Burrell, David, *Aquinas: God and Action*, Scranton: University of Scranton Press, new edn 2008.

Cunningham, Conor, *Genealogy of Nihilism* (Radical Orthodoxy), London: Routledge, 2002.

Candler, Peter and Cunningham, Coner (eds), *Belief and Metaphysics* (Veritas), London: SCM Press, 2007.

Jordan, Mark, *Ordering Wisdom: Hierarchy of Philosophical Discourses in Aquinas*, Notre Dame, IN: Notre Dame University Press, 1987.

Jordan, Mark, *The Alleged Aristotelianism of Thomas Aquinas*, Toronto: Pontifical Institute of Mediaeval Studies, 1992.

Marion, Jean-Luc, trans. Thomas A. Carlson, *God Without Being: Hors-Texte*, Chicago, IL: University of Chicago Press, 1991.

Milbank, John, *The Suspended Middle: Henri de Lubac and the Debate Concerning the Supernatural*, London: SCM Press, 2005.

Miner, Robert, *Truth in the Making* (Radical Orthodoxy), London: Routledge, 2004.

Oliver, Simon, *Philosophy, God and Motion* (Radical Orthodoxy), London: Routledge, 2005, ch. 4.

Te Velde, Rudi, *Participation and Substantiality in Thomas Aquinas* (Studien und Texte zur Geistesgeschichte des Mittelalters), Leiden: Brill, 1995.

Te Velde, Rudi, 'Understanding the *Scientia* of Faith: Reason and Faith in Aquinas's *Summa Theologiae*', in Fergus Kerr (ed.), *Contemplating Aquinas: On The Varieties of Interpretation*, London: SCM Press, 2003, pp. 55–74.

Special Edition on Scotus, *Modern Theology* 21(4), October 2005.

Questions

1. One way of understanding the distinction between philosophy and theology is to suggest that philosophy leads us to know *that* God is (*an est*), whereas theology leads us to know, in some faint way, *what* God is (*quid est*). How does Milbank deal with this distinction?

2. Although *sacra doctrina* and "that theology which pertains to philosophy" lie on a single spectrum of illumination, in what ways might they be distinguished?

3. Why is Aquinas not an "ontotheologian"?

4. Why are Scotus's voluntarism and turn to knowledge understood as representation important in distinguishing his thought from that of Aquinas?

5. How is Scotus's thought an intimation of postmodernism, and how does Pickstock see postmodernity's relation to modernity?

PART III

Theology and the secular

Introduction

The **characterization of 'modernity'** is a complex and crucial matter upon which our understanding of '*post*-modernity' obviously depends. Catherine Pickstock's book *After Writing: On the Liturgical Consummation of Philosophy* is a sustained reflection on the character of modernity as non-liturgical. Postmodernity is not the overcoming of this turn, but merely its continuance (hence Radical Orthodoxy usually refers to *late*-, rather than *post*-, modernity) to the point where its nihilism is revealed more clearly.

In making her case, Pickstock begins by challenging the account of modernity provided by one of the most influential of twentieth-century postmodern philosophers, Jacques Derrida (1930–2004). For Derrida, modernity is in part characterized by what the German philosopher Martin Heidegger (1889–1976) called 'the metaphysics of presence'. What is this? It concerns modernity's constant search for *foundations* for our knowledge: something supposedly secure and undoubtable upon which we can construct the secure edifice of epistemology. To understand why *presence* is important, think of the ways in which we try to know things, whether they be birds, people, mountains or something more abstract, say, the principles of law. In establishing knowledge, we privilege those kinds of knowledge where we are *present* to that which we seek to know in its most pure and essential nature. In other words, we attempt to see, hear, touch, taste, think or intuit the object of our knowledge in the most immediate way possible. Part of being immediately *present* to that which one seeks to know requires us to strip away anything that compromises that presence: the flux of time, prejudices or preconceptions, geographical circum-stances, prior learning, and so on. In other words, to be most fully present it is necessary to be present to an object in all its abstraction. For Derrida, this tradition of valuing presence (over absence) begins with Plato's *Phaedrus* in which Plato privileges speech over writing. Speech involves the *presence* of the speaker in the midst of the one who is addressed, and therefore apparently minimizes the mediation of the knowledge conveyed. By contrast, writing con-cerns absence – the absence, first and foremost, of the writer, and therefore the opening up of multiple interpretations of any text. So, according to Derrida, Plato is phonocentric (the privileging of the voice) and logocentric (the privileging of metaphysical foundations): he privileges speech over writing, presence over absence, and inaugurates Western metaphysics as the search for *foundations* for knowledge based on the *presence* of the knower to the known.

The first part of Pickstock's book is concerned with an extraordinary out-flanking of Derrida's reading of Plato which recognises that, in privileging speech, Plato is basing his philosophy on a liturgy which precisely does not trade in the binaries of presence and absence. Moreover, she traces the ways in which Derrida remains latently metaphysical and therefore modern insofar as he continues to search for foundations for his own critique of the metaphysics of presence. In the chapter following her critique of Derrida's reading of the *Phaedrus*, a part of which is reproduced here, Pickstock turns her attention to another aspect of modernity which is linked to presence, namely spatialization and *mathēsis*. To what does this refer? In the work of the French humanist Peter Ramus (1515–72) and the philosopher René Descartes (1596–1650), Pickstock sees another attempt to provide foundations for human knowledge, this time by 'fixing' its elements in relation to each other, much as one would draw a map of certain defined space of land. One way to think about this is in terms of the spatial layout of a university campus. Certain faculties sit along-side each other, for example classics and philosophy. Others stand at the centre, for example economics and business studies. Some are spatially far apart, for example theology and the natural sciences. The arrangement of a university campus is not accidental; it represents a very spatial and fixed understanding of the arrangement of human knowledge. This is sometimes referred to as 'architectonics'. This is spatialization – the mapping of knowl-edge onto a grid. The key problem with spatialization is that its arrangements do not conform to the reality in at least this sense: the world we investigate is characterized by constant flux, ambiguity, encounter, exchange and creativity. It cannot be straightforwardly 'mapped' onto a spatial, fixed and ossified grid. Pickstock contrasts this spatialization – the 'middle' of modernity – to the much more varied arrangements of pre-modern learning communities which, crucially, had liturgy at their heart. Liturgy is not spatial and fixed; it exhibits temporality, non-identical repetition, and praise of a donating source of life which we cannot control and therefore cannot fix on a spatial grid of knowledge. Similarly, the *mathēsis* of knowledge in Descartes is an attempt to subject a temporal and mediated human knowledge to the foundations of number, measurement and mathematical proportion.

The first chapter of John Milbank's *Theology and Social Theory*, here following Pickstock's essay, is a reflection on the outworkings of spatialization in modernity as traced by Pickstock. Just as the spatialization of knowledge was not – and could not be – anything more than an artifice, so secular society in modernity is a construct and not merely the result of the sweeping aside of the Christian theological understanding of political relations. Milbank outlines the way in which power transfers from a context of original peaceableness and *dominium*, as shared and orientated to the common good, towards a dualistic society which involves the creation of the public and private spheres. Here, power in the private sphere is entirely nominalistic and hence individualistic, and unrestrained; one could do with one's private property entirely as one chooses, regardless of the common good. Milbank sums this up:

> One can conclude that 'unrestricted' private property, 'absolute sovereignty' and 'active rights', which compose the 'pure-power' object of the new politics, are all the emanations of a new anthropology which begins with human persons as individuals and yet defines their individuality essentialistically, as 'will' or 'capacity' or 'impulse to self-preservation' (p. 183).

The notion that the individual is understood as a focus of power (a power which is protected by the peculiarly modern language of 'rights') is bolstered theologically by a modern notion of God as omnipotent will. God becomes just another power-player on the stage of human politics, and in being just another player, can be ignored. Politics can be undertaken *etsi Deus non daretur* – as if God did not exist. So, according to Milbank,

> it can be seen how theology stakes out *factum* as an area of human autonomy (that is, the *manufacture* of society as an enforced peace), by making *dominium* into a matter of absolute sovereignty and absolute ownership. This is the space in which there can be a 'secular', or secular knowledge of the secular – and it is just as *fictional* as all other human *topographies*' (p. 184, my emphases).

Chapter 5

Catherine Pickstock

Spatialization: the middle of modernity

1. The new sophistry

In the previous chapter [of *After Writing*], I argued that Derrida misrepresents one source of the metaphysical tradition, namely, Platonism. I have shown how he is mistaken in his characterization of Socratic dialectical knowledge as "domination" and as predicated upon the triumph of capital. To the contrary, Socrates critically identifies the link between sophism and both domination and capital. It has equally been shown that the Socratic preference for speech over writing is not a covertly necessary support for a metaphysics of presence, but rather its explicit rejection. And I have suggested that in presenting a new sophism, Derrida himself is exposed to all Socrates' criticisms. He is *himself* culpably "metaphysical" insofar as he celebrates sophistry and writing, just as his exaltation of the *nihil* is tantamount to an abasement before the perfect abstract and graspable object, within the context of a perverse but nonetheless perfected *mathēsis*. It is as a *metaphysician*, after all, that Derrida upholds knowledge as writing, domination, and capital, for his exaltation of absence and postponement turns out to be but the inevitably nihilistic conclusion of a rationalism indifferent to the specificities of human place, time, and desire. The perfectly present is that which will never arrive, as he himself dialectically affirms.[1] Thus he perfects, and does not refute, the Cartesian abstraction from embodiment. Not only, on the above reading, does it seem that the Derridean and entire postmodern assumption of a seamless line of development of a culpable "metaphysics" from Plato to Descartes is false; it *also* appears that Derrida *remains within* a post-Cartesian set of assumptions whose ancestry lies in sophistry and not Platonic dialectics.

If the above conclusions are substantively correct, the entire postmodern historical and philosophical perspective is called drastically into question. No longer are we the legatees of a Western logocentrism, fixated upon presence, and a domineering gaze secured by myths of transcendence. Instead it appears that it is *just those very myths* which, in ancient Athens, first radically challenged the beginnings of a technocratic, manipulative, dogmatically rationalist, anti-erotic, anti-corporeal and homogenizing society undergirded by secularity and pure immanence. And, instead of celebrating our final escape from a malign Western past, we should mourn our departure from what was once one of the most central elements in Western tradition: philosophy itself, in its revisionist Socratic variant. Finally it appears that the modem/postmodern debate is empty shadow-boxing, since nihilism is but the most extreme expression of a humanist rationalism. It should therefore cease to surprise us that postmodernism offers no new and critical politics beyond the impasse of commercialism into which modernity has led us. Instead we should consider seriously the Socratic notion that only a doxological polis and the acknowledgement of transcendence can ever liberate us from the sway of capital and linguistic debasement.

In this chapter, I examine the subsequent extension of the sophistic *mathēsis*. I contend that during the period of early modernity, with Ramism and, later, Cartesianism, which were encouraged by the facility of printing and its identical repetitions, and by the breakdown of the traditional religious order, space becomes a pseudo-eternity which, unlike genuine eternity, is fully comprehensive to the human gaze, and yet supposedly secure from the ravages of time. Through a discussion of various manifestations of spatialization in modes of scientific practice, government, and in the field of baroque poetics, I show how the attempt to bypass the intervention of human temporality and subjectivity (which a liturgical knowledge and practice had embraced) via an apparently unmediated apprehension of "objective" and "given" facts was not an eccentric or marginal phenomenon. Then in the final section of this chapter, I argue that "sophistic" spatialization has become increasingly normative, even to the extent that it has infiltrated the very structures of our language, almost obliterating its original liturgical character.

In the instances of spatialization which I discuss in this chapter, it will be seen how technological progress in writing and other modes of mechanical operation provides us with an all too seductive *facility*. If one takes this facility for "the real," one is led to imagine that the ease and predictability of operations within a new artificial sphere exhibit our true, primary relationship to the world. This is what I call a "spatial illusion." However, "technology" is not itself the prime cause at work here, for the illusions which it can encourage are only *legitimized* by an increasing denial of genuine transcendence, understood as doxological reliance upon a donating source which one cannot command. Without eternity, space must be made absolute and the uncertainty of time's source and end be suppressed. Hence, "sophistic" immanentism is the ultimate foundation of these illusions. Whilst, for Plato, the genre of the dialogue offered a remedial interlude necessary for the restoration of language as a medium of doxology, the structures of sophistry are now so boldly inscribed into our linguistic and social practices that a liturgical attitude toward reality becomes increasingly remote of access.

In seeking to expose the illusions of contemporary sophistry in this chapter, then, I trace the expansion of the unliturgical world.

2. Peter Ramus

In the Epistle to the Reader at the beginning of the *Logike* (1574), Peter Ramus boasts that his "lytle booke" will bring "more profytt" to the reader than "all thy fower yeares studie in Plato or Aristotle."[2] As well as the great utility of his book, "the facilitie and easynes of the same is not a litle to be commended."[3] The reason given for its facility and easiness is that the method, or series of ordered steps which it propounds, is applicable to every art and science, and its emphasis on clarity and simplicity is thought to open every discipline to a condition of availability and accessibility. This is accentuated by Ramus's use of diagrams and charts which apparently occupy space in a timeless domain of abstract lines, whose ability to communicate information at a single glance seems to bypass the mediation of language itself.

In seeking to supplant Plato and (especially) Aristotle, Ramus subscribes to a tradition which itself borrowed many features from Aristotelian logic and rhetoric. Indeed, the tradition itself began with Aristotle's treatise on scientific demonstration in the *Posterior Analytics*, followed by Boethius' *On the Different Kinds of Topics*, and Peter of Spain's *De locis*. This was succeeded by the development in the Middle Ages of "suppositional logic" which, by treating terms as substantives, registered the progressive visualization and spatialization of thought.[4] Rudolph Agricola's complex "place logics" continued the process of epistemological tabulation, and was assisted in this by the development of printing with which it was concurrent. Printing accelerated the drive towards spatialization because its multiplication of identical images and containment of data in abstract and apparently timeless formulations gave encouragement to the notion of the "availability" of a quantified and objectified knowledge. Furthermore, the appearance of knowledge in the impersonal arena of a printed page, in contrast to the individual and erratic scribal "hands" of the past, precipitated the notion of a pseudo-eternity of "given" reality unaffected by the human being who enacts its representation.[5]

Ramus, as Walter J. Ong has argued, carried through all these tendencies to a new extreme. He was an educational reformer reacting against scholastic subtlety which was alleged to have lost contact with the everyday world. In an attempt to make amends for Aristotelian and mediaeval obscurantism, Ramus offered a universal *mathēsis*, or calculus of reality, by which a *topos* was divided into two distinct compartments. The first, *invention*, was intended to lay bare the irreducible components of a proposition, and the second, *judgement* or *disposition*, was concerned with the proper use of these basic components or arguments in the process of reasoning. The first stage of invention entailed a division of the given topic by successive and ordered stages, beginning with the most general and progressing towards the most particular. This deductive reasoning from general principles to particularities was to be adhered to regardless of the nature of the subject under scrutiny. The first step was a brief definition in the most general terms, whose purpose was to establish clearly the extent and limits of the subject. True definition, as opposed to description, was to be as brief as possible, so as to allow the real essence of the thing being examined to be made superlatively clear. For Ramus, this meant simple classification according to genus and form. The second stage, *judgement*, comprised a division of the subject according to its principal components, a method of arrangement known as *distribution*, which was carried out in several different ways, depending on the logical relationship between the parts and the whole. Wherever possible, this distribution was to be effected by means of a *dichotomy* which split the topic down the middle, leaving two further classes upon which the operation might be repeated. When one particular distribution was exhaustively accomplished, each of the classes so obtained was to be defined in turn and subdivided following the same routine. Thus, according to a fractal epistemology, each topic, belonging to any discipline, and every aspect pertaining to that topic were seen as available to the same lateral grid of inquiry. Equally, this method presupposed that every subject is already and to the same degree "there," simply waiting to be mapped and divided, and excludes the temporal aspect of knowledge as an "event" which arrives. When the division had been carried out properly to the furthest possible degree, all the arguments appropriate to the examination of the subject were assumed to be clearly evident.[6]

The second stage, *judgement*, was itself divided into three classes: enunciation, syllogism, and *methodus*. The first, which was to be used when the truth of the matter was evident, consisted in linking one argument with another, for when truth was not in question, a mere juxtaposition of arguments was sufficient to command universal agreement. With respect to these self-evident axioms, Ramus introduced three rules. The first was the *law of verity*, by which all precepts in all arts and sciences must be true without exception. The second rule was that of *justice*, which held that each art must be contained within its own bounds, and withhold nothing appertaining to other arts: a rule, therefore, of homogeneity. The third, called the *document of wisdom*, legislated that everything be taught in accordance with its nature (i.e. that the general be taught generally, and the particular particularly).[7]

When a statement appeared to be of doubtful validity, its truth or falsehood was to be demonstrated by syllogism. Ramus details the bifurcated structure of syllogisms and lists their various types, each suited to a particular proposition (such as "symple," "affirmant," "generall," "speciall," and "proper," etc.).[8] The third procedure, *methodus*, a technique for arranging precepts in convenient order, was to be activated when many precepts were under consideration at the same time, so many that a single, synchronic glance was impossible. According to the *methodus*, the simplest notions were to precede, the more complex to come later, with the most general precepts such as definitions always being placed first.

The significance with respect to my theme of spatialization of the features of Ramism described above, are threefold, and relate to a "sophistic" negotiation of temporality: first, its epistemological construal of reality; secondly, closely linked with the first, its simplification of memory; and, thirdly, its pejoration of language.

The Ramist method has considerable implications for a construal of the perception of reality, and can be seen to prefigure the Cartesian subordination of reality to geometric *extensio*. Indeed, it is not quite right to claim, like Stephen Toulmin in *Cosmopolis*, that the modern desire to establish absolute rational certainty, focused upon method, and free from the supposed distortions of cultural particularity, is traceable first to Descartes in the seventeenth century against a background of "general crisis." For already, the successive crises of the late Middle Ages and the Reformation had engendered a search for methodological and pragmatic security, of which *humanism itself* (as Toulmin ignores) sometimes partook, especially when it sought to establish a readily usable and universally accessible "place logic." This quest reached its culmination with the work of Ramus.[9]

The philosophical emphasis of the Ramist method is upon formal arrangement rather than content or depth, and, although spatial configurations are by no means devoid of usefulness or profundity,[10] in the case of the Ramist cartographies, their purpose is purely regulative and designed for the reader's convenience. This "convenience" has a sinister aspect, for, by adopting the stance of methodizer, the pedagogue obfuscates the confusions of reality, generating an apparently objective ontology from a secretly subjective method. This subterfuge depends entirely upon a new distinction from, and elevation above, the flow of reality on the part of the subject, which alone permits reality apparently to render itself in terms of discrete definition, distribution, clarity, and distinctness. A new cultural fear, that without such imposition-disguised-as-mere-reading reality is ineluctably chaotic, is here scarcely concealed.

There is also a suggestion in this configuration of method, as distinct from the myriad complications of reality it observes and configures, that the appearance of disorder is *merely* real whilst the method and the mind which deploys it are *supra-real*. The mind is posited as a superior cipher or mirror whose systematic operation discloses a hidden regularity.[11] Furthermore, the categories, both those inherited and those devised by Ramus, assume a supra-linguistic status which bypasses all contingency, as though ordained prior to language to deliver the clear and distinct essence of reality as it really is, rather than as it merely seems, by means of a direct and yet exalted access. According to such a scheme, the Ramist charts map the divisions and subdivisions of a particular proposition in a fashion which resembles exalted mnemonic devices (where memory is defined as local recall) for the storage and re-use of data, and yet what was once a mere art of memory now serves as a method for understanding, and the logic of this method in turn usurps the place of an ontology. Thus ease of comprehension and ease of communication are compounded with the neutral delivery of a reality whose authentic mark is taken to be such instant simplicity.[12]

The second implication for epistemology of the rise of Ramist method pertains to the status of the *mathēsis* it delivers. Previously, knowledge had been associated with mythical and iconographic figures such as statues and allegorical illustrations, regarded as derived from a transcendent and constantly arriving source.[13] The "reading" of these devices was as much a part of the narrative of that arrival as the artefacts themselves, and was by no means dependent upon a singularly attestable "content." By contrast, the printed words of Ramist "reading" were connected to one another by lines in simplified binary patterns forming dichotomized charts of methodized noetic material, designed precisely to foreclose any such open-ended interpretation. Furthermore, the exhaustive dichotomization of Ramist method is a system which carries a totalizing danger. In Socratic terms, Ramism continues in the tradition of sophistic demythologization, construing knowledge as consisting in discrete items "contained" as objects in distinct and homogeneous *topoi*. Unlike the *topoi* of Aristotle, these are specifically textual, and, encouraged by the model of the manoeuvrable type of the printing press, seem infinitely transferable. Indeed, its apparently universal applicability[14] suggests that Ramism treated everything as equivalent in its availability to the *mathēsis*, which apprehended reality as an undifferentiated *given*.

According to this scheme, memory becomes a matter of simple retrieval of objects, merely a kind of stocktaking or enumeration, thus vastly reducing the reach of memory presumed by the traditional mnemonic treatises of earlier rhetorics. For, when things are "available" in such a way, epistemological activity becomes purely speculative, and memory is simply a matter of repeating the "glance," rather than an act which testifies to the temporality of knowledge and which facilitates the judgement of analogy between instances, ensuring the continuity of the knowing subject.

The final consideration of the implications of Ramist method pertains to its pejoration of language, in particular as regards its denigration of rhetoric to mere *elocutio*, which can be shown to be related to its encouragement, as described by Walter Ong, of the demise of dialogue and its commensurate exaltation of mathematics and constativity.

The chief goal of Ramist dialectic, namely pedagogic clarity, problematized the tension between the traditional categories of dialectic and rhetoric, in such a way that the classical notion of dialectic as dialogue, and the Scholastic art of disputation (according to which, both dialectic *and* rhetoric had their own respective categories of *invention* and *judgement*), were conflated into a monologic art which simply retained the name of dialectic.[15] But it is specifically a *textual* monologue which further reduces dialectic to the condition of a sophistic rhetoric,[16] that is, a rhetoric which makes no appeal beyond itself to the variable but always ethical circumstances of civic life, or that offers modes of praise and honour as the traditional rhetorics sought to do. By thus removing the dynamic poles of traditional dialectic, and the reality of sound, Ramus concomitantly displaced rhetoric itself, encouraging its relegation to the now innocuous category of *elocutio*, which, in a context where the textual is now normative, has less to do with the structures of oral delivery than with spatially construed ornamentation.[17] This further accentuates the separation of reality from the noetic categories, for this new casting of rhetoric simply involves the ornate utterance of preconstituted truths. Moreover, for Ramus, the notion of *elocutio* was doubly textual, for, in encouraging brevity, clarity, and schematization, he preferred above all, not language, but the use of spatial diagrams. And as regards language itself, he advocated the use of "plain style." This did not mean a "low style," but, rather, a synthesis of the three former styles of *elocutio*, high, medium, and low, which emerges as an expository, cerebral, and analytic style, highly depersonalized, and as close to mathematics as language can be.[18] It is ironic that a system which rejected the obscurantism of Scholasticism by seeking to assimilate "common parlance" should result in a voiceless style which presaged the Cartesian attempt to "get outside" subjectivity and language altogether, and to find the pure, unmediated *mathēsis*.[19]

Such attempts to rid language of itself were encouraged by post-Gutenberg communications, for the effect of printing was to reinforce the dominance of a linear structure of "given" arguments apprehended at a glance on the surveyable page. Agricolan place logics and Ramist diagrams encouraged a sense of discourse as something which could be manipulated, as it were, from without, as an object. With this new development, the spatial notion of "structure" or architecture came to be applied to language. And the shift is reflected in changes of syntax and punctuation. For example, whereas formerly syntax had been time-bound and aggregative in structure, and punctuation such as colons and commas had functioned to indicate pauses or emphases relating to oral delivery, with the progressive introduction of spatial models syntax and punctuation now became more abstract and logic-bound.[20]

The attempt to find a logical and voiceless discourse also bears witness to the rise of a constative construal of language as a disinterested reporter of things, constituted not in opposition to the mind, but, paradoxically, *in opposition to language itself* – since it assumes that the naturalness and immediacy of its "language" permits a conflation of language and reality. Over against ordinary language and its local prejudices stands a pristine realm of diagrams and abstractions. But this involves a contradiction: Ramism's mathematical conventions *are* still mediated, and its lines are still metaphors. The reason why this did not seem to compromise his system was perhaps that the abstract and silent formulations of its charts shared a kind of invisibility with the transcendent, and so borrowed from its authority and eternity. But in their new immanent context, authority and eternity were translated (imperceptibly) into their mundane counterparts, pedagogy and permanence.

In the following three sections, I will consider several aspects of Descartes's philosophy which reflect the continuing programme of spatialization and confirm the above diagnosis. First, I will examine the implications for my theme of his ideas on the construction of the ideal city, showing how his account of subjectivity depends upon a prior parody of the Platonic sacred polis which involves, primarily, a spatialization of the city, avoided by Plato. Then, in section four, entitled "Reality without depth," I will show how the Cartesian fulfillment of ontology in epistemology inaugurates an immanentist construal of reality as the "given," and how this gives rise to the possibility of an object; I discuss the implications of this for a theory of language and knowledge. Finally, in section five, "The written subject," I consider how the spatialization of the city and the immanentization of being together assume the dominance of a new, non-liturgical subject.

3. The Cartesian city

Whilst it is generally considered that Descartes's ontology begins with the subject and what the subject knows, I argue in this section that his theory of the subject depends upon prior moves in, first, "politico-architectonics," and, secondly, ontology. In the first case, the city is defined as purely spatial, and, in the second, being is defined as immanent. Only because the city is now spatialized and being is now transparently graspable is the city then construed as contained within the individual, and *esse* as first opened up by the *Cogito*.

First, therefore, the Cartesian city. The character of this city best emerges through a contrast with that of Plato. In the *Phaedrus*, the Socratic account of *erōs* and the contagion of the good contributes to a transfiguration of civic space, according to which the sacred polis is established wherever the philosopher–lover perceives the good. Although this means that for Plato the *polis* is instantiated in a certain sense within the philosopher–lover, it is not thereby "containable" in the manner of ordinary spatial appropriation, but is characterized by the ecstatic and interpersonal contagion of transcendent goodness. And in accordance with the good, the whole polity of the city is constructed as a dramatization of the noble and perfect life,[21] as outlined in the *Laws* and the *Republic*, where citizenship is sustained not by written contracts but through communal acts of liturgy, which ensure that subjectivity is both open and interpersonally constituted.

Whilst Plato compares the construction of the ideal city to the painter using a heavenly model,[22] for Descartes the perfect city is primarily *written*, and wholly immanent. In Part II of his *Discourse on the Method*, Descartes employs analogies of architecture, city planning, and governmental structure to describe his method for the composition and organization of knowledge. His main contention is that, in general, the singular and homogeneous is to be preferred to the multiple and diverse. In the various examples he cites, there is a suggestion also that this preference presupposes a substitution of the spatial for the temporal. He argues that buildings are "more attractive and better planned" when designed and built by a single architect than by various different craftsmen; that cities constructed by a single planner are better proportioned than those which have developed haphazardly; and that society is better governed by the laws of a single legislator than by laws which have arisen organically in response to changing circumstances. On analogy with the socially manifest priority of individually sustained consistency, the universal method in thought is devised by a man "shut up alone in a stove-heated room, where [he is] completely free to convene with [him]self about [his] own thoughts."[23] The science of many is never so closely approximated to the truth as the simple reasoning of a person led by himself alone, and a child is better guided by internal reason than by the conflicting pressures of his teachers and his own passions.[24]

The most important factor, for Descartes, in his new civic paradigm is *formal consistency*, rather than intrinsic embodiment of the good. In this fashion, he is precisely sophistic, for his model, detached both from mediations of the good and from particularity, draws significantly upon analogies of writing and draughtsmanship. These written analogies for the organization of knowledge constitute his assumed politico-architectonics: city planning, legislation, architectural design. He cites the ideal example of Sparta, arguing that if that city-state "was at any time very flourishing, this was not because each of its laws in particular was good ... but because they were devised by a single man and hence all tended to the same end."[25] Thus, he prefers the written, immanent, and homogeneous city, even when this might involve a kind of anarchy, for, in the case of Sparta, Descartes concedes that some of Lycurgus' laws were nonetheless "very strange and even contrary to good morals."[26]

Hence we have already seen that the preference for a single legislator itself assumes the priority of formal consistency, or subjection to geometric, spatial rule over the incarnation of goodness. In the second place, it can also be seen that it is linked to the sketching out of a pure interiority. Descartes's choice of Sparta, as cited above, is significant not only because of the premium which it placed on formal order and the regulation of every detail of life, but also because Sparta is known to have been organised on military lines of warfare for the defence of its own absolute interior. Indeed, not only this feature, but also the stress on the single legislator as essential to the formal consistency of the city fulfill Jacques Derrida's characterization of metaphysics as the preservation of interiority, of reason as monadic self-presence, and of the city as a pristine enclosure which must resort to the expulsion of the impure.[27] For in the case of the Cartesian city, the impure is represented as that which bears traces of time, multiplicity, and difference, in the form of the emergent structures of ancient cities, organic legal systems, and philosophical and pedagogic traditions. To such instances of impurity, Descartes responds with a violent gesture of demolition. Regarding, for instance, the traditional philosophical opinions handed down to him from the past, he writes, "I could not do better than undertake to get rid of them, all at one go, in order to replace them afterwards with better ones,"[28] thereby re-enacting, in parodic form, Plato's banishment of poets and artists from the city. But whilst, for Plato, the pretext is that mimesis is inimical to a doxological mode of life, for Descartes the axiom of singular authorship as the condition of possibility for clarity and distinctness dictates his indictment of resemblance in the *Regulae*, and of the traditions of philosophy in *The Discourse*.[29] At best, the multiple, different, and temporal can improvise as rudimentary halfway houses en route to the ideal structure. In Part Three of *The Discourse*, when Descartes describes his fourfold moral code, he explains that, before starting to rebuild one's house, having demolished the previous one, it is necessary to provide oneself with a provisional home in which to live whilst the definitive edifice is under construction. Similarly, he explains, he has devised a provisional code by which to live until his universal method has been completed. In each case, this short-term structure belongs to the past, with its concomitant multiple authorship, and is reduced to a mere convenience or formality, simply bridging the way to its own demolition. The "laws and customs" of his society are not regarded as part of a living truth enacted by a whole community, but rather as exigential grids whose gradual diffusion and purely accidental moderation will prevent him from straying too far from the truth until his final attainment of the universal method.

Descartes's suggestion that the ideal method is produced in solitude, by "the simple reasoning which a man of good sense naturally makes," as opposed to the diverse books "compounded and amassed little by little from the opinions of many different persons,"[30] or by the child guided from birth by his reason alone, presupposes that certain knowledge (*scientia*) is self-producing, ahistorical, and extra-linguistic. Like the rhetorical methods of the sophists, and Ramist calculus, Descartes's formal arrangements present a lateral ideal whose autonomy refuses the mediations of tradition, myth or transcendence. Indeed, in the Cartesian method there is no equivalent to the Platonic Forms, except to the extent that for Descartes the Forms exist as a universalized textual system which acts as an identically repeated paradigm.[31]

From the above, it can be seen that Descartes's preference for a single legislator is explained in terms of this legislation's more reliable delivery of, first, formal consistency without respect for the good, and, secondly, a pure, inviolable interiority which depends upon absolutely surveyable bounds. The city is, by the first condition, entirely predictable because immunized against new arrivals in time, and, by the second, totalized in order to be defensible. This double circumstance amounts to spatialization, since time is neutralized, and all is ordered and surveyable without remainder, within absolute borders. Hence it can be seen that the preference for a single legislator only makes sense on the assumption that legislation is itself an operation of mere formal spatial arrangement. Before the *Cogito*, already in the *Regulae*, Descartes espoused the ideal of an entirely portable method, of an *ars* that is more reliable because precontained and foreordained in the single mind. Yet this mind cannot, surprisingly, merely be first invoked in relation to private science, but, instead, the metaphoric detour via civic construction – politico-architectonics – is required, to justify the priority of the single legislator in the field of public knowledge also. (For this reflection on politico-architectonics *first* occurred to Descartes when he was alone in the stove-heated room.)[32] Why? Because knowledge is only ideally "single" if, at the outset, one's public ideal of *both* practice *and* theory is not of oral transmission through time, but of spatial, written arrangement. At the beginning, therefore, stands not the *Cogito*, but *mathēsis*, and, before even *mathēsis*, stands the spatialized city. This is precisely the portable, convertible, formalized, transferable, mercantile city which is the subject of Socrates' critique in the *Phaedrus*.

Just as this city requires, ideally, a single legislator, so also, inversely, such a legislator is able to stand alone because he pre-includes all the civic space inside himself.[33] It follows, then, that the city has now been drastically subordinated to the individual,[34] in a sense impossible for Plato, for, although, in the *Republic*, reform begins with the individual, the individual is still formed through public education and dialogue, as a member of the philosophic community. And it follows also that this prior individual is itself internally mapped like a spatialized city: there will follow absolute divisions between mind and body newly conceived as "areas," and the mind itself conceived as the spatial traverse of an inevitable order of intuited deductions.

4. Reality without depth

I shall now show how Descartes's spatialized politico-architectonics is complemented by an equally spatialized ontology which is the other precondition for his espousal of the *Cogito*. As between the two preconditions, one can assign no priority since, if, as I would claim, a spatialized ontology is without real, objective warrant, its secret motivation is the political imposition of a *mathēsis*. Yet, conversely, if "single legislation" is held by Descartes to produce not only order but also knowledge, then, before imposing spatial order by mere fiat, he must assume that his impositions of method genuinely disclose a spatialized reality.

There is some disagreement as to the chronology of Descartes's development of an ontology. Jean-Luc Marion contends that his ontology is to be found in his later work, the *Meditations on First Philosophy*, in which matter is defined as extension, and the physical world is reduced to the principles of extension, motion, and mechanical causes, whilst Jean-François Courtine argues that Descartes redefines ontology even before he arrives at his theory of the *Cogito*, in the stress in his earlier *Regulae* on clarity and distinctness as the most fundamental criteria for the existence of a thing.[35] This would suggest that Descartes follows in the tradition of Duns Scotus, for whom a being is that which is univocal and therefore graspable. In thus objectifying being, Descartes transforms the determinations of reality into purely spatial classifications, as the "given" rather than the gift of a donor through which the transcendent is mediated. And, in a sense, the disagreement between Marion and Courtine is purely formal since an ontology separated from theology is reducible to an epistemology, as I shall show in later sections of this chapter. In any case, Marion and Courtine agree in developing Etienne Gilson's analysis of Descartes, by pointing out that the turn to epistemology is pre-enabled by a radical reconstrual of ontology itself, inherited from later scholasticism. In line with their analyses, I shall now show, first of all, how this new ontology, which *naturally* fulfills itself as the primacy of epistemology, inaugurates a construal of reality as the spatial "given." I will go on to show how this objectification of reality turns the object into a sign, and how this gives rise to a contradiction in Descartes's theory of language. Finally, in section 4, I will discuss the way in which, for Descartes, secure being has become being for the *Cogito*. Such a single legislating subject, commanding both the city and being itself, is supremely a non-liturgical subject. Against Derrida, I shall show how writing, not orality, is the precondition for Cartesian subjectivity.

In the classical and early to high mediaeval periods, although truth had been regarded as unchanging, it had not been considered as graspable and available to an exact and unchanging *mathēsis*. It was thought that things "are" according to the way in which they are manifested, which can never be exhaustive. An apophatic reasoning gave play, therefore, to the mediations of memory, time, and tradition, as for Plato and Augustine. But, with Descartes's Scholastic antecedent, Duns Scotus, a new model of truth as transparently available and immanent began to emerge. Following Roger Bacon, Scotus and Ramon Lull developed the notion of an *a priori* experience of an object which is, by definition, above alteration, and univocally common to finite and infinite.[36] Accordingly, in Descartes's *Regulae*, being is defined as that which is clear and distinct, available to absolute and certain intuitions, and "perfectly known and incapable of being doubted."[37] Existence becomes a "simple" or common notion, which, along with "unity" and "duration," is univocally common both to corporeal things and to spirits.[38] Absolute and certain intuitions of such entities form part of a *mathēsis* modelled on the abstract and timeless certainty of arithmetic and geometry.[39]

Descartes delimits the knowable by ruling that one should attend only to that which manifests itself clearly and distinctly, that is, "to those objects of which our minds seem capable of having certain and indubitable cognition."[40] This departure from the pre-Scotist notion of being as something with unknowable and unanalysable depth, inaugurates the "object" as a phenomenon. There arises, therefore, an epistemological circuit whereby knowledge is based entirely on objects, whose "being" does not exceed the extent to which they are known. Representation is now prior to ontology. Furthermore, the objects which are posited as knowable are basic and simple: "We must concentrate our mind's eye totally upon the most insignificant and easiest of matters."[41] By thus excluding the difficult and multiple, Descartes is able to reduce objects to items on a consistent and formal continuum of matter in such a way that all branches of knowledge become equally available, "since they are all of the same nature and consist simply in the putting together of self-evident facts."[42]

This determination of what is knowable, and therefore of what "is," according to a set of unchanging rules, apparent to the single mind, inverts the traditional movement from ontology to epistemology, yet nonetheless *assumes* an ontological redefinition of reality as the clear and distinct. It is this assumption which undergirds the new construal of *material* reality as *extensio*, an homogeneous quantity divided into degrees of motion and mechanical causes, and grasped fully in its "givenness." Concomitantly, the qualitative and hazy differences of colour or attribute are reduced to abstract spatial quantities, by analogy "with the extension of a body that has shape,"[43] so that in a gesture not unlike the fractal epistemology of Ramism, the *Regulae* is thereby able to bring all problems into conformity with an axiomatic system. Imperfect problems are reduced, as far as possible, to perfect ones. And then perfect problems are further reduced so that they become manifest to clear and distinct intuitions. Descartes's metamathematics of order and measure is therefore a general science with no reference to particular objects, for it both precedes and establishes all other knowledge of the world.[44]

This epistemological virtual reality (which is the remote heir of the Scotist "formal distinction") therefore assumes a prior ontology which, by defining being as the unvarying, clear, and distinct, subordinates it to the measure of the knowing subject, and finally places its objectivity in doubt. But this new ontology is itself the logical outcome of an ontology prised away from theology. Descartes consummates a movement which separates being from its donating source by taking Being to be, first of all, not the divine *gift* of a participation in a plenitude of infinite actuality, but rather the mere inert *given* of a contentless "notion" of existence univocally common to the finite and the infinite. However, this prior movement requires a further movement in order for it to be secured against nihilistic nothingness. The immanent must be adequately grasped in its givenness, as fully known and transparent, and thereby secure from time and multiplicity which threaten self-identity. The given is guaranteed as never *not* present to us, since its objectified components "are all self-evident and never contain any falsity ... for if we have the slightest grasp of it in our mind ... it must follow that we have complete knowledge of it."[45]

And. yet, in spite of this gesture to secure the object, there is, after all, something nihilistic about the Cartesian "given" which at once contradicts and fulfills the project of the universal mathematics, for, as I shall show, it is above all "nothing" which fulfills the criteria of clarity and distinctness, and which is superlatively consistent.[46] First, the reality to which his *mathēsis* refers does not exceed the "virtual." Secondly, the triumph of epistemology denudes the given of its corporeality. And, thirdly, the sceptical structure of the *Cogito* ensures that before anything ever quite attains the status of the absolute given, it evaporates, under the forces of doubt, into a disqualified nothingness.

First, the Cartesian "given" colonizes a peculiar liminal space of virtuality. Even when Descartes concedes that there is another mode of knowing in addition to intuition of simple natures, namely deduction, this second mode of knowing is ultimately reducible to the spatiality or virtuality of intuition. By deduction, he means "the inference of something as following necessarily from some other propositions which are known with certainty." This form of reasoning is still able to deliver absolute knowledge, "provided (its facts) are inferred from true and known principles through a continuous and uninterrupted movement of thought in which each individual proposition is clearly intuited."[47] Following this, in Rule Five, he ordains the systematic "ordering and arranging of the objects on which we must concentrate our mind's eye" according to reduction of the complex into the simple.[48] This structuration of objects does not reflect the order in which reality arrives for everyday, confused, passional perception, but subsists only within the abstract realm of mathematics, or else in the region where mathematics corresponds to reality, which is in physics. Although it is the case that in mathematics and physics things do indeed follow from one another in the orderly manner required by Descartes's method, he insists that this orderliness alone constitutes what is relevant of fundamental reality. So although, he concedes, in Rule Twelve of the *Regulae*, in agreement with the traditional Scholastic trope, that the order in which one comes to know reality differs from the order in which it exists,[49] Descartes is concerned only with the former ideal epistemological reality, and also projects the order of knowing as a more fundamental order of being. Hence, for example, in Rule Twelve, he concedes that body, extension and shape are inseparable in being, though not in understanding, and yet proceeds to assert that bodies are really composed of such genuine "simple natures" whose mark is that they are always predicated imivocally, and never analogically. The traditional trope is hereby undone. The given is no longer in excess of what can be known by means of method, for it is now commensurate with the structures conferred upon it by Descartes's rigid and ascetically drained kind of method.

Thus, the "given" is, in one sense, supremely corporeal, consisting in matter reduced to concrete *extensio*, and, in another sense, is denuded of that corporeality by being purely an epistemological projection. This apparent contradiction arises from the separation of ontology from theology, and the concomitant removal of concealed forces from physics. In Rule Fourteen, when Descartes invokes the question as to whether the extension of a thing is different from the body itself, he attacks the Platonic aporetic mathematics of the "point," whereby a point constitutes an *ideal* reality since it has no extension, and yet the moment it is actuated, acquires breadth and so ceases to be a point. By sustaining the *aporia* according to which number is an ideal or spiritual reality, Plato implies that the true reality of material things is spiritual, thus outwitting a simple dualism of idea and matter. But Descartes suppresses the *aporia* of the "point" by contending that geometric realities constitute entirely *material* realities, thus denying that number is to any degree ideal or spiritual.[50] In a similar fashion, Descartes (unlike Nicholas of Cusa before him and Pascal after him)[51] suppresses the *aporia* of the presence of the infinite in the finite, arguing that the extension of space and its microscopic division should rather be described as "indefinite." His pious excuse is that this reserves the term "infinite" for God who is alone without limit, whereas, he avers, macro- and microscopic extension may be subject to some limit of which we do not know. But this is to prevaricate: infinite extension and division are given with the fact of space – for how, for example, could space be limited except by further space? One might further defend Descartes by arguing that God's "simple" infinity is not simply the unending. However, this objection again seeks to avoid the *aporia*: if spatial, material things are infinite, then they seem to pass over into something "spiritual," for if space is infinite "it does not, indeed, make sense (at least in terms of traditional mathematics) to ask, can infinity be halved, etc." This is an example of a "meaningless" question regarding the infinite which is mentioned by Descartes himself, in order to argue that such ineffability beyond question should be reserved for God alone.[52] But this is an arbitrary restriction: infinity *does* paradoxically invade the finite and give rise to antinomic and irresolvable questions, like that of the reality of the "point." In both cases, Descartes rejects what the tradition had always (regarding the "point") and recently (regarding the great and small infinities of the universe) taken as "traces" of the spiritual in the material.

By thus secularizing or despiritualizing geometry and physics, disallowing the *aporia*s of the "point" in its incorporeality and of finite extension in its infinity, he concomitantly drains extension or corporeality itself of all its force and power. This act of immanentizing matter is tantamount to its erasure. Paradoxically, to immanentize reality, or to insist on its exhaustive corporeality, is to turn it into an unmodified ideal, since the secular "given" of the universal method is purely formal, articulated only in abstract structures which do not coincide with any actual embodied reality. But what is an immanentized ideal except the *nihil*, something which vanishes the moment it is posited?

This nihilistic gesture of the "given" is reiterated when the implications of the *Cogito* for extended reality are considered. The two stages of this consideration are as follows. First, to think is to think *something*. Secondly, if the content of one's thoughts are to be doubted, all except the intransitive "I think," which supposedly cannot be doubted, then nothing one thinks will ever quite meet the criterion of the absolutely given, since only what is absolutely available to an intuition cannot be subject to doubt. So, the structure of the *Cogito* means that the givenness of the given evaporates. For the purposes of the *Cogito*, only the *ego* itself qualifies as "given," and the *ego* is not exactly an "item" for Descartes at all. As a pure formality which has nothing to do with what lies outside, the pre-legislated Cartesian city is contained within an interior which has no exterior, and the "given" is thus seen to be a written reality, self-consistent because empty, motionless in its superlative mobility.

We have seen how the Cartesian object is contradictory insofar as it is purportedly part of physical *extensio* and yet its materiality is seen to be reducible to immanentized ideality, equivalent to the *nihil*. This contradiction is embedded in the character of the object as *sign*. By being reduced to comply with mathematical criteria, the objects of Descartes's science acquire the symbolic value of corporeality as the incarnation of truth in a physical image. And yet this embodiment fulfills the requirements for the production of a pure, spiritual cognition in such a way that the extended realm is "eminently" present in the mind.[53] As ideal signs, Cartesian objects are above alteration, and are arbitrarily related in advance by a conventional system of order and hierarchy, in such a way that they instantiate a break with the natural order.[54] Descartes's rejection of spontaneous experience liberates reality from its perceptual limits, leading to the creation of a new manipulable *cosmos* on a theoretical plane. Its elements, because of their simplicity, abstraction, and reduction to the same transferable "substance," imply a freedom of permutation, like the exchangeable type of the printing press, suggesting that the language to which these signs belong is conceived on the lines of a visual (and typographic) analogy. Indeed, an intuition made on the basis of the Cartesian object leads to an assimilation of properties within a lateral chain of temporal metonymy always reduced in advance to prescribed synecdochic substitutions: the succession of necessitated intuitions, or explications of the primary intuition that merely masquerades as a process of "deduction." Thus, the universal *mathēsis* comprises isomorphic signs devoid of content, whose self-referential character of certitude replaces the referential character of experience, as expressed by the former principles of resemblance and difference.

With this idealization of the object as sign, it is curious that Descartes should explicitly undertake to emulate the practicality and worldliness of artisans and their ordinary crafts.[55] Similarly; he adopts an apparently Socratic position in rejecting the method of sophism on the grounds that an intuition cannot be made via empty ciphers of knowledge, and that an artificial memory encourages a lapse into mechanicalness, inimical to pure cognition.[56] For this reason, Descartes proposes an idealized *ars* which constitutes an anti-method method – a method supposedly without artifice – and yet which is in the end sophistic because of its wholly internalized, formalized, and immanent perspective. Again, like the sophists (for all that he is a "rationalist" and they were "sceptics"), Descartes seeks an extra-linguistic philosophy in and through the instrumentalization and humiliation of language, simultaneously invoking and denying the sign. For, whilst he turns the objects of his science purely and exhaustively into signs, he chooses algebra as a model for a *mathēsis* whose logical principles appear to extend beyond number, shape, and language.[57] Similarly, his emphasis on the importance of acceleration in deduction, and on fixed order, suggests a subordination of time to the spatiality of the immediate *punctum*, in an attempt to elude all the inherent problematics of both memory and representation.[58] His method, it seems, is offered as an alternative to eternity and divine ineffability. Indeed, this space is even more idealized (or immanently spiritualized) than that of Ramus, since the Cartesian intuition is fully interiorized. It does not occupy the physical space of a map or chart whose scores are surveyed in inhabited time and space, but rather, the accelerated conflation of the first and last links in a deductive series approximates an emptying of visual space in order to obtain true intellection. Thus, physical space is replaced by a purely rational, homogenous substrate which houses not "things," but idealized figures or signs which, as interior, appear to "get outside" language itself. The interiorized "flattening-out" of this new intellection thus offers an immanentized version of the angelic vision for which diverse perspectives are unified into a single omniscient gaze.[59] But the Cartesian gaze is inward and reflexive, gazing only at its own projection of order and sign, as if in its own mirrored reflection.

This withdrawal of epistemology into an interior and reflexive "space," repeating the construal of the totalized and surveyable city as a metaphor for the individual, fulfills Derrida's characterization of metaphysics as self-identity and the separation of mind from the *extensio*, although Derrida sees Descartes's prioritization of the pure interior as consistent with the production of an idealized *speech* or orality:

> We already have a foreboding that phonoceticrism merges with the histor-ical determination of the meaning of being in general *as presence*, with all the subdeterminations which depend on this general form and which organise within it their system and their historical sequence (presence of the thing to the sight as *eidos*, presence as substance/essence/ existence [*ousia*], temporal presence as point [*sigmè*] of the now or of the moment [*nun*], the self-presence of the *Cogito*, consciousness, subjectivity).[60]

But, in this characterization, he fails to recognize that, for Descartes, the pure interior is sustained through writing and not speech, as was seen above in my demonstration of the textual and contractual status of the Cartesian city. And although Derrida might argue that Descartes's writing, as alphabetic, is still meta-physical since it is always already subordinate to speech, in fact, although he does refer to alphabetic writing,[61] Descartes's emphasis on both formal order and dia-grammatic consistency suggest that his epistemological writing is closer to Derrida's supposedly non-metaphysical *hieroglyph* than to alphabetic script. Indeed, as well as the examples of knowledge as compared with architecture, building, and city-planning, he exalts the morphological arts of weaving, carpet-making, and embroidery as pic-torial and structural analogies of ideal and interior intellection.[62] His interest in order and proportion, as well as totalizing and punctiliar cognition, imply a preference for the spatial pictogram rather than the seriality of alphabetic writing.[63]

5. The written subject

The logical outcome of an immanentist ontology where epistemology is paramount is, as we have seen, the reduction of being to the "object" whose existence does not exceed the extent to which it is known by the subject. Thus the subject assumes the status of that which confers existence upon reality. But we have also seen that the subject's realm of operation contains contradictory and nihilistic aspects. In this section I will show how the Cartesian subject finds it necessary to offer a gesture of security against the void, where the given is perpetually threatened by doubt, by substituting method for memory, estranging itself from all that is material, including time, place, and particularity, and like Lysias' endeavour to sustain his metic status in the *Phaedrus*, ordering itself through writing. This textualization of the subject in turn gives rise to an *aporia* which, because of its immanentist setting, can only be "resolved" through nihilism.

After introducing the notion of the universal mathematics in Rule Four of the *Regulae*, Descartes advances the concept of order as the means for guarding against the failures of memory, and, ultimately, displacing it altogether.[64] Although he views memory as one of the perfections of the human mind,[65] he confesses to having a weak memory. His attempt to counter this via the ideal spatiality of the instantaneous and thus self-identical intuition also constitutes, as we have seen, an evacuation of his philosophical past, and, in particular, the arts of memory. Whilst Ramist method aimed at designing a simplification of education by providing new and better ways to memorize information, Descartes's enumeration functions not as a way of conserving memory, but of *abolishing* it altogether through its reduction to intuition. Although memory is necessary for the initial constitution of the concept of order, it is, by virtue of the order now established, dismissed.[66] Furthermore, and more radically, his system for the attainment of certitude (conceived as a *punctum*) challenges the prior significance of memory as a means which inseparably links knowledge, tradition, and the transcendent. Indeed, the system defies Plato and Augustine for whom the mind could only perceive "being" once it had recollected its own transcendent source, and would be unable to apprehend its object unless it was illumined by a source other than itself. Thus, for this intellectual legacy, memory was both ontologically and epistemologically necessary. Significantly, the icon of the sun in Plato, representing the transcendent bestowal of life and knowledge, becomes for Descartes the light of human reason itself.[67]

The elision of the role of memory for knowledge and ontology has sinister implications not only for the reduction of being to the object, but also for the constitution of the philosophical subject. As I argued in chapter 1 [of *After Writing*], memory is crucial for self-continuity whilst allowing for variation, and so its replacement by formal, isomorphic structures transposes the subject's continuity-with-difference into self-identity and permanence, the prime criteria, that is, for the Cartesian object itself.[68] This is also implicit in the formulation of the philosophical subject in the

Discourse, for the structure of the *Cogito*, as I discussed above, suggests that whilst all else evaporates into doubt, the *ego* alone remains indubitably "given." For all that, it cannot be given the positive quality of a real "item." And in consequence, in subjectivity, vacuity and objectivity once again coincide, for Descartes's subject is only indubitable *because* it has been emptied of its contents by its definition as pure thought, and by being differentiated from its specific modes of existence. The subject is the most certain thing there is because it is the superlative object, whose existence is a void and is thereby ideally unconstrained either by place or time.

Furthermore, the self-presence, autonomy, and lack of memory of this subject suggest that it is modelled on the text as a pure subjectivity, whose sole gesture is the act of writing itself. For subjectivity manifests itself in Descartes as the method which produces the ideal positioning of things according to their most identically repeatable characteristics. The mind which gathers itself in the (writing of) method is also an *ideal writing*, a collection of printed marks, divorced from circumstances, voice and body, occupying the achronic instant of the text, in which there is no passing, progression, or transference. Rather, the mind's writing localizes, or imprints, in the instant of intuition, outside duration, and therefore outside the act of writing too. The mind of the Cartesian subject is the purest possible text. In his deconstruction of the *Regulae*, Jean-Luc Nancy detects a supposedly hidden link between the subject and a pure interior writing when, adopting the "voice" of Descartes, he affirms that "I write while not writing in the instantaneity of the movement, describing each time different movements subordinated to the same instantaneity."[69] However, contra Nancy, it is not necessary to deconstruct the *Regulae* in order to show how the Cartesian subject depends on writing, and in particular, writing as interiority. Rather, this structure is manifest in the method itself. Writing is therefore not the opposite of Cartesian interiority, or, as Nancy insinuates, its suppressed condition of possibility, but is commensurate with it.

The radical solipsism of the Cartesian subject leads to an aporetic *mathēsis* and a contradiction within the subject itself. First, the universal *mathēsis* is identified as that which is supremely private. If the subject arrives at certain knowledge by deducing from its own existence, will this truth hold for others? How can a universal knowledge be deduced privately, in isolation from the world? Since the private *ego* is all that remains absolutely given, it alone qualifies as the warrant for the existence of truth. The *ego* thus acts as a textualized and immanentized version of the Platonic good, the sole ground for all knowledge and existence, but in privatized form. Although Descartes deems his method universal, he does concede in the Discourse that he would not necessarily advise anyone to imitate it.[70] Indeed, by definition, it could not be imitated, since it is radically subjective. Is it therefore the formality and emptiness of the *mathēsis* which qualifies it as universal? Or is it universal because the individual is all there is, and so paradoxically the individual is the universal to the extent that there is nothing "beyond" the individual? The tension between universal and private amounts to the question as to which is truly prior and foundational, given that each is a necessary metaphor for the other: the supreme individual is he who surveys a universal totality, a *"cosmopolis"* (to use Toulmin's accurate term), while this cosmopolitan universe is in turn simply that which is surveyable by a single gaze.

This tension can only be resolved by reducing the subject to an interiorized written template which bears no traces of its physical situation, and so to the scalar flexibility of the object as death. The interior of such a subject, as we have seen, has no exterior; it can only open onto itself. This is confirmed in the *Discourse* when Descartes compares the unmethodic mind to a darkened underground cellar, evoking Plato's allegory of the cave. Whilst, for Plato, illumination involves *ascent* to the sun, for Descartes there is no such avocation of the transcendent. Instead, the cellar is illumined by a lateral and instantaneous gesture of opening windows upon the cellar to admit daylight.[71] The implications of this for a Cartesian theory of the subject and epistemology are twofold. First, daylight is a diffused and diluted version of the transcendent sun as it is figured in the *Republic*. The Cartesian sun is simply "there" without need of education, or pilgrimage. And, secondly, to build windows in an underground cellar is an ambiguous act, since it is tantamount to opening windows onto the *inside*, an opening which confirms closure. A cellar is an inside with no outside, merely returning the inside to itself. Thus the image of the cellar repeats the construal of reason as monadically pure, deriving its evidence from its own self-reflection. This underground subject is surrounded by an exteriority which merely affirms its inferiority. It is enshrined in *written* form in the sense that, like the textual sign, it is outside alteration, like death itself, emplotted. And it is emplotted in another sense: it resides in firm ground, its own "ground," which is also the "ground" or warrant for the existence of all reality. Its ground is indeed so firm that it needs no Lysian contract of citizenship, because it is self-governing. Further, it is its own everything, its own universality, and so there is no authority (transcendent or otherwise) from which to borrow its own existence.

Thus, in the end, after Descartes, a spatialized written *polis*, a spatialized written being, and a spatialized written subject, cohere perfectly together, without priority or foundation, in a triadic mutual collusion, which sustains the "self-evidence" of the immanent, and its secular closure against the sun of the good only as a conspiracy, a conspiracy both cosmopolitan and esoterically concealed.

Notes

1   Jacques Derrida, *Speech and Phenomena*, trans. David Allison, Evanston: Northwestern University Press, 1973.
2   Peter Ramus, *The Logike* (1574), Leeds: The Scolar Press Ltd, 1966, p. 14; see Lisa Jardine, "Humanist Logic," in Charles B. Schmitt and Quentin Skinner (eds), *The Cambridge History of Renaissance Philosophy*, Cambridge: Cambridge University Press, 1988, 184–6.

3   Ramus, *The Logike* (see Note 2), 14–15.

4   Walter J. Ong, SJ, *Ramus and the Decay of Dialogue: From the Art of Discourse to the Art of Reason*, Cambridge, Massachusetts: Harvard University Press, 1983, 65–72.

5   On Peter of Spain and Rudolph Agricola as precursors of Ramus, see ibid., and Walter J. Ong, SJ, *Orality and Literacy: The Technologizing of the Word*, London: Routledge and Kegan Paul Ltd, 1982, chapters 3–5. On Boethius and Peter of Spain, see Etienne Gilson, *History of Christian Philosophy in the Middle Ages*, London: Sheed and Ward Ltd, 1955, 97–106 and 319–23.

6   Although, in an aside, Walter Ong writes that Ramus never really demonstrates this certainty: *Ramus and the Decay of Dialogue* (see Note 4), p. 176.

7   Ramus, *The Logike* (see Note 2), p. 74. For an exposition of this aspect of the method, see the sections on Ramus in Kenneth D. McRae, "Ramist Tendencies in the Thought of Jean Bodin," *Journal of the History of Ideas*, XVI (1955), 306–23.

8   Ong, *Ramus and the Decay of Dialogue* (see Note 4), p. 80.

9   Stephen Toulmin, *Cosmopolis: The Hidden Agenda of Modernity*, Chicago: University of Chicago Press, 1990. See also the chapter entitled 'Transition' in Catherine Pickstock, *After Writing: On the Liturgical Consummation of Philosophy*, Oxford: Blackwell, 1998.

10   See, for example, Frances A. Yates, *The Art of Memory*, London: Pimlico, 1992, 230–31, on the stimulation of the imagination by the frescoed and sculptured images in churches, such as the Fresco of The Wisdom of Thomas Aquinas by Andrea da Firenze, plate 2.

11   On the mind as a mirror, see Richard Rorty, *Philosophy and the Mirror of Nature*, Oxford: Basil Blackwell, 1980.

12   See Ong, *Ramus and the Decay of Dialogue* (see Note 4), p. 280, and Paolo Rossi, *Clavis Universalis: Arti Mnemoniche E Logica Combinatoria Da Lullo a Leibniz*, Milan: Riccardo Ricciardi Editove, 1960, p. 140, see Yates, *The Art of Memory* (see Note 10), 229.

13   Yates, *The Art of Memory* (see Note 10), pp. 230–31.

14   These "rules appertaining to the matter of every art" declare "the Methode and forme to be observed in all artes and sciences"; "No farther seeke but in this booke thy self doe exercise," Ramus, *Logike* (see Note 2), pp. 7, 2. On Aristotelian *topoi* as predicated on the spoken word, see Giorgio Agamben, *Language and Death: The Plague of Negativity*, trans. Karen E. Pinkus and Michael Hardt, Minneapolis, MN: University of Minnesota Press, 1991, p. 33.

15   In spite of this textualization of both dialectic and rhetoric, Ramus claims (emptily) that his "Dialecticke otherwise called Logicke, is an arte which teachethe to dispute well," *The Logike* (see Note 2), p. 17.

16   Walter Ong compares this textual rhetoric with Aristotelian logic which, although essentially diagrammatic, could not be reduced entirely to spatiality because it derives from aural-type analogies rather than visual. This residue of the auditory, though not made explicit by Aristotle, is inseparable from his thinking because the categories are conceived as parts of enunciations. Thus human knowledge for Aristotle exists, in the full sense, only in the enunciation, that is, in the saying of something about something, the uttering of a statement, the expression of a judgement, and the union of a subject and predicate. Concomitantly, the *topoi* of ancient rhetoric were seen as fontal sources of arguments, with such open-ended places as *relatio* and *similitudo*. With Agricola and Ramus, however, the *topoi* are presented as headings, or as entries in a classificatory finding-system to a static and given resource of information which admits of no development. This shift towards knowledge as exhaustively contained in "places" was reflected in the structure of printed books, for example as regards the introduction at this time of the *index locorum*. On the Agricolan and Ramist conceptual closure of *topoi* see Ong, *Ramus and the Decay of Dialogue* (see Note 4), pp. 104–12, and on the further implications of the format of printed books, pp. 311–15.

17   John Milbank, *The Religious Dimension in the Thought of Giambattista Vico 1668–1744*, Vol. I: *The Early Metaphysics*, Lampeter and New York: Edwin Mellen Press, 1991, pp. 278–80.

18   Whilst it is true that Aristotle's philosophy of nature was also committed to the unambiguous language of science, with much emphasis upon comparison and exhaustive definition (not similitude), there remain fundamental differences between Aristotle's philosophy and that of the new science. For Aristotle, the phenomena of nature are not homogeneous, but are governed by different kinds of causes and principles. Science cannot be any more uniform

than its subject matter. The translation of methods from one science to another leads to category-mistakes (or *metabasis*). For the new science, however, such *metabasis* no longer presented a problem because it tended to view all being as homogeneous. See Amos Funkenstein, *Theology and the Scientific Imagination from the Middle Ages to the Seventeenth Century*, Princeton, NJ: Princeton University Press, 1986, pp. 35–7.

19   "Abolyshe all tautologies and vayne repetitions, and so thus muche being done, thou shalt comprehende the rest into a litlerome," Ramus, *The Logike* (see Note 2), p. 12. See also Ong, *Ramus and the Decay of Dialogue* (see Note 4), pp. 212–13, 283–4.

20   Manfred Gorlach, *Introduction to Early Modern English*, Cambridge: Cambridge University Press, 1991, pp. 101–2,122–8; see also Ong, *Ramus and the Decay of Dialogue* (see Note 4), p. 128.

21   Plato, *Laws*, 817b.

22   "[A]nd will they distrust our statement that no city could ever be blessed unless its lineaments were traced by artists who used the heavenly model?" Plato, *Republic*, trans. Paul Shorey, *The Collected Dialogues*, VI, 500e.

23   Rene Descartes, *Discourse on the Method*, in John Cottingham, Robert Stoothoff and Dugald Murdoch (trans.), *The Philosophical Writings of Descartes*, Vol. I, Cambridge: Cambridge University Press, 1985, Part II, VI. p. 11.

24   Ibid., Part II, VI. pp. 11–17.

25   Ibid., VI. p. 12.

26   Ibid.

27   See Pickstock, *After Writing* (see Note 9), Chapter 1, Section 6 "Eros and Exteriority" and *passim*.

28   Descartes, *Discourse on the Method* (see Note 23), Part II, VI. pp. 13–14.

29   Descartes, *Rules for the Direction of the Mind*, in Cottingham et al., *The Philosophical Writings of Descartes* (see Note 23), Vol. I, "Rule One", X359–61.

30   Descartes, *Discourse on the Method* (see Note 23), Part II, VI. pp. 12–13.

31   Physicality is explicitly ruled out as a potential mediator of the truth. See Ibid., Part IV, VI. p. 37.

32   Ibid., Part II, VI. p. 11.

33   "My plan has never gone beyond trying to reform my own thoughts and construct them upon a foundation which is all my own," Ibid., VI. pp. 14–15.

34   Ibid., VI. 16.

35   Jean-Luc Marion, *Sur le prisme métaphysique de Descartes*, Paris: Presses Universitaires de France, 1986, 14–43; Jean-François Courtine, *Suarez et le système de la métaphysique*, Paris: Presses Universitaires de France, 1990, pp. 485–95; John Milbank, *The Word Made Strange: Theology, Language, Culture*, Oxford: Blackwell Publishers, 1996, p. 51 n. 16.

36   On Roger Bacon, see Gilson, *History of Christian Philosophy* (see Note 5), pp. 294–312; Umberto Eco, *The Search for the Perfect Language*, Oxford: Basil Blackwell, 1995, pp. 53–4; On Duns Scotus, see Amos Funkenstein, *Theology and the Scientific Imagination* (see Note 18), pp. 26–7, 57–9; Gilson, *Jean Duns Scot: Introduction à ses positions fondamentales*, Paris: Librairie Philosophiques, 1952; Alexandre Koyré, *From the Closed World to the Infinite Universe*, Baltimore and London: The Johns Hopkins Press, 1952/1970, 124; John Milbank, *Theology and Social Theory: Beyond Secular Reason*, Oxford: Blackwell Publishers, 1990, pp. 301–2; John Milbank, *The Word Made Strange*, pp. 9, 44; On Ramon Lull, see Gilson, 350–53, Eco, 53–72, Yates, *The Art of Memory* (see Note 10), pp. 175–96.

37   "All knowledge [*scientia*] is certain and evident cognition," Descartes, *Rules for the Direction of the Mind* (see Note 29), Rule Two, X362.

38   Ibid., Rule Twelve, X419–20.

39   Ibid., X364–5; Rule Four, X374–9.

40   Ibid., Rule Two, X362.

41   Ibid., Rule Nine, X400.

42   Ibid., Rule Thirteen, X428; Also, "We should note that comparisons are said to be simple and straightforward only when the thing sought and the initial data participate equally in a certain nature," Rule Fourteen, X440.

43   Ibid., X441.
44   For example, in Rule Thirteen, when Descartes expands mathematics to deal with physical problems through an examination of the nature of magnets, like the logicians who. presuppose the terms and matter of a syllogism, he proceeds by assuming that the question to be solved is perfectly understood, in such a way that the inferences are foreclosed in advance. In the case of the magnet, the knowledge of what is meant by the two words "magnet" and "nature" will determine the interpretation of the experiments. The reduction of the question to its basic elements thus replaces any superfluous considerations of the object. Ibid., Rule Thirteen, X431.
45   Ibid., Rule Twelve, X420–1.
46   In the next chapter [of *After Writing*], I argue that the postmodern preoccupation with death, and reduction of everything to the simple nature of "nothing", betray its metaphysics of presence.
47   Descartes, *Rules for the Direction of the Mind* (see Note 29), Rule Three, X369
48   Ibid., Rule Five, X379.
49   Ibid., Rule Twelve, X418.
50   Ibid., Rule Fourteen, X444–5.
51   "When we know better, we understand that, since nature has engraved her own image and that of her author on all things, they almost all share her double infinity." Pascal, *Pensées*, trans. A. J. Krailsheimer, London: Penguin Books, 1966,p. 199 – see also pp. 68, 201, 418; A. Koyré, *From the Closed World* (see Note 36).
52   *Principles of Philosophy,* in Cottingham et al., *The Philosophical Writings of Descartes* (see Note 23), Vol. I, VIII. A. pp. 26–7; Rene Descartes, *Principles of Philosophy*, in John Cottingham, Robert Stoothoff, Dugald Murdoch (trans.), *The Philosophical Writings of Descartes*, Cambridge: Cambridge University Press, 1984–91, Volume I, 8. A. 26–7; Volume II, *Objections and Replies* ('Author's Replies to the First Set of Objections'), 7. 113–14.
53   Descartes, *Meditations on First Philosophy*, in Cottingham et al., *The Philosophical Writings of Descartes* (see Note 23), Vol. II, *Objections and Replies*, Third Meditation, VII. p. 453.
54   Arithmetic and geometry alone "are concerned with an object so pure and simple that they make no assumptions that experience might render uncertain", Descartes, *Rules for the Direction of the Mind* (see Note 29), Rule Two, X365.
55   Ibid., Rule Eight, X397 and Rule Ten, X404. Descartes immanentizes these crafts by characterizing them as autonomous and methodized, carried out without appeal to the transcendent.
56   Ibid., X405–6, and Rule Seven, X388.
57   Ibid., Rule Four, X377.
58   On the importance of order in deductive enumeration ("so that memory is left with practically no role to play, and I seem to intuit the whole thing at once," Ibid., X388) see especially Ibid., Rule Seven; and on the merits of deductive *speed*, see Ibid., Rule Eleven, X408–9. Because of the deficiencies of memory, "I run over [the operations] again and again in my mind until I can pass from the first to the last so quickly that memory is left with practically no role to play, and I seem to be intuiting the whole thing at once," Rule Eleven, X409; see also Rule Three, X369–70.
59   Dalia Judovitz, *Subjectivity and Representation in Descartes: The Origins of Modernity*, Cambridge: Cambridge University Press, 1988, pp. 71–2.
60   Jacques Derrida, *Of Grammatology*, trans. Gayatri Chakravorty Spivak, Baltimore: The Johns Hopkins Press, 1976, p. 12; "But this violent liberation of speech is possible … only in the extent to which it keeps itself resolutely and consciously at the greatest possible proximity to the abuse that is the usage of speech – just close enough to say violence, to dialogue with itself as irreducible violence, and just far enough to live and live as speech": Derrida, "Cogito and the History of Madness," in Alan Bass (trans.), *Writing and Difference*, London: Routledge and Kegan Paul, 1990, pp. 31–78, 61.
61   Descartes, *Rules for the Direction of the Mind* (see Note 29), Rule Ten, X404–5.
62   Ibid., X404.
63   Descartes, *Discourse on the Method* (see Note 23), Part II, VI. pp. 20–21.
64   Descartes, *Rules for the Direction of the Mind* (see Note 29), Rule Four, X378–9.

65 Ibid., Rule Twelve, X441, idem, *Discourse on the Method* (see Note 23), Part I, VI. 2–3.

66 The problem of memory continued to haunt the Cartesian text, since in the *Meditations on First Philosophy* Descartes admits that only memory can separate the states of waking and sleep, and is essential to knowledge; Fifth Meditation, IX 69–70.

67 On "the natural light of reason," see Descartes, *Rules for the Direction of the Mind* (see Note 29), Rule One, X361; Rule Three, X368; Rule Four, X371. In the *Discourse on the Method* (see Note 23), Descartes compares method with daylight: Part VI, VI. 71. See further Dalia Judovitz, "Vision, Representation, and Technology in Descartes," in David Michael Levin (ed.), *Modernity and the Hegemony of Vision*, Berkeley, Los Angeles and London: University of California Press, 1993, 63–86.

68 In chapter 3 of *After Writing* (see Note 9) I show how the self-identity of the object suggests that the superlative object is death itself, as conceived in modern Western and postmodern thought. For this reason, there is a Cartesian element in postmodern "nihilism" of a Derridean kind.

69 Jean-Luc Nancy, "Dum Scribo," trans. Ian McLeod, *The Oxford Literary Review*, 3.2 (1978), 6–21, 9.

70 Descartes, *Discourse on the Method* (see Note 23), Part II, VI. p. 15.

71 Ibid., Part VI, VI. p. 71.

Chapter 6

John Milbank

Political theology and the new science of politics

O nce, there was no 'secular'. And the secular was not latent, waiting to fill more space with the steam of the 'purely human', when the pressure of the sacred was relaxed. Instead there was the single community of Christendom, with its dual aspects of *sacerdotium* and *regnum* The *saeculum*, in the medieval era, was not a space, a domain, but a time – the interval between fall and *eschaton* where coercive justice, private property and impaired natural reason must make shift to cope with the unredeemed effects of sinful humanity.

The secular as a domain had to be instituted or *imagined*, both in theory and in practice. This institution is not correctly grasped in merely negative terms as a desacralization. It belongs to the received wisdom of sociology to interpret Christianity as itself an agent of secularization, yet this thesis is totally bound up with the one-sided negativity of the notion of desacralizing, a metaphor of the removal of the superfluous and additional to leave a residue of the human, the natural and the self-sufficient. For this negative conception it is convenient that there should always have been some perception of the pure remainder, and the hybrid 'Judeo-Christianity' is cast in this role: from its inception, it supposedly removes sacral allure from the cosmos and men, inevitably, from the political, the social, the economic, the artistic – the human 'itself'.[1]

Received sociology altogether misses the positive institution of the secular, because it fully embraces the notion of humanism as the perennial destiny of the West and of human autonomous freedom as always gestating in the womb of 'Judeo-Christianity'. However, in this respect it is doomed to repeat the self-understanding of Christianity arrived at in late-medieval nominalism, the Protestant reformation and seventeenth-century Augustinianism, which completely privatized, spiritualized and transcendentalized the sacred, and concurrently reimagined nature, human action and society as a sphere of autonomous, sheerly formal power. Sociology projects this specific mutation in Christianity back to its origins and even to the Bible. It interprets the theological transformation at the inception of modernity as a genuine 'reformation' which fulfils the destiny of Christianity to let the spiritual be the spiritual, without public interference, and the public be the secular, without private prejudice. Yet this interpretation preposterously supposes that the new theology simply brought Christianity to its true essence by lifting some irksome and misplaced sacred ecclesial restrictions on the free market of the secular, whereas, in fact, it instituted an entirely different economy of power and knowledge and had to invent 'the political' and 'the State', just as much as it had to invent 'private religion'.

This consideration should govern how we view the first social theory that claimed to be a 'science', namely 'political science'. With the writings of Grotius, Hobbes and Spinoza, political theory achieved a certain highly ambiguous 'autonomy' with regard to theology. However, autonomization was not achieved in the sphere of knowledge alone; it was only possible because the new science of politics both assumed and constructed. for itself a new autonomous object – the political – defined as a field of pure power. Secular 'scientific' understanding of society was, from the outset, only the self-knowledge of the self-construction of the secular as power. What theology has forgotten is that it cannot either contest or learn from this understanding as such, but has either to accept or deny its object.

This autonomous object was, first of all, 'natural'. According to Grotius, the natural laws governing property and sovereignty could be known *etsi Deus non daretur* [as if there were no God].[2] For Aquinas, natural law had meant transcendental equity and therefore precisely that which conjoined the particular instance of justice to the divine and eternal in the surpassing of all mere regularity of convention.[3] But now, for modernity, natural law transcribes the sealed-off totality of nature, where eternal justice consists in the most invariable rules. These are not derived (as for Aquinas) from the inner tendencies of the Aristotelian practical reason towards the *telos* of the good, but rather from purely theoretical reflections on the necessity for every creature to ensure its own self-preservation. Because nature, since the Renaissance, was regarded as an 'open book' which might be almost exhaustively read, Grotius, Hobbes and Spinoza can be confident that the self-preserving *conatus* provides the universal hermeneutic key for both nature and society.[4] And the *etsi* is entirely a ruse, because the finite totality presupposes that nature is a legally governed domain, obeying completely regular laws of the operation of power and passion, which yet are wilfully laid down by the retired deity. The bond between 'natural' and 'social' science is here perfect, and present even as far back as Pierre d'Ailly, for whom an exclusively positive character of legal obligation reflects a natural causality which is the merely accidental regularity of divine, legally imposed connections between entirely discrete particulars.[5]

The autonomous object, although natural, was *also* artificial. The new political knowledge could rest on the material foundations of *conatus*, but, from then on, the knowledge of power was simply a retracing of the paths of human construction, an analysis of *factum* (the made). Here again, social science did not lag behind natural science, but rather, in both cases, the specificity of modern 'scientific' knowledge is to do with an 'artificial' method and an infallible knowledge of artifice, as the seventeenth century was universally aware (although there were divergent sceptical, rationalist and 'experimentalist' versions of this specificity).[6] Already, as far back as the *trecento*, Coluccio Salutati declared legal knowledge to be more certain than medical knowledge because it lay more within the command and insight of the human will.[7] Later, for Hobbes, Wilkins and Locke, ethical understanding is more susceptible to geometrization or probabilization than physics because here alone technical control can be coextensive with the object of understanding.[8]

The conception of society as a human product and therefore 'historical' remains one of the basic assumptions of secular social science, although it has always been aporetically crossed, as we shall see in the next chapter, by the accompanying reflection that human beings are the product of society. Not only to social scientists, but also to theologians like Harvey Cox, it has consequently seemed obvious that the sphere of the artificial, of *factum*, marks out the space of secularity. For Harvey Cox it is precisely this area of the free play of human constructive choice which formed the 'dominion' granted to Adam in Eden, as the counterpart to the individual and secret submission of the soul to God.[9]

However, the 'obvious' connection of the *factum* and the secular can and must be called into question. It is not enough just to point out, like Hannah Arendt or Jurgen Habermas, that the concentration of post-Hobbesian political science on instrumental reason tended to obscure another dimension of human action, namely Aristotelian *praxis*, where one seeks not to control with precision, but with a necessary approximation to persuade, exhort and encourage a growth in the virtues as ends in themselves.[10] This displacement of classical politics by a new political 'science' is of course very important, yet what these thinkers ignore is the fact that the sphere of the 'artificial' is not necessarily identical with that of the instrumental, any more than poetry is merely technology.

To make it appear that the scope of *factum* is necessarily identical with the rights of the secular, thinkers like Hobbes had to construct a *factum* whose essence was its formality and predictability. One can begin to grasp the contingency and the questionability of this procedure, if one considers as a contemporary counter-example the new 'conceptist' notion of the Idea in mannerist art-theory and Baroque rhetoric.[11] Here, precisely the same new recognition of the humanly artificial arises, such that the artistic or poetic 'Idea' is no longer what 'precedes' the work in the artist's mind as a reflection of the ideas of God, but instead becomes that which is conveyed as meaning to the receiver from the peculiar constitution of *the work itself*. Yet this is not a Hobbesian, nominalist move, because the Idea, though now inseparable from its own 'image', still conserves for the mannerists the full Platonic value of a participation in divine understanding. Behind this 'pragmatist' reconception of the idea one can trace, not a secularizing impulse, but rather influences of Trinitarian theology, where the Father has eternal understanding only in the 'image' of the Son. The conceptist 'Idea' is already anticipated by Nicholas of Cusa's view that *factibilitas* is the condition of possibility for human knowing and belongs to a human conjectural *explicatio* of the divine intellectual 'comprehension' in the second person of the Trinity.[12]

The mannerist counter-example shows that far from the *factum* (the made) self-evidently staking out an area of secular autonomy, it could, on the contrary, for the heirs of a Christian-humanist sensibility be seen as the gateway to transcendence. Hence just as 'obvious' as the Hobbesian move was an effortless Baroque integration of the 'modern' discovery of human making into a traditional Platonic, participatory framework. It would therefore be legitimate to look for an alternative 'Baroque' politics that was equally 'modern' yet remained both humanist and metaphysical – later one catches traces of such a thing in the writings of Giambattista Vico.[13] Both insofar as it was deemed natural and insofar as it was deemed artificial, the new autonomous object of political science was not, therefore, simply 'uncovered'. The space of the secular had to be invented as the space of 'pure power'. However, this invention was itself, as we shall now see, a theological achievement, just as only a particular sort of theology could pronounce the *etsi Deus non daretur*.

The theological construction of secular politics

For the *factum* (the made) to become identified with the secular, it was necessary that Adam's *dominium* be redefined as power, property, active right, and absolute sovereignty, and that Adam's personhood be collapsed into this redefined mastery that is uniquely 'his own'.

Dominium over oneself, 'self-government', was traditionally a matter of the rational mastery of the passions and this was also the basis for one's legitimate control and possession of external objects. One's self-identity, what was 'proper' to one and what belonged to 'propriety', was very clearly bound up with the rational and ethical management of one's 'property'.[14] Yet at the margins of this classical and medieval theme there persists the trace of a more brutal and original *dominium*, the unrestricted lordship over what lies within one's power – oneself, one's children, land or slaves – in Roman private law.

In the later Middle Ages and in the seventeenth century this original Roman sense not only returns, but for the first time advances from the margins into the centre. Originally this 'sheer power' was before and outside the city, belonging to the sphere of the household, but now, for the developers of the Roman law tradition, legal *ius*, which forms the bonds of justice within the political community, is identified with *dominium*.[15] This puts an end to Aquinas's attempt to tame Roman *dominium* by understanding Adam's *dominium* as *dominium utile*, a property right of free 'procuration and disposal' whose final justification was still *usus* by society in general.[16] Instead, *dominium* is traced by Jean Gerson to the *facultas* which possesses the power to do as it likes with its own, such that a property right is as much 'the right to exchange' as the 'right to make use of'.[17] However, this *facultas* is also for Gerson the whole root of natural law, such that a *ius* is no longer what is 'right' or just, or a 'claim right' to justice, but active right over property. As the traditional link between person and ownership remains, this means that self-identity, the *suum*, is no longer essentially related to divine rational illumination, or ethics, but is a sheer 'self-occupation' or 'self-possession'. 'Every man has a property in his own person', as Locke will later say.[18]

Dominium or 'the private', which for Roman law was at first the natural and 'chaotic', to be restrained by the laws of justice, has now so far moved into the forum as to abolish the antique public space altogether. Thus Sir Robert Filmer, who traced all political sovereignty back to Adam's private and paternal power, achieved thereby a hierocratic genealogy of an entirely *modern* sort. A fundamentally common origin for both private property and state sovereignty was also affirmed (though in a different manner) by Grotius and Hobbes.[19] The political state, for the nominalist Hobbes, is only conceivable as an 'Artificial Man' (*Leviathan*) whose identity and reality are secured by an unrestricted right to preserve and control his own artificial body.[20] The contradiction of Hobbes's State, however, resides in the fact that, while it is artificially generated through the wills of many private persons, these persons can only be public persons capable of mutual recognition, as bearers of private rights, once the 'nominal' being is really and truly enacted through the sheerly physical mechanisms of sovereign power. It is here, precisely, that one perceives the antinomic strain in the formal, instrumental and secular account of *factum*. Because it is rooted in an individualistic account of the will, oblivious to questions of its providential purpose in the hands of God, it has difficulty in understanding any 'collective making', or genuinely social process. To keep notions of the State free from any suggestions of a collective essence or generally recognized *telos*, it must be constructed on the individualist model of *dominium*.

It is in this inescapable imperative of nominalism–voluntarism that one discovers the kinship at the root of modern absolutism with modern liberalism. The same notion of *dominium* promotes both Hobbes's dictum that the sovereign power can never bind itself, *and* his view that the greatest liberty of subjects depends on the silence of the law.[21] It is precisely the formal character of state power as guaranteeing personal security and non-interference in 'private' pursuits (selling, contracts, education, choice of abode) which demands that this power be otherwise unlimited and absolutely alone. Hobbes was simply more clear-sighted than later apparently more 'liberal' thinkers like Locke in realizing that a liberal peace requires a single undisputed power, but not necessarily a continued majority consensus, which may not be forthcoming.

One can conclude that 'unrestricted' private property, 'absolute sovereignty' and 'active rights', which compose the 'pure-power' object of the new politics, are all the emanations of a new anthropology which begins with human persons as individuals and yet defines their individuality essentialistically, as 'will' or 'capacity' or 'impulse to self-preservation'.

The question then becomes, how did this anthropology ever secure legitimacy in a theological and metaphysical era? The answer is that it was theologically promoted. *Dominium*, as power, could only become the human essence, because it was seen as reflecting the divine essence, a radical divine simplicity without even formal differentiation, in which, most commonly, a proposing 'will' is taken to stand for the substantial identity of will, essence and understanding. (Although the voluntarists rejected 'participation' in favour of a theology of will, it is precisely in their treatment of will that a shadow of participation seems to lurk).[22] The later Middle Ages retrieved in a new and more drastic guise the antique connection between monotheism and monarchic unity which was affirmed in Christian tradition by the semi-Arian Eusebius and then became part of both imperial and papal ideology. For this tradition, political substance is grounded in the unity and self-identity of the rational subject, whereas the orthodox Cappadocian Father, Gregory of Nazianzus, had pointed out that it is possible for a single person to be at variance with himself and affirmed that the 'Monarchy' implied by the Christian Trinity was more 'a union of mind, and an identity of motion, and a convergence of the elements to unity'.[23] In the thought of the nominalists, following Duns Scotus, the Trinity loses its significance as a prime location for discussing will and understanding in God and the relationship of God to the world.[24] No longer is the world participatorily enfolded within the divine expressive *Logos*, but instead a bare divine unity starkly confronts the other distinct unities which he has ordained.

It is possible to dispute the precise tenor of the more extreme voluntarist statements – to the effect, for example, that God might will us to hate himself.[25] This dispute, however, is not all important; what matters is the overwhelming nominalist stress on the gulf between God's *potentia ordinata*, his declared will, which is factually, precisely known and serves as the basis for legal covenants with humanity, and his *potentia absoluta*, the infinite power of God which is absolutely unknowable for theology and knowable only formally, for *logic*.[26] No doubt thinkers like Ockham and d'Ailly understood the divine concessions in his revealed will as always in fact expressions of his *misericordia*, but this cannot disguise the point that they derive the *force* of these concessions, our obligation with respect to them (for example, our obligation to keep the natural law, if we wish to merit grace, which God is not *absolutely* bound to grant) from the formalism of a logic about power and rights.[27] Hence already for Gerson, Adam's *dominium* is in no way morally charged, but merely the consequence of Adam's *facultas*, a power greater in scope than other natural powers.[28] Yet because of the radical contingency which d'Ailly and Gerson attributed to the actual *according* of rights and obligations in natural law (as opposed to its formal truth, which holds even for God's absolute power) it is also the case for them that *dominium* is a grant of grace – but a mere *gratia gratis data* [grace freely given] not *gratia gratis faciens* [grace which makes one graceful].[29] This dominance of logic and of the *potentia absoluta* is finally brought to a peak by Hobbes:

> The right of Nature, whereby God reigneth over men, and punisheth those that break his Lawes, is to be derived, not from his creating them, as if he required obedience as of gratitude for his benefits; but from his *Irresistible Power.*[30]

In two ways, therefore, theology helped to determine the new anthropology and the new 'science' of politics. First of all, it ensured that men (*sic*), when enjoying unrestricted, unimpeded property rights and even more when exercising the rights of a sovereignty that 'cannot bind itself', come closest to the *imago dei*. Secondly, by abandoning participation in divine Being and Unity for a 'covenantal bond' between God and men, it provided a model for human interrelationships as 'contractual' ones.[31] It is not an accident that in Molina, the sixteenth-century Spanish Jesuit theologian, an identification of *dominium* with *ius* goes along with the idea that there is an area of 'sheer' human freedom in response to grace, whereas for Thomism even our freedom is mysteriously determined by God, without ceasing to be freedom.[32] Hence it can be seen how theology stakes out *factum* as an area of human autonomy, by making *dominium* into a matter of absolute sovereignty and absolute ownership. *This* is the space in which there *can be* a 'secular', or secular knowledge of the secular – and it is just as fictional as all other human topographies.

For this reason, it would be inadequate to suppose that late medieval and seventeenth-century voluntarism are 'ideological' legitimations of modern absolutism/liberalism regarded as 'really' secular and material processes. On the contrary, theology enters into the very construction of the new realities 'property' and 'sovereignty', helping to create a new space for human manoeuvre. For while it is true that there is a certain recuperation of the Roman patriarchalist notion of possession (though this shows that the *mythos* of the law is also constitutively necessary) *dominium* could only have achieved universal sway in the context of a theology of creation *ex nihilo*, reinterpreted in terms of infinite, uninhibited power.

Yet this is not to say that what mattered was theory and not practice. On the contrary, the new theory was very much a mode of action. By laying claim to a 'plenitude' of quasi-imperial power early in the Middle Ages, the Papacy embarked on a course of adjudication which more and more forced it to decide issues in terms of formal rights. Here, as Max Weber realized, 'modern' rationalization and bureaucratization were already under way.[33] Moreover, this formalization, theologically grounded in the theory of the Papacy, served as an indispensable practical and theoretical resource in a period of increasing inner-ecclesiastical disputes amongst religious orders, between religious orders and the hierarchy and finally between Pope and Pope. Hence one discovers the beginning of modern 'contractual' arrangements in canon law regulations governing the dealings between different ecclesiastical bodies and the start of entrepreneurial practices in the external transactions of certain Cistercian monasteries.[34] Perhaps in reaction to the new, power-seeking reality of monastic ownership, the mendicant Franciscans sought to redefine apostolic poverty with the concept of a *simplex usus facti* [simple use of necessities] in relation to possessions that was in no way a *dominium*.[35] The ultimate response to the radical threat inherent in this notion was not to reassert the Thomist *dominium utile* possessed by Adam even in paradise (a concept perhaps no less radical and also saner than the Franciscan one) but rather to press *dominium* back into the very construction of the subject, by founding the *ius* to anything in a natural or contractual *facultas*.[36] Modern natural rights theory had, as its 'practical' occasion, the need to declare traditional apostolic poverty and paradisal community to be, as it were, 'ontologically impossible'.

In retrospect, it appears that the *simplex usus facti* was itself also the start of a spiritualizing retreat whereby the need to disassociate the Church from formal coercive power turns into a wish also to depublicize it and separate it from any kind of rule whatsoever. The sort of poverty which is not 'a way of owning' but rather a simple 'not owning', is bound to become, in time, just 'poverty of the heart'. This retreat leaves vacant a formal, autonomous space where the Pope 'owns' the Franciscan possessions in the sense that he has the power to dispose of them.[37] Likewise, in the thought of a Franciscan conciliarist like Ockham, the Church as a collectivity has ceased to be a 'mystical' matter in the sacred sense, a corporeity focused on the Eucharist, and 'mystical body' is now so nominalized that Gerson can apply the term to the nation, France.[38] One should note here that conciliarists are on common ground with the papalists in arguing about church rule in terms of purely legal *dominium*, and the difference between a 'hierocratic absolutism' and a 'conciliar contractualism' is really an oscillation within a single *episteme*. Thus in the contrast between Aegidius Romanus's view that *dominium* is first granted by grace to the Pope, and Robert Fitzralph's view that there is a direct grant to each individual, one could say that there is already foreshadowed the contrast within a basic agreement between a Hobbes and a Locke.[39] Furthermore, the unrestricted scope of conciliar authority, especially as allowed and summoned by the Emperor, is no less a harbinger of absolutism than the canonical *plenitudo potestas* [plenitude of power] of the Pope, later invoked by Bodin in his invention of secular sovereignty.[40]

That it was first of all the Church, the *sacerdotium*, rather than the *regnum*, which assumed traits of modern secularity – legal formalization, rational instrumentalization, sovereign rule, economic contractualism – ought to give us pause for thought. In a way, it was the increasing failure of the Church to be the Church, to preserve the 'rule of the Gospel' in the monasteries, and somehow to extend this to the laity (a failure of which the Christian humanist movement was often profoundly aware), which created a moral vacuum which the *regnum* could not easily fill, because ideals of a *purely political* virtue had been half-obliterated by Christianity. In such a vacuum, it seems likely that formal instrumentalism must increasingly reign, and this becomes still more likely after the further ecclesiastical failure which led to a divided Christendom. However, this is a retrospectively interpolated likelihood; one much too easily assumes that this formalism would be inevitably forthcoming. On the contrary, one must suppose that it could only fill the gaps because it was elaborated in theological terms, and by an ecclesiastical practice increasingly ready to redraw the bounds of *regnum* and *sacerdotium* as that between public, coercive power (the hierocratic state) and private faith (the Church as consequently mere 'aggregate'). Hence it may be that the voluntarist theological legacy allowed Europe to survive the Reformation by helping to engender the extraordinary seventeenth-century discovery of a politics that might persist and grow altogether 'without virtue' and without any substantive consensus.

Modern politics as biblical hermeneutics

So far, we have seen how 'the secular' became an artificial space which was sheer *dominium*, or the sphere of the arbitrary. However, modern political science had also to cope with the secular which remained an interval of *time* (the *saeculum*) and with that ecclesial time with which it was concurrent. The new, secular *dominium* could not, according to the totalizing logic of wilful occupation which now mediated transcendence in the public realm, really tolerate a 'political' Church as a cohabitant. Hence it was first necessary, with Marsiglio and Luther, to produce the paradox of a purely 'suasive' Church which must yet involve external state coercion for its self-government.[41] It was then further necessary, with Hobbes, to exclude all 'private' inspiration from politics, by declaring the temporal 'interval' to be for the present 'the all', because the time of inspiration was over, bound and canonized, and its promises now exclusively referred to an eschatological, though literal and material, future.[42] Nevertheless, the surviving presence of the authoritative text of the scriptures within the new space of sovereign power could not be denied. It was even essentially *required* by this power, as the source of a positive divine reconfirmation of the covenantal principle, and for the truth that God stood behind the positive authority of nature. However, one use of the Bible had to be prohibited. This was its truly Catholic use, which accorded interpretative authority to a *tradition* of reading, to readers whose power proceeded not from arms, property or contract, but rather from their socially made available time for reading. It was therefore necessary for the new political science to 'capture' from Catholic Christianity the text of the Bible: to produce a new biblical hermeneutic.

   This is the reason why both Hobbes's *Leviathan* and Spinoza's *Tractatus Theologico-Politicus* comprise a political science and a biblical hermeneutics bound together in one volume. The hermeneutics, just like the politics, possesses both liberal and absolutist aspects which turn out to be really identical.

Just as the absolute State guarantees a measure of private economic freedom and of freedom of choice in things publicly 'indifferent', so, also, for Hobbes and Spinoza, its peace and security ensures some freedom of private opinion. There remains for Hobbes the possibility that the Bible speaks directly to the 'inward man' about the inward man, and he is more than happy that like-minded 'souls' should form 'independent' congregations.[43]

However, it is Spinoza who discovers that the State based on negative freedom and founded by science is also the State which permits the kind of 'free time' where science can flourish. It is not an accident that Spinoza lived for a time within a quasi-monastic community of male intellectuals; the point of freedom of opinion for Spinoza is that uncoerced people will be found to acknowledge the 'geometric' truths about *deus sive natura* [God or nature, as interchangeable] and so achieve blessedness.[44] However, in Spinoza's text, we can unmask this liberal 'freedom of enquiry' which grounds both natural and human science (including biblical criticism) at its very inception. For the promotion of the free time of quasi-monastic science is also the cancellation of the free time of monastic *lectio*. The trouble with Christianity, according to Spinoza, is that it is founded on a private and 'subtle' reading of the scriptures, whose characteristic is a false admixture of theology with philosophy, which takes time to prepare.[45] Spinoza wishes to contrast a 'total' freedom of *opinion* with an absolute unfreedom of public *action*, yet this distinction breaks down, because the traditional Catholic reading is always potentially seditious, always involves an interpretative writing which is an act of denial that all and every decree of the sovereign, must be seen to be obeyed. For decrees which negated the authority of traditional Catholic interpretation could not be obeyed by genuine Catholics, yet a mere 'opinion' against *sovereignty* counts as the action of violating the civic contract.[46] Hobbes, more logically, allows for a public censor who will deal with writings at the precise moment where opinions become actions. Opinion is free so long as it is silent, for Hobbes, but professions of faith may be commanded by *Leviathan*.[47]

If, for Spinoza, the free time of science is to replace the free time of Catholic *lectio*, then it must have as one of its central objects the 'scientific' reading of the Bible, and the possibility of biblical criticism comes close to providing the very definition of genuine 'freedom'. For the presence of a 'scientific' reading of the Bible is publicly checkable in terms of its correspondence to rational method. As Spinoza describes it, this method is universally available and accords hermeneutic priority to the most general, most accessible, most clear and most (supposedly) 'rational' meanings of scripture. Although each free individual confronts the biblical text without traditional mediation, this confrontation paradoxically *irons out* all idiosyncrasy, because the Bible, like nature, is a self-interpreting totality, a world articulated by its own widest and most unambiguous meanings, as is nature by the most general motions.[48] Yet Spinoza's rationalist hermeneutics promoted two principles – both the priority for interpretation of what is 'clear' and in accordance with philosophy, and the priority of what is most general (in the text) which may have some 'meaning' and yet, for us, no truth.[49] To make such meanings without truth only secondary, he must 'relativize' them, confine their significance to a past time and place. Hence only the 'irrational' compels a quest for context, whereas those meanings which accord with 'geometric' truths require no more historical elucidation than do Euclid's theorems.[50] And the 'scientific' content of the Bible is very restricted and precise. As it is not philosophy, it fails to uncover *deus sive natura*, but at least it inculcates obedience to a supreme power, which philosophy knows as the 'one substance'. This, for Spinoza, is the 'different' truth of the Bible, the truth of submission to sovereign will, or the revelation that one can be saved solely through obedience.[51] However, to obey God is to obey sovereign political power, for even in the case of the positive Mosaic dispensation this must have remained private (to Moses) and unknown, had not Moses been established as ruler.[52]

Hence, for Spinoza, 'free scientific enquiry' into the Bible is constituted in two ways. First, through its banishing of the other freedom of *tradition* with its metaphors, idiosyncrasies and unclarities. Secondly, through its always having as *object* of meaning, liberal freedom and absolute power – which are the only things that can be *rationally* acknowledged as *different* to reason. This second, 'absolutist' aspect of Hobbes's and Spinoza's hermeneutics is really rooted in the Lutheran *sola scriptura* which lies behind Spinoza's rule of interpreting scripture 'only through scripture'. Given the problems, as pointed out by the Catholic sceptic François Veron, of how the Bible is to authorize itself, or to provide an exhaustive guide to its own reading,[53] one is bound, in the end, to arrive at either voluntarist–formalist or rationalist solutions, or else a mixture of both. Thus for Spinoza and Hobbes, the Bible provides a kind of rational foundation which 'mirrors' the self-percipience of subjective reason ('read thyself' says Hobbes, and the ruler must 'read in himself', in the regular operations of his passions, 'Man-Kind' in general),[54] and at the same time the Bible can only legitimate itself if it is found to contain within itself the formal principle of submission to established power. It is the destiny of the *sola scriptura* to be so deconstructed as to come to mean that we must believe the scriptures because they are politically authorized.

To derive the modern doctrine of sovereignty and the 'science' of this construct, it was necessary for the new 'single' power to lay claim to the right' to interpret the Bible in all publicly significant respects and to neutralize all other acts of interpretation. This could only be done by promoting a nositivistic concept of revelation, according to which revelation is a 'present' and 'direct' occurrence interrupting the normal self-sufficiency of reason. In consequence, revelation is usually 'private' and its authority is entirely incommunicable *unless* mediated through the contractual artifice of human power: inheritances or actual transfers were equivalent to 'suppositions' of God's will according to d'Ailly.[55] Or else it is public and 'miraculous' – but miracles are at an end. What must not be allowed is for any charisma to attach to *transmission*, other than the formal circumstance of continuity. Above all, it is *allegory* that must be banished, because this traditional mode of interpretation located transcendent significance in the historical–textual syncopes between old and new covenant, and in turn between these, ecclesial time and the *eschaton*.

The traditional 'fourfold', 'spiritual' or 'allegorical' interpretation assumed and demanded a literal, historical meaning: every biblical *signum* [sign] referred to a *res* [thing]. However, it conceived the *res*, as a divine, 'natural' sign, to have a plenitude of meaning which allowed the allegorical edifice to be erected. The literal, historical 'violence' of the *res* in the old covenant effaced itself, not just vertically towards 'eternal' meanings, but horizontally in the direction of the new reality of Christ-*ecclesia* with its charity, mercy and peace.[56] This allowed the fullness of divine authority to devolve on Christ and then on the tropological interpretations of present Christians in the community of the Church. As Henri de Lubac showed, there is a link from the Antiochenes onwards between those who will admit allegory only as a very precise, 'literal' fulfilment of prophecy and those who see the more 'political'-sounding promises of the Old Testament as devolving squarely upon temporal power.[57] Thus William of Ockham's objections to applying promises of universal rule in allegorical fashion to Christ served to preserve a 'literal' and 'historical' picture of Christ's kingly sway as not only non-coercive but also not of this present world at all.[58] Both allegory and 'scholastic' interpolations were banished by Hobbes and Spinoza because they implied an uncontrollable proliferation of Christocentric meaning which inserted divine communication into the process of human historical becoming and must forever escape from sovereign mastery.

This 'capturing of the biblical text' may not seem quite so constitutive for modern politics as voluntarist theology. Nevertheless, it remains latent, and the banishing of traditional *ecclesial* time served to reinforce a commitment to the illusion of spatial immediacy and to the exorcism of the metaphorically ambiguous. Hobbes's *Leviathan* remained truly haunted by the 'Kingdom of the Fairies' who 'inhabit Darknesse, Solitudes and Graves',[59] because the latter's nominality echoes the nominality of *Leviathan* itself, and both 'engines of meaning' are equally arbitrary, although Hobbes's alone claims natural, subjective and even biblical foundations.

Polybian cycles versus ecclesial time

The abstraction of 'polities', the turning of it into a new sort of deductive science based on accident not substance and on 'artificial' and arbitrary causal connections, was the achievement of a voluntarist political theology. Here the secular as an area of human autonomy is actually promoted by a theological anthropology for which human wilfulness, in certain circumstances, guarantees divine origin. This politics is a spatial abstraction out of 'matters of fact' whose 'register', according to Hobbes, is 'civil history', not 'Books of Philosophy' like *Leviathan*.[60] Yet from the Renaissance onwards, another root of a more 'scientific' politics was historicism, which tended to the conclusion that political practice must be adapted to customs, manners, religions and times.

It is false to see in the gradual emergence of a historicist perspective a wholly sudden break with traditional modes of thought. It was not, for example, necessarily incompatible with the allegorical mode of *ecclesial* time; a humanist like Erasmus could easily contain his sense of historical distance within allegory, because the very tension involved in typological figuration between the overarching unity of divine revelation and the difference between its successive phases can actually promote such an awareness.[61] Equally, the traditional perspectives of a 'civic' politics, inherited from Aristotle and the Romans, encouraged a reflection upon the given historical circumstances in which a civic, participatory virtue (rendered redundant by Hobbes) could best flourish.

If there is a break, then it is not rightfully located (as, for example, by J. G. A. Pocock) between a timeless, Christian, hierocratic politics and a 'purely human' temporal and activist politics.[62] This is to fail to see that doing and making remained 'sacralized' for Christian humanists from Salutati onwards, and to forget, also, that monastic institutions were regarded as humanly-instituted *politeiai*.[63] Rather, one must understand what Pocock calls 'the Machiavellian Moment' as the astonishing re-emergence of pagan political and philosophical time no longer as a makeshift, nor a Thomist preparation for grace, but rather as something with its own integrity, its own goals and values, which might even contradict those of Christianity. It is, as Grabmann recognized, a parallel phenomenon to 'Averroism', where philosophical truths may be in contradiction with the truths of the faith.[64]

Here then is another and completely different root of the secular. Yet the Machiavellian secular was not an area of pure neutrality with respect to faith. On the contrary, it only came to exist as the discovery of a new sort of virtue which could not be reconciled with the Christian virtues. If the Hobbesian field of power seems to be constructed by a perverse theology, then the Machiavellian field of power is constructed by a partial rejection of Christianity and appeal to an alternative *mythos*.

The humanist and historicist legacy was no less important for the emergence of modern social theory than the natural rights legacy of liberalism/absolutism. As we shall see in the next chapter, the eighteenth-century Enlightenment was much pre-occupied with an attempt to find a new version of antique virtue. Yet, for all this, there is an important point of convergence between the two currents, which ensures that even the 'civic humanist' tradition is infected by individualism and instrumentalism. This point of convergence is the Roman stoic legacy, which directs attention to a pre-social human being which seeks sociation through an impulse belonging to its own *conatus*, or drive to self-preservation, and which also tends to redefine virtue as knowledge of, agreement with, action within or indifference to, historical *fate*.

In its Machiavellian version, civic humanism sheers off an Aristotelianism compatible with Christianity in favour of a notion of political *prudentia* as instrumental manipulation.[65] At the same time, it subscribes to a *mythos* of fate which takes it outside Christian theological bounds. Whereas, for natural rights theory, conflict is endemic to fallen human nature and this original conflict must be suppressed by a hierocratic counter-violence imposing a fearful peace, for Machiavellianism there is a simultaneous 'heroic' promotion of both internal civic solidarity and external enmity, a mixture which is most gloriously human and yet also most fatefully doomed.[66]

The Machiavellian republic emerges not gradually, through the ironic disciplines of linear time, but suddenly and sporadically in a favourable moment, against the background of an unpredictable *fortuna*.[67] For medieval Christianity, the uncontrollable reverses of fortune represented the deep-seatedness of original sin within an overall providential design, but for Machiavelli *fortuna* is again an antique and impersonal compound of chaos and fatality. The aim of political *virtiù* is to 'use' and surmount, for a time, this fortune. Machiavelli makes historicist, relativizing observations about the chances of different republics, observing that a relatively democratic republic like Venice should not make war, because the capture of foreigners will lead to the introduction of class divisions, whereas a class-divided republic like ancient Rome is well-equipped to make war and expand its population.[68] However, it is not really this relativism which makes Machiavelli a forebear of a modern and non-Christian politics. Rather, it is his explicit *preference* for the Roman option and his return to the etymological root of virtue as 'heroic manliness', to be cultivated supremely in war. This preference encompasses also the view that continued class conflict within the republic is functionally useful in preserving political 'liberty' – the habit of independence.[69] While Machiavelli by no means wishes to deny the validity of 'more moral' social virtues within their proper sphere, it is this option for internal conflict which ensures that a manipulative bias must be dominant among those who rule.

As the republic emerges 'suddenly', so its course is contained within a cyclical time. Machiavelli is heavily dependent upon the late-antique Greek-born writer Polybius, who, standing outside and at the end of Rome, interpreted its history as a progression from the rule of the few through the rule of the one to the rule of the many, culminating, through innumerable private conflicts, in an ultimate loss of aristocratic virtue.[70] Whereas the theological natural rights tradition discovered a 'self-sustaining' world of pure power without virtue, the non-Christian Machiavellian tradition derived from Polybius insisted that human power was a form of virtue, and hence just as historically precarious as the rarity of true virtue. The latter tradition ultimately lies behind the later dialectical and historicist theses of Hegel and Marx, but the eschatological 'resolutions' which these thinkers project depend, as we shall see, on the overlay of another theological programme, that of *theodicy*. For the pure Machiavellian tradition, by contrast, human meaning is 'present' and temporarily glorious – besides this there is only a lapsing back into the unmeaning fatality of history without the republic. The stance of this tradition towards Christianity is ambiguous. On the one hand it often supports a 'civil religion' – Christian or otherwise – which will 'functionally' promote civic solidarity. On the other hand, it attempts to revive, against Christianity, an antique sacrality, producing a new *mythos* of heroes without gods (though still, for Machiavelli, to be rewarded for the exercise of civic virtue by a single God) which is the second aspect of the modern 'secular'.[71]

Both the natural rights and the Machiavellian traditions in 'scientific politics' are heavily presupposed by all later social science. Yet from both a Christian *and* a metacritical perspective (meaning the historicist questioning of 'rational' foundations) it might seem that we have here only to do with heterodoxy on the one hand and the half-return of paganism on the other. For just as the first makes a perfect analysis only of its own artefact, so the second traces correctly the historical fate only of 'heroic man', which is precisely the ethical ontology which Christianity calls into question. In either case, it seems that, from the outset, the 'science of conflict' is not merely one branch of social science but rather that the 'scientific' approach seeks 'to know' power and conflict as ontologically fundamental. It follows that, if Christianity seeks to 'find a place for' secular reason, it may be perversely compromising with what, on its own terms, is either deviancy or falsehood.

Notes

1   See chapters 4 and 5 of John Milbank, *Theology and Social Theory*, Oxford: Blackwell, 2nd edn, 2006.

2   Hugo Grotius, *The Law of War and Peace*, trans. Francis W. Kelsey et al., *Prolegomena*, XI, Indianapolis, IN: Bobbs-Merrill, 1925, pp. 9–30.

3   Thomas Aquinas, *Summa Theologiae*, II.I. Q.94.

4   Robert D. Cumming, *Human Nature and History: A Study of the Development of Liberal Political Thought*, vol. 2, Chicago: Chicago University Press, 1969; Benedict de Spinoza, *A Theological–Political Treatise*, trans. R. H. M. Elwes, New York: Dover, 1951, ch. 12, p. 200.

5   Francis Oakley, *The Political Thought of Pierre d'Ailly*, New Haven and London: Yale University Press, 1964, pp. 17ff, 71–89.

6   Amos Funkenstein, *Theology and the Scientific Imagination*, Princeton, NJ: Princeton University Press, 1986, pp. 327–45; Steven Shapin and Simon Schaffer, *Leviathan and the Air-Pump*, Princeton, NJ: Princeton University Press, 1985.

7   Coluccio Salutati, *De Nobilitate Legum et Medicinae*, Florence: Vallechi, 1947, pp. 40–55, 95.

8   W. Molesworth (ed.), *The English Works of Thomas Hobbes*, vol. 1 'Elements of Philosophy: re First Section Concerning Body', London, 1845; *De Corpore Politico*, IV, p. 126, pp. 73–4, 87. John Wilkins, *Of the Principle and Duties of Natural Religion*, London, 1680, ch. 2, pp. 12–19; John Locke, *Essay Concerning Human Understanding*, Oxford: Oxford University Press, 1975, pp. 515–18, 548, 552, 643.

9   Harvey Cox, *The Secular City*, London: SCM Press, 1967, pp. 21–4.

10   Jurgen Habermas, 'The classical doctrine of politics in relation to social philosophy', in *Theory and Practice*, trans. John Viertel, London: Heinemann, 1974, pp. 41–82.

11   Sforza Pallavicino, *Trattato dello stile e del dialogo*, Rome: Masardi, 1662, ch. 10, pp. 112–18. Jean-Marie Wagner, 'Théorie de l'image et pratique iconologique', *Baroque*, 9–10, 1980, p. 71; Guido Morpurgo Tagliabue, 'Aristotelismo e Barocco', in E. Castelli (ed.) *Retorica e Barocco*, Rome: Bocca, 1955, pp. 119–95.

12 Sforza Pallavicino, *Trattato dello stile* (see Note 11), ch 1 (1662); Nicholas of Cusa, 'On actualised possibility' ('De Possest'), in Jasper Hopkins (ed.) *A Concise Introduction to the Philosophy of Nicholas of Cusa* (1941) pp. 95–7; Nicholas of Cusa, *De Docta Ignorantia*, III, 3; III, 2; Nicholas of Cusa, *The Idiot*, introduced by W. R. Dennes, Los Angeles: California State Library, 1942, p. 11; John Milbank, 'Man as creative and historical being in the theology of Nicholas of Cusa', *Downside Review*, vol. 97, no. 329, October 1979.

13 Giambattista Vico, *On the Most Ancient Wisdom of the Italians*, trans. L. M. Palmer, I i, VII, New York: Cornell University Press, 1988, pp. 45, 97–104, Idem, 'Orazioni Inaugurali', in Paolo Cristofolini (ed.) *Opere Filosofiche*, Florence: Sansoni, 1971, and idem, 'Institutioni Oratorie', in G. Ferrari (ed.) *Opere Complete*, Milan: Società Tipografica, 1852–4; Andrea Sorrentino, *La Retorica e la Poetica di Vico ossia la Prima Concezione Estetica del Linguaggio*, Turin: Bocca, 1927.

14 Cumming, *Human Nature and History* (see Note 4), pp. 129–36; Grotius, *The Law of War and Peace*, Bk. I, V, p. 35; Thomas Hobbes, *Leviathan*, Harmondsworth: Penguin, 1968, Part II, ch. 18, p. 234.

15 Richard Tuck, *Natural Rights Theories: Their Origin and Development*, Cambridge: Cambridge University Press, 1979, pp. 3–20.

16 Aquinas, *ST* II.II. Q.66.a1, a2.

17 Jean Gerson, 'De Vita Spirituali Animae', in P. Glorieuse (ed.) *Oeuvres Complètes: Lectio Tertia*, (Pierre d'Ailly collaborated on this work), Paris: Desclée et Cie, 1962, pp. 141–5.

18 John Locke, *Two Treatises on Government*, Book II, Cambridge: Cambridge University Press, 1967, ch. 5, p. 27.

19 James Tully, *A Discourse on Property*, Cambridge: Cambridge University Press, 1980, p. 58.

20 Hobbes, *Leviathan* (see Note 14), Introduction, pp. 81–3.

21 Ibid., Part II, ch 21, p. 271 (marginal summary).

22 S. E. Ozment, *Homo Spiritualis*, Leiden: E. J. Brill, 1969, pp. 25–6,54–7,83; H. A. Oberman, *The Harvest of Mediaeval Theology*, Cambridge, MA: Harvard University Press, 1963, p. 83.

23 Gregory of Nazianzus, *Theological Orations*, III, 2. E. Peterson, 'Der Monotheismus als politisches Problem', in idem, *Theologische Traktate*, Munich: Hochland, 1951.

24 Etienne Gilson, *Jean Duns Scot*, Paris: Vrin, 1952, pp. 216–306.

25 Oberman, *The Harvest of Mediaeval Theology* (see Note 22), pp. 92–8.

26 Ibid., pp. 51ff.

27 Ibid., p. 44; A. S. McGrade, 'Ockham and individual rights', in Brian Tierney and Peter Lineham (eds) *Authority and Power*, Cambridge: Cambridge University Press, 1980, pp. 149–65; Graham White, 'Pelagianisms', *Viator*, vol. 20, 1989, pp. 233–54.

28 Gerson, 'De Vita Spirituali Animae' (see Note 17), p. 145; Tuck, *Natural Rights Theories* (see Note 15), pp. 25ff.

29 Oakley, *The Political Thought of Pierre d'Ailly* (see Note 5), pp. 66–92.

30 Hobbes, *Leviathan* (see Note 14), Part II, ch. 31, p. 397; Carl Schmitt, *Politische Theologie: Vier Kapitel zur Lehre von der Souveranität*, Munich: Duncker und Humboldt, 1935, pp. 71, 49–66.

31 Oberman, *The Harvest of Mediaeval Theology* (see Note 22), p. 93.

32 Tuck, *Natural Rights Theories* (see Note 15), pp. 50–53; Jacques Maritain, *Integral Humanism*, trans. Joseph W. Evans, Notre Dame IN: Notre Dame University Press, 1968, pp. 17–21.

33 See chapter 4 of Milbank, *Theology and Social Theory* (see Note 1).

34 Randall Collins, *Weberian Sociological Theory*, Cambridge: Cambridge University Press, 1986, pp. 45–76; Oakley, *The Political Thought of Pierre d'Ailly* (see Note 5), p. 109.

35 M. D. Lambert, *Franciscan Poverty*, London: SPCK, 1961, pp. 231–2.

36 William of Ockham, *Opera Politica*, Vol. 3, Manchester: Manchester University Press, 1940, pp. 466–7; Tuck, *Natural Rights Theories* (see Note 15), pp. 22–4.

37 Lambert, *Franciscan Poverty* (see Note 35), pp. 243–4.

38 Oakley, *The Political Thought of Pierre d'Ailly* (see Note 5), pp. 55ff.

39 Ibid., pp. 71–2; Tuck, *Natural Rights Theories* (see Note 15), pp. 22-A.

40 Jean Bodin, *Six Books of the Commonwealth*, trans. M. J. Todey, Oxford: Blackwell, 1964, p. 29.

41 Marsilius of Padua, *The Defender of the Peace*, trans. Alan Gewirth, vol. 2, New York: Columbia University Press, 1956, ch. 6, pp. 24, xix, 274ff.

42 Hobbes, *Leviathan* (see Note 14), Part III, ch. 35, p. 447; Part IV, ch. 44, pp. 629–30; J. G. A. Pocock, 'Time, history and eschatology in the thought of Thomas Hobbes', in idem, *Politics, Language and Time*, London: Methuen, 1972.

43 Hobbes, *Leviathan* (see Note 14), Part IV, ch. 47, pp. 710–11.

44 Spinoza, *A Theological–Political Treatise* (see Note 4), ch. 7, p. 118; ch. 20, pp. 259–60.

45 Ibid., ch. 19, pp. 254–6.

46 Ibid., ch. 16, pp. 205, 212; ch. 19, pp. 247–8, 250, 254; ch. 20, p. 259.

47 Hobbes, *Leviathan* (see Note 14), Part II, ch. 18, p. 233; ch. 26, pp. 332–5.

48 Spinoza, *A Theological–Political Treatise* (see Note 4), ch. 7, pp. 99, 100–103.

49 Ibid., ch. 7, p. 101.

50 Ibid., ch. 7, pp. 103, 112–13.

51 Ibid., ch. 15, pp. 194–8.

52 Ibid., ch. 18, pp. 237–9; ch. 19, p. 247–8.

53 P. K. Feyerabend, *Realism, Rationalism and Scientific Method: Philosophical Papers*, vol. 1, Cambridge: Cambridge University Press, 1981, pp. 35–6.

54 Hobbes, *Leviathan* (see Note 14), the Introduction, pp. 82–3.

55 Oakley, *The Political Thought of Pierre d'Ailly* (see Note 5), p. 81ff.

56 Henri de Lubac, *Exégèse mediévale: les quatres sens de l'écriture* (4 vols.), Paris: Auber, 1964; Gerard E. Caspary, *Politics and Exegesis: Origen and the Two Swords*, Berkeley: California University Press, 1979, pp. 131–2.

57 Lubac, *Exégèse mediévale* (see Note 56), II, II pp. 198–207, 317–28, 249–352.

58 Ockham, *Opera Politico* (see Note 36), I., pp. 16–18, 41–5, 49–52.

59 Hobbes, *Leviathan* (see Note 14), Part IV, ch. 47, p. 713.

60 Ibid., Part I, ch. 9, pp. 147–8. Tito Magri, *De Cive*, Rome: Riuniti, 1981, Introduction, pp. 12–13.

61 Lubac, *Exégèse mediévale* (see Note 56), II, II, pp. 317–28, 249–352.

62 J. G. A. Pocock, *The Machiavellian Moment: Florentine Political Thought and the Atlantic Republican Tradition*, Princeton NJ: Princeton University Press, 1975, pp. 31–80.

63 Salutati, *De Nobilitate* (see Note 7), ch. 31, pp. 218–220 ; J. H. Hexter, *The Vision of Politics on the Eve of the Reformation*, New York: Basic Books, 1973.

64 A. S. McGrade, *The Political Thought of William of Ockham*, Cambridge: Cambridge University Press, 1974, pp. 197–206; Alan Gewirth, 'Philosophy and political thought in the fourteenth century', in *The Forward Movement of the Fourteenth Century*, Columbus: Ohio State University Press, 1981, pp. 183ff.

65 Niccolò Machiavelli, *The Prince*, trans. Henry C. Mansfield, Jnr., Chicago: Chicago University Press, 1985, XXV, pp. 98–9.

66 Niccolò Machiavelli, *The Discourses*, trans. Leslie J. Walker, London: Penguin, 1970, pp. 15, 16, 118–26; Pocock, *The Machiavellian Moment* (see Note 62), pp. 49–80, 156–218.

67 Ibid.

68 Machiavelli, *The Discourses* (see Note 66), 5; 6 (1970) pp. 118–26.

69 Ibid., 4; 4, pp. 113–15.

70 Pocock, *The Machiavellian Moment*, pp. 49–80.

71 Machiavelli, *The Prince* (see Note 65), XXVI, p. 103.

Further reading

Plato, trans. H. N. Fowler, *Euthyphro / Apology / Crito / Phaedo / Phaedrus*, Cambridge, MA: Harvard University Press, 1999.

Derrida, Jacques, 'Plato's Pharmacy', in idem., *Dissemination*, trans. Barbara Johnson, London: Athlone Press, 1981.

Ramus, Petrus, *The Logike* (1574), Leeds: The Scholar Press Ltd, 1966.

Descartes, René, trans. John Cottingham, Robert Stoothoff and Dugald Murdoch (eds), *The Philosophical Writings of Descartes, vol. 1: Discourse on Method,* Cambridge: Cambridge University Press, 1985.

Grotius, Hugo (ed. Richard Tuck), *The Law of War and Peace: Books 1–3*, US: Liberty Fund, Inc., 2005.

Hobbes, Thomas, *Leviathan*, Oxford: Oxford University Press, 2008.

Ferrari, G.R.F., *Listening to the Cicadas: A Study of Plato's Phaedrus*, Cambridge: Cambridge University Press, 1990.

Ratzinger, Joseph and Habermas, Jürgen, *The Dialectics of Secularization: On Reason and Religion*, San Francisco: Ignatius Press, 2007.

Taylor, Charles, *A Secular Age*, Cambridge, MA: Harvard University Press, 2007.

Toulmin, Stephen, *Cosmopolis: The Hidden Agenda of Modernity*, Chicago, IL: University of Chicago Press, 1992.

Ward, Graham, *Cities of God*, London: Routledge, 2000, especially part 1.

Asad, Talal, *Formations of the Secular: Christianity, Islam, Modernity*, Stanford: Stanford University Press, 2003.

Blond, Phillip, *Post-secular Philosophy: Between Philosophy and Theology*, London: Routledge, 1997.

Buckley, Michael, *At the Origins of Modern Atheism*, New Haven: Yale University Press, 1990

—— *Denying and Disclosing God: The Ambiguous Progress of Modern Atheism*, New Have: Yale University Press, 2004.

Funkenstein, Amos, *Theology and the Scientific Imagination from the Middle Ages to the Seventeenth Century*, Princeton, NJ: Princeton University Press, 1989.

Hanby, Michael, *Augustine and Modernity* (Radical Orthodoxy), London: Routledge, 2003.

Tuck, Richard, *The Rights of War and Peace: Political Thought and the International Order from Grotius to Kant*, Oxford: Oxford University Press, 2001.

Special Issue on John Milbank's 'Theology and Social Theory: Beyond Secular Reason', *Modern Theology* 8(4), October 1992.

Questions

1. In the section of her essay entitled 'Reality without depth', Pickstock discusses modernity's reduction of knowledge to the merely phenomenologically given. In other words, things simply *are* as they appear to be, and have no depth beyond our empirical perception. How and why is this important in the unfolding of modernity?

2.   In what ways does modernity 'spatialize' knowledge?
3.   Why is liturgy not 'spatial' in the modern sense?
4.   In what ways does secular culture today exhibit an economy of power?
5.   Is the advent of natural rights itself part of the arbitrary enforcement of peace? (See also Chapter 12 of this Reader.)

PART IV

Christ and gift

Introduction

A theme which is frequently treated within the corpus of Radical Orthodoxy writings is 'gift'. Why is this so important? A number of prominent philosophers have recently written extensively on the nature of gift-giving, notably Jacques Derrida, Emmanuel Lévinas and Jean-Luc Marion. They are provoked in part by the research of the early-twentieth-century French sociologist Marcel Mauss (1872–1950). Central to Mauss's work is the anthropology of gift-giving. He argued that, although gift-giving is central to countless cultures through history, there is no such thing as a 'free' or 'pure' gift. What does this mean? Take the example of giving a birthday present. If I were to buy you a gift on your birthday, you may very well feel obliged to return the favour on my own birthday. We are then concerned not with genuine gifts, but the exchange, or trade, of presents. In fact, Christmas could be seen not as the season of genuine gift-giving, but simply the rampant trade in goods. Mauss argued that there is always a sense of reciprocity in gift-giving; in other words, whenever we give a gift we receive something in return. Even giving to a poor stranger on the street whom one will never see again involves a kind of reciprocity of give-and-take: in response to my charity I receive the contentment and satisfaction of helping someone else.

This may seem like a rather 'academic' discussion of certain anthropological phenomena, but the nature of 'the gift' is crucial politically and theologically. It is crucial politically because the notion of giving seems to present us with the possibility of a radically different economy to the one in which we all constantly engage, namely capitalist trade. Is even gift-giving reducible to the trade of goods? Do we ever really give to each other? Is the gift, as Derrida concluded, impossible? Are we inevitably locked in some kind of capitalist exchange, or are there other forms of human reciprocal relationships?

Meanwhile, the importance of the gift for Christian theology is crucial for reasons which John Milbank spells out at the beginning of *Being Reconciled: Ontology and Pardon*. The Holy Spirit is known as 'the *donum*', the given. The Spirit imparts *gifts* (1 Corinthians 12.1–14, Romans 12.6–8, Ephesians 4.11) and the Church is characterized as the community of the gifted. Creation is the supreme gift of being (*ex nihilo*, 'out of nothing'), and grace is the continual flow of gifts to God's creation. Christ is God's supreme gift of himself in the incarnation, a gift that was finally refused at the crucifixion but given evermore abundantly and salvifically again in the resurrection. Sin is the refusal of God's gift of life and grace, and forgiveness is the gift of re-establishing our relationship with God. However, is the gift in the end reducible to 'trade'? Do Christians behave generously because they believe they will receive something in return, namely eternal life? Are we involved in some kind of exchange with God whereby he grants us life *in exchange* for our worship and praise? Or can there be a genuine theology of the gift which exceeds all secular understandings in unimagined ways and establishes the Church – the community of the gifted – as a radical alternative polity?

The discussion of Christ in the following essays by Milbank and Ward is conducted with these questions concerning the gift very prominently in the background. Does Christ genuinely *give* himself for our salvation? In what sense is that gift 'perfect' and 'once for all'? How does Christ establish again the possibility to receive, rather than refuse, the gifts of God, and therefore reconcile us to God?

Characteristically, Milbank addresses these questions by focussing on what is unique, or, in this case, *exceptional*, about Christ. This is a crucial aspect of Milbank's project, and that of Radical Orthodoxy more generally: the delineation of what is unique and irreducible in Christian theology. In a close examination of the passion narratives, we find that it is precisely the *exceptional* nature of Christ's trial and crucifixion which lend the gospel accounts their plausibility. Yet this is not just an historical exceptionality; the sacrifice of Christ uniquely puts an end to sacrifice and establishes again forgiveness in the form of our acknowledging that we *are* as a gift of God, and that our response is to acknowledge this gift Eucharistically (in thanksgiving) in the form of liturgical praise. Why is this reciprocity between God and humanity not a 'trade'? Because that which God gives is also at one and the same time our ability to respond to his gift in freedom. Because God has no need of what he is offered by humanity, and because humanity is nothing aside from God's donation of life, there can be no 'ratio' or 'common measure' (such as money) which can establish a proportion between our offering to God and what God gifts to humanity. So this cannot be trade in the strict sense, but only an expression of divine love – of charity.

Graham Ward's essay 'The schizoid Christ' is also indicative of themes which characterize his wider work. In a number of essays Ward has been anxious to stress that Christology cannot be reduced to the investigation of the life of a Jewish man who lived 2000 years ago (resisting the impact of the modern 'Quest for the historical Jesus' movement in New Testament scholarship and the associated 'turn to the subject' in philosophy). Why? Because, as Ward points out elsewhere, the identity of Christ, his corporeality, is in a state of constantly ambiguous flux through the Gospels and is continually displaced to 'fill all in all' (Ephesians 1.23): Transfiguration, walking on water, displacement into the Eucharist at the last supper, crucifixion, deposition, resurrection, ascension, the Church as Christ's body. In this particular essay, Ward, through a close reading of the healing of the haemorrhaging woman (Mark 5.24–34), is concerned with the *dynamic* aspects of Christ's *corporeality* (touch, flows of blood and power which figure Christ's kenotic yet 'pleromatic' or abundant self-donation) which contrast with the static sense of, for example, the purely historical figure of Jesus. Ward here provides a theology of the body which begins with the body of Christ. Like Milbank, Ward uses the Christology of the gift to resist a view of gift (he focuses particularly on the French philosopher Emmanuel Lévinas) as one-way and non-reciprocal, that is, not to do with exchange. For Ward, this cannot be so, for that which I give (that of which I am emptied – *kenosis*) can only be that which I have already received. Why? Because as creaturely, I am, in myself, nothing. So Ward concludes: 'That sociality … is only possible within an economy of the gift in which I am constituted in the transit of plenitudinous grace.' *Transit* is the key: to be human (and, crucially, *embodied*), as Christ revealed, is to be that through which God's grace *flows*, thereby remaining as *gift* and not being rendered a possession.

Chapter 7

John Milbank

Christ the exception

Crucifixion

I

E vil is to be overcome by forgiveness. As likewise is violence ... Yet just as violence is convertible with evil, but distinguished from it according to our *modus cognoscendi* (but not by any formal distinction), so also there is a distinction to be made by us between escape from violence and escape from evil, even though they are two entirely coinciding aspects of the same process, like the front and the back of a depthless strip.

Forgiveness restores the Good. But in another aspect, X, it restores peace. What is this other aspect? If forgiveness endures and compensates for evil, X suffers violence without violent opposition, and yet at the same time positively opposes violence with a counter-violence to violence as such, which positively reasserts peace [see the discussions in Chapter 2 of John Milbank, *Being Reconciled*]. X has no obvious name, but lies somewhere between passion and rule, exercising at once both victimhood and sovereignty [see Chapters 3 and 4 of Milbank, *Being Reconciled*].

It follows that the name of X might be cruciformity, or *imitatio Christi*. As incarnate, as we saw in Chapter 4 [of *Being Reconciled*], Christ forgave, in the sense of offering again to humans, as a gift, the possibility of their mutual reconciliation. But also, as persecuted and crucified, Christ overcame violence and restored peace. He first instituted and fulfilled X as indeed the *via crucis*, which involves in its anti-chiasmus both violence and suffering, as well as evil and negation.

But we have already spoken of sovereign victimhood. Then what is really the missing aspect?

One must recall the issue of violence and visibility. Privation theory exposes the hidden violence of autonomous self-assertion because it reads violence as negation of the infinite positive plenitude of the Good. The process of forgiveness carries out just this reading, and performs its implications.

But as we saw in Chapter 2 [of *Being Reconciled*], privation theory also calls for a discrimination amongst apparent violence: some of this truly is deprivation of the Good, and therefore also violent. Some of it is not, and therefore is not, after all, violent. The theory of radical evil, by contrast, which tends to be sheerly phenomenological, accepts the idea of a naive intuition of visible violence, and therefore defines violence merely as intrusion, as an obvious impinging upon the terrain of 'the other'. But since life consists of nothing but heteronomy, this opens the way to the terrorism of political correctness, which of course serves the purposes of liberal capitalism and the liberal state and encourages their new turn towards terroristic Fichtean policing of supposed 'natural right'. These theorists, as Alain Badiou argues in his *Ethics*, propound an ethics without politics which in fact subserves the worst politics. If violence is visible interference with the other, then it can be 'ethically' judged, without advertance to collective political purposes, questions of just distribution and so forth.

But where violence must be discriminated, there one has always a political dimension to the ethical. The aspect of violence, more obviously than the aspect of evil, concerns the realm of *visible* disturbance, and therefore the public, political realm. Evil is found in an occulted violence and so lies more within an 'interior', even if this private aspect is also, in the end, also political. But violence displays an apparent evil which seems to have the positivity of destruction, even though discrimination declares some of this 'destruction' not to be so, and furthermore decrypts real destruction as pathetically negative after all.

The 'evil' aspect, and its remedy, forgiveness, therefore are relatively ethical. But the 'violent' aspect and the *via crucis*, are relatively political, even though there is no true ethics without the polis, and no true polis without the idea of the Good. Not only is violence more visible, and in consequence more political than evil, it is also more political because here apparent violence must be collectively judged in terms of evil, whereas in the case of evil, an occulted 'private' evil (as negation) must be covertly exposed by the heroic individual operating in the back alleys of the night, also as violence.

As is well known, many apparently innocent visible processes – of the economy, of the bureaucracy, of information – are in fact violent. Inversely, many appearances of violence, such as the loud jangle of church bells, or the thrusting of a political demonstration upon people's attention, or the forceful closing down of a factory or an information network, are in fact peaceful. Both these statements are of course judgements: there is violence in one case and peace in another in relation to the justice of the ends pursued – not as extrinsic means, but as embryonic ends (this has nothing to do with ends justifying means). But this is the point: claims to see violence are always diagnostic, in relation to accounts of the political, collective Good; the apparently purely 'ethical' option of the Levinasians and advocates of radical evil (excepting Žižek here) only disguises the judgement they make in terms of their espousal of political and economic liberalism.

Therefore we need to supplement an account of forgiveness with an account of the *via crucis*. It has already been argued that forgiveness cannot be handled merely ontologically as an eternally immanent 'given' possibility, but is rather a possibility that has only arrived in history as the actuality of *an event*, which transforms the way things 'are'. This is the event of the Incarnation which revises finite ontology and more radically discloses that eternal *esse* was, from eternity, also a happening.

This event, as we also saw in the last chapter [of *Being Reconciled*], concerns the advent of the sovereign victim. But so far we have explored this notion more according to its esoteric, ethical, 'private' and ontological aspect (concerning the relations of time to eternity). This must now be supplemented by an exploration of its exoteric, political, public and historical eventual aspect – remembering always that the ethical and the political are distinct only for our *modus cognoscendi*.

What should this exploration involve? Above all a double discrimination. First of all a discrimination of the violence undergone by Christ – in what sense was he subject to violence, if at all? Who was the violent agent here? What brought about his death?

Secondly, an echoing of the discrimination Christ himself performed. If he did suffer violence, then what political project was he positively negating, and what other political project was he positively recommending? ('Political' here extends beyond the notion of legitimated violence to that of the peaceful order of the *Civitas Dei*.) What did he see and thereby suffer as violence? What did he envisage instead as perpetual peace?

II

So why did Jesus die? The Gospels present us with a very confusing and complex account. Jesus deliberately returned to Jerusalem, although he seems to have known that this was to court danger. He was 'betrayed' by one of his disciples, although it is unclear why this betrayal was necessary, nor in what it consisted. After his betrayal and seizure, he was, according to the synoptic accounts, arraigned before the Sanhedrin, who accused him of denouncing the temple, of disregarding the law and of claiming to be the Son of God. Then, however, the high priest and elders handed

Jesus over to Pilate, the Roman governor, asserting that he was a rebel who had set himself up as a king of the Jews against Caesar. Pilate subjected Jesus to enigmatic and ironic questioning, and, according to St Luke's Gospel, in turn handed him over to Herod, the Greek king of Judea and a Roman puppet. Herod could find him guilty of nothing and returned him to Pilate (Luke 23).

In an obscure decision, Pilate is then presented as having at once condemned Jesus to death in deference to the crowd's wish to release Barabbas rather than Jesus, and at the same time as having 'handed Jesus over' to the Jerusalem mob to do what they liked with: 'but Jesus he delivered up to their will. And as they led him away they seized on Simon of Cyrene' (Luke 23: 25–6). Yet this 'doing what they like' took the form of appropriating the Roman judicial punishment of crucifixion: 'Pilate said to them, "Take him yourselves and crucify him, for I find no crime in him"' (John 19: 6). In Matthew's Gospel, Pilate elaborately washes his hands before the crowd and declares 'I am innocent of this man's blood: see to it yourselves' before 'delivering' Jesus to be crucified (Matthew 27: 24–6). Even Mark's Gospel says, ambiguously, that 'Pilate, wishing to satisfy the mob ... delivered him to be crucified' (Mark 15: 15). Comparison with Matthew's version plausibly suggests that this means indeed that Pilate 'handed over' Jesus to the mob. Given this near unanimity, there is really no clear reason, as we shall further see below, to assume that the Gospel writers merely invented the role of the crowd in order to exonerate the Romans. It is true that in Mark (15: 16) it is the soldiers not the crowd who lead Jesus away, but this does not render impossible a joint mob–military action, as Mark's 'deliver' may indicate. By now we should know that Mark's brevity is no necessary sign of greater historicity, and is as literary a matter as the other Gospels' relative prolixity.

Who then really killed Jesus and why? And why did Jesus submit to this? The only consistent thread in these narratives is that Christ was constantly handed over or abandoned to another party. Judas betrayed his presence; the disciples deserted him; the Sanhedrin gave him up to Pilate; Pilate in turn to Herod; Herod back to Pilate; Pilate again to the mob who finally gave him over to a Roman execution, which somehow, improperly, they co-opted. Even in his death, Jesus was still being handed back and forth, as if no one actually killed him, but he died from neglect and lack of his own living space.

Given this strange account, the overwhelming response of modern New Testament scholars is to doubt its veracity, to such a degree that little of the Passion narrative is now seen as plausibly historical. In this chapter, however, I want to suggest a perspective from which the very strangeness of the features I have mentioned may in fact present some warrant of verisimilitude (at the very least). But at the same time this new ground for historical plausibility casts light upon the universal significance of Christ's death, as claimed by the first Christians.

Why are the Gospel accounts today viewed with so much scepticism? There are two main reasons, one critically respectable, the other less so. The first reason is that the events presented appear utterly *exceptional* and even implausible in the light of what we know from sources other than the Gospels. Most striking is the fact that nowhere else do we read of the purported Passover custom whereby the governor of Judea offered to release a prisoner every year. There is no mention of this in rabbinic sources, nor in Josephus, who was favourable to the Romans, and likely to have mentioned any instances of their mercy. Furthermore, all we know of Pilate independently of the Gospels suggests that he was a tyrannical ruler, not given to making concessions. Scholars also wonder exactly how early Christians could have been privy to private proceedings that took place between Pilate and Jesus in the Praetorium.[1] A few of them have in addition questioned the plausibility of the proceeding before the Sanhedrin: would Jesus really be thought to have transgressed Jewish law? Did he qualify as a blasphemer, since blasphemy for the Jews at this time was pronunciation of the secret name of God? If the Sanhedrin condemned Jesus, then would not they have stoned him to death, since there is evidence that they still had the power, even under Roman jurisdiction, to carry out this sentence, and in some cases did in fact do so? Scholars (such as A.N. Sherwin-White) who defend the plausibility of the Sanhedrin's condemnations and handing-over to the Roman authorities, nonetheless almost universally reject the idea that the final executioner was the mob stirred up by the chief priests and elders.[2] The ground for this rejection is twofold: first of all the lack of evidence for the Passover amnesty as already mentioned; secondly, the fact that Jesus died a Roman judicial death, which renders Pilate's real and metaphorical hand-washing either implausible or else more insincere than the Gospels seem to allow.

So the first reason for scepticism finds the events of the Passion to be so unusual as to render them most probably, in the main, ahistorical. However, if writers have embellished what is clearly intended (as scholars still allow) to be a historical account, then one must ask why? This is also a historical question. The main answer today given is that the four evangelists, writing at a time when the Christian community had become clearly separate from the Jewish one and wished to find an undisturbed place for itself within the Roman empire, desired to downplay the Roman involvement in the death of Jesus, and exaggerate the involvement of the Jewish authorities. The implication of this view is that Jesus was indeed seen as a dangerous political agitator by the Romans, and was executed as such; not, indeed, as the leader of a zealot party – or else why should the disciples not have been arrested also? – but certainly as a potential focus of popular dissent either from Rome or from the established Jewish authorities, which for Rome could be almost equally inconvenient.[3] Or, of course, from both authorities. It is notable that in St John's Gospel the high priest Caiaphas is presented as fearing that Jesus could become just such a focus, and eventually incite a terrible Roman reaction (John 18: 14).

The second reason for scepticism concerning the Passion narratives also concerns the issue of false attribution of blame to the Jews, but is much more driven by a presumption that the early Christians were anti-Semitic, and that any continued attribution of responsibility for Jesus's death to any Jews in Jerusalem at this time is a perpetuation of such an attitude. In particular, any taking-seriously of the role of the mob is seen as politically reprehensible.[4] However, even if one profoundly sympathizes with the underlying motivations for this attitude, there is no logic in any automatic presumption of anti-Semitism as constitutive of Christianity as such, and still less logic in the view that segments of a people too often victims cannot in certain instances have been themselves the persecutors. Therefore we are returned to the first reason for scepticism: the sheer atypicality of the events which the Gospels narrate.

It is possible, I think, to whittle away the plausibility of this first reason, before stating my positive reason for believing what the Gospels tell us. There is, first of all, a general methodological point to be made, and secondly, a series of considerations about details. The general point is that arguing against exceptions primarily as exceptions is highly dubious historiographical procedure. It is only resorted to when there is a significant lack of confirmation that an event did in fact occur. For, in point of fact, well-attested and yet extraordinary and unpredictable events do occur: as I first wrote this chapter I was just receiving news that the World Trade Center in New York and a part of the Pentagon in Washington had been destroyed by hijacked aircraft. The immediate aftermath of this event illustrates the truth that we are often far more certain that something has happened, than why it has happened. The surprisingness and often inexplicability of precisely the most outstanding events renders them the most typical events – since an event, to be recordable, and so to be an event, must to some degree be an exception to 'the normal course of events', for which in reality only 'the course' (the instance of a particular culture, etc.) is really an 'event' in human history. This constitutive exceptionality of the event means that the most event-like events are necessarily surprising and very often inexplicable, since they exceed the normal expectations of causality. Indeed one can go further: given the complexity of human reasoning, human lack of reason and the contagion of mass behaviour, it may be true to say that the biggest events – those that most shape our experience and understanding – occur literally without sufficient causation. Causal explanation of, for example, the First World War, runs the danger of seeing it as, with hindsight, an inevitable event. In reality it is much more plausibly seen in Tolstoyan terms as arriving according to the gathering pace of its own mad momentum. There were preceding occasions, for this as for other greatest and most event-like events, but no causes in the strict sense.[5]

Of course, where events are insufficiently well attested, then the problem is not simply one about cause and occasion, but a fuller reconstruction both of what took place and of what led up to this taking-place. In the absence of much evidence, one has to resort to what is known in general about the circumstances in which the events are alleged to have taken place, in order to establish analogies and plausibilities and so forth. Nevertheless, one should only do so in a tentative spirit, and should try to discriminate between more-or-less possible exceptions on the one hand, and more-or-less-impossible exceptions on the other, while remembering that this exercise is itself more impossible than possible, given the foregoing methodological caution regarding the exceptional character of all events as such.

This caution is especially pertinent in the case of the Gospels; one could argue that here it is most of all pertinent. For the Gospels themselves assume that the events they are describing are unique and remarkable, even that they are the most exceptional and singular events that have ever occurred. In addition, they are also held to be the most important and the most meaningful; so much so that they are now to be regarded as the frame of reference within which everything else is to be understood. So here we have a purported hyperbolic instance of an event which is so exceptional and singular that it vastly exceeds, as effect, its own occasioning causes: just as Mary's fiat allowed but did not cause the Incarnation – not even in any degree (given that she could do nothing *in addition* to God) and John the Baptist's baptizing of Jesus allowed but did not cause the first hypostatic descent of the Holy Spirit at 'the down-rusher's ford' (the expression is David Jones's in his *Anathemata*). There can be no question that hyperbolic, uncaused events do occur, nor can one rule out a priori the possibility of a supreme instance of such an event, which renders all other events only instances within its own down-rushing course.

The claim that such a supreme instance has arrived in actuality and therefore belongs to real (not merely logical) possibility is an aspect of the claim that God has become incarnate. It follows, in consequence, that liberal criticism of the Bible is in double methodological peril; not only does it tend to rule out as historical what is different and unprecedented, it also can only contest orthodoxy by begging the very question that is at issue between itself and orthodoxy: namely, did Christ constitute an absolutely unique exception? The very 'evidence' which orthodoxy can cite for this claim, although it is indeed without genuine evidential warrant in a strict scientific sense, is seen by liberalism as evidence against the claim, but equally without genuine evidential warrant. (Of course liberal criticism veers also into the opposite error, when it dismisses any Gospel event described in terms of typological repetition as *deficient* in the exceptionality that guarantees real historicity – here one makes the opposite methodological rejoinder: no entirely unique event can register with human beings.)

Even if one were to set aside the claims of orthodoxy to recognize in the life of Christ a hyperbolic and final event (announcing already the end of history), one would still be left with undeniable evidential warrant for the instance of an event in the strong sense of something unique and unprecedented. Without question, the Gospels constitute, if not the record, then at least some sort of trace of the arrival of, an in many respects entirely new sort of religious institution, practice and belief. The danger, then, for liberal criticism, if it loses its sense of discriminatory balance, is that it will so disallow all that is exceptional in the Gospel narratives that it will merely have postponed the problem of manifest exception for the consideration of the historical fact of the Church, and in such a way that the Christocentric aspect of this phenomenon will have to be implausibly played down or evaded – a mistake which is as great as trying to conceive of a Christ-event which prescinds from the always-already given presence of the reception of Christ by the Church, beginning with Mary and the disciples. (Here also the issue arises of why one should treat Josephus and rabbinic texts as independent background sources, and not accord the Gospels the same status; is this to privilege official and established literature over insurrectionary and emergent voices?)

So much, then, for the first, general methodological point. As for the details, the objections cited are perhaps less convincing than is usually imagined. Regarding Pilate's known character, bread and circuses were proverbially never adverse to Roman tyranny, and the idea that a cruel and non-concessionary ruler would never have been obliged to let the populace have their way in certain circumstances is simply naive. As to conversations that could not have been overheard, there is simply no way of knowing what may or may not have leaked out of the Praetorium, but the main point is that one must allow for ancient historiographical conventions of reconstructed dialogue which by no means betray a cavalier disrespect for historicity. With respect to Jesus's infringements of Jewish law, certainly some but not others of the Pharisees at the time would have objected to things like Sabbath-breaking; from Philo we know that blasphemy could be extended to any impious invocation of God; it is *not* the case that calling oneself 'Son of God' or 'Messiah', or invoking the coming of the 'Son of Man' were never seen as blasphemous – it depended on context and fortune. Certainly Jesus's metaphorical threats to the temple might have been taken non-figuratively and regarded gravely.[6] One can also imagine that if Jesus claimed to be the Son of God identifying himself with a pre-existent emanation of divinity like wisdom or the eternal law or the *Logos* (and we have no real grounds to doubt this, outside the bias against exception) this extraordinary claim would have met with ordinary judicial hostility.

When it comes to the executive powers of the Sanhedrin, then the scholarly consensus now is that they did not enjoy undisputed and autonomous powers to put to death; instances where they did fell during vacancies in the procuratorship and otherwise (as Simon Légasse notes) Josephus records two cases where, indeed, the Sanhedrin tried to get self-appointed prophets executed by Rome for essentially Jewish offences – one of them another man named Jesus. Sherwin-White explained how, as wielder of *imperium*, Pilate would have been able to try the crimes of non-Roman citizens by a process of personal *cognitio* that was *exceptional* to the regular *ordo iudiciorum publicorum*, without jury-courts or specific criminal laws and with absolute personal licence as to the punishments that could be meted out. (This process was significantly only allowed at the margins of empire; it was not permitted at the centre even for the Emperor himself – revealing the paradox that the optimum arbitrary power of the centre only appears at the boundary.) Nevertheless, both the presence of accusers and the answering of a charge were normally demanded: Pilate's demurral and then deferral to the Sanhedrin in the face of Jesus's silence is highly plausible. Yet if *cognitio extra ordinem* could easily extend by fiat to the recognition of alien religious and other charges in the interests of good order and appeasement, it does not seem to have been the case that it allowed powers of sovereign (rather than mandated) sentencing and capital execution themselves to be alienated. 'Pliny', says Sherwin-White, 'did not understand the charges against the Christians in Pontius, but he condemned them to a Roman execution without hesitation.'[7] It is then broadly agreed that there is little reason to doubt at least *this* 'handing-over' procedure.

This still leaves us with the problem of the Passover amnesty. Before discussing this, however, let us consider briefly the historical explanation given for the evangelists purported falsification of history. Is it really plausible? Certainly it is highly speculative, because we do not really know whether the synoptic Gospels were written by Christians with a clear and distinct sense of their separation from Jewry. In addition, even John's Gospel, let alone the Synoptics, still attributes a great deal of blame to Pilate, and indeed presents him as cynical, sceptical, vacillating and submissive to the mob, rather than as tolerant and concessionary. (The Gospel writers fall well short of the later occasional elevation of Pilate to a *figura* of the Church, and in the Coptic case, to sainthood.) If Rome was to be exonerated, could not the job have done better? One can protest here that the Gospel writers could not evade the undeniable fact of a Roman execution, but there remains their superfluous presentation of Pilate as uncertain (especially in Luke), as cruelly playful (especially in John) and as a witness to the truth merely despite himself. (By contrast, the apocryphal *Report of Pilate the Procurator Concerning our Lord Jesus Christ*, and other similar fragments, presents Pilate as writing to Tiberius Caesar concerning the positive evidence of Jesus's astonishing powers.) Most of all it is striking that no attempt was made to present Pilate as indeed simply acceding to the Sanhedrin's wishes, even though the idea that Christ died under the Jewish law is expressed within Pauline theology and is semi-implied by the Gospels themselves. Notably, the Gospel writers do *not* present the Romans as executors of Jewish sovereign will, and in this respect they accord with what we know of circumstances in the technically 'unfree' city of Jerusalem under the Roman jurisdiction.

If the evidence of a desire to exonerate Rome is after all not so clear, then what of the evidence for anti-Semitism? Again it is far weaker than usually claimed. Certainly John's Gospel speaks of 'the Jews' in general as an actor, but this may reflect only the distance from Jewry of a Hellenistic or Hellenized Christian community. But even if the anti-Semitism of John's Gospel is allowed, no general case is thereby established, since the Synoptics report basically the same structural feature of the Passion proceedings – that is to say, a handing-over by accusing Jewish authorities to the Romans, and a later semi-handing-over by Pilate to the mob. A recent study by Jon A.

Wetherby of the attitude of Luke-Acts towards the Jews concludes that there is no evidence of anti-Semitism, and that these books specifically make the leaders and people *in Jerusalem* in part responsible for Jesus's death and certainly not the Jews as a whole.[8] Indeed Luke (if it is he) in Acts is careful to record the defence of Paul by some Pharisaic scribes (Acts 23: 9). Wetherby also notes that Luke is, amongst the Gospel writers, especially concerned to portion out the guilt also to Pilate, Herod (a non-Jew) and the Roman soldiers. What Luke stresses is the division of Israel with regard to Jesus, just as in Acts he stressed the division of the whole of the known world. Of course the idea that all nations are complicit in the death of Jesus, just as this very event brings all nations together (Acts 2) is in Luke a theological theme, but this does not prove that it is not also a meditation upon the actual course of events. As to his recording in Acts of repeated Roman defences of Paul against some Jewish elements, since Paul was a Roman citizen and the case in question would have been seen by the Romans as a Jewish sectarian dispute, there is little reason to ascribe this repetition to theological motives *rather* than the protractedness of the proceedings which Paul really underwent.

One can conclude that if Luke evinces no especial drive to blame the Jews, nor any in exonerating the Romans (which is unlikely, given his evident concern for the distressed and marginalized), then the shared structural features of the Passion procedure cannot really be accounted for by ideological motivations. In that case, at the very least, we cannot be so sure that the Passover amnesty is a typological construct based, for example, on the freeing of Jehoiachin in II Kings and Jeremiah, or written as a fictional fulfilment of Isaiah 53's prophecy concerning the suffering servant taking the punishment of the criminal upon himself. Even sceptical critics allow that 'Barabbas' is not an invented name, and that his release, if not under a regular amnesty, and not as a result of a plebiscitory choice, may well have occurred.[9]

These positions are adopted by Simon Légasse in the most recent and extensive book-length treatment of the trial of Jesus, portions of which have been translated by John Bowden for SCM Press. Much of what I have contended up till now is not so far removed from what Légasse is prepared to accept. However, along with the general consensus, he denies the historical plausibility of the Passover amnesty, the large role of the mob, and the dispensing with responsibility by Pilate. In doing so he considers the 1965 work of the Belgian classicist Jean Colin, entitled *Les Villes litres de l'orient Gréco-Romain et l'envoi du supplice par acclamations populaires*.[10] Unusually, Colin defended the crucial role of the mob in the Passion narrative. He showed that in the 'free cities' of the Oriental empire, the Romans dealt with the fierce Greek sense of legal autonomy by a practice known as *epiboesis*, whereby people could be condemned and executed by popular vote and reclamation (including instances of preference between two people accused). He cites the later example of the Christian Attale of Pergamon, who, although a Roman citizen, was thrown to the beasts in the arena by the Roman governor to be 'agreeable to the multitude'.[11] Colin suggested that precisely *epiboesis* was resorted to the case of Jesus. Légasse, however, summing up the general consensus of the New Testament academic guild's reaction to this book, declares Colin's appeal to the Greco-Oriental rather than to the Jewish or Roman world to be irrelevant. He points out the obvious: Jerusalem was not a free city, and there is absolutely no evidence of this legal usage being deployed by Palestine. Naturally though, Colin knew this, and Légasse does not discuss the case he made out in its despite.

This was as follows: Pilate is known to have been in Caesarea, a free city, where he could have become acquainted with the practice; Herod must certainly have known of the practice from the Decapolis, the ring of free cities surrounding Galilee, where Herod held sway. Colin suggests that we take seriously Luke's Gospel's presentation of Pilate as being at his wit's end when faced with Jesus; in such a state he might have resorted to an alien practice that was nonetheless countenanced within the *imperium*. Perhaps he thought of the idea himself; more plausibly, suggests Colin, it was suggested to him by the Greek Herod during the episode, recorded only by Luke, when Jesus is shuttled to and fro between the two Roman jurisdictions. Here it is notable that Pilate first hands Jesus over to Herod because he realizes that Jesus is a Galilean. Alternatively, one might claim that Luke – from the free city Antioch – fabricated the whole episode from his experience. This conclusion, however, conflicts with the structural consonance of the four Gospel accounts, and the generally accepted historical secondariness of the Lukan version.

Once again, therefore, the issue concerns the question of an exception. In the face of the problems raised by Jesus's exceptionality, did Pilate resort to a locally exceptional legal procedure? It seems that one can only conclude that Colin's solution is not impossible, and perhaps more plausible than the now orthodox ones. As to the question of the supposed Passover custom of amnesty, it is perhaps significant that Luke *does* not mention a custom, which would be consistent with the notion that this release of Barabbas was *also* an exception; taken along with the Herod episode, this may imply that Luke's account is the most accurate one. (Nonetheless, given the paucity of available evidence, the silence of Josephus, Philo and rabbinic sources concerning the amnesty custom is not really conclusive, and one has no real warrant to doubt the witness of the other Gospels.)

Another peculiarity of the Lukan account is the absence of the crowd welcoming Jesus into Jerusalem on Palm Sunday: at Luke 19: 36 it is the *disciples* who spread their garments. This might appear to betoken a Lukan bias against the mob, which would compromise his witness. However, Luke equally and inversely is unique in his recording of support for Jesus by 'a great multitude of the people' *after* he had been condemned by the mob, and they had led him away (Luke 23: 27). So here again Luke is the most notably even-handed of the Gospel writers, perhaps out of historical fairness as well as symbolic appropriateness. According to him, a large number of people condemned Jesus and a large number of people wept for him.

This may seem to be all that one can really say on this topic. However, there is a way of going further, of increasing the plausibility of Colin's solution by showing that precisely *exceptionality* was paradoxically typical of Roman rule in general.

III

Although *epiboesis* was confined to the Eastern empire, a somewhat parallel phenomenon was recorded in the case of Rome itself and Roman law in general by Pompeius Festus, the late antique grammarian. In his treatise *On the Significance of Words,*[12] he tells us that, after the secession of the plebs in Rome, it was granted to the plebeians to have the right to pursue to the death (singly or collectively it is implied) someone whom they have as a body condemned. Such an individual was declared *homo sacer* [sacred man], and his irregular death was not exactly homicide, nor punishment, nor sacrifice, since, unlike regular capital punishment, it had to be carried out without purification rites. Such a person was *sacer*, simply in the sense of cast out, utterly abandoned, a sense of the word which may be more ancient than the connotation 'sacred', deriving from the specific sending forth which is sacrifice. This is the conclusion of the Italian philosopher and scholar of late antique philology Giorgio Agamben, in his recently translated book, itself entitled *Homo Sacer.*[13]

Agamben argues that there are isomorphic parallels between the recorded *homo sacer* procedure and other Roman practices: first of all, the *patria potestas*, or absolute right of the Roman father over the life and death of his son. One should note here that the law described by Deuteronomy 21: 18–21 presents a certain analogy to the *patria potestas*: here a drunken and gluttonous son who habitually disobeys his father and mother is to be handed over by both parents to the elders at the gate of the city, who in turn hand him over to all the men of the city to be stoned outside the gate. This exceptional action is deemed to be purgative in its effect; though whether it was ever actually effected is debatable. Nevertheless, such a concept may have provided a kind of residual background for a fusion of cultural horizons in terms of the kind of enacted exception which (I shall further argue below) was the death of Jesus.

The second parallel claimed by Agamben is the 'devotion' of oneself and one's enemies to a sacrificial death offered to the gods of the underworld in battle. If these enemies were not killed, then simulacra of them had to be offered instead, while the dedicated enemies from thenceforwards occupied a kind of ontological no-man's land, having no place amongst either the living or the dead. A similar thing was true, Agamben argues, of a dying Roman emperor, whose real life was also transferred to a simulacrum, ensuring the fiction of uninterrupted sovereignty. Here again, there are certain Israelite parallels which could have formed the basis for a hermeneutic fusion. Robertson Smith noted (and in this case Agamben notes also) that the Old Testament speaks of a dedication (*herem*) unto utter destruction, and avoidance on pain of death (that is, contagion of such dedication) of a person, place or thing so dedicated or 'anathematized' (Micah 4: 13: 'You shall beat in pieces many people, and devote their gain to the Lord').[14]

Of all these parallels, the closest and most crucial is the *patria potestas*. For this power was absolute: to kill a son was to kill what naturally belonged to you – it was not murder, nor execution, nor sacrifice. And, upon this mythical and real foundation, Roman notions of political sovereignty, unlike those of ancient Greece, were themselves founded.

Agamben characterizes all these legal instances, and especially *homo sacer* itself, in terms of the notion of exception. Here, normal legality is suspended: someone is reduced to bare life, to sub-humanity, and can be killed indifferently, yet not murdered, sacrificed nor executed, since the Roman power is *indifferent* to merely plebeian judicial decision. From certain parallels with *patria potestas*, however, Agamben argues that the exception is the secret foundation of Roman authority. What establishes legality is the power of authority to break its own law, and sometimes to abandon those whom it is normally self-bound to protect. At bottom, as Augustine realized, in Roman logic legality is the self-bestowal of normativity by the *de facto* possessor of power. This means that, at the limit, naked power will keep reasserting itself, and even the citizen must be (never mind the sub-citizen), by definition as a citizen, reducible to sub-human, natural, quasi-animal status, in such a way that he can be hunted down like a werewolf. For Agamben, therefore (here invoking both Carl Schmitt and Alain Badiou), *homo sacer* is to be correlated with the aporetic structure of sovereignty as such: it works by including only what is simultaneously excluded, namely illegal exceptionality. And one can add to Agamben here a second *aporia* which applies not only to sovereign will, but to will as such: for a will to be effective, something other than will must carry out the will's order – if my hand will not move, I cannot throw. So for political will to be effective, someone else must always perform the sovereign's will – every sovereign needs an executive. Yet this executive is unavoidably other, and therefore always a potential rival sovereign power in itself; in addition its difference from sovereignty must be one of interpretation and delegation, as well as execution, so it is also necessarily a partially actual lesser sovereignty. In this way the 'handing over' to the plebs involved in *homo sacer* belongs to any logic of a single sovereign centre. Such a centre, by its very claim to singleness, is doomed to duality.

One detail of Agamben's analysis can, however, be called into question from his own evidence. Is it so clear that *homo sacer* is not offered as a sacrifice? All that is certain is that he was to be killed without ritual purification – but this is still consistent with a total offering, as indeed the Israelite examples attest: totally unclean towns were to be offered to Yahweh. Agamben himself at one point says that the *homo sacer* was delivered over to chthonic gods.[15] Perhaps the difference from more ritualized expulsions concerned precisely a degree of impurity, or else, to the contrary, official indifference one way or the other. In either case, total absence of ritual still belongs to ritual, especially as the event was to take place within certain circumstances and therefore was brought within regularity, yet not within a punitive response to officially criminal irregularity. It would also follow that to 'sacralize' in the mode of expulsion might always have had sacrificial connotations. Certainly one should not confuse all banishing, including scapegoating, with vertical sacrifice (after the tendency of René Girard); nonetheless, a horizontal banishing could often be construed as a sending downwards and occasionally as a sending upwards.

IV

So now the inevitable question: was Jesus a *homo sacer*? Not, most probably, in any consciously identified way, but possibly in a way conforming to the deep structure of Roman law which Agamben diagnoses. For this structure, the exception proves the rule; the exception is the ultimate paradoxical basis of order, always liable to erupt. When it does so, it re-enacts the foundational banishment – and Agamben notes that in Greece, as in other ancient legalities, the ban was the oldest form of punishment and of community self-definition and regulation.[16] Thus it would follow that liberal Biblical criticism is doubly guilty of *petitio principii*: once, because it assumes the non-verisimilitude of exception with respect to Christ, when this is the very thing at issue; and, twice, because it does the same thing with Roman law, when again the role of exception is what needs to be debated. And in the second case it is up against a certain amount of hard evidence and not simply faith.

Jesus is certainly presented by the Gospels in a way that conforms with *homo sacer*. In fact he is presented as *homo sacer* three times over. Once, because he is abandoned by Jewish sovereignty to the Roman executive. Twice, because he is abandoned by Roman sovereignty to the sovereign–executive mob; three times (at least according to Luke and John), because he is in some obscure fashion handed over by the mob to the Roman soldiers and executed after all in a Roman fashion. But did he really and exactly undergo Roman execution? It is much more as if the mob were allowed to lynch him after the fashion of a Roman execution, and to place him among those truly executed according to the sovereign but exceptional power of *cognitio*. In like fashion, Jesus was only addressed and arraigned in mock fashion as King of the Jews by Pilate, but on the cross named really King of the Jews, as if (without a simulacrum) Jewish rule were thereby really destroyed. Again, was Jesus really condemned by Jewish law, or did the Sanhedrin altogether substitute for this condemnation the accusation that he had offended Caesar? But then the Romans sarcastically rejected this, and, apparently accorded plebiscitory authority to the mob. Yet, by a final twist, it seems as if the mob enjoyed no real delegated executive power, as in the instance of *homo sacer*. Instead, Jesus was crucified only virtually, even though this really killed him; for neither Jewish nor Roman law had succeeded in condemning him. (In chapter 2 of *Being Reconciled* it is argued that real violence always is ritual violence, a gaze upon abandonment.) Only the mob did this – *they* became in effect the sovereign power (under instigation from the priests and elders) and the Romans in a certain sense their irregular executive. But in this way sovereign power and plebiscitory delegation were uniquely collapsed into each other. The necessary exception of mob lynching coincided precisely with regular execution. Accordingly, one could argue that the Cross exposed the structure of arbitrary sovereign power in its ultimate exceptional yet typical instance (Matthew 26–27; Mark 14–15; Luke 22–23; John 18–19). This is its act of discernment of the worst human violence.

Did the Gospel writers really fabricate these features (as most New Testament critics now think)? If so, then how did they alight upon a narrative which makes such sense in terms of the structures of Roman law and the interactions between incompatible, yet forcibly supplementary, Roman and Jewish jurisdictions? There seem to be good reasons at least to suspend one's doubts.

Atonement

I

Even were one unable to accept my arguments for the historicity of the Passion narratives in the previous chapter, one would still have to take seriously the surface structure of the texts, and their implications for the interactions of *ecclesia* with *imperium*. Does that mean that these arguments are only an interesting curiosity as far as theology is concerned? No, for two reasons.

First of all, even in the case of mythical and fictional thought, meanings and events are normally inseparable. There are no events outside the assignment of meanings, and there are no construable meanings not ultimately including some reference to an active rearrangement of things in time. The salt passes after I have asked for the salt to be passed: it is a mineral, but also a condiment, subject to meaningful convention. The situations where one deliberately drains events of meaning in order to confront their strangeness, as in physical or even historical science, or inversely one abstracts events from the normal course of events through mimicry in order to heighten meaning, as in drama, are clearly secondary and parasitic. Thus, in the case of new legends, ideologies and fictions, one legitimately asks after the real occasions that have helped to give rise to such novel configurations of sense.

Secondly, there is the question of genre. Despite the normativity of a coincidence of meaning and action, there is always also a perceived interval which allows both science and drama to emerge: I know the salt lay for countless ages in fathoms indifferent to humanity; I know that it is the subject also of superstition and metaphor. So — given that all human language must ultimately partake of both, event and meaning being originally inseparable — do the Gospels ally their narrations more to the side of science or of drama? The simple answer 'drama' entirely misses the point of the specific drama which the Gospels restage. For the entire content of this *unique* drama is the presentation of a situation in which, for the first time, there is no interval whatsoever between meaning and action. What they seek to present is the *Logos* become flesh: a situation in which the surplus of fictional and metaphoric meaning is here *none other* than the surplus of unknown consistency and causation. None of Jesus's imaginings are ineffectual, unlike ours; none of his actions lack an infinite depth of meaning. There is no possibility that the consistency and causes of his actions might be meaningless for humanity, since the depth of Jesus is God, the eminent locus of meaning and exemplar for our humanity. Even though Jesus in his humanity necessarily followed human examples, in his divine personhood, which means his ultimate singularity of character, he was without example, and imbued his human mimesis with an absolutely original creative power able to hold together without any interval between sense and occurrence.[17]

It follows that every claim that the Gospels are 'merely legendary' must ironically rebound. For it entirely begs the claim of the Gospels to present an absolutely exceptional phenomenon. Normally, a suggestion of fictive drama must count against scientific and historical accuracy, but if (although only if) the Gospels' presentation of 'Incarnation' is successful, then here alone, where fictionality abounds, historicity must all the more abound. Of course the reverse equally applies.[18]

The implication of this unique state of affairs is that the Gospel is immune to an idealist reading. Its meaning is that meaning has sloughed off its fallen impotence and is now fully actual and effective. If Christ be not raised, then our faith is in vain, because the new meanings offered in Christ only have significance (unlike all other meanings) if they are entirely effective. They must have arisen originally as events, indeed as hyper-events that more truly occurred than any other occurrences, else they would have no power now to be effective and to generate the event of reconciliation.

So, theologically speaking, given the second reason, the broad accuracy of the Gospels with respect to the Passion narratives is not dispensable. But, given the first reason, even a secular outlook, besides a theological one, has to be concerned with the active occasioning of new significance. *Something* must have occurred to create a new exposure of the violence and terror latent in given social and political structures, and to give rise to a new social alternative. I have already tried to show that the alternative 'somethings' of New Testament critics are not adequate to the scale of the new irruption, unlike the Gospels' own understandings of what this something was.

So let us ask again about the implications of the surface structure of the texts for the interaction of *ecclesia* with *imperium*, given that, theologically speaking, these surfaces must be understood as immediately conveying (without the usual interval of suspension of assent) the full depth of actual occurrence.

II

What are these implications? First of all, that Christ, the God–Man, died precisely a purely divine and a purely human, or even sub-human, death. He did not die the death of a martyr, as a witness for a universal cause, although later martyrs have died in cause of *him*. For his 'infringements' of the law were not such for many Jews; his apocalyptic prophecies were misunderstood; all that was comprehended and denied was his claim to be God. Herein lies nothing typical, nor inevitable. Two of the synoptic Gospels declare that the high priests (Mark 15: 10) and the people (Matthew 27: 18) resented Jesus – they envied him his unique status, his absolute unreachability, his absolute height beyond height. No creature is in principle unreachable; hence God alone inspires ontological envy. All real envy is of God, and Jesus was envied because he was God in the flesh. The people screamed out their resentment to Pilate. It is true that it is only Matthew who appears to suggest that the crowd caught the contagion of envy from the high priests and elders. And perhaps to the contrary they warned the crowd that Jesus would destroy the temple, and it was this fear, and not resentment, which moved them. However, Jesus's subversiveness with regard to the law and the temple economy had been visibly demonstrated and Jesus had at first been welcomed by the people to Jerusalem. If the people now viewed themselves as protectors of the temple, then they shared a posture with the high priests and elders which both Mark and Matthew diagnose as in the latter case being but a cover for envy (since Jesus clearly was protecting the temple's integrity and was not out to destroy it). If supposed defence of the temple was a self-deceit for the high priests and elders, then it would logically be a self-deceit for the people also. Jesus was truly hated for his awesome elevation.

Nevertheless, Jesus did not die only a divine death. He also died the most sheerly human death – or a kenotic death of utterly emptied-out humanity. For he was not Socrates, dying for the truth: jesting Pilate denied him this dignity. Even if the Gospels ironically know that Jesus did die for the truth since he was the truth, there is no clear question of truth being publicly displayed here; neither can the disciples see why Jesus has to die. Nor was he seen as leader of a party, since his disciples were ignored. Indeed the first handing-over by Judas seems to have been required because Jesus was seen as belonging only to this private group, within which alone he had influence, and to which alone one had to resort, in order to know about him. No, in the end, he died at what was possibly the whim of a drunken mob. To try to give Jesus a dignified death, like that of St Thomas More, is to miss the point: in his death, Jesus entered into absolute solidarity with each and every one of us. He died the death which any of us, under sovereign authority, in exceptional circumstances which always prove the rule, may possibly die. He died as three times excluded: by the Jewish law of its tribal nation; by the Roman universal law of empire; by the democratic will of the mob. In the whole summed-up history of human polity – the tribe, the universal absolute state, the democratic consensus – God found no place. He was shuttled backwards and forwards, with an undercurrent of indifference, as though not really dangerous, between their respective rules. He became *homo sacer*, cast outside the camp, abandoned on all sides, so that in the end he died almost accidentally. He died the death of all of us – since he died the death that proves and exemplifies sovereignty in its arbitrariness.

In this respect, it is ironically only by disallowing an anti-Semitic bias to the Gospels (which is supposed to account for the story about the mob) that one can directly relate the death of Jesus to the death of those who died in the Holocaust. For Agamben points out that the Holocaust victims became in a sense *homo sacer*: killed in a way that was characterized neither as murder nor execution nor indeed – now for certain – sacrifice (despite the misnomer 'Holocaust'). Jesus imbued with his divine height precisely the death of absolute innocence, the death of the outcast, of people reduced beneath humanity into half-animality. Moreover, Agamben rightly warns us not to be sanguine about the end of totalitarianism, because the line between totalitarianism and liberal democracy is not after all so distinct. The liberal notion of natural rights guaranteed by a sovereign state itself plays directly into a first constitutive *aporia* of sovereignty. If these rights are 'natural' (and follow from certain given facts regarded as prior to valuation) as if they belonged to an animal, yet are only operative and recognized – and therefore existent – within the State, then the State assumes to itself a power over nature, a right even to define nature, and indeed defines itself by this power, and therefore secretly reserves to itself alone a supreme *de facto* right of pure nature prior to contract, by which in exceptional circumstances it may withdraw any right whatsoever. If you accord people 'human rights' by nature, it means (as Alain Badiou argues in his *Ethics*), that you already envisage people *primarily* as passive if freely wandering animals, who *might* be victimized: the ban actually creates the space for its own violation, just as St Paul saw was the case with all law outside the counter-law of charity. Agamben cites instances of reduction to half-life by liberal democracies and especially the United States: dangerous experiments upon prisoners condemned to death; drug testing in the Third World; the dubious treatment of brain-dead organ donors – and one could of course add experiments upon foetuses and late abortion which is but disguised infanticide. Recently we have had instances of American politicians declaring that Taliban prisoners or suspected terrorists enjoy *neither* the rights of criminals *nor* the rights of prisoners of war. They have therefore become *homo sacer*, denied contradictorily *as* humans (since we would not really treat animals like this) any humanity whatsoever, and any mark of the *imago dei*.

Christ, then, in Agamben's terms, was reduced to this bare life. Agamben struggles nobly but perhaps futilely to imagine an escape from the *aporias* of sovereignty. He suggests that we exit this structure which seems to encompass humanity as such, and instead identify with the outcast position of abandonment. Yet Agamben also seems to believe that the aporetic constitution of sovereignty is echoed at the ontological level: Being, like sovereignty, is itself nothing save through its inclusion of beings, whose contingency it must of course also exclude from itself as Being as such – as the reality that there is Being at all, whose secret every particular being assumes but can never disclose. Therefore beings, for Agamben following Heidegger, are abandoned by the Being that discloses them, and in this sense are in a condition like that of *homo sacer*.[19]

But in that case, one may well ask, just what is the point of identifying oneself with bare life in order to escape earthly sovereignty, only to fall into the hands of cosmic tyranny? Is not the latter bound always to reincarnate itself politically? And why do we still accept the metaphysical projections of semi-Nazi ideologues like Heidegger and Schmitt, however brilliant? And however much we can learn from their philosophies concerning the ways in which Nazism and Fascism were unfortunately rooted in aspects of the Western legacy?

Here it is notable that Agamben does seem to elide the Christian Middle Ages from his purview. Even the presentation of Roman law seems somewhat exaggerated, since however much the *patria potestas* operated as a reserved foundation, Roman rulers were also bound by customary and cooperative limitations upon their powers. True, unlimited sovereignty is rather a modern doctrine, developed by Bodin and Hobbes, which assumes a metaphysical background unknown to Rome of an infinite God, denned mainly by an unlimited will. Yet this new political theology – of which Carl Schmitt was the ultimate (one might vainly hope) legatee – was itself erected within the ruins of a Christocentric understanding of politics and sociality.

This understanding maintained consistency with the New Testament itself. What are the main features of the New Testament's understanding of our solidarity with Christ, the God abandoned as *homo sacer* upon the Cross?

III

First of all, the main stress is that, upon the basis of the rejected one, a new sort of community is to be built. But this is only possible because the rejected one is, bizarrely, also the most envied, unrepeatable one. If abandonment is the last word, then, as with Agamben, there is no real hope. Mere identification with a victim as victim confirms victimhood and diminishes us all. But Christ was never merely abandoned, even for a single instance. Even though all his friends deserted him in the garden of Gethsemane and he suffered thereby the worst extremity of human agony, he still did not endure ontological desertion. The cry of dereliction upon the cross recorded by Matthew and Mark (Matthew 27: 46; Mark 15: 34) involves no abandonment by the Father, but rather Jesus's deepest entering into the self-separation of sinful humanity from God: hence it is to God, not the Father ('My God, my God') that Jesus as Son in his humanity cries out. When, by contrast, Jesus in his divine nature speaks as the

Son to the Father, it is a question of serene deliverance in contrast to the cruel human handings over: 'Father, into thy hands I commit my Spirit!' (Luke 23: 46).

(I owe this point to David Hart. Yet one must also mention here that Luke does admittedly present a uniquely stoical dispassionate Jesus, and that Christ's 'bloody sweat' in Gethsemane, recorded only by Luke (22: 44), is not found in some early manuscripts and therefore is very likely an interpolation. Perhaps Luke had a semi-docetic worry about ascribing suffering to Jesus, and perhaps this was later detected by the redactor – though one can scarcely be sure. But this does not affect Hart's point about the exactly 'Chalcedonian' use of terminology by the Gospel writers: Luke's serene commending to the Father is scarcely inimical to the spirit of the other writers, while it remains notable that they locate the anguished alienation as lying between manhood and Godhead, not between Son and Father.)

Christ failed to resist human power and went freely to his death because he knew that a merely human counter-power is always futile and temporary. But he also went to his death, and therefore was innocent of suicide (and perhaps only innocent for this reason) in trust of his return, his resurrection. Hence the New Testament does not speak of Jesus's death as a sacrifice in the rabbinic sense of a death atoning for sins, nor as something lost to earth to compensate for what we have taken from God. Nothing can be taken from the impassable God, and nothing can be added to his sum. This is why John's Gospel is always ironically instilling the point that Jesus is the real initiator who gives himself, even when he appears to be constantly handed over. This does not at all denote an indifference to the historical causality of the latter pro-ceedings (into which, to the contrary, John offers us a certain unique insight), but rather the coincidence of Christ's personhood with that of the *Logos*, so that Christ, moving genuinely in the realm of secondary causes, is also himself the first cause behind the very being of these causes. Jesus only submits to being handed over because he is in himself the very heart of all transition as really loving gift, and thereby able to subvert every betrayal and abandonment.

St Paul therefore speaks not of the offering of Christ to the Father, with whom he is really identical, but, instead, of our dying to sin and purely finite obsessions, including negative legality, *with Christ*, in order that we might immediately pass with him into a new sort of life. Christ and we ourselves are both killed by evil, which is nothing, and so, in dying to evil, we die to nothing whatsoever. Fully to die, for St Paul, means already and automatically to be resurrected (II Corinthians 5: 14: 'we are convinced that one has died for all, yet therefore all have died'; Romans 6: 5–6; Ephesians 2, Galatians 2, Philippians 2; Colossians 1–2; 3: 1–3 and 9; see also I Peter 4: 1–2). If any 'ransom' is offered by Christ, then it seems indeed that, for St Paul, as the Fathers divulged, it is granted to the chthonic gods who are really demons, and to the demonic intermediate powers of the air (Galatians 4: 3–5: 'we were slaves to the elemental spirits of the universe. But ... God sent forth his son ... to redeem those who were born under the law'; and see Colossians 2: 14 plus Ephesians 4: 9). As *homo sacer*, Christ is delivered over to the corrupt (or semi-corrupt?) angelic forces who are the guardians of laws and nations; yet Paul's point is that these powers are nothing, are impotent, outside the divine power which they refuse: hence such a sacrifice becomes, in Christian terms, absurd. Only in a comical sense was Christ, strictly speaking, a sacrifice. In a serious sense he was an effective sacrifice because he overcame sacrifice once and for all – because, in the absolute kenotic impotence of refusing to fight finite potency with finite potency, the ultimate of infinite irresistible power was disclosed. In refusing violence, Christ also exercised a militant opposition to violence. However, this counter-violent violence was disclosed as consisting in utter self-giving which is immediate return, as resurrection, and therefore also gift-exchange. Already, in dying, because he is God, Christ is not truly abandoned, but through apparent abandonment is finally and inexorably returned to us. In dying, as God, he already receives back from us, through the Holy Spirit which elevates us into the life of the Trinity, our counter-gift of recognition. Though to God we can really give nothing, by the humanization of the *Logos* we are given that hypostatic indwelling of the Spirit which is the ground of our deification, in such a way that we can, after all, in the Spirit, return the divine gift. Hence the divine answer to the original human refusal of his gift is not to demand sacrifice – of which he has no need – but to go on giving in and through our refusals of the gift, to the point where these refusals are overcome. Christ's abandonment offers no compensation to God, but when we most abandon the divine donation it surpasses itself, and appears more than ever, raising us up into the eternal gift-exchange of the Trinity.

It is the same for the *Epistle to the Hebrews*: sacrifice implies multiplicity, repetition, appeasement, whereas Christ the true Priest puts an end to sacrifice. He does this not really by offering a one all-sufficient sacrifice (this is to read over-literally and naively) but by passing into the heavenly sanctuary as both priest and victim, and making an 'atoning offering' there – in the one place where it is absurdly unnecessary, since offerings are only sent up to this altar from earthly ones. The point is that Christ's earthly self-giving death is but a shadow of the true eternal peaceful process in the heavenly tabernacle, and redemption consists in Christ's transition from shadow to reality – which is also, mysteriously, his 'return' to cosmic omnipresence and irradiating of the shadows (Hebrews 9: the Middle Platonic element here is essential). If nevertheless the heavenly altar must be cleansed, then once again this must be from the impurity of the cosmic powers, which infect even the very portals of Godhead (all that is not absolutely God). Yet though Christ's offering is even here unto death, the death that the *Logos* dies is a showing, within a death-dreaming cosmos, of that utter ecstatic self-giving which is eternal life itself. The heavenly altar that is purified is, for the author of the *Epistle to the Hebrews*, the psychic realm: 'your conscience'; and purification of this realm consists not in one more sacrificial 'work' – even a final such work – but rather in the final removal of the illusion of the need for such works. The 'blood of Christ will purify your conscience from dead works to serve the living God'.

This offering of his blood is made by Christ, not as incurring a subtraction from his own resources, but instead 'through the eternal Spirit', which is to say out of and within the eternal mutually sustaining *donum* that holds together the Father and the Son (Hebrews 9: 14 and see Philo, *De Sacrificiis Abelis et Cain*, XXV, XXX, iii). Therefore, in pouring himself as an apparent oblation upon the heavenly altar – which is the upper terminus for the escalating smoke of oblation, not its basement origin in bloodletting – Christ in truth passes as peaceful gift-that-returns beyond this altar to the right hand of the Father.

Both St Paul and the author of the *Epistle to the Hebrews* speak of Christ rather than the law as fulfilling the 'will' of Abraham. Both argue that a 'will' only becomes effective when someone dies (Hebrews 9: 17; Galatians 3–4, esp. 3: 15–18). It seems to me that something more than a banal legal reference is intended here. What is surely being invoked is something akin to my second *aporia* of sovereignty, which regards the relation of will to execution. For this *aporia*, a will is only effective in its own absence, when its wishes are carried out by another, just as a political sovereign requires, but is weakened by, a relatively distant executive, and an economic mono-poly must bifurcate into two relatively independent parts in order to remain effi-cient – as symbolized for Jean Baudrillard by the erstwhile World Trade Center, whose sinister monopolistic character and Babelistic height made it an easier target, while its bifurcation weakened its solidity.

Hence the final guarantee of will, and for our *respect* for human wills, is death. This is exactly why we have legal wills, whose reality is poised somewhere between human worth and human terror (human freedom and human bondage, the honour due to father and mother, and enslavement to the past). Yet this reproduces constantly the entire sovereignty/executive problematic. By contrast, for the *Epistle to the Hebrews*, Christ's will is indeed ratified by death and by blood, but not in a way that leaves it at the mercy of an executive. Instead, Christ's will is a new sort of self-emptying will that consists *entirely* in its passing out of itself to be non-identically repeated in another. It is only, in appearance and for a finite gaze, the blood of a deadly sealed contract, because it is secretly the infinite blood of life that flows in the firmament (Hebrews 9: 9–12). Likewise, for St Paul, the will of Abraham cannot really be fulfilled in the carrying out of injunctions which only keep us from worse wrongs, suggest to us temptations, and tend to impose on us over-precise categories, but only in the single living heir who fulfils the spirit of Abraham's legacy from the eternal Father. So whereas, as we saw in Chapter 1 [of *Being Reconciled*], Kant projects the separation of powers into the Godhead, the New Testament incarnates a new divine polity which uniquely abolishes all such separation, yet equally without any 'confusion' of the distinct powers, pre-cisely because it reconceives 'unity' beyond 'singularity'.

In both St Paul and the *Epistle to the Hebrews*, one finds the tendency, as throughout the New Testament, and supremely in its Pneumatology, to promote the category of 'life'. It is almost as if it is suspicious of categories of human cultural institution and of the culture/nature divide.[20] The carrying through of 'will' involves a continuity and yet rupture between 'living' voice and 'cultural' inscription. The very order of sovereign arbitrary control depends upon this. Yet, for the New Testament, there is neither 'natural' will nor regular conventional performance of will. Instead there is created will which participates in God, wherein life and *Logos* (Spirit and Son) communicate as one. Such a will is never the presupposed 'pure nature' of sovereignty and liberal rights theory. Instead it is already a will to reciprocity and to harmony with others according to an ineffable order and measure, which is yet not the measure of law. Such a will does not consist sovereignly in itself, and so cannot be betrayed by any executive – instead it only win its always-already othering as execution: always for furtherance and not termination of life. Therefore by offering ourselves in and with Christ, we do not really lose ourselves, but live the genuine and eternal absolute life that returns as it proceeds outward.

This same promotion of life informs also the New Testament's overcoming of the first *aporia* of sovereignty. This concerns the rule of exception and the logic of inclusion which is also exclusion. For the Church is founded on Christ who was *entirely* excluded: by imperial Rome, by tribal-cum-city-state Israel, by modern democracy. But were Christ only the abandoned one, this would constitute a politics of naturalistic nihilism, a kind of cynicism in the antique sense, to which the New Testament stress upon uncontaminated natural life is curiously akin. Yet, to the contrary, Christ as purely excluded is risen: therefore the life he is risen to is the possibility of life after exclusion from life, of a life beyond inclusion versus exclusion. If Christ is supremely exceptional, this is because he is the exception even to the law of exception: after Christ there is no more of that oscillation between norm and exception which paradoxically establishes the sphere of the norm. There is now only – so to speak – a series of exceptions, of pure outstanding and emanating (not caused) 'events' which are nonetheless consistent with each other. This is equally the new 'usual' beyond the usual: in truth an endless process of *variation*, since without the usual usual, there can be no real exception any longer. As for David Jones at the end of the *Anathemata*, Christ works in the mode of what has 'always been done', yet performs through this something 'other'. And, as for W.H. Auden in *For the Time Being*, redemption is like the extraordinary event of stepping into the room behind the mirror: it entirely is, and entirely is not, the same room.

The New Testament is here very direct: Christ's blood makes peace, Christ's blood makes possible harmony between people; in Christ, there is no longer the inclusion/exclusion logic of race, nor of economics, nor of gender. There is in Christ no more black and white, master and slave, male and female. But this inclusion of differences does not mean their exclusion! No, they remain, as pure relations, pure passages of harmonious will. To the disappointment of liberal democrats, but the delight of Socratic (and socialist) critics of liberal democracy, hierarchical relations also remain: the subordinate are to obey freely, but masters to rule generously and with care. This is not to endorse the specific hierarchies of gender and slavery which Paul within his limited historical perspective was likely to endorse, and duly did, but it is to insist that Paul rightly recognizes the necessary 'educative' and architectonic hierarchies of the transmission of harmonious life which no culture can ever truly dispense with. [See Chapters 7 and 9 of *Being Reconciled*.]

At the centre of this new social and even 'political' institution lies an absolute mystery: the insistence on Christ's specificity. For if there can be more to social life and hierarchy than arbitrariness, if there can indeed be 'harmony' or a passing of events in the 'right' way like music, then this suggests that there is a real 'affinity' to be constantly produced, discovered and enacted. Were this unnecessary, then Christ would be unnecessary; a mere command to 'be reconciled' would do, or a set of legal recipes, or books of wisdom. Of course we are to imitate Christ and to live ecstatically through exchange, losing our lives in order to gain them. But if only Christ reconciles us to each other – nation to nation, race to race, sex to sex, ruler to subordinate, person to person (and this is not because he has achieved something forensic outside our sharing in Christ, a reading of Paul that E.P. Sanders has forever destroyed)[21] – then this can only mean that the specific shape of Christ's body in his reconciled life and its continued renewal in the Church (where it is authentic, which must also be ceaselessly discerned) provides for us the true aesthetic example for our reshaping of our social existence.

We live in Christ because Christ as *homo sacer* was archetypally a human being as a *creature* and not simply the *bios theoretikos* who is both inside and outside the *polis* – half animal of passions, half man [*sic*] of political reason. We also live in Christ because this typical abandoned man was nonetheless God, in whom we participate and from whom we all have our life. Our new political life in Christ is once more a merely natural life in the sense of created life, and of specifically human life which is orientation to supernatural deification. The Middle Ages started to think through the possibility of this life, but cut itself short by a dual development which invented a forensic reading of the atonement and a voluntaristic doctrine of sovereignty in a single gesture (this is well attested by the theology of Grotius, but has earlier roots in Ockham and further back still). In the earlier mediaeval model, we are not ruled from above by a sovereign source which includes yet excludes us, but by blood flowing from the past which we imbibe, so that the outside is also the inside. For this vision we submit to the will of the past and its living hierarchical representatives, yet in such a way that we are to fulfil this will in the spirit not the letter, and carry it beyond and above the shoulders of the giants on whom we stand – as depicted in the overwhelming blue of the windows of Chartres Cathedral. [See further Chapter 7 of *Being Reconciled*.]

Today we must take up this project again and insist that the body of Christ is the true universality – against both the taboos of tribes (even though the law of Christ extends as well as abolishes taboos: see Chapter 10 of *Being Reconciled*) and the universality of enlightenment, whose dark gothic secret is *homo sacer*. We must espouse and oppose the abandonment of potentially all of us to half-animality. We must oppose also the sacrifice without return of individuals to the state, to globalization, to the future, to ethical duty, to pagan fatality. Unlike Dante's Ulysses we must not once more abandon Penelope, sailing heroically beyond the pillars of Hercules, without hope of return, to the foot of Mount Purgatory, without hope of ascent. Instead, beyond the mediaeval venture, we must give ourselves to voyaging, unto death if necessary, like the English sailors John and Sebastian Cabot of Bristol (whose statue still stands there by the quayside) and before them the Portuguese sailors Magellan, Vasco de Gama and Columbus. Supremely we must follow the example of the Portuguese King Sebastian, lost at sea in one of Fernando Pessoa's poems (whom the Portuguese have believed will return to save them, as the British have believed of the Romano-British King Arthur) yet in sure knowledge that the created world is round – the world not only of sacrifice, but also of returning. So Pessoa invokes him: 'I spy through fog your dim shape turning back' (*Vejo entre a cerracao tue vulto baco que torna*).[22]

Notes

1   See, for example, John Dominic Crossan, *Who Killed Jesus? Exposing the Roots of Anti-Semitism in the Gospel Story of the Death of Jesus*, San Francisco: HarperCollins, 1995, p. 111. I am indebted to discussions with Harry Gamble of the Department of Religious Studies, University of Virginia, on the current state of scholarly thinking concerning these points.

2   The view that the Sanhedrin had strong autonomous powers of judgement and execution was put forward by Lietzmann and Juster and repeated by Paul Winter in his book *On the Trial of Jesus*, Berlin: De Gruyter, 1961. It is demolished by A.N. Sherwin-White in his *Roman Society and Roman Law in the New Testament*, Oxford: OUP, 1961 and Simon Légasse, *The Trial of Jesus*, trans. John Bowden, London: SCM, 1991, pp. vi and 52ff. However, they both still reject the historicity of the role of the mob (Sherwin-White with Anglican discretion – or cynicism? See *Roman Society*, 26: 'One may here leave aside the worked-up sections concerning the release of Barabbas, and other material, such as the story of Pilate's wife in Matthew, and the sending of Christ to Herod in Luke, none of which is part of the *cognitio* proper.')

3   See Légasse, *The Trial of Jesus* (see Note 2), pp. 65ff.

4   Again, this is Winter's view. And Légasse's at p. 69. See also Crossan, *Who Killed Jesus?* pp. 82–133. (See Notes 1 and 2 for citations.)

5   See Jean-Luc Marion, *Etant Donnée*, Paris: Presses Universitaires de France, 1997, pp. 169–251.

6   See A.C. Harvey, *Jesus on Trial*, London: SPCK, 1976, p. 77.

7   Sherwin-White, *Roman Society*, p. 35. And see Légasse, *The Trial of Jesus* (see Note 2), p. 138. I am indebted to Russell Hittenger for the point about *cognitio extra ordinem* being only exercised by Governors at the margins. On the dangers of leaving things to judges' solo authority, see Thomas Aquinas, *S.T.* II. II. Q.95 a 1 AD 2.

8   Jon A. Wetherby, *Jewish Responsibility for the Death of Jesus in Luke-Acts*, Sheffield: Sheffield Academic Press, 1994.

9   Légasse, *The Trial of Jesus* (see Note 2), pp. 68, 144.

10 Jean Colin, *Les Villes litres de l'orient Gréco-Romain et l'envoi au supplice par acclamations populaires*, Brussels: Latonus, 1965.

11   Ibid., p. 16.
12   See Giorgio Agamben, *Homo Sacer: Sovereign Power and Bare Life*, trans. Daniel Heller-Roozen, Stanford, CA: Stanford University Press, 1998, p. 71.
13   Ibid., passim.
14   Ibid., pp. 76–7.
15   Ibid., p. 96.
16   Ibid., pp. 104–12.
17   I am indebted here to conversations with Regina Schwartz concerning Milton's *Paradise Regained*. The present chapter should be related always to chapter 4 of *Being Reconciled* and to my earlier piece, 'The Name of Jesus', which is chapter 6 of my *The Word Made Strange: Theology, Language, Culture*, Oxford: Blackwell, 1997, pp. 145–71.
18   See J.R.R. Tolkien, 'On Fairy-Stories' in J.R.R. Tolkien, *Poems and Stories*, London: George Allen and Unwin, 1980, pp. 75–113. Tolkien here famously speaks of the gospels as uniquely true fairy-stories. However, since for him all genuine fairy-stories truly invoke what is in some sense a real other world of faerie, what he says more precisely is that in the gospel story Divine 'primary creation' and human 'secondary creation' uniquely coincide. This means that whereas normally a fairy-story dimly discloses an impinging yet absent world, where all is rearranged by enchantment, the gospels record a fully actualized entrance of enchanted transformation into our everyday reality. This renders the events they record a genuinely magical drama; whereas normally, for Tolkien, drama is suspiciously pseudo-magical, mere stage-magic. By contrast, third-person narrative evokes an absent true enchantment, which the imagination can reach beyond the range of vision, yet reach without reaching, in a fashion that sustains the mystery of distance. By appearing to render the enchantment present, drama tends to betray the imagination and the real power of literature.
      Tolkien's suspicion of Shakespeare here is fascinating. Yet surely he might have remarked that Shakespeare's non-classicism deconstructs dramatic presence; that he tends to refuse the visual closure of either tragedy or comedy, and that he accords a great role to fetishized or magical objects. (Tolkien rightly complains that most drama is too personalist, and downplays the role of symbolic objects which outlast humans through time. Perhaps the Ring-Master envisages himself as in competition with Wagner as well as Shakespeare here.)
      In future work on the Gift, I will include an analysis of this astonishing essay: its account of fairy-story as supreme 'sub-creation', of creative imagination as entry into a real world of faerie; and its subtle critique of drama as pseudo-magic which falsely entrances us in a frozen presence, compared with the liberating effects of diegesis, and its theory of the special status of 'things'.
19   Agamben, *Homo Sacer* (see Note 12), pp. 59ff., 188.
20   See Michel Henry, *C'est moi la verité: pour une philosophie du Christianisme*, Paris: Editions du Seuil, 1996.
21   E.P. Sanders, *Paul and Palestinian Judaism*, Philadelphia: Fortress, 1977, pp. 502–8. But Sanders fails to disprove Paul's antinomian bent (in a certain sense). Sanders rightly asserts: (1) that justification in Paul means participation in the body of Christ; (2) that death does not for Paul, as for the rabbis, atone for transgressions, but that we are to die to the power of sin and live to another power; and (3) that Paul denies the salvific efficacy of the Jewish covenant. Sanders goes wrong in (1) arguing that participation in Christ, though it substitutes for the old covenant, does not involve belonging to a new group; he argues that ecclesia does not imply 'Church' in the later sense, whereas 'Church' meant later (at least up till the late Middle Ages) precisely participation in the Body of Christ; (2) exaggerating the non-legalism of the rabbis regarding salvation: see Donald A. Hagner, 'Paul and Judaism', in Peter Stuhlmacher, *Revisiting Paul's Doctrine of Justification*, Downers Grove: IVP, 2001, pp. 86ff.
22   Fernando Pessoa, 'The Last Ship', in *O Mar sem Fin/ The Boundless Sea*, Lisbon: Instituto Portugues de Patrimonio Arquitectonico/Mosteiro des Jeronimos, 2000 [unpaginated].

Chapter 8

Graham Ward

The schizoid Christ

The term 'Godhead' is significant of operation, and not of nature.

(Gregory of Nyssa)[1]

Despite the allusion to a certain psychopathology – schizophrenia – this is not an essay attempting to psychoanalyse Jesus of Nazareth. In fact, nothing could be further from the intention of this essay than an investigation into the historical Jesus and what consciousness he may or may not have had of being the Christ. Such investigations assume the autonomy of the liberal individual, that consciousness is a unified field, and that this individual, in possession of this consciousness, forms a specific sense of self: an identity. This is the subject-in-control; the subject of liberal understandings of freedom who is in subjection to no one. The focus of this essay is working against these assumptions, for the essay is concerned with sketching certain operations in which Jesus is the Christ. 'Operations' is the key term here and is employed synonymously with the word 'economy'. To rehearse Christology in terms of operations and economies raises all sorts of questions and dogmatic enquiries about the nature of the God-Man or the nature of the bodies of Christ (the historical and distinctively gendered Jew, Jesus of Nazareth, and the body of the incarnate God) and their co-inherence. These questions and enquiries have courted the opprobrium of 'heresy' in the past. Since the turn to the subject and the cult of the human that emerged as a dominant cultural theme from the seventeenth century onwards, Christology has been treated in terms of defining the subjective personhood of Christ – his consciousness, his autonomy, his history, his mission, his embodiment of the Godhead. But I wish to step out of that way of understanding and examining the incarnate God and think Christology from another direction; to step outside of the turn to the subject and the cult of the human. I wish to avoid reducing 'Jesus', 'Christ' or 'body' to identifiable and locatable entities, and to examine this profound theological nexus as a mobile site for the production of desire and belief, love and hope. For Deleuze and Guattari, the schizo is a desiring-machine:

> continually wandering about, migrating here, there, and everywhere as best he can, he lunges further into the realm of deterritorialisation, reaching the furthest limits of the decomposition of the socius on the surface of his own body without organs.[2]

This essay is an attempt to view Christology in terms of the operations of the schizo, whose desire is liquid and viscous, passing through 'relationships of intensities' in a way that demands the surrender of the ego, of the subject-in-control.[3] It takes up Deleuze and Guattari's challenge that 'schizophrenisation' is therapeutic; and examines the operations of Jesus the Christ as performing such a form of healing.

There are points where Deleuze's thinking about space and flows touches on Scriptural reasoning and narrative, enabling us to reconnect the ministry to the person and view Christology as a relational praxis. In other words, our thinking-through of central concepts in a doctrine of Christ – incarnation, atonement and community – emerges from a participation in which we are responding to representations of this figure. This participation and responding I will call the Christic operation. And that is where I wish to begin, developing three characteristics of this Christic operation – touch, flows and relations – on the basis of Scriptural exegesis. Let us take the account in Mark (5.24–34) of the woman with the unstoppable flow of blood:

> a great crowd pressed upon [Jesus]. Among them was a woman who had suffered from haemorrhages [*en rusei aimatos*] for twelve years; and in spite of long treatment by many doctors, on which she had spent [*dapanesasa*] all she had, there had been no improvement. On the contrary, she had grown worse. She had heard what people were saying about Jesus, so she came up from behind and touched him; for she said to herself 'If I touch even his clothes, I shall be cured.' And there and then the source [*pege*] of her haemorrhages dried up [*exeranthe*] and she knew in herself [*egno en somati*] that she was cured of her trouble. At the same time [*euthus*] Jesus, aware [*epignous en eauto*] that power [*dunamin*] had gone out of him [*exelthousan*], turned round and asked, 'Who touched my clothes?' His disciples said to him, 'You see the crowd pressing upon you and yet you ask, "Who touched me?"' Meanwhile he was looking round to see who had done it. And the

woman, trembling with fear when she grasped what had happened to her [*eiduia o gegonen aute*], came and fell at his feet and told him the whole truth [*pasan ten aletheian*]. He said to her, 'My daughter [*thugater*], your faith [*he pistis sou*] has cured you [*sesooken se*]. Go in peace, free for ever from this trouble.'

Matthew (9.20–2) reduces this complex and detailed scene to three verses and completely erases the extended use of the metaphor of the flowing spring that proceeds from the woman and is met by a force proceeding from Jesus which dries it up.[4] Luke (8.43–8) reduces it to five verses but maintains the metaphor (*en rusei ... he rusis*) which in fact is a citation from the Septuagint of Leviticus 12.7 concerning the purity laws. Luke also turns into a highly reflective form of direct speech what had been only a description in Mark: 'Jesus said, "Someone did touch me, for I felt that power had gone out of me [*ego gar egnon dunamin exeleluthuian*]".'[5] The comparative reflexivity of Luke's over Mark's Greek draws attention to the action and the subject with respect to it: the strong presence of the 'I' with respect to a passive verb and a dynamic object (power). By its self-consciousness, it constitutes a highly significant insight not only into Jesus as a person but also into the operations in which he is situated, operations that pass through him. Luke recognises that, telescoping the encounter with the woman with the haemorrhages into that one observation. But it is Mark's account that remains more subtle. For Mark maintains a balance of relations between the woman and Jesus. Being ritually unclean means social as well as religious ostracisation – which is why both Augustine and Ambrose saw in this woman a figure for the Gentile Church.[6] The woman is alienated, but Mark's attention to both persons in this exchange culminates in the relational term 'daughter'. The 'cure' effected, the 'peace' found, the 'trouble' resolved – the whole economy of the woman's salvation [*sesooken*] – is captured, even produced, in the intimacy of his words to her and the new relationship that is established between them. The redemption lies in the translation from alienation and anonymity ('You see the crowd pressing in on you and yet you ask, "Who touched me?"') to kinship. And it is with this translation, I suggest, that we can come to understand the Christological operation; the divine as it works in, through, with and as the body of this Jewish man who is the Christ. For, after all, the Messiah in Jewish and then Christian thinking is not just a person but an eschatological operation. The person is identified only in the mission. But more of this later. For the moment, I wish to make a number of observations about the flows of blood and power, and their different economies, as this passage suggests them to us.

First, there is a relation between the flow of blood and the spending of money. Both operations, the biological and the economic, represent the woman's life and livelihood. She is being drained or undergoing a kenosis, in emptying out. This is something that is happening to her. Her body is situated in these two consumptions. Nevertheless, she responds to what she hears about Jesus and actively places herself within another operation – the movement of the entourage around Jesus as he walks from the shores of the Sea of Galilee to the house of Jairus, one of the rulers of the synagogue. The whole event takes place in transit between two points. What links the two points, passing through the woman herself, is water, touch (for Jairus wishes Jesus to lays hands on his daughter) and the kinship of father and daughter. For Jesus was 'nigh unto the sea' (5.21) and the water motif is picked up by the metaphors of the spring and the stream of blood [*rusis* – flow, stream; *pege* – running water, spring], and he is on his way to heal Jairus's daughter. The encounter occurs, then, at an intersection of several movements; movements within which the woman is caught. The salvation of the body takes place *en passant*. The body is never stationary. It is never there as such. Perhaps it is because the physicians try to treat the body as a static thing that they fail to heal the woman; they fail to recognise that the body only lives in transit. It is profoundly locked into temporality, located in a 'space of flows'. It comes to an understanding of itself only in terms of the webs of relation (constantly changing) that are produced and displaced in its being borne by and placing itself within these operations.

The body of Jesus is also situated within various fluid operations. Having no 'place to lay his head', constantly sought after by the multitude and followed after by his disciples, he moves from place to place. Being 'on the way' is a prominent theme in Mark's Gospel.[7] Frequently in the first part of Mark's Gospel Jesus crosses and recrosses the Sea of Galilee. He is connected to flows of water, bodily fluids like blood and spit (Mark 8.23) and a force, authority or bodily strength (*dunamis*) that passes through him.[8] But he is always in command of these flows and the initiator of operations. That is why this encounter with the woman is so remarkable. For it is the woman's touch that initiates the healing that is discharged through the body of Jesus.[9]

Second, there is a relation between the mobility of these bodies and knowledge. The woman immediately recognises the staunching of the flow of blood, she '*egno en somati*'. And when Jesus is touched in this particular, even intimate way, immediately he *epignous en eauto* – he learns of, recognises an alteration in the currents within which his body is situated. These operations within and between bodies constitute a somatic form of knowing that is not unrelated to physical sensation but the interpretation of which transcends merely registering such sensation. In fact, Mark describes two moments in the woman's understanding. For having known in her body what has taken place – '*egno en somati*' – she then grasps what has happened to her – '*eiduia o gegonen ante*'. This second moment is also an embodied knowing, for she is 'trembling with fear'. What takes place in this move from *ginosko* to *oida* [both Greek terms could be understood as 'coming to know']? Are they synonyms or is Mark suggesting a move from apprehension to comprehension, a move marked by an outward physical manifestation (trembling) of an inner physical event (the staunching of the flow of blood)? Certainly there is a grammatical move from a past historic to a punctiliar aorist – the second knowing is quite specific and epiphanic – but, either way, this process of knowing and the contents of what is known are both related to the body. For both Jesus and the woman there are significant moments of recognition, there is a knowledge and a knowing that are somatic. Recognition issues from altered states in the flows within which each body is located (and continually being relocated). For the woman this issues in her being able to tell him the whole truth [*pasan ten aletheian*] – where *aletheia* in Mark's Gospel is reserved for the Christ alone.[10]

Third, it is touch that effects these alterations. There is a movement through the senses in this passage. First, the woman has heard of Jesus (always in Mark a precondition for believing), then she sees Jesus as one of the crowd, then she touches him. The movement of the senses implicates the woman in an economy of distance – of which more later. It is touch that bridges the different flows within which each body is situated and lives. The bridging disturbs and redistributes the currents. In Mark's Gospel there are 11 references to touch (*apto*) but several scenes in which touch is implied by descriptions of what Jesus does with his hands. In each case bar one there is a cleansing (1.41) or a making whole (3.10; 6.56; 7.33; 8.22). The one exception is 10.13 where Jesus desires that the children are brought to him 'that he should touch them'. Touch initiates transference, involving each in an economy of response that is rooted in the body and calls forth somatic knowledges of recognition. Sometimes, as with the haemorrhaging woman, the recognition is sealed by a naming that indicates a new relation – the woman becomes 'daughter'. Touch gives particular direction to a body continually being situated relationally; it orientates and focuses the various fluid operations. Touch triggers a divine operation, an eschatological operation. It is an operation in which the messianic is performed.[11] The making-whole of the body is a salvific act that translates the recipient into a citizen of the Kingdom. Proleptically, each one cleansed[12] or made whole receives intimations of their resurrected body. This is significant in a gospel like Mark's where there may be no resurrection scene of the body of Christ. Related to touch is faith, for Jesus redirects each recipient of healing away from the touch to a participation that the touch is an expression of: 'Your faith has cured you.' Faith here is a practice, a form of acting, not a state of mind. For touch enacts trust. To pass over from one's own body to another is an act of entrustment. Entrustment is believing as an action; a believing that the body knows (*ginosko*) and performs before the intellect grasps (*oida*). Faith draws each into the energy flows within which Jesus is situated.[13] Only in Christ in this way can the pronouncement be made of 'Peace', *Shalom*.[14] The levels of entrustment become more pronounced when what is touched is not the garments but the body itself. Consider these two other passages in Mark:

> And they brought to him [Jesus] a man who was deaf, and had an impediment in his speech; and they besought him to lay his hand upon him. And taking him aside from the multitude privately, he put his fingers into his ears, and he spat, and touched his tongue. (7.32–3)

And they came to Bethsaida. And some people brought to him a blind man, and begged him to touch him. And he took the blind man by the hand, and led him out of the village; and when he had spat upon his eyes, and laid his hands upon him, he asked him, 'Do you see anything?' And he looked up and said, 'I see men; but they look like trees, walking.' Then again he laid his hands again upon his eyes; and he looked intently and was restored, and saw everything clearly. (8.22–5)

There are degrees of intimacy here not found in the passage concerned with the haemorrhaging woman. Flesh makes contact with other flesh, and no doubt this intimacy is possible because the miraculous healing involves two men. Significantly, neither Matthew nor Luke makes any use of these two miracle stories. The personal withdrawal of each man into a secluded space and away from the anonymity of the 'they' who bring these persons to him – 'he took the blind man by the hand' – emphasises that intimacy. Touch is again related to a certain discharge of salvific power. Although in these passages there is no allusion to *dunamis*, the power is materialised instead in terms of a discharge of Jesus's own bodily fluids. But the touch in both accounts is specific. It is directed to the area of the body that is damaged: Jesus reaches into each man's pain, identifies it (and with it). In the first case he actually penetrates the other man's body, crossing into the flesh of the other. The pain is assuaged by the love, care and attention that each is drawn into by that touch. Touch translates the negative into the positive. Touch is a reaching beyond the boundaries of oneself to find a place not yet given, a future not yet received. It is a gesture of overflow.

From the following piece of exegesis we can proceed to develop theologically the three interconnected *topoi* I draw attention to – touch, flows and relation – that will facilitate an understanding of the logic of the incarnation that Christ inaugurates and conducts for the salvation of the world. Touch, flow and relation enable us to develop a Christology in which doctrines of incarnation and atonement become inseparable from doctrines of creation and the Church.

Touch

Let me clarify at the beginning here the mode of touch that I am treating and what I am investigating in this treatment. First: the mode of touch is directly related to the healing of the woman's haemorrhage and any number of uses of touch by Jesus to heal. It is significant in Mark's account of the haemorrhaging woman that two forms of touch are identified, for the woman's touch is distinguished from mere contact. It is the disciples (always in various states of ignorance throughout Mark's Gospel) who draw attention to contact: 'You see the crowd pressing upon you and yet you ask,

"Who touched me?'" I am not concerned here with forms of contact – and neither is Mark's Gospel. Aristotle's attention to touch in *De Anima* has been criticised for its 'exclusive concentration on passive rather than active touching'[15] or 'contact sense'. I am far from sure this is a correct evaluation of Aristotle, but it serves to emphasise that the treatment of touch here is exclusively concerned with active touching. In German one can distinguish between two types of body, *Körper*, that is inert, and *Leib*, that is not. *Körper* can refer to the physical bodies of people or animals and can be extended metaphorically to speak of the body of a text (*Textkörper*), for example. *Leib*, on the other hand, bears several interrelated senses. First, it is the precondition for perception. As such it is the German translation of what Merleau-Ponty calls 'body' – that site of crossing between the seeing body and that which is seen, the touching body and that which is touched. Self-reflexivity is the very condition for *Leib*. Second, *Leib* refers on a social level to the complex matrix of relations and circumstances in which individual bodies are implicated. As such, it is only because of this body (as *Leib*) that community becomes possible. The body as *Leib* is political because the body as *Leib* lives (*bios*) whereas the body as *Körper* subsists (*zoe*).[16] Thirdly, *Leib* is, theologically understood, the dwelling-place of the soul.[17]

This examination of touch concerns, then, bodies in the German sense of *Leiber*. Furthermore, it is concerned with the active touching between persons.[18] In the active touching between persons we are examining the intentional structure of touching. 'Intention' here is not simply the conscious motivations for the subject as agent. I use intention in a way developed by Husserl in the fifth of his Logical Investigations – the experience of an object of my directed attention (*Gerichtetheit*), an object made meaningful for me.[19] These intentions are constitutive of the experience of the perception (apperception) and there is an indeterminacy about them intrinsic to what is being presented as such. Intentional experiences involve interpretative relations and may become the basis upon which volitional intentions to act are made by an agent, but are prior to such intentions. Intentional structures, as Husserl wrestled to point out, are complex and multilayered. An examination of such structures attempts to clarify some of these layers. The intentional structure of touching cannot simply be examined from the point of view of the one touching. For it is the nature of this mode of touch (and Aristotle was certainly aware of this) to affect whatever is touched – as the example of Jesus's response to the haemorrhaging woman makes plain. As a swimmer one quickly comes to recognise an accidental 'brush' against another swimmer and a touch whose intentions are, in some subtle way, communicated (that is, delivered and received). Those intentions can take on various communicative shadings – sexual suggestion, aggressive warning, competitive edge, etc. The context is important: both bodies are exposed, each to the other. The nakedness renders them both open to the world, vulnerable to suggestion. What is important for this analysis (and returns us to the object of this investigation into touch) is how a 'recognition' of the intentional structure of that touch is produced.

What is the operation of such knowledge, what are its effects, and what are the implications of both that operation and its effects for a theological anthropology? These are some of the questions I wish to examine. In the pool much is communicated between two swimmers about each other, but without words or often distinctive gesturing (for the swimming proceeds through a steady rhythm of strokes that neither wishes to disrupt). Nevertheless temperament, present mood, past training, ability, and even levels of intelligence are all communicated through mutual observation (which has always an element of voyeurism about it). Jean-Louis Chrétien speaks of how 'The flesh listens. And the fact that it listens is what makes it respond.'[20] The addition of intentional touch, though, dramatises this communication. It is this dramatisation that is being investigated below.

Origen in *Contra Celsum* 1.48 writes: 'And they touched the Word by faith so that an emanation came from him to them which healed them ... [Jesus's] truly divine touch.' He refers to 1 John 1.1 in which the 'Word of life' is apprehended or 'handled' by three senses: hearing, seeing and touching – handling 'the Word of life'. 1 John continues that there is a bearing witness that can take place by describing what the followers of Christ have seen and repeating what they have heard. These acts of representation also disseminate a power that will bring those who picture and hear them into a fellowship, a participation that is ultimately Trinitarian (1 John 1.3). We analysed this *poiesis* and its association with mimesis in the previous essay [in Ward, *Christ and Culture*: cited in Note 7]. But what the witnesses cannot communicate is their touching Christ; for representation distances and renders into a general vocabulary that which was personally experienced. And touch individuates by a bringing into contact and proximity. Touch cannot distance and does not submit to a general vocabulary without ceasing to be what it is. Touch communicates only to the other being touched. It cannot communicate to a third party. A third party may witness touch and draw inferences about it, but s/he has not entered into what was being communicated in the touch. Touch can be described in terms of pleasure, pain, pressure, warmth, etc., but that which has been brought into being by the touching cannot be brought into being through the representation of that touch. Touch intimates, it does not speak. Speaking of the child's early tactile experience, the psychologist David Katz uses the term *Eindruck*, an impression, a prehension.[21] The intimacy it creates communicates not a knowledge but a knowingness, an intentionality that expects a response. It brings this knowingness into existence not as creation from nothing but as the realising of the singularity of that which exists. It announces that it is I, in my very corporeal individuality, who is knowing (rather than who knows) you in your very corporeal individuality. As such, this singularising is a bringing forth from an indifference, an indeterminacy, an anonymity. It is not a bringing to identity, for identity is too strong a word for what is only intimated. Rather, it is a bringing into relation because of an intimation of difference. This relational difference is recognised only in a belonging, only in the interchange that in intimating something brings about a transformation in what is perceived and under-stood in and between the touching and the touched; though the substance of this transformation is only realised in a subsequent reflection.

I would, then, modify what Maurice Merleau-Ponty (for whom also embodied perception is a locus of mystery and enigma) observes about touch and perception when he writes:

> The moment perception comes my body effaces itself before it *and* never does the perception grasp the body in the act of perceiving. If my left hand is touching my right hand, and if I should suddenly wish to apprehend with my right hand the work of my left hand as it touches, this reflection of the body upon itself always miscarries at the last moment: the moment I feel my left hand with my right hand, I correspondingly cease touching my right hand with my left hand. But this last-minute failure does not drain all truth from that presentiment I had of being able to touch myself touching: my body does not perceive, but it is as if it were built around the perception that dawns through it.[22]

Merleau-Ponty, here as elsewhere in his work, while wishing to move beyond the dualism of mind and body, nevertheless draws a distinction between the body and reflection in which perception is already cognition and prejudgement. This is a model of perception founded upon seeing[23] and I would accept what both Heidegger and Wittgenstein have taught us that we 'see as'. But I suggest that in touch the body does not efface itself. There is an intimation of its very corporeality; as if the body is brought into being by that touch. In fact, in his earlier work *Phenomenology of Perception*, Merleau-Ponty points exactly to that when he writes that in touch,

> I do not only use my fingers and my whole body as a single organ, but also, thanks to this unity of the body, the tactile perceptions gained through an organ are immediately translated into the language of the rest ... Each contact of an object with part of our objective body is, therefore, in reality a contact with the whole of the present or possible phenomenal body.[24]

And so I would correct Merleau-Ponty's later phrase, writing: 'my body does perceive and is built around that perception'. The body perceives itself in relation and knows the nature of that relation. If Merleau-Ponty misses that, it may well be because in the left hand touching the right there is no other, both hands are mine. They are 'one sole organ of experience'.[25] There is what he elsewhere calls the criss-crossing 'of the touching and the tangible',[26] but the touching does not enter a field of intentions and an economy of response, because there is no *eros*.[27] Consider a different kind of touching of oneself in which there is *eros*: masturbation. Here the body is effaced and there is no experience of 'touching myself touching', for a distance is opened up by fantasy, erotic scenarios into which the body is inserted; not the physical body but one of the many fantasised bodies we live with. Fantasy consumes the body's perceptions. The body cannot be intimate with itself. Though it can pleasure itself, it cannot singly enjoy the pleasuring of itself without withdrawing from the fantasised scene that supports the pleasuring. The body cannot intimate things to itself.[28] The *eros* that is conjured in masturbation has first to project and maintain a body image elsewhere. It has to manufacture a distance, an exteriority, for itself such that touching and being touched can take place.

If then the body comes to a sense of itself as different, as singular, as a unity through touch, the economy of that response is governed by desire. Desire issues in a play of nearness and separation, availability and inaccessibility, masking and revealing. If desire can only be desire through an economy of distance, then the economy of response is intertwined with an unfolding of distances, differences, exteriorities that pass in and out of inferiorities. This movement in and out, separation and penetration,[29] is not only the heartbeat of the economy of response; it is an exchange, a giving and reception, and a communication. One recalls that the word 'intimate' in its verbal form comes from the Late Latin verb *intimo* – to flow into (Julius Solinus, AD 250), to communicate to the spirit (Tertullian AD 160–240), to put into, but also by AD 400 to narrate, tell, describe, relate. Its adjectival form comes from the earlier Latin *intimus* – innermost or most secret. It is used by Cicero (43 BC) to describe a form of relationship, even a close friend. One might also add, a little more felicitously, a relation to *in-timeo*, where *timeo* means to dread, to fear and the prefix *in* negates that experience. I add this last conjectural possibility because intimacy is always ringed with fear, even when it most excludes, and this is part of the way in which desire and distance are interrelated. For intimacy demands the body's openness, its vulnerability. The calibre, or profundity of the giving or reception, depends upon recognising the possibilities of fear, of dread, and negotiating them. The negotiation involves a suffering because I am not the other, and intimacy, while fearing absorption by the other, also suffers the longing for an integration. In Emily Brontë's *Wuthering Heights*, at the climax of an argument between Catherine Earnshaw and Nelly Dean concerning Cathy's obsession with Heathcliff, Cathy shouts out 'I *am* Heathcliff.'[30] But she is not, and that is both her triumph, as a character who epically takes her place at Heathcliff's side, and her tragedy. Intimacy causes a tearing apart, to expose the suffering of longing. Distance, difference are figurations of longing (long-ing) – without them there would be stasis.

Intimacy and distance then require flows, movements, operations and economies. Aquinas provides us with a theological account of this state of things when discussing the divine governance of creation:

> Thus this God does work in every worker, according to these three things.
> First as an end. For since every operation is for the sake of some good, real

or apparent; and nothing is good either really or apparently, except insofar as it participates in a likeness to the Supreme Good, which is God; it follows then that God Himself is the cause of every operation as it ends. Again, it is to be observed that where there are several agents in order, the second always acts in virtue of the first: for the first agent moves the second to act. And thus all agents act in virtue of God Himself: and therefore He is the cause of action in every agent. Thirdly, we must observe that God not only moves things to operate, as it were applying their forms and powers to operation ... but He also gives created agents their forms and preserves them in being. Therefore He is the cause of action not only by giving the form which is the principle of action, as the generator is said to be the cause of movement in things heavy and light; but also as preserving the forms and powers of things ... And since the form of a thing is within the thing [*est intra rent*], and all the more as it approaches nearer to the First and Universal Cause, and because in all things God Himself is properly the cause of universal being which is innermost of all things [*quod inter omnia est magis intimum rebus*], it follows that in all things God works intimately [*in omnibus intime operatur*]?[31]

We will return to this passage. Distance here has only to do with spatiality insofar as spatial images are used to conceive it. But distance cannot be reduced to some mathematical measurement separating two bodies in some pure or idealised space. Bodies can be in close proximity, touching, even interpenetrating, and yet nevertheless distance is experienced. Distance cannot in fact become an identifiable object. Perhaps the closest we get to distance as such is the identification of difference. The distance is intimated to those differences that compose it. This distance is implicated, then, in a common participation, a common recognition of exteriority: I am not the other; the other is not I; the other is not reducible to or measurable by me; and I am not reducible to or measurable by the other. What is intimated in this distance is an excess; the mystery of alterity. Every representation made of this distance must fail if the aim of such representation is to define. For there is no place from which an exhaustive representation is possible, no neutral locus – which again appeals to an ideal, mathematically conceived spatiality. Even the notions of exteriority and inter-iority lose their meaning, as neither subject has access to this distance outside of participating in it. The memory of that participation may attempt to re-present it – but at best it will be an echo of the experience bouncing back from the walls of a single consciousness. It is not that the distance escapes representation, in fact it demands representation because the distance constitutes a command to communicate. Distance precedes and haunts all communication. But what is intimated in this dis-tance exceeds chains and combinations of signifiers. At best it can imbue signs with a semantic plenitude – like the phrases 'I know you' or 'You know me', spoken by those participating in what Jean-Luc Marion describes as an 'intimate alterity'.[32] These phrases are bridges of suspended steel that open up the distance, sway in the wind and expand and contract with the rise and fall of temperature. The knowledge of distance and its negotiation as it arises in intimacy is a knowledge of difference-in-relation. But, again, this is not a conceptual knowledge, for 'the relation' itself is rendered indefinable in this distance. The relation is always in play, always under construction. Like the distance itself, the relation is never there as an object as such. This is not a conceptual knowing; it is a bodily knowing that is received, given and lived prior to any reflection. The reflection cannot erase the traces of what the body has received, given and lived. In fact, it is these traces that call forth reflection – or rather, meditation, or what the prayerful understand as contemplation.

We must distinguish here between reflection, as Merleau-Ponty (after Husserl) understands it, and contemplation.[33] For it is in this distinction that the theology of embodiment (and touch as the most fundamental mode of joining to an understanding of being embodied) announces itself most clearly. Following Descartes, to reflect is always to grasp one's own knowing (*cogito ergo sum*), to recognise it as such. Reflection conceptualises and therefore represents certain states and conditions to itself. Its movement is circular in the way phenomenologists since Hegel have recognised the dialectic of In-Itself and For-Itself. To contemplate is to transcend the circularities of rejection; for it is a movement towards the other – a movement that is facilitated, even solicited by that other. It is to be drawn to the other, who is drawn to you. It is a movement without concepts – though images may be used in the first instance (as with an icon). As the goal of reflection is understanding, so the goal of contemplation is a mutual discerning – to know even as I am known. There is not a content to this knowledge. The knowing is a condition of being, a condition in the Johannine texts that is often described as abiding (*meno* – to stay, to stand, but transitively to await, to expect).

Intimacy is mutual abiding, what in John's Gospel is described as the centre of Messianic relationality – I in you and you in me.[34] This relationality participates in and reveals the logic of the incarnation. As the Prologue in the Gospel of St John describes it through a complex combination of prepositions: 'he came into [*eis*] the world. He was in [*en*] the world, and the world came to be [*egeneto*] through him [*di'autou*]' (John 1.9–10). Christ in-dwells that which is already in Christ – the world that was made through him. And so the only-begotten of God begets. The one who, as Origen expounded it,[35] is eternally generated by the uncreated God creates, and then indwells his creation. In this sense we can speak of God's profound touch; the intimacy of his presence as that which touches through maintaining our very existence as an emanation of his own essence. This is at the heart of Aquinas's understanding of divine operations above in which he employs the adjectival form '*intimo*'. He also explicitly relates the intimacy with the cognates of the verb – to flow into, to communicate to the spirit. In *Summa Contra Gentiles* he observes: 'one finds a diverse manner of emanation of things [*diversus emanationis modus invenitur in rebus*] and, the higher a nature is, the more intimate to the nature is that which flows from it [*et quanto aliqua natura est altior, tanto id quod ex ea emanat, magis ei est intimum*].[36] Gregory of Nyssa in his Eleventh Homily on the *Canticum Canticorum* describes this intimacy as the 'perception of his presence [*aesthesis parousias*]':[37] a perception or feeling (*aesthesis*) in which the remoteness of the uncreated *ousia* of God effects in the soul a profound closeness. If this tension of intense proximity and distance is the very nature of human beings created in the image of God, it issues from the logic of the incarnation. Salvation is to become enfolded within this enfolding logic – to attain the condition of being incarnate as the Word is incarnate, or what Gregory and others termed *theios*. More clearly, human beings have to participate in becoming flesh as he became flesh. Human beings are not truly themselves, are not truly flesh, until they have become flesh as he became flesh. We are, then, seeking a body; through intimacy we seek an intimacy with that source of the 'emanation of things'. It is a body being prepared for us. According to Paul's letter to the Ephesians,[38] it is 'his body, the fullness [*to pleroma*] of him that fills all in all' (Ephesians 1.23).[39] It is a condition of enfleshment that is eschatological – a resurrection body, a new kind of embodiment that in its very singularity indwells or is, to use a term coined by Merleau-Ponty, 'transcorporeal'. Giorgio Agamben describes this condition as being at 'ease':

> The Provençal poets (whose songs first introduce the term into Romance languages in the form of *aizi, aizimen*) make ease a *terminus technicus* in their poetics, designating the very place of love. Or better, it designates not so much the place of love, but rather love as the experience of taking-place in a whatever singularity.[40]

Touch is an orientation towards being incarnate and it finds its true-self-understanding in love. Even the touch involved in violence towards, in abuse of, oneself or the other is a call for love, a recognition of its absence. To cut oneself is an attempt to attain some recognition of an embodiment that seems constantly to be under threat of disappearing. It is the mark of the wish to feel again; the recognition of being in a frozen state, without desire. Touch is always an action, an activity – as distinct from seeing, which is more passive and at my command. As Merleau-Ponty observes:

> In visual experience, which pushes objectification further than does tactile experience, we can, at least at first sight, flatter ourselves that we constitute the world, because it presents us with a spectacle spread out before us at a distance, and gives us the illusion of being immediately present everywhere and being situated nowhere.[41]

Seeing invokes the possibility of pure separation, of exteriority, of rampant individualism, of social atomism, of the society of the spectacle. But touch, adhering as it does 'to the surface of the body',[42] disrupts the 'spectacle' as 'spectacle'. Theologically understood, it disrupts the production of idols – it forestalls reification by the instauration of an economy, a movement, an action. It is at this point that touch is related to flows, for the movement described above as the economy of response (that is inseparable from touching and loving) is a profoundly kenotic movement – the emptying of one towards the other, that is ongoing and endless.

Flows

Two Greek terms are at the theological heart of understanding motion and flows: *kenosis* [self-emptying] and *pleroma* [fullness]. These terms are also the theological heart for our third, *topos* [relation]. This is a giving of oneself that can only come from the ongoing and endless reception of the other. This outpouring, both divine and human, is only possible, and for human beings only sustainable, in terms of the infinite plenitude of God's *ousia* [substance]. Here lies the basis for a sociality that is the burning vision in all ecclesiological practice. This is very important today, because the unprecedented rise in refugees, exiles, and homeless and stateless people finds an echo in the growing popularity of ideas like kenosis, emptying, exile and the nomadic among some postmodern philosophers:[43] Michel de Certeau,[44] for example, Mark C. Taylor,[45] Jean-Luc Nancy,[46] Gianni Vattimo,[47] Emmanuel Lévinas[48] and Jacques Derrida.[49] It is, as we shall see, a kenosis or emptying without telos, an infinite kenosis, a kenosis also that issues from and into absence, not *pleroma*. I will develop what is at stake here with reference to the work of Lévinas.

What characterises philosophy, for Lévinas, is totality: the going out from and the return to the Same in some Hegelian feedback loop. This takes narrative form in the story of Ulysses 'whose adventure in the world was only a return to his native island'.[50] What his own work defines is the wounding mark or trace of the infinite, the transcendent, an exteriority that forever disrupts this return to the homeland of the Same and therefore totality. This is a thinking orientated towards the wholly other [*autre*], a

> departure with no return, which, however, does not go forth into the void, [but] would lose its absolute *orientation* if it sought recompense in the immediacy of its triumph ... As an orientation towards the other ... a work is possible only in the patience, which, pushed to the limit, means for the agent to renounce being the contemporary of its outcome, to act without entering the Promised Land.[51]

The orientation towards the other – in which oneself is hostage to the other, totally responsible before this other, accused in the eyes of the other – means for Lévinas that we forever live beyond ourselves. This is the basis for ethics, for him. Not simply an ethics of moral prescriptions, but an ethics commanded by a Good beyond being whose infinity calls all our human productions and fabrications into question. We are summoned to live beyond our home-making, to leave the cities of refuge. This wholly other, in whose wake we follow, is recognised in the face of the stranger, the widow, the orphan; it calls each of us in turn to 'go forth', even if that going forth is not 'into the void'. There is redemption only in this movement out to the other. In a passage entitled '*Pièces d'identité*' Lévinas writes: 'A Jew is accountable and responsible for the whole edifice of creation. Something engages man even more than the salvation of his soul. The acts, utterance, thoughts of a Jew have a formidable privilege of destroying or restoring worlds.' '[A]s responsible,' Lévinas writes, 'I am never finished with emptying myself of myself. There is infinite increase in this exhausting of oneself, in which the subject is not simply an awareness of this expenditure, but is its locus and event ... *The glory of a long desire!* The subject as hostage.'[52]

If I am critical of Lévinas, and even more so of other modern philosophers of the kenotic, or endless self-emptying, it is because of the lack of attention they pay to reception. I do not accept that kenosis is the basis of sociality. As the host must receive her guests, the guests must receive the hospitality offered. For Lévinas, this omission is explicable in terms of the attention given to receptivity in Kant and also Husserl's phenomenology; he wishes to examine that which is prior, for him, to receptivity: being obligated or *subjectum* to the other. Lévinas is also wishing to describe an economy, a work towards the other, that 'requires the ingratitude of the other'; since gratitude would be the 'return of the movement to its origin'.[53] In other words, in Lévinas's understanding of the economy of the gift there cannot be mutuality or reciprocity. The economy envisaged, and Lévinas is emphatic about this, is 'a one-way movement'. It is not, in my own terms, an economy of response. What this other brings or evokes is desire; 'desire for the other'[54] is key to Lévinas's account of oneself, one's neighbours, God and ethics. The other is recognised in the economy of the desire it evokes. But sociality is not simply desire *for* the other, it is also the other's desire for me. Lévinas conceives that in the unending emptying of oneself, in the way the other empties me, I discover 'ever new resources. I did not know I was so rich'.[55] But from where can these resources spring if the ego is always a hostage, always accused? They can only come from that which is continually being given, such that what I am being emptied of is that which I am being given: the infinite generosity or fullness of God's grace that St Paul conceives in terms of *pleroma*. That sociality, which moves beyond ourselves and into a permanent journeying towards the other, is only possible within an economy of the gift in which I am constituted in the transit of plenitudinous grace. Only then can my desire for the other avoid being endless sacrifice, on the one hand, or a lust that only consuming the other would satisfy. *Pleroma* as infinite, divine generosity makes possible a relationality beyond self-abnegation and beyond appetite. There are alternative economies of the gift that do not figure mutuality in terms of a return to the same.[56] This is an economy of the gift that Lévinas inherits from Marcel Mauss, in which giving incurs a debt to be repaid.[57] Giving is fundamentally associated with exchange, so non-reciprocity is needed to forestall a return.[58] But the economy of giving that I am outlining is more akin to the situation between the host and his guests when Abraham welcomes the three strangers into his camp at Mamre (Genesis 18.1–15).[59] Abraham does not give to the strangers because he will get something in return. Though he later receives the promise of Isaac, the service and the welcome he offers are prior to this promise. He receives the strangers as God and in faithfulness to the God who has been with him throughout his journeying. Being faithful is an orientation of being towards God; it determines but is prior to action. Faithfulness is not part of an exchange system. It is excessive to any system since, when nothing appears to be given and one has to live for a future in which others will enter the Promised Land, not you, faithfulness remains.

The giving that operates between oneself, other people (*autrui*) and God as wholly other (*autre*) transcends exchange. Lévinas is right to point out how we do not own ourselves, but I believe his understanding of God as absolutely other is wrong. It is a God who is always absent, whose mark upon creation is only a trace of his passing on ahead; a God who does not return the infinity of one's desire but, in order to remain God and other must be indifferent to our continual attention to his intention in creating us. Now while I hold to the importance of the apophatic tradition in cutting through our projections and fetishes of God, nevertheless I would maintain that the infinity of our desire for the other is only possible on the basis of the infinity of the other's desire for me, and that it is only on that basis of participation in that prior divine erotic giving and receiving, that each of us is able to give to each other. Not that this economy of reception between the divine and human is equal, for the God who created and sustains me, and in whose Triune life I live, is both the origin and the end of my desire. But within what John Milbank has rightly termed 'the asymmetrical reciprocity'[60] we are each of us both constituted and all our relationships likewise. Human beings are gifts to each other in an endless economy of God's grace whereby we are given in order to give.

Now why has this investigation into Lévinas's thinking been important? Because this account of the endless journeying into exile, this account of kenosis in which one is always a stranger, is very popular among postmodern philosophers. With de Certeau and with Lévinas it is developed in a theological context such that Lévinas can remark that this 'departure with no return ... however, does not go forth into the void'. It is the theological context alone that saves this journeying from nihilism. Nihilism issuing from an account of being in exile can do nothing for the plight of the refugee. The work of Derrida, Vattimo and Taylor simply announces that we are all dispossessed persons and in a continual state of being dispossessed; we are all nomads. The corollary of that confronts the refugee with the claim: 'You are nothing special. You merely give poignant expression to the condition of being human.' While there is some truth in that, as I have argued above, that is not the whole of the story. As Edward Said has pointed out in his examination of the experience of being the migrant or the refugee, 'To live as if everything around you were temporary and perhaps trivial is to fall prey to petulant cynicism as well as a querulous lovelessness.'[61] That is not a recipe for sociality; only for indifference and accelerated social atomism. Abraham journeys into deeper and deeper exile but always within the context of God's grace and promise towards him. He journeys within the economy of divine giving, of divine loving that is not impassive to Abraham's desire to be faithful. It is this participation that enables him, in exile, to be the host: to welcome the stranger into all the temporary conditions of his own dwelling. Let me put this in another way: Abraham can befriend the strangers because he knows that his true dwelling lies in God's love for him, and the strangers can accept and return Abraham's reception for exactly the same reason. The economy of faithful response is excessive to (because prior to) economies of exchange. In such an economy, to give hospitality also requires us to recognise how we are receiving hospitality: the reception of what is given is also a hosting in oneself of the other. There is no superiority between host and guest. For to host is to allow the guest to be as oneself; and to be a guest is to receive the host as oneself. True justice only operates in obedience to the economy of faithful response that recognises the question in every encounter, 'Who is the stranger?', and realises the answer is: 'Neither of us – while we have each other.' This is the economy of love – that aims always at the perfection and righting of relation. There is no justice, just as there is no beauty, truth or goodness, outside the divine ordering of all relation (or what Pseudo-Dionysius understood as 'hierarchy' and Gregory of Nyssa termed 'order' or *akolouthia*). From the human body in right relation issues the body politic and ecclesial.

We will treat relation itself more fully below. For the moment let us continue this meditation through the association between 'flows' and kenosis (through the metaphorical suggestiveness of the verbs *kenoo* – to empty – and *pleroo* – to fill or make full). This association draws attention to the different forms of flow and flux within Mark's text. For throughout we have been talking about 'operations', 'movements', 'productions' and 'economies'. What is the relationship between the physical issue of blood (which eventually turns into the issue of Christ's own blood, which in terms of the Eucharistic outpouring continues to haemorrhage until his body is complete), the corresponding and countering issue of power and these other dynamisms? Theologically, motion is governed by a teleology – salvation.[62] What is this salvation that physical healing is analogically related to? We can only appreciate the nature of salvation when we understand the origin and end of motion – that is, why there should be a divine creating at all and how that is related to God's own desiring. Motion is ecstatic and ultimately Trinitarian; and the condition for its possibility is distance. We saw above that it is distance that gives intimacy and enables participation. What salvation is then, and what the operations of grace move towards, is an ever-deepening

participation in God – the source of life in abundance, resurrection life. Eschatological concepts such as 'peace', 'abiding', 'rest' (as eternal Sabbath) are intimations of the
content of this participation, like Agamben's 'ease'. The ecstatic nature of motion requires
continual self-abandonment. What Paul calls being a 'living sacrifice' (Rom. 12.1). It
stands in contradistinction to what Paul describes as hardening the heart (Rom. 9.18,
11.7, 11.25) – that is, the stasis, the paralysis that issues from self-protection, fear,
resentment, anger, narcissism. In fact there is only one motion because there is only
one telos – and that motion is, depending upon perspective, kenotic or pleromatic (to
coin a word). It is either emptying towards the other or filling with respect to
receiving the other. Any notion of participation requires understanding this economy.
Not that there is a reciprocity here, finally. For we are given before we learn to give
and receive within that ultimate givenness. Divinely understood, there is response not
reciprocity proper (though we can use Milbank's felicitous phrase 'asymmetrical reciprocity'). But insofar as God accommodates himself to that which is human, and
insofar as we human beings as his creation are 'necessarily … framed of such a kind
as to be adapted to the participation of such good',[63] then it follows that there are
both operations of God in the world and discernments of them and a reciprocity of
relation among all things mundane (of the created order). In Barth's language, in
creation there is both an external and an internal covenant. Christ, as the mediator of
God to humankind and humankind to God, makes possible both the asymmetrical and
symmetrical reciprocity, for the movements of Christ are both participations in the
perichoresis that constitutes the impassable triune Godhead and the economic operations of that perichoresis with respect to creation itself. Creation in and through the
Word is caught up in the flows, emanations and energies that not only keep that
creation in existence but also maintain its orders. Gregory of Nyssa, commenting
upon a traditional Trinitarian analogy of the relationship of the Father to the Son
being like the relationship between mind and word, puts it thus:

> the Word of God has been shown not to be this actual utterance of speech,
> or the possession of some science or art, but to be a power [dunamis]
> essentially and substantially existing, willing all good, and being possessed of
> strength to execute all its will; and, of a world that is good, this power
> [dunamis] appetitive and creative of good is the cause.[64]

With the word dunamis we return to the Gospel passage of the haemorrhaging
woman's miraculous healing. Both kenoo and pleroo, as descriptions of the divine
economy and the response it calls forth, are related back to dunamis. In the Introduction [to Christ and Culture] I commented upon how this word, like oikonomia and
energeia, was central to early Christologies as found in the Apologists. Let me take this
further in developing a Christology in terms of flow and motion on the basis of the
citation from Gregory. As Jean Daniélou points out, following the early Apologists,

'the *dunamis theou* came to be thought of in two successive stages: first, as an impersonal power inherent in the divine nature, and, secondly, as the Son of God brought forth specifically for the work of creation'.[65] But this led to varieties of subordinationist thinking. It was Origen who corrected some of the early apologetic (and Gnostic) thinking in which *dunamis* and *energeia* figured by making the generation of the Son from the Father eternal. But, as Michel Barnes has commented, 'where Athanasius and his contemporaries use the doctrine of divine generation to prove that the Father and the Son share the same nature or essence, Gregory uses generation as the basis for distinguishing the Persons [of the Trinity]'.[66] Power is the expression of essence or *ousia*. Christ shares in the power of God (as does the Spirit), and it is the unity of the operations of this power that demonstrates the singleness of their nature (*ousia*). We will return to the generation and production of difference in several other essays [in *Christ and Culture*]. For the moment I only wish to pay attention to the way the Godhead is conceived as endlessly appetitive and creative in its operations; and how all these operations are good. Christology has to be conceived in terms of this power and these operations. As such, salvation comes as human beings recognise they exist within this economy of response, this 'eternal power of God which is creative of things that are, the discoverer of things that are not, the sustaining cause of things that are brought into being, the foreseeing cause of things yet to be'.[67] The woman's spring of blood (that has caged her in a concern with herself, with her health, with spending all she has on the care of that self and trying to restore that health) dries up – because she enters into the flows of God's power. Participating now in a new, dynamic economy – living out that appetitive and creative kenosis and *pleroma* – issues in new asymmetrical and symmetrical reciprocities: the relations that constitute the body of Christ. As such, as we saw, some early commentators saw her as a figure of the Church.

Relation

Let us at this point return to the New Testament, and to another account in which touch, flows and relations coincide with Christology. This account is, in some way, the reverse of the scene of the woman with the haemorrhages as it concerns an extravagant outpouring towards Jesus:

> Six days before the Passover, Jesus came to Bethany, where Lazarus was, whom Jesus had raised from the dead. There they made him supper [*deipnon*]: Martha served [*diekonei*], and Lazarus was one of those at table with him. Mary took a pound of costly ointment of pure nard [*pistikes polutimou*] and anointed [*deipsen*] the feet of Jesus and wiped his feet with her hair; and the house was filled [*eplerothe*] with the fragrance of the ointment. But Judas

Iscariot, one of the disciples (he who was to betray [*paradidonai*] him), said, 'Why was this ointment not sold for three hundred denarii and given to the poor?' This he said, not that he cared for the poor but because he was a thief, and as he had the money-box he used to take what was put into it. Jesus said, 'Let her alone, let her keep it for the day of my burial. The poor you always have with you, but you do not always have me.' (John 12.1–8)

We have been concerned with relation throughout the examinations of touch and flows, but from this passage I wish to point to three things pertaining to the Christic operation. The extent to which this Johannine account is related to the accounts in Mark (14.3–9), Matthew (26.6–13), Luke (7.36–50) or some independent source has been fiercely debated by New Testament scholars.[68] I do not intend to enter those debates, which often tend to result in judgements about John's confused blend of traditions. And in moving from the account in Mark's Gospel to John's I have no other purpose than recognising different Christological elements, evident in Mark, pro-nounced in John.[69] As Rudolf Schnackenburg points out, with John 'the construction and direction of the story ... [has] its clear Christological tendency'.[70] This account allows me to make a number of points on the economy of relational exchanges; these points draw together the themes of this essay.

First, an economy of love constitutes the relations here (an 'extravagant act of love' – Bultmann[71]). There is a profound return of that which Mary had received. If, with the haemorrhaging woman in Mark's Gospel, *dunamis* flows out from Jesus through touch, here something is bestowed upon Jesus through the pouring of the ointment over his feet. What is bestowed is costly [*polutimou*], much valued, but it is the act itself that bestows most. For it not only anoints Jesus as the Messiah King,[72] and (as the different accounts of the story in the other Gospels express) anoints him proleptically for his burial. There is also here an act of sacrificial worship that confers on Jesus the glory of God. This glorification is important. Throughout the Gospel Jesus glorifies God and God glorifies Jesus. This co-glorification as an economy of response is central to the identification of Jesus as the Christ. Mary's act of glor-ification, intensified because it takes place in silence and is witnessed in silence, is a participation in the salvific presence (*kabod*) of the divine. Hence the act issues in a perfume that fills the house, akin to the smoke of the glory of God that fills the temple. There is an operation in this economy and a participation in that operation. Throughout the Gospel this divine operation is figured in terms of movements of descent and ascent.[73] Here in Mary's act is a profound obeisance, a descent that imitates and responds to Christ's own kenotic descent. She enacts, at another level, Martha's own serving (*diekonei*). In her descent Christ receives. His passivity is deeply receptive of the acknowledgement of who he truly is. He is lifted up, exalted, by her descent – the pouring of the ointment is a metonymy of the flow of her very self towards him.[74] This letting go occurs in several stages: the anointing of the feet, not the head (that parallels Jesus's own lowliness in the following chapter, where he stoops to wash the feet of the disciples at the Last Supper);[75] the smearing of the feet with the oil; and the letting down of her hair, a thing prostitutes did in the ancient world – as in the Lukan account. This act is, of course, related to the theme of reception and refusal that occurs throughout the Gospel. John insists it is not enough that Christ come to his own; his own must receive him.

But in this reciprocity we must always observe a difference that introduces us to the second observation about the Christic operation. The divine reaches out to the human, first and foremost; the human responds and, cooperating with the divine, glorifies God. The reciprocal relation issues from and is sustained by God. There is a priority here and that means there is a politics. Let me begin to define politics with an observation made by Michel Foucault: 'Power is only a certain type of relation between individuals.'[76] I would wish to take this further and suggest all power concerns relations as such. We will return to the question of reciprocity in a moment, but I suggest every relation (and power can only be powerful with respect to relations) is a power relation insofar as all relation involves the distribution of differences, and some of the differentials (perhaps many) involve inequalities. The inequalities may relate to biology (one having higher energy levels than another), physiology (one being stronger than another), psychology (levels of self-confidence or self-assertiveness), intellectual capacity, economics, class, professional hierarchy, etc. No relation is equal. Reciprocity, then, is either the ideal horizon towards which all relations aspire, or of a different order to personal and social standings; or perhaps both. There are two sets of the politics of relation in this story. There is the politics of what some commentators call the 'family circle' within which this supper takes place. The relations are deliberately politicised. It is uncertain whether Lazarus is both host and guest[77] but Martha's serving and both her and Mary's female presence at such a meal 'is surprising to the Jewish–Christian reader'.[78] But before we jump to the idea of a democratisation we have to recognise social levels of servitude that the Gospel writer disrupts by giving greater prominence to the female characters than the male ones (other than Jesus himself). The second set of political relations concerns the emphasising of differentials implicit in various hierarchical structures in the encounter between Mary and Jesus. There is the reclining male and the female at his feet; there is the teacher and the disciple; there is Christ and one of his believers; there is, theologically conceived, God and a human being, the creative Word and the creature. Touch, which here is not a momentary event but a continued action involving anointing and wiping [*exemaxen*],[79] establishes an exchange that does not overthrow the hierarchies; in fact, it confirms them as the order of things – it subtends them. Economies of gift and response constitute a relation in which both figures participate. It is in the participation itself that a reciprocity beneath or beyond personal, social or even theological standings operates. Power is continually displaced because the mutual affirmation that takes place in this event demands a co-dependency. To employ Louis Althusser's term 'interpellation', this event names Jesus as Christ as surely as it names Mary as the lover of Christ, a disciple, a bride, a figure of the Church as the bride. This co-dependency and co-constitution of identity allows for the reversal of roles – which is what occurs in the chapter that follows, when, at the Last Supper, Jesus lays aside his garments and both washes and wipes [*ekmassein*] the feet of the disciples. Touch establishes flows of love concretised in perfumed ointment and water that while affirming difference, are excessive to it.

The radical nature of the relation, the economy of exchange and touch in this passage, are emphasised through a contrasting relation and economy of response introduced with Judas Iscariot. There is a social equality established between him and Jesus, issuing in the way both are able to articulate judgements: Judas's observation that the ointment could have been sold for the poor is countered by Jesus's observation that there will always be poor people. The contrasting judgements about the situation can only be made, for both protagonists, from a position of assumed authority. Judas challenges Jesus and it is in the assumed right to challenge that a social equality is announced. But it is a *primus inter pares* [first amongst equals] that makes this reciprocity (that democratises Jesus as a man like Judas is a man), and therefore both relation and touch are impossible. Exchange is reduced to a simple material and financial one that is impervious to personal and theological economies of response. Rather than power being displaced it is reified in two antithetical positions. The move from the material specificities of 'this ointment' to the vague abstraction of 'the poor', in Judas's question, is indicative of the disembodiment that accompanies the establishment of political contestation and the hypostasising of democratised differences. This disembodiment is figured in terms of 'theft'. For Judas is a thief on many levels, most profoundly in being unable to return that which most truly belongs to the Christ (in contrast to Mary's sacrificial giving). In the foot-washing of chapter 13 Judas is included in a liturgy of incorporation ('If I wash you not, you have no part with me': John 13.8). Jesus, then, as the Messianic servant, refuses the disembodiment and distance from relation that Judas's refusal to engage installs. But then it is after the foot-washing that Judas 'went out immediately. And it was night' (John 13.30).

These observations on what we might term Christic relations or relations *en Christo* put a different gloss on Paul's statement in the Letter to the Galatians: 'There is nei-ther Jew nor Greek, there is neither slave nor free, there, is neither male or female; for you are all one in Christ Jesus' (Gal. 3.28). For that sentiment is read today in terms of a democratising of differences: Christ the leveller of hierarchies, the lib-erator of the subjugated. And what my reading has sought to point out is how that is not so. The oneness is in Christ and it does not concern the equality of social posi-tions. Jews remain Jews, Greeks Greeks, slaves slaves, freeborn freeborn, males male and females female and all relations between them will reflect levels of social and cultural power, its distribution, its waxing and waning. The Christic operation is not apolitical; it concerns power and its authorisation. The oneness concerns the submission of all social positions (and the politics of identity) to Christ, and the new orders of power (and its polity) that are engendered by this submission. It is an order and a polity that participates in the same oxymoronic condition found in the apophatic observations on knowing by unknowing, grasping by surrendering, fuelling a passion that is apathetic. Here in this economy of descent and ascent, service and kingship, vulnerability and power, framed by a coming crucifixion that is simultaneously a glorification, a giving that is receiving, an intimacy that distances, a kenosis that is plenitude, a laying down that is an exaltation.

The schizoid Christ

By way of conclusion, let me return to the 'schizophrenisation' that Deleuze and Guattari view as therapeutic.[80] In a chapter, called (after Engels and Freud) 'The Holy Family', they offer a characterisation of one who lives as a schizo:

> These men of desire – do they live yet? – are like Zarathustra. They know incredible sufferings, vertigos, and sicknesses. They have their spectres. They must reinvent each gesture. But such a man produces himself as a free man, irresponsible, solitary, and joyous, finally able to say and do something simple in his own name, without asking permission; a desire lacking nothing, a flux that overcomes barriers and codes, a name that no longer designates any ego whatever. He has simply ceased being afraid of becoming mad. He experiences and lives himself as the sublime sickness that will no longer affect him.[81]

The person is given over to the operations he performs, the desiring he produces and reproduces; as such this one is radically deterritorialised and gives way to the body without organs. What I am suggesting is that Christian theologians might rethink this figure in terms of Jesus as the Christ – viewing Christology as concerned with tracing and understanding the operations of Christ. I make such a proposal on the basis of trying to recover something of the 'otherness' of Christ for contemporary Christology. If Christ reveals to us what it is to be human, we cannot simply project our images of being human onto the figure of Christ. We have then to wrestle with and deconstruct the language and the categories we use to speak about this incarnate one. The early Church Fathers like Tertullian and Athanasius were emphatic that at every moment of his historical existence Jesus Christ did not cease being God.[82] It was by not ceasing to be God that human beings could become deified. The figure of the schizo I take, then, as a figure for the rethinking of what is human – 'do they live yet?' Of course, for Deleuze and Guattari, this experience of schizoid living is the product of capitalism's liberation of the flows of desire. But there is a correlation between the spirit of Christianity and capitalism that Marx, Weber and Benjamin (among others) have noted. Elsewhere I have argued how Marx understood capitalism as fundamentally an idolatrous form of religion – a religion in which the operations of a transcendent God become fetishised in terms of money or gold.[83] But the true schizo living – that Deleuze and Guattari recognise as intrinsic to any social production and reproduction, even in precapitalist times/places,[84] because inseparable from the *socius* as such – transgresses such fetishism, transgresses all codings of desire. There might then be theological value in examining further this schizo Christ who produces, through his unique operations, the deterritorialised Church – which, if not exactly a body without organs, might, in terms of Paul's first Letter to the Corinthians (12.12–31), be understood as a body in which the differences between organs are only epiphenomenal: 'many members, yet one body'. A schizo Christology, already announcing a theological anthropology, would lead then to a schizo ecclesiology: a true *socius*. But that is another essay.

Notes

1   'On "Not Three Gods"' in *Select Writings and Letters of Gregory, Bishop of Nyssa*, trs. William Moore and Henry Wilson, Oxford: Parker and Company, 1893, p. 333.

2   Deleuze and Guattari, *Anti-Oedipus: Capitalism and Schizophrenia*, tr. Robert Hurley et al., London: Athlone Press, 1984, p. 35. See Philip Goodchild, *Gilles Deleuze and the Question of Philosophy*, London: Associated University Presses, 1996, pp. 59–65 and his *Deleuze and Guattari: An Introduction to the Politics of Desire*, London: Sage Publications, 1996, pp. 73–105, 165–9 for commentary upon this notion of the schizo as developed by Deleuze and Guattari. In English 'schizo' may have derogatory connotations. I am certainly not wishing to use it in that way. I use the word here and throughout only because it is their word and the same word is employed in all secondary discussion.

3   I need to add here that unlike Deleuze and Guattari I am not suggesting the dissolution of the subject. I wish to retain notions of self, subject, personhood and identity. But I wish to make these notions radically relational – both in their nature and in the way in which we come to understand them. The surrender of the ego is not its disappearance, but it does mean that all our understandings of what that ego is are mediated, are interpretations that are mobile insofar as they arise from being continually contextualised and recontextualised. It is not then that Christ does not have a divine nature, but we can only gain understanding of that nature (and our own) through observing and participating in interpretations of his operations. To a certain extent this accords with the first part of Karl Barth's Christology in which Christ's divinity lies in his radical subjection to the Father. Revisiting Christology in terms of kenosis, Barth views Christ's humanity in terms of the surrender of his will to be in control. '[W]e must determine to seek and find the key to the whole difficult and heavily freighted concept of the "divine nature" at the point where it appears to be quite impossible ... the fact that Jesus Christ was obedient unto death' (*Die Kirkliche Dogmatik*, IV. 1, p. 218; *Church Dogmatics*, IV.I, p. 199). In terms of a more traditional dogmatic division, we only come to understand the nature and work of Christ through an economy of response.

4   Matthew nevertheless does observe the relation between touch and the distribution and reception of divine power: 'They besought [Jesus] that they might only touch the hem of his garment: and as many as touched were made perfectly whole' (14.36).

5   Nevertheless, it is Luke who records unambiguously what is central to my interpretation of this passage in Mark: 'And the crowd sought to touch him [Jesus], for power came forth from him and healed them all' (6.19). In both 6.19 and 8.46 Luke uses different prepositions

to describe the passage of the power – *para* (with the genitive) in 6.19 and *apo* (with the genitive) in 8.46, where Mark uses *ex* (with the genitive). Each can mean 'from' but, as Morna Hooker observes with respect to the Markan account, *ex autou* is difficult to render into English because 'the phrase "out of him" belongs to power and not to the verb: Jesus is the source of the power and does not simply act like the conductor of an electric current' (Morna Hooker, *The Gospel According to St Mark*, London: A. & C. Black, 1991, p. 149).

6   For an account of the early Church's exegesis of this passage, see what is the most detailed study of it: Maria J. Selvidge, *Woman, Cult and Miracle Recital: A Redactional Critical Investigation on Mark 5.24–34*, Lewisburg, PA: Bucknell University Press, 1990.

7   See chapter one of Graham Ward, *Christ and Culture*, Oxford: Blackwell, 2005, pp. 49–52.

8   See Ludwig Bieler, *Theios Aner: Das Bild des 'göttlichen Menschen' in Spätantike und Frühchristentum*, Darmstadt: Wissenschaftliche Buchgesellschaft, 1967: 'Was *dunamis* ist, lehrt am besten die Geschichte von der Heilung der Blutflüssigen … *dunamis* hier die "Kraft" ist' (pp. 80–1). For the relationship between touch, power and the *theios aner* see also K. Kertelge, *Die Wunder Jesu in Markusevangelium: Eine redaktionsgeschkhtliche Untersuchung*, Munich: Koesel, 1970, p. 114; and H.-W. Kuhn, *Altere Sammlungen im Markusevangelium*, Göttingen: Vanderhoeck & Ruprecht, 1971, pp. 192–200.

9   A number of commentators have remarked upon how distinctive is this physical touch. We can take Bultmann as illustrative: *The History of the Synoptic Tradition*, tr. John Marsh, Oxford: Blackwell, 1963, p. 214.

10 See Maria J. Selvidge, *Woman, Cult and Miracle Recital* (see Note 6), who also notes that 'blood' is only used in connection with both Jesus and this woman in the Gospel.

11 For the relationship between Christology and performance see chapter one of Ward, *Christ and Culture* (see Note 7), pp. 43–9.

12 There is a substantial body of literature that treats the uncleanliness issue in this passage. In fact both Tertullian and Chrysostom observed that this woman's condition made her unclean according to the cultic laws laid down in Leviticus 15.25–31. What is not often observed is the enormous importance purity laws give to touch. The Leviticus text explicitly warns against touching anything associated with the woman, for anything touched by her in this condition is rendered unclean. Her touching his garment (Matthew and Luke render this as the hem of his garment and some commentators have made much of the symbolic tassels about the hem of a rabbi's garment) is a sacrilegious act that Jesus turns into a salvific one. The scandal of the touching is another example of the irony and crisis of representation in Mark's Gospel. The borders crossed far exceed the permeability of one body by another – as well as the crossing of theological difference (creator–creation) there is also the crossing of sexual difference (man–woman) and cultic difference (clean–unclean).

13 Without discussing the economy of the response, Dietrich-Alex Koch remarks on this passage: 'Nicht mehr Jesu automatische wirkende *dunamis*, sondern die *pistis* ist der Grund der Rettung' (*Die Bedeutung der Wundererzählungen für die Christologie des Markusevangeliums*, Berlin: de Gruyter, 1975, p. 137). Power does not operate coercively, it inspires and completes faith, it incorporates. It is in the incorporation that the salvation that Christ brings becomes her salvation (and healing). There has been much discussion among commentators about the role faith plays in this miracle. Kertelge (*Die Wunder Jesu in Markusevangelium*, p. 115), Koch (p. 137) and Nineham (*The Gospel of Mark*, London: A. & C. Black, 1963, p. 158) wish to make faith the dynamic for her healing and suggest Mark does too in order to counter the *theios aner* tradition that emphasised the operation of *dunamis*. But this fails to recognise that the economy of response has two poles – *dunamis* and *pistis*. The woman is healed and knows it before Jesus pronounces that it was her faith that made her whole. Jesus only names the practice in which the woman participated such that the *dunamis* was effective.

14 Only in Mark's account do we find this confirmation of the woman having come to a new place and well-being.

15 Cynthia Freeland, 'Aristotle on the Sense of Touch', in Martha C. Nussbaum and Amelie Oksenberg Rorty (eds), *Essays on Aristotle's* De Anima, Oxford: Clarendon Press, 1992, pp.

227–248, p. 230. See also Jean-Louis Chrétien's excellent examination of Aristotle on touch, 'Body and Touch' in *The Call and the Response*, tr. Anne A. Davenport, New York: Fordham University Press, 2004, pp. 83–131. He agrees that Aristotle is not talking about 'contact' (pp. 116–17), rather 'Touch is the perpetual place of exchange' (p. 117).

16   For an important discussion of the politics of *bios* and *zoe* and the logic of sovereignty that seeks to produce a biopolitical body, see Giorgio Agamben, *Homo Sacer: Sovereign Power and Bare Life*, tr. Daniel Heller-Roazen, Stanford University Press, 1998.

17   For an exposition of my view of the soul see chapter 3 of *Christ and Culture* (see Note 7).

18   One could examine intentional touch between persons and animals, for example, though one would have to define how 'intentions' are ascribed to forms of animal behaviour.

19   See *Logical Investigations*, vol. 2, tr. J.N. Findlay, second edition, London: Routledge & Kegan Paul, 1970, pp. 533–659, particularly pp. 552–96.

20   'Body and Touch' (see Note 15), p. 130.

21   David Katz, *Der Aufbau der Tastwelt*, Leipzig: Verlag von Johann Ambrosius Barth, 1925, p. 160.

22   Maurice Merleau-Ponty, *The Visible and the Invisible*, ed. Claude Lefort, tr. Alphonso Lingis, Evanston, IL: Northwestern University Press, 1968, p. 9.

23   Chrétien views Merleau-Ponty as making touch fit into his understanding of sight; 'Body and Touch' (see Note 15), pp. 100–101.

24   Maurice Merleau-Ponty, *Phenomenology of Perception*, tr. Colin Smith, London: Routledge, 1962, p. 369.

25   Ibid., p. 141. In his late essay 'The Intertwining: The Chiasm' (in *The Visible and the Invisible*, see Note 22), very briefly Merleau-Ponty broaches again the question of 'touching the hand of another' and coins, elliptically, the term 'intercorporeality'. But the model of what he calls 'the circle of the touched and the touching, the touched takes hold of the touching' (p. 141) is founded upon a synergy in which because the organs of my body communicate with each other therefore a transitivity is founded from one body to another (p. 143). In the handshake, then, where each experiences being touched in touching, I 'touch in it the same power to espouse the things that I have touched in my own' (p. 141). In this there is a transcending of difference as each 'address themselves to the body in general and for itself' (p. 143). His account of incorporeal touching is, as he himself claims, curiously locked into the logic of Narcissus. My own account emphasises that touching and being touched by a sentient other goes beyond reflexivity. There is a sense in which Merleau-Ponty's own vocabulary performs a transcendence that he does not investigate beyond an allusive Spinozistic monism; he uses descriptors like 'magical', 'mystery', 'enigma', 'surpassing' and 'miracle'. Even 'vision' in the late essays takes on the gravity of disclosure, revelation and epiphany. He never manages to shake off his Catholic imagination, but he does not reflect upon it either.

26   Ibid., p. 133.

27   Desire arrives late in the economy of perception for Merleau-Ponty. In 'The Interwining', he describes 'the patient and silent labour of desire' (p. 144) that follows touching and is related to articulation. We see this move in much more detail in *Phenomenology of Perception* (see Note 24), where, in the development of his phenomenology of the body, 'The Body in its Sexual Being' (pp. 178–201), he lays the foundation for 'The Body as Expression, and Speech' (pp. 202–32). Although Merleau-Ponty suggests in that volume (p. 178) that an analysis of 'desire or love' will enable us to understand 'the birth of being for us', he views desire as a mode of affectivity, not, as I suggest, the condition for affectivity itself.

28   Chrétien concludes: 'Self-touch cannot be the truth of touch'; 'Body and Touch' (see Note 15), p. 118.

29   Merleau-Ponty observes: 'my own body's "invisibility" can invest the other bodies I see. Hence my body can assume segments derived from the body of another, just as my substance passes into them'; 'Eye and Mind', tr. Carleton Dallery, in Maurice Merleau-Ponty, *The Primacy of Perception*, Evanston, IL: Northwestern University Press, 1973, p. 168.

30   *Wuthering Heights*, Harmondsworth: Penguin Books, 1965, p. 122.

31   Aquinas, *Summa Theologiae*, 1a.105.5 responsio.

32   Jean-Luc Marion, *L'Idol et la distance*, Paris: Grasset, 1977, p. 199.

33   We can associate this difference with the difference I allude to in the Introduction [of *Christ and Culture* (see Note 7)] (p. 20) concerning the categories 'understanding' and 'discernment'. With discernment and contemplation (rather than understanding and reflection) a religious metaphysics begins to take shape; in this case, a Christian epistemology.

34   See chapter three of my *Christ and Culture* (see Note 7) for a developed exposition of this Johannine theme.

35   Origen, *De Principiis*, 1.2.2.

36   Aquinine, *Summa Contra Gentiles*, IV. 11.1.

37   Werner Jaeger and Hermann Langerbeck (eds), *Gregorii Nysseni in Canticum Canticorum*, Leiden: Brill, 1960, p. 324.

38   I am aware of the arguments among commentators as to whether this letter can in fact be attributed to Paul, but these arguments have no bearing on the Christology announced in this letter.

39   For a further exposition of the importance of *pleroma* and its association with *kenosis* see chapter nine [of *Christ and Culture* (see Note 7)], pp. 257–61.

40   Giorgio Agamben, *The Coming Community*, tr. Michael Hardt, Minneapolis, MN: University of Minnesota Press, 1993, p. 24.

41   Merleau-Ponty, *Phenomenology of Perception* (see Note 24), p. 369.

42   Ibid.

43   There is an interesting collection of essays concerning this theme in contemporary continental philosophy: Onno Zijlstra (ed.), *Letting Go: Rethinking Kenosis*, Bern: Peter Lang, 2002.

44   See the later chapters of Michel de Certeau, *The Mystic Fable*, vol. 1: *The Sixteenth and Seventeenth Centuries*, tr. Michael B. Smith, Chicago, IL: University of Chicago Press, 1992.

45   See Mark C. Taylor, *Altarity*, Chicago, IL: University of Chicago Press, 1987.

46   See his notion of the endless diremption of the body: 'Corpus' in Jean-Luc Nancy, *The Birth to Presence*, tr. Claudette Sartiliot, Stanford, CA: Stanford University Press, 1993, pp. 189–207.

47   See Gianni Vattimo, *Beyond Interpretation: The Meaning of Hermeneutics for Philosophy*, Cambridge: Polity Press, 1997, and *Belief*, tr. Luka Disanto and David Webb, Stanford, CA: Stanford University Press, 1999.

48   This is a profound and recurrent theme throughout Lévinas's work. It perhaps best finds expression in the section treating 'The Substitution' that began as an essay in 1968 but was incorporated into Lévinas's book *Otherwise than Being or Beyond Essence*, tr. Alphonso Lingis, The Hague: Martinus Nijhoff, 1981.

49   See in particular 'Sauf le nom' in Jacques Derrida, *On the Name*, tr. John P. Leavey Jnr., Stanford, CA: Stanford University Press, 1995, pp. 35–85.

50   'Meaning and Sense' in Emmanuel Lévinas, *Collected Philosophical Papers*, tr. Alphonso Lingis, The Hague: Martinus Nijhoff, 1987, p. 91

51   Ibid., p. 92.

52   Ibid., p. 169.

53   Ibid., p. 92.

54   Ibid., pp. 94, 97.

55   Ibid., p. 94.

56   I am aware here of the extensive debate between Jacques Derrida and Jean-Luc Marion on the gift, John Milbank's rigorous theological analysis of the debate and his own richly suggestive contribution. I have learnt much from engaging with this material, particularly Marion's phenomenological account of donation and reduction in *Reduction and Givenness: Investigations of Husserl, Heidegger, and Phenomenology*, tr. Thomas A. Carlson, Evanston, IL: Northwestern University Press, 1998, and *Being Given: Towards a Phenomenology of Givenness*, tr. Jeffery L. Korsky, Stanford, CA: Stanford University Press, 2002 (both of which are profoundly theologically informed) and Milbank's provocative challenges to it in the name of deeper appreciation of Trinitarian participation.

57   Marcel Mauss, *The Gift*, tr. Ian Cunnison, New York: Norton, 1967.

58   See Jacques Derrida, *Given Time: I Counterfeit Money*, tr. Peggy Kamuf, Chicago, IL: University of Chicago Press, 1992.

59   'Then the Lord appeared to him [Abraham] by the terebinth trees of Mamre as he was sitting in the tent door in the heat of the day. So he lifted his eyes and looked, and behold, three men were standing by him; and when he saw them, he ran from the tent door to meet them, and bowed himself to the ground, and said, "My Lord, if I have now found favour in your sight, do not pass on by your servant. Please let a little water be brought, and wash your feet, and rest yourselves under the tree. And I will bring a morsel of bread, that you may refresh your hearts. After that you may pass by, inasmuch as you have come to your servant." And they said, "Do as you have said"' (Genesis 18.1–5). One notes how the three strangers constitute for Abraham 'the Lord'. His response is gratitude at being able to serve and the meal he prepares subsequently far exceeds water and 'a morsel of bread'.

60   See John Milbank, 'The Soul of Reciprocity Part One: Reciprocity Refused', *Modern Theology* 17 (3), July (2001), pp. 335–91 and 'The Soul of Reciprocity Part Two: Reciprocity Granted', *Modern Theology* 17 (4), October (2001), pp. 485–507.

61   Edward Said, 'Reflections on Exile' in idem, *Reflections on Exile and Other Literary and Cultural Essays*, London: Granta Books, 2001, p. 183.

62   For an excellent genealogy of motion in relation to the divine, see Simon Oliver, *Philosophy, God and Motion*, London: Routledge, 2005.

63   Gregory of Nyssa, 'The Great Catechism' in *Select Writings and Letters of Gregory, Bishop of Nyssa* (see Note 1), p. 478.

64   Ibid.

65   Jean Daniélou, *A History of Early Christian Doctrine*: Volume Two, *Gospel Message and Hellenistic Culture*, tr. John Austin Baker, London: Darton, Longman & Todd, 1973, p. 352.

66   Michel René Barnes, 'Divine Unity and the Divided Self: Gregory of Nyssa's Trinitarian Theology in Its Psychological Context', *Modern Theology* 18 (4), October (2002), pp. 475–96, p. 483. See an earlier article by Barnes for a discussion of the hierarchical process involved in the terms *ousia, dunamis, energeia* and *ergo*, and how Gregory goes against this trend by viewing power as the natural expression of essence – 'The Background and Use of Eunomius' Causal Language', in Michel Barnes and Donald Williams (eds), *Arianism after Arius: Essays on the Development of the Fourth Century Trinitarian Conflicts*, Edinburgh: T. & T. Clark, 1993, pp. 217–36. For a much more detailed and fascinating study of *dunamis theou* with particular reference to the theology of Gregory of Nyssa, see Barnes, *The Power of God: Dunamis in Gregory of Nyssa's Trinitarian Theology*, Washington, DC: Catholic University of America Press, 2001.

67   Gregory of Nyssa, 'The Great Catechism' (see Note 1), V, p. 478.

68   All commentators enter the debates, cite the various possibilities and come to their conclusions.

69   Specifically, these concern the paradoxical nature of all relations *en Christo* that participate in the *kenosis/pleroma* economy, as I hope to show. To some extent Mark offers an account that could have achieved most of the same ends insofar as there is a touching, a liturgical pouring out of oil and a relational exchange that is public. This account too then can be viewed as paralleling the account of the haemorrhaging woman. But the woman in Mark anoints Jesus's head, while the anointing is explicitly related to his burial (where he does not receive any anointing). In John, Mary anoints Jesus's feet – it is not an anointing for burial in the same way, since Nicodemus and Joseph of Arimathea anoint Jesus's dead body (John 19.38–40). To my mind, the verbal echoes and explicit mention of location (Bethany) point to John's knowledge of the Markan text. Though some have suggested that the account in Mark is a later addition indebted to John, most see the Markan text as expressing the earliest tradition. My interpretation is foregrounding the Christology here.

70   Rudolf Schnackenburg, *The Gospel According to St John*, vol. 2, trs Cecily Hastings et al., London: Burnes & Oates, 1980, p. 371.

71   *The Gospel of John: A Commentary*, tr. G.R. Beasley-Murray, Oxford: Blackwell, 1971, p. 415.

72   I am aware some commentators have questioned the kingship theme (championed by C.K. Barrett, *The Gospel According to St John*, 2nd edn, Philadelphia, PA: Westminster Press, 1978, p. 409) because, unlike in Mark, it is the feet not the head that are anointed. But this ignores the fact that John (unlike Mark and Matthew) strategically situates this story before Jesus's

Messianic entrance into Jerusalem and associates it directly with the repeated motif of kingship in John's account of the Passion (John 18.33–40; 19.1–6, 12–16, 19). Some have noted that John's attention to the days on which the supper took place (six before the Passover) may be an allusion to the Habdalah, the supper concluding the Jewish Sabbath – a supper which came to be associated with Elijah and the welcoming of the Messiah. See Barrett, p. 411. Furthermore, I argue that the anointing of the feet is an important aspect of the lowliness theme in John's Gospel. Bultmann (*The Gospel of John*, p. 415) and Raymond Brown (*The Gospel According to John*, vol. 1, London: Geoffrey Chapman, 1971, p. 452) both point to the feet having theological significance but fail to elaborate the nature of that significance.

73   For an excellent theological interpretation and historical account of the exaltation and glorification in John's Gospel see Schnackenburg, *The Gospel According to St John* (see Note 70), pp. 398–410.

74   Brown, *The Gospel According to John* (see Note 72), notes that *myron* came as either a powder or a liquid (p. 448).

75   Bultmann notes a rabbinic parallel to this anointing of the feet (*The Gospel of John* (see Note 72), p. 415). The association of this account with the Last Supper is strengthened through the term for the meal (*deipnon*) that is found in John only here, 13.2, 4 and 21.20.

76   Michel Foucault, 'Pastoral Power and Political Reason' in Jeremy Carrette (ed.), *Religion and Culture by Michel Foucault*, Manchester: Manchester University Press, 1999, p. 134.

77   See Brown, *The Gospel According to John* (see Note 72), p. 448.

78   Ernst Haenchen, *John*, vol. 2, tr. Robert W. Funk, Philadelphia, PA: Fortress Press, 1984, p. 84.

79   Again some commentators have observed how this account must be a 'confused amalgamation of details' (Brown, *The Gospel According to John* (see Note 72), p. 452) from the synoptic Gospels because why would someone pour the oil and then wipe it away again. But as my reading emphasises that the pouring and the wiping mirror the washing and the wiping in chapter 13, John is drawing a parallel to make a theological point.

80   Deleuze and Guattari, *Anti-Oedipus* (see Note 2), p.68.

81   Ibid., p.131.

82   See Tertullian, *Adversus Marcionem*, ii.27, and Athanasius, *Contra Arianos*, I, 42.

83   See 'The Commodification of Religion or the Consummation of Capitalism', in Slavoj Žižek and Creston Davis (eds), *Political Ontologies*, Durham, NC: Duke University Press (forthcoming).

84   Deleuze and Guattari, *Anti-Oedipus* (see Note 2), p.139.

Further reading

On Christ

St Anselm of Canterbury, 'Why God became Man', in Davies, Brian and Evans, Gillian (eds), *The Major Works*, Oxford: Oxford University Press, 1998.
St. Thomas Aquinas, trans. R.J. Hennessey, *Summa Theologiae*, 3a.1-6 (vol. 48), Cambridge: Cambridge University Press, 2006.

Agamben, Georgio, trans. Daniel Heller-Roazen, *Homo Sacer: Sovereign Power and Bare Life*, Stanford, CA: Stanford University Press, 1998.
Milbank, John and Pickstock, C., *Truth in Aquinas*, London: Routledge, 2000, ch. 3.
Milbank, John, *Being Reconciled: Ontology and Pardon*, London: Routledge, 2003.
Ward, Graham, *Christ and Culture*, Oxford: Blackwell, 2005.

On Gift

Mauss, Marcel, trans. W.D. Halls, *The Gift: Form and Reason for Exchange in Archaic Societies*, London: Routledge, 2001.
Caputo, John D., Dooley, Mark and Scanlon, Michael J., *Questioning God*, Bloomington, Indiana: Indiana University Press, 2001.

Horner, Robyn, *Jean-Luc Marion: A Theological Introduction*, Aldershot: Ashgate, 200, ch. 6.
Royle, Nicholas, *Jacques Derrida* (Routledge Critical Thinkers), London: Routledge, 2003, pp. 138–42.
Sykes, Karen, *Arguing with Anthropology: An Introduction to Critical Theories of the Gift*, London: Routledge, 2005.

Derrida, Jacques, trans. David Wills, *The Gift of Death*, Chicago, IL: University of Chicago Press, 1996.
Derrida, Jacques, trans. Peggy Kamuf, *Given Time: Counterfeit Money v.1*, Chicago, IL: University of Chicago Press, 1994.
Leask, Ian and Eoin Cassidy (eds), *Givenness and God: Questions of Jean-Luc Marion,* New York: Fordham University Press, 2005.
López, Antonio, *Spirit's Gift: The Metaphysical Insight of Claude Bruaire*, Washington, DC: The Catholic University Press of America, 2006.
Marion, Jean-Luc, trans. Jeffrey Losky, *Being Given: Toward a Phenomenology of Givenness*, Stanford, CA: Stanford University Press, 2002.
Milbank, John, 'Can a Gift Be Given? Prolegomena to a Future Trinitarian Metaphysic', *Modern Theology* 11 (1) (January 1995), pp. 119–61.
Milbank, John, 'The Soul of Reciprocity Part One: Reciprocity Refused'. *Modern Theology* 17 (3), July (2001), pp. 335–91 and 'The Soul of Reciprocity Part Two: Reciprocity Granted', *Modern Theology* 17 (4), October (2001), pp. 485–507.
Milbank, John, 'The Gift and the Mirror: On the Philosophy of Love', in Kevin Hart (ed.), *Counter-Experience: Reading Jean-Luc Marion*, Notre Dame, IN: University of Notre Dame Press, 2007.

Questions

1. In what ways does Milbank point to the exceptionality of Christ?
2. For Milbank, Christ did not die as a martyr or hero. What kind of death did Jesus die, and why is this important?
3. The New Testament seems to imply that, in Christ, distinction (between, for example, slave and free, Jew and Greek, male and female) is erased (Galatians 3.28). How do Milbank and Ward understand this teaching?
4. How does Ward understand 'relation' and 'sociality' in terms of Christ?
5. In what ways is *desire* crucial to Ward's Christology and theology of the body?

PART V

Church and Eucharist

Introduction

In introducing Part III of this Reader, I referred to Derrida's claim that Plato inaugurated modern metaphysics by privileging presence over absence, and speech over writing. Let me explain again something of what this difficult thesis means. There is currently a book on my desk. I am 'present' to the book. I know what the book *is* by its appearance, or the *phenomena* which are given to my senses. This means that, in being 'present' to the book (it is here in front of me on my desk), I can know it, apparently in all its fullness. In a similar way, I can be present to someone in the room with me and hear their voice, thus coming to know that person without mediation (the mediation, say, of reading a letter from that person), for I hear them presently (and not, say, mediated through a letter). Now, take the case of the book. Am I really fully 'present' to everything the book *is* and *signifies*? In one sense, the book is just an object. But someone wrote the book. Someone else proofread the book and someone typeset the book. Then there are the potentially infinite number of readers of the book who are part of the book's reception. So I am not truly and fully present to the book, if one understands that the book is more than a material object on my desk. It exceeds the phenomenologically given – it is more than it *appears* to be. It has a history and a 'life'. Crucially, it is a *sign* that points beyond itself, and what the book signifies is part of what the book *is*.

It is Derrida's contention that an emphasis on presence constitutes an attempt in modernity to make knowledge certain and to fix the meanings of things (rather in the way that the modern dictionary tries to 'fix' the meanings of words – another example of Pickstock's spatialization, for the dictionary is a 'space' ordered by the alphabet). How is this so? By suggesting that we can be fully present to that which we know, we can claim that we fully know by being present. But Derrida points out that objects are not merely inert things. They are signs which point beyond themselves. Even the book on my desk is a sign of its author and all those who might have read it. In fact, the meaning of anything (words and things) is, for Derrida, infinite and therefore endlessly *deferred*. I never could finally pin down the thing on my desk even as a book (it could, for example, be used as a coaster). So whereas modernity fixes knowledge by fixing meaning by privileging presence, Derrida disrupts this by privileging absence – the constant deferral or absence of meaning in our attempt to know the world. The 'meaning' of the book on my desk, and what the book is, is infinite and therefore, in the end, *absent* – it could never finally be pinned down.

Some theologians see in Derrida's work a profound contribution to theology in the form of an association with the apophatic tradition. Aspects of Graham Ward's work indicate this appreciation, particularly his early book *Barth, Derrida and the Language of Theology* (1995). Meanwhile, as we saw in Part III, Pickstock roundly rejects Derrida's identification of Plato as the beginning of the privileging of presence over absence. But Pickstock goes one crucial stage further: she claims that, in privileging the constant deferral and flux of meaning in language – in other words, in privileging absence – Derrida remains in precisely the modern metaphysical dualism he seeks to overcome: the distinction between presence and absence. It is simply the case that, rather than opt for presence, he opts for absence. But Pickstock thinks that the very distinction between presence and absence needs to be completely subverted. How is this done?

On the face of it, Pickstock opts for that which appears most unpromising: the Eucharist. Why is this perplexing? Because certain understandings of the Eucharist seem to privilege presence – the presence of Christ, the *real presence*. It seems that we want to 'lock down' and fix Christ as the foundation for a particular way of knowing the world. Certain Counter-Reformation understandings of transubstantiation certainly understand the Eucharist in this way; it is no longer a sign, participating in that which it signifies, but simply *is* Jesus Christ understood as a bounded and fetishized object lying on the altar. Yet Pickstock refers back to pre-modern understandings of transubstantiation, particularly that of St Thomas Aquinas. Here she finds in the Eucharist the provocation of *desire*. Put simply, the Church is what Graham Ward has called 'the erotic community' in which God's people are drawn towards the reception of that which is most alluring and beautiful, namely the Bread of Life and the Cup of Salvation. For Pickstock, the Eucharist – the consecrated bread and wine at the altar – is a sign, but a sign which is not separated from the real and from that which it signifies. In fact, because she follows Aquinas, the sign participates most intimately in that which it signifies (the Body and Blood of Christ) in such a way that it becomes transparent to faith. That sign subverts presence and absence because, although it nourishes us with Christ's body and blood, nevertheless it nourishes us with that which is infinite and utterly inexhaustible, namely the life of God. There is always infinitely more to be given. So it is not that Christ is 'present', because his 'presence' is inexhaustible; there is always infinitely more to be given. Yet we do nevertheless receive the presence of Christ, so Christ is not absent or, to put it in Derridean terms, constantly deferred. It is, quite simply, a presence in which there is infinitely more yet to be given. So we do not have to opt either for a modern fixity of meaning in Christ's presence, not a constant deferral as if Christ were always around the next corner on our Christian journey. Each reception of the Eucharist carries with it a crucial extra: there is more to be given. Pickstock likens this to the literature of the high Middle Ages which associated the Eucharist with the quest for the Holy Grail, the cup which Christ used at the Last Supper. The Eucharist is a focus of human desire, but it is not a desire frustrated; it is a desire which, in its very fulfilment, provokes desire for what is more and new. Unlike addiction, however, it is not desire for the *same* again and again. Christ is continually given in what Pickstock calls (coining a term of Kierkegaard) nonidentical repetition. In every Eucharist, one receives a different and new gift through the one, inexhaustible body of Christ.

Graham Ward's essay 'The ontological scandal' is similarly concerned with the presence of bodies, particularly the body of Christ. Referring to a peculiarly modern materialistic and atomistic understanding of the body, Ward writes: 'For now what is important is to recognise that with this emphasis upon the world as fully given, fully *present*, mediation, the act of representation itself ... is downplayed at best, but certainly on the road to being forgotten.' 'With positivists and radical empiricists, it [materialism] announces a fluorescent world of fully *presenced* certainties – indifferent to time, agency and mediation' (my emphases). He is particularly concerned with the association of 'body' with the material object which Descartes thought was somehow inhabited by a mind. For Ward, bodies are fractured and variegated. Their identity is constantly in flux. This is apparent with regard to the body of Christ in the gospels. Here, we find an 'ontological scandal' which cannot be reduced to metaphor, icon or simple identity: 'This', says Christ before a piece of bread, 'is my body'. This is displacement (one of many in the Gospels) of the identity of Christ into the

Eucharist. This is recapitulated very clearly in the accounts of the resurrection appearances, for Christ's presence is extremely strange – he appears from nowhere, eats fish and can be touched, and yet is not recognized by his disciples and disappears. Finally, Christ ascends to 'fill all in all'. There is, again, a subversion of presence and absence. Finally, for both Pickstock and Ward, following Henri de Lubac, the twentieth-century theologian who has influenced Radical Orthodoxy more than any other, the Church is made by the Eucharist, and the Eucharistic celebration is the Church. The Church is, therefore, at once the body of Christ and the questing community of Eucharistic desire. Christ is neither simply present or absent in the Church, but is *given*.

Chapter 9

Catherine Pickstock

Thomas Aquinas and the quest for the Eucharist

I n his speculation on the noun-phrase "landscape" in Paragraph 65 of the *Pensées*, Pascal explains how language fixes or designates reality and at the same time surrenders to the indeterminacy and flux of signifieds: "A town or a landscape from afar off is a town and a landscape", he writes, "but as one approaches, it becomes houses, trees, tiles, leaves, grass, ants, ants' legs, and so on *ad infinitum*. All *that* is comprehended in the word 'landscape'."[1] A single noun-phrase is shown at once to conceal and yield an infinite asymptotic analysis of reality, and here Pascal intimates how our words remain always undefined until we actually use them, even though there is always something we know of a word's meaning which enables us to use it in the first place. However, it is clear from Pascal's analysis that even when we have used a particular word, we can never be entirely certain of its exhaustive definition.

In the Port-Royal treatise on the categorical theory of propositions, *Logic or the Art of Thinking*, Antoine Arnauld and Pierre Nicole invoke precisely this discussion of the infinite divisibility of the world and the difficulty this presents for our use and understanding of words. They explain how every word we use summons at best a confused idea of the signified, which will always be accompanied by what they call "incidental ideas" which the mind perforce adds to the meanings of words. Such confusion is at an absolute maximum in the case of the demonstrative pronoun *hoc*, "this", used instead of a proper noun. When the supremely indeterminate pronoun "this" is used to display, say, a diamond, the mind does not settle on conceiving it as a present apparent thing, but adds to it the ideas of a hard and sparkling body having a certain shape, besides connotations of wealth, beauty, romance and rarity.[2]

This qualification of our certainty regarding the meaning of words forms the basis of Arnauld and Nicole's attack on the Calvinists' metaphorical interpretation of the Eucharist. The Calvinists, they argue, assume in full nominalist fashion (probably influenced by the French Calvinist humanist Petrus Ramus), that the word "this" establishes a firm attachment to a determinate referent, namely, in the case of Jesus's assertion, "This is my body", a firm attachment to the bread. If one detaches the demonstrative pronoun from its obvious referent, as is the case, the Calvinists claim, when Jesus says "This is my body", then it must be intended metaphorically. Arnauld and Nicole argue against this by drawing attention to the Calvinists' error of assuming that the demonstrative pronoun "this" is anchored to a determinate specificity. To the contrary, they argue, specific application is only made possible in this case because of the term's maximum of indeterminacy, its unlimited transferability. For the word "this" always remains susceptible of further determinations and of being linked to other ideas.[3] In addition, even when something apparently determinate is invoked by the pronoun "this", that specificity is itself infinitely divisible and in consequence retains an open-ended and mysterious character. One might think, in the case of the bread to which the pronoun "this" refers in Jesus's assertion, that there is at least some limit to the open-endedness of our mental compassing of the bread. But later in the *Logic*, again invoking Pascal, Arnauld and Nicole protest that even "the smallest grain of wheat contains in itself a tiny world with all its parts – a sun, heavens, stars, planets, and an earth – with admirably precise proportions; that there are no parts of this grain that do not contain yet another proportional world."[4] Thus, even the most literal-seeming reference in fact preserves an infinity of mystery even as it seems to command or delimit that extension.[5]

It should of course be added that behind these assertions of the infinite divisibility of matter lies the seventeenth-century disciplining and enhancement of the senses provided by such devices as the microscope, telescope and air-pump, which revealed things that were previously invisible, and cautioned against relying upon the observations of unassisted sense.[6] Thus Pascal and his allies deployed aspects of the New Science *against* nominalism and the cruder variants of empiricism. And they brought into apologetic alignment the scene of experimentation with the scene of sacrificial offering to the extent that both are read as exposing and releasing unexpected depths within seemingly brute matter.

For the Port-Royal grammarians, therefore, there is a triple bond between the theory of physical matter, the question of how language operates and the theology of the Eucharist, and in particular the doctrine of transubstantiation. Echoing this threefold concern I will demonstrate in this essay how discernment of the Body and Blood of Christ in the material species of bread and wine in the Eucharist allows for – even demands – the greatest inexhaustibility of meaning, but, at the same time, overcomes the problem of a sheer indeterminacy of sense.

But, before going on to consider this oxymoronic status of meaning and language in the Eucharist, one should perhaps ask why, having referred to the Port-Royal critique of how the Calvinist "fixing" of language ignores language's indeterminacy, one should regard "sheer indeterminacy" without qualification as a problem – for surely the attempt to secure meaning is inherently futile. Is not this view, after all, a key feature of postmodern – especially Derridean – philosophy which hails *différance* and the eruption of flows and postponement of meaning as the ineliminable out-witting of metaphysical attempts to secure present truth from the ravages of time and indeterminacy. Such a position exalts the release of language into a play of traces which, far from being "commanded" or fixed by the person wielding signs, rather ensures that that person is commanded by those signs.[7] Moreover, this command is a strange anarchic sort of command, which never finally declares what is commanded, since meaning is held forever in abeyance by the postponing protocol of *différance*. So, given this rigorous release of language, why should one reinvoke a nostalgia for even the relatively determinate? There is not time to investigate at length the Derridean sign within the compass of this essay, but, put briefly, the problems, as I see them, with the Derridean sign as they relate to my theme are as follows.

In the first place, by cleaving to absence, Derrida leaves the metaphysical correla-tion of meaning and presence in place, even as he claims that presence is that which is perpetually postponed. For the vehicle of Derridean *différance*, namely the sign, must perforce remain the same in its repeatedly pointing to something which never arrives. This renders both signification and repetition transcendentally *univocal*, precisely because they point to the nothing of postponed presence – and it should perhaps be noted that nothing is more identical than nothing is to nothing. In this way the very unmedia-bility of an absolute radical difference, immune to any likeness, must collapse into its opposite, into identity, sameness and indifference. It resolves, as a transcendental category, into absolute equivalence which comprehends or measures each difference after all.

The second problem with the Derridean theory is that when difference is held at such optimum pitch, each assertion of discontinuity is identically superlative and attains a kind of homogeneous heterogeneity. Indeed, in the third place, for all his high talk, this in some way reduces the Derridean sign to the ideality of a perennially available and wordless thought which overcomes its own mediations and cleaves to presence. In the logic of deconstruction, there is no mediating relationship between *différance* and the various appearances of meaning which it organises or disorganises. In consequence, the universality of the "grammatological flux" is perhaps to be seen as a saturation of language which empties language of itself. As John D. Caputo explains, meanings are allowed "to slip loose, to twist free from their horizons, to leek and run off".[8] Thus, the Derridean sign relinquishes commitment to any specific epiphanies of meaning, or preferences for the lure of certain metaphors, and substitutes a uni-versalised, autonomous and impersonal *mathesis* for language as such (as Gillian Rose rightly argued). For true difference and openness to the Other demand a sensitivity to the fact that some things are more alike than others, or are driven by the provocation of preference or desire which celebrates that difference all the better.

In the fourth place, one might even say that, grammatically speaking, the Derridean sign, in privileging absence which becomes after all the superlative present object, is cast in the indicative mood of the present tense, which is the very prototype of all language, only for a specifically *Cartesian* linguistics. One should add here that Derrida invokes the category of the middle voice to suggest that *différance* nonetheless does exceed the dichotomy of active and passive. However (as I have argued elsewhere), because for Derrida the sign commands the subject bespeaking or inscribing language, however much a speaker or writer intends a meaning, the infinite play of autonomous "corridors of meaning" by definition always arrives over-against the subject to cancel the specificity of his or her desire.[9] In this way the impersonally objective rules, but such a notion of the objective, from Descartes onwards, is only available for the dispassionately representing *subject*. Hence any suggestion of postmodernism that the Cartesian subject has been erased is a ruse: in fact what it removes is the situated, embodied, specifically desiring historical subject, whereas it must secretly retain a transcendental subject who merely knows, since otherwise the indifferent rule of the sign would never "appear" as a transcendental truth.

Finally, one should perhaps say a little more about the *subject*, as Derrida sees him or her. Insofar as Derrida hastens to undo any substantiality on the part of the subject's intention or desire when he or she elects a meaning in language – by insisting upon meaning as being withheld in an abstruse realm of postponement and by subjugating the speaking self to the sway of the grammatological flux – he after all assumes that the subject's intentionality is something that *requires* cancellation. In other words, he simply repeats the assumption that human will can only be construed as something that issues from a self-identical subject which commands all that it wills. He here enthrones a voluntarist subjectivity which wields dominion over all that it surveys, even as he insists upon the inevitable abdication of that subjectivity. His fear of the engulfing power of human desire – that same fear which forces Derrida to deny the giving or receiving of a gift, or any reciprocal relationship with the Other – too much equates desire with exhaustive *acquisition*, and suggests that there are no modalities other than that of the indicative and the imperative, even if these modalities are consummated through deconstruction in Derrida's sceptical discourse. And if one can have no intimation at all of the postponed meanings of a sign through anticipation or desire – just as one cannot for Derrida ever present oneself, as oneself, to the Other, either with one's gifts, praise or prayer – then, like the air which surrounds us, that postponed meaning has in fact no distance from us at all. In refraining from every risk of reducing meaning to presence, one in fact finds that meaning is accorded a kind of hyperpresence which surrounds us with its untouchability. The preciosity of Derrida's demur accords absent meaning a stifling inaccessibility and unmediable enclosure within a revered guarded fortress. Such a construal renders absence dialectically identical with an all-too-metaphysical fetishization of presence.[10]

Now, the foregoing critique of Derrida's account of the sign is by no means exhaustive, but what I have been trying to show is that it is neither presence as such nor absence as such which is culpably metaphysical, but rather the dichotomy itself, and that, for all Derrida's exaltation of the indeterminacy and flux of meaning, by simply inversing the metaphysical structure of the sign, he stays within its paradigm, and ends up fetishizing presence after all.

At this point, we must return to the theme of the signs of the Eucharist and ask whether by contrast they in any way outwit this difficult dichotomy of presence and absence. If *all* they do is render explicit the indeterminacy of a sign, then there would be no contribution that Eucharistic theology could make to semiotics surplus to that of a sceptical philosophy. However, one might also entertain an opposite anxiety: a cursory glance at the history of postmediaeval Catholic theology, and its focus upon transubstantiation and "real presence", might seem to suggest that the Eucharistic signs clearly privilege presence over absence. But if one looks further back to mediaeval theology and some of its later refractions, such as the work of the Port-Royal grammarians already mentioned – despite their Cartesian aspects – one can construct a different account of the theological signs of the Eucharist which – beyond the postmodern – genuinely outwits the metaphysical dichotomies of presence and absence, life and death, continuity and discontinuity and so forth. In order for such an account to be possible, however, one must understand the Eucharist, following the work of Henri de Lubac, as an essential action within the Church which constantly reproduces the Church, and not simply as either an isolated authoritative presence or merely illustrative symbol, which came, following the early modern period, to be the dominant readings.[11]

Briefly, the key to the transcending of the dichotomy of absence and presence in the Eucharist lies in the "logic" – if one can here use such a term – of *mystery* which, according to patristic negotiations of the word *musterion*, implies a positive but not fetishizable *arrival* in which signs essentially participate, but which they cannot exhaust, for that mystery arrives by virtue of a transcendent plenitude which perfectly integrates absence and presence. Thus, a more positive account of the sign is suggested, for the sign here is neither emptily "left behind" through postponement, nor is it the instrumental Ramist sign which secures the real in an artificial exactitude.

What this amounts to is an ontological coincidence of the mystical and the real, a coincidence which, as de Lubac shows, lies at the heart of mediaeval Eucharistic theology. If this coincidence becomes fissured, the Eucharistic signs perforce become either a matter of non-essential, *illustrative* signification which relies upon a non-participatory and conventional (if mimetic) similitude between the bread and the Body, and the wine and the Blood, or else the site of an extrinsicist miracle which stresses the alienness of bread from Body and wine from Blood. These alternatives, in disconnecting the symbolic from the real, in an attempt to prioritize either one or the other, are *both* equally reducible to a synchronic mode of presence which fails to allow the sacramental mystery its full, temporally ecstatic potential within the action of the *ecclesia*, namely, the continuing coming-to-be of the Church as Christ's body through an ingesting of this same body which is at once a real and a symbolic consuming. Without such a context, the merely static localized presences of instrumental sign or intrusive miracle are ultimately situated within the order of the sign mentioned already in association with philosophical privileging of either presence or absence, for, in being disconnected from ecstatic ecclesial action, the Eucharistic signs must implicitly separate the signifier from the signified.[12] Even in the case of an arbitrary miraculous presence, the exclusive prioritization of the "real" over the merely "symbolic" gives rise to a tendency to think of the Eucharist as an arbitrarily present sign concealing an equally present meaning (the giving of a merely extrinsic "grace") subsisting within a synchronic or rationalized realm of logical demonstration on the basis of certain authorized assumptions.

So, by stressing the *ecclesial* and *relational* context of the Eucharist, and its character as linguistic and significatory *action* rather than extra-linguistic presence, one can start to overcome the logic of the secular Derridean sign. But in doing so, one finds also that one has – almost by default – defended an account of transubstantiation. For it is when the Eucharist is hypostasized as either a thing or a sign in separation from ecclesial and ecstatic action that it becomes truly decadent. Thus, Jean-Luc Marion, implicitly building upon de Lubac, convincingly argues that transubstantiation *depends* upon the idea that Christ's Body and Blood are "present" only in the sense of the ecstatic passing of time as gift, and *not* in the mode of a punctual moment abstracted from action, under the command of our gaze. And he shows furthermore that modern theories of transignification presuppose a mundane temporality in which Body reduced to meaning is fully "present" to us, rendering such theories crudely metaphysical in a way that transubstantiation avoids.[13]

To explain further how one can construe the theory of transubstantiation in terms of a theory of the sign as mediating between presence and absence, two points can be emphasised. First, following Louis Marin, there is the question of the relation between this theory and a general philosophical scepticism. On the fact of it, transubstantiation seems to collude with the sceptical notion that the way things *appear* to be is no guarantee as to how they really are. For here, it seems, we have an absolute denial of the apparent presence of bread and wine, and an affirmation, by faith, of the presence of the Body and Blood of Christ, despite the fact that none of the normal sensory indicators of such phenomena is present at all.[14] Does one have here, then, a fideistic denigration of vision, and of the reliability of sensory evidence as indicators of truth? It might seem so, since there is discontinuity and rupture between the bread of the Body, or between wine and Blood. However, the sceptical disruption of normal certainty in the case of transubstantiation is balanced by the certainty of the affirmation of faith: here is the Body and Blood. Moreover, the appearances of bread and wine are not disowned as mere illusions. To the contrary, it is allowed that they remain as accidents, and indeed as accidents which convey with symbolic appropriateness their new underlying substance of Body and Blood. One might say that only the symbols of an outpoured body nourishing us give us an expanded sense of the character of this divine body: disclosing it as an imparted and yet not exhausted body quite beyond the norms and capacities of an ordinary body.[15]

Hence although one passes here through a moment of the most apparently extreme philosophical scepticism – this thing is not at all what it appears to be; its reality is radically absent – this is only to arrive at a much more absolute guarantee of the reliability of appearances. For now it is held that certain sensory phenomena mediate and are upheld by a divine physical presence in the world (though this is invisible). The extreme of scepticism has been entertained in one instant, only comprehensively to overcome all possible scepticism and to arrive at a more absolute trust in our material surroundings. Through the faithful reception of the Eucharist we can now experience these surroundings as the possible vehicle of the divine. And the only mode of scepticism thereby finally endorsed is a benign, doxological one. If bread and wine can be the vehicle for the divine Body and Blood, then we must now assume that nothing exhaustively is as it seems.[16] But instead of this unknown surplus being construed as the threat of deception, it is now the promise of a further depth of significance: of a trustworthiness of appearances even beyond their known, everyday predictable trustworthiness. And, since the fact of an unknown depth behind things is unavoidable, it really is only this benign scepticism upheld by a faith in a hidden presence of God which could ever fully defeat the more threatening scepticism of philosophy.

In the second place, one can note that there is still a rupture here of the normal functions of sense and reference. Under ordinary circumstances, one can present a sense or a meaning in the absence of any anchoring reference(at least of a specific sort): for example, one can speak of an imaginary town, and still make sense. Inversely, if one is to *refer*, there has to be something palpable one can point to: if one says "London", then one knows that this is a place one can visit, somewhere one can point to on a map of a real place, "England". However, in the case of the words of institution, it seems that sense and reference peculiarly change places, or collapse into each other. Thus, pointing to a piece of bread and saying "This is my Body" does not even make fictional or imaginative sense, as we do not imagine an unknown body as bread. The phrase only makes sense if it does, however absurdly, actually *refer*: that is, there is only a meaning here if the words *do* point to the Body via the bread; only a sense if the bread has been transubstantiated. Inversely, however, the phrase "This is my Body" does not refer in the normal sense, because it does not indicate anything palpable which fulfils the expectation of the words – as would be the case if one used them while pointing back at oneself. In the latter case, "reference" would be satisfied because one could then look at the Body and say "ah, it's like that": one would have *identified* it. But in the case of the reference of the words of institution, no ordinary identification can take place, since there is no immediately manifest Body: reference is here affirmed without identification, since sense – the imaginative supposition of 'Christ's Body' – must continue to do all the identifying work. Thus, while sense is drained of its usual absence, since there is only sense via specific reference, equally reference is drained of its usual presence, as we are presented with no palpable content.[17]

This second point about the collapsing together of sense and reference (in such a way that both appear to be missing) can now be brought together with the first point about a faithful trust in the bread and wine as disclosing an invisible depth of Body and Blood. Combining both points, it can now be seen that "this is my Body" – as said while pointing to bread – means that a missing sense for Body (how can it be bread?) and a missing identifying reference for Body (we do not see it) are both simultaneously supplied when we take the bread as symbolically disclosing an inexhaustible Body (or wine as disclosing the Blood); in other words, when we re-understand Christ's divine–human body as what nourishes our very being.

However, this does not mean that sense and reference are exhaustively supplied. To the contrary, if we say that the real sense and reference of this bread and wine are the Body and Blood of Christ, then since the latter are ultimately mysterious, sense and reference here are only supplied in being simultaneously withheld. Yet, once again, this faithful trust is the most guarantee of sense and reference one could ever obtain. This is the case because, ontologically speaking, for anything to be "here" it must be in excess of here; for something to arrive, it must withdraw. And the strange effect of such withdrawal into the inaccessibly real is to return reference to the "surface" of signification, to the realm of interpretation of senses or of meanings. For this reason, the Eucharistic collapse of sense and reference into one another only dramatises a situation which always obtains: sense and reference are never discrete, since even the fictional city is only imaginable because we identify it by reference to some real cities, while inversely London will be diversely identified according to the different senses we make of its appearances (including where we draw its boundaries). Thus reference is not denied, but secured in the only way possible, when, in the case of transubstantiation, it ceases to be that "other" of language which anchors all signs, but instead becomes that which folds back into sense, into language. For here, instead of the referent being confirmed by our glance towards the bread, it is confirmed by Jesus's phrase itself, uttered with a simple authority which kindles our trust.

So, whereas, according to Derrida, Christian theology privileges something pure outside language, it is on the contrary the case that the Eucharist situates us more inside language than ever. So much so, in fact, that it is the Body as word which will be given to eat, since the word alone renders the given in the mode of sign, as bread and wine. Not only is language that which administers the sacrament to us, but, conversely, the Eucharist underlies all language, since, in carrying the absence which characterizes every sign to an extreme (no body *appears* in the bread), it also delivers a final disclosure, or presence (the bread *is* the Body), which alone makes it possible now to trust every sign. In consequence we are no longer uncertainly distanced from "the original event" by language, but, rather, we are *concelebrants of that event* in every word we speak (the event as transcendental category, whose transcendentality is now revealed to be the given of the Body and Blood of Christ).

We have discussed how the use of the word *hoc* or "this" hovers between specific designation and an open expectancy of infinite arrival. Such a hesitation brings together a specificity of presence – *this* tomato, etc. – with a generality of absence, where "this" may denote anything whatsoever. This point can be further elaborated by realizing that this indicated hovering is in fact a linguistic presentation of the general epistemological problem of the aporia of learning, namely the question first articulated in the *Meno* as to how, if one is ignorant of something and *knows* one is ignorant of that thing, one can already know something of it in order to know that one is ignorant of it. At what imperceptible moment is the barrier of ignorance pierced? And, once one has reached the stage of knowing one is ignorant of something, how does one know that there is more to be known, beyond this initial revelation? One of the ways in which Augustine resolves the aporia of learning is by recourse to the mediations of desire which not only provoke the knower ever forward without quite knowing what he or she is looking for, but also issue from the thing to be known, drawing the knower towards it, as if electing to be known by a particular person. But it should be noted that desire – which is divine grace in us – offers a resolution to the conundrum of knowledge only insofar as it lets it stand *as* a conundrum. For the provocations of desire reveal that the truth to be known is never exhausted, but is characterised by a promise of always more to come. Now, one can suggest that there is a linguistic variant of this Augustinian thematic, for, when one uses words, one perforce uses them without quite knowing the true proportions of their referent, for those true proportions lie ever beyond our grasp. To a certain extent, they imply, words remain undefined until one elects a particular path for them, until one *uses* them, and yet this indeterminate or half-arbitrary specification is not wholly defined by us, for there always remains in the words we use some *lure* by which we can infer the paths of their meaning.

In a similar way, the simultaneous indeterminacy and specificity always involved in the deployment of the word "this" is mediated by the desire provoked by an initial indeterminacy in pronouncing the word "this" which yet requires a specific instantiation. Moreover, this work of mediation is doubled in an instance where one uses the word "this" in a seemingly redundant way by saying "This is" of something which is manifestly bread. And, yet again, this element of desire is here trebled because, if one continues by saying "This is bread from the bakery", the dimension of desire would drop away with the satisfaction of one's curiosity about what was going to be said. However, where one pronounces a seemingly bizarre identification, desire *remains*, partly because one wishes forever to penetrate this mystery, and partly because the specification is itself of something infinite, and therefore not exactly specific at all. So whereas in every specific use of the word "this", the indeterminate horizon remains, in this instance that is all the more the case.[18]

One can further illuminate this peculiar situation by mentioning an alternative use of the phrase "This is". Not only might it precede a statement of identification, which can often include an element of derivation as in "This is my grandmother's ring", it might alternatively precede a statement of re-identification or unmasking, as in "This painting is a forgery". However, in the case of "This is my body", neither of these seemingly exhaustive alternatives pertain. As we have already seen, one is not here giving accidental information, as in the first example, where the fact that the ring used to belong to my grandmother does not displace its essential and visible ringness (which does not require to be identified, except in the initial learning of language). This contrasts with the Eucharistic scenario, because when the priest says "This is my body", although he is not saying "This bread is not really bread", he is not attributing an accidental property: instead it would seem that he is providing an absurd identification, where actually no identification at all need be rendered. On the other hand, there is no suggestion of exposure of false appearances, as if Jesus had said "This bread is really Body". Thus when Aquinas claims that transubstantiation has been effected in such a way that the accidents of bread and wine nonetheless remain, one could say that he is strictly adhering to the peculiar linguistic pragmatics of this New Testament usage.

Nevertheless, there does seem to be one major problem about Aquinas's interpretation, namely that it runs counter to common sense. The natural reaction to the claim that the bread is more essentially Body is one of tremendous shock, because no Body can be seen.[19] Why does this shock not lead to rejection? The answer here is manifold, because it has to do with the complex circumstance in which this phrase is uttered. For one thing, the sheer plainness of the phrase tends to produce trust, and, for another, the circumstances in which it is uttered – the ceremonial context, the priestly authority, the echoing of the original institution at an evening banquet, the choice of simple elements – which as Aquinas says possess a natural sweetness – all tend to ensure our consent. Although the shock could not be greater, it nonetheless concerns the conjoining of the supernatural with the ordinary in such a way that we are persuaded of a certain analogical continuity which makes us desire the claimed presence of the Bread and Body of Christ. In short, the shock is acceptable because desire, instead of being cancelled, as in the case where one's expectations are fulfilled, as when one says "This was my grandmother's ring", is here sustained and intensified. Aquinas repeatedly observes that it is actually desire for the Body which ensures discernment of the presence of the Body.[20]

Thus in Aquinas's description of the liturgy surrounding the Consecration, it seems that there is a determined effort to *incite* passions. These allusions to emotion can be divided into two categories, (1) relating to preparing the right sort of feelings during the liturgy leading up to the Consecration, in keeping with the solemnity of the mysteries about to be celebrated; and (2), related to the first kind, a more intense, even physical, stirring of emotions, which, as we will see later, is closely linked to Aquinas's theology of the Eucharist.

The first set of allusions can be surveyed quite briefly. Aquinas introduces the theme of emotional preparation with an invocation of the Old Testament injunction to "Keep thy foot when thou goest into the house of God" (Eccles. iv:17). The celebration of this mystery, he writes, "is preceded by a certain preparation in order that we may perform worthily that which follows after",[21] which would seem to suggest that liturgy is not an end in itself, but an act of preparation, very closely allied to human desires. The first stage of this preparation, he writes, is divine praise, and, for Aquinas, this meant the singing of an Introit, usually taken from the Psalms; this is followed by are calling of our present misery, and an invocation of divine mercy, through the recitation of the *Kyrie*. Next, heavenly glory is commemorated in the *Gloria*, so that, as Aquinas puts it, such glory becomes that towards which we might incline ourselves or tend. And, finally, before the next main stage of this long act of preparation, the priest prays on behalf of the people that they may be made worthy of such mysteries. What this final prayer amounts to is in fact a prayer for emotional preparation, a preparation for preparation, a desire for there to be desire. What one might call this incipient stage, then, is a liturgical liturgy.

The second advance towards preparation is, as Aquinas puts it, the instruction of the faithful, which is given dispositively, when the lectors and subdeacons read aloud in the church the teachings of the prophets and apostles. At this point, we notice a slight change in the provocation of right desire. Whereas, in the first stage, as we have already seen, the desires provoked were immediate responses or solicitations of joy, misery, glory and so on, now the passions of the people are lured via the mimetic enactment by choir or priest of certain spiritual or elevated emotions: for example, a sense of progress towards God, which is a sense of spiritual delighting or, sometimes, of spiritual sorrowing, according to Aquinas. Thus, after the Lesson, the choir sings the Gradual, which Aquinas says is to signify "progress in life"; then the Alleluia is intoned, and this denotes "spiritual joy"; or, if it is a mournful Office, the Tract is intoned, which, he writes, is "expressive of spiritual sighing". So, it seems that having first elicited the raw and uninstructed passions of joy and sorrow, the liturgy then provides a spiritual model whereby these emotions might be guided to make the people worthy of the mysteries to come. It is as if desire is at first fulfilled only by a reinforcing and increasing of desire which we must learn from the desired goal itself. It might at first sight seem strange that liturgical progress here runs from initially spontaneous and authentic emotions towards feigned and borrowed ones. For this inverts the normal assumed sequence whereby first one learns by copying and then one grows into authentic possession. However, the placing of *mimesis*, in this case ahead of the autonomous, suggests that, for the liturgical point of view, a borrowing is the highest authenticity that can be attained. For, where all desire for God and praise of God must come from God, imitation is no mere pedagogic instrument which subserves a more fundamental self-originating substantiality. Here, to the contrary, one must copy in order first to begin to be, and one continues to be only *as* a copy, never in one's own right. However, as has been seen, what we first imitate and copy in the divine is desire or love. And here again normal expectations are subverted. For just as being does not here precede copying, so also the apprehension of the thing copied does not precede our copying. We do not first apprehend and *then* desire and imitate; rather we first apprehend in acts of desiring which alone begin to disclose, through mimesis, that which is imitated. This liturgical logic of imitation in fact performs a theology of creation for which it is the case that, outside participation in the divine, the creature is, of itself, precisely "nothing". Later in this chapter I will show how the narrative logic of imitation in the liturgy is underpinned by a metaphysical logic of participation, and how the culmination of the Mass in the transformation and reception of the elements displays the fusion of these two levels. For now, one can note that Aquinas's logic of imitation both anticipates and surpasses in advance a postmodern treatment of mimesis. For the latter also, imitation is constitutive of the imitator and precedes the original. And yet postmodernism, as if still echoing negatively a suspicion of all mimesis which it (falsely) attributes to Plato, regards these circumstances as entirely disruptive of all identity. More radically, Aquinas thinks of identity as reception, and of perception *as* receiving.

The third stage in preparation of emotions is to proceed to the celebration of the Mystery, which, as Aquinas explains, is an oblation and a sacrament. Both of these dimensions of the mystery, the sacrificial and the sacramental, entail their own respective passions as well. Regarding the Mystery insofar as it is an oblation, the peoples' praise in singing the Offertory is now realised as they imitate in turn the mimetic performances of the choir or priest, for, as Aquinas says, this expresses the joy of the offerers. Insofar as the Mystery is to be seen as a sacrament, he declares that

> the people are first of all excited to devotion in the Preface … and admonished to lift up their hearts to the Lord, and therefore when the Preface is ended the people devoutly praise Christ's Godhead, saying with the angels: Holy, Holy, Holy; and with His humanity, saying with the children, Blessed is He that cometh.

Now one might think that after all this elevating and instructing of the passions, the people would finally be ready to receive the Mysteries. And we have seen how this involved a turning away from the rawness of spontaneity and a sublimation to a higher kind of passion. This would surely seem an appropriately elevated moment for proceeding to the Mysteries. But not so. At this most mysterious of moments, just prior to receiving God into one's body, the people are reminded of more earthly emotions; far from this being a moment to look into a spiritual and abstruse realm of higher desire, the people are now reminded of their desire and love for one another. This is done by the communal recitation of the Lord's Prayer, in which the people ask for their daily bread and by the exchange of the *Pax* [peace] which is then given again with the concluding words of the *Agnus Dei*. In this final intrusion of community, we can see a further elaboration of the logic of *mimesis*. The doubling of the choir's imitation of God and the angels by the peoples' imitation of the choir reveals that the inversions of copy and original involved in relation to God are repeated at an interpersonal level. For our existing only as first created, as first an imitation of God, is repeated through the passage of time, as we exist (naturally and culturally) only through first receiving our specific mode of human existence, the mediation of our forebears and contemporaries. They indeed give birth to us, and speak us into articulate being. Hence *metaphysical* participation extends to the political domain, ensuring that here a participation in the *social* sense precedes the individual self. Thus once the people have been restored to themselves in earthly proximity to one another, after the earlier elevation of desire, they are now ready to receive the sacrament.

When Aquinas has thus narrated the modulations of desire during the liturgy, he then turns to more local observations in his replies to the various objections. And one or two of these replies are relevant to our theme. In his Reply to the Sixth Objection, Aquinas notes the way in which the liturgy seems to involve a great many different genres and perspectives, and that each of these seems to have a corresponding purpose linked to the provocation of desire. He writes that the Eucharist is a sacrament which pertains to the entire Church, and, consequently, every different quarter of the Church must be included. Consequently, "some things which refer to the people are sung by the Choir, so as to inspire the entire people with them" and there are other words which the priest begins and then the people take up, the priest then acting as in the person of God, and so on. And even when the words which belong to the priest alone, and are said in secret, are to be uttered, he calls the people to attention by saying "The Lord be with you" and waiting for their assent by saying "Amen". At all times, it seems, the desire of the people is provoked, channelled and maintained. This is no automatic ritual, but one which, like the order of ancient sacrifices, must be accompanied by the right devotion in order to be acceptable to God.[22] So much is this the case, in fact, that at the Consecration, the priest does not seem to pray for the consecration to be fulfilled, but, as he says, "that it may be fruitful in our regard". Here Aquinas cites the words of the priest, "That it may become 'to us' the body and blood".

But just why is the Body of Christ so desirable? I have already mentioned that this is partly to do with its infinite absence and inexhaustibility, but it would be a mistake to suppose that this is the only reason. To do so would be to associate the instigation of desire with lack and frustration. On that account, desire is primarily a *possibility*. However, this account of desire, although a common one, is false, because, if desire is primarily instigated by frustration, it reduces to the mere epistemic imagining of a *possible* satisfaction. But, in order for desire to be felt at all, it must be granted at least some scope of expression, which amounts to some measure of fulfilment, since desire expresses itself only in response to some reception of the desired object. Were such reception to be withheld, then no desire could be expressed, nor any desire felt. Moreover, while it is true that we may appear especially to want the impossible, the knowledge that something is impossible always in some fashion blocks the spontaneity of desire in such a manner that one is not really relaxed in desiring, and remains self-conscious in a way which inhibits ecstasis or else forces one to contrive an artificial or rational *mathēsis* of desire. In the opposite situation of a desire that can be fulfilled, it is true that familiarity can breed a slackening of interest. But all that this implies is that for desire fully to operate, there must be both the possibility of fulfilment, and a sustained strangeness and distance. In this optimum and therefore defining situation, desire is something primarily *actual* rather than *possible*, because it is maximally in existence when flowing freely, as well as being continuously provoked.

Such a construal of desire as primarily actual accords with a Thomistic under-standing of desire in relation to the Eucharist. For us to desire Christ's Body in the Eucharist, according to Aquinas, it must not only be withheld but also, in a measure, be given. Thus Aquinas places great stress on the analogical appropriateness of the elements of bread and wine right down to the details of the multiplicity of grape and grain being compressed into a unity and so forth.[23] He also stresses how the elements of the Eucharist taste and smell good, and regards this as part of a complex rhetoric whereby the Eucharistic presentation of Christ is made attractive to us.[24] Indeed, one could argue that Aquinas implies a Eucharistic reworking of what it is to know. On the one hand, it would seem, as we have seen, that transubstantiation accords with an optative scepticism about sensory evidence. Normally this would preface a spir-itualizing or idealist philosophy which takes refuge in the certainty of ideas or logic. However, Aquinas denies sensory evidence only to announce that the real concealed substance is nonetheless manifest in sensory appearances if these are now reconstrued as both metaphors and sources of delectation. The elements are reduced to accidents, and yet their accidentality is then seen as all-important. One can go so far as to say that having denied knowledge by sensory evidence, Aquinas then affirms a knowledge by sensual enjoyment. Beyond the disciplining of desires by reason lies a higher desire for God only made possible when God conjoins Himself with the seemingly most base forms of sensory delighting in the form of bread and wine. There is no induction of God *a posteriori* and there is no deduction of God *a priori*, and yet there is a tasting of God through direct physical apprehension, conjoined with a longing for the forever absent. Thereby, one can see that the ultimate reason for the acceptance of the shock of the phrase of institution is that it is one's body which here guides one's reason in the name of an infinite reason. Such a pedagogic order is, for the patristic inheritance which Aquinas received, strictly in keeping with the kenotic logic of salvation history: since it was the higher, Adam's reason, which first betrayed the lower, his body, redemption is received in reverse order through the descent of the highest, God, into our bodies which then start to reorder our minds.

So far, in the foregoing, we have seen how one can read the Eucharist as a particularly acute resolution of the aporia of learning in terms of the category of desire. This reading also has the advantage of showing just how fundamentally in line with Augustinianism Aquinas's thinking about transubstantiation really is. Something similar can be glimpsed in a fourth example of mediation between presence and absence, namely the persistence of the accidents after the event of transubstantiation. This phenomenon, it turns out, is only comprehensible for Aquinas in terms of his somewhat Neoplatonic ontology of participation in Being which surpasses Aristotelianism in seeking to do justice to the doctrine of creation.

Not often noted in Aquinas's account of the Eucharist is the way in which, besides transubstantiation, at least two subsidiary miracles are involved, although they are all part of the same miracle.[25] One of these is the conversion of water – representing the people – into wine, as at the wedding feast at Cana, occurring before the transubstantiation of the wine into Christ's Blood.[26] This is important, because it shows that the Body of Christ is a nuptial body which is always already the unity of Christ with the Church, His people; in a similar fashion, Aquinas emphasizes that bread and wine include a vast synthesis of disparate human labours, including the labour of transport and trade.[27] All these features tend to confirm the idea that, in the Eucharist, God is only made apparent in a sensual fashion which involves the mediation of all human physical interactions. Now, this exaltation of the sensual runs parallel with the glorification of the accidents which is the second subsidiary miracle involved.[28] It might seem that if bread and wine are reduced from substance to accident, that their natural materiality is thereby degraded. However, one can only think this if one remains ignorant of just how transubstantiation relates to Aquinas's most fundamental ontology. This is a matter ignored, for example, by P. J. FitzPatrick. I shall elaborate this presently. The miraculous character of the remaining accidents is patent for Aquinas in the fact that, since the persisting accidental properties of bread and wine go on having a generative effect – for example, nourishing and delighting us – God causes the accidents to act as if they were substantive. This means that here the operation of matter in a *normal* fashion has been rendered miraculous. It is as if Aquinas is here saying that the rendering of the normal and continuous as miraculous is the greatest miracle of all, and helps us to reunderstand the miraculously created reality of the everyday.[29]

Under normal circumstances, the accidents of bread and wine – for example, their shape and their taste – would manifest the substance of bread and wine, but now they have to be taken as directly manifesting God in whom they subsist. However, they are not accidents *of* the Body and Blood of Christ, since Christ being God, and therefore being simple, cannot be the subject of accidents. Nor, however, does this mean that they are simply signs of the divine, as if they were mere persisting miraculous appearances. This cannot be the case because Aquinas insists that the bread and wine remain as ontological accidents even though they are no longer accidents of any substance.[30] This is the point objected to by FitzPatrick on the grounds of its utter incoherence in terms of Aristotelian philosophy.[31] But what he ignores is that Aquinas's metaphysic is not ultimately Aristotelian.[32] Aquinas is quite explicit; in question 77, article 1 of the *Summa*, he raises the question of whether free-floating accidents are not utterly simple and therefore blasphemously like God in character.[33] But the answer he gives is that although they are torn away from the composition of substance and accident, they still retain a composition of existence and essence, since their essence, unlike that of God, does not cause them *to be*. This invocation of the real distinction between essence and existence constitutive of all creaturehood explains how it is possible for accidents to persist without substance, for they possess a ground in which to inhere, namely created being, *esse commune* [being 'in common', or shared being – i.e. creatures], which is nonetheless only ever displayed in specifically characterized formations. The real distinction displays a deeper ontological level than that of substance and accident, because substance is always present in its own right as this or that kind of creature which can be accidentally qualified; whereas created being [*esse commune*] is not present in its own right at all, but only as this or that kind of being, whether substance or accident, since created being is really only a participation in Being as such, which belongs to God alone. Hence, paradoxically beyond substance, which is self-standing, lies something, for Aquinas, *not* self-standing, namely *esse commune*, which only exists in an improper borrowed fashion, just as earlier we saw that the human creature is imitative without remainder.[34] But since participation in being is the most fundamental ontological dimension of creation, the real distinction of essence and existence can in theory sustain finite reality before and without the division of substance and accident. And this explains why free-floating accidents are possible, although it would probably be better to say that the remaining accidents have passed beyond the contrast of substance and accident. They are neither essential – since they are not God – nor are they non-essential – since they manifest God and are His creation.

Once one has understood that the remaining accidents exceed the contrast of substance and accident, one can also see that they are not relegated beneath the level of substance. On the contrary, they are now promoted to a character that most essentially reveals the condition of createdness, and they are accorded the honour of directly subsisting in Being which is the most immediate divine created effect. For this reason, one can say that merely accidental bread and wine have become more themselves than ever before, and this coheres with the fact that they have also become completely attuned to a signifying and spiritually active purpose.[35] So much is this the case that Aquinas insists that partaking of the Body and Blood of Christ under the species of bread and wine has become the means of deification. It is as if one is saying that bread and wine now remain eschatologically alongside God in such a way that the most ordinary is here exalted, and it becomes not absurd to adore a mere piece of bread.[36] This is especially the case because the remaining accidents are no longer like food that only becomes food when we take it up and eat it, and otherwise is only *potential* food. Rather, to exceed the contrast between substance and accident is to attain to createdness as pure transparency, as pure mediation of the divine. At this point the underlying metaphysical logic of participation as it were surfaces or erupts into the narrative logic of *mimesis* which it supports. For as purely subsisting in the divine, the accidents also achieve a pure flow of ceaseless and self-sustaining creative mimicry. Thus, the bread and wine which persist as accidents, have become always and essentially *food* – figurative food which shapes our imitative humanity – and, in this way, they are the appropriate vehicles of the *Logos*, since, like the *Logos*, they now exist in a pure passage, or relationality. For this reason, Aquinas repeats Augustine's statement that the Eucharistic food is not like ordinary food which is cancelled as food by being incorporated into our nature when we eat it. It is rather the other way about: we are incorporated into the food.[37] This implies that we are speaking here about an essential food which never starts to be food and never ceases to be food, because it is entirely the mediation of a God who is in Himself mediation.

The fifth way in which the contrast of presence and absence is outwitted by the Eucharist concerns the operation of desire. We have already seen how desire mediates the usage of the word "this" in the case of the Eucharist; now I will show how for Aquinas the central role of desire helps to ensure that for the whole phenomenon of the Eucharist and the liturgy there is no fetishization of presence or absence.

First of all, the Eucharist might seem to risk a fetishization of presence if all that mattered for the sake of salvation were to receive the elements, since this is authorized by the Church. And indeed such a fetishization was risked by many Counter-Reformation approaches. Aquinas, by contrast, insists that what is primarily salvific, even if one does receive, is *desire* for the Body and Blood of Christ.[38] And this tends to make sense of the fact that we can never receive once and for all, and have to go on receiving. If there is no end to receiving the Eucharist, and we have never received enough, this does indeed imply that desire is as good as receiving, just as receiving the Eucharist in the right desire is essential.[39] Thus Aquinas repeatedly suggests that the whole of the liturgy is primarily directed towards preparing in people a proper attitude of receptive expectation.[40] Everything is intended to affect us in an appealing manner directed towards every aspect of our common humanity, including the more sensory aspects; and as we have seen, if anything, an appeal is made to our minds *through* our bodies, *rather* than the other way around.

Indeed, Aquinas construes the circumstances of the instauration of the Eucharist – the drama of the late evening supper, the unexpected directness of the words used –

as deliberate rhetorical means deployed to fix truths in his disciples' memories and our memories, and incite true desire in our hearts.[41] Nevertheless, Aquinas insists that the primacy of desire does not mean that abstention is as good as reception, for it is in the very nature of desire that it should want what it desires, just as we have already seen that desire is only actualized when it is in part fulfilled and can flow freely, not when it is frustrated or contrived. Thus while avoiding a fetishization of presence, and insisting that it is the personal desire for God which is salvific, rather than adherence to ecclesial authorities, Aquinas nonetheless avoids an opposite fetishization of absence and postponement.[42] Thus God does provide us with a fore-taste of His eschatological presence, and indeed Aquinas insists that we only have desire for Christ, not because of some *abstract* promise, but because our imaginations have been engaged right from the outset of the first Maundy Thursday by the use of beguiling verbal and sensory devices.[43]

It will be recalled that in the background of this interest in desire lies the Augus-tinian deployment of desire to resolve the aporia of learning. Desire is the answer to this aporia, but not desire alone. It has to be desire *for* God, for only if God is real can we trust that a desire for further knowledge will be fulfilled and that signs are not empty. However, the question of desire for God should not be taken merely in an individualistic way, but rather in collective and historical fashion. Human beings have only been able to believe in God through the mediation of signs conveying His reality which they believe they can trust. Indeed, one might describe our fallenness as a situation of the absence of such trustworthy signs. The Passion of Christ drives that situation to an extreme because here one has a maximum visibility of the divine presence in humanity that is nonetheless destroyed. This can provoke a kind of death of God nihilism which affirms that we glimpse the truth in and through destruction. However, such nihilism is qualified in the Christian gospel because it offers, even in the extreme of the death of the divine, an image of something trust-worthy. The death of Christ becomes a sign of promise since in the resurrection, the shedding of Christ's Blood is transformed into the gift of the Eucharist. And in every Eucharist, the extreme contrasts that one sees in the Passion are repeated, and repeated in their reconciliation. Every Eucharist is a representation, a reactualization of the sacrifice of Christ, therefore it is a continuation of His loss and destruction. However, since this loss *feeds* us, this ultimate dereliction is also revealed as the pure essential food that is substantive passage. And this death as food can therefore act as the ultimate trustworthy sign – the passage of the Eucharistic food is also the unique Christian passage of sacrifice to sign which constitutes the very nature of a sacrament.

One can sum up this balancing of the Eucharist as presence with a non-elided desire for the Eucharist by invoking the mediaeval allegorical linking of the Eucharist with the quest for the Holy Grail. And this invocation is far from being arbitrary, because the period of emergence of grail literature (roughly 1170–1220) is contemporary with the increasing articulation of a doctrine of transubstantiation.[44] The allegory of the Grail helped to ensure that the seemingly most commonly available thing in every Church in every town and village was made the object of a difficult quest and high adventure, a quest indeed so difficult that it was almost impossible to attain, as if it were scarcely possible even to locate and receive the Eucharist. Nonetheless, the ultimate vision accorded Sir Galahad ensures that the postmodern fetishization of pure postponement is also here avoided.

In the above, we have seen how the Eucharist is situated between presence and absence. Because of this situation, it does not pretend that indeterminism of meaning can be cancelled by pure presence; on the other hand, since presence is not denied, the Eucharist remains something meaningful. But now the further question arises as to how this can possibly benefit meaning in general. In conclusion, I will try to indicate the outlines of an answer to this question.

Outside the Eucharist, it is true, as postmodern theory holds, that there is no stable signification, no anchoring reference, and no fixable meaning. This means that there is no physical thing whose nature one can ultimately trust. We have seen how the Eucharist dramatizes this condition, pushes it to an extreme, but then goes beyond it. The circumstance of the greatest dereliction of meaning is here read as the promise of the greatest plenitude of meaning. However, if we do trust this sign, it cannot be taken simply as a discrete miraculous exception, if we are true to a high mediaeval and Thomistic construal of the Eucharist. First of all, we have seen how Aquinas sees bread and wine as the most common elements of human culture. Hence, if these become the signs of promise, they pull all of human culture along with them. Secondly, "This is my body" cannot be regarded as a phrase in isolation anymore than any other linguistic phrase. Here, the Saussurean point holds true, that every phrase of language in some sense depends for its meaningfulness upon the entire set of contrasts which forms the whole repertoire of language, such that, for example, "this" only makes sense in contrast to "that", "my" in contrast to "your" and "his", "is" in contrast to "is not" and "was" and the other verbs, and so forth *ad infinitum*.

For this reason, if this phrase is guaranteed an ultimate meaningfulness, it draws all other phrases along with it.

In the third place, these words and events only occur in the Church. And we only accept real presence and transubstantiation because the giving of Body and Blood in the Eucharist gives also the Body of the Church. The Eucharist both occurs within the Church and gives rise to the Church in a circular fashion. In consequence, a trust in the Eucharistic event inevitably involves trusting also the past and the future of the Church. In receiving the Eucharist, we are in fact receiving an entire historical transmission which comprises the traditions of the Church and then those of Greece and Israel. This tradition includes the Bible in which it is declared that God is in some fashion manifest to all traditions and in the physical world as such. Thus, trust in the Eucharist draws all historical processes and then every physical thing along with it.

One could even say that just as the accidents remain, so the supreme event of the Eucharist, which other things anticipate, is only present in a kind of dispersal back into those very things. One is referred back to a primitive trust in the gifts of creation. For all peoples, these things have enabled a beginning of trust in the divine, even if it is only the incarnation, the Passion and the gift of the Eucharist which ensure that this trust does not run into an ultimate nihilistic crisis.

This idea, according to which the Eucharistic fulfilment of prophecy turns one back towards the original prophecies and ennobles them (just as reception does not cancel desire; just as the accidents remain; just as the body teaches the mind) is dramatized in the mediaeval allegorical text, *The Quest of the Holy Grail*, which reflects a Cistercian spirituality focused upon desire, and which reads devotion to the Eucharist in terms of a search,[45] just as Aquinas said that we are "wayfarers" who can only discern the Body of Christ through faith.[46] On their way to the Grail castle, the knights in the story are led to a mysterious ship which has been voyaging since the time of King Solomon. This ship has a mast made of the Tree of Life from the Garden of Eden and other insignia which foreshadow Christ. It had been built by Solomon's wife who was concerned that future times should know that Solomon had prophesied Christ's coming. Her female left-handed *ingenium*, which is a crafty capacity to make things, is contrasted to Solomon's male contemplative wisdom.[47] The ostensible concern in the story is that we should recognize the prophetic power of our ancestors, but surely the deeper point is that, if there were no record of the anticipation of Jesus and the Eucharist, we would not recognise them as significant at all, nor discern them, for they are only meaningful as fulfilment; without the record of Israel, there could be no manifest incarnation. It follows that Jesus and the Eucharist are in some way a ship, just as the Tree of Life was read allegorically in terms of the God-man. The ship is already the Church and the Eucharist, as a tentative human construction, whereas the fulfilled Eucharist is perfect human and yet divine art. Inversely, one can say that the Eucharist remains the ship because it persists as quest despite fulfilment. This allows us to link the notion of non-cancelled desire with the idea that trust in the Eucharist points us back towards a trust in everything, and especially the ordinary and the everyday. For, if we are to go on questing, then all the things pointing towards the Eucharist retain their pregnant mystery without cancellation. We are still knights looking for the Grail, just as we are still Israel on pilgrimage. Since knowledge consists in desire, we must affirm that the aporia of learning is resolved all the time in the promise of everyday human practices. We are usually unaware of this recollection, and yet in a way we do have a certain inchoate awareness of it. Thus we can see that what the Eucharist is is desire. Although we only know via desire, or wanting to know, and this circumstance alone resolves the aporia of learning, beyond this we discover that what there is to know is desire. But not desire as absence, lack and perpetual postponement; rather, desire as the free flow of actualization, perpetually renewed and never foreclosed.

Notes

1   Blaise Pascal, *Pensées*, trans. A J Krailsheimer, Harmondsworth: Penguin Books, 1966, § 65.

2   Antoine Arnauld and Pierre Nicole, *Logic or the Art of Thinking*, trans. Jill Vance Buroker, Cambridge: Cambridge University Press, 1996, pp. 70–71, and p. 231 re Pascal § 72.

3   Ibid., p. 72. See also G. W. F. Hegel, *Phenomenology of Spirit*, trans. A V Miller, Oxford: Oxford University Press, 1977, § 109.

4   Arnauld and Nicole, *Logic or the Art of Thinking* (see Note 2), p. 231.

5   Ibid., p. 71.

6   Steven Shapin and Simon Schaffer, *Leviathan and the Air-Pump: Hobbes, Boyle, and the Experimental Life*, Princeton, NJ: Princeton University Press, 1985, pp. 36–7; Steven Shapin, *A Social History of Truth: Civility and Science in Seventeenth-Century England*, Chicago, IL: University of Chicago Press, 1995, pp. 194–5; Maurice Mandelbaum, *Philosophy, Science, and Sense Perception: Historical and Critical Studies*, Baltimore, MD: The Johns Hopkins University Press, 1964, ch 2; B. J. Shapiro, *Probability and Certainty in Seventeenth-Century England: A Study of the Relationship between Natural Science, Religion, History, Law, and Literature*, Princeton, NJ: Princeton University Press, 1983, pp. 61–2; Albert van Helden, "'Annulo Cingitur': The Solution of the Problem of Saturn", *Journal of the History of Astronomy*, 5 (1974), pp. 155–74.

7   Catherine Pickstock, *After Writing*, Oxford: Blackwell, 1998, pp. 35–7, 116–18.

8   John D. Caputo, *The Prayers and Tears of Jacques Derrida: Religion Without Religion*, Bloomington and Indianapolis, IN: Indiana University Press, 1997, p. 13.

9   Jacques Derrida, "Plato's Pharmacy" in *idem.*, *Dissemination*, trans. Barbara Johnson, London: Athlone Press, 1981, pp. 63–171, 95–96.

10 Pickstock, *After Writing* (see Note 7), chapter 3.

11 Henri de Lubac, *Corpus Mysticum: L'Eucharistic et l'eglise au moyen-age*, Paris: Aubier-Montaigne, 1949; Michel de Certeau, *The Mystic Fable*, trans. Michael B. Smith, Chicago, IL: University of Chicago Press, 1992; Pickstock, *After Writing* (see Note 7), pp. 158–66.

12 de Lubac, *Corpus Mysticum* (see Note 7), pp. 253–4, 266–7.

13 Jean-Luc Marion, *God Without Being*, trans. Thomas A. Carlson, Chicago, IL: University of Chicago Press, 1991, pp. 161–83.

14 Arnauld and Nicole, *Logic or the Art of Thinking* (see Note 2), p. 211; see further, Marin, in *idem.*, *La Parole Mangée et autres essais théologico-politiques*, Paris: Méridiens Klincksieck, 1986, pp. 12–35.

15 *Summa Theologiae (S.T.)*, III. q. 75 a. 1; III. q. 76. a. 7.

16 Marin (see Note 14), pp. 23–5.

17 *S.T.*, III. q. 78 a. 6.

18 *S.T.*, III. q. 78 a. 5.

19 *S.T.*, III. q. 75 a. 1; q. 76 a. 7.

20 *S.T.*, III. q. 80 a. 4.

21 *S.T.*, III. q. 83 a. 4.

22 *S.T.*, III. q. 83 a. 4 AD 8.

23 *S.T.*, III. q. 73 a. 1–a. 2; q. 74. a. 1; a. 4; a. 5; q. 75 a. 8 AD 1; q. 76 a. 2 AD 1; q. 77 a. 6; q. 79 a. 1.

24 *S.T.*, III. q. 74 a. 3 AD 1; q. 79 a. 1; q. 81 a. 1 AD 3; q. 83 a. 5 AD 2.

25 *S.T.*, III. q. 74 a. 8.

26 *S.T.*, III. q. 74 a. 6; a. 8; q. 77 a. 5.

27 *S.T.*, III. q. 74 a. 1; a. 3.

28 *S.T.*, III. q. 75 a. 8 AD 4; q. 77 a. 1 AD 4; q. 77 a. 3 AD 2; a. 5.

29 *S.T.*, III. q. 75 a. 8; III. q. 78 a. 2 AD 2; III q. 77 a. 3; a. 5.

30 *S.T.*, III. q. 77 a. 1 especially AD 2.

31 P. J. FitzPatrick, *In Breaking of Bread: The Eucharist and Ritual*, Cambridge: Cambridge University Press, 1993, pp. 12–17.

32 See further Mark Jordan, "Theology and Philosophy", in Norman Kretzman and Eleonore Stump (eds), *The Cambridge Companion to Aquinas*, Cambridge: Cambridge University Press,

1993, pp. 232–51; A. N. Williams, "Mystical Theology Redux: The Pattern of Aquinas "Summa Theologiae", *Modern Theology*, 13.1 (January 1997), pp. 53–74.

33   *S.T.*, III. q. 77 a. 1, esp. AD 2.

34   *S.T.*, III. q. 77 a. 1 AD 2.

35   *S.T.*, III. q. 73 a 1; a. 2; q. 74 a. 1; a. 4; a. 5; q. 75 a. 8 AD 1; q. 76 a. 2 AD 1; q. 77 a. 6; q. 79 a. 1.

36   *S.T.*, III. q. 75 a. 8; q. 78 a. 2 AD 2.

37   *S.T.*, III. q. 73 a. 3 AD 2.

38   *S.T.*, III. q. 73 a. 3 AD 2; q. 78 a 3; q. 79 a. 3; q. 80 a. 1 AD 3; a. 2 AD 1; a. 9 AD 1.

39   *S.T.*, III. q. 80 a. 4.

40   *S.T.*, III. q. 76 a. 8; q. 78 a. 1 especially AD 4; q. 79 a. 4; a. 5; q. 80 a. 11; q. 83 a. 2; q. 83 a. 4 AD 1; AD 6; AD 7.

41   *S.T.*, III. q. 73 a. 5; q. 83 a. 2 AD 3.

42   *S.T.*, III. q. 80 a. 11 AD 1.

43   *S.T.*, III. q. 75 a. 1.

44   Ronald Hutton, *The Pagan Religions of the Ancient British Isles: Their Nature and Legacy*, Oxford: Blackwell, 1991, 1993, p. 319.

45   Sister Isabel Mary SLG, "The Knights of God: Citeaux and the Quest of the Holy Grail", in Sister Benedicta Ward SLG (ed.), *The Influence of Saint Bernard*, Oxford: SLG Press, 1976, pp. 53–88; Andrew Sinclair, *The Discovery of the Grail*, London: Century, 1998, passim.

46   *S.T.*, III. q. 76 a. 7.

47   P. M. Matarasso (trans.), *The Quest of the Holy Grail*, Harmondsworth: Penguin, 1969, esp. p. 230.

Chapter 10

Graham Ward

Transcorporeality: the ontological scandal

The floating signifier relates to the body, this crucible of energy mutations. But what goes on there remains unknown – and will remain so until an adequate semiology (one that can take account of transsemiotic fields) is established. In particular, it would be important to make a large part of this deal, not only with the capacity of the body to send and receive signs and to inscribe them on itself, but also with the capacity to serve as a base for all communicative activity

(Gil: 1998, 107)

Corpus

In Michigan, a man named David wanted his union of twelve years with Jon blessed by a representative of God before he died. David lay on the couch while Jim, a gay Presbyterian minister who also has AIDS, moved his hands to the silent sounds of peace. He spoke nourishing words of blessing on these two lives bound by God's grace: 'Those whom God hath joined together, let no one put asunder ... ' And then, as the minister began to celebrate the Communion for those who were present, he spoke the familiar words: 'This is my body, broken for you ... ' and that was the point at which David died. 'Do this in remembrance of me' (Brantley: 1996, 217). These are not my words. They belong to another voice, an American voice; the voice of a Christian journalist himself dying of AIDS. I ventriloquise his voice, because I want to begin by outlining a Christian construal of the body with respect to the brokenness of bodies in postmodernity. The brokenness of these bodies is a continuation of the logic (and, ironically, humanism) of modernity. Postmodernity does not transcend but deepen, and bring to a certain terminus, the hidden agendas of modernity (Toulmin: 1990). And so the corpses and carnage of Ypres and the genocides of Belsen, are repeated, variously, at Pol Pot and Bosnia. The bodies, modern and postmodern, are concrete and also symptomatic. Where culture can be understood as a language, as an open field of shifting symbols, these pilings up of the dead are metaphors of cultural disintegration.

In this chapter I want to examine the racked and viral-ridden bodies of the sick, the engineered bodies of the beautiful, the power-hungry and disenfranchised bodies of the polis, the torn and bleeding body of the Church, the poisoned and raped body of the world and the abused body of Christ. What Christian theology has to offer any discussion of corporeality is not simply in terms of the way its discourses have informed our past understanding (and neglect) of the experience of embodiment. Christian theology also offers a profound thinking about the nature of bodies through the relationship it weaves between creation, incarnation, ecclesiology and eucharist. As Elizabeth Castelli observes, 'From the very earliest Christian texts and practices, the human body functioned as both a site of religious activities and a source of religious meanings' (Castelli: 1991).The work on epistemology by feminist philosophers such as Sandra Harding and Bat-Ami Bar On emphasises that subjects construct 'knowledges' or make claims about the way things are from specific situations and these subjects need to acknowledge their standpoint if, together, we are to move towards what Harding terms 'maximizing objectivities' (Harding: 1993, 49–82, On: 1993, 83–100, Longino: 1993, 101–20). Standpoint epistemology is not perspectivalism (Anderson: 1998, 73 – 87), but moves out from a position in the margins, with a certain knowledge learnt as marginal, towards new negotiations with non-marginal knowledges. I begin then from a tradition-bound knowledge.

I want to examine the broken bodies of postmodernity through the discourses which access them for us. As Judith Butler reminds us, ' "To matter" means at once "to materialize" and "to mean"' and, elsewhere, 'the materiality of the signifier (a "materiality" that comprises both signs and their significatory efficacy) implies that there can be no reference to a pure materiality except via materiality' (Butler: 1993, 32, 68). We have no knowledge, and no acknowledged experience of, the material world outside of the way we represent that world to ourselves. Furthermore, that recording of what is physical, that representation, is going to be saturated with cultural meaning. For we have been taught how to represent the world to ourselves – our descriptions are culturally and historically embedded. But through these representations we inhabit the broken fragments of these contemporary bodies; they are mapped onto our bodies through their 'signs and significatory efficacy'. The narratives of their tearing and violation, as we read them, involve themselves in the narratives of our own embodiment. Through these narratives these bodies, and our bodies also, scream and rage for resurrection.

'Take, eat, this is my body' The shock-wave in these words emerges from the depths of an ontological scandal; the scandal of that 'is'.[1] The literary nature of this demonstrative identification cannot be accurately catalogued. There is no avowed element of similitude or comparison: it is not a simile, it is not a metaphor. There is no element of substitution or proportion to indicate synecdoche or metonymy: it is not a symbol. A piece of bread is held up for view and renamed: this is my body. A is not A in a logic of identification. A is B and, possibly (for there is no stated reason why this should not be the implication) A could be renamed again as C or D or E: this bread is my … whatever; or this … whatever is my body. What is being perceived and what we are being told is the nature of what is being perceived are out of joint. The phrase has the literary structure of allegory or irony: something which seems to be the case is so, but otherwise.

The scandal of that 'is', what I call the ontological scandal, raises a question to do with the naming, nature and identification of bodies. The question runs somewhat parallel to a question raised in the title of an (in)famous essay by the critical theorist Stanley Fish. Fish asked 'Is There a Text in This Class?' in order to demonstrate that the stable identification of a text is contingent upon the context. '[B]ecause it is set not for all places or all times but for wherever and however long a particular way of reading is in force, it is a text that can change' (Fish: 1980, 274). Similarly, I am asking 'Is there a body in this room?', the upper room, that is, the room in which the Last Supper of Christ was eaten. This is not to deny embodiment. I am not per-forming some postmodern act of prestidigitation in which what is disappears in clouds of philosophical obscurity But I am asking, like Fish, about the stability of the identity and identification of bodies. Is it that bodies are beyond our ability to grasp them and that we deal only with imaginary and symbolised bodies – our own and other people's? What does that ontological scandal in that upper room announce about bodies? What kind of bodies occupy what kind of spaces and in what kind of relationships to other such bodies? This is the constellation of questions being orbited here. If, from the specific standpoint of Christian theology, orderings and accounts of the world proceed from that which has been revealed; and if, therefore, this Eucharistic and Christic body informs all other understandings of 'body' for Christian teaching, then what kind of bodies is Christianity concerned with?

The shock-wave of the Eucharistic phrase has to be calibrated according to our conceptualisations of the body Our conceptualisations of the body depend, in turn, upon the way the word is used; upon the discursive practices in which 'body' has been and is now employed. If we take Mark's Gospel as a certain delineated context, then 'body' (soma) occurs four times – three of those occasions in the last, Passion section. On three of those occasions 'body' is used to designate the physical and biological organism – of the woman whose haemorrhage of blood is healed (5.29), of Jesus when he is anointed with the precious ointment (14.8), of Jesus when Joseph of Arimathaea requests the corpse from Pilate for burial (15.43). Only the Eucharistic 'This is my body' of 14.22 differs, fissuring the consistent employment of 'body' throughout Mark's text. But the dissonance that it registers in the context of that one text may not reflect the dissonance registered in the wider Greco-Roman culture of

Paul's use of soma in his letters to the Church at Corinth or the wider context of the New Testament (Robinson: 1952; Martin: 1995). The dissonance registered in Mark will not be the same as that even four hundred years later when a new concept of the body was emerging governed by the ideals of fasting and penance (Brown: 1998). The dissonance will differ further from the manner in which bodies were imaged in the Middle Ages with its notion of the *corpus mysticum* or the dissonance registered today when the meaning of 'body' is so governed by medical materialism and scientific discourses (Sawday: 1995; Laquer: 1990). Perhaps the ontological scandal is greater today, following a long period in which bodies have become discrete, self-defining, biological organisms. A change is certainly evident in the use of the word, for 'body' comes from an Old English word, *bodig*, meaning corpse, inert thing. Today it is used much more in the sense of a living, active form of life. Bodies are measured and identified according to strict, scientific criteria. And so to the logical positivist the demonstrative identification 'this is my body' with reference to an observable piece of bread is simply nonsense, a misidentification.

The ontological scandal of 'This is my body' today lies particularly in the confidence with which the misidentification is made. The grammar (whether English or Greek) announces an unequivocal logic – pronomial object (this) related to possessive subject (my body) through the cupola (is) – but the isomorphism of bread = body defeats the logic. Furthermore the logic of A = A expresses no knowledge; it has the sense only of a tautology. This phrase seems to express a knowledge of bread as body, but it is not a knowledge that can be read off from the sense-data of bread and body The phrase, then, presents the same structure as, in the context of holding a wedge of Edam aloft, an authoritative subject-position pronounces: 'Here is the moon.' It is an act of madness. But why and was it always?

Corpuscularity

It is an act of madness today because demonstrative identification is linked to perception. That is, philosophically, the way words (and mental conceptions) hook up to the world. As one leading analytical philosopher has remarked,

> Most of us are inclined to suppose that there are close connections between demonstration and perception; and some of these could be brought out by principles of the form "If conditions are G, then if a person makes a statement which demonstrates an object, the person perceives that object"' (Wallace: 1979, 319).

But even he then goes on to say, 'But I do not know how to spell out the conditions'. For example, the person making the statement could be blind or the object at a considerable distance. But it is not only the conditions which make the association between demonstration and perception difficult, it is the act of naming and the nature of perception itself. Naming relies upon social consensus and memory of past, confirming, acts of identification. People, generally and contemporaneously, call this a church and that a frog. They have learnt it. Social consensus does not call 'bread' 'body'. To call 'bread' 'body', to rename the world, requires an Adamic act, an act at the origins of the world:

> And out of the ground the Lord God formed every beast of the field and every fowl of the air; and brought them unto Adam to see what he would call them: and whatsoever Adam called every living creature, that was the name thereof (Genesis 2.19).

Despite modernity's several attempts to think back to and then from beginnings – witness Descartes, Locke, Kant and Hegel, to name a few – with language we always begin after the beginning. Margaret Thatcher may have attempted to rename 'community' those people who are allowed to vote and live in dwellings they have paid a tax on; but older views of community persisted and successfully resisted such distortions. Furthermore, as Gareth Evans points out with reference to Strawson's belief that a subject can identify an object demonstratively if he [sic] can pick it out by sight, hearing or touch, 'the ordinary concept of perception is vague' (Evans: 1982, 144). Perception involves a certain ego-centred orientation and evaluation of objects in a specific spatiality. Each subject position perceives, and in perceiving evaluates (hot/cold, dry/damp, dark/light) differently. I am, at first, alone in what it is that I perceive. Perception is always mediated – we see something as something (a chair *as* a chair, the garden *as* a garden), we do not simply see. Sometimes we are blind to what we see. Most of us have experienced what is common to dyslexics, or children learning to write who reverse letters/numbers – that something looks right, when in fact it is not: we are blind to an error we cannot perceive while staring at it. Authors make bad proof-readers of their own work. Only when something is pointed out do we see what it is we are perceiving. More generally, critical assessment – of a painting or a building, a poem or a state of mind – is illuminating to the extent that it brings to light things we have not considered before or things we intuited but did not articulate. Demonstrative identification is, as Gareth Evans emphasises 'an information-based thought' (Evans: 1982, 145), it is not a form of description. But, if naming is taught and perception is both relative and mediated, then what the statement 'This is my body' effects when the person saying it is holding a loaf of bread is a scepticism. Do I see aright? Do I orientate myself correctly insofar as 'this' implies a 'here', implies a certain spacing, a certain understanding of place such that I can identify this place? Have I learnt to use 'body' and 'this' aright? The I, in its self-certainty, is undermined and has to seek confirmation for what it sees and has learnt from the responses of others.

The scepticism is the product of the metaphysical framework within which we today assess a demonstrative statement. It is evident from Gareth Evans' analytical approach in his essay 'Demonstrative Identification' that what is presupposed in this analysis is the following: first, an independent ego (in order to create the 'egocentric space' from which one perceives); secondly, concepts of space and representation such that a distinction can be drawn between the internal spacing of objects and the external or public spacing of those same objects (so that the latter makes possible the former); thirdly, concepts of relations between objects filling and creating that public space such that a subject 'has an idea of himself as one object among others' (Evans: 1982, 163); fourthly concepts of materiality or what Russell called 'the ultimate constituents of matter' (Russell: [1917] 1994, 121–39) and, fifthly, a notion of the faculties of the mind and their operation to account for memory (of previous encounters with the object) and perception (such that object x can be deemed to be x because it constantly has the properties of x as seen over a period of time). Overall, what is privileged throughout (whether by logical positivists, empiricists or materialists) is the experience of what Ayer called sense-data as they access the objective properties of the particular object being indicated (Ayer: 1959, 66–104, 125–66; 1963, 58–133, 229–74). This privileging has certain consequences. It assumes that the full presence of the object, all that the object is, was and will be, is available for observation. The 'is' of demonstrative identification dissolves as a word, suggesting direct access to the presence of the object through the assertion. 'This is a table', 'This is a chair'. A commodity is born – the possessable reification of a certain individual's perceptual labour. The name sticks so close to the object named – and it is the sticking close which enables 'identification' and 'verification' – that they become indistinguishable. It is only as such that the communication can be understood as information- (or misinformation-)based.

Read from a Christian theological standpoint, one could say that the metaphysical framework here is a secularised doctrine of realised eschatology – the condition of resurrected and permanent dwelling within the fully illuminating presence of the divine. Even Wittgenstein himself seems to make this very same emphasis in insisting in *Philosophical Investigations* that 'everything lies open to view', that what is called for is 'complete clarity' and that 'nothing is hidden' (Wittgenstein: 1953, nos 126, 133, 435; Cunningham: 1998). As Wittgenstein stated: 'The truth of the matter is that we have already got everything and we have got it actually present, we need not wait for anything' (Wittgenstein: 1979, 138). Putnam has recently pointed out that: 'Materialists think the whole universe as a "closed" system, described as God might describe it if he were allowed to know about it clairvoyantly, but not allowed to interfere' (Putnam: 1990, 49). We will return to the monism of this 'closed' system in a moment. For now what is important is to recognise that with this emphasis upon the world as fully given, fully present, mediation, the act of representation itself, the performance of referring itself, is downplayed at best, but certainly on the road to being forgotten. For what is paramount is the relation of the concept to what John McDowell calls 'the myth of the given' (McDowell: 1994, 21). It is not the statement which acts to bring the object into being as a certain object; it is the object which acts, provoking the assertion. The world asserts its own reality; it is self-grounded. Behind such a view lies an atomism: ultimate reality is found in the independence of each atom asserting its own self-enclosed being. Bodies, as such, dissolve into their distinct properties or sense qualia. A form of dissection is performed as the list of distinctive predicates lengthens. A form of death is performed; death as also the dissolution of the body into its composite elements. So that the care to identify an object through perception and perception's correlation with naming, in fact collapses upon itself – the object is torn up into its various compounds, *Speragmos*.[2] The body is a collection of organs, a binding of chemicals, a grouping of molecular structures, etc. Jean-Luc Nancy observes the strong connection between atomism, individualism and claims to unqualified veracity:

> the individual is merely the residue of the experience of the dissolution of community. By its nature – as its name indicates, it is the atom, the indivisible – the individual reveals that it is the abstract result of a decomposition. It is another, and symmetrical, figure of immanence: the absolutely detached for-itself, taken as origin and as certainty (Nancy: 1991, 3; see also Freudenthal: 1986).

With certain ancients, like Leucippus and Democritus, this soulless materialism – materialism without mystery – announced a void, a nihilism. With positivists and radical empiricists, it announces a fluorescent world of fully presenced certainties – indifferent to time, agency and mediation: the eternity of matter, like the ancient *hyle*. To the post-Einsteinian scientist, since matter and energy at root are interchangeable, matter is defined as the contingent but specific focusing of energy. And this is, as McDowell points out in his description of the teaching of modernity, 'devoid of meaning [since] its constituent elements are not linked to one another by the relationships that constitute the space of reasons' (McDowell: 1994, 97).

Corporeality

Within such a metaphysical construal 'This is my body' makes three responses possible: observational self-doubt; a judgement about the mental abilities of the one who has made the misidentification; an ontological scandal (a 'miracle' as certain rational approaches to the philosophy of religion would understand it). Within such a metaphysical construal, because of the independence of the object from the assertion and the one who asserts, the second of these responses would be privileged. The first would be ruled out by appeal to the experience and memory of objects having normative predicates; an appeal to normativity extended through calling upon the experience of other people. The third would be ruled out on Hume's ground that a 'miracle' can only be demonstrated to have occurred when it occurred with a regularity that would make its occurrence normative and, therefore, no longer a miracle (Hume: [1777] 1975, 109–31).

If then we can understand the demonstrative identification involved in 'This is my body' as suggestive of madness (within the current metaphysical construal and its priorities), can we say that this was always so or need be so? What if self, space (place), representation, perception and materiality are conceived otherwise such that 'I', 'here' and 'body' are only contingently stable and identifiable? What if transmutation is written into the fabric of the way things are? What if we take 'becoming',[3] take contingency, seriously such that the *nunc* as the 'is' of Jesus' demonstrative identification constitutes a different kind of ontological scandal?

Take, for example, the theological construal for the interpretation of 'I', 'here' and 'body' in the work of Gregory of Nyssa, a fourth-century bishop living in the province of Cappadocea – and the implications of this construal for understanding self, space (place), representation, perception and materiality. It might seem from the following that Gregory would concur with our contemporary analysis of the ontological scandal of 'This is my body':

> if one were to show us true bread, we say that he properly applies the name to the subject: but if one were to show us instead that which had been made of stone to resemble the natural bread, which had the same shape, and equal size, and similarity of colour, so as in most points to be the same with the prototype, but which yet lacks the power of being food, on this account we say that the stone receives the name of 'bread', not properly, but by a misnomer (Nyssa: 1979, 403).

But such a reading would be mistaken. The clues to the Christian metaphysics framing this passage are there in phrases like 'the same with the prototype' and 'lacks the power of being'. The emphasis is not upon the object as such but upon the failure of the object to be part of a power-economy which nourishes, and upon the act of naming. Later in the same treatise, he can write:

> I, however, when I hear the Holy Scripture, do not understand only bodily meat, or the pleasure of the flesh; but I recognise another kind of food also, having a certain analogy to that of the body, the enjoyment of which extends to the soul alone: 'Eat of my bread', is the bidding of Wisdom to the hungry; and the Lord declares those blessed who hunger for such food as this, and say, 'If any man thirst, let him come unto Me, and drink' ...

'famine' is not the lack of bread and water, but the failure of the word (Nyssa: 1979, 409).

What is is governed here by the operation of the Word, not the perceived predicates of objects existing in and of themselves in a world consisting also in and of itself. The divine, the spiritual, principle prioritises. Nature exists in and through this prioritisation such that even within the human being the intellectual as spiritual is the animating principle that enables nature to prosper 'according to its own order' (Nyssa: 1979, 404). The 'stone' imitating bread in the first passage cannot nourish (and so become a form of bread) because 'it lacks the power of being food'. It is inanimate. But in and of itself as matter it could be animated and therefore become a source for food. The turning of stones into bread is a distinct possibility for the Messiah, as Satan points out in the temptation of Christ in the wilderness. This potential is not contained within the material but 'in and around it'. Nature cannot be natural without the spiritual informing it at every point. The perceptually sensed can give knowledge, but Gregory distinguishes between 'knowledge' – which is mixed because its source is the tree of knowledge of good and evil in Paradise – and 'discernment' – which skilfully separates the good from the evil and 'is a mark of a more perfect condition of the "exercised senses"' (Nyssa: 1979, 410). Without the exercise of discernment human beings cannot understand or see correctly. Building upon the Old Testament story of the fall of Adam and Eve into sinfulness (Genesis 3), Gregory reasons that the progenitors of humankind, having eaten the fruit of the tree of mixed knowledge, incline all subsequent generations towards a dependence upon the material order. This condition of being fallen expresses itself in the reification (and idolatry) of the objects perceived; a forgetting that they are continually in a state of being gifted to us, animated for us, by God himself. Materiality, for Gregory, is a manifestation of divine *energia*, a mode of Trinitarian *dunamis*.[4] The danger of the fallen condition, whose disposition is not towards that which is blessed and divinely good, is self-gratification – a certain aestheticisation of the senses such that one can be gratified through them. We will meet this again when examining Augustine on time and presence in Chapter 7 [of Ward, *Cities of God*]. A certain solipsism ensues, a self-subsistence which is not merely illusory but destructive: the material orders are used and exploited for self-gratification, they are reduced to atoms of potential pleasure or pain, their form (which theologically is in harmony with the form of the good) is dissolved.

Corporeality has to be read spiritually, that is, allegorically (Ward: 1999). Creation, as the manifestation of God through His Word, is a text which it is the vocation of the human being, made in the image of that God, to read and understand. Allegorical reading takes representation seriously, it has to; takes agency seriously for the point of reading and understanding is the perfection of the good life (blessedness). Allegorical reading disciplines the naming and therefore the identification of the material world – deception is the structure of evil, where a name and an appearance coalesce.

Positivism is therefore evil. The world has to be read with discernment. Even bodies have to be read: 'thou wilt read, as in a book, the history of the works of the soul; for nature itself expounds to thee' (Nyssa: 1979, 422).

Matter is not eternal, it is brought into being by God, *ex nihilo* (Genesis 1.2) and *ex libertate* (through God's sovereign free will). Matter is temporal and transmutation is structured within its very possibility – it came from nothing. Bodies will change until they attain their perfect, impassible state, post-resurrection. It is this transmutational potential that makes miracles possible – turning water into wine, the healing of the sick, the raising of the dead, etc. Within this theological construal of corporeality 'This is my body' is another such miracle. The ontological scandal here concerns God's uncreated power to call something into being from nothing, bring flesh from bread. The scandal is the giftedness of being itself – that something should be rather than not be – which the transformative Word of God announces. The very assertiveness of the statement is a practice of authority – authority to rename, refigure – the performance of the transaction. What is involved in this transaction? Gregory writes that 'our nature is twofold, according to apostolic teaching, made up of the visible man and the hidden man' (Nyssa: 1979, 421). So which body is being pointed to, transposed, represented in that statement 'This is my body'? For Gregory, who takes a grain of wheat as an example of his understanding of a body, in which the whole potential of the plant lies still hidden, the 'body' of the wheat is its totality of transformations, the totality of its becoming. Not the object of one moment, but the *skopos*,[5] the whole of the work that it performs, the unfolding of its natural order, defines the nature of a body. By 'natural' here is meant that which is in accordance with the telos of divine blessedness which animates, maintains and perfects creation.

The observation of the outward qualities of an object, what Gregory termed *poiotes*,[6] is not an end itself. The end is the underlying reality of a thing, what Gregory termed *upokeimenon*.[7] This is approached when we see things in relation to God, *epinoia*,[8] when we view what is through our desire towards God. Because we are, and all created things are, subject to time, then this process can never come to a conclusion. Hence, we can never know the *upokeimenon* itself. And so, as one of Gregory's more recent commentators has stated, 'Gregory draws the conclusion that we cannot know the essences of things, even our own soul and body, or the elements of creation' (Harrison: 1992, 38). What we occupy is a certain intellectual processing that operates within a generative semiosis. Since the essence of things cannot be known, the displacement of their identity is endless. The *poiotes* become signs to be read by the intellect and yet their meaning is endlessly not deferred but protracted, extended out of the material order of this world and into what Gregory termed the *aion*.[9]

> Now that which is always in motion, if its progress be to good, will never
> cease moving onwards to what lies before it … it will not find any limit of

its object such that when it has apprehended it, it will at last cease its motion' (Nyssa: 1979: 410–11).

All created things push on towards their final dissolution (in death) and recomposition (in resurrection).

This multiplicity, this fragmentation and dissemination of identities differs from modernity's atomism, insofar as all proceeds from and participates in God, the Lord as the one simple *upokeimenon*, the one *ousia* which is not the same as our *ousia*.[10] 'For according to the diversity of his activities (energies) and of his relations to the objects of his gracious activity, he also gives himself different names' (Nyssa quoted in Harrison: 1992, 40). An object's identity, its intelligibility, only consists in its being an object of God's activity. It has no autonomous identity outside of these divine energies. Gregory writes in his book *The Life of Moses*:

> none of those things which are apprehended by sense perception and contemplated by the understanding really subsists, but only the transcendent cause of the universe, on which everything depends. For even if the understanding looks upon any other existing things (*ousin*), reason observes in absolutely none of them the self-sufficiency by which they could exist without the participation in true being (*metousias tou ontos*) (Nyssa: 1978, 60).

To experience the world in this way is to experience a profound vertigo.

> For here there is nothing to take hold of, neither place nor time, neither measure nor anything else; it does not allow our minds to approach. And thus the soul, slipping at every point from what cannot be grasped, becomes dizzy and perplexed and returns once again to what is connatural to it' (Nyssa: 1979: 127–8).

Since we live in and through metaphors of the real, which are never stable as the nature of the objects they name are never stable, from one moment to the next; since, for Gregory, allegoriesis is the character of creation: we can name this vertigo, semiosis. Semiosis here is the opening up of words to their infinite possibilities to mean. But *this* semiosis, unlike the semiosis argued for by Philippe Lacoue Labarthe where 'madness is a matter of mimesis' (Labarthe: 1989, 138; see also Ward: 1995, 131–58) is not the nihilism of soulless materialism, but a divine not-knowing working within what is seen and disciplining a discernment that sees beyond what it is given to who it has been given by and for what purpose. God is not substance here; God is distinct from substance as created matter is distinct from uncreated, creation from creator. God is transcendent and materiality is suspended.

It has caused some surprise among scholars that Gregory has little explicit discussion on the Eucharist, and yet might this not be because, within his doctrines of creation and incarnation, the world is a Eucharistic offering? The world is maintained and sustained as a giving of thanks for its very givenness. In a way which drives a stake through the heart of the contemporary vampirisms and viruses discussed in the last chapter, all things feed each other – that is the nature of their participation in God. Christ as the bread of life feeds our rational beings that we might continue to discern and desire God in all things.

Bodies here are frangible, permeable; not autonomous and self-defining, but sharing and being shared. When I give I give myself, even though what I give is flowers, a smile, a sweet word, an academic account such as this one. The body itself serves 'as a base for communicative activity' (Gil: 1998, 107). It is the transducer of signs. Communication is embodied giving, and what I give is consumed by the others to whom I give. I touch upon their bodies by the presence of my own body heard and seen, smelt and sometimes tasted by them. The fluidity of time itself is the fluidity of identity 'This is my body. Take, eat. This is my blood. Drink.' The body is always in transit, it is always being transferred. It is never there, as a commodity I can lay claim to or possess as mine. This is the ontological scandal announced by the Eucharistic phrase – bodies are never simply there (or here).

Corpus mysticum

It is the scandal of Mark's Gospel – taking the ending that most New Testament scholars advise (16.8) – that the resurrected body makes no appearance. And, even though in the other gospels, as in the second century appendix to Mark's, the resurrected Christ makes an appearance, it is neither a stable body nor a permanent one. The body takes on different properties – the propensity to appear and disappear at will, a transformation of its appearance such that even disciples do not immediately recognise who it is who is with them. Finally, the body disappears back to heaven in the ascension. The body of Christ – the archetypal incarnate being, the body given over totally in its witness to God, in its manifestation of God – is a body which constantly exceeds itself, figured forth in signs (the sacraments and liturgies, the scriptures and lives of the saints). As Ephesians puts it, 'The Church is Christ's body, the completion of him who himself completes all things everywhere.' We will say more about this in the next chapter [of Cities of God]. Here, as we lay the foundations for a Christian metaphysics of the body, it is sufficient to delineate how the body, any body, disseminates itself through a myriad other bodies, which are themselves other signs where tissue is also text. As such, each of us can affect, for good or ill, the world around us. As belonging to other, larger corporations, we necessarily impact upon the world we live in, for good or ill. Similarly, that which I exclude from my body, or that which is excluded in my name from the corporations to which I belong, will affect me, for good or ill. The ghettoisations and the segregations of racism, sexism, class, and ageism done in my name, condoned by my silence, injure me. 'To matter' is 'to materialise' and 'to mean', to return to Judith Butler's comment.

We can call this view of the body transcorporeality It is a feature of intratextuality and *vice versa*. The body is fractured endlessly, by the Spirit, and yet also, simultaneously, gathered into the unity of the Word and the unity of the Word with the triune God [see Chapter 7 of Ward, *Cities of God*]. The Eucharistic 'This is my body' performs that first act of dissemination, that first transcorporealism. Michel de Certeau notes that this was the understanding of '*corpus mysticum*' until the middle of the twelfth century when 'the expression no longer designated the Eucharist ... but the Church'. He adds, significantly, that 'The Church, the social "body" of Christ, is henceforth the (hidden) signifier of a sacramental "body" held to be a visible signifier, because it is the showing of a presence beneath the "species" (or appearances) of the consecrated bread and wine' (Certeau: 1992, 82). The meaning and scandal of the Eucharistic 'This is my body' begins now to make its increasing move towards an emphasis on what is visible (rather than what is hidden). The trajectory of modernity begins, which will culminate, as we saw, in the positivism (and nihilism) of the statement's scandal today. The move can be paralleled with the need in the Lacanian subject to enter the law of the Father, the law of the symbolic as a substitute for the lost real body of the mother, the ineffable and irrecoverable *réel* as Lacan defines it. Certeau points out what is forgotten here, or what (taking the Lacanian picture) is being repressed – the loss of the body as the very possibility for its dissemination. 'Christianity was founded upon the *loss of a body* – the loss of the body of Jesus Christ, compounded with the loss of the "body" of Israel, of a "nation" and its genealogy. A founding disappearance indeed' (Certeau: 1992, 81). It is the loss which prepares the way for the mystical; the kenosis which prepares the way for a semantic diffusion of naming gathered together under him who will be given the Name above all Names.[11] Rather than loss, I wish to speak of 'displacement' – the kind of displacement which accompanies expansion. The displacement of the one, archetypal body, which engenders a transcorporeality in which the body of Christ, is mapped onto and shot like a watermark through the physical bodies, social bodies institutional bodies, ecclesial bodies, sacramental bodies. All these bodies are available only in and through textual bodies (discourses, gestures to be interpreted, social semiotics). But bodies cannot be reduced to signs, they are always excessive to signs, resistant, insistent upon a presence which eludes and discharges signs. The symbolic issues from the demands of the real and the desires of the imaginary. In the logic of demonstrative identification the impenetrability and discreet autonomy of the physical body provides the concrete means whereby these other bodies can be deemed metaphorical. But in the analogical account of bodies, within an account of incarnation and creation, only the body of Christ (hidden, displaced and yet always pervasive for always disseminated) is the true body and all these other bodies become true only in their participation within Christ's body. Christ's body as the true body is the pure sign – the only sign which is self-defining. I recall one of the controversial hymns of the tenth-century Syrian monk, Symeon the New Theologian: 'I move my hand, and my hand is the whole of Christ / since, do not forget it, God is indivisible in His divinity ... / ... all our members individually / will become members of Christ and Christ our members' (Maloney: 1976, 54).

We need to go one step further – a highly important clarifying step. For there have been recent attempts to figure transcorporeality as a description of what is 'removed from any mystery' (Nancy: 1994, 31). This attempt, frequently owning its indebtedness to a Christian doctrine of incarnation – 'The *spirit* of Christianity is incorporated here in full. *Hoc est enim corpus meum*' (Nancy: 1994, 22). – is more fundamentally indebted to Spinoza's and Hegel's secularisation of this doctrine. (See chapter 6 of Ward, *Cities of God*.) 'There was a spirituality of Christ's wounds. But since then, a wound is just a wound' (Nancy: 1994, 22). Jean-Luc Nancy's justly acclaimed essay 'Corpus' presents such a picture. Here, in a way which seems to push beyond the soulless materialism evident in the logic of demonstrative identification, Nancy writes: '*The body has the same structure as spirit*, but it has that structure *without presupposing itself as the reason for the structure*. Consequently, it is not self-concentration, but rather the ex-concentration of existence' (Nancy: 1994, 26). Bodies are no longer discrete entities, they are disseminated. Body is always and only a community of bodies – textual, social and institutional – touching each other 'separated but shared [*partage*]' (Nancy: 1994, 29). 'This body has no longer any members, if members are the functional parts of the whole. Here, each part is the whole, and there is never any whole. Nothing ever becomes the sum or the system of the corpus' (Nancy: 1994: 28). In Spinoza, there is only one body or substance and everything else is a modification of that One, a part within the whole. Here the body is fractured and disseminated endlessly through the spirit and thus allows for a place of 'ab-solution' (Nancy: 1994, 29), a deepening absence. 'We should lead community towards this disappearance of the gods ... community inscribes the absence of communion' (Nancy: 1991, 143). 'Thus, the body has been turned into nothing but a wound', Nancy concludes (Nancy: 1994, 30).

As Nancy realises the wound here has lost its mystery. It is the final expression of soulless materialism.[12] The piles of corpses at Ypres, Belsen and Cambodia will not go away. This is a fatal wound that bleeds eternally. There is no life here. There may be room for a liberal notion of tolerance – we belong to one another, so bring out the social contract that all may sign. But there is no telos for this tolerance, no good life to which it tends, no commonality which subtends its possibility. In fact, Spivak criticised the essay for its adoption of a position which 'is not yet articulated into the ethical, and calculated into the moral and the political' (Spivak: 1994, 36). But what ethics or politics can this position support? Like Levinas, Nancy moves to another, a meta-level. He offers a politics of politics, an ethics of ethics in a transcendental freedom of being (Nancy: 1993; Ward: 2000). Furthermore, human bodies are gendered and there is no account of what that gendering practises or how that gendering is produced in Nancy's 'communities of bodies'. Spivak asks if Nancy is 'performing an Augustine who cannot himself undo the *metalepsis* of the Eucharist' (Spivak: 1994, 47).[13] Slavoj Žižek also takes Nancy to task for 'the whiff of the incarnation' that lingers about the essay (Žižek: 1994, 52). But this essay announces endless crucifixion, Hegel's endless death of God.[14] There is nothing here to stop the eternal haemorrhaging. The all too real wound will only endlessly replicate itself in other all too real wounds. As I pointed out earlier, this nihilistic monism stands within the trajectory of secularism, the logic of modernity, where all objects are seen as present to themselves. This announces the postmodern brokenness of bodies as much as the paintings of Francis Bacon or the sculptures of Ron Mueck or the fibreglass creations of Jake and Dinos Chapman.[15] This is the fracture of atomism, not of the *corpus mysticum*.

To understand this is fundamental for this project. The postmodern move can only be made from the other side of modernity, as a critique of modernity. There is only one radical critique of modernity – the critique that denies the existence of the secular as self-subsisting, that immanent self-ordering of the world which ultimately had no need for God.[16] The secular to be secular requires a theological warrant. Otherwise the secular implodes; its values collapse in upon themselves. We will discuss the implosion of secularism in Chapter 9 [of Ward, *Cities of God*] when we take Nancy's dematerialisation of the body one step further – into cyberspace. The Christian doctrines of incarnation and creation stand opposed to closed, immanentalist systems. They stand opposed to positivism's simulation of realised eschatology. They stand opposed also to the endless deferral and unquenchable grief for a lost body. The body is absent yet present, that is what *mysticum* announces. In Christ's ascension his body is expanded to become a space in which the Church will grow. Paul's *en Christo* is a locative use of the dative. Eschatology is both not yet and being realised in our midst, through our labourings. Christ is both broken and given so that we become partakers in him and yet Christ also gathers us together, calls us to each other as fellow members of his multi-sexual body. Our transcorporeality is towards resurrection, not endless 'ab-solution' (or dissolution). Nancy states how, in transcorporeality, his 'community of bodies', 'Bodies call again for their creation' (Nancy: 1994, 23). But there can be no account of either such a creation or such a re-creation; only, to use Simone Weil's term, de-creation (Weil: 1952). All creation is seen to groan in Nancy's notion of embodiment, but no salvation or redemption can be offered it. The Slovenian philosopher Žižek comments, with reference to Nancy's notion of the body (which he develops in terms of the Lacanian *objet petit a* – an immanent antagonism of the psyche whereby the subject rejects the Real) that the self-positing itself as an object 'appears as an antagonism of God's prehistory, which is resolved when God speaks out of his Word' (Žižek: 1994, 77). In other words,

Nancy's body exists on a plane of endless dispersal, the Real, figured as the *nihilo* out of which creation will emerge. But this creation is only possible when conceived theologically, as an act of God's Word. Without this the body will dissolve into what Nancy describes as 'millions of scattered places' (Nancy: 1991, 137).

We cannot afford the disappearance of the body. Too many bodies have disappeared already. Ultimately, Nancy announces a metaphysical genocide. While refusing the full, self-realised presence of the body, we must also refuse its endless dissemination.[17] With transcorporeality, as I am conceiving it theologically, the body does not dissolve or ab-solve, it expands *en Christo*. While always located within specific sociological and historical contexts, it nevertheless is continually being opened up, allowing itself to open up, in acts of following which affect the transferral, the transduction. Transcorporeality is an effect of following in the wake of the eternal creative Word. Discipleship becomes transfiguring. The body accepts its own metaphorical nature – insofar as it is received and understood only in and through language. Only God sees and understands creation literally. We who are created deal only with the seeing and understanding appropriate to our creatureliness. We only negotiate the world metaphorically. The body as metaphor, moves within and along the intratextual nature of creation. As such metaphor becomes inextricably involved with participation within a divine economy – *metousia, metexein, metalambanein* and *metanoia*.[18] Continually called to move beyond itself, the transcorporeal body itself becomes Eucharistic, because endlessly fractured and fed to others. It becomes the body of Christ broken, given, resurrected and ascended. The body does not disappear. In fact, it realises its own uniqueness, its own vocation, its own irreplaceability, as offering a space for the meeting and mapping of other specified bodies, a sacred site. The transcorporeal body expands in its fracturing, it pluralises as it opens itself towards an eternal growth. Only, as such, can the wounding, can the differences, be redemptive – constitutive of the endless desire to know (where both knowledge and desire correlate with love). Only as such can the wounding, can the differences, image the intradivine wounding, the intradivine differences, of the Godhead. Through the brokenness of the transcorporeal body God's grace operates through his creation. As such 'This is my body' announces, for the Christian, the scandal of both crucifixion and resurrection, both a dying-to-self-positing and an incorporation into the city of God.

Here is announced a theology for the disabled, the sick, the racked, the torn, the diseased, the pained. Only in the context of the Presbyterian minister, the liturgies of marriage and communion, the sanctification of practised love as worship, does the brokenness of David's AIDS and Jon's bereavement become redemptive; redemptive for those of us who bear something of their body weight (with something of its pain) within our imaginaries. For these broken bodies too, perhaps especially, are transcorporeal. Especially, because the body that lives out such a brokenness understands more clearly a living in and through others, a dependency. It is a dependency that the (always relatively) able-bodied need to accept as a gift, as a spiritual food they cannot live without. This Christian theology of the body bespeaks the need to bear the weight of the body's uniqueness. For the Christian, the giving and receiving of our bodies constitutes human beings in Christ; the transcorporeality of all flesh makes possible its transfiguration. We need now to explore the Christology implicit here.

Of course, as I said at the beginning of this chapter, all this is from the standpoint of Christianity Other standpoints – even within Christianity – are inevitable. Those occupying these other standpoints will read (and write) the experience of embodiment (and the brokenness of so many bodies) differently. What we know, or what we believe we know (and its representations), is always situated – historically, culturally, economically – and sexed. But if we are to make moves towards a 'maximizing objectivity' we need to begin by surveying the scene from where we are, while being open to the resonance and resistance of other voices. For me, something of that standpoint is composed of the fact that I am a male, Christian theologian who openly advocates same-sex unions, who has friends dying or living with the fear of AIDS, and a family that lives in the shadows, embarrassments and sufferings of a genetic disorder. But we, each of us, move out from where we are placed and place ourselves, and in doing so understand that we are also elsewhere.

Notes

1   For another discussion of this scandal, as it was discussed by the Port-Royal grammarians of the seventeenth century, see Louis Marin's essay 'The Body of the Divinity Captured by Signs' (Marin: 1989, 3–25).

2   This return to a Dionysian ecstasy which seizes the present while tearing it apart is a recurrent theme in contemporary writing. See Thomas Pynchon: 1963 and Donna Tartt: 1992. In all these novels *speragmos* plays an important, ritualistic role where immanence turns upon itself. In pure immanence all bodies are dissolved.

3   I place this word in inverted commas because of the way 'becoming' is axiomatic in immanent economies whether Spinozas', Hegel's, Marx's or process theologians'. I do not intend 'becoming' in such a way. I intend the activation, the *dunamis*, of being; a being that is gifted by a God who is the pure actantial giving. My 'becoming' should be read theologically. That is, as process associated with Trinitarian procession. See Chapters 7 and 8 [of Ward, *Cities of God*].

4   *Energia* is often translated as 'operation' or 'working', from the Greek verb *energeo* 'to be operative' or 'to be at work'. *Dunamis* is often translated as 'power', power, that is, which resides in a thing by virtue of its nature. Both these terms are used technically and philosophically first by Aristotle. For the relationship between Aristotle's ideas and Gregory's see Ward: 1999.

5   The Greek word used by Gregory is often translated as the 'mark' or the 'goal' one has in view. The English word 'scope' derives from it.

6   Translates as 'those things which compose or make up any object' from the Greek verb *poieo*, to make.

7   *Upo* is a Greek suffix meaning 'under' and *keimai* is the Greek verb 'to lie'. The noun *upokeimenon* has a philosophical use approximating to what might be translated 'the ultimate reality'.

8   This is a very important word for Gregory – as it was also for Basil, another of the Cappadocian fathers. It translates often as 'conception' but refers to the faculty in the mind which

operates upon what the senses immediately perceive. For a further, and more detailed, examination of this word see Schaff and Wace: 1979, 249.

9   This Greek word is often translated as 'age' or 'from of old'. From Plato's *Timaeus* onwards it took on the associations of a realm independent of time, the eternal realm, and this is how Gregory uses the term.

10   This is the Greek word for 'Being' because it derives from the participle form of the verb *eimi* – to be. But the word is freighted with philosophical usage and is sometimes translated 'substance'.

11   The Christian doctrine of kenosis issues from a baptismal hymn incorporated into Paul's letter to the Church at Philippi (Philippians 2.5–11). Here is described the descent of Christ from heaven to earth and, following his death, his return to the Father who gives him 'a name which is above every name'. For a further examination of the association of kenosis with naming and discourse see Ward: 1999.

12   This, of course, raises an highly important question: why does Nancy continually make appeal to Christian rhetoric in order to describe his concept of the body or the community? Why does the Inoperative Community move, inexorably, towards a final chapter, entitled 'Of Divine Places' where he insists that 'we shall not call this presence "god", we shall not even say it is divine' (Nancy: 1991, 150)? Why does this demythologising discourse which attempts the stripping away of mystery operate through and upon Christian discourses concerning the mysteries of incarnation and transubstantiation? Is this the repressed other of French intellectualism, a Catholic imaginary informing the symbolic at every level? As theologians we have hardly yet begun to ask these questions. See Ward: 2000.

13   'Metalepsis' is the Greek word for 'a taking' or 'participation'. With Quintilian it became a term in rhetoric, rather like metonymy – it means an act of substitution (of one word for another).

14   See Ward: 1999 for a discussion of Hegel in the context of modernity's fascination with taxidermy.

15   See the catalogue for Sensation: Young British Artists from the Saatchi Collection (Saatchi: 1998).

16   To a certain extent, this will also be a critique of postmodernism in its philosophical guise. It can point up the way philosophical postmodernism pushes beyond the secular and employs theological language to do so, but it will also have to announce the impossibility of philosophy to move beyond itself. Postmodern philosophy eventually flounders upon an implicit metaphysics which it is continually trying to avoid and evade.

17   I find illuminating here a comment made by Conor Cunningham on an earlier draft of this chapter: 'Postmodernity dissolves the body and modernity ossifies it.'

18   These are all words employed theologically by the Greek Fathers in the basis of New Testament texts. *Meta* is the Greek suffix for 'with', *metousia* is the sharing in one substance, *metexein* is the verb 'to participate', *metalambanein* is the verb 'to be made a partaker of and *metanoia* often translates as 'repentance', but more accurately means a transformation of one's mind.

Bibliography

Anderson, Pamela Sue (1998) *A Feminist Philosophy of Religion: The Rationality and Myths of Religious Beliefs.* Oxford: Blackwell.

Ayer, A. J. (1959) *Philosophical Essays.* London: Macmillan.

——(1963) *The Foundation of Empirical Knowledge.* London: Macmillan.

Brantly, William F. (1996) 'Thunder of New Wings: AIDS: A Journey Beyond Belief', in Stephen B. Boyd *et al.* (eds), *Redeeming Men: Religion and Masculinities.* Louisville: Westminster John Knox Press.

Brown, Peter (1998) *The Body and Society: Men, Women, and Sexual Renunciation in Early Christianity.* London: Faber and Faber.

Butler, Judith (1993) *Bodies that Matter: On the Discursive Limits of 'Sex'*. London: Verso.

Castelli, Elizabeth (1991) '"I will make Mary Male": Pieties of the Body and Gender Transformation of Christian Women in Late Antiquity', in Julia Epstein and Kristina Straub (eds), *Body Guards: The Cultural Politics of Gender Ambiguity*. London: Routledge: 49–69.

Certeau, Michel de (1992) *The Mystic Fable*, tr. Michael B. Smith. Chicago: University of Chicago Press.

Cunningham, Conor (1998) 'Language: Wittgenstein after Theology', in John Milbank, Catherine Pickstock and Graham Ward (eds), *Radical Orthodoxy*. London: Routledge: 64–90.

Evans, Gareth (1982) *The Varieties of Reference*, John McDowell (ed.). Oxford: Oxford University Press.

Fish, Stanley (1980) *Is There a Text in this Class? The Authority of Interpretive Communities*. Cambridge, MA: Harvard University Press.

Freudenthal, Gideon (1986) *Atom and the Individual in the Age of Newton: On the Genesis of the Mechanistic World View*, tr. Peter McLaughlin. Dordrech: D. Reidel Publishing Company.

Gil, José (1998) *Metamorphoses of the Body*, tr. Stephen Muecke. Minneapolis: University of Minnesota Press.

Harding, Sandra (1993) 'Rethinking Standpoint Epistemology: "What is Strong Objectivity?"', in Linda Alcoff and Elizabeth Porter (eds), *Feminist Epistemologies*. London: Routledge: 49–82.

Harrison, Verna E. F. (1992) *Grace and Freedom According to Gregory of Nyssa*. Lampeter: Edwin Mellen Press.

Hume, David (1975) *Enquiries Concerning Human Understanding and the Principles of Morals*. Oxford: Clarendon Press.

Labarthe, Philippe Lacoue (1989) *Typography: Mimesis, Philosophy, Politics*. Cambridge, MA: Harvard University Press.

Laquer, Thomas (1990), *Making Sex: Body and Gender from the Greeks to Freud*. Cambridge, MA: Harvard University Press.

Longino, Helen (1993), 'Subjects, Power and Knowledge', in Linda Alcoff and Elizabeth Potter (eds) *Feminist Epistemologies*. London: Routledge: 101–20.

McDowell, John (1994) *Mind and World*. Cambridge, MA: Harvard University Press.

Maloney, George A. (tr.) (1976) *Hymns of Divine Love by St. Symeon the New Theologian*. New Jersey: Denville.

Marin, Louis (1989) *Food for Thought*, tr. Mette Hjort. Baltimore: John Hopkins University Press.

Martin, Dale (1995) *The Corinthian Body*. New Haven: Yale University Press.

Nancy, Jean-Luc (1991) *The Inoperative Community*, tr. Peter Connor *et al*. Minneapolis: University of Minnesota Press.

——(1993) *The Experience of Freedom*, tr. Bridget McDonald. Stanford, CA: Stanford University Press.

——(1994) 'Corpus', tr. Claudette Sartiliot in Juliet Flower MacCannell and Laura Zakarin (eds) *Thinking Bodies*. Stanford, CA: Stanford University Press.

Nyssa, St. Gregory of (1978) *Life of Moses*, tr. Abraham J. Malherbe and Everett Ferguson. New York: Paulist Press.

——(1979) 'One the Making of Man', in Philip Schaff and Henry Wace (eds) *Gregory of Nyssa, Dogmatic Treatises, etc*. Michigan: Wm. B. Eerdmans.

On, Bat-Ami Bar (1993) 'Marginality and Epistemic Privilege', in Linda Alcoff and Elizabeth Potter (eds), *Feminist Epistemologies*. London: Routledge: 83–100.

Putnam, Hilary (1990) *Realism with a Human Face*. Cambridge, MA: Harvard University Press.

Pynchon, Thomas (1963) *V*. London: Picador Books.

Robinson, John A. T. (1952) *The Body: A Study in Pauline Theology*. London: SCM.

Russell, Bertrand [1917] (1994) 'The Ultimate Constituents of Matter,' in *Mysticism and Logic*. London: Routledge: 121–39.

Saatchi, Charles (1998) *Sensation: Young British Artists from the Saatchi Collection*. London: Thames and Hudson.

Sawday, Jonathan (1995) *The Body Emblazoned: Dissection and the Human Body in Renaissance Culture*. London: Routledge.

Schaff, Philip and Wace, Henry (eds) (1979) *Gregory of Nyssa, Dogmatic Treaties, etc*. Michigan: Wm. B. Eerdmans.

Spivak, Gayatri Chakvarorty (1994) in Juliet Flower MacCannell and Laura Zakarin (eds) *Thinking Bodies*. Stanford: Stanford University Press.

Tartt, Donna (1992) *The Secret History*. London: Penguin Books.

Toulmin, Stephen (1990) *Cosmopolis: The Hidden Agenda of Modernity*. Chicago: Chicago University Press.

Wallace, John (1979) 'Only in the Context of a Sentence do Words have any Meaning', in Peter A. French *et al.* (eds), *Contemporary Perspectives in the Philosophy of Language*. Minneapolis: University of Minnesota Press.

Ward, Graham (1995) *Barth, Derrida and the Language of Theology*. Cambridge: Cambridge University Press.

——(1999) *Theology and Contemporary Critical Theory*, first edition, London: Macmillan.

——(2000) *Theology and Contemporary Critical Theory*, second, enlarged edition. London: Macmillan.

Weil, Simone (1952) *Gravity and Grace*, tr. A. Wills. New York: Putnam.

Wittgenstein, Ludwig (1953) *Philosophical Investigations*, G. E. M. Anscombe (ed.). Oxford: Blackwell.

——(1979) *Wittgenstein and the Vienna Circle: Conversations recorded by F. Waismann*. Oxford: Blackwell.

Žižek, Slavoj (1994) 'How to Give a Body a Deadlock', in Juliet Flower MacCannell and Laura Zakarin (eds) *Thinking Bodies*. Stanford: Stanford University Press.

Further reading

De Lubac, Henri, *Corpus Mysticum: The Eucharist and the Church in the Middle Ages*, Laurence Paul Hemming and Susan Frank Parsons (eds), tr. Gemma Simmonds *et al.*, London: SCM, 2007.

Nancy, Jean-Luc, 'Corpus', trans. Claudette Sartiliot, in Juliet Flower MacCannell and Laura Zakarin (eds) *Thinking Bodies,* Stanford, CA: Stanford University Press, 1994.

St Thomas Aquinas, trans. William Barden O.P., *Summa Theologiae*, 3a.73–78 (vol.58), Cambridge: Cambridge University Press, new edn, 2006.

St Thomas Aquinas, trans. Thomas Gilby O.P., *Summa Theologiae*, 3a.79–82 (vol.59), Cambridge: Cambridge University Press, new edn, 2006.

McPartlan, Paul, *The Eucharist Makes the Church: Henri de Lubac and John Zizioulas in Dialogue*, London: T & T Clark, 1994.

Oliver, Simon, 'The Eucharist before Nature and Culture', in *Modern Theology* 15(3), 1999: 331–53.

Special edition on the Eucharist, *Modern Theology* 15(2), 1999.

Astell, Anne, *Eating Beauty: The Eucharist and the Spiritual Arts of the Middle Ages*, Cornell: Cornell University Press, 2006.

Cavanaugh, William T., *Torture and the Eucharist: Theology, Politics and the Body of Christ*, Oxford: Wiley-Blackwell, 1998.

Rowland, Tracey, *Culture and the Thomist Tradition After Vatican II* (Radical Orthodoxy), London: Routledge, 2003.

Rubin, Miri, *Corpus Christi: The Eucharist in Late Medieval Culture*, Cambridge: Cambridge University Press, 1991.

Questions

1. How does desire overcome the aporia of learning?
2. What are the implications of transubstantiation (or the incarnation) for the material natures in general?
3. What, for Pickstock and Ward, is the scandal of the Eucharist?
4. How does the Eucharist inform Ward's theology of the body?
5. How does the Eucharist make the Church?

PART VI

Politics and theology

Introduction

A **large number of writings** in the broad sphere of Radical Orthodoxy refer to politics and the nature of human society. Today, our politics is dominated by the nation state. This dominance is so considerable that the nation state defines for us all the aspects of human society, from law to commerce to education and religion. With regard to religion, the nation state has a particular story to tell, and this is the focus of William Cavanaugh's essay.

Cavanaugh sees that the State emerged in the wake of the Wars of Religion as a supposed 'keeper of the peace'. The story is quite straightforward: as the so-called Wars of Religion erupted in sixteenth- and seventeenth-century Europe, so the State emerged in order to keep the peace in the midst of a religions environment which is intrinsically violent. The result of the State's rise to dominance over religion is the restriction of the religious to the purely private sphere (along with, say, leisure and child-rearing), while the public sphere – *explicitly* governed by the State – concerns politics, the law, commerce and business. This newly founded political liberalism suggested that religious disagreements were a purely private and therefore a relatively trivial matter. Religion need no longer demand one's supreme loyalty; the State should be the individual's ultimate focus. In sixteenth-century England, one could see this in the rule of Elizabeth I. Regarding religion, she did not wish to make windows into men's souls. Yet there was one variety of religious expression which could not be tolerated: public confession of Roman Catholicism. Why? Not because there was a particular objection to transubstantiation or some other doctrine, but because Roman Catholicism suggested an allegiance to a political authority higher than England's State, namely Rome. Thus was inaugurated the sense that Roman Catholicism is a peculiarly *unEnglish*, exotic mode of Christianity.

Cavanaugh suggests that this very common narrative 'puts the matter backwards'. He argues that 'religion' was used as an excuse during the rise of the States of Europe in which land and rule became increasingly contested. In fact, the State emerges not as a keeper of the peace, but as the locus of violence and coercion. In the social contract theory of politics, exemplified in England in the work of Thomas Hobbes, each individual gives to a central, sovereign authority the means of coercion: the law (including the police and courts) and the armed forces. In exchange, the individual gains protection of his or her private property rights. In this context, argues Cavanaugh, religion is no longer worth dying for. However, it is perfectly laudable to kill and die for one's country, one's nation state. So far from being a peacekeeper, the State becomes that for which one must be willing to die, and that which (violently) enforces a peace upon an intrinsically violent society. This article marks the beginning of Cavanaugh's extensive and highly influential work in theological politics in recent years. His mature views, in which the history included in this article is investigated in more detail, will soon be available in his *The Myth of Religious Violence* (Oxford: Oxford University Press, forthcoming).

As with many others, Cavanaugh finds connections and disagreements with writings which lie at the heart of Radical Orthodoxy. He describes himself as 'an admirer and fellow traveller'. The connections between his work and that of John Milbank will perhaps be clear with reference to Milbank's essay 'The gift of ruling: secularization and political authority'. Here, Milbank uses the work of the French Catholic liberal Pierre Manent to underline his thesis that the secular is an invention. In this particular essay, he critiques Manent's view that the secular was somehow latent within the practices of mediaeval Christianity and had to be 'released'. Milbank rejects this view, not least because he sees in liberalism the invention of a wholly new and quite bizarre anthropology: the human being understood as an asocial, asexual and utterly non-specific wilful individual to whom one attaches 'rights'. Milbank contrasts the language of 'rights' and 'property' with the theological category of 'gift' which we encountered in Part IV of this Reader. Rights and property are held by individuals and are regarded as inalienable until the State decides that, in the common interest, those rights and property no longer apply. Thus, for example, Milbank cites the work of the American anthropologist Talal Asad to the effect that the legal imperative against torture as a violation of human rights has singularly failed to stop instances of torture in even the most liberal of Western democracies. Rights and property can be arbitrarily suspended by the State when its own absolute right of rule in relation to its citizens is perceived to be threatened (viz. Guantanamo Bay).

In our current political and liberal environment, in which all difference is flattened and political hierarchy neutralized (see the general introduction to this Reader), the State rules by a kind of reversal of 'divide and conquer': individuals are treated as part of a uniform conglomeration of people who can only express two or three different opinions on any given grand issue such as health or education. In the cult of the mass media and opinion polls, we now have politicians responding only to 'public opinion', an opinion arrived at by meaningless polls which might in fact be no *one*'s opinion at all.

Milbank contrasts the liberal-democratic politics of the nation state with the Christian notion that to rule is a gift *exchange*. A monarch (Milbank gives the example of a sixteenth-century French monarch) might bestow gifts on a city in recognition of its *share* in his rule, and in return the city anoints the king as its ruler. It gives the gift of ruling. More generally, Milbank explores the way in which the theological category of gift can help us to understand the ways in which the violence and decadence of modern liberal democracy (witness the financial crisis of 2008 and 2009) can be replaced by a different kind of polity orientated towards a theological doctrine of creation as divine donation.

Chapter 11

William T. Cavanaugh

"A fire strong enough to consume the house"

The Wars of Religion and the rise of the nation state

I n September of 1993, the Parliament of the World's Religions in Chicago issued a declaration called "Towards a Global Ethic" meant to locate ethical values common to the world's religions. One of the most emphatic parts of the statement is that condemning wars waged in the name of religion.

> Time and again we see leaders and members of religions incite aggression, fanaticism, hate and xenophobia——even inspire and legitimize violent and bloody conflicts. Religion often is misused for purely power-political goals, including war. We are filled with disgust.[1]

Is the Parliament of the World's Religions taking a pacifist stand? Well, no. While violence in general is condemned, the document stops well short of calling religious people out of the armies of the world. Only killing in the name of religion is damned; bloodshed on behalf of the State is subject to no such scorn.[2] What is wrong, then, with killing in the name of religion? The answer can be derived from the definition of "religion" implicit in the declaration. Religion is assumed to be a matter pertinent to the private sphere of values. The individual's public and lethal loyalty belongs to the State.

My purpose in this essay will be to focus on the way revulsion to killing in the name of religion is used to legitimize the transfer of ultimate loyalty to the modern State. Specifically I will examine how the so-called "Wars of Religion" of sixteenth- and seventeenth-century Europe are evoked as the founding moment of modern liberalism by theorists such as John Rawls, Judith Shklar, and Jeffrey Stout.[3] I will let Shklar tell the familiar tale:

liberalism ... was born out of the cruelties of the religious civil wars, which forever rendered the claims of Christian charity a rebuke to all religious institutions and parties. If the faith was to survive at all, it would do so privately. The alternative then set, and still before us, is not one between classical virtue and liberal self-indulgence, but between cruel military and moral repression and violence, and a self-restraining tolerance that fences in the powerful to protect the freedom and safety of every citizen ... [4]

In Jeffrey Stout's view, the multiplication of religions following on from the Reformation produced appeals to incompatible authorities which could not be resolved rationally. Therefore

liberal principles were the right ones to adopt when competing religious beliefs and divergent conceptions of the good embroiled Europe in the religious wars ... Our early modern ancestors were right to secularize public discourse in the interest of minimizing the ill effects of religious disagreement.[5]

In other words, the modern, secularized State arose to keep peace among the warring religious factions.

I will argue that this story puts the matter backwards. The "Wars of Religion" were not the events which necessitated the birth of the modern State; they were in fact themselves the birthpangs of the State. These wars were not simply a matter of conflict between "Protestantism" and "Catholicism," but were fought largely for the aggrandizement of the emerging State over the decaying remnants of the medieval ecclesial order. I do not wish merely to contend that political and economic factors played a central role in these wars, nor to make a facile reduction of religion to more mundane concerns. I will rather argue that to call these conflicts "Wars of Religion" is an anachronism, for what was at issue in these wars was the very creation of religion as a set of privately held beliefs without direct political relevance. The creation of religion was necessitated by the new State's need to secure absolute sovereignty over its subjects. I hope to challenge the soteriology of the modern State as peacemaker, and show that Christian resistance to State violence depends on a recovery of the Church's disciplinary resources.

I. The rise of the State

In the medieval period, the term *status* had been used either in reference to the condition of the ruler (*status principis*), or in the general sense of the condition of the realm (*status regni*). With Machiavelli we begin to see the transition to a more abstract sense of the State as an independent political entity, but only in the works of six-teenth-century French and English humanists does there emerge the modern idea of the State as "a form of public power separate from both ruler and the ruled, and constituting the supreme political authority within a certain defined territory."[6] In the medieval period the Church was the supreme common power; the civil authority, as John Figgis put it, was "the police department of the Church."[7] The net result of the conflicts of the sixteenth and seventeenth centuries was to invert the dominance of the ecclesiastical over the civil authorities through the creation of the modern State. The chief promoters of this transposition, as Figgis makes plain, "were Martin Luther and Henry VIII and Philip II, who in reality worked together despite their apparent antagonism."[8]

It is important to see that the origins of civil dominance over the Church predated the so-called "Wars of Religion." As early as the fourteenth century, the controversy between the Papalists and Conciliarists had given rise to quite new developments in the configuration of civil power. Marsilius of Padua had argued that the secular authorities had sole right to the use of coercive force. Indeed, he contended that coercive force by its very nature was secular, and so the Church could be understood only as a moral, and not a jurisdictional, body.[9] Luther took up this argument in his 1523 treatise *Temporal Authority: To what Extent it Should be Obeyed*. Every Christian, Luther maintained, is simultaneously subject to two kingdoms or two governances, the spiritual and the temporal. Coercive power is ordained by God but is given only to the secular powers in order that civil peace be maintained among sinners. Since coercive power is defined as secular, the Church is left with a purely suasive authority, that of preaching the Word of God.[10]

Luther rightly saw that the Church had become worldly and perversely associated with the wielding of the sword. His intention was to prevent the identification of any politics with the will of God, and thus extricate the Church from its entanglement in coercive power.[11] In sanctifying that power to the use of secular government, how-ever, Luther contributed to the myth of the State as peacemaker which would be invoked to confine the Church. While apparently separating civil and ecclesiastical jur-isdictions, the effect of Luther's arguments was in fact to deny any separate jurisdiction to the Church. Luther writes *To the Christian Nobility of the German Nation*,

> I say therefore that since the temporal power is ordained of God to punish
> the wicked and protect the good, it should be left free to perform its office
> in the whole body of Christendom without restriction and without respect to
> persons, whether it affects pope, bishops, priests, monks, nuns or anyone else.[12]

Christ has not two bodies, one temporal and one spiritual, but only one.

The Lutheran doctrine of the two kingdoms signifies, therefore, the defeat of the medieval metaphor of the two swords. The entire edifice of ecclesiastical courts and canon law is eliminated. As Quentin Skinner puts it, "The idea of the Pope and Emperor as parallel and universal powers disappears, and the independent jurisdictions of the *sacerdotium* are handed over to the secular authorities."[13] Because the Christian is saved by faith alone, the Church will in time become, strictly speaking, unnecessary for salvation, taking on the status of a *congregano fidelium*, a collection of the faithful for the purpose of nourishing the faith. What is left to the Church is increasingly the purely interior government of the souls of its members; their bodies are handed over to the secular authorities.

It is not difficult to appreciate the advantages of this view of the Church to the princes of Luther's time. It is important to note, however, that the usurpation of papal perquisites in the first half of the sixteenth century was not limited to those princes who had embraced Protestantism. The Catholic princes of Germany, the Habsburgs of Spain and the Valois of France all twisted the Pope's arm, extracting concessions which considerably increased their control over the Church within their realms. As Richard Dunn points out, "Charles V's soldiers sacked Rome, not Wittenberg, in 1527."[14] When Charles V, Holy Roman Emperor, finally turned his attention to the Protestants in 1547, igniting the first major War of Religion, his attack on the Lutheran states was an attempt to consolidate Imperial authority rather than an expression of doctrinal zealotry. This fact was not lost on the princes, both Catholic and Protestant, whose power was growing in opposition to that of the Habsburgs and the Church. When in 1552–53 the Lutheran princes (aided by the French Catholic King Henry II) defeated the Imperial forces, the German Catholic princes stood by, neutral.[15] The war ended in 1555 with the Peace of Augsburg, which allowed the temporal authority of each political unit to choose either Lutheranism or Catholicism for its realm: *cuius regio, eius religio*.

Historians often claim that the Reformation and Counter-Reformation retarded the secularizing trend towards the modern State by making politics theological. It is certain that both reformers and their Catholic adversaries in the sixteenth century agreed that the idea of the State should include upholding the true religion. This in itself was, however, a radical departure from the medieval idea of the proper ordering of civilization. Pre-sixteenth century Christendom assumed, at least in theory, that the civil and ecclesiastical powers were different departments of the same body, with the ecclesiastical hierarchy of course at the head. The sixteenth century maintained the conception of a single body, but inverted the relationship, setting the good prince to rule over the Church. The eventual elimination of the Church from the public sphere was prepared by the dominance of the princes over the Church in the sixteenth century.

The policy of *cuius regio, eius religio* was more than just a sensible compromise to prevent bloodshed among the people, now divided by commitment to different faiths. It was in fact a recognition of the dominance of secular rulers over the Church, to the extent that the faith of a people was controlled by and large by the desires of the prince. G.R. Elton puts it bluntly: "The Reformation maintained itself wherever the lay power (prince or magistrates) favoured it; it could not survive where the authorities decided to suppress it."[16] There is a direct relationship between the success of efforts to restrict supra-national Church authority and the failure of the Reformation within those realms. In other words, wherever concordats between the Papal See and temporal rulers had already limited the jurisdiction of the Church within national boundaries, there the princes saw no need to throw off the yoke of Catholicism, precisely because Catholicism had already been reduced, to a greater extent, to a suasive body under the heel of the secular power. In France the Pragmatic Sanction of Bourges had accomplished this in 1438, eliminating papal collection of the Annate tax, taking away the Pope's right to nominate candidates for vacant sees, and giving the crown the formerly papal prerogative to supplicate in favor of aspirants to most benefices. The Concordat of Bologna in 1516 confirmed the French kings' control over Church appointments and revenues. In Spain the crown was granted even wider concessions between 1482 and 1508. France and Spain remained Catholic. Where such concordats were not arranged, as in England, Germany, and Scandinavia, conflicts between the Church and the secular rulers——which, it must be remembered, predated Luther——contributed significantly in every case to the success of the Reformation.[17]

After the Concordat of Bologna, the French kings and Catherine de Medici saw no advantage to Reformation in France. The early settlement of civil dominance over the Church was a crucial factor in the building of a strong, centralized monarchy during the rule of Francis I from 1515 to 1547. When Calvinism began to challenge the ecclesiastical system in France, it therefore formed a threat to royal power. The rising bourgeoisie in provincial towns, anxious to combat centralized control, joined the Huguenots in large numbers. Moreover, as many as two-fifths of the nobility rallied to the Calvinist cause. They wanted to reverse the trend toward absolute royal authority and coveted power like that of the German princes to control the Church in their own lands.[18]

For the main instigators of the carnage, doctrinal loyalties were at best secondary to their stake in the rise or defeat of the centralized State. Both Huguenot and Catholic noble factions plotted for control of the monarchy. The Queen Mother, Catherine de Medici, for her part, attempted to bring both factions under the sway of the crown. At the Colloquy of Poissy in 1561, Catherine proposed bringing Calvinist and Catholic together under a State-controlled Church modeled on Elizabeth's Church of England. Catherine had no particular theological scruples and was therefore stunned to find that both Catholic and Calvinist ecclesiologies prevented such an arrangement. Eventually Catherine decided that statecraft was more satisfying than theology, and, convinced that the Huguenot nobility were gaining too much influence over the king, she unleashed the infamous 1572 St. Bartholomew's Day massacre of thousands of Protestants. After years of playing Protestant and Catholic factions off against one another, Catherine finally threw in her lot with the Catholic Guises. She would attempt to wipe out the Huguenot leadership and thereby quash the Huguenot nobility's influence over king and country.[19]

The St. Bartholomew's Day massacre was the last time it was easy to sort out the Catholics from the Protestants in the French civil wars. By 1576 both Protestant and Catholic nobles were in rebellion against King Henry III. In that year the Catholic League was formed, whose stated goal was "to restore to the provinces and estates of this kingdom the rights, privileges, franchises and ancient liberties such as they were in the time of King Clovis, the first Christian king."[20] The League wished to check the power of the crown by appealing to the medieval doctrine of sovereignty, in which kingship was based on the will of the people. The Catholic League was opposed by another Catholic party, the *Politiques*, who pushed for an absolutist vision of the State. For the *Politiques* the State was an end in itself which superseded all other interests, and the monarch held absolute sovereignty by divine right. They advocated a Gallican Catholic Church and liberty of conscience in the private exercise of religion. Most *Politiques* allied themselves with the Protestants following the formation of the Catholic League.[21]

Ecclesial loyalties were complicated further by the entrance into the fray of Spain's Phillip II, who wanted to place a Spanish *infanta* on the French throne. Phillip financed the Guises's attack on Paris in 1588, thus compelling the Catholic King Henry III to ally himself with the Protestants under Henry of Navarre. Upon the King's death in 1589, Henry of Navarre took the throne as Henry IV, and conveniently converted to Catholicism four years later. The war ended in 1598 when Phillip II finally gave up Spanish designs on the French throne.[22]

The end of the French civil wars is seen as the springboard for the development of the absolutist vision of sovereign power unchallenged within the State which would come to full fruition in seventeenth-century France. It is common to maintain that a strong centralized power was necessary to rescue the country from the anarchy of violence produced by religious fervor. My brief sketch of these wars should make clear that such a view is problematic. The rise of a centralized bureaucratic State *preceded* these wars and was based on the fifteenth-century assertion of civil dominance over the Church in France. At issue in these wars was not simply Catholic versus Protestant, transubstantiation versus spiritual presence. The Queen Mother who unleashed the massacre of St. Bartholomew's Day was not a religious zealot but a thoroughgoing *Politique* with a stake in stopping the nobility's challenge to royal pretensions toward absolute power.[23]

In the seventeenth century, the success of the French example of a centralized State was not lost on the Holy Roman Emperor, who had long wished to make his nominal power real over the lesser princes. The result was the Thirty Years War (1618–1648), the bloodiest of the so-called "Wars of Religion." Emperor Ferdinand II's goal was to consolidate his patchwork empire into a modern state: Habsburg,

Catholic, and ruled by one sovereign, unrivaled authority. To accomplish this Ferdinand relied on shifting alliances with lesser princes, mercenary soldiers, and his Spanish Habsburg cousins. Again, ecclesial loyalties were not easy to sort out. On the one hand, Ferdinand relied on the Lutheran elector of Saxony to help reconquer Bohemia, and his troops were commanded by the Bohemian Protestant soldier of fortune Albrecht von Wallenstein. On the other hand, the Catholic petty princes opposed Ferdinand's attempts to centralize his power and his neglect of the imperial Diet.[24]

The war's tide turned against Ferdinand in 1630 when Sweden's Gusta vus Adolphus entered the conflict against him. Sweden's effect on the war was great, in large part because France under Cardinal Richelieu had decided to subsidize an army of thirty-six thousand Swedes in German territory. Presumably the Catholic Cardinal was not motivated by love of Luther to support the Protestant cause. France's interest lay in keeping the Habsburg empire fragmented, and France's interest superseded that of her Church. In 1635 the French sent troops, and the last thirteen years of the war——the bloodiest——were essentially a struggle between the Habsburgs and the Bourbons, the two great Catholic dynasties of Europe.[25]

II. The creation of religion

Historians of this period commonly point out that religious motives are not the only ones at work in fueling these wars. As J.H. Elliot comments, whether or not these are in fact "Wars of Religion" depends on whether you ask a Calvinist pastor, a peasant, or a prince of this period.[26] The point I wish to make, however, goes beyond questions of the sincerity of personal religious conviction. What is at issue behind these wars is the creation of "religion" as a set of beliefs which is defined as personal conviction and which can exist separately from one's public loyalty to the State. The creation of religion, and thus the privatization of the Church, is correlative to the rise of the State. It is important therefore to see that the principal promoters of the wars in France and Germany were in fact not pastors and peasants, but kings and nobles with a stake in the outcome of the movement toward the centralized, hegemonic State.

In the medieval period, the term *religio* is used very infrequently. When it appears it most commonly refers to the monastic life. As an adjective the "religious" are those who belong to an order, as distinguished from lay Christians or "secular" clergy. When "religion" enters the English language, it retains these meanings and refers to the life of a monastery or order. Thus around 1400 the "religions of England" are the various orders.[27]

Thomas Aquinas devotes only one question of the *Summa Theologiae* to *religio*; it names a virtue which directs a person to God. St. Thomas says that religion does not differ essentially from sanctity. It differs logically, however, in that religion refers specifically to the liturgical practices of the Church. Thus, according to St. Thomas, "The word religion is usually used to signify the activity by which man gives the proper reverence to God through actions which specifically pertain to divine worship, such as sacrifice, oblations, and the like."[28] In response to the query "Does religion have any external actions?" Thomas answers affirmatively and emphasizes the unity of body and soul in the worship of God.[29] As a virtue, *religio* is a habit, knowledge embodied in the disciplined actions of the Christian. In Aquinas's view virtuous actions do not proceed from rational principles separable from the agent's particular history; virtuous persons instead are embedded in communal practices of habituation of body and soul that give their lives direction to the good.[30]

Religio for St. Thomas is just one virtue which presupposes a context of ecclesial practices which are both communal and particular to the Christian Church. Wilfred Cantwell Smith notes that during the Middle Ages, considered by moderns the "most religious" period of Christian history, no one ever thought to write a book on religion.[31] In fact he suggests that "the rise of the concept 'religion' is in some ways correlated with a decline in the practice of religion itself."[32] In other words the rise of the modern concept of religion is associated with the decline of the Church as the particular locus of the communal practice of *religio*.

The dawn of the modern concept of religion occurs around the late fifteenth century, first appearing in the work of the Italian Renaissance figure Marsilio Ficino. His 1474 work entitled *De Christiana Religione* is the first to present *religio* as a universal human impulse common to all. In Ficino's Platonic scheme, *religio* is the ideal of genuine perception and worship of God. The various historical manifestations of this common impulse, the varieties of pieties and rites that we now call religions, are all just more or less true (or untrue) representations of the one true *religio* implanted in the human heart. Insofar as it becomes a universal impulse, religion is thus interiorized and removed from its particular ecclesial context.[33]

The second major shift in the meaning of the term religion, which takes shape through the late sixteenth and seventeenth centuries, is toward religion as a system of beliefs. Religion moves from a virtue to a set of propositions. Political theorist Hugo Grotius, in his *De Ventate Religionis Christianae*, can therefore write that the Christian religion teaches, rather than simply is, the true worship of God. At the same time the plural "religions" arises, an impossibility under the medieval usage.[34]

In sixteenth century France, *Politiques* and humanists began to provide a theoretical reconfiguration of Christianity which fitted it into the generic category of "religion." In his 1544 work *The Concord of the World,* Guillaume Postel provided an argument in favor of religious liberty based on the construal of Christianity as a set of demonstrable moral truths, rather than theological claims and practices which take a particular social form called the Church. Christianity, according to Postel, is based on common, universal truths which underlie all particular expressions of "religious belief." Liberty of conscience in matters of "religion" is essential because all rational people are able to recognize these universal truths.[35]

The *Politique* political theorist Jean Bodin also advocates liberty of conscience in religion as part and parcel of a plan for an absolutist State with a centralized sovereign authority. In his landmark *Six Books of the Commonwealth* (1576), religion is treated under the heading "How Seditions may be Avoided." "Even atheists agree," according to Bodin,

> that nothing so tends to the preservation of commonwealths as religion, since it is the force that at once secures the authority of kings and governors, the execution of the laws, the obedience of subjects, reverence for the magistrates, fear of ill-doing, and knits each and all in the bonds of friendship.[36]

Religion for Bodin is a generic concept; he states directly that he is not concerned with which form of religion is best. The people should be free in conscience to choose whichever religion they desire. What is important is that once a form of religion has been embraced by a people, the sovereign must forbid any public dispute over religious matters to break out and thereby threaten his authority. Bodin cites with approval some German towns' prohibition of "all discussion of religion" on pain of death after the Peace of Augsburg. Religious diversity is to be allowed only where it is too costly for the sovereign to suppress it.[37]

The concept of religion being born here is one of domesticated belief systems which are, insofar as it is possible, to be manipulated by the sovereign for the benefit of the State. Religion is no longer a matter of certain bodily practices within the Body of Christ, but is limited to the realm of the "soul," and the body is handed over to the State. John Figgis puts it this way:

> The rise and influence of the *Politiques* was the most notable sign of the times at the close of the sixteenth century. The existence of the party testifies to the fact that for many minds the religion of the State has replaced the religion of the Church, or, to be more correct, that religion is becoming individual while the civil power is recognized as having the paramount claims of an organized society upon the allegiance of its members. What Luther's eminence as a religious genius partially concealed becomes more apparent in the *Politiques*; for the essence of their position is to treat the unity of the State as the paramount end, to which unity in religion must give way.[38]

Among the founders of the modern State, no one is more blunt than Thomas Hobbes in bringing religion to the service of the sovereign. He defines religion as a binding impulse which suggests itself to humans in the natural condition of their ignorance and fear. "Gnawed on by fear of death, poverty, or other calamity,"[39] and unaware of secondary causes, there develops in all parts of the globe a belief in powers invisible, and a natural devotion to what is feared. Some worship according to their own inventions, others according to the command of the true God Himself through supernatural revelation. But the leaders of both kinds of religions have arranged their devotions "to make those men that relied on them, the more apt to obedience, laws, peace, charity, and civil society."[40] Religion for Hobbes derives from fear and need of security, the very same root from which springs the social contract and common-wealth. Where God has planted religion through revelation, therefore, there also has God established a "peculiar kingdom," the kingdom of God, a polity in which there is no distinction of spiritual and temporal. The "kingdom" of God is no mere metaphor; by it is meant the commonwealth, ruled over by one sovereign who is both "ecclesiastical and civil."[41]

Hobbes's aim in uniting Church and State is peace. Without universal obedience to but one sovereign, civil war between temporal and spiritual powers is tragically inevitable.[42] Its inevitability lies in Hobbes's ontology of violence. The war of all against all is the natural condition of humankind. It is cold fear and need for security, the foundation of both religion and the social contract, that drives humans from their nasty and brutish circumstances and into the arms of Leviathan. This soteriology of the State as peacemaker demands that its sovereign authority be absolutely alone and without rival.

In Hobbes it is not so much that the Church has been subordinated to the civil power; Leviathan has rather swallowed the Church whole into its yawning maw. Scripture is nothing less than the law of the commonwealth, such that the inter-pretation of Scripture is the responsibility of the sovereign. The Christian king is supreme pastor of his realm, and has power to preach, to baptize, to administer the Eucharist, and even to ordain.[43] The sovereign is not only priest but prophet; the king reserves the right to police all charism and censor any public prophecy. The "private man," because "thought is free," is at liberty in his heart to think what he will, pro-vided in public he exercise his right to remain silent.[44] In a Christian commonwealth, Hobbes denies even the theoretical possibility of martyrdom, since he defines martyrs as only those who die publicly proclaiming the simple doctrine "Jesus is the Christ." A Christian sovereign would never impede such a simple (and contentless) profession of faith. As for other more specific doctrines or practices for which a Christian might die, these could only go under the title "subversion," never martyrdom, since the sovereign has the sole right to determine proper Christian practice and sanction any public deviations therefrom. Those Christians who find themselves under a heathen regime Hobbes counsels to obey, even unto public apostasy, provided they maintain the faith in their hearts, since Christian faith is wholly interior and not subject to external coercion.[45]

"A Church," Hobbes writes, "is the same thing with a civil commonwealth, consisting of Christian men; and is called a *civil state*."[46] It follows, therefore, that there is no one Church universal, but only as many Churches as there are Christian States, since there is no power on earth to which the commonwealth is subject. Along with denying the international character of the Church, Hobbes makes another crucial move. He contends that the members of a Church cohere as in a natural body, but not to one another, for each one depends only on the sovereign.[47] The Body of Christ is thereby severely nominalized, scattered and absorbed into the body of the State.

Hobbes and Bodin both prefer religious uniformity for reasons of state, but it is important to see that, once Christians are made to chant "We have no king but Caesar," it is really a matter of indifference to the sovereign whether there be one religion or many. Once the State has succeeded in establishing dominance over, or absorbing, the Church, it is but a small step from absolutist enforcement of religious unity to the toleration of religious diversity. In other words, there is a logical progression from Bodin and Hobbes to Locke.[48] Lockean liberalism can afford to be gracious toward "religious pluralism" precisely because "religion" as an interior matter is the State's own creation. Locke says that the State cannot coerce the religious conscience because of the irreducibly solitary nature of religious judgment: "All the life and power of true religion consist in the inward and full persuasion of the mind."[49] But for the very same reason he categorically denies the social nature of the Church, which is redefined as a free association of like-minded individuals.[50]

Toleration is thus the tool through which the State divides and conquers the Church. Locke's ideas were enshrined in England's Toleration Act of 1689, drawing an end to what is considered the "Age of Religious Wars."[51] Catholics, of course, were excluded from the Toleration Act, not because of lingering religious bigotry, but because the Catholics in England had as yet refused to define themselves as a "religion" at all. The English Catholics had not yet fully accepted that the State had won.

Perhaps the best way to get a flavor for the "religious" wars of the seventeenth century is to read the words of one of the interested parties. The following is from a 1685 English anti-Catholic tract penned by the Earl of Clarendon:

> No man was ever truly and really angry (otherwise than the warmth and multiplication of words in the dispute produced it) with a man who believed *Transubstantiation* ... but when he will for the support of this *Paradox* introduce an authority for the imperious determination thereof ... it is no wonder if passion breaks in at this door, and kindles a Fire strong enough to consume the House. This is the Hinge upon which all the other controversies between us and the English Catholicks do so intirely hang.[52]

Clearly the Pope can inspire deadly passion in a way that Eucharistic doctrine cannot because at stake in the conflict is the loyalty of the Christian to the State; doctrine is being defined as a matter of internal conscience, not available for public dispute. Clarendon continues

> Their opinions of *Purgatory* or *Transubstantiation* would never cause their *Allegiance* to be suspected, more than any other error in Sence, Grammar or Philosophy, if those opinions were not instances of their dependance upon another Jurisdiction foreign, and inconsistent with their duty to the *King*, and destructive to the *peace* of the *Kingdom*: and in that sence and Relation the Politick Government of the Kingdom takes notice of those opinions, which yet are not enquired into or punished for themselves.[53]

I do not wish to argue that no Christian ever bludgeoned another over dogma held dear. What I hope to have shown, however, is how the dominance of the State over the Church in the sixteenth and seventeenth centuries allowed temporal rulers to direct doctrinal conflicts to secular ends. The new State required unchallenged authority within its borders, and so the domestication of the Church. Church leaders became acolytes of the State as the religion of the State replaced that of the Church, or, more accurately, the very concept of religion as separable from the Church was invented.

III. Discipline and discipleship

Liberal theorists such as Rawls, Shklar, and Stout would have us believe that the State stepped in like a scolding schoolteacher on the playground of doctrinal dispute to put fanatical religionists in their proper place. Self-righteous clucking about the dangers of public faith, however, ignores the fact that transfer of ultimate loyalty to the nation state has only increased the scope of modern welfare. Anthony Giddens has shown how, for example, the new sixteenth-century doctrine of the State's absolute sovereignty within a defined territory carried with it an increase in the use of war to expand and consolidate borders. Traditional polities were bounded by frontiers, peripheral regions in which the authority of the center was thinly spread. The territories of medieval rulers were often not continuous; one prince might own land deep within the territory of another. Furthermore, the residents of a territory might owe varying allegiances to several different nobles, and only nominal allegiance to the king. Only with the emergence of nation states, according to Giddens, are States circumscribed by borders, known lines demarcating the exclusive domain of sovereign power, especially its monopoly over the means of violence. Attempts to consolidate territory and assert sovereign control often brought about violent conflict. More importantly, borders in the nation-state system include the assumption of a "state of nature" existing between States which increases the possibility of war.[54]

The conception of the State as peacemaker was given theoretical form by Immanuel Kant, intellectual forebear to many of today's liberal political theorists. For Kant the State is the condition of possibility of morality in history because it ensures that people do not infringe the freedom of others and are thereby free to develop as rational beings.[55] The modern republic is the agent for bringing about perpetual peace because it will allow people to transcend their historical particularities, e.g. Lutheran vs. Catholic, and respect one another on the basis of their common rationality. If a "powerful and enlightened people" can form itself into a republican State, it can act as a "fulcrum" for other States to follow suit and join it in a federation of States towards the goal of peace. It is conceivable that this leverage will include war, but only to bring liberal republicanism to other States, thereby furthering the aim of peace.[56]

The problem is that the State, as guarantor of freedom and peace, takes on the character of an end in itself which has as its goal, as Kant says, to "maintain itself perpetually."[57] For this reason Kant forbids categorically any type of rebellion or even resistance to the legislative authority of the State, since to oppose the lawfully constituted authority is to contradict one's own will.[58] A pluralism of conceptions of the good is protected by the liberal State, but in fact this pluralism exists only at the private level. In the public sphere, the State itself is the ultimate good whose prerogatives must be defended coercively. As Ronald Beiner has shown, the liberal State is by no means neutral. It defends and imposes a particular set of goods——e.g. the value of the market, scientific progress, the importance of choice itself——which excludes its rivals.[59] Wars are now fought on behalf of this particular way of life by the State, for the defense or expansion of its borders, its economic or political interests.

Far from coming on the scene as peacekeeper, we have seen that the rise of the State was at the very root of the so-called "religious" wars, directing with bloodied hands a new secular theater of absolute power. The wars of the nineteenth and twentieth centuries testify that the transfer of ultimate loyalty to the liberal nation-state has not curbed the toll of war's atrocities. Liberal theorists and the Parliament of the World's Religions both assume that public faith has a dangerous tendency to violence, and thus preclude the possibility of any truly social Christian ethic. I will argue, however, that the Church needs to reclaim the political nature of its faith if it is to resist the violence of the State. What this may mean, however, must go beyond mere strategies to insinuate the Church into the making of public policy. If this essay is a plea for the social and political nature of the Christian faith, it is also a plea for a Christian practice which escapes the thrall of the State.

There have been a number of recent attempts, both Catholic and Protestant, to diagnose and overcome the claustrophobia induced by the Church's confinement to the private sphere. Most take the form, predictably enough, of arguing for the public potential of religion and encouraging Christians to get off the sidelines and into the game. The rules of the game are assumed to be fixed. In this final section I will try to show that being "public" is a game at which the Church will inevitably lose, precisely because the very distinction of public and private, as we have seen, is an instrument by which the State domesticates the Church.

In his *The Naked Public Square*, Richard John Neuhaus makes his case for the public nature of religion by defining religion as "all the ways we think and act and interact with respect to what we believe is ultimately true and important."[60] Politics is a function of culture, and at the heart of culture is religion. Neuhaus argues that it would be foolish therefore to try to denude the public square of religion, for it is very much a part of what drives our life together. Law derives its legitimacy from the fact that it expresses "what people believe to be their collective destiny or ultimate meaning."[61] The law of the land is thus the embodiment of the network of binding obligations, the *religare*, from which is derived the word "religion."[62] Granted, Neuhaus admits, religion in the past has been banned for fear of the kind of fanaticism that tore apart Europe in the era of the religious wars, but he argues that today the only way to prevent politics from degenerating into a violent struggle for power is by constructing a public ethic built on the operative values of the American people, "values that are overwhelmingly grounded in religious belief."[63] Religion is not to be narrowly understood, however, for religion and culture are impossible to distinguish sharply; Neuhaus draws on Clifford Geertz to argue that religion is the "ground or depth-level of culture"[64] and must therefore be present in building a common political culture based on peaceful consensus.

If consensus is the goal, however, Neuhaus claims that religion must gain access to the public sphere with arguments that are public in nature. The problem with the Moral Majority is that "*it wants to enter the political arena making public claims on the basis of private truths*," that is, arguments "derived from sources of revelation or disposition that are essentially private and arbitrary."[65] Another recent attempt at "public theology," that of Michael and Kenneth Himes, is more sanguine about the possibility of using the revelation claims of a particular tradition as public discourse. Theological symbols, insofar as they are "classics," (David Tracy's phrase), may bear disclosive possibilities to all persons in the public sphere, even those who do not share one's explicit faith tradition.[66] Nevertheless, both Neuhaus and the Himeses agree that once we step into the public arena we are bound to common standards of plausibility by which the public assesses any truth claims. As the Himeses put it, "truth in the public realm will be fundamentally a matter of consensus."[67]

For public theologians the lessons of the Wars of Religion dictate that, if religion is to emerge from the punishment corner of privatization and rejoin the public game, it will need to do so chastened, with an enhanced sense of pursuing peaceful consensus. Crucial to the public theologians' project, therefore, is the distinction between State and civil society, which they pick up from John Courtney Murray. The State relates to the society as a part to a whole. The State is that limited part of society which is responsible for public order.[68] As the State maintains a monopoly on legitimate coercion, the Church will not hope to intervene directly in State affairs, lest the specter of religious warfare once again show its cadaverous face. The State is, as Neuhaus says, "not the source but the servant of the law,"[69] and the law derives from the deepest moral intuitions of the people. It is here, outside the State, that the Church goes public in the broader sense of its participation in the free public debate and the formation of religious sensibilities of its members. "The activity of the U.S. Catholic bishops on nuclear weapons and abortion, for example, is often directed toward policies which are established by the state, but the bishops' involvement in these issues occurs in and through the channels a democratic society provides for public debate," writes Richard McBrien. "In such a society voluntary associations play a key role, providing a buffer between the state and the citizenry as well as a struc-tured means of influencing public policy. In the U.S. political system the church itself is a voluntary association."[70]

Now the first problem with the attempt to make religion public is that it is still religion. Neuhaus, the Himeses, and McBrien all abide by McBrien's "working assumption" that "religion is a universal category (genus) and that Christianity is one of its particular forms (species)."[71] Talal Asad's critique of Geertz's work provides us with a useful antidote to these universalist constructions of religion. Asad shows how the attempt to identify a distinctive essence of religion, and thus protect it from charges that it is nothing more than an epiphenomenon of "politics" or "economics," is in fact linked with the modern removal of religion from the spheres of reason and power.[72] Religion is a universal essence detachable from particular ecclesial practices, and as such can provide the motivation necessary for all citizens of whatever creed to regard the nation state as their primary community, and thus produce peaceful con-sensus. As we have seen, religion as a transhistorical phenomenon separate from "politics" is a creation of Western modernity designed to tame the Church. Religion may take different cultural and symbolic expressions, but it remains a universal essence generically distinct from political power which then must be translated into publicly acceptable "values" in order to become public currency. Religion is detached from its specific locus in disciplined ecclesial practices so that it may be compatible with the modern Christian's subjection to the discipline of the State. Echoes of Bodin resound in the public theologians' attempt to make religion the glue that holds the commonwealth together. Religion, that is, and not the Church, for the Church must be separated entirely from the domain of power.

Even in the Himeses' attempt to maintain the distinctive language of Christian symbols such as the Trinity in public discourse, the search for publicly accessible ultimate truths which obey the "standards for public conversation"[73] ensures that any "disclosive possibilities" that theology bears to individuals does not challenge the individual's loyalty to the State. Christianity becomes a varied symbol system which stands at one remove from the reality it represents. Thus, for the Himeses, Christian symbols can elicit transformations quite apart from the individual's participation in a disciplined Church body. As Asad argues, however, religious symbols do not, as Geertz contends, produce moods and motivations in the individual believer which are then translatable into publicly available actions. Religious symbols are rather embedded in bodily practices of power and discipline whose regulation belong to the authoritative structure of the Church, or at least did until modern times. In the modern era, Asad points out, "discipline (intellectual and social) would abandon religious space, letting 'belief,' 'conscience' and 'sensibility' take its place."[74] This does not mean, however, that discipline has disappeared, only that it is now administered by the State, which is assumed to possess an absolute monopoly on the means of coercion.

Part of the difficulty here is that the public theologians' theory of State and society obscures the way that the production of consensus in our society is anything but peaceful and uncoerced. In this regard political scientist Michael Budde's comments on John Courtney Murray, on whom all the Catholic public theologians draw, apply with equal force: "Murray's theory of the state, such as it is, can only be described as naive, almost a direct transferral from civics texts to political description."[75] McBrien claims, following Murray, that collapsing the distinction of State and society is a case of conceptual confusion.[76] In a society in which up to a third of the work force labors directly or indirectly for the State, however, it is simply empirically false to claim that the State is a small and limited part of the wider societal whole, regardless of the intentions of the Founding Fathers. In fact the supposedly free debate of the public square is disproportionately affected by the State. What counts as news is increasingly determined by spin doctors and media handlers. The media looks for its sources among government spokespersons and various "experts" closely linked with the State apparatus.

Beyond the issue of "big government," however, political scientists writing on the State in late capitalism tend to emphasize the extent to which civil society and the State have been fused into different moments of a single complex.[77] The economic, political, social and cultural spheres have merged to such an extent that culture obeys the logic of the market and the political apparatuses in turn create spaces for capital to operate. What is permissible as public discourse increasingly obeys the logic of accumulation; State-funded school lunch programs are defended in terms of increasing students' performance and thus enhancing America's position in the global economy vis-à-vis the Japanese.[78] In this way the State-society complex comes to disempower and coopt other forms of discourse, such as that of the Church. Fantasizing that the State is a limited part of society only makes the Church more vulnerable to its own debilitation.

The State is not simply a mechanism for the representation of the freely gathered general will, nor is it a neutral instrument at the disposal of the various classes. It is rather, in the words of Kenneth Surin, an institutional assemblage which has as its task "the modification and neutralization, primarily by its symbolic representations of social classes, of the efforts of resistance on the part of social subjects." The State, as

Surin puts it, "subserves the processes of accumulation by representing the whole world of social production for its subjects as something that is 'natural,' as an inevitability."[79] Thus, for example, the "laws" of supply and demand and maximization of self-interest are presented as responding to human nature, and economists' predictions are held to be descriptive of reality rather than prescriptive, when they are in fact both.

In an article entitled "War Making and State Making as Organized Crime," sociologist Charles Tilly explores the analogy of the State's monopoly on legitimate violence with the protection rackets run by the friendly neighborhood mobster. According to Tilly

> a portrait of war makers and state makers as coercive and self-seeking entrepreneurs bears a far greater resemblance to the facts than do its chief alternatives: the idea of a social contract, the idea of an open market in which operators of armies and states offer services to willing customers, the idea of a society whose shared norms and expectations call forth a certain kind of government.[80]

States extort large sums of money and the right to send their citizens out to kill and die in exchange for protection from violence both internal and external to the State's borders. What converts war making from "protection" to "protection racket" is the fact that often States offer defense from threats which they themselves create, threats which can be imaginary or the real results of the State's own activities. Furthermore, the internal repression and the extraction of money and bodies for "defense" that the State carries out are frequently among the most substantial impediments to the ordinary citizens' livelihood. The "offer you can't refuse" is usually the most costly. The main difference between Uncle Sam and the Godfather is that the latter did not enjoy the peace of mind afforded by official government sanction.[81]

Building on Arthur Stinchcombe's work on legitimacy, Tilly shows that historically what distinguished "legitimate" violence had little to do with the assent of the governed or the religious sentiments which bind us. The distinction was secured by States' effective monopolization of the means of violence within a defined territory, a gradual process only completed in Europe with the birth of the modern State in the sixteenth and seventeenth centuries. The line between State violence and banditry was a fluid one early in the State-making process. Eventually the personnel of States were able to purvey violence more efficiently and on a wider scale than the personnel of other organizations.[82]

The process of making States was inseparable from the pursuit of war by the power elites of emergent States. As Tilly tells it, "the people who controlled European states and states in the making warred in order to check or overcome their competitors and thus to enjoy the advantages of power within a secure or expanding territory."[83] To make more effective war, they attempted to secure regularized access to the money and the bodies of their subjects. Building up their war-making capacity, and the birth of standing armies, increased in turn their power to eliminate rivals and monopolize the extraction of these resources from subject populations. These activities of extraction were facilitated by the rise of tax-collection apparatuses, courts, and supporting bureaucracies, in short, the rise of the modern State capable of realizing administrative sovereignty over a defined territory.[84]

The assent of the governed *followed*, and is to a large extent *produced by*, State monopoly on the means of violence within its borders. As a general rule, people are more likely to ratify the decisions of an authority that controls substantial force, both from fear of retaliation and, for those who benefit from stability, the desire to maintain that stability.[85] As Tilly puts it, "A tendency to monopolize the means of violence makes a government's claim to provide protection, in either the comforting or the ominous sense of the word, more credible and more difficult to resist."[86]

The attempt to construct religion as an actor subject to the rules of the public debate destroys the disciplinary resources of the Church and its ability to resist this discipline of the State. The price of entrance to the public square is acceptance of the myth of the State as peacemaker, as that which takes up and reconciles the contradictions in civil society. By recognizing the legitimacy of the State's monopoly on coercive authority, by handing our bodies over to the State, the Church renounces forever the specter of religious warfare and in turn is granted the freedom of soul to pursue influence in the public sphere outside the confines of the State.[87] This public realm outside the State is, however, largely a fiction, as is therefore the ideal of a noncoercive public marketplace of ideas. The State is unlimited in another sense as well, for it demands access to our bodies and our money to fuel its war making apparatus. The State is implicated in much more than the maintenance of public order. The State is involved in the production, not merely the restraint, of violence. Indeed the modern State depends on violence, war and preparations for war, to maintain the illusion of social integration and the overcoming of contradictions in civil society.[88]

If the Church accedes to the role of a voluntary association of private citizens, it will lack the disciplinary resources to resist the State's *religare*, its practices of binding. The use of the Church's own practices of binding and loosing is not, however, a call for the Church to take up the sword once again. In fact, it is precisely the opposite. I have contrasted Church discipline with State discipline in order to counter violence on behalf of the State, which has spilt so much blood in our time. Contesting the State's monopoly on violence does not mean that the Church should again get a piece of the action, yet another form of Constantinianism. What I have tried to argue is that the separation of the Church from power did nothing to stanch the flow of blood on the West's troubled pilgrimage. The pitch of war has grown more shrill, and the recreation of the Church as a voluntary association of practitioners of religion has only sapped our ability to resist. The discipline of the State will not be hindered by the Church's participation and complicity in the "public debate." Discipline must be opposed by counter-discipline.

What the term "discipline" refers to here is essentially control over the body. According to Hugh of St. Victor, "it is discipline imposed on the body which forms virtue. Body and spirit are but one: disordered movements of the former betray outwardly (*foris*) the disarranged interior (*intus*) of the soul. But inversely, 'discipline' can act on the soul through the body———in ways of dressing (*in habitu*), in posture and movement (*in gestu*), in speech (*in locutione*), and in table manners (*in mensa*)."[89] There is no disjunction between outer behavior and inner religious piety. The modern construction of religion interiorizes it, and makes religion only a motivating force on bodily political and economic practices. The modern Church thus splits the body from the soul and purchases freedom of religion by handing the body over to the State.

The recovery of the Thomist idea of religion as a virtue is crucial to the Church's resistance to State discipline. The virtues involve the whole person, body and soul, in practices which form the Christian to the service of God. Furthermore the virtues are acquired communally, within the practices of a disciplined ecclesial community which, as the Body of Christ, retains the authority to tell vice from virtue, or violence from peace. Christian "political ethics," therefore, is inseparable from an account of how virtues such as religion and peaceableness are produced and reproduced in the habitual practices of the Church. Christian "politics" cannot be the pursuit of influence over the powers, but rather a question of what kind of community disciplines we need to produce people of peace capable of speaking truth to power.

The virtues are acquired by disciplined following of virtuous exemplars. Discipline is therefore perhaps best understood as *discipleship*, whereas the discipline of the State seeks to create disciples of Leviathan, the discipline of the Church seeks to form disciples of Jesus Christ, the Prince of Peace. For this reason our discipline will more often resemble martyrdom than military victory. Oscar Romero, the day before he was martyred, used his authority to *order* Salvadoran troops to disobey orders to kill.[90] Romero understood that the discipline of Christian discipleship was in fundamental tension with that of the army. He put it this way:

> Let it be quite clear that if we are being asked to collaborate with a pseudo peace, a false order, based on repression and fear, we must recall that the only order and the only peace that God wants is one based on truth and justice. Before these alternatives, our choice is clear: We will follow God's order, not men's.[91]

What I am pointing to is not the discipline of coercion but its antidote, to be found in all those practices of the Christian Church which bind us to one another in the peace of Christ. Recall that Hobbes's two crucial moves in domesticating the Church were to make individuals adhere to the sovereign instead of to one another, and to deny the international character of the Church. In contrast, as some Latin American churches have shown us, the Christian way to resist institutionalized violence is to adhere to one another as Church, to act as a disciplined Body in witness to the world. As Romero wrote, "The church is well aware that anything it can contribute to the process of liberation in this country will have originality and effectiveness only when the church is truly identified as church."[92] The ecclesial base communities in Latin America come together as Church to incarnate disciplined communities of peace and justice without waiting for an illusory influence on the State while the poor go hungry.[93] And the very Eucharistic practices by which the world is fed in turn join people into one Body which transcends the limits of the nation state. To recognize Christ in our sisters and brothers in other lands, the El Salvadors, Panamas and Iraqs of the contemporary scene, is to begin to break the idolatry of the State, and to make visible the Body of Christ in the world. We must cease to think that the only choices open to the Church are either to withdraw into some private or "sectarian" confinement, or to embrace the public debate policed by the State. The Church as Body of Christ transgresses both the lines which separate public from private and the borders of nation-states, thus creating spaces for a different kind of political practice, one which is incapable of being pressed into the service of wars or rumors of wars.[94]

Notes

1   1993 Parliament of the World's Religions, "Towards a Global Ethic," p. 3, available at: http://www.parliamentofreligions.org/_includes/FCKcontent/File/TowardsAGlobalEthic. pdf (accessed 16 December 2008).

2   Nonviolence is put against the backdrop of what is possible. For example, the declaration states, "Persons who hold political power must work within the framework of just order and commit themselves to the most non-violent, peaceful solutions possible. And they should work for this within an international order of peace which itself has need of protection and defense against perpetrators of violence" ("Towards a Global Ethnic," p. 6). Did the Parliament of World's Religions have in mind here an endorsement of the U.S.'s prosecution of the Gulf War?

3   See, for example, John Rawls, "Justice as Fairness: Political not Metaphysical," *Philosophy & Public Affairs* (Summer 1985), p. 225; Judith Shklar, *Ordinary Vices*, Cambridge, MA: Harvard University Press, 1984, p. 5; Jeffrey Stout, *The Flight from Authority: Religion, Morality, and the Quest for Autonomy*, Notre Dame, IN: University of Notre Dame Press, 1981, pp. 13, 235–42.

4   Shklar, *Ordinary Vices* (see Note 3), p. 5.

5   Stout, *The Flight from Authority* (see Note 3), p. 241.

6   Quentin Skinner, *The Foundations of Modern Political Thought*, Cambridge: Cambridge University Press, 1978, vol. II, p. 353.

7   John Neville Figgis, *From Gerson to Grotius, 1414–1625*, New York: Harper Torchbook, 1960, p. 5.

8   Ibid., p. 6.

9   Marsilius of Padua, *Defensor Pacis*, trans. Alan Gewirth, Toronto: University of Toronto Press, 1980, pp. 113–26.

10   Martin Luther, *Temporal Authority: To what Extent it Should be Obeyed*, trans. J.J. Schindel in *Luther's Works*, vol. 45, Philadelphia: Fortress Press, 1962, pp. 75–129.

11   Uwe Siemon-Netto argues this in "Luther Vilified – Luther Vindicated," *Lutheran Forum*, vol. 27 (1993), no. 2, pp. 33–9 and no. 3, pp. 42–9.

12   Martin Luther, *To the Christian Nobility of the German Nation*, trans. Charles M. Jacobs in *Three Treatises*, Philadelphia: Fortress Press, 1966, p. 15.

13   Skinner, *The Foundations of Modern Political Thought* (see Note 6), vol. 11, p. 15.

14   Richard S. Dunn, *The Age of Religious Wars: 1559–1689*, New York: W.W. Norton & Company, 1970, p. 6. Dunn adds that "when the papacy belatedly sponsored a reform program, both the Habsburgs and the Valois refused to endorse much of it, rejecting especially those Trentine decrees which encroached on their sovereign authority. In refusing to cooperate with Rome, the Catholic princes checked papal ambitions to restore the Church's medieval political power."

15   Ibid., pp. 48–9.

16   G.R. Elton, "The Age of the Reformation," quoted in Dunn, *The Age of Religious Wars* (see Note 14), p. 6.

17   Skinner, *The Foundations of Modern Political Thought* (see Note 6), vol. 11, pp. 59–60.

18   Dunn, *The Age of Religious Wars* (see Note 16), p. 24. See also Skinner, *The Foundations of Modern Political Thought* (see Note 6), vol. 11, pp. 254–9.

19   Dunn, *The Age of Religious Wars* (see Note 16), pp. 23–6.

20   Quoted in Franklin C. Palm, *Calvinism and the Religious Wars*, New York: Henry Holt and Company, 1932, pp. 54–5.

21   Ibid., pp. 51–4.

22   Dunn, *The Age of Religious Wars* (see Note 16), pp. 27–31.

23   See J.H.M. Salmon, *Society in Crisis: France in the Sixteenth Century*, London and Tonbridge: Ernest Benn Limited, pp. 189–90. After the massacre, a flood of Huguenot literature explored the influence of Machiavellianism on the Queen Mother's actions.

24   Dunn, *The Age of Religious Wars* (see Note 16), pp. 69–73.

25   Ibid., pp. 73–8.

26   J.H. Elliot, *Europe Divided: 1559–1598*, New York: Harper & Row, 1968, p. 108. Elliot quotes the words of the sixteenth-century Venetian ambassador as to the secular motivation behind the French civil wars: "In like manner as Caesar would have no equal and Pompey no superior, these civil wars are born of the wish of the cardinal of Lorraine to have no equal, and the Admiral (Coligny) and the house of Montmorency to have no superior."

27   Wilfred Cantwell Smith, *The Meaning and End of Religion*, New York: The Macmillan Company, 1962, p. 31.

28   St. Thomas Aquinas, *Summa Theologiae*, ed. Blackfriars, New York: McGraw-Hill, 1964, II–II.81.8.

29   Ibid., II–II..81.7.

30   Ibid., I–II.49–55.

31   Cantwell Smith, *The Meaning and End of Religion* (see Note 27), p. 32.

32   Ibid., p. 19.

33   Ibid.

34   Ibid., pp. 32–44.

35   Skinner, *The Foundations of Modern Political Thought* (see Note 6), vol. 11, pp. 244–46.

36   Jean Bodin, *Six Books of the Commonwealth*, trans. and abr. M.J. Tooley, Oxford: Basil Blackwell, n.d., p. 141.

37   Ibid., pp. 140–42.

38   Figgis, *From Gerson to Grotius, 1414–1625* (see Note 7), p. 124.

39   Thomas Hobbes, *Leviathan*, New York: Collier Books, 1962, p. 88.

40   Ibid., p. 90.

41   Ibid., pp. 94, 297–9.

42   Ibid., pp. 340–41.

43   Ibid., pp. 395–8. In chapter 42 of *Leviathan* Hobbes provides a lengthy explanation of why sovereigns have this power without needing to bother with such inconveniences as apostolic succession and the imposition of hands.

44 Ibid., p. 324.

45 Ibid., pp. 363–6.

46 Ibid., p. 340.

47 Ibid., p. 418.

48 John Milbank also points to the kinship of modern absolutism and modern liberalism in slightly different terms: "It is precisely the formal character of state power as guaranteeing personal security and non-interference in 'private' pursuits (selling, contracts, education, choice of abode) which demands that this power be otherwise unlimited and absolutely alone. Hobbes was simply more clear-sighted than later apparently more 'liberal' thinkers like Locke in realizing that a liberal peace requires a single undisputed power, but not necessarily a continued majority consensus, which may not be forthcoming," John Milbank, *Theology and Social Theory*, Oxford: Basil Blackwell, 1990, p. 13.

49 John Locke, *A Letter Concerning Toleration*, Indianapolis: The Bobbs-Merrill Company, 1955, p. 18.

50 Ibid., p. 35.

51 Although William of Orange has often been presented as a religious zealot, fervent Calvinist and scourge of papists, recent scholarship makes him out to be a "thoroughgoing politique" for whom theology was but a tool of statecraft. On the eve of the Glorious Revolution, William and the Dutch States General embarked on a lobbying campaign aimed at convincing Catholic Europe that they had no Protestant motives for invading England, and that Catholic worship would be protected. The Dutch were at the brink of war with France, and were convinced that their chances of winning hinged on turning the English against the French. At the same time, French propagandists sought to paint the conflict as a *guerre de religion*, not a *guerre d'état*. At least one English pamphleteer thought that interpretation unlikely, writing in 1688 "none that know the religion of the Hollander would judge the Prince or States would be at the charge of a dozen fly-boats or herring busses to propagate it." See Jonathan I. Israel, "William III and Toleration", in Ole Peter Grell, Jonathan I. Israel, and Nicholas Tyacke (eds), *From Persecution to Toleration*, Oxford: Clarendon Press, 1991, pp. 129–42.

52 Earl of Clarendon, *Animadversions upon a Book, Intituled, Fanaticism Fanatically Imputed to the Catholick Church, by Dr. Stillingfleet, And the Imputation Refuted and Retorted by S.C.*, London: Rich. Royston, 1685, p. 12.

53 Ibid., p. 11.

54 Anthony Giddens, *The Nation-State and Violence*, Berkeley: University of California Press, 1987, pp. 50–51, 86–90. Borders imposed by the nation-state system continue to cause conflict. The 1991 Gulf War was largely a product of artificial borders drawn by the British after World War 1, which divided the Arab world into artificial and often mutually antagonistic nation-states. The Iraq–Kuwait border was drawn arbitrarily by the British High Commander, Percy Cox, deliberately denying newly created Iraq access to the sea in order to keep it dependent on Britain. See Glenn Frankel, "Lines in the Sand", in Micah L. Sifry and Christopher Cerf (eds) *The Gulf War Reader*, New York: Times Books, 1991, pp. 16–20.

55 Immanuel Kant, *The Metaphysics of Morals*, trans. Mary Gregor, Cambridge: Cambridge University Press, 1991, pp. 57 [231], 123–6 [311–15].

56 Immanuel Kant, *Perpetual Peace*, Indianapolis: Bobbs-Merrill Company, 1957, p. 12. In *the Metaphysics of Morals* Kant explains that war is always fought to eliminate war. "Right during a war would, then, have to be the waging of war in accordance with principles that always leave open the possibility of leaving the state of nature among states ... and entering a rightful condition" (p. 153 [347]). Kant's myth of perpetual peace is often invoked by U.S. foreign policy makers; if we "assist" other countries to adopt liberal democracy, they will have no more reason to go to war. Of course, this position only gives us bigger wars, since now wars are not limited by historical particularities. Now any people in any part of the globe is a potential enemy if it has not chosen to govern itself rationally.

57 Kant, *Metaphysics of Morals* (see Note 55), 136 [3261]. Ralph Walker notes that Kant "clearly regards the stability of the state as an end which the Theory of Right requires us to pursue (though he does not put this in so many words, so that the contradiction with his other remarks about ends does not become obvious)," Ralph C.S. Walker, *Kant*, London: Routledge, 1978, p. 161.

58   Kant, *Metaphysics of Morals* (see Note 55), p. 131 [320].

59   Ronald Beiner, *What's the Matter with Liberalism?*, Berkeley, CA: University of California Press, 1992, pp. 20–28. Beiner also describes how the rhetoric of pluralism masks a numbing uniformity in American life. We eat the same things, wear the same clothes, talk the same, worship the same, coast to coast. Toqueville made similar observations 150 years ago. In private life people tried to assert their independence through "numerous artificial and arbitrary distinctions"; Alexis de Toqueville, *Democracy in America*, New York: Mentor Books, 1956, p. 248. In public, however, uniformity reigned and the opinions of the majority were a "species of religion" (pp. 148–9). The medieval consensus on the good did not simply fragment into a pluralism of different conceptions. Pluralism exists on the private level. The medieval consensus was replaced by a new consensus, that of liberal society.

60   Richard John Neuhaus, *The Naked Public Square*, Grand Rapids, MI: William B. Eerdmans Publishing Company, 1984, p. 27. Public theologian Richard McBrien similarly defines religion as "the whole complexus of attitudes, convictions, emotions, gestures, rituals, symbols, beliefs, and institutions by which persons come to terms with, and express, their personal and/or communal relationship with ultimate Reality (God and everything that pertains to God)", Richard McBrien, *Caesar's Coin*, New York: MacMillan Publishing Company, 1987, p. 11. For their definition of religion, Michael and Kenneth Himes quote McBrien; see *Fullness of Faith: The Public Significance of Theology*, New York: Paulist Press, 1993, pp. 19–20.

61   Neuhaus, *The Naked Public Square* (see Note 60), p. 256.

62   Ibid., pp. 250–1.

63   Ibid., p. 37.

64   Ibid., p. 132.

65   Ibid., p. 36.

66   Himes and Himes, *Fullness of Faith* (see Note 60), pp. 15–19.

67   Ibid., p. 18.

68   Ibid., pp. 19–20.

69   Neuhaus, *The Naked Public Square* (see Note 60), p. 259.

70   McBrien, *Caesar's Coin* (see Note 60), p. 42.

71   Ibid., p. 17.

72   Talal Asad, *Genealogies of Religion: Discipline and Reasons of Power in Christianity and Islam*, Baltimore: The Johns Hopkins University Press, 1993, pp. 27–54.

73   Himes and Himes, *Fullness of Faith* (see Note 60), p. 18.

74   Asad, *Genealogies of Religion* (see Note 72) p. 39.

75   Michael L. Budde, *The Two Churches: Catholicism and Capitalism in the World System*, Durham, NC: Duke University Press, 1992, p. 115.

76   McBrien, *Caesar's Coin* (see Note 60), p. 25; p. 42.

77   See, for example, Bob Jessop, *State Theory*, University Park, PA: The Pennsylvania State University Press, 1990, pp. 338–69; Antonio Negri, *The Politics of Subversion*, trans. James Newell, Cambridge: Polity Press, 1989, pp. 169–99; and Kenneth Surin, "Marxism(s) and the 'Withering Away of the State,'" *Social Text no. 27* (Durham, NC: Duke University Press Journals, 1990), pp. 42–6.

78   I owe this example to Professor Romand Coles of Duke University.

79   Surin, "Marxism(s)" (see Note 77), p. 45.

80   Charles Tilly, "War Making and State Making as Organized Crime," in Peter B. Evans, Dietrich Rueschemeyer and Theda Skocpol (eds), *Bringing the State Back In*, Cambridge: Cambridge University Press, 1985, p. 169.

81   Ibid., pp. 170–71.

82   Ibid., pp. 170–5.

83   Ibid., p. 172.

84   Ibid., pp. 172–86.

85   Ibid., pp. 171–5.

86   Ibid., p. 172.

87   See Neuhaus, *The Naked Public Square* (see Note 60), pp. 8–9; Himes and Himes, *Fullness of Faith* (see Note 60), pp. 19–20.

88   See Surin, "Marxism(s)" (see Note 77), pp. 45–9, and Paul Virilio, *Popular Defense and Eco-logical Struggles*, trans. Mark Polizzotti, New York: Semiotext(e), 1990.

89   J.C. Schmitt, "Me geste, la cathedrale et le roi," quoted in Asad, *Genealogies of Religion* (see Note 72), p. 138.

90   Archbishop Oscar Romero, "The Church: Defender of Human Dignity," in *A Martyr's Message of Hope*, Kansas City: Celebration Books, 1981, p. 161. The relevant part of his sermon on March 23, 1980 reads as follows: "I would like to issue a special entreaty to the members of the army, and specifically to the ranks of the National Guard, the police and the military. Brothers and sisters, you are our own people; you kill your own fellow peasants. Someone's order to kill should not prevail; rather, what ought to prevail is the law of God that says, 'Do not kill.' No soldier is obliged to obey an order against the law of God; no one has to fulfill an immoral law ... Why, in the name of God, and in the name of this suffering people whose cries rise up to the heavens every day in greater tumult, I implore them, I beg them, I order them, in the name of God: Cease the repression!"

91   Archbishop Oscar Romero, homily, July 1, 1979, quoted in James R. Brockman (trans. and ed.), *The Church is all of You: Thoughts of Archbishop Oscar Romero*, S.J., Minneapolis: Winston Press, 1984, p. 88.

92   Archbishop Oscar Romero, "The Church's Mission amid the National Crisis," in idem, *Voice of the Voiceless*, trans. Michael J. Walsh, Maryknoll, NY: Orbis Books, 1985, p. 128.

93   For an extended discussion of the base communities as alternative ecclesial polities, see William T. Cavanaugh, "The Ecclesiologies of Medellin and the Lessons of the Base Communities," *Cross Currents* vol. 44, No. 1 (Spring 1994), pp. 74–81.

94   This essay is an expanded version of a paper entitled "The Wars of Religion and the Fiction of Pluralism" which I delivered to the History of Christianity section at the American Academy of Religion Annual Meeting in Washington in November 1993. I would like to thank Frederick Bauerschmidt, Michael Baxter, Daniel Bell, Stanley Hauerwas, Reinhard Hütter and D. Stephen Long for their comments on various drafts of this paper.

Chapter 12

John Milbank

The gift of ruling

T oday, it seems, all the ancient global realities have fallen under a kind of
  secular last judgement, heralded by the onset of a secular Armageddon. What is
Islam and is it violent and intolerant? What is Catholicism and is it sexually hypo-
critical and sadistic? What is Christianity and is it an irrational sect? What is Europe,
and is it inherently bureaucratic and decadent? What is America and is it inherently
violent and expansionist? What is the West and is it inherently greedy and imperialist?

In the midst of all this questioning though, rather strangely we do not seem to
question the abstract ideas carried by the Western instances amongst these ancient
realities. We still seem to believe in what we have transported, if not very much in
the modes of transport. Thus we do not often question the ideas of liberal democracy
or of human rights, but assume rather that the actual collective realities that we have
inherited may now be, in various ways, threatening the instantiation and further extension
of these ideals. In the United States, many people lament the apparent start of a
transformation of republic into empire and of democracy into the rule of manipulative elites. Less often do they ask whether the American modes of republic and
democracy have of their very nature always nurtured both imperialism and oligarchy.

Rather, the story we tell ourselves is that since 1945, and even more since 1990,
the dark demons of the past have been put to rout. Now, however, they are returning
in the form of fundamentalist religion which is producing both a dangerous mutation
in Islam and a dangerous mutation in American conservatism. Once more, irration-
alism is asserting itself. We should not be surprised: humans have always been mas-
sively prone to superstition, and enlightenment is history's late and most fragile

bloom. Once again we must be vigilant – although the rationally illumined divide as they have done ever since the 18th century between advocacy of a vigilance through intensified deployment of regulatory economic and legal institutions (the Franco-German way) or else a military heroism whose ancient spirit liberalism must somehow keep alive against its own deepest inclinations (the new American way, much inspired by Leo Strauss and Carl Schmitt).

I do not believe this relatively comforting story. I do not want to deny that all our major inherited collective realities deserve to come up for judgment. They do. But I want to argue that that which seems above reproach, namely liberal democracy, should now most of all come under our judging scrutiny.

Let us ask, first of all, why the West gave birth to liberalism? Not why the West and nowhere else, because this assumes that it was likely to arrive everywhere sooner or later. Rather we should ask why the West gave birth to anything so fantastically peculiar and unlikely. Liberalism is peculiar and unlikely because it proceeds by inventing a wholly artificial human being who has never really existed, and then pretending that we are all instances of such a species. This is the pure individual, thought of in abstraction from his or her gender, birth, associations, beliefs and also, crucially, in equal abstraction from the religious or philosophical beliefs of the observer of this individual as to whether he is a creature made by God, or only material, or naturally evolved and so forth. Such an individual is not only asocial, he is also apsychological; his soul is in every way unspecified. To this blank entity one attaches 'rights', which may be rights to freedom from fear, or from material want. However, real historical individuals include heroes and ascetics, so even these attributions seem too substantive. The pure liberal individual, as Rousseau and Kant finally concluded, is rather the possessor of a free will. Not a will determined to a good or even open to choosing this or that, but a will to will. The pure 'nature' of this individual is his capacity to break with any given nature, even to will against himself. Liberalism then imagines all social order to be either an artifice, the result of various contracts made between such individuals considered in the abstract (Hobbes and Locke) or else as the effect of the way such individuals through their imaginations fantastically project themselves into each other's lives (roughly the view of the Scottish Enlightenment).

Why did thinkers in the West, from Machiavelli, through Hobbes and Locke to Montesquieu, embark on such a seemingly unreal approach to human association? According to Pierre Manent, the French Catholic liberal political thinker, this was because of the so-called 'Theologico-Political problem' bequeathed to it by Christianity.[1] The Western Middle Ages inherited from Plato, Aristotle and Cicero the idea that political life is natural, and that a civilized political life most of all fulfills human practical nature when we participate in the political process, make friends amongst the like-minded, and achieve a balanced economic independence exercised by magnanimity towards others. The high-born man in the city is a respected owner, only in so far as he is a judicious and generous giver. Christianity, however, posited above this natural political goal for human beings a supernatural end: for the righteous the life of heaven and the vision of God face to face. According to Manent these two goals, natural and supernatural, came into conflict in three different ways. First of all, Christianity was relatively indifferent to the mode of secular political order and its dignity: its job was simply the disciplining of sin and the ordering of things destined to pass away. Secondly, however, in a countervailing tendency, the superiority of the supernatural order could be used to justify interventions of the Church in secular rule and indeed the doctrine of the *plenitudo potestatis* of the Pope legitimated a final overruling of kings in all matters and in all circumstances – even if before 1300 or so this overruling was not deemed to be coercive and was not founded on a Papal claim to eminent *dominium* even over material things; yet after 1300 even these claims were made by some.[2]

Thirdly, in Manent's opinion magnanimity and humility could not sit easily together: Western Christendom was divided in its admiration both for the prideful hero and the self-abnegating saint.[3]

On this view then, there was nothing stable about medieval order. Kingdoms and city states, the realms of feudal warfare and trade, were always champing at the bit, searching for more secular pasturage. However, nearly everyone remained Christian; they accepted the superiority of the supernatural, and therefore could not simply reassert the autonomy of politics from theological considerations and ecclesiastical control, without seeming to revert to paganism. Although pagan political participation, heroism, friendship and magnanimity were still affirmed, they were considered, following Augustine, but 'glittering vices' if not informed by supernatural humility, patience, forbearance, forgiveness, faith, hope and charity.

This appears to leave the secular nowhere to go if it wishes to expand its breathing space: neither the order of nature, nor the order of grace. It is just for this reason, according to Manent, that it was therefore forced to invent a third, artificial realm, built on a consideration not of humanity as it really is, nor as might ideally become, but rather as it most generally and abstractly and minimally might be considered. In this way no rival *ideal* to Christianity was proposed, even if an amoral nonevaluative rival to traditional theological reflection was nonetheless put forward. Henceforward the realm of politics was thought of not as the realization of a natural *telos*, nor as the abetting of a supernatural one, but simply as the most efficient co-ordination of competing wills, and their summation into one common, powerful collective will. From a theological point of view, this meant that the human individual was not here thought of as a creature, as a divine gift, as defined by his sharing-in and reflection-of divine qualities of intellect, goodness and glory, but rather as a bare being, existing univocally no more and no less than God himself taken as an abstract possibility and not as the creator. The only thing that now distinguishes this bare existence from a blade of grass or an asteroid, was its reflexive capacity for self-moving: its will, which might be equally for good or for evil.

Such a choice was now politically irrelevant. Or rather, as Manent says, if anything, there was, from Machiavelli through Hobbes to Montesquieu and Hegel, a bias towards the primacy of evil.[4] Respect for the good was now seen as the everyday unexceptional reality, but no longer as the normative defining one: that rather belonged to the exceptional suspension of normality in the moment of crisis that reveals a deeper truth and on that basis makes founding civil gestures. This truth emerges in circumstances of pure anarchy and of threat to the city or its rulers: then evil assumes priority precisely in the face of violence. All lies, subterfuges and resorts to counter-violence then become justified. Manent is the only liberal I have read who admits that liberalism is at bottom Sadeian and Satanic. (This seems strange for a Catholic, but then sometimes in French Catholicism a Catharist streak still lurks ...)

What is impressive in Manent's genealogy is his insistence on the *contingency* of Western liberalism. Even though he is a liberal, liberalism is not for him the sane, common-sense residue that remains once one has sloughed off gothic superstitions. Instead it is rather shaped by the Christian gothic crisis, and therefore remains perpetually haunted by it.

Nonetheless, I believe that he does not push this approach far enough. The odd thing about all his writings is that though his central theses revolve around religion and theology he says very little about either. In particular, his treatment of the Middle Ages is cursory and I would argue in some crucial ways inaccurate. Let us examine the three aspects of his theologico-political crisis.

The first two concern tensions between the natural and supernatural ends. Here Manent associates attempts to merge the two with the Baroque, whereas to the contrary, if certainly the Baroque sometimes attempted this, it was only trying to heal its own, not a medieval wound. Overwhelmingly the research of historical theology in the 20th century showed that the Middle Ages did not tend to recognize a natural end that was actually, as opposed to formally, independent of the supernatural one. In political terms this means that Manent wholly overstates ecclesiastical indifference to the modes of secular rule: if permitted political forms within Christendom might be either aristocratic or monarchic with a certain indifference according to relatively democratic circumstance, then this was true of pagan thought also. But there was no indifference to the substantive exercise of justice, or a 'Lutheran' tolerance of any enforced peace so long as it was formally peace. Manent is on far surer ground when he stresses the perpetual interference of the supernatural claims in those of the nat-ural: from Augustine onwards, the Church showed a desire to infuse secular practices of warfare, punishment, trade and feudal tenure with the exercise of mercy and for-bearance. Even in relation to the function of doing justice, it is arguable that Chris-tianity had an innovative impact: Oliver O'Donovan plausibly contends that St Paul for the first time made *judgement* (the provision of equity) the sole legitimating ground of government and no longer also the guarding of a terrain which paganism had always included. This renders rule purely active and donative rather than reactive and defensive. (Another way in which Paul is more Nietzschean than Nietzsche.) And if Christianity asked the state to attend more closely to mercy and justice, inversely its own 'household' communities from the outset took over in part from the *polis* the 'political' function of *Paideia*: training in ultimate virtues.[5] Moreover, salvation itself was not simply an individual matter in the Patristic and Medieval period: redemptive charity, for example, was a state pertaining *between* people, not simply a virtue exercised by an individual. The Church itself was a complex multiple society and not simply the administrative machinery for the saving of souls which it later tended to evolve into. Hence to speak of 'secular' and 'sacred' concerns in this period can be to overlook the fact that monasteries were also farms, that the church saw to the upkeep of bridges which were at once crossing places and shrines to the Virgin and that the laity often exercised economic, charitable and festive functions in confraternities that were themselves units of the Church as much as parishes, and therefore occupied no unambiguously 'secular' space. Indeed the first freely shaped voluntary associations in the Christian West tended to be religious ones: the various religious and lay orders did not see constitution-making (any more than canon law itself) as at variance with the idea that the constituted body was itself a divinely instituted gift and event of grace. Hence while indeed it is true that Christianity, unlike Judaism and Islam, enforces no detailed religious law, and even instills a 'law of charity' beyond legality as command and restriction, this did not so clearly open up the space of the secular as is often thought. For the greater free play given to human social inventiveness opened by the displacing of the notion of divine law from the centre of religious consciousness applied also or more within the religious sphere than within the sphere of worldly rule. In the latter case, Christianity more positioned what it regarded as the regrettably necessary use of coercion outside the redemptive sphere, yet even this was relative and qualified by degrees – the church also directly exercised some coercion, while the theological warrant for its just exercise even in secular instances was finally assistance to redemptive processes. Moreover, if the *sacerdotium* could also be coercive, the *regnum* could also exercise a positive pastoral concern in the material sphere, for the *regnum* fell at least half within the *ecclesia*.[6]

One should remember too, of course, that the supreme laymen, namely kings, were anointed, and assumed that they had thereby received a Christic office in another aspect to that received by the priesthood: Christ being understood following the New Testament as fulfilling the offices of prophet, priest and king.[7]

So to speak of the secular in the Middle Ages can be problematic. For this period the *Saeculum* was not a space but the time before the eschaton: certainly some concerns that were more worldly belonged more to this time, but this did not imply quite our sense of sheer 'indifference' and 'neutrality' as concerns religious matters when we speak of 'the secular.' Indeed one can go further: 'temporal' concerns existed in ontological contrast to eternal ones, but both were 'religious' as falling under divine judgement. Manent writes too much as if the secular *in our sense* was frustrated during the Middle Ages, perpetually struggling to express itself, just waiting for the right language. But surely his own insights show that there *is* no secular in our sense outside liberalism, and that therefore before the invention of this discourse, there was nothing waiting to be articulated.[8] (The same point applies to the question of 'religious tolerance'. Again this was not something 'frustrated' in the Middle Ages, since it was as yet inconceivable as compatible with social and political order. Apart from Judaism – in which Christendom, like Islam, saw a complex and unique case – there *were* no other religious points of view seeking expression. Heresies were the work of minorities themselves seeking hegemony, and the forms they took often – as with Catharism – appeared to threaten not simply the Church's authority, but the sanctity of the body, the significance of our compromised life in time, the offer of salvation to all and the general mediation of the sacred in nature, image, word and event.)

A direct way to instance this issue is Manent's example of the Italian city republic. He simply takes it for granted that they were always somewhat secular, neo-pagan realities, trying to escape church control because overwhelmingly preoccupied with the secular business of manufacture, trade, politics and warfare. However, recent research (for example, by Augustine Thompson OP) utterly belies this: the earlier Italian republics were not founded on pagan models, but were more like 'confraternities of confraternities'; citizenship was liturgically linked to baptism (as the free-standing baptisteries of Italian cities still attest today) and participation in local church and civic life (often astonishingly and directly democratic in character) were so complexly interwoven as to be inseparable. Suspicion of the Pope and even of the clergy does *not* here amount to 'secularity' as Manent's modern conservative French piety appears to assume. Moreover, the emergence of a more pagan republicanism with Machiavelli coincided with an evolution of the city-states towards princedoms and local imperialism.[9]

We are starting then to see that liberalism is yet *more* contingent than Manent allows. It is not so clear after all that the Middle Ages contained an entirely irresolvable tension. If it had done, one must then ask why should *not* it have been possible to reassert the independence of pagan virtue? Manent's claim that this was impossible seems actually to concede that there was no real notion at this time of an entirely independent natural end. Besides it is clear that some thinkers, notably Dante, did try to make this assertion. One can say perhaps that the attempt failed, but if it did then again this was because the notion of a substantive natural end valid in its own right could not yet easily find favour. (And one should also add that, as Dante's case shows, even such a purely natural end remained 'religious').[10]

Finally, Manent can only insist on the incompatibility between magnanimity and humility by explicitly denying Aquinas's own opinion to the contrary.[11] In effect, Manent says that Christian virtue is the abject reception of divine gift; Aquinas, by contrast, says that we should recognize greatness of soul as the crucial divine gift as our sharing in God's generous rule. In possession of magnanimity, a man may even 'deem himself worthy of great things', but only 'in consideration of the gifts he holds from God'. For ourselves, nevertheless, in humble consideration of our weakness we should not boast, because we are deluded if we think we are sure of the range of our powers or their stability. We should rather more strongly acknowledge magnanimity in others and its source in God, since we are its beneficiaries — since it helps to mediate divine grace to us. Aquinas therefore sees no problem in the Christianization of the notion of a governing and generous dispersal. If he does qualify the goodness of magnanimity, it is more in terms of charity than of humility: supreme ethical virtue is now not to be independent of the help and assistance of others (as Manent, to be fair, also notes, yet strangely fails to link to charity as friendship) and so friendship no longer ornaments magnanimity. Rather magnanimity promotes friendship.[12] So it is less that supernatural humility and natural magnanimity are in tension for Aquinas, as that supernatural charity elevates and perfects natural (Aristotelian) friendship, stressing more its mutuality and its scope, namely downwards beneath humanity and upwards beyond him to God. (It is clear from the example of St Francis and others that a new stress on 'befriending creatures' was itself allied to transformed social practices.)

Within these perspectives, the invention of liberalism appears still more of a mystery. What can one suggest instead of Manent's thesis or rather in modification of it? First of all, one should take more seriously Charles Péguy's view, which Manent mentions, that despite the bridges and the confraternities, the orders of chivalry and the at times semi-baptized cults of erotic love, the Medieval church did not *adequately* incarnate Christianity in the lay and material orders. Lay paths to salvation were seen as more perilous than clerical ones; increasingly the laity were removed (often understandably in the name of anti-corruption, yet still with exclusive effect) from influence over specifically clerical and sacramental matters. It never quite worked out how, if contemplation is the highest end of human life, then leisure could be 'the basis of culture' for every individual as well as for the whole of society. Nor did it question a theory/practice duality or come to the realization that work also can be contemplative. This was also a failure to grasp adequately its *own* reality; it took Chateaubriand, Hugo, Pugin and Ruskin in the 19th century to point out that medieval contemplation was also the work of the church masons, the composers and the poets. One can sum this up by saying that the Middle Ages never quite understood that if liturgy stands at the summit then this is at once a humanly crafted work (involving in the end all of society, lay and clerical) and a divinely received gift; here we both shape and see.

Thus Christianity, one could argue beyond Manent, was not inherently prone to duality; rather its contingent modes of clerical development encouraged such duality.

A second point is linked to the first one. The more the clergy tended to see themselves as specialists in salvation and sacramental mediation, then the more the mediation of the transcendent by symbols, by nature, by society and by reason was played down. Instead, the resources of scripture, tradition, hierarchy, sign and sacrament started to be viewed as so many positive, given, revealed facts. In this perspective the clergy became like shadows of the wielders of physical force – they were now the quasi-literal exponents of quasi-literal circumstances.[13] This attitude went along with a new theology which stressed the inscrutability of the divine will. This was still a giving, generous will, but the gifts of material well-being or of salvation now tended less to be seen as disclosing to us the very inner-life of the Trinity. In consequence, life on earth and the process of salvation started less to be seen as an entering into this Trinitarian life.[14]

I think that in our current circumstances, it is here important not to overlook the fact that these new developments involved certain echoings of Medieval Islam – even when paradoxically the aim was to escape just this influence. First of all, the tension between revealed word and Greek reason was far greater in Islam, which never arrived at the kind of synthesis achieved by Aquinas: indeed, the latter, like most thinkers in the Latin West *never* saw himself as a philosopher in the way the great Arabic developers of Aristotle and Neoplatonism did. Secondly, the Islamic world tended to resolve this tension in the political world by minimizing the role of natural equity: the Caliph's inscrutable word was law because he had been appointed by the inscrutable command of Allah. This voluntarist approach to political rule later became dominant in the West also, wherein it encouraged first papal and later royal absolutism.

It may seem to us that absolutism and liberalism are opposites, but in fact they spring from the same root since they both have to do with the primacy of the will. In the early modern West, the competition of individual wills was only resolved by investing all political rule for the first time in a single sovereign will. This applies whether or not this will was seen as ruling by divine right or by contract or both, and whether it was seen as the will of the king or as the democratic will of the people. If this entire tendency both echoes Islam and foreshadows enlightenment, then that is less surprising when one remembers that Islam saw itself as a more final religion than Christianity, since it is more manifestly a universal monotheism, purged of the mysterious mystical and unfathomable (Trinity and Incarnation) and reinstating the practical order of law beyond the anarchy of love. A rational as well as pious stress on unity paradoxically promoted the arbitrariness of a willing source – since this is one of the strongest paradigms of unity – all the way from Mohammed to Montesquieu. Hence the whole line of thought which goes 'Islam needs the enlightenment which Christendom has passed through' is somewhat shallow. In a certain sense one can say that, while Islam failed to engage with the Christian other and went into a decline, Christianity *did* engage with the Islamic other with multiple consequences and *even the Enlightenment* (think of deism) is in some degree an upshot of a subtle 'Islamification'. (Certain *philosophes* spasmodically admired Islamic despots, just as they did the greater 'rationality' of both Islam and Judaism.)[15]

So although Manent is right to stress the importance for liberalism of Machiavelli's neo-pagan cult of heroic virtue and the free but mortally doomed republic, he is wrong to ignore additional ecclesiastical and theological roots of liberalism. Even though the latter eventually enshrines secularity, the invention of an autonomous secular realm is perhaps mainly the paradoxical work of a certain kind of theology. This theology tends to lose sight of the fact that created being is only a gift; only exists as *sharing* in divine existence and as perpetually *borrowing* this existence. Instead, God is now idolatrously regarded as a kind of very big literal fact, who established other facts alongside himself and grants to these facts certain autonomies, certain areas of purely free decision – like a government decreeing that 'normally' police cannot enter a private house or say what should go on there. (The qualifier 'normally' being also relevant to the nature of that kind of theology.) The same norms of non-interference now pertain between individuals: already Duns Scotus substituted for the 'common good' contractually agreed upon conventions as sufficiently guaranteeing the civil peace.[16]

So liberalism is not witness to a kind of tragic truth or fantasized Manichean Christianity. Instead it witnesses the failure of the Church regarding the laity and the growth of a somewhat positivist and formalist theology of divine power which itself helped to invent liberalism. Manent significantly ignores the echo of this theology in Hobbes and Locke who were by no means yet purely secular thinkers but more like Christian heresiarchs.[17]

But what is wrong with the liberalism which this theology engendered? Here I have nothing to add to the profundity of Manent, the chastened liberal.[18] With Manent let us note the following: liberalism assumes the greater reality of evil over good; liberalism begins by suppressing the soul, or rather by assuming a gross psychology largely for the sake of administrative convenience. Liberalism, as the liberals Rousseau, Constant and Tocqueville further diagnosed in practice bifurcates the soul, by ensuring that it must submit to a tyranny of mere opinion, given that no opinion is for liberalism inherently right or wrong. As a result, it is perpetually swayed away from its 'own' opinion which remains elusive. Furthermore, as Montesquieu gleefully pointed out, under liberalism, since only what is generally represented is publicly valid, the spectacle of representing always dominates the supposedly represented people, ensuring that what they think is always already just what they are represented as thinking. Thus Tocqueville noted that in America, the freest society on earth, there is least of all public debate, and most of all tyranny of general mass opinion.[19] Instead of debate, as Manent also points out, one has *competition*, not just in the economic realm but in the cultural realm also. In the absence of collective standards, or even a collective search for standards, the only standard is a regulated *agon* according to formalized procedures.

Beneath all of these woes of liberalism lurks one fundamental point: it lacks any extra-human or any extra-natural norm, and this ensures that it revolves in an empty circle. As Manent says, for liberalism it is nature alone that *gives* although she cannot command, cannot authorize, before the arrival of the State. Inversely, the sovereign State, or the effectively sovereign free market can alone command, but it does not give: it only lays down boundaries or offers products or opportunities. Apparently it does not *force* us, but equally by the same token it *provides* us with nothing. The State legislates, the market exchanges, on behalf of human nature which it represents, yet without the State or market this human nature is not really *entitled* to be represented. Therefore representing and represented compose an empty hall of mirrors: in the middle, the soul of humanity is no longer there where we suppose it to be. And since there are no more souls with intrinsic destinies and purposes, no *projects* can be allowed: opinions cannot be permitted any influence. In theory the Church can offer to people its rule of charity and reconciliation; in practice its scope for doing so is limited by the sovereign state. If for example the citizens of New York chose to run their city according to that liturgical order which its gothic skyscrapers so strangely intimate (indeed Manhattan constitutes one gigantic cathedral-castle) with a third of the days off a year for worship and feasting neither state nor market would permit this. Liberalism allows apparent total diversity of choice; at the same time it is really a formal conspiracy to ensure that no choice can ever be significantly effective. Already Tocqueville noted that in the United States nothing really happens; its apparent dynamism conceals an extraordinary stasis. (And if change does occur Americans tend quickly to deny that anything was ever any different; today, for example, if shops in the USA cease to stock a product, they will often deny that they ever *have* stocked it.)

Without souls or purposes, equally victim to mass manipulation, there is no longer anything for people to share. Under liberalism we no longer really meet each other; establish connections yes, truly make friends, almost never. There is no longer anyone to be friends with, as a hundred novelists have told us. Removed from society and friendship, liberal man focuses like Locke's Adam on dominating nature. But even here he does not escape empty circularity. His business with nature is to be guided by nature, by an accurate science of nature; this, however, is always incomplete, so he fantasizes complete stories of evolutionary genetics whose real truth is the under-girding of unlimited programmes for self-alteration and the commodification of the biosphere. But even were the full story apparently known, how would the fact of evolutionary drift tell him how to modify himself, and how would he be sure this was a pure goalless drift unless a legitimation of random modification, obedient only to choice, was just what he secretly sought out?

Manent, like many others, contrasts these phenomena with the antique pursuit of natural virtue, but he also contrasts them with the Augustinian idea of the rule of grace. Grace itself, for Augustine in the *Confessions*, was at once gift and rule: it 'orders what it gives, gives what it orders'. But just as the market divides purely contracted exchange from the realm of the free-giving that expects no return, so also the liberal state sunders ruling which gives nothing, but formally and disinterestedly mediates, from a free giving which can no longer command the other. Thereby though, both rule and gift are, from a Christian point of view, denatured. 'Rule', means for theology, 'provide good order' and so to give something. Indeed for

Augustine and Aquinas it means to give ruling itself – to give a share in ruling. When my mind rules my body, my body acquires the habit of self-control, so body also commands body. Similarly, political rule is for Aquinas *communication,* an imparting of power which must take place if it can, else power falsely reserved will fester.[20] This means that every time one rules, one *loses* ruling in part except in the sense of fully retaining the capacity for ruling, or even increasing it through its very exercise. Even in the case of God he loses no rule, because in utterly sharing it, he is sharing ruling, which is in itself a mode of sharing. Thus God the supreme ruler is within himself an imparting of the *Verbum* and *Donum.* But liberal sovereignty is not like this: because it gives nothing, it entirely reserves all power to itself as a sinister stagnant pond of pointless possibilities.

One can see the contrast by a brief illustration. Prior to 1548, the kings of France gave privileges of trade and manufacture to the city of Lyons after visiting it and first receiving tributes of presents and pageants from the city. The king, though superior, thereby acknowledged Lyons's share in his ruling; hence when he delegated ruling power to the city he appropriately received something back from it. The rule of the traditional anointed king was therefore not just a giving, it could even be exercised as a mode of gift-*exchange* in which to some extent the city obligated the monarch. But in the year 1548 Henry II decided that the partying had to stop: he stayed in Paris, received nothing and merely issued the privileges as written documents. Lyons understood that what it had received it might also not have received, that it was no longer ruled, but commanded. That what it had received were no longer gifts but devices of state policy, manipulated by murderous *politiques.*[21]

In such modes the traditional ruler shared his sovereignty and thereby ruled. His sovereignty – whether that of medieval kings or Roman senators – was not just a lone impotent word prior to action; it was also already an action: the king really went to Lyons. In this way the sovereign was always already an executive. The executive forces that existed apart from him were multiple and beneath him, mediating his crowned rule. But under fully developed liberalism, starting with Montesquieu, the sovereign is apparently qualified at the centre by the independent executive.[22] Is this really wise and benign? Not entirely; in some ways it is highly sinister. For the fact that the executive is now at the centre confirms and does *not* qualify the monopoly of sovereign power at the centre. For it confirms and further reveals that this sovereign commands and does not truly rule or give. Just because the sovereign word is absolute and empty, speaking only the freedom of the individual and its own freedom, none of its words *ever mean anything,* and therefore never devolve in action. For precisely this reason, the very sovereignty of the sovereign needs the supplementation of the executive. The latter must both interpret and act, although both aspects are bound in the circumstances to involve a certain individual arbitrariness. For the modern executive does not share in ordering, and therefore what he gives is blind, banal and empty like a fact or a bare univocal existence.

From the outset – despite the protestations from different political wings of John Adams and Thomas Jefferson – the American division of powers was intended to balance out oligarchic forces and limit the power of the masses. The federalists, like Machiavelli, envisaged a republic sustaining its strength and freedom by the muted encouragement of internal agonisms. (For this reason Leo Strauss was wrong in ostensibly regarding the American principle as the opposite of the Machiavellian one although the current actions of his many students now in power suggests that they may have had direct access to one of those opposite esoteric meanings of which he was so fond.)[23] It is not surprising then, that the republic defined as regulatively free should go on needing external enemies, nor that the sustaining of the internal agonism should seek out endless new frontiers. As with ancient Rome, as Augustine in effect diagnosed, the empire may have corrupted the *republic*, but it was still the republic with its agonistic and defensive understanding of virtue that generated the empire. (In any case talk of a specifically 'republican empire' has a long pedigree in the United States: for example, in some writings of Walt Whitman.)[24]

I am of course hinting at reasons why liberal democracy, with and not against its own nature, can turn internally oppressive and externally expansionist. But surely I am missing out on a whole dimension here regarding our present global troubles? This is the renewed role of religion. What has that to do with the historical course of liberalism?

Well, here again Manent is of considerable help. He argues, as we have seen, that liberals themselves have sooner or later become aware of the empty 'hall of mirrors' factor that I have invoked. He gives the crucial example of the period in French thought after the French Revolution and before 1848. Suddenly, in that period, *all* political thought – conservative, liberal and now socialist – became obsessively *religious* in one way or another.[25] Why this break with 18th-century norms? Manent argues that once Rousseau had defined the liberal individual as pure will, it became clear that this will is in excess either of the economic market (civil society) or the sovereign political state, precisely because these two will nothing, or else will each other in a futile circle. Suddenly what Rousseau's 'general will' willed became the nation, history, society or culture. Because there was a certain new realization (especially in Tocqueville – and there are British and German parallels to this) that politics could not be *about* anything without the recognition of superhuman norms, the nation, history, etc., started to be imbued with quasi-religious values. These were brutally deconstructed much later by Charles Péguy – who showed, for example, that the historical point of view suppresses the inexplicability (beyond a certain point) of every historical event by fantasizing an exhaustive circumstantial or causal account (one thinks of those admirable 1,000 page *Annales* volumes ultimately inspired by Michelet whom Péguy partially had in mind) which idolatrously seems to mimic the mind of God. Likewise, Péguy saw that the very idea of sociology supposed that one had fantasized a kind of eternal normative society which displaced the function of God himself.[26]

Manent follows Péguy in dismissing the 'quasi-religions' of historicism, sociology, *Bildung* and national development. However, his assumptions regarding the supposed Christian dilemma, means that like Leo Strauss (who is a strong influence), but for somewhat different reasons, he continues to espouse both political liberalism and political economy as better than any possible alternative, even though, again as with Strauss, the antique *polis* with an elite in charge remains for him the irreplaceable guide to genuine human nature. To both Strauss and Manent one can here validly pose the question: does not this mean that one requires *slavery* (at least in some form) to reveal true human nature and sustain the pursuit of real excellence, not negative freedom alone? (And this may well be another esoteric view covertly entertained by the scions of the neo-Roman empire, north as well as south of the Potomac.) And why is a more widely dispersed pursuit of excellence not in principle possible? Why outside the sheltered bubble of the American campus is resignation to the mass pursuit of only negative freedom inevitable?

In addition, one can point out that, while Manent is refusing the quasi-religions of sociology and historicism, he is still embracing the quasi-religions of the Machiavellian Hobbesian republic and the Hobbesian–Lockean translation of theological voluntarism. By contrast, the new early-19th-century attention to society, history and culture sometimes – as with Coleridge, the Oxford Movement the Catholic Tubingen School, Chateaubriand, Lamennais and Ballanche in France and the French and English Christian socialists (Pierre, Buchez, Ludlow, Ruskin, Thomas Hancock) – involved a genuine recovery of Christianity which newly stressed both its links to poetic, not literal language, and the Patristic idea of the Church as a new kind of society.[27] These efforts were taken up again by Péguy, and setting to one side his often unjustifiable nationalism, it is hard to agree with Manent that he is *confusing* the mystical with the political. To the contrary, Manent is here misled by his own failure to see how grace in the Middle Ages already sought to sanctify the material realm; hence, he also fails to see that much 19th-century neo-Gothicism tried to take this process further. Christianity has gradually redefined virtue as existing primarily in the charitable exchange of gift throughout the cosmos and human society and between the creation and its maker. In this way the invocation of grace has democratized virtue and sug- gested a deepening embodiment of this virtue in the social order as a truly Christian project. Indeed without such an embodying, how can day-to-day life perpetually raise us up into the supernatural?

Already in the Middle Ages John Wyclif had said that, since God is One, *whenever* he gives his natural gifts, he also gives us his supernatural gift.[28] Wyclif, building on the more valid aspects of the Franciscan vision thereby suggested that all ownership and rule is by grace (by borrowing from God) and that the justification of both property and government is communicative distribution: just as the priest receives the gift of dispensing the sacrament in order to induct others into the *common* life of grace, so, also, the property owner owns in order to induct others into the common material life and the ruler rules in order to induct others into the shared life of society.[29] This was a valid radicalisation of Augustine, and it was a pity that Wyclif's Franciscan separation of 'spiritual' ownership of the life of interior grace from material *dominium* reinstituted a duality which his theory of *dominium* by grace tended to negate. Because of this duality he was led into a doubtful Erastianism which disallowed any actual material ownership to the Church.

The same duality sets in motion again the voluntarist logic of the other English Franciscan legacy which Wyclif in general resisted: if the Church is too pure to 'own' things, then owning is thereby downgraded and a drastically secular domain is encouraged.[30] By contrast, if owning is by grace, then a just appropriation ought to permit genuine private property which is thereby not impure and can be ascribed (as by Aquinas) to Adam in paradise.[31] The same consideration applies also to a non-coercive ruling linked to a natural hierarchy of talents: such a rule also could be exercised by the unfallen Adam.

However, the later English thinkers John Fortescue (in the 15th century) and Richard Hooker (in the early 17th century) tended creatively to blend somewhat Wyclif-like notions of owning and ruling by grace and gift-giving with Thomist notions of natural possession and natural hierarchy. This allowed them further to elaborate Aquinas's own synthesis of Aristotle and Augustine: there is a natural 'ownership' based on use and a 'political government' that existed before the Fall, founded in sociability, differential endowments of ability and consensual association (the 'Whig' element that Aquinas already adds to Aristotle). On the other hand, somewhat arbitrary property ownership and 'royal' government are necessities consequent upon the Fall. Nevertheless they are both for Fortescue and Hooker founded in natural law, not the *ius gentium*, since they both perpetuate, in straitened circumstances, the prelapsarian goals of communication of material goods and the benefits of peaceful order. Likewise the natural principle of tacit consent is perpetuated in the importance given by both thinkers to 'parliaments, councils and the like assemblies' (Hooker). Here then a certain line of English political theory linked Germanic common law principles of free association with a Latin and realist sense of intrinsic equity – avoiding the rational barbarism of nominalism and voluntarism. This same synthesis (with Thomist input) avoided also the ambiguity of Wyclif's Franciscan-derived spiritualism, along with his drift (albeit less marked than with Ockham) to a notion of subjective not objective right. (This notion in Wyclif is linked to the idea both of a sheerly material pure possession and to a certain Pelagian independently human reception of grace. It is also completely linked to his very extreme, almost Platonic mode of realism. Here the shared essence is *so* common and hypostasized that it leaves the individual *external* to the essence: so radically free and singular.)[32]

Wyclif's notions had politically radical consequences: the heir of a king *not* ruling by giving should be deposed; the heir of a property not dispensing its bounty should be ousted. In this scheme then there was nothing merely otherworldly about the impact of grace, but these worldly consequences were a logical elaboration of Augustinian principles.

In many ways the 19th-century Christian socialists took up again the spirit of Wyclif, but, whereas he had spoken of ruling and owning by receiving the divine gift and passing it on, they now spoke also of the *worker* as receiving the gift of craft and passing it on, and furthermore argued that all human ruling, owning, agriculture and trading are kinds of working: not only a receiving of the gift of creation, but an extension of the divine creative process itself.[33] These thematics are in fact supremely well summed up by Péguy.[34]

But in all this, Manent seems only to discern a contamination of religion with an attempt to fill the empty heart of liberalism with the pseudo-religion of society, history and culture. It is exactly here though that Christian socialism can contest his (very subtle and chastened) Christian liberalism. For if one argues that the Middle Ages already practiced and promoted a political rule by giving, a mode of freedom in which one gives what one commands, and commands what one gives, then there was no inherent Christian problem that needed the liberal invention of the empty negative freedom of a mythical individual. Grace *can* validly be incarnated as the exchange of gifts according to a mutual and continuous discovery of what should be given and what should be received. In shaping and constructing new gifts, we constantly rediscern our human teleology; here Manent also fails to see that Christianity had already historicized nature, since the fullness of human nature only arrived with the event of the God-man and is further unfolded in the life of the Church. Christianity does not inevitably encourage liberal democracy; yet it always should encourage another mode of democracy, linked to the idea of the infallible presence of the Holy Spirit in the whole body of the Church and by extension humanity across all times and places. (Since all human society in some degree foreshadows *ecclesia* and in this way always mediates some supernatural grace.) Unlike liberal democracy, this Christian democracy has a hierarchic dimension: the transmission of the gift of truth across time, the reservation of a non-democratic educative sphere concerned with finding the truth, not ascertaining majority opinion. Without this sphere democracy will not be able to debate about the truth, but will always be swayed by propaganda: mass representation will represent only itself not the represented. Christian democracy though should also be Christian socialism – not the somewhat limited Christian democracy of so-called Christian-Democratic parties. (Or, one can say, it should be 'Christian social democracy' and one should add that there can be Jewish and Islamic democracy also and that in many parts of the world – France perhaps imminently – we shall need hybrids. I believe that within the more metaphysically realistic Platonic–Aristotelian and mystical versions of these three monotheisms, a large shared social ground can emerge.) It should not be resigned to the existence of poverty as a field for the reactive exercise of personal charity; instead it should see the eradication of poverty as the chance for the fuller arrival of a festive charitable exchange.

I have been writing intermittently about the nature of the 19th-century revival of religion and its links with the dilemmas of liberalism. In the later 19th century though, the quasi-religious nature of this tendency became more marked and one had the paradox of secular religions: notably of positivism and Marxist socialism. In the latter case, Marx perpetuated Rousseau's attempt to discover something substantive within the immanent terms of liberalism itself: the gap between individual and state could be closed, because the general productive will of all was to be identified with the general productive will of each. This, however, elevates the emptiness and purposelessness and illusory transparency of production as such: this general pursuit of production is bound to result in tyranny and is only a variant, after all, of liberal political economy. Positivism was both more honest and more sinister: it promoted at once liberal science and the formal inescapability of the rule of the will, with indifference as to content. Inevitably, positivism mutated into fascism, Nazism and Stalinism (which had a strong component of Georgian fascism: the Georgian *Khvost* carried out a purge of Jews and Leninists and it was Hitler who broke his pact with Stalin, not *vice versa*). These phenomena were bizarrely both ultra-modern and atavistically mystical. But this contradiction is only the extreme and most telling variant of the attempt to fill the empty heart of liberalism with society, culture, history, etc. It is now an attempt made in strictly immanent terms consistent with liberalism itself: thus the new dark heart espoused is patently arbitrary, even to many of its espousers. If it is a myth to supplement formal emptiness, it is also itself a myth of apocalyptic emptiness – a myth of will, of the will to power, which reaches back into our animality under the banner of race.

Since 1945 and 1990, however, liberal democracy has been restored. So what happened to the great endeavour from 1800 to 1865 to infuse psychic and bodily content into liberalism's hall of mirrors? The attempt seemed discredited by totalitarianism. This is partly why, since 1970, we have seen the reinstatement of 18th-century modes of liberalism, of the pure empty echo-chamber – though it is also in part because the forced submission of capital to the demands of labour was creating a crisis of profitability. But is there any stability here, any Hegelian end of history in liberal mutual recognition of human rights? The answer is no, for several reasons. First of all, between 1945 and 1990 communism still existed. The stability of liberal democracy in the West partly *depended* upon its existence. Why? The answer is that fear of the communist alternative helped to keep capitalism reasonable – it tended to protect both trade union rights and the welfare state. Also it gave to the West a binding purpose: oppose the gigantomachy of totalitarian regimes.

After the collapse of communism we had exactly twelve short years of liberal democratic stability. It seems then that it cannot really bear its own hegemony. Without the external state socialist alternative to both modify and negatively define it, the central *aporia* of liberalism tends to reappear: which is primary, the representing state or the represented market? In Europe, once again, the 'middle' of society and history has been reinterpreted, this time as the project of Europe itself, whose nature and fate remain very uncertain. But once more we note a certain neo-Gothicism: already Europe has become a bewildering maze of interlocking and overlapping jurisdictions, in some ways once again like Christendom with a relative disregard for nation-state sovereignty, although the question of its submission to a sovereignty writ large definitely remains. Meanwhile, the United States, which was only ever a *nation* state through racist attempts to invent a 'white' nation finds its statehood and economic hegemony in dire crisis: undercut by other rising nations or transnational political realities, by international corporations and by those using the free market and freedom of information only to subvert the market and the trade in knowledge. (For example, the US recently stemmed the decline of its manufacturing base by encouragement of the inflow of foreign capital; this, however, has generated a massive and unprecedented national debt. At the same time, a long-term response to over-production in the face of rival producers overseas has been the diversion of capital into finance; this in turn, however, has caused a 'realization' crisis – there is too little that one can viably invest in. Both the resisting of creditors and search for new investment fields tends to dictate an imperial solution.[35] The United States' response, perhaps inevitably given its history, and the nature of its polity, is to seek to safeguard itself by exporting itself and rendering itself a globally pervasive reality. Here economic, political and symbolic dominance are inseparable. If the increasingly free market is potentially vulnerable to those increasingly disadvantaged by it, then it must be extended everywhere; as it is vulnerable and porous it must also be *politically* imposed everywhere and relentlessly policed. Finally, since neither the market nor policing can suppress opinion and acting on opinion, the American market way of life, the spectacle of its capitalist order, must be ceaselessly displayed with every product, every police manoeuvre. This is the more possible because, increasingly, America is less an actual place with roots and history than it is a virtual microcosm of the globe. By one set of statistics, it is the most powerful nation on the earth, by another – for example, infant mortality – it is just another third world country. Within the United States, a mass of dispossessed are kept in thrall by the image of America – by the idea of aspiration, by the notion that failure is their fault and yet contradictorily that tomorrow may still bring a golden dawn.

However, the myth of America, the myth of the market, is not enough. America and the market must *stand* for something – otherwise one would once again have fascism. It is clear that we do not have this, but something new and different. State socialism, positivism, fascism and Nazism all embraced, but severely qualified, the values of the market and of abstract production. Since 1970 though, we have had a revived and purified liberalism, a neo-capitalism. This neo-capitalism, in postmodern style, openly exults in the liberal hall of mirrors. However, the pure empty reflection is always in some sense impossible – not necessarily the real, but at least more positive symbolic values always cast their shadow, even in the fairground. So neo-liberalism does not seek, like fascism, to fill liberalism's empty heart with darkness; rather it rejoices in this emptiness and yet *still* at some level seeks to escape it. Not to fill the middle, but at once to celebrate and yet *exit* the vicious circle of representing and representation.

This, in my view, is just the role of fundamentalist or else extreme evangelical Protestantism. Everywhere a revival of the latter has accompanied the emergence of neo-capitalism, or else Jewish, Islamic and even Buddhist and Hindu parodies of Protestant evangelicalism have performed the same job.[36] Fundamentalism has its roots partially in theological voluntarism – so here we see a certain return to the religious roots of liberalism itself. God has given us the creation for our free use; he handed over a material and social world to private ownership without gift and to merely formal and contractual regulation, yet this regulation itself echoes the arbitrary covenants God has established for our salvation. A contract is literal and unambiguous, supposedly. So is God's word to us, supposedly. Here the freedom of the State and of the individual remain, and remain unbridged; yet they are sacralized as echoing the sovereign freedom of God. This is not classical fascism, but if one wants to speak of a new 'religious market fascism' then I would not demur.

It is not an accident that this tendency is most marked in the United States and has its headquarters there. For in a sense the US *never had* a 19th century – never had historicism and the cult of society and culture and socialist populism. It remains in a way up to the present 18th century in character, but a specific, different 18th century noted by Tocqueville. Moreover, this difference has itself always bifurcated: on the one hand, Tocqueville noted that the most liberal country was in fact *not* liberal at all – not most essentially driven by the market, by the state, nor even by the trade in polite civility that he also recorded.[37] At bottom, because Americans were the real settlers of Eden, they had given the lie to liberalism, by showing that at the outset lay not the lone individual but rather the art of association – always for concrete, and so religious, purposes. The United States was first of all a bizarrely plural neo-Gothic multitude of churches and sects. Here was the source of a genuine Christian republicanism and of the exchange of real gifts. And this source remains today. However, Tocqueville also noted the tendency of American religion towards the *ersatz*: people embraced religion in the US he suggested often for half-admitted *pragmatic* reasons – *this* is the American version of filling up the empty heart of liberalism.[38] Religion in the US, he observed, tends to be simplified and non-intellectual, popular rather than learned (in Europe today it is just the opposite), acting as a safety valve to ensure that Americans, unlike Frenchmen and women do not use their freedom to question bourgeois ethical values which indeed became in America further banalized. Religion in the US had already decided on all the big questions and this tended (and tends) to shore up the bizarre notion that the American constitution has decided forever on all the big political questions.

As I have already indicated, there are today Islamic and Jewish partial parallels to this quintessentially Protestant fundamentalism. Islamic fundamentalism tends to be urban and middle class; opposed to material and sacramental mediation of the sacred, pro-capitalist, and textually literalist. Conservative Zionism likewise qualifies Judaism to embrace a modern race-based state, the unrestricted market economy and a relentlessly literal reading of the Hebrew Bible, which ties prophecy to land in perpetuity.

All these fundamentalisms are modern. Modern science insists on literalism as regards facts, and Protestant fundamentalism was born (around 1900) in a construal of the Bible as presenting a parallel universe of revealed facts alongside the realm of natural facts.[39] Catholic, orthodox Christianity, by contrast, insists that the abiding truth of the Old Testament is allegorical: literal violence points figuratively to a future revelation of embodied peace in Christ.[40] In science, the literal, observable thing tends to incite dissection, vivisection, stasis and death; this alone permits control and regularity. Likewise, in religion, a revealed word which is both arbitrary and literal can only be ascertained in its instance when it is not the communication of gift, but rather the imposition of violence, of an ending and a death-dealing. Science and fundamentalism can then readily collude with each other.

Hence today the world is increasingly governed and fought over by a fearful combination of literal readers of the Hebrew scriptures together with out-and-out post-modern liberal scientific nihilists who shamelessly rejoice in the ceaseless destruction of every rooted and ancient tradition and even the roots and long habits of *nature* herself.

So, if today there is a problem of the recrudescence of intolerant religion, this is not a problem that liberalism can resolve, but rather a problem that liberalism tends to engender. We cannot oppose it in the name of liberal human rights, because this notion also revolves in a futile circle: these rights are supposedly natural, yet inert uncreated nature has never heard of them. They only exist when the State proclaims them, yet the State alone cannot legitimate them, else they cease to be natural and so general and objective.

A person's right is only a reality when recognized by another. But in that case, the *duty* of the other is the inner reality of right. Why should a person not be tortured? Because he owns his body by right? But in that case the liberal state will always exert its right of eminent domain in an emergency when the 'rights' of the majority can be said to justify this, as today in the case of the pursuit of terrorists and 'terrorists'. Talal Asad has pointed out that the liberal idea that torture 'transgresses human rights' has *in no way* prevented nearly all liberal States from resorting to torture. The real difference from non-liberal states is that they *torture in secret*. Asad explains this in terms of the history of the West's attitude both to evidence and pain: once, direct confession was regarded – quite reasonably, since circumstances and witnesses may always mislead – as the crucial factor in truth, in a period when neither the inflicting nor the suffering of measured pain (witness asceticism) was regarded so negatively as it is today. From the Enlightenment onwards, though, increased horror at pain, and its exhibition in an era now more confined to notions of imminent and palpable happiness, was conjoined with a greater trust (linked to an empiricist sensibility) in circumstantial evidence: a trust which then and ever since has in fact led to horrendous miscarriages of justice. This betrays the fact that at bottom liberalism cares more about ravages to the body then violations of the spirit. The former nevertheless, as Asad so precisely notes, *are* still admitted, and in fact on an *unparalleled* scale where they can be quantified and made part of a utilitarian calculus: thus reasons of state in modernity have permitted massive civilian casualties in war, and continue to permit for the same reason torture in secret (and now in the open) – in fact an augmentation of pain's intensity where the circumstances are deemed to warrant this.[41]

A person should not be tortured rather because of her intrinsic value, because she resides in the image of God or something like that. Such a view recognizes that spiritual and bodily integrity are inseparable, and that the body is more than a possessed domain which may be troubling to its mental owner. For the former view the body confesses as much as the mind, and therefore must not be violated – for the sake of truth as well as mercy. Torture may be often carried out by religions, but only genuine religion, not liberalism, can promise a rationale to stop torture.

Likewise, there is no 'right' to freedom of religious opinion or expression, as if truth were something one could own and develop at random; rather, truth requires free consent else it is not understood, and a freely consented-to partial error displays more truth than an obviously or subtly coerced, or even a mechanically habitual opinion. But this principle that truth requires free consent, that profound truth is irreducibly subjective, is *itself* entirely religious: indeed fully at home only, one could argue, in Judaism, Christianity and Islam. As with the prohibition of torture, only the religious notions of these traditions which insist on 'consent of the heart to truth' fully safeguard free-consent, since if this is only a 'property we have in our person' a government will always appropriate this private property for 'general use' in an emergency – suspending religious liberties along with other freedoms. Indeed Asad also argues that in a situation where biotechnical companies 'own' human genetic material, the question of when the human is in the subjective 'owning' position, including owning rights, and when he is in the object-position of a thing possessed, becomes itself something that only the market decides. Hence it becomes clear that the entrepreneurial capitalist rights which international human rights agreements also underwrite are the only real serious rights of rights discourse.[42]

What really guarantees human dignity and freedom, I have just argued, is something like the idea that the individual is in the image of God. This image is for Christians restored to luster by baptism and chrism. Christic anointing renders us all kings, all rulers. As kings we are not impotently free with no necessary influence, but more realistically we are dangerously free with inevitable influence. We are free as givers: to give a gift is to run the risk of violence; it is always something of an imposition. But if every free act proceeds outwards it is itself both always a gift and something of an imposition. Nobody ever asked me 'to say just that', 'do just that' and it *may* hurt, indeed it may rankle forever. Inversely, though, we *cannot* be free only by trying to dominate: every time I act and give I am somewhat bound to the people who suffer my actions, receive my gifts.

For this reason, Pope John Paul II has stressed in his political thinking, as Russell Hittenger has pointed out, that while Christian kings have mostly vanished, the kingship of all remains the key to Christian politics. For Christianity the human being is a *Basilikon Zoon* (Eusebius of Caeserea) before he or she is a *Zoon Politikon*. Each Christian occupies a *munus*, which is an office linked to gift in the sense of talent. This talent exists for others as well as herself – it must be communicated. Thus the Pope points out, in a way that seems commensurate with Wyclif, that human political rule commences not just in Adam's dominion over nature, but also in the mutual bestowing on each other of Adam and Eve. After the Fall, this mutuality and bestowing were contaminated and women especially were subordinated and degraded. But Christ the King restores to us the idea that to rule is to serve – he gives us to us again the *munus regale* itself.[43]

Today then, we need to surpass liberal democracy and search again for the common good in ceaseless circulation and creative development, a search that may involve laws, but more fundamentally involves charity beyond the law. Our poles of reference should not be the fantasized pure individual nor the pure sovereign state (natural or globalized) nor the pure free market. Instead we should both locate and form real groups pursuing real goods and exchanging real gifts amongst themselves and with each other according to measures judged to be intrinsically fair. We need to acknowledge the place and point of families, schools, localities, towns, associations for genuine production and trade (not the mere pursuit of profit), and transnational bodies.[44] However, if we conceive this within immanence or theological voluntarism (as with Calvinist versions of corporatism: Kuyper, etc.) then these groups will themselves be reduced to quasi-individual mutually contracting entities and we will be back in the empty liberal echo-chamber.

Instead all these groups can communicate and exchange with each other only if all are conceived as operating under grace; only if we can come to regard corporate bodies as receiving the objective and subjective gifts of created realities that are already imbued with pre-human meaning;only if we can conceive the work of these bodies as further realising the natural order in order to offer the gift of Creation back to a God who is no arbitrary sovereign but a giver who can order what he gives because it is intrinsically true, good and beautiful.

Only a global liturgical polity can save us now from literal violence.

Notes

1   Pierre Manent, *An Intellectual History of Liberalism*, trans. Rebecca Balinski (Princeton, NJ: Princeton UP, 1995), Ch. 1 'Europe and the Theologico-Political Problem', pp. 3–10.

2   See Oliver O'Donovan and Joan Lockwood O'Donovan, *From Irenaeus to Grotius: A Sourcebook in Christian Political Thought*, 100–1625 (Grand Rapids, MI: Eerdmans, (1999) pp. 231–40, 362–87; Henri de Lubac, 'L'autorité de L'Eglise en matière temporelle' and 'Augustinisme Politique?' in idem, *Théologies d'Occasion* (Paris: Desclée de Brouver, 1986), pp. 217–40.

3   Pierre Manent, *The City of Man*, trans. Marc A. LePain (Princeton, NJ: Princeton UP, 1998), pp. 25, 200–201.

4   Manent, *An Intellectual History of Liberalism* (see Note 1), Ch. 11, 'Machiavelli and Fecundity of Evil', pp. 10–20.

5   O'Donovan and O'Donovan, *From Irenaeus to Grotius* (see Note 2), pp. 1–228; Oliver O'Donovan, *The Desire of the Nations: Rediscovering the Roots of Political Theology* (Cambridge: Cambridge University Press, 1999), pp. 193–285. For the point about St. Paul and ruling by judgement alone, see p. 148. For the *oikos* and *paideia*, see John Milbank, *Theology and Social Theory* (Oxford: Blackwell, 1991), p. 399.

6   For a synthesis of research on this question, see Catherine Pickstock, *After Writing: On the Liturgical Consummation of Philosophy* (Oxford: Blackwell, 1998), pp. 140–58.

7   See O'Donovan and O'Donovan, *From Irenaeus to Grotius* (see Note 2), pp. 169–231; Ernest H. Kantorowicz, *The King's Two Bodies: A Study in Medieval Political Theology* (Princeton, NJ: Princeton UP, 1997), pp. 42–273.

8   See John Milbank, *Theology and Social Theory: Beyond Secular Reason* (Oxford: Blackwell, 1993), pp. 9–27.

9   Manent, *An Intellectual History of Liberalism* (see Note 1), pp. 5–7; Augustine Thompson, *Cities of God: The Religion of the Italian Communes, 1125–1325* (Penn State, PA: Penn State University Press, 2005).

10 Dante, *Monarchy*, ed. Prue Shaw (Cambridge: Cambridge U.P., 1996), esp. III xvi, pp. 91–4.

11 Manent, *The City of Man* (see Note 3), pp. 200–201; *S.T.* II-II Q. 129 a3 AD 4; Q 161 a1.

12 Milbank, *Theology and Social Theory*, (see Note 8), pp. 359–62; *S.T.* II.-II. Q8 a1; Q23 aa 1–7.

13 De Lubac, (see Note 2 above); John Milbank, *Being Reconciled: Ontology and Pardon* (London: Routledge, 2003), p. 105.

14 See Pickstock, *After Writing* (see Note 6), pp. 121–40.

15 See O'Donovan and O'Donovan, *From Irenaeus to Grotius* (see Note 2), 423–76, 517–30; Milbank, *Theology and Social Theory* (see Note 8), pp. 9–27; John Neville Figgis, *From Gerson to Grotius, 1414–1625* (Cambridge: Cambridge University Press, 1907) and *The Divine Right of Kings* (Cambridge: Cambridge University Press, 1914). And see Charles-Louis de Montesquieu, *Lettres Persanes*, ed. Jean Goldzink (Paris: Presses Universitaires Francaises, 1989) where he displays a certain fascination for the absolutism of the seraglio. The *Encyclopédie* speaks of Islam as a more rational faith, though Voltaire eventually came to see it as intrinsically despotic. I am grateful for discussions with David Hart here.

16 See Isiduro G. Manzano O.F.M., 'Individuo y Sociedad en Duns Escoto' in *Antonianium*, Jan.–March 2001 LXXVI, fasc. I, pp. 43–79.

17 See Milbank, *Theology and Social Theory* (see Note 8).

18 See Manent, *An Intellectual History of Liberalism* (see Note 1), Chapters III–X, and conclusion, pp. 20–119; Manent, *The City of Man* (see Note 3), esp. Part Two, pp. 111–207; Pierre Manent, *Modern Liberty and its Discontents*, ed. Daniel J. Maloney and Paul Seaton (Lanham, MD: Rowman and Littlefield, 1998), pp. 79–117, 197–231.

19 Manent, *An Intellectual History of Liberalism* (see Note 1), pp. 65–119. Manent disallows that Rousseau is a liberal, since he seeks, albeit within modern, liberal terms, once again a mode of the positive liberty of the ancients, a coincidence of individual with civic virtue. However, the coincidence, whereby the liberty of each would be immediately the liberty of all, is still put forward by Rousseau in terms of modern negative liberty of pure choice and survival whether of the city or the individual. Certainly Manent admits that Rousseau and Marx after him were trying to resolve the *aporia* of liberalism – which comes first, represented civil society, or the representing state? – and to this extent their 'ideological' excesses were the consequences of liberal presuppositions. Yet because, at the limit, he himself accepts these presuppositions, Rousseau and Marx became for him non-liberals by virtue of their continued quest for antique *sittlichkeit* in modern guise. Yet if this quest leads logically to terror

(and one can agree with Manent it does) and the problem is the perverted hybrid of liberalism with *sittlich keit*, then the fault *may* lie with the impossibility of positive liberty in modern circumstances, or it *may* lie with liberalism itself, since an aporetic reality must periodically (or even ceaselessly) seek to resolve the dilemmas it generates. The latter view appears more logical, and on this understanding Rousseau and Marx represent part of the inevitable *continuum* of liberal philosophy. Manent's own Straussian perspective which appears to combine a tragic recognition of the truth but impossibility of antique virtue, with a resignation to liberal *aporias*, appears every bit as 'postmodern' as the views of the *soixante-huitards* he would reject since he is resigned to a kind of endless undecidability. But if this is indeed the end of history, it will always generate new perturbations beyond this end, and new post-liberal terrorisms. For Montesquieu, see Manent, *An Intellectual History* (see Note 1), pp. 53–65; for de Tocqueville, see Manent, *An Intellectual History*, pp. 103–14, and Alexis de Tocqueville, *Democracy in America*, trans. George Lawrence (New York: Doubleday, 1969), p. 235.

20   Thomas Aquinas, *Contra Impugnantes*, I cap 4 para 14. Here he cites Augustine in *De Doctrina Christiana*: 'Everything that is not lessened by being imparted, is not, if it be possessed without being communicated, possessed as it ought to be possessed.' Russell Hittenger notes that Aquinas always mirrors 'every analogous use of the word *societas* by uses of the word *communicatio*: *communicatio oeconomica, communicatio spiritualis, communicatio civilis*, and so forth.' – see Hittenger's unpublished article, 'The *Munus Regale* in John Paul II's Political Theology', p. 24.

21   See Natalie Zemon Davis, *The Gift in Sixteenth Century France* (Madison, WI: University of Wisconsin Press, 2000), pp. 90–95.

22   One can contrast Montesquieu with James Harrington (the cavalier turned republican; never a roundhead) on this point. For Harrington 'the Senate' is not a sovereign legislative power sundered from the executive; it is rather an aristocratic assembly of the wise that offers disinterested advice to the sovereign democratic power. But the constitution of the United States was finally based more on Montesquieu than on Harrington. See James Harrington 'A System of Politics' Chap. V, 28–32, esp. 28, in idem., (ed. J. G. A. Pocock), *The Commonwealth of Oceana and a System of Politics*, Cambridge: Cambridge University Press, 1992: 'If a council capable of debate has also the result, it is oligarchy. If an assembly capable of the result has debate also, it is anarchy. Debate in a council not capable of result, and result in an assembly not capable of debate is democracy'. Hence democracy, as opposed to anarchy for Harrington/ Toland contains an educatively 'aristocratic' moment.

23   See Milbank, *Being Reconciled* (see Note 13), pp. 192–3, and Ted V. McAllister, *Revolt Against Modernity: Leo Strauss, Eric Voegelin and the search for a postliberal order* (Kansas City: University Press of Kansas, 1995), pp. 160–61. See also Seymour M. Hersch's 'Annals of National Security' column in *The New Yorker*, 12 May 2003, entitled 'Selective Intelligence: How the Pentagon Outwitted the CIA,' 44–52. Hersch points out that many of the neo-conservative 'cabal' who have set up their own intelligence network – Abram Schutz, Paul Wolfowitz, William Kristol and Stephen Camtone are Strauss's pupils and that Schutz together with Gary Schmitt had already developed in print a 'Straussian' approach to intelligence gathering, which of course stressed that these are always more hidden secrets than one imagines. These are the very people who *overrode* the professional expertise of the CIA and the DIA to insist that Iraq had massive concealed stores of Weapons of Mass Destruction! Pointing out the predominance of German and German-Jewish names here is surely not racist, but rather a necessary indication of profoundly terrible and tragic historical ironies at work. Strauss was a German Jew who fled Hitler, yet his heirs along with many others have helped to insinuate an element of Germanic authoritarianism and paranoia at the heart of an Anglo-Saxon polity. Nor has Israel – perhaps from the outset – escaped this taint. Meanwhile a chastened Germany now has much politically to teach the Anglo-Saxon world.

24   See David Brooks' article on Whitman's essay 'Democratic Vistas' in *The Atlantic Monthly*, May 2003, pp. 32–3. Brooks cites Whitman: 'So will individuality, and unimpeded branchings, flourish best under imperial republican forms.' Brooks appears however – like increasingly many left of centre supporters of the US Democratic Party – unperturbed by this sort of rhetoric.

25 Manent, *An Intellectual History of Liberalism* (see Note 1), pp. 80–114. See also Milbank, *Theology and Social Theory* (see Note 8), pp. 66–71, 196–203, 408.

26 Pierre Manent, 'Charles Péguy: Between Political Faith and Faith', in idem, *Modern Liberty and its Discontents*, (see Note 18), pp. 79–81. And see Romain Rolland, *Péguy*, vol. I (Paris: Albin Michel, 1944), pp. 137–9, 309.

27 Milbank, *Theology and Social Theory* (see Note 8), pp. 66–71, 196–203, 408; Alexander Dru, *The Church in the Nineteenth Century: Germany 1800–1918* (London: Burns and Oates, 1963). One can also note here that Augustine's new definition of a *res publica* as forgathered around the object of its desire *already* tends to make the political a sub-category of the social: see Milbank, *Theology and Social Theory*, pp. 400–401.

28 John Wyclif, 'Civil Lordship' Book I, Chap. 7 15 C, in O'Donovan and O'Donovan, *From Irenaeus to Grotius* (see Note 2), p. 488: 'God gives only in the best way of which the recipient is capable; but every righteous man is capable of the best gift in general; so God bestows only in that way, for as long as one is righteous ... and so God cannot give a creature any created good without first giving uncreated good'; Chap. 716c: 'God gives no gifts to man without giving himself as the principal gift?'

29 Wyclif, 'Divine Lordship Book 3 Chap. I 70, Chap. 4 78 a, in O'Donovan and O'Donovan, *From Irenaeus to Grotius* (see Note 2), pp. 487–8.

30 See the O'Donovans' commentary on Wyclif in ibid., pp. 482–7 and O'Donovan, *The Desire of the Nations*, (see Note 5) again on Wyclif at p. 26, and on the ambivalence of Franciscan poverty at p. 207. See also on the same subject Milbank, *Theology and Social Theory*, (see Note 8), pp. 15–16.

31 See Hilaire Belloc, *An Essay on the Restoration of Property* (Norfolk, VA: IHS Press, 2002). Belloc's distributist notions were clearly of more Dominican than Franciscan inspiration.

32 See O'Donovan and O'Donovan, *From Irenaeus to Grotius* (see Note 2), pp. 530–41, 743–57; On Wyclif and the late post-Ockham Oxford neo-realism, see Alain de Libera, *La Querelle des universaux: de Platon à la fin du Moyen Age* (Paris: Editions du Seuil, 1996), pp. 402–10. One can sympathize strongly with O'Donovan's predilection for what one might call 'very early modern' conciliar realists: Fortescue, Nicholas of Cusa, Hooker, etc. In their fusion of Ancient natural law and modern constitution-making they seem to offer an alternative to either the medieval or the modern. But is it correct to speak as he does of 'early modern liberalism' here, and to assimilate such currents to the undoubted liberalism (founded in subjective rights) of Grotius? In these currents there is no subjective right proceeding primarily from the ground of will in the Hobbesian–Lockean sense, and no social contract in the Hobbesian–Lockean sense of an agreement between previously sovereign individuals and establishing a primarily formal legitimacy. Fortescue's 'mystical "compact"' is rather the issuing of the Aristotelian social impulse at the very 'origin' of any conceivable humanity in the collective enterprise of shaping artificial and historically contingent institutions that nevertheless seek to express a substantive equity.

33 See Milbank, *Theology and Social Theory* (see Note 8), pp. 197–200.

34 See Charles Péguy, *Basic Verities*, trans. Ann and Julian Green (London: Kegan Paul), pp. 75–95, 101–19.

35 See Giovanni Arrighi, 'Tracking Global Turbulence' in *New Left Review* 20, 2nd Series, March–April 2003, pp. 5–73.

36 The ongoing researches of Paul Morris (of Victoria University, Wellington, New Zealand) are tending to show this. For further reflections on the relation between religion and the nation-state, and the way the latter always has to rerecruit and define the former, see Talal Asad, *Formulations of the Secular: Christianity, Islam, Modernity* (Stanford, CA: Stanford University Press, 2003).

37 Manent, *An Intellectual History of Liberalism* (see Note 1), pp. 104–5; de Tocqueville, *Democracy in America* (see Note 19), p. 364.

38 Manent, *Modern Liberty and its Discontents* (see Note 18), p. 105.

39 See James Barr, *Fundamentalism* (London: SCM, 1984).

40 See Milbank, *Theology and Social Theory* (see Note 8), p. 20 and John Milbank, Review of M.S. Burrows and Paul Rorem (eds), *Biblical Hermeneutics in Historical Perspective*, *Journal of Theological Studies*, October 1995, vol. 46, Part 2, pp. 660–70.

41   Asad, *Formations of the Secular* (see Note 36), pp. 100–127.

42   Ibid., 127–59.

43   See Hittenger, 'The *Munus Regale*' (see Note 20). And see the Papal encyclicals, *De Familiae Christianae Muneribus*, para. 63; *Lumen Gentium*, para 3b; *Christifidelis Laici*, para. 14.

44   See Hittenger, 'The *Munus Regale*' (see Note 20) for the correct comment that the principle of 'subsidiarity' is *not* a liberal one that means 'do everything that can possibly be done at a local level, only resorting to higher levels or the centre in extreme necessity'. Rather it means 'do everything at the *appropriate* level'. Hence, as Hittenger also says, liberals who think that subsidiarity should be applied to Church government as a liberal principle are wrong, but conservatives who think that it should *not* be applied are also wrong, since it is not averse to hierarchy. Of course, Hittenger and I would probably disagree about 'appropriate levels' in the case of Church government.

Further reading

Asad, Talal, *Formations of the Secular: Christianity, Islam, Modernity*, Stanford CA: Stanford University Press, 2003.
——*Genealogies of Religion: Discipline and Reasons of Power in Christianity and Islam*, Baltimore: The Johns Hopkins University Press, 1993.
Hobbes, Thomas, *Leviathan*, Oxford: Oxford University Press, 2008.
Manent, Pierre, *An Intellectual History of Liberalism*, trans. Balinski, Rebecca, Princeton: Princeton University Press, 1996.
Stout, Jeffret, *The Flight from Authority: Religion, Morality, and the Quest for Autonomy*, Notre Dame, IN: University of Notre Dame Press, 1981

Cavanaugh, William T., *Theopolitical Imagination*, London: T& T Clark, 2003.
——*Being Consumed: Economics and Christian Desire*, Grand Rapids, MI: Wm. B. Eerdmans Publishing Company, 2008.
——*The Myth of Religious Violence*, Oxford: Oxford University Press, forthcoming.
Hauerwas, Stanley, *The Hauerwas Reader*, ed. Michael Cartwright and John Berkman, Durham, NC: Duke University Press, 2001, especially part III.
Scott, Peter and Cavanaugh, William T. (eds), *The Blackwell Companion to Political Theology*, Oxford: Wiley-Blackwell, 2006.

Bell, Daniel, *Liberation after the End of History: The Refusal to Cease Suffering* (Radical Orthodoxy), London: Routledge, 2001.
Cavanaugh, William T., *Torture and the Eucharist: Theology, Politics and the Body of Christ*, Oxford: Wiley-Blackwell, 1998.
Davis, Creston, Milbank, John and Žižek, Slavoj (eds), *Theology and the Political: The New Debate*, Durham, NC: Duke University Press, 2005.
Long, Stephen, *Divine Economy: Theology and the Market* (Radical Orthodoxy), London: Routledge, 2000.
O'Donovan, Oliver, *The Desire of the Nation: Rediscovering the Roots of Political Theology*, Cambridge: Cambridge University Press, new edn 2008.

Questions

1. Is liberal 'tolerance' of religion in western Europe and the US in fact liberal 'indifference' to religion? If so, what are the consequences?
2. How, according to Cavanaugh, should the Church overcome its confinement to the 'private' sphere?
3. What, for Milbank, are the problems lying at the heart of political liberalism?
4. How does rule come to be understood as 'command' rather than 'delegated and mutually granted authority'?
5. How might a polity of gift result in a radically different society?

Afterword

John Milbank

The grandeur of reason and the perversity of rationalism: Radical Orthodoxy's first decade

1. Introduction

Within ten years Radical Orthodoxy has succeeded in transforming the face of Anglo-Saxon theology and today helps to shape most of its serious agendas. Its international influence also increases at a rapid rate. But it remains a project that has scarcely begun and whose boundaries are fortunately fuzzy; many who are 'close' to the movement are not necessarily 'in' the movement and this is a fundamentally healthy thing. Uniquely, it was an ecumenical theology from the outset: fundamentally Catholic in its orientation, yet attracting many who would consider themselves as 'post-Protestants'. Uniquely also, it is a collectively undertaken project not dominated by any one person, even if there are certain texts that can be regarded as 'foundational'. Yet even that is open to revision – it could well be that in years to come the initial writings will fade into the background. They possess no canonical status.

Let me try to say in this postface how RO has developed within a decade. The most important shift is from being basically an academic movement to being an embryonic cultural and political movement. To this, however, I will return at the end. The other shifts are intellectual in character. And they are less shifts than consistent developments brought about through deeper reflection and in response to new exigencies.

2. Radical Orthodoxy and twentieth-century theology

Initially, Radical Orthodoxy took the view that what was to be salvaged from twentieth-century theology was mainly the contribution of the *nouvelle théologie* and above all the work of Henri de Lubac. (More recently we have stressed the importance of Sergei Bulgakov and the Sophiological tradition.)

The *ressourcement* carried out by this school has an initial priority, because most modern theology since the seventeenth century has been captive to a false grace/nature, faith/reason dualism that is itself partially responsible for ushering in secularisation. The resulting 'extrinsicism' assumes that first one must prove God by reason, then show that revelation is possible *de jure* and finally provide 'sound reasons' (miracles, proof of historical facticity, evidence of transformation, etc.) for revelation *de facto*. Since Vatican II, this triple approach has been formally eschewed within most Roman Catholic thinking. However, both in the case of Rahnerianism and of the so-called 'theological turn' within phenomenology, traces of the second aspect of this approach still persist – along with a strong separation of philosophy from theology in both doctrine and ethics that is not really compatible with the recovery of the ancient and paradoxical 'natural desire for the supernatural'. Meanwhile, in Anglo-Saxon countries, one is witnessing a lamentable desire to question Lubac's historical findings and return to a neo-scholastic paradigm.

On the other hand, within Protestantism and then in Catholicism also under Protestant influence, the Barthian insistence on knowing God from revelation alone did not escape a hidden negative determination of what revelation must mean by the seemingly abandoned extrinsicist framework. A double sense that revelation involves something 'positive' in contrast to the deliverancies of reason and yet that it discloses knowledge beyond the scope of reason was not entirely expunged. Admittedly, as Johannes Hoff has argued, this took the subtle form of the notion of 'self-revelation'.[1] Here the at-once positive and cognitive content is thoroughly subjectivised: God shows only himself and his showing of himself is himself. This is of course an admirable advance: no longer does God communicate to us 'information' and no longer do we accept this communication because it is *a priori* plausible. And indeed the idea of 'self-revelation' also accords with pre-modern ideas of the emanation of divine glory in the creation which is one and the same with God as such.

However, there is a post-Kantian nuance in the Barthian notion that throws everything askew, as Hoff suggests. Kant's thought is itself one ultimate outcome of the late medieval separation between reason and faith: 'pure reason' can know only its own limits, only its own subjective capacity, only the way in which being 'appears' to it. Hegel was able to reinscribe a (heterodox) version of Christian doctrine within this scheme, first by identifying God himself with the historical sequence of the way in which things appear to the human spirit and then by projecting onto God himself a model of spiritual subjectivity taken from the circumstances of a sheerly finite human subject, bereft of the lure of faith and of analogical participation in transcendence. This, then, is the God who 'reveals only God' and whose immanent identity is collapsed into his revealed identity, in a forgetting of all genuine apophaticism. For the pre-modern view by contrast, though God was at one with his glory, this glory was itself, as theophanic, the disclosure of unsoundable mystery. It was not primarily the disclosure of knowledge – not even the knowledge that God is an infinite self-determining subjective structure. Instead, it was a mediated revelation through creatures – inorganic, organic, human – and in consequence involved 'always already' a creaturely response of gratitude and praise to the wonder of divine revelation. This meant that the most primordial event of revelation was *liturgical* – it already involved a new human *habitus*, something that humans must consistently do, something which they have already begun consistently to perform. This is one reason why Catherine Pickstock's 'liturgical turn' is so crucially foundational for Radical Orthodoxy.

By contrast, the Hegelian paradigm places something cognitive first, still in keeping with modern extrinsicism. This thing to-be-known before it is worshipped is the self-becoming of divine subjectivity which is one and the same with the self-positing of God as free. The usual undergraduate contrast of 'necessity' and 'divine liberty' is here irrelevant: Barth remains entirely Hegelian in his celebration of the sovereign freedom of God. The infinite subjectivity is 'immediately' present to us within our finitude, in accordance with his post-Kantian perspective.

Hence, even though, for Barth, revelation must include our acknowledgment of revelation and indeed is only possible through the full acknowledgment made by the God-Man, he tended to confine this to recognition of a hyper-cognitive disclosure, absolutely (and apocalyptically) relativising his own self-understanding, and not to see that it must include also the active poetic response of liturgical praise if this is to be the disclosure of *mystery*. (He implicitally reduces mystery to the empty arbitrariness of the revealing God.) Precisely in poetic action we are 'sur-prized' by something that comes to us unexpectedly from things which we have produced and which we may have imagined that we controlled. It is in this moment of address to us from within our own fashionings that the 'fetish', the 'icon', the 'revelatory' and the 'liturgical' are all born.[2] Were the liturgical merely a response to a revelation already given, in a Barthian fashion, then the concealed mediator (for mediation of God cannot really be denied) would be cognitive recognition alone, whereas if revelation is from the very outset liturgical (the event commemorated already a commemoration, like The Last Supper), then also our emotions, also our imaginations, also our senses, also our bodies and also the collective human body also mediate. In short, revelation becomes a fully personal event, which is must be, if it is centrally the event of the Incarnation.

Paradoxically then, it might seem, the playing down of human mediation and exaltation of human passivity reduces the revelation event to the scope of categories of reason, whilst inversely the insistence that the human response is strangely there 'with' what it is responding to, permits us to see revelation as an 'excess' emergent through human action and so as exceeding any human rational grasp — even of a formally negative kind. In relation to finite causes, response concides with prompting; it is the very mark of the strange absolute remoteness of divine revelation that here active response is co-original with passive being-prompted, because the latter entirely overwhelms the former — just as when we receive the Eucharistic elements all our offering of them is taken up into this receiving and we realise that the offering was a receiving from the outset. So as Dom Odo Casel rightly realised, divine mystery is only communicated through *the mysteries*.[3]

Failure, in Barth, to grasp this primacy of liturgical mediation is directly linked to his equal failure to embrace the traditional structure of analogy and participation which overarched the reason–faith divide and so disallowed either pure rational foundations for faith, which Barth refused, or the kind of (rationalist, after all) fideism which he perpetuated.

For this traditional structure, in one of its most acute realisations in Eriugena's *Periphyseon*, the things of this world are paradoxical *symbola*, hybrid 'grotesques' like to God in their very unlikeness, and leading us back to God who is more like to ourselves than ourselves in his utter incomprehensible infinite difference.[4] Our traverse through this benign perplexity must be one of liturgical persistence and of reaching towards a goal which we can only respond to in astonishment beyond the scope of conceptualising reason. To be 'fallen' is to have strayed from this traverse — but the theophanies recorded in the Bible and finally the descent of God himself show us once more how to read the world as a thicket of perplexing yet *redemptive* signs. Christ himself does not disclose the truth about God, even the subjective truth. All he does is exemplify perfectly a true seeking: hence, as to his humanity, he is at one with the *Logos* in his 'character', his *persona*, 'how he does things', his habitual performance. All we see is this humanity, this perfect following and worship of God. So 'revelation' here is nothing but the inauguration of a perfect worship, as Pierre de Bérulle taught, since now, thanks to the hypostatic union, the response to revelation that necessarily occasions revelation is fully included within the event of revelation itself. But this is no Hegelian becoming of the infinite as finite — no, the infinite qualitative difference between these two is still respected within the being of Christ, and to know that his finite 'expression' of the Father is also an infinite expression is to acknowledge that 'infinite expression' and so 'infinite reason' is now a much a mystery to us as is that 'infinite source' which is the Father.

But given the Barthian immediacy of self-revelation, the sheerly personal or hypostatic mediation (which includes a communication of idioms) of the infinitely distanced Christological natures cannot really be respected. Nor can the reserved mystery of the infinite Trinity, and the excess of Trinitarian person-as-relation over any mere self-becoming and reflexivity — or, inversely, interpersonal dialogue.

Much of twentieth-century Catholic thought remains a hybrid between persistences of the older extrinsicism and an importation of Barth. Rahner notoriously reworked older extrinsic prologues to faith, demonstration of the possibility of revelation and of the reasonableness of actual revelation in terms of an aspirational rational anthropology, the supernatural existential and a transcendentalist Christology. The shift to the 'intrinsic' here, though proclaimed, was in part illusory (in contrast with Lubac), because it was really a Kantian subjectivisation of the structures of extrinsic argument, leaving one with the empty formalism of 'going beyond' every boundary, a foreshadowing of grace untraceable in time ('anonymous Christianity') and the need for an 'absolute' saviour – which need must then determine Christ's actual content, rendering him a projected and spectacularised *führer*, not a genuine divine deliverer.

Of course this emptiness has to be complemented by a fideism that will alone deliver content, still in keeping with the extrinsicist model. But the fideism is also now subjectivised, in essential consistency with Barth: what God shows is his self insofar as this self is manifest to us: hence the persons are but 'modes' and the immanent is more-or-less collapsed into the economic Trinity (rather than the other way round). This is the truth that lies behind the fashionable view that the theology of the later Rahner has little to do with transcendentalist presuppositions: they are either still there in the shadowy background, or else the transcendentalism has migrated, after Barth, within a somewhat fideistic purview.

By comparison, the work of Hans Urs von Balthasar is infinitely preferable to all this and predominantly points in the right directions, consistent with Lubac. Yet he does not at crucial points entirely escape the same extrinsicist/Barthian mix that we find in Rahner. At times he still concedes too much to a *natura pura*. The structure of his theology involves unnecessary and completely unpatristic metaphysical prologues and theological foundations to doctrine proper. Ocasionally he speaks in non-Christological terms of a self-authenticating divine revelation that seems to be so 'over-against us' that it is in principle unmediated by creation and humanity. His selection of drama rather than liturgy as paradigmatic likewise risks rendering revelation an event which we first regard before we respond. In places he speaks of 'the aesthetic experience' in over-categorial and phenomenological terms which sunders it from experience in general and from ontological structures. And a residual Kantianism ensures that the beautiful still tends to be but a prologue to the good as the 'dramatic'. This is in keeping with a highly modern Fichteen mutation of subjective constructivism into dialogicism that can never be anything but the banal mutual saluting of two self-constructing subjectivities. This banality notoriously distorts his theologies of the Trinity and of the cross, where the modern intersubjective inevitably becomes host to the neo-mythical and the gnostic.[5]

What is unfortunate here is that these distortions then get pounced upon by neo-neo-scholastic Neanderthals (mostly located in the US) who both ignore the finer things in Balthasar and fail to see that these distortions are themselves ultimately traceable to modern philosophical assumptions rooted in the very late scholastic decadence to which they long to return – imagining, bizarrely, that this will somehow shield the Catholic Church against deviant sexual practices by which, in theory, they are much troubled.

In contrast it is safer to take Lubac as the exemplary exponent of the *nouvelle théologie*. And this permits the welcome discovery that precisely Lubac's more 'liberal' (in the true sense) humanism, which goes along with the greater Christological grounding of his theology (only Christ, as God, is the true man, just as only deified man is natural man, yet it is indeed a *man* who alone shows God, just as it is only *nature itself* which is exceeded) renders him the more orthodox thinker. And one can add here that Joseph Ratzinger's theology in its sparkling sobriety is thoroughly in keeping with the Lubacian perspective.

Of course Lubac is not alone. Perhaps the most authentic Christian theology of the twentieth century resides in the contributions of others, who like Lubac himself offered only something fragmentary, though on a smaller scale: Odo Casel, Eric Peterson, Erich Przywara, Romano Guardini, Pierre Rousselot, Paul Claudel, Jean Daniélou, Louis Bouyer, G. K. Chesterton, Charles Williams, D. L. Sayers, Conrad Noel and many others, besides the names of more philosophical and more exclusively literary figures.

Above all one should mention here the critiques offered of Barth by Erich Przy-wara and Eric Peterson – who showed respectively that he had ignored both the genuine ancient analogical and liturgical–pedagogical structures of Christian theology, rooted in a contemplative practice which transcended the reason–faith divide. Thereby, they rightly contended, he remained essentially the prisoner of German idealism. One could suggest that this was perhaps the death-knell of Protestant theology as such, with Peterson's conversion highly symbolic – for since then it has enjoyed a merely cadaverous survival in the writings of figures who are already but little read on a global scale.

The only alternative to this verdict would be to take seriously a revived Hegelian-ism. And as Hoff again points out, in effect all the later attempts to salvage Barthian 'self-revelation' – Pannenberg, Moltmann, Jüngel – have taken Barth back towards absolute idealism. However, Hoff agrees with me that Slavoj Žižek is right to contend that in the end, read rigorously, the Hegelian position is atheistic. He also agrees that it lacks any genuine account of mediation, since it is rather an endless collusive shuttle between identity and difference, unable to think the analogical, paradoxical mystery of the *metaxu,* William Desmond's (anti-Hegelian) 'between'. Others, however, within or near to Radical Orthodoxy – especially Rowan Williams (at least at one stage of his writing) – would see Hegel as open to a construal far more in keeping with genuine Christian mediation. This is an important and fruitful debate – in which even anti-Hegelians like myself will be forced to admit that in certain ways they *are* still trying to do what Hegel was trying to do. Certainly, if this means: take more central account of history, society and *poesis* than was the case for pre-modern tradition, then this is true. But I would contend that these essentially post-Renaissance emphases are subtractable (and indeed must be subtracted fully to emerge) from the structures of modern philosophy and especially transcendentalist philosophy that are rooted in late scholasticism and not in the best Christian humanism.

But if Hegel fails, then the game is up for a strictly speaking Protestant theology. It is clear that the greatest anti-Kantian Lutheran pietist, Johann Georg Hamann, already in effect re-Catholicised theology (thereby assisting the Catholic conversion of several later German romantics) and that a return to the reformers is not an option, since they were compromised by the same proto-modern philosophy whose errors they but partially saw and which already contaminated their own Christological orthodoxy, as Newman correctly intimated. (Luther veers towards monophysitism, Calvin towards Nestorianism.)

But the point here for Radical Orthodoxy is not at all intra-ecclesial polemics. It is rather to transcend ecclesial chauvinism by realising that Protestants and Catholics alike are the victims of errors deeply inscribed far back in a shared Christian history. This even applies to Orthodox theology: not only was it historically affected by the bad manual theology of the West, one can also see certain parallels between the Scotist 'formal distinction' in God and the Palamite over-rigid construal of the essence/energies distinction (parallels sometimes noted in the Christian East at the time). In either case, there is a resulting loss of a true participatory vision and a concomitant rise in fideism and extrinsicism.

From here onwards though, things get more difficult. Is *ressourcement* enough? Is it enough to recover, after Lubac and many others, an authentic paleo-Christianity? Clearly not, and clearly the thinkers of the *nouvelle théologie* thought of *ressourcement* as but the prelude to a new speculative and constructive effort. It is, in a sense, the task of this 'next phase' which Radical Orthodoxy has sought to take up, though in a wider ecumenical context.

Three questions in particular impose themselves here. First, if the illusion of *natura pura* has distorted philosophy as well as theology, reason as well as faith, then just what stance did the *nouvelle théologie* really take towards philosophy? Secondly, is all of theology/philosophy since Scotus (roughly) to be regarded as a mistake, so that all we need to do is to return to Aquinas and before, in such a manner that Radical Orthodoxy, metaphorically like the pre-Raphaelites, would paint theologically always in antique dress, being unable as yet to think something tropically like artistic 'modernism'? Thirdly, just what sort of philosophical/theological synthesis should Radical Orthodoxy now be attempting?

3. The *nouvelle théologie* and philosophy

The answer to the first question is murky: for this was one of the constructive tasks that the *nouvelle théologie* never really got round to. However, both Lubac and

Balthasar saw clearly (unlike Rahner) that refusal of the *natura pura* entailed an anti-Kantianism. Today, in the wake of complex researches in intellectual history (by Honnefelder, Muralt, Courtine, Marion, Boulnois, Schmultz and others) we are able to realise more precisely how Kant is still operating within a Scotist/Ockhamite paradigm whose assumptions were yet more theological than they were philosophical. This means that the new generation of early twenty-first-century theologians clearly sees that it is no longer a matter of supposing that Kant puts unavoidable 'critical' questions to theology on the basis of a validly autonomous philosophy. To the contrary, it is a question of calling into question a Kantian 'package' which is every bit as much (no, in fact more) theological than it is philosophical. Once again, it now appears that the immediately previous theological generation was unnecessarily cowed by an intellectual phenomenon which they failed to realise was but a rival theology in disguise.

But the philosophical alternative to this anti-Kantianism of the two leading 'new' theologians tended to be somewhat eclectic. Balthasar blended Thomas and Bonaventure not always coherently, and too much embraced the tendency of many German Catholics to think that Heidegger could be corrected with a small twist and made to provide a new rational foundation for belief in God. Balthasar indeed sees that Heidegger in fact *suppresses* the ontological difference and in refusal of transcendence (which even the ancient Greeks did not affirm through reason alone, as Eric Voegelin showed) reduces 'being' to an identification with the sheerly ontic flow of time. However, Balthasar still thought of the difference between 'Being' and 'existences' as something belonging basically to the pre-theological metaphysical purview, and therefore tended too much to speak of Thomistic *esse* as if this could be identified with Thomistic *ens commune*. A corrected Heideggerean perspective ought, therefore, according to Balthasar, to conclude to the groundlessness of 'abstract' being as well as the sheer contingency of existences. Therefore it should invoke an absolute transcendent freedom and a difference between God and creation beyond the merely ontological difference.

However, there are no purely philosophical arguments which can refute the secular decision to reduce Being as such to nullity – even if this decision needs to be more consistently thought-through than in the case of Heidegger's arbitrary attachment of 'nullification' to temporal becoming. Being is only more than nothing when theology has already intervened to identify it as eternal plenitude on the grounds of a rational inference which alone saves reason from a self-abolishing nihilism, and yet which can only finally be supported by the gesture of faith. (The most which apologetic can do here, though it is by no means insignificant, is to argue that the 'rational' decision of nihilism against the final ontological reality of reason is 'irrational' insofar as it points to a contradiction that cannot – like the attribution of contradiction to God – be the mask of hypereminent sense, inaccessible to us.)

For Aquinas, somewhat in contrast to Balthasar, the 'real distinction' (his version of the ontological difference) concerns not merely the difference within each existent thing between its essence and (abstract, quasi-generic) *ens commune*, but also the difference between its contingent essence and the divine *esse* in which it participates. Therefore the ontological difference is not simply something which philosophy should correctly describe as a prelude to the theological invocation of transcendent freedom; it is rather something which, from a Christian perspective, only theology can correctly decipher in theological terms – in such a way that Being is saved both from ontic reduction and from collapse into a non-existential *henos* (Plotinus) or into nullity. Certainly this involves the further complication that God, as the coincidence of being and essence (and so as eminently including all essential differences) also exceeds the ontological difference, yet it is just this exceeding which also resolves, in theological terms, the conundrum of the ontological difference: that which is 'being itself' is also infinitely and supereminently every 'determination'. Moreover, this is for Aquinas (I would argue) fully a matter of *sacra doctrina* and not just 'the theology of the philosophers'. This is because *esse* as hyper-generic (unlike *ens commune*) is as much exemplified (as Michel Corbin and Philipp Rosemann have stressed) in contingent accidents and events as it is in generic or specific essences. The God who is *esse ipsum* is the God of revelation, for whom a particular historical manifestation can take priority over the generic schemes of ontology. This is precisely why, for Aquinas, the incarnate Christ, although utterly specific, possesses existentially *only* the infinite *esse* of God, just as he possesses personally only the *hypostasis* of the Son.[6]

With Balthasar, however, there is too great a tendency to see the *differentia specifica* of Christian theology as being the invocation of an ultimate ground of freedom. Whilst indeed this cannot be completely false, for Christianity does indeed see infinite liberty as convertible with being, it is also inadequate. For one thing, it too much falls into the modern Christian trap which Johannes Hoff rightly identifies, of supposing that one has to argue that something vital for Christianity is not at all found elsewhere – whereas, as he says, pre-modern Christianity was entirely at ease with finding anticipations of the Trinity, etc., outside this specific faith. In the present case one can be in danger of ignoring certain intimations of personal freedom as applying to the One even in Neoplatonism – for example in the case of 'gift' and 'grace' language applied to emanations (*dosis*, etc.) or of the language of divine self-disclosure in the oracular texts to which they granted a quasi-scriptural status. But more crucially, finite notions of 'freedom' are qualified when an infinite freedom is seen as coinciding with an infinite intelligence, power of judgement and fidelity to being. Balthasar of course knows this, and yet he still tends to give an explicit (and unwarranted) priority to the moment of freedom and love within God, in a Franciscan rather than Thomistic mode. It is for this reason that he appears too readily inclined to see the divine 'decision' to create as contingent in precisely the way a finite decision would be contingent, thereby risking a reduction of the ontological excess purely to the ontic.

For this reason also, he in the end regards with suspicion the three perhaps most rigorous of all Christian theologians: Eriugena, Eckhart and Cusanus. He accuses them of reducing the divine act of creation to the unfolding of an inner necessity, despite the fact that Aquinas himself saw this act with all its specific contents as included from all eternity within the Paternal uttering of the *Logos* – which involves an absolute ineffable coincidence of freedom with necessity. They are also accused of confusing the beings of creator and creation, whereas in truth they were simply thinking through the paradoxical implications of the truth that the difference of God from the world is not a merely inner-worldly ontic difference. In this light one can regard them as the most *extreme* exponents of the divine difference and distance. Balthasar, however, anachronistically conflates their perspectives with those of German idealism, for which God's existence indeed reduces to the process of 'self-revelation'. This is to ignore the historical situation of idealism both after Boehme's positivisation of evil and insertion of even this positivity within God, and after the Kantian *hiatus*, which then suggested the dialectical identity of God with the finite – which as finite and often also as 'evil' is entirely alienated from God. Hence the rationalistic dialectical shuttle of idealism – God as entirely other to the world *is* only the detritus of this world after all – is entirely other to the unresolved *paradoxical* tensions of the three great pre-modern 'extremists'.[7] Their paradoxical statements were after all but the hyperbole of analogy which, as refusing either univocity or equivocity, requires the 'contradictory' coincidence of likeness and unlikeness without any rational resolution, including a dialectical one. Hence, as Hoff argues, even Cusa's theological mathematics (which is in a strictly Augustinian lineage) concludes to praise and wonder and not to the sort of identification with the divine through self-abolition which would render all prayer otiose. The latter circumstance is rightly the nub of Balthasar's quarrel with idealism – yet he fails in the end to see that the source of this lies not just in the refusal of transcendent freedom, but more simply in the refusal of authentic transcendence *per se*, which can only be known through faith as well as reason.

The final irony here is that, having cast unnecessary suspicion on certain ancient Christian masters, Balthasar himself renders too much obeisance to Fichte and Schelling. This is because the hypostasisation of lone freedom is of course one figure that idealism itself tended to take. It is perhaps the ultimate way of thinking through the projection of the self-determination of the epistemological subject onto God – the ground of all subjective being and reasoning, theoretical and practical, is the practical thinking-through of its own freedom, even if this can be deemed by Balthasar to take place intersubjectively and dialogically.

A further problem with Heidegger, as Balthasar himself recognised, was his relative disinterest in the physical universe and in biology, and consequent (Cartesian) failure to account for manifest 'self-organisation' beneath the level of the consciously rational or to link the 'opening' of *Dasein* to human animality. The obliteration from sight of 'unconscious' autopoetic and teleological processes in organic and even inorganic matter, of course renders an impersonal construal of being far more plausible – as again Balthasar astutely points out. But here Lubac's continued (both explicit and

covert) closeness to the thought of Maurice Blondel, besides his cautiously enthu-
siastic interest in Teilhard de Chardin, is significant. For Blondel stood clearly in the
French tradition of 'spiritual realism' or 'spiritual positivism' which stretches from
Maine de Biran through Ravaisson, Lachelier and Boutroux to Bergson and Merleau-
Ponty. What is significant about this lineage is that it is by and large non-Kantian and
non-transcendentalist. It is rather Cartesian, in the sense that it affirms fully the
reality of a material world out there as explored by science and yet at the same time
the 'other' reality of mind or soul. And herein lies the deepest reason for Radical
Orthodoxy's consistent Francophilia – nothing to do with trends and fashions, but
rather a preference for this French 'common sense' over against a Germanic idealist
tendency to deny the reality of the material world and equally an Anglo-Saxon tendency to reduce everything to the material and the sensuous.[8] (Though at its best a
combination of Platonism and empiricism has given Anglo-Saxon thought an equivalent to French spiritual realism, whilst the same applies to the Germanic 'radical pietist'
tradition stemming from Hamann, Jacobi and Wizenmann and reaching its – albeit
slightly skewed – apogee in Kierkegaard.)

Of course Radical Orthodoxy, along with *tout le monde*, denounces Cartesian dualism, geometrisation of space, retreat into solipsism, etc., etc. Yet the 'allowing for
both' of Descartes (albeit in over aprioristic terms) remains important and clearly
connects him back to medieval realism in a way that it is not true for Kant, whilst
also concurring more with the implicitly realist assumptions of modern science, as
Quentin Meillassoux has argued. It is also the case that Michel Henry has shown that
Descartes's dualism is far more qualified than the usual reading suggests, whilst Jean-
Luc Marion has demonstrated a greater *reserve* towards paradigmatic modern univocity and representation in Descartes than in Suarez, allied to a certain reinvocation
of the older Dionysian tradition of reflection upon the divine names, besides a new
(albeit distorted) re-inscription of Augustinian themes.

Moreover, the significance of the work of Maine de Biran and Félix Ravaisson is
that they sought to overcome the admitted dualistic aspect of Cartesianism, whilst at
the same time trying to incorporate an evolutionary sense of the dynamism within
nature. Hence their attempts to update Aristotle by making the concept of 'habit'
fundamental for theoretical as well as practical reason. This gives a nuanced version of
panpsychic vitalism in which a self-organising habituating power operates with different degrees of intensity at every level of physical reality from the inorganic to the
consciously rational. Thus a 'habitual' process can paradoxically be the most automatic
and the most spontaneous, free and flexible – as in the case, for example, with bal-
letic art. (In many ways Kierkegaard's equally anti-Kantian reflexions on 'repetition' –
already important in Pickstock's work and for Radical Orthodoxy in general – were
exploring the same paradox.) Such a perspective has the advantage of seeing something spiritual at every level of the universe and so of denying that the conscious mind
is an anomaly. Indeed these thinkers already boldly asserted that 'natural laws' are

merely reportage on contingent settled processes that are sedimentations of natural habit (a theme which Meillassoux has recently taken up in a nihilistic guise which is yet not without a certain spiritual, religious resonance).

But most significantly for the trajectory of the *nouvelle théologie,* Ravaisson realised that the paradox of a 'fundamental' habit, when 'habit' is something that by definition has to be established, approximates *all* habit to the *habitus* of grace – which is for Aquinas a 'supernatural infused habit'.[9] He could, indeed, have gone in the direction of subordinating the actuality of habit to the virtual force of habit, which is the line later followed by both Bergson and Deleuze. But instead he remained strictly with the paradox of 'foundational habit' in its bare actuality, and therefore was forced to invoke an *ur*-habit which is nothing other than the grace of the transcendent God. He accordingly cited Fénelon – 'all nature is prevenient grace'. For habit to 'get going' it must be lured beyond itself; for it to be able to seek for that which it does not as yet know (the Meno problematic is cited), there must be divine kenotic descent, which is later echoed in the kenotic descent of our own reason 'back' to the automatism of matter the more it become firmly established – as in the case of the practised keyboard-player who thinks entirely through her hands.

The exact influence of Ravaisson upon Blondel remains unclear. However, it is unarguable that the latter's initial 'transgression' of the nature/grace boundary derives from the tradition of French 'spiritual realism' in which Ravaisson stood and that Lubac also is at least indirectly indebted to this tradition; only later did he succeed in showing that such transgression was in reality paleo-orthodoxy. So it seems legitimate to seek to build up the latent philosophical dimension in Lubac with reference to the exponents of spiritual realism – which includes of course Charles Péguy's recension of Bergson.

For reasons which I have tried to indicate, this tradition can be seen as having a certain authentic continuity with the Christian pre-modern – what it adds to the pre-modern perspective is not a transcendentalism grounded in univocity of being and knowledge as representation, but rather a greater sense of time and dynamic alteration in the course of time. It is this very emphasis on 'historicity' and the dynamic which tends to *increase* a theological stress on the continuity between nature and grace – for the 'middle' between the two, which is the obscure natural drive towards the supernatural must naturally become associated with the altering power of nature and the transformative power of human culture. Hence Ravaisson can suggest that primary habit is in some sense already grace. Blondel can similarly suggest that the surplus in every human act over rational control is the obscure anticipation of grace which only the Incarnation will elucidate. Likewise Blondel can assert that the mysterious 'binding factor' that ensures the relative stability of every finite substance, the inter-relation between substances, the bond between body and soul and the co-ordinated power which generates new substances (Leibniz's *vinculum substantiale*), is an anticipation of the transubstantiated presence of Christ in the Eucharist which manifests and realises ever-again the hypostatic unity of God and humanity which alone finally guarantees and secures the finite ontological order.[10] (There are clear parallels here to Catherine Pickstock's argument that only the event of transubstantiation finally secures linguistic meaning against scepticism.)

This reflection on the links between the *nouvelle théologie* and the tradition of 'spiritual realism' is important for the third question of what sort of philosophical/ theological synthesis Radical Orthodoxy should be aiming for. But relevant for that also is the second question of whether late scholasticism is to be simply regarded as a mistake.

4. Genealogy and complexity

To answer this question however, more needs to be said about the adequacy or otherwise of the Radical Orthodoxy genealogy. This can be crudely summed up as 'it all went wrong with Scotus'. Of course, Duns Scotus is only here regarded as the figure who brings to a head and decisively synthesises several already well-established currents of thought, particularly those that have to do with the 'Avicennised Augustinianism' which the Franciscan scholastics tended to favour. These currents include: the loss of analogy and the substitution of univocity or equivocity of being; the substitution of knowledge by representation for knowledge by identity; the primacy of possibility over actuality; the cooperation or 'concurrence' of uncreated and uncreated causes (losing the sense that these operate at incommensurable levels); the plurality of forms in a single created substance; matter as a quasi-form; the switch in meaning of the term 'transcendental' from an ontological to an epistemological focus; the separation of the operations of the intellect and the will; the abandonment of participation in divine exemplars; the denial of the Augustinian theory of illumination; the refusal of the Dionysian *via negativa*; the attack on the adoration of images; the formal distinction in God; the denial of the definition of the Trinitarian persons by relation; a quasi-Nestorianism in Christology and finally a priority of the will over the intellect in God.

It has to be stressed that there is nothing peculiar to Radical Orthodoxy whatsoever about this Scotus-centred genealogy, despite the disingenuous insinuations of Richard Cross and his ilk. To the contrary, the idea that Scotus is the real turning-point in the history of Western theology and philosophy is now the received wisdom of historians of ideas. They have abundantly demonstrated how Descartes and even Kant are still working within a late scholastic conceptual space and how the 'subjective turn' is latent within the very 'metaphysics' which Kant is criticising, whereas the authentic position of the tradition that culminates in Aquinas is simply not considered by Kant at all, because it was not known to him. But to espouse this genealogy is not of course to be 'anti-Scotus' – indeed many of those espousing it are either pro-Scotus or ambivalent.

Radical Orthodoxy is rather offering a theological response to this newly accepted genealogy. It adds perhaps an emphasis on the theological aspects of the shift and it adds certainly a negative attitude towards the post-Scotist paradigm, which it believes is subject to a theological critique on the basis of this perceived priority of the theological in forging the new perspective.

New nuances are however being added to the genealogy all the time. Within Radical Orthodoxy Adrian Pabst has stressed (in his as yet unpublished Cambridge doctoral dissertation) the importance of developments towards nominalism and the plurality of forms in early Latin scholasticism even before the encounter with Avicenna – a circumstance which places limits on any sort of 'Arab corruption of the West' thesis. Lydia Schumacher, who is working towards a doctorate at the University of Edinburgh, is developing a comprehensive account of how Augustine's theory of illumination involves no alienation of the human intellectual powers and no notion of *a priori* conceptual determinants.[11] These elements were rather introduced to the reading of Augustine by the Franciscans under Avicennian influence. Nor did Aquinas abandon the Augustinian doctrine as is often said – instead he deploys a Procleanised Aristotle to restore against the Franciscans an authentically Augustinian view, even if he puts a yet stronger emphasis on the role of sensory and imaginative mediation. The doctrine is rather finally abandoned by Scotus, who sees the divine influence, when seen in various ways as alienating human powers, to be superfluous. This leaves 'illumination' as only applying to faith and helps to encourage a nature/supernature duality. Schumacher's genealogy of illumination shows Bonaventure to be clearly culpable: he both apriorises the presence of illumination in the human mind and tends to reduce the divine causation of human mental light to mere efficiency. In this respect he is notably *less* committed to Platonic participation than Aquinas (!), who construes the agent intellect as continuously partaking of the divine intellectual power.

The more one traces corruptive tendencies prior to Scotus, however, then the more perhaps the question arises about a dangerously 'rationalist' bias of the Latin West. One approaches this issue with extreme caution, because there have been so many crude 'yes' answers given in the past. All the same the question persists, and has often been subtly raised by David Hart, an Orthodox theologian close to Radical Orthodoxy who is unusually free of anti-Latin biases. But perhaps the most significant probing of this issue has come recently from outside Radical Orthodoxy in the work of the French historian of philosophy Olivier Boulnois.[12] There *is*, he argues, a tendency in Augustine to see the image of God in man as residing primarily in the intellect, in conformity with the idea that God himself is eminently comprehensible, and will be seen directly by the deified intellect in the beatific vision without mediation of any image. All these positions, as he shows, were sometimes construed within the West, as in the case of the *Libri Carolini*, as favouring a support for semi-iconoclasm. Perhaps indeed, as Rowan Williams recently suggested to me, it is their author,

Theodulf of Orleans, who is the ultimate villain of Western theology. This would be hyperbolic, and yet the suggestion makes sense to the degree that the common factor underlying all the 'currents of perversity' which I listed above is indeed a 'rationalism' which refuses the need for mediation via the inscrutable 'density' of the image and fails to see that it is this density which must stand between us and any direct perception of the ineffable deity. All of the 'currents' tend to accept as concepts only that which can be univocally and distinctly grasped, in refusal of real phenomena which cannot be so clearly conceptualised and can be but obscurely intuited. A certain refusal of our dependency on the concretely envisaged tended to oust the real in favour of the rational and to model the real on the basis of the rational.

Of course this should be seen as a corruption of Augustine – and one could argue that Boulnois downplays the evidence that Augustine saw the divine image as reflected at every level of created reality and as also present in human embodiment. All the same, his Trinitarian approach to the *imago dei* can indeed be contrasted, as Boulnois points out, with the more Christological approach of the Christian East. This assures that the image is seen to reside in the entire human *persona* – just as the icon's participation in the divine–human *persona* of Christ (and of the saints through participation) is what justified its worthiness of adoration. The impenetrable 'density' of the image is linked in Dionysius and then yet more strongly in Eriugena (who sought to synthesise Eastern perspectives with Augustine) with a Proclean sense of the way in which the material order refracts something of the simplicity of the One beyond the intellect which the reflexivity of reason cannot grasp.

Boulnois probes in fine scholarly detail the paradox whereby the greater Western sense of mediation within God (the equality of the Son and the Spirit with the Father) goes along with construal of this medium as reason, which ensures that material images are seen as merely illustrative or superfluous, whilst conversely the Eastern sense of a divine simplicity beyond mediation (the Paternal *monarchia*, an ineffable Proclean Unity) requires that our access to the divine is *always* mediated by impenetrable density, even in the case of the beatific vision. The latter remains an *epectasis*, an infinite approximation precisely because God cannot be fully grasped and mediation by images can never be left behind.

Again though the contrast between West and East still seems slightly overdrawn; both are internally more diverse than Boulnois sometimes implies. There is really no Unity beyond the Trinity in Dionysius, no strong stress on the *monarchia* and no detectable doctrine of *epectasis* (though there is in Eriugena). But he is right to stress the Nyssan–Dionysian view that God is 'in-comprehensible' even to himself. Perhaps it is just this view which permits a certain East/West synthesis which Boulnois himself half-indicates as present in Eckhart. The beatific vision can be considered as mediated only, but crucially, in the sense that we enter into Trinitarian mediation. The *Logos* itself however has a certain 'dense' image-like character, which is captured by the fact that for Augustine 'thought' is now also 'inner word' which points intentionally beyond itself. Whilst the 'intentional' character of thought as sign tends, as Boulnois argues, to render thought transparent, the very necessity and yet self-negation of 'word' for thinking incorporates more of an image-like density than he perhaps allows. Given that the *Logos* is eminently 'image' as well as eminently thought, it then becomes possible to combine the 'Western' sense of an absolute mediation in God with the 'Eastern' sense that all approaches to God are 'densely' mediated. Prior to the beatific vision, as both Eriugena and Aquinas emphasised in different (but equally Proclean) ways, reasoning always passes through the detour of the body, the senses and the imagination – since the latter three also echo the infinite *Logos* and in ways which reflexive reason cannot grasp.

So carefully handled, Boulnois's researches (from which he deliberately draws no theoretical conclusions himself) can suggest that an overly 'rationalist' reading of Augustine is the long-term source of later perversity, whilst even Augustine himself requires supplementation by the stronger Byzantine articulation of Christology, along with the theurgically-tinged theology of icons and the view that infinite reason no longer 'comprehends' itself in a way that would only be possible for a finite reflection – this leads later, in Eckhart and Cusanus, to the Proclean-inspired insistence that God lies beyond the range of the law of non-contradiction. (Augustine's thoughts about infinity are very rudimentary.) Whilst Boulnois over-insists on the 'Plotinian Augustine' versus 'Proclean Dionysius' contrast (for Augustine makes, in his own Christian terms, the equivalent of the Iamblichan gesture of refusing the undescended soul and presents Christological worship as a kind of 'theurgic' resolution of the *aporias* of time), it remains the case that Augustine had a deficient sense of the sacrality of matter and space as compared with the Christian East.

Several allusions to Proclus in the above paragraphs indicate a further long-term genealogical issue which is enjoying increasing attention within Radical Orthodoxy. This is the ultimate *Plotinian* parentage of the shift to a subjectivist and epistemological and aprioristic starting point for understanding. In brief: Plotinus denied the 'full descent' of the individual soul into the human body. This eventually encouraged Avicenna's proto-Cartesian argument that one could be totally self-aware without bodily mediation. The influence of Avicenna in turn led, as Gilson already noted, to an over-interiorising reading of Augustine in the Latin West and eventually, through Scotus and then the nominalists to the rationalist and idealist notions that knowledge is essentially an 'internal construct'.

A contrast of this lineage with the theurgic, Proclean one, allows a somewhat different comparison to be made from the usual one between idealism and realism. Where the soul is deemed (as with Iamblichus and Proclus) to have 'fully descended' into the body, then, correspondingly, the constructive efforts of the human mind will be seen as more collaborating with the imagination and the senses and the bodily organs and so as occurring not internally (between mind and sensory information) but externally, in terms of our modification of material and signifying reality. The

Proclean perspective, therefore, is emphatically realist, yet much *more* links human construction to creative and historical novelty. Hence the 'Proclean' lineage would run: Cusa, Vico, Hamann, Novalis, Coleridge. American pragmatism (though never, even in Peirce, sufficiently free from utilitarianism) is also more allied to this intermittent tradition than to the 'Plotinian' one.

And as already intimated, the Proclean line is also linked to the notion that the 'simplicity' of matter discloses something of the One or of God that the 'doubling' innate to intellectual reflection cannot reach. This permits then a much stronger account of the ineffable dimension of the sacramental, whilst it also invites (in the wake of Proclus himself) more consideration of the irreducibly obscure 'sympathies' that must obtain between mind and matter if mind is spiritual and yet the two are able to interact with each other. The latter topic, when combined with the question of analogy as inhabiting an 'impossible' domain between identity and difference and of the necessity of liturgy as a 'theurgic' atunement of the self with God also invites a revisiting of Christian exploration of the Hermetic and the naturally magical, all the way from Pico della Mirandola to Arthur Machen and Charles Williams. (It is clear that Rowan Williams's reflections on the last two authors hovers about such questions.)

This set of considerations – and no doubt many others like it – are required in order to enrich and extend the Radical Orthodoxy genealogy, besides incorporating more comparative and ecumenical dimensions.

Moreover, if one identifies in the West the persisting danger of a 'rationalist' bias, a 'logocentrism' as Jacques Derrida put it (which may of course go along with an insufficiently *sophisticated* exercise of reason), then one also needs to ask about the practical and institutional dimensions of this tendency. Here Charles Taylor's *A Secular Age* is of inestimable importance, even though this importance has scarcely yet been grasped. At the end of his book he suggests that his cultural genealogy is compatible with Radical Orthodoxy's intellectual one, with which he is broadly in agreement. He rightly denies that the Radical Orthodoxy 'intellectual deviation' narrative (ID) can be the primary explanation for secularisation – but exponents of Radical Orthodoxy would agree about this.[13] We have only been claiming partially to account for secularisation in the intellectual realm and we do not espouse the idealism of, say Michael Buckley in his brilliant (and largely correct as regards intellectual history) *At the Origins of Modern Atheism.*

Hence I more than welcome Taylor's complementary and in many ways more fundamental cultural genealogy – what he calls his 'Reform Master Narrative' (RMN). Taylor's claim here (often following the thoughts of that now neglected Catholic genius and accidental guru of the 1960s, Ivan Illich), is that the post-legal 'inter-personal' governance suggested and partially realised by Christianity was perverted in the Latin West by the very eagerness for reform which ensured an over-institutionalisation of charity and resulted in too much 'help as control', as extensively charted by Michel Foucault.[14] Part and parcel of this tendency was the gradual extirpation of the more 'festive' aspects of lay piety and a mistaken attempt to make lay piety over-conform to a monastic model – whilst the latter itself could suffer from over-regulation, loss of its 'holy folly' aspect and a tendency after John Cassian (as Michael Hanby has argued from within Radical Orthodoxy), to make stoic self-control substitute for openness to the unpredictable workings of the divine *eros*. Where 'discipline' itself becomes an end, formalism tends to replace substance and finally, as in the stoic-dominated Renaissance period, the 'ethical' starts to be seen as an end in itself and the religious as dispensable. Taylor rightly points out how 'dark' romanticism then rebelled against the Enlightenment as 'all too Christian' because 'all too exclusively ethical'. But as against this Nietszchean reaction, one can place the Christian romantic Kierkegaardian one – the loss of the ecstatically more-than-ethical will lose also the ethical, because the role of the 'good' will then get reduced to the inscribing of a pointless circle of regulated behaviour, whose order will be indistinguishable from the exercise and prevalence of arbitrary power.

Because the 'disciplinary' policies of the Latin West were largely the work of elites, ID is perhaps a more integral aspect of RMN than Taylor allows. Nevertheless, his historical considerations are even more fundamental than those of Radical Orthodoxy or of Boulnois. Has Christianity as such – in defiance of its own credal orthodoxy – tended to 'excarnate' almost from the outset? In particular, has it succeeded in providing an *ascesis* compatible with lay, married, family and working life? In many ways the medieval laity itself sought to invent such an *ascesis* in the modes of cults of romantic love, of chivalry and trade guilds, but their efforts were ultimately undermined by a practical rationalism which was as suspicious of 'festive' practices of sexual, martial and economic exchange as it was of theophanic mediation. The emerging regime (from the late Middle Ages onwards) of separation of private gift from public formal contract, of juridically arriving grace from a public physical world drained of meaning, is entirely rooted in an ecclesially imposed disciplinary practice linked to an anti-participatory theology.

All these emerging supplements to the Radical Orthodoxy ID genealogy suggest a slightly modified approach to Scotist and nominalist theologies. For their extreme carried-through rationalism can be seen to be in part an extension of tendencies as old as scholasticism itself – the danger of subordinating *lectio* to *questio* and the danger of 'spatialising' and so rationalising *lectio* itself by separating it from collective liturgy and private meditative memorisation in the wake of the increased practice of silent reading. Or even tendencies as old as the Latin West. Or even, again, tendencies as old as Christianity itself. The sin of Ockham could be our very own 'original' sin.

From this perspective Scotus, Ockham and the rest performed a very important and skilful negative work. One can sees this especially in six ways:

1. They question how, if finite being is simply analogical participation in God, it can enjoy integral, independent existence;

2. They ask whether analogy of attribution as lying 'between identity and difference' does not violate non-contradiction;

3. They ask the same thing in the case of real universals and real relations: how can a particular thing be 'also' a universal thing?; how can a particular thing be 'also' that which it is not?;

4. They point out that what we take to be 'universals' are always linguistically constructed;

5. They suggest that if being is univocal then, like God himself, creatures may be able in some measure to bring being into existence; and

6. They also suggest that God, *de potentia absoluta*, could create another infinite reality.

Why do these six points represent an important negative work? They do so because they indicate the kind of theology that emerges on the basis of 'pure reason' which must rationally reduce revelation to that which concerns the only 'extra-rational' which reason can recognise, namely the purely positive and 'factual'. Once these points have been made, it is impossible to return entirely to Aquinas, or even to the intellectual tradition preceding him. This is because, whilst Aquinas and his forebears certainly operated with a concept of reason which assumed that we can only 'see in a glass darkly' and whilst there are many implicit rhetorical and poetic aspects in their thought (as Olivier-Thomas Venard has superbly articulated in the case of Aquinas) there is still not a strong enough sense that thought depends upon the extra-rational contribution of the senses, the imagination, imaging and language – what Bruno Pinchard, in his work on Vico, calls the *dédoublement* of reason. Of course one can exaggerate this point – several recent theologians, including Joseph Ratzinger and Radical Orthodoxy's Peter Candler, have rightly stressed the humanist dimension of the monastic tradition and the way in which faithful persistence in listening to the Word of God demands a careful and intense cultivation of letters with the attendant question of the images they invoke and the musical sounds by which they may be intensified. Yet when theology moved into the city with the mendicants, it also tended gradually to leave this humanism behind – especially in the Franciscan case.

It is striking therefore that the defence and reworking of the great tradition against the Scotists and the nominalists occurs through a new combination of theology with a now laicised humanism. One could say that laicised humanism is also radicalised humanism, because it inevitably demands a greater linking of letters to the entire range of human corporeal life in time. Often, indeed, such humanism was dominated by a Stoic corruption, but at its best this was not the case: one can cite Dante, Salutati, Eckhart, Cusanus, Pico della Mirandola through to Pierre de Bérulle in the early seventeenth century. Sometimes this humanism, under Thomistic more than Franciscan inspiration (Sara Nair James having reversed E. R. Curtues' verdict on this point in her book *Signorelli and Fra Angelico at Orvieto*) encouraged a new support for *theologica poetica*, with a newly generous attitude towards pagan mythology. (Within humanism one can discover both an acceptance of nominalism, which tends in consequence to reduce grammar and rhetoric to instruments of social and ethical use and alternatively (as Michael Allen Gillespie ignores in his *Theological Origins of Modernity*), as with for example Pico, a return to metaphysical realism which at times suggests a certain dialectical relation to nominalism – a new sense that human language and human shaping is involved in our grasp of both immanent universals and the unchanging divine ideas.)

In short, it was discovered that in order to defend classical Christian metaphysical orthodoxy one must allow far more for the ineffable mediations carried through by the density of material images – and this could legitimately, as with Pico, as already indicated, include a Christian engagement with ideas of 'natural magic' and esoteric 'affinities' derived from the *corpus hermeticum*. (This is being explored within Radical Orthodoxy by Joshua Ramey.) The defence of Christianity through appeal to the 'imagination' and the mysterious extra-rational creativity of the human spirit in effect began here – even though this reached a new specificity in the pre-romantic and romantic eras. It is precisely our recognition of all this which ensures that Radical Orthodoxy is not in any sense a 'nostalgic' movement. We acknowledge that both the aesthetic and the poetic have to be 'brought out' of the earlier tradition.

Yet at the same time we are also on our guard against many dominant notions of the aesthetic and of 'art'. For the Middle Ages rightly considered that it is truth itself that is 'manifest' and 'attractive' – both revealing itself as 'good' and only showing itself to a rightly ordered will. The 'beautiful' is here a shadowy mediation between the apparent and the desirable, an assumed background of 'appropriateness' and 'convenience'. All the same, in the face of 'rationalism' it became necessary to more explicitly foreground this background and to insist on the primacy of its esoteric connecting links through all of reality. But this has nothing to do with the eighteenth-century 'science of the aesthetic' whose negative significance is that 'aesthetic experience' had emerged as a residual mental idiom not readily assignable either to the rational *a priori* or to empirical sensory enjoyment. This engenders eventually – sometimes following Hume's reduction of both logical reasoning and empirical induction to imaginative 'fictioning' – a new sense in the proto-romantic and romantics (Vico, Hamann, Jacobi, Novalis, Schlegel, Coleridge, etc.) of the ineffable fusion of the rational and the corporeal as governing *all* our cognitive processes.

Likewise in the case of 'art': as Boulnois argues, this notion is a bastard offspring of iconoclasm, which desecularised the image and so left us with the idea of merely secular images that are either instructive or diverting. If 'art' is to be more than illustration of an abstract idea or mere than merely self-referential ('its own truth') then it has to be returned to the condition of the icon where one particular unique image is nonetheless generally disclosive, just as the enigma of individual 'character' can be universally binding and compelling. Nevertheless, this demand that the artwork return to the condition of the icon is inseparable from a new, retrospective sense that iconicity is entirely central for theology as such.

A certain initial recognition of the theological need for a 'supplement to logo-centrism' is evident in the responses of Eckhart and Cusanus to the six Scotist/nominalist points listed above. These can be listed as:

1. Not indifferently either infinite or finite being, but instead purely infinite being is univocal, and the existence of created finite being must be seen as irreducibly paradoxical and as linked to the mystery of Trinitarian difference;

2. The infinite and the infinite/finite relation involves a logic outside the law of identity (though infinite and finite do not 'coincide' as for Hegel);

3. Universals and real relations must be considered in terms of the paradoxes of numbers and geometric figures which reveal how indeed every particular 'is' also an encompassing generality and every reality also 'tends' infinitely towards a completely different one. In this way the paradigmatic numerical reference point for the law of identity is itself undermined;

4. Linguistic construction may itself participate in ontological universals whilst our notions even of 'individuals' are also linguistically constructed;

5. We cannot create in the full sense that God does, because we do not originate being which is infinite; yet just as our very being is shared, so also all our actions can be seen as participating in the divine creative and 'linguistic' act of bringing about being. Hence in technology and art (though the extension from technology to art in the sense of 'the fine arts' is post-Cusa) we do not merely imitate nature and through nature the divine exemplars (as for Augustine), but share in the divine originating capacity (after Proclus's gloss on certain passages in Plato's *Republic* – as Boulnois has shown);[15]

6. Though God cannot create another infinity without doubling himself and so impossibly denying his own simplicity, his unlimited generosity involves a self-giving such that the bounds of finite reality are none other than his own bounds – hence the infinite bounds of the universe symbolise God, but they are not really 'there' as the bounds of the universe, though neither are they merely 'possible' (as for the Aristotelian conception of the infinite). Rather the universe tends infinitely (by a kind of transfinitude earlier spoken of explicitly by Robert Grosseteste) towards the true simple infinite which it 'is' at its (absent) heart.

In these ways Eckhart, Mirandola and Cusanus responded to later medieval theology with a newly problematised sense of the Creator/Creation distinction linked to a more 'modern' awareness of immanent dynamism, human self-construction and unlimited cosmic scope. In place of a rationalism tending to lose sight of the real, they replied in favour of a realism that has an intensified sense of extra-rational paradox within the real, of ineffable but real ontological 'connectors' and the primacy of spiritual shaping-forces in the cosmos and in humanity (extending the Augustinian account of *rationes seminales*) over mere 'representation' of the already given.

5. Radical Orthodoxy and twentieth-century philosophy

Hence, to turn now to the third question, Radical Orthodoxy sees its task of philo-sophical/theological synthesis as taking forwards the Renaissance/Romantic rethink-ing of authentic Christian tradition. This is one crucial aspect of the 'radicalism' of its orthodoxy. In loyalty to the most authentically Christian aspects of the R/R tradition, Radical Orthodoxy seeks to integrate into a metaphysically realist perspective a greater attention to 1. Sign, 2. Aspect and 3. Number.

In the first case it regards the linguistic turn as fundamentally correct, but does not read this in a quasi-transcendentalist way (after Wittgenstein, in the end, as Conor Cunningham has shown) as confining us all the more within finite limits, but rather as rendering the Kantian basis of securing these limits 'impossible' by undoing the Kan-tian 'correlation' between *a priori* categories and *a posteriori* appearances, respectively established from independent sources. For in language there can be no such inde-pendence: there is rather an original confusion. So if words are not 'destined' for sensory things in the way that concepts supposedly are for appearances, nor things for words, but rather words arise originally as a hermeneutic response to the world 'speaking' to us (as for Hamann), then we cannot dogmatically say that words are not obscurely disclosive of the infinite. And the indetermination to which our fundamentally hermeneutic circumstance gives rise (as 'postmodern' philosophies tended to imagine) does not in any way free us from metaphysics. Rather the reverse: it obligates a choice between a nihilistic metaphysics on the one hand – indeterminate unmeaning is more fundamental than meaning and it (un)discloses to us an originary void – and a (probably Christian) theological metaphysics on the other – indeterminate meaning points us, with a certain privileged, hierarchic trajectory, towards an 'unknown reason', the infinite of meaning in God which for Christians is the second person of the Trinity. The Radical Orthodoxy critique of the secular (and some pseudo-religious – Caputo, etc.) postmodern is, in essence, that it sometimes obfuscates the metaphysically optional character of its nihilistic vision, presenting it as the ineluctable outcome of theoretical rigour. (Derrida did this, but less clearly Deleuze, and today Badiou not at all.)

The attitude of Radical Orthodoxy to phenomenology runs rather parallel to its attitude towards 'linguistically based' philosophy (analysis, semiotics, deconstruction). If, in the latter case, sign and the interpretation of sign needs to be woven into metaphysical realism, then the same applies to 'the description of aspects'. Not *all* of the Renaissance discovery of 'perspective' was to do with either or both the reduction of thing to measurable object or the confinement of sight to the structures of sight itself.[16] Rather in some paintings (Piero della Francesca, for example) it could also be to do with a new sense of the variety of finite angles upon the infinite. This is 'the perspective upon perspective' that is echoed philosophically by Nicholas of Cusa. We see God always from a certain unique angle, just as we see finite things from a certain unique vantage. Modern phenomenology legitimately turns this round to stress that 'things themselves' only exist through the multiple (and in principle infinite) 'aspects' by which they are shown forth. That 'to be' is 'to affect' as well as 'to be affected' was something already announced by Plato. In this sense every ontology must also be an open-ended phenomenology, concerned with the unending task of describing how things 'show themselves forth' in the world.

However, what Radical Orthodoxy resists in this case also is the dominant 'transcendentalism' (or 'correlationism') of twentieth-century philosophy. We cannot, as Husserl and his heirs have imagined, arrive at any fundamental or framing phenomena, with the question of their underlying ontological base either bracketed or rendered superfluous. This is because the idea that we can have a 'pure' phenomenology, describing appearances only in terms of appearances, of 'how things show themselves', according to Husserl's 'principle of principles', is quite simply impossible. For every description, in order to be a description and not simply a mute regarding, has to describe what appears in terms of something *other* than what appears – description is ineluctably metaphorical. So characteristically, as Ray Brassier has argued, phenomenology since Heidegger has tended to select a dominant metaphor which it then regards as an 'arch-phenomenon' in terms of which everything else appears: 'Being', 'the Other', 'Auto-Affection', 'Saturation' and so forth. All the 'rigour of reduction' here is spurious, barely concealing what are obviously ungrounded elective preferences.[17]

What then, are the consequences for Radical Orthodoxy of rejecting the continental version of 'foundationalism'? What is the role of an 'impure' phenomenology? First, one is returned, after all, to 'the natural attitude'. There are only multiple phenomenologies of contingent natural-historical worlds whose description of affects includes our contingent response to those affects – hence also our interpretations of affects-as-signs. Secondly, without a Cusan 'conjecture' as to the invisible dimension of what appears (the 'ontological'), nothing does ever really appear to us. So whereas a pure phenomenology imposes transcendentalist boundaries through operation of the principle of principles, an impure phenomenology is already also in itself an ontology, also a metaphysics – even if it is one that is now problematically unfinished and always revisable. (The later work of Maurice Merleau-Ponty had more or less arrived at this position, which is much imbued with the influence of the 'spiritual realist' tradition.) Thirdly, a 'pure' phenomenology that has taken 'the theological turn' tends still, in neo-scholastic fashion, as with Jean-Luc Marion, to suppose that it can demonstrate the *a priori* possibility of revelation and even of a revelation taking a specifically Christian shape. Hence if the phenomenologists of the 'theological turn' accuse Radical Orthodoxy of 'neo-scholasticism', then this is a charge which we would cordially return. Nor do we see any real analogy here between their moves and those of Maurice Blondel, who stood within the avowedly metaphysical tradition of spiritual realism – as did the more recent French Catholic philosopher Claude Bruaire. For both thinkers spoke of a real foreshadowing of grace in its primary, self-establishing actuality. But this is what the transcendentalism of pure phenomenology would disallow. So the third point is that an impure phenomenology (which is also a hermeneutics, or a linguistic pragmatics) has no way of either discounting actual anticipations of grace, nor the idea that the irruption of specific grace with the Incarnation will result in an entire revision of phenomenology and philosophy as such. Radical Orthodoxy specifically seeks to dissolve the philosophy/theology disciplinary boundary in its modern academic form as both the offspring of bad theology and as the entrenchment of secular reason. Often one feels that the defences of this boundary are institutionally and professionally rather than intellectually motivated.

6. Radical Orthodoxy and the return of metaphysics in the twenty-first century

Broadly speaking, Radical Orthodoxy has tended then to endorse Rorty's deconstruction of analysis and Derrida's deconstruction of phenomenology. This has left the field clear for philosophies of indeterminate signs (Rorty and Derrida themselves), creative vital forces (Deleuze, reviving both Bergson and Whitehead), equally real 'possible worlds' (David Lewis) and anarchically selected numbers and figures (Badiou, Laruelle and Meillassoux, plus their British epigones).

The latter examples remind us that the dimension of 'number' also needs to be integrated into a modern metaphysical realism, because physics since Galileo has newly and repeatedly shown how mathematics can illuminate physical structures. This has positive implications for Christian theology for three reasons: first, it can be integrated with a longstanding Christian Pythagorean tradition of seeing the world as ordered according to 'weight and number' after the Biblical wisdom tradition. Secondly, Cusa inaugurated a tradition of showing how number, the very paradigm of identity, is yet subject to *aporias* (as shown yet further by modern set-theory) which reveal to us the primacy of the infinite and the imponderability of both the infinite and the infinite/finite relation. Thirdly, the problematic inseparability of qualitative from quantitative difference, as seen by Leibniz, newly suggests the dynamic, relational and perspectival character of all of reality. Giving due place to number, therefore – as one can already see in Augustine – tends to give an equal weight to relationality alongside substance within ontology.

There can nonetheless be a certain tension – as we see in the debates between Badiou and Deleuze – between a stress on the numerical and a stress on the vital, between mathematics and biology. But as the most recent work of Badiou tends to indicate, whilst numbers can support both fluidity and paradox, they are of themselves inert, incapable of accounting for the actuality even of physical motion, which is one reason (as Simon Oliver within Radical Orthodoxy has shown) why it is impossible to demonstrate the primacy of mechanical motion or its normativity for all forms of motion. Thus even Badiou, it would appear, has to have recourse in the end to his own form of the *élan vital*, to account for the emergence of 'appearing worlds' and of human 'truth-processes'.[18] Likewise his follower (in part) Quentin Meillassoux reverts, in a nihilistic mode, to Ravaisson and Lachelier's nineteenth-century argument that physical laws are entirely contingent, subordinate to the chance stabilisation of physical forces. But here, of course, Radical Orthodoxy, after Ravaisson, reads paradoxical 'primary habit' as incipient grace.

This reading bears a strong relation to Radical Orthodoxy's focus upon the postmodern exposure of indeterminacy. The latter privileged 'difference' over 'sameness' and, in refusing any subordination of difference to 'resemblance', inevitably read the univocal plane within which difference arises as a plane of conflict. For, if what justifies a difference is only itself, then it is only different by virtue of pure aggressive assertion. Yet this entire rendering is a mere wager upon the primacy of ontological violence. To wager otherwise, with Radical Orthodoxy, on ontological peacableness, is to reinvoke 'resemblance' as genuine analogy. This is not, as Deleuze would have it, the triumph of the same, but on the contrary that which allows there to be differences at all without an *agon* that must be incipient mutual abolition. It is also that which allows differences to be there at all *in actuality,* as opposed to the mere *possibility* or at best *virtuality* of 'sheer' difference, which is what the ontology of primary difference must require, since no 'absolute' difference, without relation, could ever be visible. (Both Derrida and Deleuze are very clear about this.)

In searching again for a logic of analogy, Radical Orthodoxy asserts the primacy of mediation, or of 'the between' – though not necessarily after Hegel, as already stated. Sometimes, following Catherine Pickstock, this has been spoken of as 'non-identical repetition'. But it could also, following the lead of spiritual realism, be called 'paradoxical habit'. Habit is that which is prior to either identity or difference, undergirds both substance and relation, mediates matter and mind, motion and meaning. And reason and grace.

Alongside sign, aspect and number then, habit transferred from Thomistic practical to Thomistic theoretical reason also assists the re-thinking of metaphysical realism in an era aware of temporality, evolution and historicity. All four can be seen as working at inorganic and pre-human organic levels if one accepts, after Ravaisson, the primacy of habit over law and so the priority of something like Whitehead's 'prehension' over the operation of efficient causality.

It has to be admitted though, that there is some truth in the criticism made by many (including some Barthians, for example Michael Banner, now of Trinity Cambridge) that Radical Orthodoxy was originally in danger of making postmodern philosophy an 'apologetic' starting point in an all too liberal manner. One can see this now more clearly in the wake of philosophers like Badiou, Laruelle and Brassier who accuse even Derrida and Deleuze of having essentially 'humanistic' preoccupations.

What they mean quite simply is this: it is all very well to speak of the primacy of the linguistic, the semiotic or the figural over human beings, but all these categories derive from the human, all too human 'liberal arts'. But if 'material' and inhuman forces are really in control, nothing really justifies the view that linguistic processes disclose anything real, not even the primacy of unmeaning.

So it is arguable that the 'apologetic' task for Radical Orthodoxy is thereby shifted one stage backwards. Before beginning with the 'given' indeterminacy of language, one must construct an argument about the status of this 'givenness' – for all that this remains undeniable, at least at the phenomenal level. And this argument clearly has to deal with the issue of 'mind' and 'soul' as well as with the issue of language. For despite the postmodern talk of the primacy of language over thought, it is clear (as Derrida himself came to stress) that language is through and through 'psychic'. If linguistic meaning is epiphenomenal, then that is because mind is so likewise. Therefore inversely, defending the primacy of language means defending the irreducibility of the psychic. Here various strategies are open: one can point out that physicalist reductionism leaves a sheer unexplained mystery as to why we have the illusion of thinking and receiving phenomenal disclosures or 'qualia'; one can also suggest that 'thinking' may be in some sense a dimension of all of reality – an option increasingly favoured within analytic philosophy by those rightly bothered by the just-mentioned anomaly.

I have now said enough, I hope, to indicate why initial Radical Orthodoxy preoccupations with language and culture have recently been supplemented (in the work of Simon Oliver, Conor Cunningham, Michael Hanby, Robert Miner and others) with diverse explorations of physics, biology and the mind/brain relation. (It should be mentioned here that Nicholas Lash and John Cornwell of Cambridge much earlier saw the importance of these dimensions for contemporary theology.) I also hope that I have indicated why there is here continuity rather than rupture.

At the start of the twenty-first century, therefore, Radical Orthodoxy finds itself alongside those who are breaking with the main versions of twentieth-century philosophy and seeking to 'return to metaphysics' whether in a naturalistic or a spiritualistic guise. With Pope Benedict therefore, we proclaim the 'grandeur of reason' in its unlimited reach, beyond the transcendentalist confines of the finite, which can only be insinuated by a philosophy that is 'metaphysical' in the bad sense of reducing the ontological to the univocal and ontic and finally the epistemological and thereby seeking to corral it against theology.[19] A true metaphysical confidence in reason, on the other hand, only enjoys this confidence because it has a *faith* in the infinity of unknown reason beyond our grasp – the infinity of the *Logos* which is participatively mediated to us by our liturgical journey through time. The grandeur of reason is therefore also the nobility of faith, the primacy of habit and desire and the essential role of matter and the senses. This grandeur, is, as Benedict has clearly expounded, anything but rationalism and is severely impaired and finally undermined by the latter, in the fashion that I have tried to indicate.

7. What makes Radical Orthodoxy radical?

But having said all that I have said so far, readers may still be asking the old and valid question: just what is it that makes Radical Orthodoxy radical? The answer is that, not only is this title deliberately paradoxical, but also the combination works in paradoxically different ways.

On the one hand, what is meant is the radicalism of orthodoxy as such. The idea that orthodox Christianity brought about a shift so fundamental than all later 'radicalisms' are but phony makeshifts by comparison. Christianity placed love above law; it put the person-in-relation before either the collective or the isolated individual; it made the habit of association primary and yet it never instrumentally subordinated the person to collective interests. It did not, like antique materialism, refuse the noble in the name of the many and the general; instead it redefined nobility in such a way as to place it within the reach of all, yet it did not thereby abolish the hierarchy of example. It produced 'community' through the common ingesting of the 'mystical' Body of Christ which engendered a 'true' body of ecclesial unity-in-diversity, neither atomically individualist nor collectively universalising on an abstract basis. It led in all these ways to a new sort of 'interpersonal' society, fused throughout by pastoral, economic ('household') concerns. Hence the Western world of individual liberty, of developed 'personality', of free association, of obsessive 'care' and 'welfare' remains entirely a Christian world.

The case of Radical Orthodoxy is that, to have all this in the most radical and least perverted form, it is always necessary to go back to Christian 'roots', because otherwise the whole thing will eventually collapse — towards individualism, a neo-pagan enslavement and a post-Christian utilitarian control through false 'care' of merely material bodies — without the quite specific Christian metaphysical underpinning.

In this sense a 'radical' orthodoxy means a militant orthodoxy in the sense of a proper integrity. Unlike many modern religious people, we are not playing disingenuous games — we are not for example pretending that secularity is a providential blessing-in-disguise, like Bonhoeffer at his worst. To the contrary, we are arguing that in the end secular dominance will undermine all the goods that it has inherited from Christendom, including those goods (like female emancipation) which clearly and admittedly have been able to develop more freely (if distortedly) outside clerical and Church-institutional oversight. Therefore we believe that secular order must be overcome and a new mode of 'Christendom' invented. (Given that 'Christianity' and 'Christendom' are the same word, and any separation of the two suggests a disincarnate, asocial, acultural, early-modern derived 'belief' that could not possibly be Christian at all.)

However, 'radical orthodoxy' *also* implies a radicalisation of orthodoxy. Some dimensions of this have already been alluded to. It seems to me that there is considerable truth in the Illich/Taylor argument that *agape* got over-institutionalised in the Latin West – even if one might argue that it was equally *under*-institutionalised in the Greek–Slavic East. The over 'disciplinary' society in the Latin West also connects to an increasing over-emphasis on sexual sins (as charted by historians like Jean Delumeau and John Bossy) as well as to a 'culture of fear' (traced by Delumeau) that is directly connected to an equal Latin over-stress on hell and a too-restricted account of its harrowing by Christ. Here the sympathies of Radical Orthodoxy tend to be Origenist and Nyssan – emphasising at least the eternal openness of divine love to spiritual repentance and perhaps also (in my own case, definitely) arguing the view that God simply cannot be God (omnipotent goodness) if in the end the 'impossibility' of evil and suffering is not entirely overcome – or banished as corrosive illusion. Nothing finally can *be* corroded, if being is 'to be' at all.

This is an example of how, at some points, Radical Orthodoxy is prepared to contest what 'orthodoxy' precisely is. But more generally, we seek a 'radicalisation' of orthodoxy in a double sense. First, we do not regard the development of doctrine as over – for example, I think that the exact implications for the Father and the Holy Spirit of the Incarnation, given that the Son is entirely constituted by substantive relations to the other two persons, remain under-explored. Nor, of course, will we have ever have finished with drawing 'new things' from the infinite plenitude of meaning contained in the Scriptures. The unfinishedness of *doctrina* is a direct consequence of the primacy of the Church's liturgical, contemplative and 'spiritual' reading (according to the traditional 'four senses') of the Scriptures over any more abstract reflection designed to guard the boundaries of acceptable belief and practice. For this reason we regard very sympathetically the attempt of the Russian 'sophiologists' (from Soloviev to Bulgakov) to think through the implications of Biblical statements about hypostasised Wisdom beyond the what Christian tradition has so far entertained.

Second, we tend to favour renewed attention to those thinkers whom I would describe as 'hyperbolically orthodox'. I am thinking primarily of Eriugena, Eckhart and Cusanus, but to a degree I would also include Anselm, Kierkegaard and Chesterton. What these thinkers have in common is an attempt to think in a 'concentrated' form the logic that runs through all of Christian doctrine, besides a willingness to probe deeply the paradoxes implied by doctrine itself – in such a way that they can seem to the superficial to be deviating from orthodoxy in this very attempt. (If they do at all deviate, then this is on account of the integrity of their orthodoxy which has to raise questions even about the meaning of orthodoxy at certain obscure points.) I would myself make a distinction between the 'broad' Christian theologians who are *more* paradigmatic because of their reach, complexity and supple variety – Augustine, Maximus, Aquinas – and the 'concentrated' thinkers whom I have already mentioned who may be more secondary and yet consistently 'push things further' in a way that we cannot now ignore. They also tend to favour a vision of universal cosmic salvation that is more compatible with the glory of God and more likely to deliver us in practice from 'disciplinary' aberrations.

It is quite likely that the majority of those who like the sound of our 'radicalism' in the first sense will be suspicious of our radicalism in the second. And vice-versa. But that is just why we exist – to attract those rare and finely-tuned souls who see that the double radicalism is both crucial and authentic. For a Christian radicalism not promoting orthodoxy cannot be radical; but equally an orthodoxy that does not seek to radicalise itself continuously cannot be orthodox.

As to those for whom the very notion of an 'orthodoxy' is anathema, I can only direct them to certain remarks of W. H. Auden. It is not 'doctrine' that is the prime source of authoritarian violence. Rather the very failure of a religion to define its boundaries is a licence to the sectarian to become intolerant through insistence on adherence to inessentials or to eccentric distortions of a tradition.[20] A contemporary gloss might conclude that it is Islam, Judaism and Protestantism's *lack* of a magisterium which encourages both anarchic and state terror to be conducted falsely in their name.

And one could add that this terror is also linked to the most iconoclastic, most unmediated and deracinated modes of these faiths. Their very complicity with modern rationalism and denial or trivialisation of the image ensures the extreme literal positivity and non-negotiability of their religious message, which is deemed to fall from a clear sky with the same clear drop into the treeless urban desert, wherever on the earth's surface one may happen to be.

8. Radical Orthodoxy and the Church today

I hope that everything which I have said so far gives some sense of the intellectual developments and self-clarifications that Radical Orthodoxy has recently undergone. However, those who attend the conferences of the Centre of Theology and Philosophy, set up to promote Radical Orthodoxy and the debates which it has instigated, will testify that Radical Orthodoxy has become more than an academic tendency. It is also a network of friends and an ethos – an ethos that extends its embrace to many who scarcely agree with Radical Orthodoxy at all, but who resonate with some of its aspects or feel that it has instigated important questions and inspired interesting reflections. On this basis it is not going too far to suggest that it is already a cultural movement in embryo.

This is already bearing two fruits – both of them the linked concern of the think-tank *Cosmopolis*, which exists to promote Radical Orthodoxy's more public and practical goals. These are the pursuit of Church unity and the promotion of a global Christian order. The two are seen as intimately linked, because the divisions between Protestantism, Catholicism and Orthodoxy are closely echoed in current divisions between the Anglo-Saxon world, continental Europe and Russia. Accordingly, we reject the views of those who think that institutional Church unity is of no importance, because it is clear that the division of institutions is inseparable from cultural tensions and ideological disagreements. On the other hand, we consider that future unity under the *aegis* of Rome, which is what should be sought, must allow a proper place also for the operation of conciliar principles and for creative cultural diversity.

But what Radical Orthodoxy may specifically have to contribute to the ecumenical cause is twofold. First, a genealogy of 'what went wrong', besides one of 'what went right', that tends to cut across denominational divides, by pivoting upon a focal point in time – roughly the year 1300 – that long preceded the Reformation and even the full consolidation of East/West divisions. Secondly, an extreme scepticism about any ecumenical advance achieved through official 'dialogue' and interconfessional documents (whose compromises are too often dishonest and fail therefore to be accorded any wide credence). Rather what is needed is an extension of the activity of inter-confessional cultural bodies like Radical Orthodoxy itself, which will tend to encourage an *ad hoc* increase in intercommunion, on the basis of an increasingly shared theology and spirituality rather than a vague well-meaning. Also important is an increased practice of different denominations sharing the same sacred places – in England and Wales this is especially important to the continued role of its medieval parish church buildings and can also serve to rebuild local cohesion. If reunion under Rome can finally be achieved, then this will be because it has already become a *de facto* reality. Very important here is the increasingly 'post-Protestant' disposition of most of the more reflective Protestants – to which I believe the Vatican will accord a careful attention.[21]

It might be added here that ecumenism needs a greater sense that the existing episcopally ordered churches are *already* parts of the one Church – that ontologically speaking, disunity is more of a delusory appearance than a reality. Then the task becomes one of denying in reality that false seeming. The old lady who might attend her Catholic Mass in the morning and Anglican evensong in the evening in double-acknowledgment of both Pope and historic parish would be doing just that.

Moreover, with the full support of Radical Orthodoxy, Rowan Williams has recently shown that he realises that the only way out of the 'Anglican gay crisis' is to play the 'Catholic' card – including a sense of the potential conciliar authority of the Rome–Constantinople–Canterbury triangle – in order to outmanoeuvre both the evangelical extremists (indifferent to all Church order) and the liberals (indifferent to everything except indifference). This inspired but difficult strategy can surely allow the Anglican Church to play a creative role in the kind of ecumenical process which I am talking about. Nor are its early wrestlings with – if, arguably, premature theological resolutions of – those issues of gender and sexuality which face us all today, necessarily any disqualifications for this role.

9. The politics of paradox

The second sphere of Radical Orthodoxy's practical involvement is the political. As Phillip Blond has suggested, there are now three crucial global forces in the world:

capitalist rationality, Islam and Christianity. And of the latter two, the global reach of Christianity is far more serious and far more likely to prevail in the long-term. This means that the anomaly pointed out almost a century ago by Hilaire Belloc is likely to pose its cultural contradiction ever more strongly upon the world stage. This is the manifest gap between the teachings of Christianity which still undergird Western morality on the one hand and the theory and practice of capitalism on the other.[22]

Radical Orthodoxy believes that only the Church has the theoretical and practical power to challenge the global hegemony of capital and to create a viable politico-economic alternative. We stand thereby in a long tradition of Anglican and Catholic Christian socialism which has always insisted on the necessity of the 'Christian' component for the 'Socialist' one. In that sense we have always stood proudly amongst those who see themselves as 'conservative theologically, radical politically'.

But over the years we have become more aware of the potential for smugness and inertia in that perspective. One can gently challenge it in three ways. First, there is a dimension that I have already hinted at. Can Christians really, fundamentally, categorise themselves as either left or right? Surely, as André de Muralt has argued, both the ideas of 'the rule of one', of the sovereign centre, and of the 'rule of the many', of individuals either in contracted dispersion or collective unity are equally 'nominalist' – both genealogically and ontologically? For both deny primary real relation, the real universal that is 'the common good' and the role of 'the few', whether that of the guiding virtuous elite or of the mediating institutions of civil society. But 'right' and 'left' define themselves variously in terms of either 'the one' or 'the many'. Today, of course, what we really have is two versions of a 'left' celebration of the many either as individuals or as a democratically voting mass. For reasons still not yet sufficiently accounted for by historians and social theorists, we have a 'liberal right' stressing economic negative liberty and a 'liberal left', stressing cultural and sexual negative liberty. In reality, of course, the two liberalisms are triumphing both at once and in secretly collusive harmony – perhaps what still sustains party conflict is alternating anxieties amongst the populace about the inevitable insecurities generated by now economic and now cultural 'freedom' in different temporal phases.

It follows that the very division of left and right assumes a nominalist social ontology which of course Radical Orthodoxy rejects. And it is also critically important to remind oneself that this division only postdates the French revolution. This has created a curious historical delusion from which almost no one is really free. For we suppose that the pre-modern is somehow allied with 'the right', just as barbarous journalists frequently imagine that the divine right of kings was a medieval theory, when it was in reality an early-modern one. But pre-nominalist modernity was neither left nor right, neither 'progressivist' nor 'reactionary' – it was simply 'other' to most of our assumed socio-political categories.

There is a further point to be made here. When the French revolutionaries invented 'left' and 'right', they arguably took us back to paganism and indeed they often explicitly supposed that they were doing so. For characteristically, the ancient Greeks lined-up philosophies of the spirit and of 'ideal forms' with aristocracy and philosophies of matter with democracy. It is as if they assumed that the latter was always a matter of LCD and not of HCF. But as I have already suggested, the Christian revolution cuts right across this categorisation. Instead of siding with 'the noble' over against 'the base', or inversely 'the base' over against 'the noble', it paradoxically democratises the noble: hence Paul addresses his interlocutors as 'all kings'. Yet at the same time, if there is now a new possibility of the spread of virtue (virtue being redefined as the more generally possible attitudes of love and trust, immune to the instance of 'moral luck' as usually understood), there is still a political place for the superior role of the more virtuous and of those appointed to be the 'guardians' of virtue, the virtuosos of *charisma*.

But unlike those paradigms of virtue hitherto, 'the heroes', these Christian 'pastors' (who are 'shepherds' like Plato's guardians) will frequently remain both mocked and invisible, since they may lack the glamour of obvious 'honour', and may need to retain a hidden 'outlaw' status in order both to escape the need to appease the masses upon whose adulation manifest power depends and to directly execute a summary justice which the procedures of inevitably inflexible law might foil. This is the theme brilliantly explored in Christopher Nolan's Batman film, *The Dark Knight*, with its explicit Platonic resonances concerning the noble lie and so forth. But the film leaves us with the Platonic *aporia* of a division between the ignoble hero-ruler (a J. F. Kennedy figure) whom the people must *believe* to be noble if they are to have any ideals and the genuinely noble outlaw-guardian who must pursue virtue in uncorrupted secrecy (thereby passing the test of Gyges ring). The only dimension that can in part resolve this aporetic tension is the Christian one of sacramental ordination and anointed monarchy. The ideal symbolic dimension of the pastoral role implicitly corrects with its equitable outlawry any abuse of legal authority – it also to an extent permits the enactment of such equity to the degree that awe at sacred charisma can override the blandishments of popular concession to which mere democracy must remain prone. And yet – save for the example of Lear on the heath in the storm, or Walter Scott's Richard the Lionheart in Sherwood Forest – the priest-as-apostle rather than the monarch surpasses even this possibility of visible purity by stepping, like Paul, in and out of visibility, in alternation of command and vagabondage. Thus likewise there is still a monarch at the summit of the *ecclesia* – but it is the crucified, resurrected, ascended and so apparently absent Jesus, who died as a king but had nowhere on earth to lay his head, and it is this pattern which should be followed by the Church hierarchy which mediates his authority.

The politic-ecclesial pattern suggested by the NT is therefore democratic/aristocratic/monarchic. Following the norms of antique political thought, this has often in Christian history implied that one or the other stress should dominate according to the prevalence or otherwise of virtue. One could validly say that the ultimate bias of

Christianity is democratic, because its aim is that all should love and trust, all should become virtuous. In this sense it has a populist slant 'to the left'. But this is not exactly 'the modern left', because Christianity (unlike Bush and Blair) sees no automatic merit in democracy in all circumstances, nor any validity in the notion that the will of the majority should always prevail. Its reasons for favouring democracy are rather that the entire truth of Christianity exists in harmonious dispersal amongst the body of Christ (eschatologically the entire human race and the entire cosmos) and that agreement in the truth requires ideally a free consensus.

The post-revolutionary 'left' however, tends to revive a pagan sense of democracy as LCD: it links democracy to naturalistic materialism and to a sophistic individualism. One can contrast this with John Ruskin's genuinely Christian and explicitly at once 'Tory' and 'communist' desire to extend norms of nobility, of self-regulation of standards of behaviour, work, outcomes and protection of members from the 'liberal' professions also to mercantile and artisanal pursuits.

It is mainly for this reason that 'a Christian left' is not really situated within the same spectrum as the secular left – for it both aspires to democratise excellence and to grant an educative and political role to the exponents of excellence in order to balance-out the verdict of the many. (I would, for example, favour a *genuinely* aristocratic House of Lords including the representation of key corporate bodies, but certainly not an elected House of Lords which would only increase the power of party machines and cripple the ability of the Lords to check the passage of deleterious legislation – a capacity that has recently been often exercised in favour of the 'left' as much as in favour of 'the right'.) But this requirement does not compromise democracy – rather it enables it. For democracy is not an infinite regress – no one finally votes on the *dominant options presented to people*, and if these are not the work of disciplined elites, educated towards virtue as well as knowledge, then they will be the work of propagandists, of a corrupted elite, as now prevails.

The second reason for questioning an over-glib 'conservative in theology/radical in politics' equation is that one has to integrate one's politics with one's ecclesiology. The Lamennaisian combination of hierarchy in metaphysical truth, democracy in pragmatic politics, will not quite do. Of course it is by no means entirely false: in Church affairs what matters is truth, not opinion, and so hierarchy must prevail. In secular affairs, though, a second-best pragmatic peace may usually be the priority and therefore consensus must prevail at the cost otherwise of unacceptable violence and outright inhumanity. Yet in the end there can be, for Christianity, no such absolute contrast. The earthly city is valid insofar as it serves the heavenly and from the outset Christianity has modified the role of the political ruler in a 'pastoral' direction (sometimes for ill as well as good, as I have mentioned). He becomes more a kind of ecclesial pastor of material affairs – which always have an implication for our salvation. Here also we need to balance Western with Eastern perspectives: the 'monarch' may be properly subordinate to 'the priest', and his dealing in law and coercive violence is now (uniquely by Christianity) desacralised because of its ambivalence – and yet the 'kingly' role remains Christological insofar as it foreshadows the integrity of the resurrected body, when the material will fully shine with the glory of the spiritual. In the end Christ's priesthood fades, and his kingship remains. Perhaps therefore something authentically 'Byzantine' has shone out in the Anglican stress upon the 'incarnational' aspect of socio-political transformation – even if this has often been perverted by support for the modern sovereign and disciplinary State.

The sense that the secular arm is 'within' as well as 'outside' the Church accords then with the need also for secular hierarchy for the reasons which I have explained. But inversely, one can also argue that we need more democracy inside the Church. This is because, as Newman pointed out, the 'correctness' of doctrine must finally be tested in practice by the assent of all. This is because Christian truth abides more fundamentally in the entirety of liturgical and pastoral life than it does in abstract reflection.

Political theory and ecclesiology must finally then be of one piece. Both involve a classical mixture of democracy, aristocracy and kingship, even if the Christian *demos* is paradoxically anointed and Christian kingship is paradoxically kenotic.

The third reason for questioning a facile Christian leftism is circumstantial. In the face of the ever-increasing triumph of capitalism in our times, secular socialism has all but vanished and the left increasingly understands itself as liberal, and frequently in addition as atheist and anti-religious. The minority who continue seriously to question the free market have increasingly begun to realise that in some measure an opposition to this can only be 'conservative' – and indeed I have always argued that originally in France socialism itself was somewhat 'counter-Enlightenment' in character. This is because only what is 'sacred', what possesses a value that reason cannot fully fathom – that which, therefore is validated only by modes of usually religious tradition – is truly immune from commodification. Equally, a non-nominalist politics, stressing the role of 'the few' both in the mode of mediating associations and of virtuous elites, must perforce appeal back to the Middle Ages and seek to recommence what Belloc referred to as its unfinished project of freeing people from antique slavery by assuring the widest possible distribution of land and capital which will allow both individual creativity and collective sharing and conviviality (the latter being something which Belloc's overly modern liberal perspective – despite everything – failed properly to emphasise. It is for this reason that one can correct his 'distributism' with the articulation of a 'distributist socialism').

It is also the case that a secular liberal left is unable metaphysically to validate even its own liberalism, because its abandonment of any belief in the spiritual reality of 'mind' or 'soul' leaves it with only a sham belief in either freedom or ideals worth struggling for. Inevitably it plays more and more lip service to 'scientific' diagnoses of human behaviour and more and more favours a utilitarian state-plus-market control of human beings designed to facilitate their maximally efficient collective functioning.

With these provisos, Radical Orthodoxy on the whole stands within that tradition of non-statist Christian Socialism which regards modern statism as involving the support of the very rich, a guarantee of their finances and an enabling additional support through 'welfare' of their dispossessed workforce. However, one needs also to recognise a wider family resemblance with many variants of Christian social teaching which characteristically stress subsidiarity (the distribution of money and power to appropriate levels, not necessarily the lowest) and the break-up of central sovereignty through the operation of intermediary associations. These theories can appear as relatively more 'left' or 'right', yet all in reality question the left/right distinction in its secular form. In relation to the latter Christians must pursue a politics of seeming paradox from apparently 'opposite' vantage points. Thus some within Radical Orthodoxy may follow Phillip Blond in his espousal of a new British form of 'Red Toryism'. Others, currently the majority, will follow my own brand of 'Blue Socialism' – socialism with a Burkean tinge, now common to many of the more reflective on the left, including some within the centre-left (anti-New Labour) British Labour party 'Compass Group' like John Cruddas.

But these differences may not be what matters. In either case the debate is about how one would bring about a just distribution that would render reactive State 'redistribution' mostly redundant and how this would be sustained. These debates concern the role of cooperatives, of trade-guilds, of mutual banks, housing associations and credit unions and of the law in setting firewalls between business practices, defining the acceptable limit of usury and the principles that must govern the fair setting of wages and prices. Above all perhaps they concern how we can turn all people into owners and joint owners, abolishing the chasm between the mass who only earn or receive welfare and so are dependent and the minority who own in excess.

This abolition will then allow a more genuine, multi-stepped and educationally dynamic hierarchy of virtue to operate. For in the economic sphere also there needs to be a mixture of the democratic and the paternalistically guided: some enterprises are adapted to the cooperative, others require more hierarchical corporations. But the corporation based upon Christian principles must, like the units of 'feudalism' in the Middle Ages, combine political and economic functions, since the engineered indifference of these to each other is not a division of spheres preserving liberty, but rather an abuse which permits both 'the purely economic' and the 'purely political' to enjoy a nihilistic sway. For defined in purity apart from each other they both cease to involve moral concern and oversight and instead come to have an exclusive regard for the positive power of money as such or the positive power of law as such. By contrast, exchange for the social good must also be 'political' in character, whilst legislation for the social good has to have regard to the economic in all its aspects.

This mention of a 'corporatist' aspect is bound of course to raise charges of fascism as are those paradoxical titles which seem to invoke a crossover of left and right. But this is ahistorical – the Christian Democratic parties at the end of the Second World War for a short time (before they succumbed to the lure of liberalism) sought to recapture from fascism principles of Catholic social teaching which it had perverted. For fascism involves a secular cult of state, race or military power that really lines up with modern political nominalism: it is bound in reality (as experience has always proved) increasingly to eradicate the role of the few and so both to exalt the One at the sovereign centre and to disguise through *ersatz* paternalistic pretence the market manipulation of the many at the margins. It should be added here that *religion* can provide the element of tacit binding ethos that prevents both distributism and corporatism from drifting back towards the twin dominance of the State and monopoly capitalism. More specifically one needs the *Church* as an organisation is continuous excess of the State in order to coordinate without suppressing the diverse activities of intermediate associations. (Lack of this, as William Cavanaugh has argued, has often led to the perversion of Christian Democratic projects in Latin America.)

Radical Orthodoxy is by no means alone in coming to some of the above insights. Hence various of its members have been recently involved in behind-the-scenes cross-party interactions between 'old Labourites' and 'old Tories' striving to forge a new common anti-liberal and radical alternative. The point here though is not necessarily the formation of a new political party, because party politics is so stuck in the nominalism of left/right. It is rather about the creation of a new 'movement' that might eventually encourage the formation of a new 'ethos'.

This ethos is radically Catholic rather than radically Protestant. An aspect of the deadlock in British and American politics today is the way in which the hinterland of the left's assumptions remain determinatively Protestant. Indeed its subjectivism, emotionalism, restrictive Puritanism, iconoclasm and opposition to high culture owe more in the end to the Reformation than they do to the Enlightenment. These attitudes are all powerless to resist capitalism and bureaucracy, because both are profoundly promoted by the mainstream Protestant legacy. Even the radical Protestant legacy is in the end unable to think beyond individualism, sectarian isolation and collectivism – which is but individualism dialectically inverted or else writ large. Anabaptism also is usually mired in the social metaphysics of the *via moderna*, or else its anti-metaphysical perpetuation – though one can allow that certain British dissenting radicals, like William Blake (as Peter Ackroyd has suggested) were strangely echoing, in a newly creative way, the suppressed British Catholic past.

By contrast, it is only a 'Catholic centre' more extreme than either of the extremes, because it points metacritically to a different plane, which can think and act its way out of our current heretical, immoral and neopagan political morass.

10. Conclusion

Politically, culturally, ecclesially, theologically, Radical Orthodoxy is just one of the new 'creative minorities' spoken of by Pope Benedict, whose youthful and spontaneous spirit is renewing Christendom throughout the world. But it is already playing its part and I trust will continue to do so.

Notes

1   In this initial section I am immensely indebted to Johannes Hoff for his as yet unpublished paper, delivered at the 5th Radical Orthodoxy/Centre of Theology and Philosophy (RO/COTP) conference in Rome in September 2008: 'Self-revelation as Principle of Christian Theology? Critical Considerations on Modern Responses to the Conundrum of Faith and Reason'.

2   See Bruno Latour, *Pandora's Hope: Essays on the Reality of Science Studies* (Cambridge Mass: Harvard University Press, 1999), esp. ch. 9.

3   Odo Casel, *The Mystery of Christian Worship* (London: DLT, 1962) and see Louis Bouyer, *Life and Liturgy* (London: Sheed and Ward, 1978), pp. 86–98. Bouyer's scepticism, in partial criticism of Casel, about any possible influence of Greek Mystery Religions on the NT, seems itself now open to question in terms of recent scholarship. One can now argue about whether the Greek mysteries were, as Bouyer said, originally 'just rites' without much cognitive or contemplative dimension; whether the gods whose death was celebrated in them were without any active agency in their own resurrections and finally why, exactly, this influence being denied, Paul used the word *mysterion*.

4   On Eriugena in this respect, see Olivier Boulnois, *Au-délà de l'image: une archéologie du visuel au Moyen Âge Ve–XVIe siècle* (Paris: Seuil, 2008).

5   See John Milbank, *The Suspended Middle* (Grand Rapids/London: Eerdmans/SCM, 2005).

6   See John Milbank and Catherine Pickstock, *Truth in Aquinas* (London: Routledge, 2001); Michel Corbin, *Le Chemin de la théologie chez Thomas d'Aquin* (Paris: Beauchesne, 1972); Philipp W. Rosemann, *Omne ens est aliquid; Introduction à la lecture du "système" philosophique de saint Thomas d'Aquin* (Louvain/Paris: Peeters, 1996).

7   See John Milbank, 'The Double Glory or Paradox versus Dialectics: on not quite agreeing with Slavoj Žižek' in John Milbank and Slavoj Žižek, *The Monstrosity of Christ: Paradox versus Dialectics* (Boston: MIT, 2009).

8   See Dominque Janicaud, *Ravaisson et la métaphysique: une généalogie du spiritualisme français* (Paris: Vrin, 1997).

9   Félix Ravaisson, *De l'habitude* (1957[1838]) (Paris: Presses Universitaires Francaises, 1957). [Recent English translation with dual-text: *Of Habit*, trans. Clare Carlisle and Mark Sinclair (New York: Continuum, 2008)]; and *Testament Philosophique* (2008 [1901] (Paris: Allia, 2008).

10   See David Grummett's first-rate article, 'Blondel, Modern Catholic Theology and the Eucharistic Bond' in *Modern Theology*, Vol. 23 No. 4 Oct. 2007, 561–77.

11   A similar reading of Augustine on illumination was offered in a paper (now lost) by Rowan Williams to the first RO conference in Oxford in 2002.

12   See Boulnois, *Au-délà de l'image* (see Note 4).

13   Charles Taylor, *A Secular Age* (New Haven: Yale University Press 2007). See also my review-article on the book, 'A Closer Walk on the Wild-Side', in *Studies in Christian Ethics*, Vol. 22 No. 1 Feb. 2009, 89–104.

14   There are also hints of such a thesis in the work of Peter Brown.

15   Boulnois, *Au-délà de l'image* (see Note 4), 355–62.

16   See, classically, Erwin Panofsky, *Perspective as Symbolic Form* (New York Zone, 1997). But see also, James Elkins, *The Poetics of Perspective* (Ithaca NY: Cornell University Press, 1994).

17   Ray Brassier, *Nihil Unbound: Enlightenment and Extinction* (London: Palgrave, 2007), 26–31.

18   Alain Badiou, *Logique des mondes: l'être et l'événement 2* (Paris: Seuil, 2006).

19   One can argue with some plausibility, like Jean-Luc Marion, that, historically speaking, 'metaphysics' can *only* have this 'bad' sense. Then one would need another word for the kind of theologically linked metaphysical realism that I am talking about. This is a largely semantic issue, but there would seem still to be enough precedent for my usage in the way that Aquinas and other pre-moderns spoke of the 'metaphysical' without according it the full autonomy of an independent discipline.

20   Auden declared that, 'if no one knows what is essential and what is unessential, the unessential is vested with religious importance (to dislike ice cream becomes a proof of heresy)'.

Or not wearing a headscarf, or wearing one, one could now add. This passage is cited by the contemporary English poet Sean O'Brien in his review headed 'Ice Cream Tests' of *The Complete Works of W.H. Auden: Prose Volume Three 1949–1955* (Princeton Conn: Princeton University Press, 2008) in *The Times Literary Supplement*, No. 5502, 12 September 2008, 3–5.

21   How to counteract the phenomenon of the dominant Pentecostalism and excessive Biblicism of *unthinking* Protestantism, with its increasing alliance to capitalist success culture and its ever-increasing anti-Christian fissiparous tendencies, is a huge problem to which I do not pretend to have any easy answer – save to suggest that we must promote far more vigorously the centrality of parish life and its importance to all aspects of the local community. See John Milbank, 'Stale Expressions: the Management-Shaped Church' in John Milbank *The Future of Love: Essays in Political Theology* (Eugene OR: Wipf and Stock, 2009).

22   See for this and some of what follows, Hilaire Belloc, *The Servile State* (New York: Cosimo, 2007).

Index

Abraham 223, 243, 244, 255n59
absence 262, 267, 269, 273, 279, 281, 283
absolutism 182, 184, 188, 190, 345
accidents 92, 278, 279–81
Adam 295, 347, 351, 358; beatific vision 128; *dominium* 181, 182, 183, 185; naming of the world by 291; reason 279
Adams, John 349
aesthetics 131, 386
Agamben, Giorgio 213–14, 215, 219–20, 240
agnosticism 97, 100
Agricola, Rudolph 156, 174n16
d'Ailly, Pierre 179, 183–84, 188
allegory 189, 190, 295
Althusser, Louis 248–49
analogy 12, 130–31, 376, 383; Aquinas 100, 113n110, 139–40, 143n4; of attribution 15–17, 18, 26n28, 122, 126, 129, 139, 385; Duns Scotus 120, 136; faith/reason relationship 370; language use 96, 97; of proportion 15, 26n26, 73, 100; revelation 127
Anselm, St. 87, 121, 394
anti-Semitism 206–7, 210–11, 219
Apologists 245–46
aporia of learning 42, 273, 279, 282, 284
Aquinas, St. Thomas 12, 13–17, 42, 116, 345, 394; analogy 15–17, 139–40; Ango-American scholarship 46; Augustinianism 380; *communicatio* 360n20; creation 67, 132, 134, 237–38, 376; Cross on 142n4; defence of 41; difference 374–75; *dominium* 182;

Eucharist 263, 274–82; exegesis 127; existence 33; faith/reason relationship 69–74, 86–89, 93; freedom 124; God as subject of metaphysics 126; grace 378; imitation 276; infinity 123; intellect 121, 137; intimacy 239; magnanimity 343–44; materialism 128; matter 144n31; motion 38; natural law 179; negativity 136; ownership 351; participation 18; political rule 348; reason 382; religion 320–21; religious language 26n22, 26n26; return to 373, 385; *sacra doctrina* 27n36, 65, 66, 68, 69–72, 74–86, 89–101, 107–8; subject matter of theology 19; transubstantiation 27n31; Trinity 101–7, 134, 138; univocity of being 21, 22; use of the term 'metaphysical' 403n19; *see also* Thomism
architectonics 152; Cartesian city 162, 164; metaphysics 85–86, 89, 90, 92, 107
Arendt, Hannah 180
Aristotelianism: accidents 280; Aquinas 87, 91; civic humanism 191; knowledge 139; teleological determination 124
Aristotle 5, 43, 89, 118, 129; categories 94; cosmology 11; forms 138; gift 106; Islamic philosophers 345; knowledge 174n16; law of excluded middle 130; metaphysics 90, 129; nature 174n18; political life 339; Ramus on 156; substance 78; touch 234; transcendence 171; universals 83
Arnauld, Antoine 265–66
art 386

Asad, Talal 312, 328–29, 356–57
Athanasius 246, 250
atomism 293, 297, 301
atonement 55, 57, 225
Attale of Pergamon 211
attribution, analogy of 15–17, 18, 26n28, 122, 126, 129, 139, 385
Auden, W.H. 224, 395, 403n20
Augustine, St. 42, 58, 140, 295, 340, 394; Church as sacrifice to God 56; desire 59–60; divine image 381; Duns Scotus's reading of 119; Eucharist 281; existence 33; good and evil 11; grace 347–48; illumination 135, 379, 380; knowledge 273; 'musical' ontology 52; negativity 136; peaceful community 53; reason 87; Roman law 214; thought 381–82; Trinity 60, 137, 138; violence 7; Wyclif's radicalization of 351
Augustinianism 40, 145n37, 178–79; Aquinas 78, 79, 102; 'Avicennized' 379; good and evil 11–12; 'postmodern critical' 49–62; transubstantiation 279; truth 73
Austin, J.L. 133
authoritarianism 29
authority 39, 40, 189, 316
Averroës 120, 122, 140
Avicenna 33, 116, 119, 120, 139, 140, 380, 382
Ayer, A.J. 292

Bacon, Roger 33, 116, 138, 165
Badiou, Alain 118, 203, 214, 219, 388, 390–91
Balthasar, Hans Urs von 43, 45, 371, 374, 375–76
banishment 215
Banner, Michael 391
baptism 343, 357
Bar On, Bat-Ami 288
Barfield, Owen 35
Barnes, Michel 246
the Baroque 100–101, 125, 180, 181, 341
Barth, Karl 44, 251n3, 369, 370–71; creation 245; critique of 372; hermeneutics 136; modernity 112n75; post-Kantian mediation with Aquinas 75–76
Baudrillard, Jean 223
beatific vision 86, 88–89, 92, 108, 127, 128, 380, 381
beauty 73, 97, 109n14, 386
becoming 17–18
Beierwaltes, Werner 105–6
Beiner, Ronald 326, 336n59
being 29, 118–19, 387; absolute 106; Agamben 220; analogy of 16–17; Aquinas 75, 82, 83–84, 89–90, 99, 142n4; community of 78; Descartes 165–66; Duns Scotus 120–21, 126; finite 101; Heidegger 98, 374; participation in God 384; Plato 79; transcendent source of 171; transgeneric 89–90, 91–92, 93; see also esse; ontology; univocity of being
Belloc, Hilaire 397, 400
Benjamin, Walter 250–51
Bergson, Henri 378, 390
Bérulle, Pierre de 41, 370, 385
Bible 32, 283; biblical hermeneutics 186–89; liberal criticism of 208; metaphorical speech 14; Protestant fundamentalism 356; rejection of dualistic violence 53–54; see also Gospels; New Testament; Old Testament
Biran, Maine de 377
Blake, William 402
blasphemy 206, 209
Blond, Phillip 396–97, 401
Blondel, Maurice 376–77, 378–79, 389
blood: Eucharist 263–64, 266, 269–73, 277–81; Mark's account of the bleeding woman 229–33; peace made by Christ's blood 224; purification 222–23
Bodin, Jean 185, 220, 322, 324, 328
body 231, 240, 287–307, 333; brokenness 287–88, 301, 302; discipline over the 332; Eucharist 263–64, 266, 269–74, 277–81; Merleau-Ponty on 253n29; ontological scandal 289, 290, 294, 296, 298, 299; of the State 324; torture 357; touch 234, 236, 237
Bonaventure 33, 116, 119, 121, 124, 131, 140, 374, 380
Boulnois, Olivier 35, 116–17, 118, 120, 138, 380–82, 386
Bouyer, Louis 372, 403n3
Boyle, Robert 10
Brassier, Ray 389, 391
bread 263, 266, 269–72, 274, 278, 279–81; Gregory of Nyssa 294–95; ontological scandal 289, 290, 294, 296, 298
Breton, Stanislas 58
Brontë, Emily 237
Bruaire, Claude 389
Buckley, Michael 34, 38, 383
Budde, Michael 329
Bulgakov, Sergei 34
Buridan, Jean 116
Burrell, David 26n22, 107, 113n103, 131
Butler, Judith 288, 299

Calvin, John 39, 373
Calvinism 266, 267, 318, 358

Candler, Peter 385
capitalism 203, 250–51, 354, 357, 397, 402, 404n21
Caputo, John D. 267
Cartesian city 161–64, 170
Casel, Dom Odo 370, 372
Cassian, John 384
Castelli, Elizabeth 288
categories 94
Catharism 341, 343
Catherine de Medici 318–19
Catholic League 319
Catholicism see Roman Catholicism
causality 13, 25n9, 129–30; Aquinas 81–82; Duns Scotus 34, 117, 124; exceptional events 207; sacra doctrina 86
Cavanaugh, William 9, 311–12, 314–37, 402
celestial body 7–8
Certeau, Michel de 241, 243, 299
charity 106, 117, 125, 132, 201; Aquinas 106, 344; Duns Scotus 123, 136; over-institutionalization of 383; poverty eradication 352; redemptive 342
Charles V, Holy Roman Emperor 317
Chesterton, G.K. 372, 394
Chrétien, Jean-Louis 32, 235
Christ, Jesus 60, 202–27, 228–29, 250–51, 342, 398; blood of 222–23, 224, 244, 263, 266, 270–73, 277–81; body of 225–26, 231, 263–64, 266, 270–74, 277–81, 298–301, 324, 333, 393; Christic relations 246–50; corporeality 201; descent from heaven to earth 304n11; disciples 332; divine authority 189; Eucharist 262–64, 270–73, 277–81; as founder 59; gift 200; glorification of 247; grace 128; incarnation 57, 239; infinite esse 375; infinite expression of the Father 370; kingship 400; Lubac's humanism 372; Mark's account of the bleeding woman 229–33; Newton's understanding of 37, 38; Passion narrative 200, 204–13, 215–16; persona 370, 381; political rule 358; power of God 246; reciprocity 245; resurrection 264, 282, 298; self-offering 54–55; Summa Theologiae 108; touch 232, 233, 235, 248, 249; see also Christology; Trinity
Christendom movement 30
Christian socialism 352, 397, 400–401
Christianity 4, 24, 44–45, 396–97; Augustine 59; Balthasar 375; bodies 288, 289, 303; boundaries 53; and capitalism 250–51; civic humanism 191; community 56; concept of religion 321, 328; consensus 52; defence of 386; desacralization 6, 178; difference 51–52;

discipleship 332; duality 344; Hobbes 323–24; law of charity 342; Machiavellianism 192; Milbank 28, 29, 32, 40; Neoplatonism 7–8; nobility 398; orthodox 393, 394; peace 7; poetic language 350; politics 358, 398–402; postmodern theology 50–51; rejection of dualistic violence 53–54; sin 55–56; social principles 41; sociological approaches 178–79; Spinoza 187; temporal processes 50; 'Theologico-Political problem' 339–40, 341–42; Trinity 108; see also Church; Protestantism; Roman Catholicism
Christic operation 229, 230, 247, 248, 249–50
Christology 201, 228–29, 245–46, 250–51, 381; Aquinas 76, 89, 105, 108; Augustine 382; Barth 251n3; 'high' 59; John's Gospel 247; Luther/Calvin 39; quasi-Nestorianism 379; transcendentalist 371; see also Christ, Jesus
Chrysostom 252n12
Church 40, 44, 60, 185–86, 395–96; as community of the gifted 200; deterritorialized 251; differentiated body of the 11; domestication of the 333; as erotic community 262–63; Eucharist 264, 269, 277, 283; Hobbes 10, 323–24; laity 344, 346; Neoplatonic understanding of hierarchy 7, 8; ownership 351; political authority 316, 317, 318, 402; private sphere 326; privatization of the 320; secular space 342; sexual practices 371–72; and State 323, 325, 326–29, 331–32, 347; subsidiarity principle 362n44; transcorporeality 299; see also Christianity
Cicero, Marcus Tullius 237, 339
civil society 327, 329, 397
Clarendon, Earl of 324–25
Claudel, Paul 372
Cogito 161, 164, 165, 167, 168–69, 172
Coleridge, Samuel Taylor 41, 350, 383, 386
Colin, Jean 211–12
common good 133, 346, 358, 397
communism 353
community 52–53, 56, 58, 60, 78, 291, 393
Consecration 274–75, 277
consensus 52
Constant, Benjamin 346
contemplation 239
Conti, Antonio 144n31
Corbin, Michael 77, 78, 82, 92, 107, 108, 375
Cornwell, John 392
corporatism 401, 402
corporeality 167, 168, 169, 201, 236, 288, 293–98; see also body; transcorporeality

corpus mysticum 299–300
Cosmopolis 395
cosmos 38, 93; Descartes 169; Duns Scotus 123; Greek cosmology 11
Counter-Reformation 39, 262, 281, 317
Courtine, Jean-François 35, 116, 118, 164–65
Cox, Harvey 180
creation 25n9, 33–34, 60, 129–30, 301, 387; allegorical reading 295; Aquinas 67, 71, 93, 101, 132, 134, 237–38; Balthasar 375–76; difference 10–11; Duns Scotus 123; *ex nihlio* 11, 18, 27n34, 51, 52, 54, 60, 107, 132, 184; gift of 18, 41, 60, 93, 200, 313, 358; God's understanding of 302; pantheism 17; participation 17, 18, 19; speaking of God 13; Trinitarian ontology 104; univocity of being 22; violence 7
Cross, Richard 123, 142n4, 145n46, 145n47, 146n48, 379
crucifixion 200, 205, 215–16, 250
Cudworth, Ralph 39, 41
culture 133–34, 223–24, 327
Cunningham, Conor 392
Cusanus *see* Nicholas of Cusa

Daniélou, Jean 245–46, 372
Dante Alighieri 343, 385
The Dark Knight 398
deduction 167
deification 54
Deleuze, Gilles 121, 388, 390, 391; habit 378; nihilism 129; schizophrenization 229, 250, 251; univocity of being 117, 118, 140
democracy 352, 398, 399, 400
demonstrative identification 290, 291–92, 294, 299, 300
Derrida, Jacques 118, 121, 241, 243, 388, 391; deconstruction 54, 390; *différance* 25n11, 267; gift 199, 200; language 268, 272, 392; 'logocentrism' 383; metaphysics 154–55, 162, 170; modernity 151; on Plato 261; presence 152, 262, 267; signs 267–69; speech 176n60
desacralization 5, 6, 178
Descartes, René 42, 118, 152, 153, 158, 377; Cartesian city 161–64; epistemology 166–70; late scholastic conceptual space 379; mind 263; ontology 164–66; reflection 239; written subject 171–73
desire 58–60, 102, 273–74, 392; Eucharist 262, 275, 277–78, 281–82, 284; touch 237; Trinitarian ontology 103–4
Desmond, William 372
dialectic 159–60
différance 25n11, 267

difference 7, 9, 51–52, 267, 374–75, 391; creation 10–11; Duns Scotus 119; intimation of 235–36; ontological 22, 99, 123, 131, 375
Dionysius the Pseudo-Areopogite 7–8, 119, 136, 140, 244, 381
discernment 254n33, 295, 296, 297
discipline 331–32, 384, 394
distance 100, 237, 238–39, 244, 250
distribution 157
distributism 400, 402
divine perfection 78–80, 97, 100, 135–36; *see also* perfection
divine simplicity 89, 104, 381
Dominican order 113n98
dominium 181–85, 340
dualism 53–54, 69, 131, 377
Dunn, Richard 317, 334n14
Duns Scotus, John 21–22, 46, 66–67, 116–47, 379; conventions 346; Descartes following on from 165; end of ontotheology 121–25; finite being 119–20; finite essence 83; illumination 380; impact on theology 121; knowledge as representation 23, 138–39; Milbank's critique of 29, 32–33, 34, 43; and postmodernism 135–40; theological dimension of univocity 125–35; Trinity 183

Eckhart, Meister 375–76, 381, 382, 385, 387, 394
ecumenism 395–96
Edwards, Jonathan 39
Elizabeth I, Queen of England 311
Elliott, J.H. 320, 334n26
elocutio 159, 160
Elton, G.R. 318
embodiment 240, 288, 289, 301
emotions 274–75, 276
empiricism 125, 131, 139, 263, 266, 377
Enlightenment 5, 29, 34, 40, 117, 190; as 'all too Christian' 384; culture of 'civility' 10; Islamification of Christianity 345; postmodern nihilism 51; rejection of bad theology 41; Scottish 339; Williams on 39
ens 121–22, 123, 128
ens commune 71, 75, 82–85, 89–90, 99, 374
entrustment 232
epistemology 23, 29, 31, 35, 40, 41; Aquinas 82–83; Descartes 161, 165, 166–70, 173; Duns Scotus 117, 118; postmodernity 151; Ramus 157, 159; shift from ontology to 118–19, 166; standpoint 288; *see also* knowledge
equality 8
equivocity 96, 97, 119, 120, 139–40

Eriugena 136, 370, 375–76, 381, 382, 394
eschatology 32, 46, 87, 245, 292
esse 71, 78–79, 83–85, 89–91, 99–100;
    Balthasar 374; forms 111n50; God's essence
    81; Incarnation 204; individuation 144n31;
    participation 96, 97, 122, 128, 129, 375;
    scholasticism 94; transgeneric 93; Trinity
    103; univocity 119; *see also* being; ontology
essence: Aquinas 16, 21, 72, 81–82, 84, 99,
    128, 280, 374–75; *dominium* 183; Duns
    Scotus 120, 137; finite 83, 85; Trinity
    102–3
essentia 71, 81, 84–85, 90, 99, 103, 123, 128
Eucharist 27n31, 135, 185, 262–64, 265–86,
    370; Blondel 378–79; blood of Christ 244;
    Gregory of Nyssa 298; ontological scandal
    288–89, 290, 298, 299; ship allegory 284;
    transcorporeality 299
Europe 353–54
Eusebius 183
Evans, Gareth 291–92
evil 55, 56, 202, 295–96, 376, 394; primacy
    of 341, 346; rejection of dualistic
    conception of 11–12; theory of radical 203
excluded middle, law of 122, 130
existence: Aquinas 16–17, 21, 33, 78, 79, 99,
    280; Descartes 165, 166; Duns Scotus
    122–23; logic 128–29
experimental science 5
'extrinsicism' 123, 128, 368, 369, 370, 373

Fabro, Cornelio 132
factum 180–81, 182, 184
facultas 182, 183
faith 39, 61, 232, 392; creation 101; leap of
    67; reason relationship 20, 43, 65–66,
    69–74, 86–89, 93, 368, 370; Trinity 106
the Fall 116, 128, 351, 358
fascism 353, 354, 355, 401–2
Fichte, Johann Gottlieb 106, 376
Ficino, Marsilio 321
Figgis, John 316, 322
Filmer, Sir Robert 182
finitude 119–20
first mover 83
Fish, Stanley 289
FitzPatrick, P.J. 279, 280
Fitzralph, Robert 185
flow 229, 230–31, 233, 241–46
forgiveness 200, 202, 203, 204
forms 17–18, 91, 107, 111n50, 138; creation
    238; Descartes 163; Trinitarian ontology
    103
Fortescue, John 351, 361n32
Foucault, Michel 248, 383

foundationalism 389
free market ideology 354
freedom 123–24, 131, 132, 184, 187, 375,
    376
French Revolution 349, 397–98
friendship 344
fundamentalism 338, 355–56

Geertz, Clifford 327, 328, 329
generation 246
Gerson, Jean 182, 183–84, 185
Giddens, Anthony 325
gift 106–7, 125, 132–33, 199–201, 222; of
    being 17, 124, 126, 130; causality 81–82;
    Christian democracy 352; communication
    as embodied giving 298; of craft 352; of
    creation 18, 41, 60, 93, 200, 313, 358;
    Derrida 268; Descartes 165, 166; Eucharist
    284; free acts 357–58; of grace 18, 200,
    347–48, 350–51; Lévinas 242–43;
    magnanimity 343–44; redefinition of virtue
    350; of ruling 312, 313, 347–48;
    transgeneric 104; Wyclif 350–52, 361n28
Gil, José 287
Gilson, Étienne 99, 118, 144n31, 165, 382
Gnosticism 11, 12
God: 'bracketing' of 22; community 52, 58;
    creation 11, 17, 25n9, 33–34, 60, 67, 129,
    237–38, 387; declared will 183; deification
    54; Descartes 168; desire for 282; divine
    image 380, 381–82; Duns Scotus 124, 126;
    envy of 218; Eucharist 278–79, 281, 282;
    existence of 16–17, 78, 122–23; faith/
    reason relationship 74, 86, 93;
    fundamentalism 355; gift-giving 200–201,
    361n28; glorification of 247; goodness
    14–16, 80, 91; Gregory of Nyssa 296, 297,
    298; Hobbes 184, 323; idealism 376;
    imitation of 276, 277; immanence 132;
    impossibility of humanism without 45; 'in
    himself' 80, 81; incarnation 55–56, 57,
    208; individual as image of 357; infinite
    reality 385, 387; intellect 380; intimacy
    240; knowledge as representation 24;
    knowledge of 75–76, 88–89, 142n4, 368,
    369; Lévinas 243; as literal fact 346;
    magnanimity 343–44; mediation within
    381, 382; Middle Ages 28–29; naming 121;
    Newtonian physics 38; Nicholas of Cusa 8;
    omnipotence 130, 153; omnipresence 87,
    130–31; ontological difference 375;
    participation 17–19; perfection 78–79, 100,
    107; postmodern theology 50–51; power of
    7, 246; in rational creatures 112n73;
    revelation 368–69; *sacra doctrina* 66, 67–68,

75, 77, 92, 110n44; secularism 4, 12; sin
55–56; speaking of 13–15, 26n22, 33;
substance 110n37; *Summa Theologiae* 108;
Trinity 57–58, 102, 104; truths about
110n43; univocity of being 21–23, 66–67;
Word of 301–2; *see also* Trinity
goodness 11–12, 91, 93, 121, 131; Aquinas
79–80, 110n39; Duns Scotus 120; speaking
of God 14–16
Gospels 205–7, 208–9, 210, 216, 217, 218,
256n79
grace 44, 122, 358, 389–90; Aquinas 87–88,
89, 93, 107, 108; Christ-centred treatment
of 39; *dominium* 184; Duns Scotus 127; gift
of 18, 200, 347–48, 350–51; habit 378,
391; knowledge 109n15; Middle Ages 350;
and nature 43, 112n75, 378; operations of
244–45; rule of 347–48; univocity of being
123; Wyclif on 350–52
Gregory of Nazianzus 183
Gregory of Nyssa 228, 240, 244, 245, 294–95,
296–98
Gregory the Great 80
Grosseteste, Robert 131, 387
Grotius, Hugo 179, 182, 225, 321, 361n32
Guardini, Romano 372
Guattari, F. 229, 250, 251

Habermas, Jurgen 180
habit 377–78, 391, 392
Hadot, Pierre 32
haecceity 144n31
Hamann, Johann Georg 41, 98, 373, 383
Hanby, Michael 384, 392
Hankey, Wayne 105–6
Harding, Sandra 288
Harrington, James 360n22
Hart, David 221, 380
Hauerwas, Stanley 36
heaven 53
Hegel, G.W.F. 31, 121, 239, 372–73, 387;
God 368–69; incarnation 300; Machiavellian
tradition 191; nihilism 106, 108; rationalism
40
Heidegger, Martin 31, 70–71, 121, 136, 236,
389; being 98–99, 220; correction of 374;
failure to account for 'self-organization' 376;
presence 151
Henry, Michel 377
Henry of Ghent 33, 116, 140
Henry VIII, King of England 316
hermeneutics 136, 186–89, 388
Herod 205, 212
hierarchy 7–8
Himes, Michael and Kenneth 327, 328

historicism 40, 50, 134, 190, 350
Hittenger, Russell 358, 360n20, 362n44
Hobbes, Thomas 179, 189, 190, 346; biblical
hermeneutics 186–87, 188; domestication
of the Church 333; ethical understanding
180; God's power 184; liberal peace
335n48; religion 322–24; social contract
theory 312, 339; sovereignty 220; State
182; 'state of nature' 10
Hoff, Johannes 368, 372, 375, 376
Holocaust 219
Holy Grail 263, 282–83, 284
homo sacer 213, 214–15, 219, 220, 221–22,
225, 226
Honnefelder, Ludwig 35, 116
Hooker, Richard 351, 361n32
Huculak, Benedykt 135
Hugh of St. Victor 332
human rights 219, 338, 353, 356, 357; *see also*
natural rights; rights
humanism 31, 45, 178, 190–91, 373, 391;
Augustine 42; laicized 385–86; Lubac 372;
method 158; rationalist 155
Hume, David 10, 81, 133, 294, 386
humility 47, 343–44
Husserl, Edmund 234, 242, 389

Iamblichus 106, 107
idealism 17, 70, 139, 372, 376
identity 8, 130, 139, 385, 387
illumination 43, 58, 65–66, 121, 135, 379,
380
imitation 143n4, 275–76, 277
immanence 20, 132, 168, 171, 173, 301
incarnation 55–56, 57, 135, 204, 208, 301;
Aquinas 89, 105; logic of 240; relationality
239; transcorporeality 300
individualism 9, 44, 182, 190, 293, 393, 402
individuation 144n31
infinity 15, 34, 122–23, 390; Descartes 168;
Duns Scotus 126, 131, 135; univocity of
being 22
influence 124
Inglis, John 110n24, 112n98
intellect 72–74, 77, 101–2, 122, 134, 379;
created 112n77; divine 136, 137, 139; and
grace 87–88; illumination 121; Lonergan
95; and soul 109n8, 111n61
'intellectual deviation' narrative (ID) 383, 384
intention 102, 234
intimacy 235, 237, 239–40, 250
intuition 92, 95, 97, 100, 101, 107
invention 157, 159–60
Islam 11, 342, 345, 355–56, 395, 396–97
Italian city republics 343

Jacobi, Friedrich Heinrich 386
Jefferson, Thomas 349
Jenkins, John 72
Jews 206–7, 210–11, 360n23; *see also* Judaism
John 210, 221, 239, 247–48, 255n69, 255n72
John of St. Thomas 134–35
John the Baptist 208
Jones, David 208, 224
Jordan, Mark 102
Judaism 11, 52, 54, 342, 343, 345, 355–56, 395; *see also* Jews
Judas Iscariot 246–47, 249
judgement 157, 159–60, 341
justice 157, 181–82

Kant, Immanuel 35, 76, 122, 136, 139, 223; free will 339; late scholastic conceptual space 379; proportionality 100; reason 81, 101, 368; receptivity 242; rejection of 113n103; scholasticism 118; Scotist/ Ockhamite paradigm 374; State 326; Theory of Right 335n57; war 335n56
Katz, David 235
kenosis 241, 242, 244, 246, 250, 304n11, 378
Kerr, Fergus 44
Kierkegaard, S. 377, 394
Kleutgen, Joseph 70
knowledge 31, 88–89, 174n16, 231–32; 'aporia of learning' 42–43; Aristotelian view 139; Cartesian city 164; Derrida 154; and desire 273; of distance 239; Duns Scotus 125, 127, 134, 139, 145n47, 379; eschatological vision 87; Gregory of Nyssa 295; illuminated 43, 58, 66; as 'internal construct' 382; *mathēsis* 153; metaphysical 75–76; political 179, 180; presence 151–52, 262; printed 156; Ramus 159; as representation 23–24, 34–35, 45–46, 117, 119, 138–39; revelation of grace 109n15; *sacra doctrina*/philosophy relationship 66, 67–68; standpoint epistemology 288; *see also* epistemology
Körper 234

Labarthe, Philippe Lacoue 297
Lachelier, Jules 391
language 13, 26n22, 156, 265, 283, 388; Aquinas 26n26, 95–97, 98; Descartes 169; *différance* 25n11; Eucharist 272–73; indeterminacy 266, 267, 273–74, 392; Milbank 30–31; naming 291; Ramus 159, 160; subjectivity 268
Laruelle, François 390, 391
Lash, Nicholas 30, 36, 47, 94, 392
Last Supper 248, 249, 263, 289, 369

Latour, Bruno 117
law 10, 54, 327, 328; Roman 181–82, 213, 214, 215, 216, 218, 220
Lazarus 246–47, 248
Légasse, Simon 209, 211–12
Leib 234
Leibniz, G.W. 107, 134, 378, 390
Lévinas, Emanuel 199, 241–43
Leviticus 252n12
Lewis, David 390
Libera, Alain de 140
liberal democracy 219, 224, 313, 335n56, 338–39, 349, 352, 353
liberalism 51, 184, 204, 312, 335n48, 353; contingency of 341; critique of 346–48, 352, 356–57; 'early modern' 361n32; founding moment of 314–15; invention of 339, 344; left 397, 400; Lockean 324; natural rights legacy of 190; neo-liberalism 354–55; nominalism-voluntarism 182; political 125, 311, 326, 350; primacy of the will 345; right 397; roots of 345–46, 355; Rousseau 359n19; Satanic nature of 341; subsidiarity 362n44
liturgy 108, 152–53, 274–76, 277, 281, 344, 369, 383
Locke, John 180, 182, 324, 339, 346
logic 127, 128–29, 138, 139, 184; algebraic 113n106; Aquinas 94–95, 140; Duns Scotus 140; suppositional 156
Logos 5, 59, 128, 183, 224; bread and wine 281; Christ's character 370; creation 376; desire 60; divine image 381–82; illumination 58; incarnation 56, 57; infinity of 392; Trinity 103–4, 106–7
Lonergan, Bernard 72, 94, 95, 102, 113n103
love 56, 240, 247, 393
Lubac, Henri de 44–45, 88, 368, 371, 373–74, 376–77; allegory 189; Eucharist 264, 269; humanism 372; salvation 43; spiritual realism 378
Luke 211, 212, 221, 230, 233, 247, 251n5
Lull, Ramon 165
Luther, Martin 39, 186, 316, 322, 373
Lyotard, J.-F. 51

Machen, Arthur 383
Machiavelli, Niccolò 190–92, 315–16, 339, 343, 345, 349
MacIntyre, Alasdair 36, 125
MacKinnon, Donald 28, 30, 31, 47
magnanimity 343–44
Manent, Pierre 312, 339–47, 349–50, 352, 359n19

Manicheanism 11, 12
mannerism 181
Manzano, Isiduro 121–22, 123–25, 126, 132–33
Marin, Louis 270
Marion, Jean-Luc 35, 90, 100, 118, 270, 377, 389; being 84, 99; causality 81, 82; Descartes 164–65; Duns Scotus 117, 136; gift 199
Mark 218, 220, 229–33, 247, 251n5, 252n12, 252n13, 255n69, 289–90, 298
Marshall, Bruce 89
Marsilius (Marsiglio) of Padua 186, 316
martyrdom 323
Marx, Karl 191, 250–51, 353, 359n19
Mary 246, 247, 248, 249
masturbation 236–37
materialism 128, 263, 292, 293, 300, 399
mathematics 77, 83, 390; Descartes 167, 176n44; Plato 167–68
mathēsis 152, 153, 154, 155; Derrida 267; Descartes 164, 165, 166, 169, 172; of desire 278; Ramus 157, 159, 160
matter 91, 144n31, 266, 292, 296, 379, 383; see also substance
Matthew 218, 220, 230, 233, 247, 251n4
Mauss, Marcel 199, 243
McBrien, Richard 328, 329, 336n60
McDowell, John 125, 293
mediaeval period see Middle Ages
Meillassoux, Quentin 377, 378, 390, 391
memory 42, 58, 159, 171, 177n66, 292
'Meno problematic' 86–87, 104, 135, 378
Merleau-Ponty, Maurice 234, 236, 239, 240, 253n25, 253n27, 253n29, 389
metaphorical speech 14
metaphysics 24, 30–31, 35, 139, 388, 390–92; Aquinas 75–78, 82–86, 89–92, 94–95, 100, 107, 113n103, 126, 140; Aristotle 129; Baroque rationalism 100–101; categories 94; causality 82; Derrida 154–55, 162, 170; Duns Scotus 120, 121, 126; Plato 261; premodern 50; sacra doctrina 89; semantic issues 403n19; substance 26n30; univocity of being 94, 122
methodus 157, 158
Middle Ages 4–5, 12, 28–29, 40, 117, 225; bodies 290; Church/papal authority 70, 316; crises 158; Eucharist 269; grace 350; knowledge 35; liturgy 344; philosophy 32; political order 340; power 181; religion 320, 321; revelation 39; secularism 342–43; State concept 315; supernaturalism 340, 341; suppositional logic 156; truth 386

Milbank, John 3, 6–7; 'asymmetrical reciprocity' 243, 245; Christ 202–27; conversation with 28–48; development of Radical Orthodoxy 367–404; difference 10–11; gift 200; participation 17, 18; politics 178–95, 312–13, 338–63; 'postmodern critical Augustinianism' 49–62; sacra doctrina/philosophy relationship 65–66, 67–68, 69–115; spatialization 153; state power 335n48; theology 20, 21, 24
mimesis 143n4, 275–76, 277
mind 58, 88, 171, 263, 292, 377, 383
Miner, Robert 392
miracles 279, 294, 296
modernity 6–7, 23–24, 41, 44, 151, 155; atomism 297; bodies 287–88, 304n17; critique of 301; Duns Scotus 118, 125, 140; end of 49; evil and violence 12; 'flattening' tendency of 9; knowledge 262; ontological scandal 299; origins of 117
Molina 184
monotheism 53–54, 91, 106, 183, 345
Montag, John 39
Montesquieu, Charles de Secondat, Baron de 339, 346, 348, 360n22
More, Thomas 41, 218
motion 37, 38, 83, 107, 244–45, 390–91; see also kenosis
Muralt, André de 397
Murray, John Courtney 327, 329
music 52, 60, 77
mystery 135, 269, 276–77, 370

names 96
naming 96, 291, 295
Nancy, Jean-Luc 172, 241, 293, 300–302
Narcisse, Gilbert 107
natural law 44, 45, 133, 179, 182, 183–84, 351
natural rights 185, 190, 191, 192, 219; see also human rights; rights
nature 46, 179, 295, 387; Aristotle 5, 174n18; and grace 43, 112n75, 378; man's domination over 347
'negative' theology 14, 385
neo-conservatism 360n23
neo-Gothicism 350, 354, 355
neo-liberalism 354–55
Neoplatonism 12, 32, 87, 102, 118, 375; causality 13, 34, 81, 129; Duns Scotus 145n46; finite reality 59; hierarchy 7–8; Islamic philosophers 345; Ockham 130; participation in Being 279; Pickstock 36; Proclean 84; theurgic 107, 135; Trinitarian reflection 105–6; truth 73; Unity 98

neo-scholasticism 73, 389
neo-Thomism 70, 113n103
Neuhaus, Richard John 327, 328
New Testament 212, 220, 223–24, 298;
    atonement 55; body 290; Christology 201,
    246–47; Christ's death 221; Passion
    narrative 205, 216; understanding of Christ
    342; *see also* Bible
Newman, John Henry 42
Newton, Isaac 10, 37–38
Nicholas of Cusa (Cusanus) 361n32, 382, 383,
    387, 394; creation 375–76; critique of
    rationalism 41; *factibilitas* 181; hierarchy 8;
    humanism 385; identity 130; number 390;
    ontological difference 131; perspective 388;
    proportion 15
Nicolas, J.-H. 88
Nicole, Pierre 265–66
Nietzsche, Friedrich 342
nihilism 98, 99, 243, 374; death of God 282;
    Derrida 154; Descartes 166, 171; Hegel
    106; humanist rationalism 155; liberal
    scientific 356; materialism 293, 297;
    postmodern 50, 51, 54, 151; Scotist 129
nobility 398, 399
Noel, Conrad 372
nominalism 9, 94, 178–79, 182, 380;
    Calvinism 266; and humanism 386; political
    401–2; Trinity 183
nouvelle théologie 43, 368, 372, 373–79
Novalis 383, 386

Ockham, William of 116, 123, 130, 183, 185,
    189, 225, 384
O'Donovan, Oliver 361n32
Old Testament 189, 213–14, 295, 356; *see also*
    Bible
Oliver, Simon 3–27, 151–53, 392; conversation
    with 36–38, 42–43, 45–47; gift 199–201;
    motion 37–38, 390; politics 311–13
Olivi, Peter 116, 124
omnipotence 130, 153
omnipresence 87, 123, 130–31
oneness 249–50
Ong, Walter J. 156, 159, 174n16
ontology 29, 31, 35, 93, 389; Aquinas 82–83,
    101; Descartes 161, 164–66; Duns Scotus
    118, 120; 'musical' 52; shift to epistemology
    118–19; theology separation from 167;
    Trinitarian 60, 103; *see also* being; *esse*
ontotheology 85, 117, 120, 121–25, 126, 136
operations 228, 230–31, 247
Origen 235, 239, 246
original sin 191
otherness 241, 243

Pabst, Adrian 380
paganism 54, 89, 192, 340, 397–98
pantheism 17
Papacy 70, 184–85, 318, 340
participation 12, 17–19, 21, 22, 61, 244–45,
    384; Aquinas 73, 84, 85, 96, 97, 143n4,
    279; Duns Scotus 122, 123, 136, 379;
    faith/reason relationship 370; in God's own
    knowledge 66, 68; Gregory of Nyssa 297;
    incompatibility with Augustinianism
    145n37; law of excluded middle 130;
    metaphysical 277; Proclean hierarchy 129;
    transcendence 132
Pascal, B. 265, 266
Passion 200, 204–13, 215–16, 282
Paul 219, 221–23, 225, 242, 301, 398;
    judgement 341–42; *kenosis* 304n11; Letter
    to the Corinthians 251, 289–90; Letter to
    the Galatians 249; 'living sacrifice' 245;
    Roman defences of 211; Sanders on
    227n21
peace 7, 11, 53, 202, 323, 335n48, 335n56
Péguy, Charles 344, 349–50, 378
perception 236, 290–91, 297
perfection 78–80, 97, 107, 121, 135–36;
    absolute 105; Duns Scotus 139; finite 100;
    as reflexivity 106; triple 111n60
persona 59, 128, 370, 381
Peterson, Eric 372
phenomenology 47, 98, 100, 117, 136, 368,
    388–90
Philip II, King of Spain 316, 319
philosophy 23, 24, 35–36, 41; Duns Scotus
    29, 136; modernity 118; *nouvelle théologie*
    373–79; postmodernism 155; theology
    relationship 32, 42–43, 65–68, 69–72,
    74–86, 89–101, 105, 116–17, 368, 390;
    twentieth-century 388–90; univocity of
    being 67; *see also* epistemology; metaphysics;
    ontology; reason
physics 37–38, 46, 83, 139, 390, 391
Pickstock, Catherine: 'aporia of learning' 42;
    critique of Derrida 151, 152, 154–55, 262,
    267–69; Duns Scotus 22, 33, 67, 116–47;
    epistemology 23; Eucharist 262–63, 264,
    265–86; 'liturgical turn' 369; participation
    17, 18; on Plato 36; 'repetition' 377, 391;
    spatialization and modernity 154–77, 262;
    transubstantiation 27n31, 379
Pickstock, John 42
Pico della Mirandola, Giovanni 41, 383, 385,
    386, 387
Pilate, Pontius 205, 206, 209, 210, 212, 218
Pinchard, Bruno 385
place logic 156, 160

Plato 36, 46, 135, 389; Aquinas's Aristotelian critique of 91; being 79; cave allegory 173; city 161, 163, 164; creation 11; Derrida on 152, 261; dialogue 156; knowledge 42; mathematics 167–68; mimesis 276; participation 17; political life 339; realm of becoming 18; transcendence 171; Trinity 108; *see also* Neoplatonism

Platonism 11, 32, 43, 87, 91; Anglo-Saxon thought 377; Derrida 154; participation 17–18; *see also* Neoplatonism

pleroma 241, 242, 246

Pliny 210

Plotinus 106, 107, 135, 140, 382

Pocock, J.G.A. 190

Poinsot, Juan 134–35

politics 69, 189–90, 311–13, 338–63; as biblical hermeneutics 186–89; Christ 204; construction of secular 181–86; Machiavellianism 190–92; political theory 179; Radical Orthodoxy 396–402; secularism 4; 'state of nature' 10; violence 203; *see also* State

Polybius 191

Pompeius Festus 213

Pope Benedict 392, 402

Pope John Paul II 358

Porreta, Gilbert 33, 116

positivism 70, 126–27, 263, 296, 299, 301, 353

Postel, Guillaume 321–22

postmodernism 45, 50, 55, 60, 154–55, 388; Cartesian subject 268; critique of 304n16; dualism 54; Duns Scotus 117, 118, 121, 135–40; indeterminacy 267, 391; meaning 31; mimesis 276; Spinozistic 131–32

postmodernity 49, 50, 136, 140, 151, 287–88, 304n17

power 6–7, 153, 246, 252n5, 316; Christic operation 249–50; divine 346; *dominium* 181–85, 340; Machiavellianism 190, 191; relations of 248; Roman law 214; sovereign 10, 182, 214, 216, 319, 360n22; State 335n48; theocratic theories 70

pre-modernity 49–50

presence 151–52, 170, 261–62, 267, 268–69; Christ 263; Eucharist 273, 279, 281, 283

private sphere 4, 153, 311, 326, 333

privation theory 203

Proclus 106, 107, 129, 130, 135, 140, 382–83, 387

progress 6, 118

property ownership 350–51

property rights 123, 143n15, 182

prophecy 74, 284

proportion, analogy of 15, 26n26, 73, 100

Protestantism 43, 368, 395, 396, 404n21; authoritarianism 29; death-knell of Protestant theology 372, 373; fundamentalist 355, 356; liberal 44; neo-orthodoxy 38; politics 402; 'Wars of Religion' 315, 317, 318–20

proto-modernity 121

Przywara, Erich 84, 96, 372

purification 222–23

Putnam, Hilary 292

Quine, W.V.O. 125

radicalism 393–95

Rahner, Karl 370–71

Ramey, Joshua 386

Ramus, Peter 152, 156–61, 174n16, 266

ratio 58, 72, 77, 100; *see also* reason

rationalism 44, 46, 125, 131, 384, 395; Augustine 380–81, 382; Baroque 100–101; critiques of 41; Duns Scotus 118, 125; Hegel 40; humanist 155; negative theology 385; Western rationalist bias 383; *see also* reason

Ratzinger, Joseph 372, 385

Ravaisson, Félix 377, 378, 391

Rawls, John 314, 325

realism 139, 382, 387, 388, 390, 391; Descartes 377; Pico della Mirandola 386; Platonic 121, 351; spiritual 377, 378, 379, 389, 391

reality: atomism 293; Descartes 165, 166, 167, 168; Ramus 158–59

reason 5, 6, 36, 41–42, 131, 382; Aquinas 123; Duns Scotus 122–23; early modern science 9–10; Enlightenment 40; 'extrinsicism' 368; faith relationship 20, 43, 65–66, 69–74, 86–89, 93, 368, 370; 'grandeur of' 392; Kant 81, 101; negative theology 385; and nihilism 374; and revelation 32, 33, 121; *sacra doctrina* 75, 78; Trinity 101; truths about God 110n43; *see also* rationalism

reciprocity 106, 199, 200, 242, 243, 245, 248

reflection 239

reflexivity 106

'Reform Master Narrative' (RMN) 383–84

Reformation 29, 39, 40, 158, 178–79; political authority 317–18; Protestantism 402; Roman Catholic Church 44

refugees 241, 243–44

relation 233, 239, 246–50

religion 4, 311, 312, 314, 349–50; bodily practices 332; creation of 320–25; definition of 336n60; fundamentalist 338,

355–56; public nature of 327; United States 355; universalist construction of 328; 'Wars of Religion' 117, 314, 315, 316, 317, 318–20, 327
representation 23–24, 34–35, 45–46, 117, 119; Descartes 165–66; distance 238; divine intellect 139; univocity of being 125, 138
resurrection 56–57, 108, 264, 282, 298
revelation 19, 38–39, 80, 122, 125, 368–70; analogy 127; Aquinas 74, 110n43; Duns Scotus 126, 136; 'extrinsicism' 368; neo-scholastic accounts 73; nositivistic concept of 188; positivism 126–27; Rahner 371; and reason 32, 33, 121
rhetoric 159–60, 174n16
rights 312–13, 339, 356, 357; see also human rights; natural rights
Rogers, Eugene 89
Roman Catholicism 40, 44, 70, 373; authoritarianism 29; Duns Scotus 136; Elizabethan intolerance of 311–12; 'extrinsicism' 368, 370; fundamentalism 356; politics 318, 402; Spinoza on 187; transubstantiation 324; 'Wars of Religion' 315, 317, 318–20
Roman law 181–82, 213, 214, 215, 216, 218, 220
Romanus, Aegidius 185
Romero, Oscar 332, 333, 337n90
Rorty, Richard 35, 125, 390
Rosemann, Philipp 375
Rousseau, Jean-Jacques 339, 346, 349, 353, 359n19
Rousselot, Pierre 372
Ruskin, John 399
Russell, Bertrand 292

sacra doctrina 27n36, 65–66, 67, 69–72, 74–86, 89–101, 107–8, 375
sacralization 6
sacrifice 53, 54, 213, 214, 222, 226
Said, Edward 244
Salutati, Coluccio 180, 385
salvation 57, 240, 244–45, 246, 342; Eucharist 281; lay paths to 344; Trinity 345
Sandel, Michael 125
Sanders, E.P. 225, 227n21
Sanhedrin 204–5, 206, 209–10
Santer, Mark 30
Sayers, D.L. 372
scepticism 139, 270, 271
Schaffer, Simon 10
Schelling, Friedrich 106, 376
Schlegel, Friedrich von 386
Schmitt, Carl 214, 220, 339

Schnackenburg, Rudolf 247
scholasticism 39, 40, 118, 371, 373, 379; esse 94; neo-scholasticism 73, 389; obscurantism 160; plurality of forms 380
Schumacher, Lydia 380
Schwöbel, Christoph 33
science 5, 6, 38, 46, 69, 356; Aristotle 174n18; early modern 9–10; sacra doctrina 75, 77–78, 92
scientia divina 66, 67, 77
scripture 76, 77, 92, 136, 188, 394
secularism 153, 178, 181, 184, 393, 400; Church's role 185–86; 'intellectual deviation' narrative 383; invention of the secular 3–12, 21, 22, 24; liberalism 346; Machiavellian secular 190; Middle Ages 342–43; nihilistic monism 301; rise of the State 117, 317; voluntarist political theology 189–90
self-interest 9, 10
self-offering 54–55
self-revelation 368, 370, 372, 376
Sellars, Wilfrid 125
semiosis 297
senses 232
Shapin, Stephen 10
Sherwin-White, A.N. 209, 210
Shklar, Judith 314–15, 325
Shortt, Rupert 28–48
signs 189, 238–39, 282, 298, 388; Bacon 138; bodies 299–300; Derrida 261–62, 267–69; Descartes 169; Eucharist 269–70, 272–73, 283; Poinsot 134–35
simplicity 89, 104, 381
sin 55–56, 105, 200
Skinner, Quentin 317
Smith, Wilfred Cantwell 321
social contract 9, 10, 312
social norms 41
socialism 352, 353, 397, 400–401
sociality 241, 242
society 9
sociology 178–79, 349, 350
Socrates 42, 83, 95, 154, 164
sophistry 156, 169
soul 42, 45–46, 84, 135, 322; descent of the 382; discipline 332; as divine gift 343; dwelling-place of the 234; and intellect 109n8, 111n61; liberal suppression of the 346, 347; Neoplatonism 107; spiritual realism 377
space 37–38
spatialization 152, 153, 155, 262; Cartesian city 161–64; Descartes 170, 173
speech 152, 154, 170

Spinoza, Benedict de 179, 186–88, 189, 300
Spirit 42, 57, 58, 137, 222, 394; Aquinas 102, 105, 106, 107; gift 200; *see also* Trinity
spiritual realism 377, 378, 379, 389, 391
Spivak, Gayatri 300, 301
St. Bartholomew's Day massacre 318–19
State 117, 311–13, 314–37; creation of religion 320–25; liberalism 346–47; natural/human rights 219, 356; as peacemaker 325–26; rise of the 315–20; social contract 9; *see also* politics
'state of nature' 10, 325
stoicism 190
Stout, Jeffrey 314, 315, 325
strangers 244
Strauss, Leo 339, 349, 350, 360n23
subjectivity 172, 268
subsidiarity 362n44, 401
substance: and accidents 92, 280, 281; Aquinas 75, 78, 79, 85, 92, 110n37; Aristotelian terms 26n30; Blondel 378; divine 88; Duns Scotus 379; law of excluded middle 130; Trinitarian ontology 103
suffering 54, 55–56
supernaturalism 340, 341
Surin, Kenneth 329–30
syllogism 42, 157–58, 176n44
symbols 328–29, 344–45
Symeon the New Theologian 300

Taylor, Charles 4, 383–84
Taylor, Mark C. 241, 243
technology 155
Tertullian 250, 252n12
Thatcher, Margaret 291
theocracy 70
Theodulf of Orleans 381
theology 19–21, 24, 27n36, 36–37; Duns Scotus 29, 121, 125, 126, 136; Eucharist 269; 'extrinsicism' 368; Milbank on 30, 31–32, 47, 49; 'negative' 14, 385; *nouvelle théologie* 43, 368, 372, 373–79; ontology separation from 167; philosophy relationship 32, 42–43, 65–68, 69–72, 74–86, 89–101, 105, 116–17, 368, 390; political 179; postmodern 50–51, 60; science separation from 38; *see also* ontotheology
Thomism 47, 70, 123, 134–35, 391; *dominium* 185; freedom 184; Lonergan 95; metaphysics 75; participation 145n37; *see also* Aquinas, St. Thomas
Tilly, Charles 330–31
time 145n48, 186, 190, 378
Tocqueville, Alexis de 346, 347, 349, 355

Todisco, Orlando 121–22, 123–25, 126, 128, 130, 132–33
tolerance 343
Tolkien, J.R.R. 227n18
topos 241
torture 356–57
touch 232, 233–41, 248, 249, 252n12, 253n25
Toulmin, Stephen 158, 173
Tracy, David 47
transcendence 99, 132, 155, 171, 173, 181, 376
transcendentalism 93, 94, 371, 373, 378, 379, 389, 390
transcendentals 89, 119, 120, 121
transcorporeality 240, 299–300, 301–2, 303; *see also* corporeality
transubstantiation 27n31, 266, 269, 270–72, 324, 325; Aquinas 274, 279; Blondel 378–79; Counter-Reformation understandings of 262; Holy Grail 282–83
Trinity 57–58, 60, 181, 222, 370, 394; academic disbelief 30; Aquinas 71, 76, 101–7, 108, 134; creation 10, 11; divine generation 246; divine simplicity 89; Duns Scotus 137–38; mediation 381; 'Monarchy' implied by 183; Rahner 371; salvation 345; and Unity 8
Trouillard, Henri 80, 98
Trouillard, Jean 32
truth 58, 131, 165; Aquinas 69, 72–73, 104; early modern science 9–10; free consent 357; Middle Ages 386; postmodernity 49; universal truths 321–22

uncertainty 32
uncleanliness 252n12
United States of America 4, 328, 338, 346–47, 349, 354–55, 360n22
universals 83, 139, 385, 387
univocity of being 21–23, 33, 35, 46, 385, 387; Ango-Saxon questioning of 125; Duns Scotus 66–67, 116–17, 118, 119–20, 122–24, 125–35, 140, 379; representation 138; transcendental being 94

Vattimo, Gianni 241, 243
Velde, Rudi te 71, 81, 84, 111n50
Venard, Olivier-Thomas 385
verbum 102, 103, 104
verity, law of 157
Veron, François 188
Vico, Giambattista 40, 41, 181, 383, 385, 386

violence 7, 9, 202–4, 222, 314; Hobbes 10, 323; ontological 52; rejection of dualistic 53–54; State 315, 325, 326, 330–31
virtue 190–91, 321, 332, 343–44, 347, 350, 398
vision 97–98
voluntarism 183, 184, 189, 225, 358; fundamentalism 355; Hobbesian-Lockean translation of 350; Islam 345; liberalism 182; scholasticism 40; theocratic theories 70; theological legacy of 186; Wyclif's resistance to 351

Walker, Ralph 335n57
Wallace, John 290
war 314, 323, 325, 326, 330–31, 335n56
Ward, Graham: bodies 263, 287–307; Christ 201, 228–57, 263; Church as erotic community 262–63; Eucharist 264; Hegel 372
'Wars of Religion' 117, 314, 315, 316, 317, 318–20, 327
water 231
Weber, Max 184, 250–51
Weil, Simone 301
Wetherby, Jon A. 210–11

Whitehead, A.N. 390, 391
Whitman, Walt 349, 360n24
Wilkins, John 180
will 153, 183, 223–24, 225, 340, 379; culture 133–34; general 349, 353; inscrutability of the divine will 345; liberal individual 339, 349; primacy of the 345; reason distinction 132; Scotism 138; Trinity 137
William of Ockham 116, 123, 130, 183, 185, 189, 225, 384
William of Orange 335n51
Williams, Charles 372, 383
Williams, Rowan 30, 31, 39–41, 47, 372, 380–81, 383, 396
wine 263, 269, 270–71, 272, 278, 279–81
wisdom 157
Wittgenstein, Ludwig 30, 94, 236, 292, 388
the Word 235, 240, 245, 295, 296, 299, 301–2, 385
writing 152, 154, 155, 170, 172
written subject 171–73
Wyclif, John 350–52, 358, 361n28

Yale School 47

Žižek, Slavoj 301, 372